Microsoft®

# Expression®
# Web 2

## Comprehensive Concepts and Techniques

# Gary B. Shelly
# Jennifer T. Campbell
# Ollie Rivers

**Shelly Cashman Series®**

*An imprint of Course Technology, Cengage Learning*

COURSE TECHNOLOGY
CENGAGE Learning™

Australia • Brazil • Japan • Korea • Mexico • Singapore • Spain • United Kingdom • United States

# COURSE TECHNOLOGY
## CENGAGE Learning™

**Microsoft® Expression® Web 2:**
**Comprehensive Concepts and Techniques**
Gary B. Shelly, Jennifer T. Campbell, Ollie Rivers

Executive Editor: Kathleen McMahon

Product Manager: Klenda Martinez

Associate Product Manager: Jon Farnham

Editorial Assistant: Lauren Brody

Director of Marketing: Cheryl Costantini

Marketing Manager: Tristen Kendall

Marketing Coordinator: Julie Schuster

Senior Print Buyer: Julio Esperas

Director of Production: Patty Stephan

Senior Content Project Manager: Jill Braiewa

Developmental Editor: Amanda Brodkin

Copy Editor: Troy Lilly

Proofreader: Andrew Therriault

Indexer: Alexandra Nickerson

QA Manuscript Reviewers: John Freitas, Serge Palladino, Chris Scriver, Danielle Shaw, Marianne Snow, Teresa Storch

Art Director: Marissa Falco

Cover and Text Design: Joel Sadagursky

Cover Photo: Jon Chomitz

Compositor: GEX Publishing Services

For product information and technology assistance, contact us at
**Cengage Learning Customer & Sales Support, 1-800-354-9706**
For permission to use material from this text or product, submit all requests online at **www.cengage.com/permissions**
Further permissions questions can be emailed to
**permissionrequest@cengage.com**

ISBN-13: 978-1-4188-5977-0

ISBN-10: 1-4188-5977-X

**Course Technology**
20 Channel Center Street
Boston, Massachusetts 02210
USA

The resort photographs used in Chapters 1 and 2 are included with the permission of the Inn at Twaalfskill. The art in Chapter 4 is included with the permission of Mimei Thompson. All other photos are the property of the author of this text.

Cengage Learning is a leading provider of customized learning solutions with office locations around the globe, including Singapore, the United Kingdom, Australia, Mexico, Brazil and Japan. Locate your local office at:
**international.cengage.com/region**

Cengage Learning products are represented in Canada by Nelson Education, Ltd.

To learn more about Course Technology, visit **www.cengage.com/coursetechnology**
To learn more about Cengage Learning, visit **www.cengage.com**
Purchase any of our products at your local college bookstore or at our preferred online store **www.ichapters.com**

Printed in the United States of America
1 2 3 4 5 6 7 15 14 13 12 11 10 09

# Microsoft®
# Expression® Web 2
Comprehensive Concepts and Techniques

# Contents

Preface     viii
To the Student     xiv

## Microsoft EXPRESSION WEB 2

### CHAPTER ONE
### Creating an Expression Web Site

| | |
|---|---|
| **Objectives** | **EW 1** |
| **What Is Microsoft Expression Web?** | **EW 2** |
| **Project — Home Page** | **EW 2** |
| Overview | EW 4 |
| **Starting Expression Web** | **EW 5** |
| To Start Expression Web | EW 6 |
| **Expression Web Workspace** | **EW 7** |
| The Workspace Window | EW 7 |
| Toolbars | EW 8 |
| To Reset Workspace Layout | EW 9 |
| **Creating a Web Site** | **EW 10** |
| To Create a Web Site | EW 10 |
| To Open a Web Page | EW 14 |
| **Setting Page Properties** | **EW 14** |
| To Set Page Properties | EW 15 |
| **Entering Text** | **EW 20** |
| To Add a <Div> Tag | EW 20 |
| To Add Paragraph Text | EW 23 |
| To Add a Bulleted List | EW 25 |
| To Complete Page Content | EW 28 |
| **Saving Individual Web Pages** | **EW 30** |
| To Save a Web Page | EW 30 |
| **Applying Formatting and Styles** | **EW 30** |
| To Use the Quick Tag Selector | EW 31 |
| To Apply a Heading Style | EW 33 |
| To Center Text | EW 36 |
| Applying Font Characteristics | EW 36 |
| To Change Font Color | EW 37 |
| Changing Font Sizes | EW 38 |
| To Change Font Size | EW 39 |
| To Indent Text | EW 41 |
| To Italicize Text | EW 42 |
| Choosing a Font | EW 43 |
| To Change a Font | EW 44 |

| | |
|---|---|
| **Spell Checking Pages** | **EW 45** |
| To Spell Check a Page | EW 46 |
| **Switching Views** | **EW 48** |
| To Show Code and Split Views | EW 49 |
| Visual Aids and Quick Tags | EW 51 |
| To Hide and Display Visual Aids | EW 52 |
| **Previewing in Browsers** | **EW 54** |
| To Preview in a Browser | EW 54 |
| **Printing a Web Page** | **EW 55** |
| To Print a Web Page | EW 56 |
| **Closing Expression Web** | **EW 57** |
| To Close a Web Page | EW 57 |
| To Quit Expression Web | EW 58 |
| **Chapter Summary** | **EW 58** |
| **Learn It Online** | **EW 59** |
| **Apply Your Knowledge** | **EW 59** |
| **Extend Your Knowledge** | **EW 61** |
| **Make It Right** | **EW 62** |
| **In the Lab** | **EW 63** |
| **Cases and Places** | **EW 68** |

### CHAPTER TWO
### Working with Images and Links

| | |
|---|---|
| **Objectives** | **EW 71** |
| **Introduction** | **EW 72** |
| **Project — Enhancing the Boon Mountain Resort Web Site** | **EW 72** |
| Overview | EW 73 |
| Choosing Images and File Types | EW 74 |
| Technical Considerations for Image Files | EW 74 |
| **Accessibility Properties** | **EW 75** |
| **Inserting an Image** | **EW 76** |
| To Start Expression Web | EW 77 |
| To Open a Web Site | EW 77 |
| To Insert an Image | EW 80 |
| **Adjusting the Workspace Layout** | **EW 84** |
| Task Panes | EW 84 |
| To Close a Task Pane | EW 85 |
| To Display the Ruler | EW 87 |
| **Adjusting Proportions** | **EW 89** |
| To Resize an Image | EW 89 |

**Positioning an Image** **EW 93**
To Align an Image EW 94
Adding Borders and Spacing EW 95
To Add a Border to an Image EW 95
To Modify Image Margins EW 97
**Enhancing an Image** **EW 98**
To Add Transparency to an Image EW 99
The Clipboard EW 103
To Copy an Image to Other Pages EW 103
To Crop an Image EW 107
**Controlling Image Files** **EW 112**
Thumbnail Images EW 112
To Create a Thumbnail EW 113
To Create a Folder for Images EW 118
**Adding Navigational Links to a Site** **EW 121**
To Add an Internal Link EW 122
To Test Internal Links EW 126
To Copy and Paste Internal Links EW 128
To Add an External Link EW 130
To Test External Links EW 132
To Add a Bookmark EW 133
To Add an E-Mail Link EW 135
To Add a ScreenTip EW 137
To Preview the Site EW 138
To Close a Site and Quit Expression Web EW 139
**Chapter Summary** **EW 140**
**Learn It Online** **EW 140**
**Apply Your Knowledge** **EW 141**
**Extend Your Knowledge** **EW 142**
**Make It Right** **EW 144**
**In the Lab** **EW 145**
**Cases and Places** **EW 149**

**CHAPTER THREE**
**Working with Templates and Styles**
**Objectives** **EW 151**
**Introduction** **EW 152**
**Project — Personal Portfolio** **EW 152**
Overview EW 153
**Starting a New Web Site Using a Template** **EW 154**
To Start Expression Web and Reset the
Workspace Layout EW 156
Placeholders EW 156
To Create a New Web Site from a Template EW 157
**Specifying the Structure of the Site** **EW 160**
To Rename a Folder EW 161
To Rename a Web Page EW 162
**Modifying the Structure of a Web Site** **EW 163**
To Delete a Web Page EW 164
To Delete a Folder EW 166
To Add a Folder EW 167
To Add a Web Page EW 169
**Entering and Editing Text** **EW 172**
To Replace Template Placeholder Text EW 172
Pasting Text EW 177
To Paste Text EW 177

To Close Microsoft Word EW 182
Editing Text EW 182
To Edit Text EW 183
To Find and Replace Text EW 186
**Dynamic Web Page Template Pages** **EW 189**
To Make Global Changes to a Template EW 190
**Defining Styles and Style Sheets** **EW 193**
Style Sheet Types EW 194
Style Rule Syntax EW 194
To Modify a Style EW 195
To Create a Style EW 198
To Apply a Style EW 201
To Preview the Site EW 203
To Close a Site and Quit Expression Web EW 204
**Chapter Summary** **EW 204**
**Learn It Online** **EW 205**
**Apply Your Knowledge** **EW 205**
**Extend Your Knowledge** **EW 207**
**Make It Right** **EW 209**
**In the Lab** **EW 210**
**Cases and Places** **EW 215**

**EXPRESSION WEB DESIGN FEATURE**
**Web Design Basics**
**Objectives** **EW 217**
**Introduction** **EW 218**
**Web Site Purpose, Target Audience, and
Structure** **EW 218**
Establishing Your Site's Purpose EW 219
Identifying Your Site's Target Audience EW 220
Types of Web Pages EW 220
Site Structure EW 222
**Site Navigation System** **EW 224**
**Color Schemes and Page Layout** **EW 227**
Color Schemes EW 228
Page Length and Content Positioning EW 230
Balance, Proximity, Alignment, and Focus EW 232
**Writing Web Page Text** **EW 234**
**Web-Ready Images and Multimedia** **EW 236**
**Pre- and Post-Publishing Testing** **EW 237**
**Feature Summary** **EW 237**
**In the Lab** **EW 238**

**CHAPTER FOUR**
**Creating Styles and Layouts with CSS**
**Objectives** **EW 241**
**Introduction** **EW 242**
**Project — Gallery Web Site** **EW 242**
Overview EW 243
**Using CSS to Control Formatting and Layout** **EW 244**
CSS Syntax EW 244
**Using CSS to Prioritize Rules** **EW 246**
To Open a Web Site and Web Page EW 247
To Define an ID-Based Style EW 249
To Position Content Using a Class-Based Style EW 254
To Use the CSS Properties Task Pane EW 256

**Creating and Attaching Style Sheets** **EW 259**
To Create an External Style Sheet EW 260
Font Families EW 262
To Create a Font Family EW 262
Entering CSS Code EW 265
To Modify a Page in Code View EW 266
To Attach a Style Sheet EW 268
Pre-Built CSS Layouts EW 271
To Use Pre-Built CSS Layouts EW 271
To Copy and Paste Elements EW 274
To Complete Page Content EW 276
To Attach Multiple Style Sheets EW 280
To Add a Hyperlink EW 283
To Organize Style Sheets EW 284
To Create a CSS Report EW 286
To Preview the Site EW 288
**Chapter Summary** **EW 289**
**Learn It Online** **EW 290**
**Apply Your Knowledge** **EW 290**
**Extend Your Knowledge** **EW 292**
**Make It Right** **EW 294**
**In the Lab** **EW 295**
**Cases and Places** **EW 299**

**CHAPTER FIVE**
**Working with Data Tables and Inline Frames**
**Objectives** **EW 301**
**Introduction** **EW 302**
**Project — Hair Salon** **EW 302**
Overview EW 304
To Create a New Web Site and Web Page EW 305
**Using a Preformatted Style Sheet** **EW 309**
To Create a New Style Sheet EW 310
To Create a New Page and Attach a Style Sheet EW 314
**Creating Data Tables** **EW 316**
Working with Data Tables EW 316
To Insert a Data Table EW 316
**Table and Cell Properties** **EW 319**
To Change Table and Cell Properties EW 320
**Entering Text into Cells** **EW 323**
To Add Text to a Table EW 323
**Adding Images into Cells** **EW 326**
To Add Images to a Table EW 327
**Adding Rows and Columns** **EW 329**
The Tables Toolbar EW 329
To Add Rows and Columns EW 330
Table Fill EW 333
To Use Table Fill EW 334
**Merging and Splitting Cells** **EW 336**
To Merge Table Cells EW 337
To Split Table Cells EW 338
**Formatting Table Text** **EW 340**
To Apply Styles to Table Text EW 340
**Converting Text to a Table** **EW 342**
To Convert Text to a Table EW 342
To Distribute Rows and Columns EW 345

**Table AutoFormat** **EW 346**
To Use Table AutoFormat EW 347
**About Inline Frames** **EW 348**
To Create an I-Frame EW 349
To Target Links in an I-Frame EW 352
**Using Frames and Tables to Lay Out a Web Page** **EW 354**
**Chapter Summary** **EW 354**
**Learn It Online** **EW 355**
**Apply Your Knowledge** **EW 355**
**Extend Your Knowledge** **EW 358**
**Make It Right** **EW 359**
**In the Lab** **EW 360**
**Cases and Places** **EW 365**

**CHAPTER SIX**
**Adding Interactivity**
**Objectives** **EW 367**
**Introduction** **EW 368**
**Project — Farm Stand Web Site** **EW 368**
Overview EW 370
**Creating an Interactive Navigation Area** **EW 372**
Interactivity and Web Browsers EW 372
To Create an Interactive Button EW 373
To Duplicate an Interactive Button EW 379
**Editing and Organizing Interactive Buttons** **EW 379**
To Edit an Interactive Button EW 380
To Test Interactive Buttons EW 382
To Copy and Paste the Navigation Area EW 385
To Organize the Button Images into Folders EW 387
**Defining Behaviors** **EW 390**
Creating a Jump Menu EW 391
To Add a Jump Menu Behavior EW 391
Creating a Status Bar Behavior EW 396
To Add a Status Bar Behavior EW 397
Creating a Swap Image Behavior EW 398
To Add a Swap Image Behavior EW 399
To Modify a Swap Image Behavior EW 402
**Creating Image Maps** **EW 405**
To Add an Image Map EW 405
**Chapter Summary** **EW 409**
**Learn It Online** **EW 410**
**Apply Your Knowledge** **EW 410**
**Extend Your Knowledge** **EW 413**
**Make It Right** **EW 414**
**In the Lab** **EW 416**
**Cases and Places** **EW 420**

**E-COMMERCE FEATURE**
**E-Commerce**
**Objectives** **EW 423**
**The Role of E-Commerce in Today's Business Environment** **EW 424**
**E-Commerce Business Models** **EW 424**
Business-to-Consumer (B2C) EW 425
Business-to-Business (B2B) EW 425
Consumer-to-Consumer (C2C) EW 426
Consumer-to-Business (C2B) EW 427

Business-to-Government (B2G)   EW 427
Business-to-Employee (B2E)   EW 428
**Web Site E-Commerce Elements**   **EW 429**
Product Catalog   EW 429
Shopping Cart   EW 430
Payment Processors, Payment Gateways, and
    Merchant Accounts   EW 432
Order Fulfillment   EW 434
Customer Support   EW 435
Transaction Security   EW 435
**Adding E-Commerce Capability to a Web Site**   **EW 436**
Third-Party Payment Processor Solution   EW 436
All-in-One E-Commerce Solution   EW 437
**Feature Summary**   **EW 439**
**In the Lab**   **EW 439**

**CHAPTER SEVEN**
**Working with Forms**
**Objectives**   **EW 441**
**Introduction**   **EW 442**
**Project — Farm Stand Web Site**   **EW 442**
Overview   EW 444
**Defining Forms and Form Controls**   **EW 445**
Understanding Databases   EW 445
Defining Form Controls   EW 446
To Create a Page from Another Page   EW 448
To Create a Form Area   EW 450
To Create a Table   EW 452
**Adding Form Controls**   **EW 453**
Text Box Controls and Text Areas   EW 454
To Add a Text Box Control   EW 455
To Assign Properties to a Text Box Control   EW 457
Drop-Down Boxes   EW 458
To Add a Drop-Down Box Control   EW 459
Group Boxes   EW 462
To Create a Group Box Control   EW 463
Using Check Boxes and Radio Buttons   EW 464
To Add Checkbox Controls   EW 465
To Add a Radio Button Group Box Control   EW 468
To Add Radio Button Controls   EW 469
To Add a Text Area Control   EW 471
**Submitting and Collecting Data**   **EW 472**
To Add a Submit Button   EW 473
To Create and Apply a New Style   EW 475
To Add a Link to a Page   EW 478
To Test the Form   EW 481
**Chapter Summary**   **EW 483**
**Learn It Online**   **EW 483**
**Apply Your Knowledge**   **EW 484**
**Extend Your Knowledge**   **EW 486**
**Make It Right**   **EW 488**
**In the Lab**   **EW 489**
**Cases and Places**   **EW 496**

**CHAPTER EIGHT**
**Testing and Publishing Your Web Site**
**Objectives**   **EW 497**
**Introduction**   **EW 498**
**Project — Farm Stand Web Site**   **EW 498**
Overview   EW 500
**Running and Reviewing a Site**
    **Summary Report**   **EW 500**
To Run a Site Summary Report   EW 502
To Fix an Unlinked File   EW 503
To Organize Site Folder Contents   EW 507
To Verify External Hyperlinks   EW 509
To Save a Report as an HTML Page   EW 512
**Running and Reviewing an**
    **Accessibility Report**   **EW 516**
To Create an Accessibility Report   EW 518
**Running and Reviewing a**
    **Compatibility Report**   **EW 518**
To Create a Compatibility Report   EW 519
**Understanding Web Site Hosting**   **EW 522**
**Defining Web Server Types**   **EW 523**
**Setting Publishing Options**   **EW 524**
To Set Publishing Options   EW 525
**Optimizing HTML**   **EW 526**
To Optimize HTML   EW 526
To Publish Files to a Remote Folder   EW 528
To Manage Files on a Remote Server   EW 530
**Chapter Summary**   **EW 534**
**Learn It Online**   **EW 534**
**Apply Your Knowledge**   **EW 535**
**Extend Your Knowledge**   **EW 537**
**Make It Right**   **EW 538**
**In the Lab**   **EW 540**
**Cases and Places**   **EW 545**

**CHAPTER NINE**
**Building a Web Site with**
**CSS-Based Templates**
**Objectives**   **EW 547**
**Introduction**   **EW 548**
**Project — Juice Bar Web Site**   **EW 548**
Overview   EW 550
To Create a New Web Site and Add
    Web Pages   EW 551
**Creating a New Dynamic Web Template**   **EW 554**
To Create a New Dynamic Web Template   EW 554
**Importing Files**   **EW 555**
To Import Files into a Site   EW 556
**Adding Background Images**   **EW 557**
To Add a Background Image to a Page   EW 558
To Add Page Content   EW 561
**Creating ID-Based Styles**   **EW 567**
**Using List-Based Navigation**   **EW 568**
To Create a List-Based Navigation Area   EW 569
To Add CSS Rules to the List   EW 571
To Create Rollovers   EW 574

**Adding Sidebars** **EW 579**
To Add a Sidebar Element EW 580
**Using Typography to Improve Readability** **EW 584**
To Specify Line Height EW 584
To Specify Line Length EW 586
**Adding Drop Cap Styles** **EW 588**
To Add a Drop Cap Style EW 589
**Defining Editable Regions** **EW 590**
To Define Editable Regions EW 590
To Attach a Dynamic Web Template to
Existing Pages EW 592
To Insert and Format Home Page Text EW 594
To Preview a Web Page in a Browser EW 600
**Chapter Summary** **EW 601**
**Learn It Online** **EW 602**
**Apply Your Knowledge** **EW 602**
**Extend Your Knowledge** **EW 606**
**Make It Right** **EW 608**
**In the Lab** **EW 610**
**Cases and Places** **EW 617**

**WEB SITE MARKETING FEATURE**
**Marketing and Maintaining**
**a Web Site**
**Objectives** **EW 619**
**Introduction** **EW 620**
**Online Marketing Tools** **EW 620**
Search Engine Optimization (SEO) EW 620
Search Tool Submission EW 621
Search Tool Paid Placement Programs EW 622
Link Exchange EW 625
Online Ads and Advertising Networks EW 625
Affiliate Marketing Programs EW 627
Business Blogs EW 628
Permission-Based E-Mail Advertising and
Newsletters EW 628
**Offline Print and Word-of-Mouth**
**Advertising Tools** **EW 629**
**Web Site Maintenance** **EW 629**
**Web Site Performance Evaluation** **EW 629**
Web Server Log Analysis EW 630
Web Analytics EW 630
**Feature Summary** **EW 631**
**In the Lab** **EW 631**

**APPENDIX A**
**Using Microsoft Expression Web 2 Help**
**Introduction** **APP 1**
To Open the Expression Web 2 Help Window APP 2
**The Expression Web 2 Help Window** **APP 3**
Browsing Help Topics APP 3
To Browse Help Topics APP 4
The Toolbar APP 5
To Browse Help Topics Using the Table of
Contents Pane APP 7
The Search Bar APP 8
To Search Help Topics Using the Search Bar APP 9
**Using Help** **APP 11**

**APPENDIX B**
**Web Standards and Accessibility**
**Introduction** **APP 12**
**Web Standards** **APP 12**
**Web Accessibility** **APP 14**

**APPENDIX C**
**Publishing Content to the Web**
**Introduction** **APP 16**
**Publishing Your Site Using Expression Web** **APP 19**
Setting the Remote Web Site Properties APP 19
Remote Web Site View APP 21
**Publishing Your Site Using FTP Client Software** **APP 23**

**APPENDIX D**
**Microsoft Expression Studio 2**
**Introduction** **APP 25**
**Expression Web** **APP 25**
**Expression Design** **APP 26**
**Expression Media** **APP 27**
**Expression Blend** **APP 28**
**Expression Encoder** **APP 30**

**APPENDIX E**
**Using Expression Web in Windows XP**
To Start Expression Web APP 33
To Open an Existing Web Site APP 34
To Close a Web Site APP 36

**APPENDIX F**
**Changing Screen Resolution**
To Change the Screen Resolution APP 38

**Index** **IND 1**

**Quick Reference Summary** **QR 1**

# Preface

Shelly Cashman Series® offers the finest textbooks in computer education. We are proud of the fact that our textbooks have been the most widely used books in education. *Microsoft Expression Web 2: Comprehensive Concepts and Techniques* continues with the innovation, quality and reliability that you have come to expect from the Shelly Cashman Series.

Microsoft Expression Web is known as the standard in web authoring. Microsoft Expression Web 2 enhances the work experience for users by providing a WYSIWYG design environment that can be used to create complex, standards-compliant, multi-page Web sites using tools such as dialog boxes, task panes, and dynamic Web templates without needing to enter HTML or CSS code.

In this Microsoft Expression Web 2 book, you will find an educationally sound and easy-to-follow pedagogy that combines a step-by-step approach with corresponding screens. All projects and exercises in this book are designed to take full advantage of the Microsoft Expression Web 2 enhancements. The Other Ways feature offers in-depth knowledge of Expression Web. The popular Q&A feature provides answers to common questions students have about the Web design processes. The Learn It Online page presents a wealth of additional exercises to ensure your students have all the reinforcement they need. The project material is developed carefully to ensure that students will see the importance of learning Expression Web for future coursework.

## Objectives of This Textbook

*Microsoft Expression Web 2: Comprehensive Concepts and Techniques* is intended for a course that includes an introduction to Expression Web 2. A basic understanding of the Internet, computers, data entry, and program tools such as dialog boxes and menu bars is assumed. The objectives of this book are:

- To teach the fundamentals of Microsoft Expression Web 2

- To expose students to the planning and decision-making process involved in creating Web pages, Web sites, dynamic Web templates, and style sheets

- To acquaint students with the proper procedures to create Web pages, Web sites, and dynamic Web templates that include text, images, hyperlinks, tables, I-frames, interactivity, and forms, and are suitable for coursework, professional purposes, and personal use

- To help students use the Expression Web tools and user-interface to create Web pages, Web sites, and style sheets that are easy to create, maintain, and use

- To develop an exercise-oriented approach that allows learning by doing

- To teach students the necessary steps to prepare a completed Web site for beta testing, publication, and Web site hosting, using Expression Web reports and tools

# The Shelly Cashman Approach

Features of the Shelly Cashman Series Microsoft Expression Web 2 books include:

- **Project Orientation** Each chapter in the book presents a project with a practical problem and complete solution in an easy-to-understand approach.

- **Plan Ahead Boxes** The project orientation is enhanced by the inclusion of Plan Ahead boxes. These new features prepare students to create successful projects by encouraging them to think strategically about what they are trying to accomplish before they begin working.

- **Step-by-Step, Screen-by-Screen Instructions** Each of the tasks required to complete a project is clearly identified throughout the chapter. Now, the step-by-step instructions provide a context beyond point-and-click. Each step explains why students are performing a task, or the result of performing a certain action. Found on the screens accompanying each step, callouts give students the information they need to know when they need to know it. Now, we've used color to distinguish the content in the callouts. The Explanatory callouts (in black) summarize what is happening on the screen and the Navigational callouts (in red) show students where to click.

- **Q&A** Found within many of the step-by-step sequences, Q&As raise the kinds of questions students may ask when working through a step sequence and provide answers about what they are doing, why they are doing it, and how that task might be approached differently. Q&As also help students troubleshoot any problems or inconsistencies they might encounter.

- **Experimental Steps** These new steps, within our step-by-step instructions, encourage students to explore and experiment. These steps are not necessary to complete the projects, but are designed to increase the confidence with the software and build problem-solving skills.

- **Thoroughly Tested Projects** Unparalleled quality is ensured because every screen in the book is produced by the author only after performing a step, and then each project must pass Course Technology's Quality Assurance program.

- **Other Ways Boxes and Quick Reference Summary** The Other Ways boxes displayed at the end of many of the step-by-step sequences specify the other ways to do the task completed in the steps. Thus, the steps and the Other Ways box make a comprehensive reference unit. A Quick Reference Summary at the end of the book contains all of the tasks presented in the chapters, and all ways identified of accomplishing the tasks.

- **BTWs** These marginal annotations provide background information, tips, and answers to common questions that complement the topics covered, adding depth and perspective to the learning process.

- **Integration of the World Wide Web** The World Wide Web is integrated into the Expression Web learning experience by (1) a Quick Reference Summary Web page that summarizes the ways to complete tasks (mouse, shortcut menu, and keyboard); (2) the Learn It Online section at the end of each chapter, which has chapter reinforcement exercises, learning games, and other types of student activities; and (3) text annotations that refer students to the Expression Web site, /scsite/ew2, for more information on specific topics.

- **End-of-Chapter Student Activities** Extensive student activities at the end of each chapter provide the student with plenty of opportunities to reinforce the materials learned in the chapter through hands-on assignments. Several new types of activities have been added that challenge the student in new ways to expand their knowledge, and to apply their new skills to a project with personal relevance.

---

**Q&A**

What is the red, wavy line under Arborwood?

Expression Web underlines a word with a red, wavy line to indicate that the word is not in its dictionary. You will learn more about checking spelling later in Chapter 1.

**Other Ways**

1. As you are typing, right-click a flagged word to display a shortcut menu that includes a list of suggested spelling corrections

2. Press the F7 key to start the spell checker

**BTW**

**File Extensions**
HTML files can be saved with either the .html or .htm file extension. DOS-based operating systems restricted file extensions to three letters, necessitating the abbreviation of .html to .htm. All of today's browsers recognize both file extensions.

## Organization of This Textbook

*Microsoft Expression Web 2: Comprehensive Concepts and Techniques* consists of nine chapters on Microsoft Expression Web 2, three special features, six appendices, and a Quick Reference Summary.

## End-of-Chapter Student Activities

A notable strength of the Shelly Cashman Series Microsoft Expression Web 2 books is the extensive student activities at the end of each chapter. Well-structured student activities can

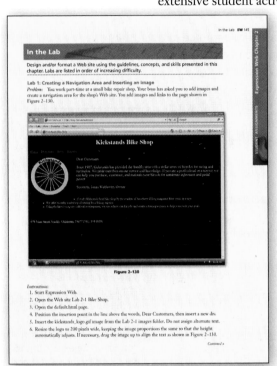

make the difference between students merely participating in a class and students retaining the information they learn. The activities in the Shelly Cashman Series books include the following.

**CHAPTER SUMMARY** A concluding paragraph, followed by a listing of the tasks completed within a chapter together with the pages on which the step-by-step, screen-by-screen explanations appear.

**LEARN IT ONLINE** Every chapter features a Learn It Online section that is composed of six exercises. These exercises include True/False, Multiple Choice, Short Answer, Flash Cards, Practice Test, and Learning Games.

**APPLY YOUR KNOWLEDGE** This exercise usually requires students to open and manipulate a file from the Data Files that parallels the activities learned in the chapter. To obtain a copy of the Data Files for Students, follow the instructions on the inside back cover of this text.

**EXTEND YOUR KNOWLEDGE** This exercise allows students to extend and expand on the skills learned within the chapter.

**MAKE IT RIGHT** This exercise requires students to analyze a document, identify errors and issues, and correct those errors and issues using skills learned in the chapter.

**IN THE LAB** Three all new in-depth assignments per chapter require students to utilize the chapter concepts and techniques to solve problems on a computer.

**CASES AND PLACES** Five unique real-world case-study situations, including Make It Personal, an open-ended project that relates to student's personal lives, and one small-group activity.

## Instructor Resources CD-ROM

The Shelly Cashman Series is dedicated to providing you with all of the tools you need to make your class a success. Information about all supplementary materials is available through your Course Technology representative or by calling one of the following telephone numbers: Colleges, Universities, and Continuing Ed departments, 1-800-648-7450; High Schools, 1-800-824-5179; and Career Colleges, Business, Government, Library and Resellers, 1-800-477-3692.

The Instructor Resources CD-ROM for this textbook include both teaching and testing aids. The contents of each item on the Instructor Resources CD-ROM (ISBN 1-4239-1232-2) are described on the following page.

**INSTRUCTOR'S MANUAL** The Instructor's Manual consists of Microsoft Word files, which include chapter objectives, lecture notes, teaching tips, classroom activities, lab activities, quick quizzes, figures and boxed elements summarized in the chapters, and a glossary page. The new format of the Instructor's Manual will allow you to map through every chapter easily.

**SYLLABUS** Sample syllabi, which can be customized easily to a course, are included. The syllabi cover policies, class and lab assignments and exams, and procedural information.

**FIGURE FILES** Illustrations for every figure in the textbook are available in electronic form. Use this ancillary to present a slide show in lecture or to print transparencies for use in lecture with an overhead projector. If you have a personal computer and LCD device, this ancillary can be an effective tool for presenting lectures.

**POWERPOINT PRESENTATIONS** PowerPoint Presentations is a multimedia lecture presentation system that provides slides for each chapter. Presentations are based on chapter objectives. Use this presentation system to present well-organized lectures that are both interesting and knowledge based. PowerPoint Presentations provides consistent coverage at schools that use multiple lecturers.

**SOLUTIONS TO EXERCISES** Solutions are included for the end-of-chapter exercises, as well as the Chapter Reinforcement exercises.

**TEST BANK & TEST ENGINE** In the ExamView test bank, you will find our standard question types (40 multiple-choice, 25 true/false, 20 completion) and new objective-based question types (5 modified multiple-choice, 5 modified true/false and 10 matching). Critical Thinking questions also are included (3 essays and 2 cases with 2 questions each) totaling the test bank to 112 questions for every chapter with page number references, and when appropriate, figure references. A version of the test bank you can print also is included. The test bank comes with a copy of the test engine, ExamView, the ultimate tool for your objective-based testing needs. ExamView is a state-of-the-art test builder that is easy to use. ExamView enables you to create paper-, LAN-, or Web-based tests from test banks designed specifically for your Course Technology textbook. Utilize the ultra-efficient QuickTest Wizard to create tests in less than five minutes by taking advantage of Course Technology's question banks, or customize your own exams from scratch.

**DATA FILES FOR STUDENTS** All the files that are required by students to complete the exercises are included. You can distribute the files on the Instructor Resources CD-ROM to your students over a network, or you can have them follow the instructions on the inside back cover of this book to obtain a copy of the Data Files for Students.

**ADDITIONAL ACTIVITIES FOR STUDENTS** These additional activities consist of Chapter Reinforcement Exercises, which are true/false, multiple-choice, and short answer questions that help students gain confidence in the material learned.

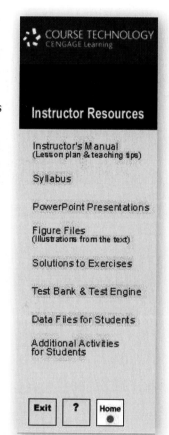

## SAM 2007: Assessment & Training and Project Grading Solutions

SAM 2007 now contains Assessment, Training, and Projects assignments. Instructors may choose to assign any or all of these assignment types based on the needs of the course. The SAM system includes robust reporting, classroom management, section management, and scheduling to help instructors manage their classes with ease. The newest addition to the SAM family is SAM Projects. SAM Projects is live-in-the-application grading software that enables students to complete projects in Word, Excel, and PowerPoint 2007 and have them graded instantly. SAM Projects assesses a student's ability to connect skills and complete tasks in the context of real-world projects. SAM Projects evaluates whether or not a student can complete a document, spreadsheet, or presentation, allowing them to solve a problem or make a sound business decision. This tangible experience prepares today's learners for success in the workplace. Designed to be used with the Shelley Cashman series, SAM 2007 includes built-in page references so students can print helpful study guides that match the textbooks used in class.

## Student Edition Labs

Our Web-based interactive labs help students master hundreds of computer concepts, including input and output devices, file management and desktop applications, computer ethics, virus protection, and much more. Featuring up-to-the-minute content, eye-popping graphics, and rich animation, the highly interactive Student Edition Labs offer students an alternative way to learn through dynamic observation, step-by-step practice, and challenging review questions.

## Content for Online Learning

Course Technology has partnered with Blackboard, the leading distance learning solution provider and class-management platform today. In addition to providing content for Blackboard and WebCT, Course Technology provides premium online content for multiple learning management system platforms. To access this material, simply visit our password-protected instructor resources available at www.cengage.com/coursetechnology. The resources available for download may include topic reviews, case projects, review questions, test banks, practice tests, custom syllabi, and more. For additional information or for an instructor username and password, please contact your sales representative.

## CourseCasts Learning on the Go. Always Available...Always Relevant.

Our fast-paced world is driven by technology. You know because you are an active participant — always on the go, always keeping up with technological trends, and always learning new ways to embrace technology to power your life. Let CourseCasts, hosted by Ken Baldauf of Florida State University, be your guide into weekly updates in this ever-changing space. These timely, relevant podcasts are produced weekly and are available for download at http://coursecasts.course.com or directly from iTunes (search by CourseCasts). CourseCasts are a perfect solution to getting students (and even instructors) to learn on the go!

## CourseNotes

Course Technology's CourseNotes are six-panel quick reference cards that reinforce the most important and widely used features of a software application in a visual and user-friendly format. CourseNotes serve as a great reference tool during and after the student completes the course. CourseNotes for Microsoft Office 2007, Word 2007, Excel 2007, Access 2007, PowerPoint 2007, Windows Vista, and more are available now!

**course|notes**™
quick reference guide

## To the Student . . . Getting the Most Out of Your Book

Welcome to *Microsoft Expression Web 2: Comprehensive Concepts and Techniques*. You can save yourself a lot of time and gain a better understanding of Expression Web if you spend a few minutes reviewing the figures and callouts in this section.

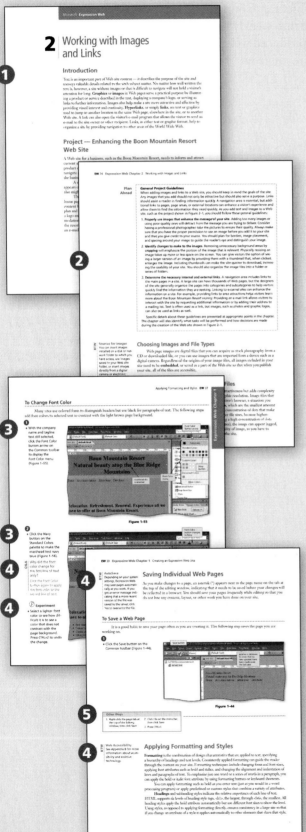

### 1 PROJECT ORIENTATION

Each chapter's project presents a practical problem and shows the solution in the first figure of the chapter. The project orientation lets you see firsthand how problems are solved from start to finish using application software and computers.

### 2 PROJECT PLANNING GUIDELINES AND PLAN AHEAD BOXES

Overall planning guidelines at the beginning of a chapter and Plan Ahead boxes throughout encourage you to think critically about how to accomplish the next goal before you actually begin working.

### 3 CONSISTENT STEP-BY-STEP, SCREEN-BY-SCREEN PRESENTATION

Chapter solutions are built using a step-by-step, screen-by-screen approach. This pedagogy allows you to build the solution on a computer as you read through the chapter. Generally, each step includes an explanation that indicates the result of the step.

### 4 MORE THAN JUST STEP-BY-STEP

BTW annotations in the margins of the book, Q&As in the steps, and substantive text in the paragraphs provide background information, tips, and answers to common questions that complement the topics covered, adding depth and perspective. When you finish with this book, you will be ready to use Expression Web to solve problems on your own. Experimental steps provide you with opportunities to step out on your own to try features of the programs, and pick up right where you left off in the chapter.

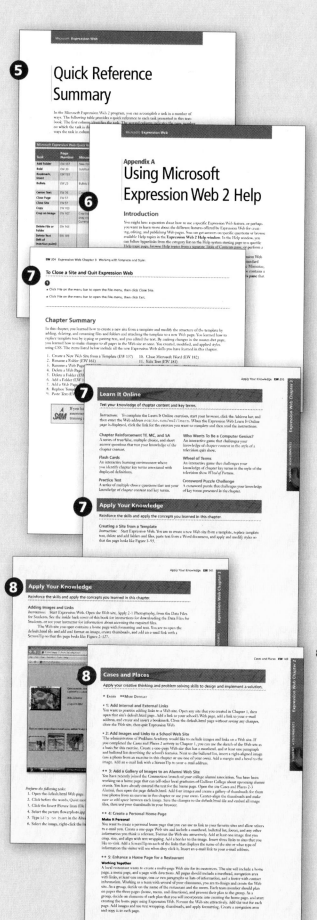

**5 OTHER WAYS BOXES AND QUICK REFERENCE SUMMARY**
Other Ways boxes that follow many of the step sequences and a Quick Reference Summary at the back of the book explain the other ways to complete the task presented, such as using the mouse, shortcut menu, and keyboard.

**6 EMPHASIS ON GETTING HELP WHEN YOU NEED IT**
Appendix A shows you how to use all the elements of Expression Web Help. Being able to answer your own questions will increase your productivity and reduce your frustrations by minimizing the time it takes to learn how to complete a task.

**7 REVIEW, REINFORCEMENT, AND EXTENSION**
After you successfully step through a project in a chapter, a section titled Chapter Summary identifies the tasks with which you should be familiar. Terms you should know for test purposes are bold in the text. The Learn It Online section at the end of each chapter offers reinforcement in the form of review questions, learning games, and practice tests. Also included are exercises that require you to extend your learning beyond the book.

**8 LABORATORY EXERCISES**
If you really want to learn how to use the programs, then you must design and implement solutions to problems on your own. Every chapter concludes with several carefully developed laboratory assignments that increase in complexity.

Learning styles of students have changed, but the Shelly Cashman Series' dedication to their success has remained steadfast for over 30 years. We are committed to continually updating our approach and content to reflect the way today's students learn and experience new technology.

This focus on the user is reflected in our bold new cover design, which features photographs of real students using the Shelly Cashman Series in their courses. Each book features a different user, reflecting the many ages, experiences, and backgrounds of all of the students learning with our books. When you use the Shelly Cashman Series, you can be assured that you are learning computer skills using the most effective courseware available.

We would like to thank the administration and faculty at the participating schools for their help in making our vision a reality. Most of all, we'd like to thank the wonderful students from all over the world who learn

# 1 | Creating an Expression Web Site

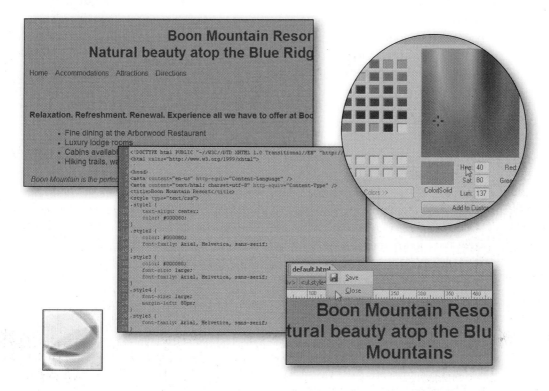

## Objectives

You will have mastered the material in this chapter when you can:

- Start and quit Expression Web
- Describe the features of Expression Web's main window
- Create a new Expression Web site
- Set page properties
- Enter and format text
- Create headings and lists

- Switch views
- Spell check a page
- Save a page
- Show and hide visual aids
- Use Quick Tag Selectors
- Display a page in a browser
- Close an Expression Web site

# 1 | Creating an Expression Web Site

## What Is Microsoft Expression Web?

**Microsoft Expression Web 2** is a full-featured Web site authoring program that allows you to create professional looking Web sites. A **Web site** is a collection of connected Web pages that contain text, images, or video. With Expression Web, you can create any type of Web site, from a one-page personal site to a sophisticated professional site consisting of hundreds of pages. Expression Web provides a **What You See Is What You Get (WYSIWYG)** design interface; in Design view, you can see exactly how the layout and formatting will appear in a browser and make necessary changes while editing. Expression Web provides automated tools for creating Web pages and Web sites.

You can use Expression Web to create and edit HTML files that contain the content of a page, and Cascading Style Sheets (CSS) files that control the formatting and layout of text and objects on a page or on multiple pages. Expression Web tools such as the design interface, task panes, and dialog boxes assist you in entering content and defining the style rules, without you having to know CSS and HTML codes. Expression Web also provides a full-featured HTML/XHTML editor for viewing and entering code, and allows you to view and modify the CSS code.

Expression Web is part of the **Microsoft Expression Studio 2** program suite. Appendix D provides more information on the various products in Expression Studio and describes how they work together.

**Project Planning Guidelines**

> Before you can begin to create a Web site, you must do some initial planning and get approval on the plan from your client or colleagues. You will need to establish the goal or purpose of the Web site, the type of site (such as informational or e-commerce), and identify the target users you want to attract to your site. Next, you should conduct research to learn how comparable sites are designed. With these elements defined, you should create a plan that specifies the content and layout of your site. After establishing the basic structure and content of your site, you will be ready to develop the site and test it with multiple browsers. Finally, after the site is complete, you can publish it to a Web server and begin marketing your site to attract visitors. Each project in this book provides practical applications of these guidelines.

## Project—Home Page

Boon Mountain Resort is located in Redhat, Georgia. The resort has been in business for one year and now would like to have a Web site to promote its many features. The resort has an excellent restaurant, luxury lodge rooms, and individual cabins located throughout the property. Nearby hiking trails and water sports are available for guests. The resort intends to promote itself to potential guests through a Web site with pages for accommodations, attractions, and directions, along with a home page.

The project in this chapter follows general guidelines and uses Expression Web to create the home page shown in Figure 1–1. This home page is the entry to the Boon Mountain Resort's Web site, and will need text and formatting, and, eventually, graphics and hyperlinks. You will create a navigation area to which you will add links to other site pages in the next chapter. In Chapter 1, you will create the text for  Boon Mountain Resort's home page, and in the next chapter, you will enhance your Web site by adding pages, images, and links.

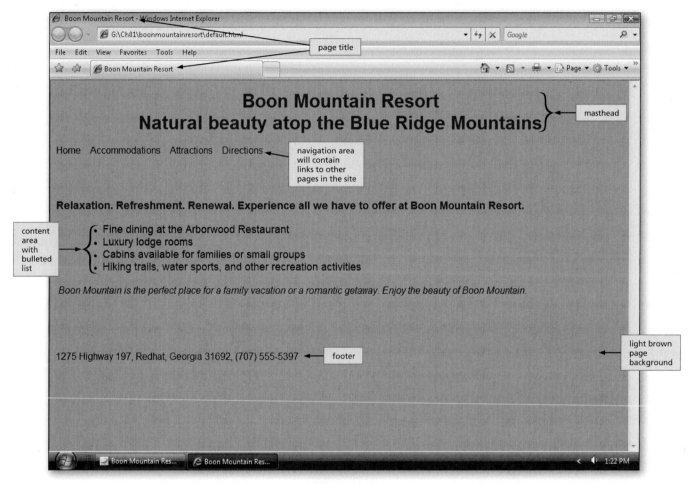

**Figure 1–1**

Figure 1–2 illustrates a plan showing site layout and content for Boon Mountain Resort.

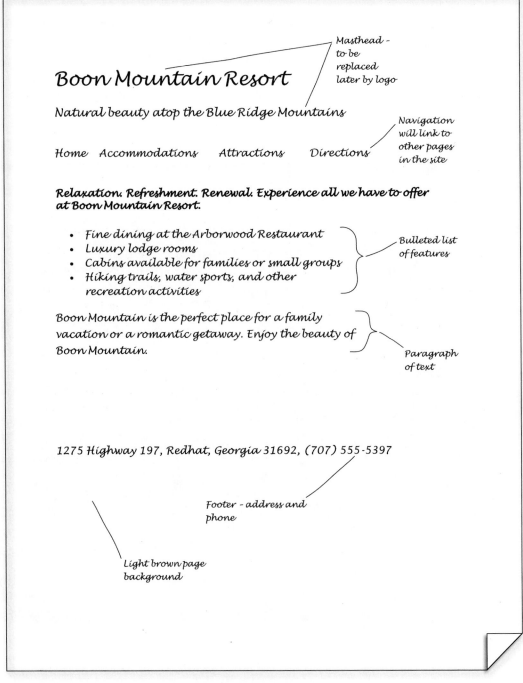

*Boon Mountain Resort*

*Natural beauty atop the Blue Ridge Mountains*

*Home   Accommodations      Attractions        Directions*

**Masthead - to be replaced later by logo**

**Navigation will link to other pages in the site**

**Relaxation. Refreshment. Renewal. Experience all we have to offer at Boon Mountain Resort.**

- *Fine dining at the Arborwood Restaurant*
- *Luxury lodge rooms*
- *Cabins available for families or small groups*
- *Hiking trails, water sports, and other recreation activities*

**Bulleted list of features**

*Boon Mountain is the perfect place for a family vacation or a romantic getaway. Enjoy the beauty of Boon Mountain.*

**Paragraph of text**

*1275 Highway 197, Redhat, Georgia 31692, (707) 555-5397*

**Footer - address and phone**

**Light brown page background**

**Figure 1–2**

# Overview

As you read this chapter, you will learn how to create the Web site shown in Figure 1–1 by performing these general tasks:

- Open the Expression Web program.
- Create an Expression Web site.
- Set page properties.
- Add page divisions.
- Enter text on the page.

- Format text on the page.
- Use visual aids and tags.
- Save the page.
- Preview the page.
- Print the page.

---

**General Project Guidelines**

When creating an Expression Web site, the actions you perform and decisions you make will affect the pages and links included in the site. As you create a Web site, such as the project shown in Figure 1–1, you should follow these general guidelines:

1. **Choose a Web site structure to use as the starting point for the site.** A Web site consists of one or more Web pages. Determine the purpose of the site, such as commercial or personal, then determine the number of pages and how site users will navigate to the pages.

2. **Determine folder structure and location and file naming conventions for the Web site files.** You must save all of the related files and folders for the Web site in one location.

3. **Determine the page properties or settings that will apply to the pages.** You can choose page settings, such as page title and keywords, using the Page Properties dialog box.

4. **Decide what the page layout will look like.** Page **layout**, which is the placement of text and objects, contributes to the look and consistency of a site. Well-arranged elements, such as a company logo or a navigation bar with links to the main pages of a site, keep the visitor interacting with the site longer and give the site a professional look.

5. **Determine the text content for the page.** Use text to convey the message with as few words as possible. Easy-to-read content encourages visitors to consider your product or service.

6. **Design the format for the text elements on the page.** The use of headings, fonts, lists, and color helps to identify important content and assists the visitor when scanning the page for specific content.

When necessary, specific details about these guidelines are presented at appropriate points in the chapter. The chapter also will identify the tasks performed and decisions made during the creation of the Web site shown in Figure 1–1.

**Plan Ahead**

---

# Starting Expression Web

If you are using a computer to step through the project in this chapter, and you want your screen to match the figures in this book, you should change your screen's resolution to 1024 × 768. For more information about how to change a computer's resolution, read Appendix F.

**BTW**

**File Extensions**
HTML files can be saved with either the .html or .htm file extension. DOS-based operating systems restricted file extensions to three letters, necessitating the abbreviation of .html to .htm. All of today's browsers recognize both file extensions.

## To Start Expression Web

The following steps, which assume Windows Vista is running, start Expression Web based on a typical installation. You may need to ask your instructor how to start Expression Web for your computer.

**Note:** If you are using Window XP, see Appendix E for alternate steps.

- Click the Start button on the Windows Vista taskbar to display the Start menu.

- Click All Programs at the bottom of the left pane on the Start menu to display the All Programs list (Figure 1–3).

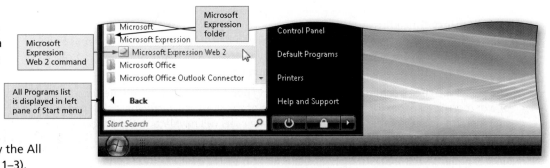

**Figure 1–3**

- Click the Microsoft Expression folder on the All Programs list to display the Microsoft Expression list.

- Click Microsoft Expression Web 2 to start Expression Web and display a new blank Web page in the Expression Web editing window (Figure 1–4).

**Q&A** Why does Expression Web sometimes open a Web site and other times open with a blank Web page named Untitled_1.html?

When you quit Expression Web without closing the Web site you are working on, Expression Web remembers the site and auto- matically opens it the next time Expression Web starts. If no pre- vious site is in Expression Web's memory, it starts with a blank page named Untitled_1.html.

**Q&A** Sometimes when opening Expression Web, an error message displays. What does that error mean?

If you quit Expression Web without closing a Web site first, Expression Web will try to open that site the next time Expression Web is started. If the site was saved on an external drive such as a USB flash drive, Expression Web looks for that drive address; if the location is not available (such as when the USB flash drive has been removed), the server error is generated. Just click OK to proceed.

**Figure 1–4**

| Other Ways |
| --- |
| 1. Double-click the Microsoft Expression Web 2 icon on the desktop, if one is present    2. Click Microsoft Expression Web 2 on the Start menu |

# Expression Web Workspace

Expression Web opens with a menu, toolbar, status bar, editing window, and four task panes for adding components and managing site content. When you first open Expression Web, a new blank HTML page displays with the name, Untitled_1.html.

## The Workspace Window

The workspace window shown in Figure 1–5 is where you build your Web site. The **workspace** contains the tools necessary to edit and manage Web pages. You can customize the workspace to contain the tools you use most often.

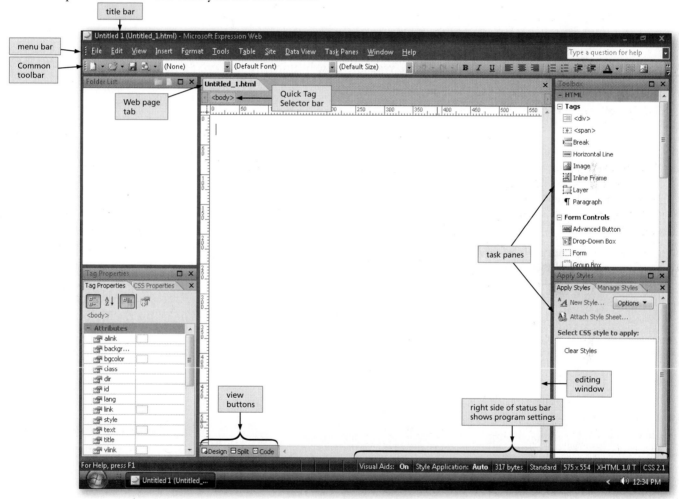

**Figure 1–5**

**Title Bar** The **title bar** at the top of the screen shows the application name and filename of the current Web page.

**Menu Bar** The **menu bar** at the top of the workspace contains all of the Expression Web commands.

**Common Toolbar** The **Common toolbar** is located below the menu bar and contains buttons for the most commonly used commands.

BTW

**Other Views**
When the Web Site tab is active, the views change to Folder, Remote Web Site, Reports, and Hyperlinks. Folder view is used to manage files and folders. Remote Web Site shows files located on a remote server. Reports show content and status of site elements, and Hyperlinks view shows links to pages within the site.

**Editing Window**   The **editing window** is where you create your Web page using the various Expression Web tools.

**Web Page Tab**   The **Web page tab** shows the filename of the page being edited as well as any other open pages.

**Quick Tag Selector Bar**   The **Quick Tag Selector bar**, located just below the Web page tab, shows the underlying HTML tags generated as you add content to the page.

**Task Panes**   There are four default **task panes:** two on the left (Folder List and Tag Properties) and two on the right (Toolbox and Apply Styles). Task panes are moved or replaced to reflect the current task.

**View Buttons**   The **view buttons** are located at the lower left of the editing window and change depending on which tab is active (Web Site tab or Web page tab). When a Web page is open, the available view buttons are Design, Split, and Code. Design view is the WYSIWYG view. Split view shows the HTML tags at the top of the screen and the WYSIWYG page on the bottom. Code view shows only the HTML code.

**Status Bar**   The right side of the **status bar** shows the status of visual aids, style application settings, download statistics, rendering mode, page size dimensions, and the XHTML and CSS versions Expression Web is using to code your pages.

## Toolbars

Expression Web's default toolbar is the Common toolbar. To display the menu of toolbar options, right-click a toolbar (Figure 1–6). In addition to the Common toolbar, Expression Web has 10 other task-specific toolbars that you can display when needed to perform a specific task, such as working with a table. When Expression Web opens for the first time, the Common toolbar is the only one visible. When you open a toolbar, it remains open each time the program is started, until you close it manually. Depending on past usage, your toolbar buttons may differ slightly. A check mark next to the toolbar name indicates it is visible. To show a toolbar, click the toolbar name to add a check mark. To hide a toolbar, click the name that contains the check mark to remove the check mark.

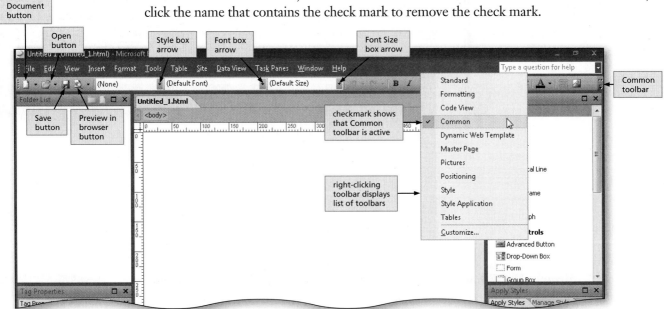

**Figure 1–6**

## To Reset Workspace Layout

As you work with Expression Web, you may rearrange the toolbars and task panes by opening, moving, maximizing, or closing them. To make your screen match the figures in this book and to ensure that you start from the same point during each work session, you should reset the workspace to the default layout, and close any open sites. The following steps restore all task panes and content areas to the default sizes and locations, and close any open sites.

- Click Task Panes on the menu bar to open the Task Panes menu (Figure 1–7).

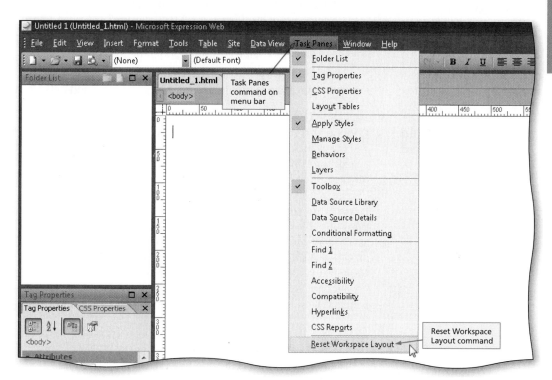

**Figure 1–7**

❷

- Click Reset Workspace Layout to restore the task panes to their default layout.

- If a site is open, click File on the menu bar to open the File menu, and then click Close Site to close the site (Figure 1–8).

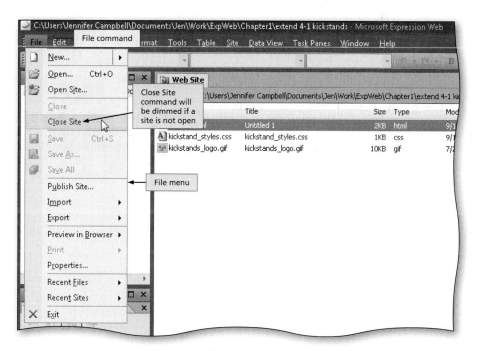

**Figure 1–8**

**Naming files and folders**

The site name, which is the folder that contains the site contents, can include spaces. Within the site, folders and filenames cannot contain uppercase letters, spaces, or certain characters, such as the pound sign (#) or an asterisk (*). You can separate words in a filename by using an underscore (_), such as in the folder name assets_images or the filename web_page2.html.

# Creating a Web Site

A Web site consists, at minimum, of a folder and an HTML file. Once these two basic components are created, you can enhance the site with additional HTML files, embed images and style sheets, and organize the files into folders and subfolders. The first Web page in the site is the **home page**. The home page provides access to the other Web pages in the site by including hyperlinks in a navigation bar.

When creating an Expression Web site, you are actually creating a root folder to store all the files and subfolders for your site. When you create a new one-page Web site, Expression Web creates a root folder and a file named default.html, which serves as the home page for the site. Expression Web uses the default.html name because the Web servers on which Web pages are stored look for a home page named default.html or index.html.

**Plan Ahead**

**Choose the Web site structure to use as the starting point for the site.**
You must first decide whether to begin your Web site using a blank Web site, by modifying an existing Web site, using a template, or by importing an existing site from the Internet or other location into Expression Web.

**Determine folder structure and location and file naming conventions for the Web site files.**
Saving an Expression Web site is different from saving an individual file created in another program. A site consists of HTML files that store content, style sheets that indicate how formatting is applied, and elements such as graphics and media files. It is important to plan how you will name and organize the files and folder structure where you will store the site's pages, style sheets, and graphics and media files.

## To Create a Web Site

If you need your site to be portable so that you can work on it on different computers, you should store the site on an external storage device such as a USB flash drive. The following steps create the Web site folder for the Boon Mountain Resort site and a one-page blank HTML file, and save them to the USB flash drive.

**1**

• With a USB flash drive connected to one of the computer's USB ports, click File on the menu bar to open the File menu, then point to New (Figure 1–9).

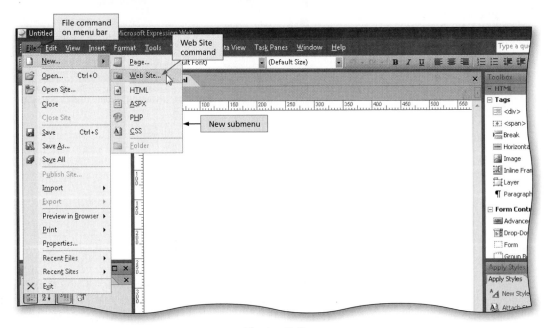

**Figure 1–9**

**2**

- Click Web Site on the New submenu to display the New dialog box (Figure 1–10).

**Figure 1–10**

**3**

- In the middle pane, click One Page Web Site.

- Click the Browse button to open the New Web Site Location dialog box (Figure 1–11).

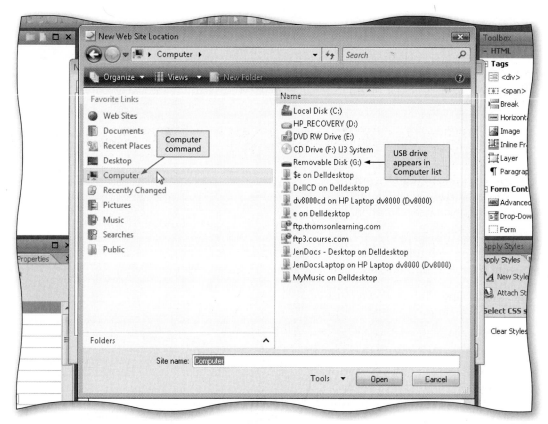

**Figure 1–11**

- Click Computer in the Favorite Links section to display a list of available drives (Figure 1–12).

**Q&A** My dialog box is different.

If your dialog box shows a Folders List below the Folders button, click the Folders button. If Computer is not displayed in the Favorite Links, drag the top or bottom edge of the Save As dialog box until Computer is displayed.

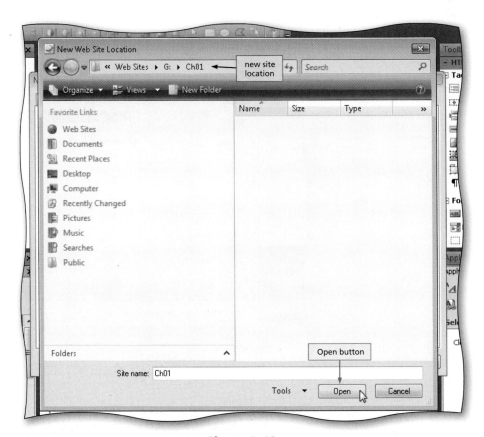

**Figure 1–12**

- If necessary, scroll until USB (G:) appears in the list of available drives.

**Q&A** Do I have to use a USB flash drive?

No. You can save to any device or folder. Use the same process, but select your device or network folder from the Computer list.

- Double-click USB (G:) to select the USB flash drive, Drive G in this case, as the new save location.

- If necessary, navigate to or create a folder on your drive into which you will save your Data Files.

- Click the Open button to return to the New dialog box (Figure 1–13).

**Q&A** What if my USB flash drive has a different name or letter?

It is likely that your USB flash drive will be named differently and be connected to a different port. Use the device, folder, or drive where you save your files.

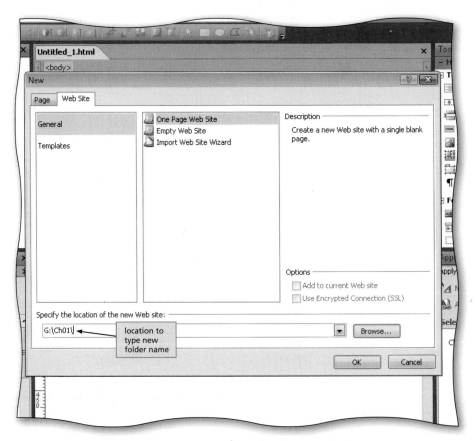

**Figure 1–13**

**6**

- Click after the text in the Specify the location of the new Web site box.

- Type `boonmountainresort` to specify the site folder name (Figure 1–14).

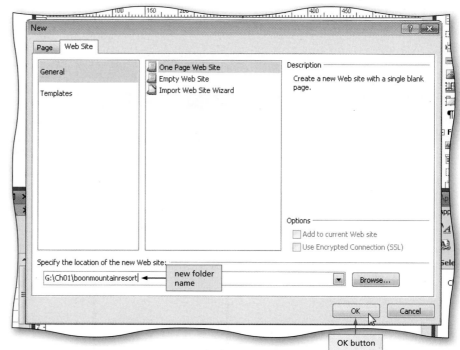

**Figure 1–14**

**7**

- Click the OK button to close the New dialog box and open the Web site folder for the site and create the default.html page (Figure 1–15).

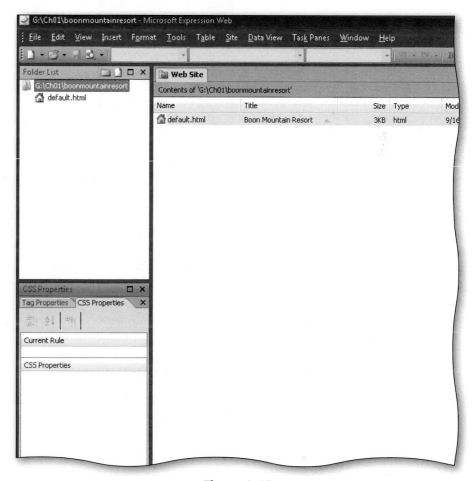

**Figure 1–15**

## To Open a Web Page

Now that you have created the Web site, you are ready to add content to the home page. The home page will contain links to the other pages in the site and information about the Boon Mountain Resort. The following step opens the HTML file that will contain the home page content.

- Double-click default.html in the Folder List to open the page (Figure 1–16).

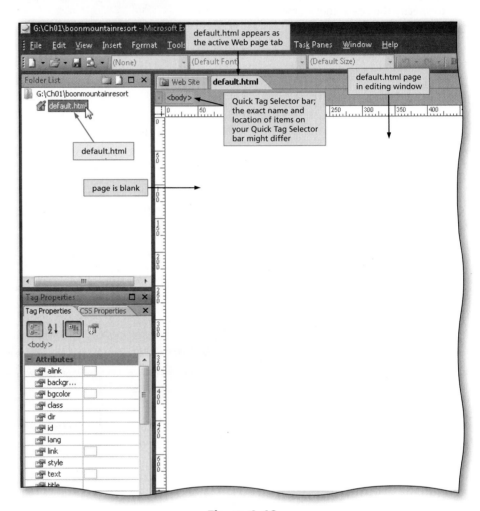

**Figure 1–16**

| Other Ways | | |
|---|---|---|
| 1. Double-click the filename in the Web Site tab | 2. Click File on the menu bar, then click Open to open the Open dialog box. Click the filename, then click the Open button. | 3. Press CTRL + O to open the Open dialog box. Click the filename, then click the Open button. |

# Setting Page Properties

Each page in the site can have unique page properties. These properties include file location, page title, page description, keywords, background sound, background image, hyperlink colors, and margins. Such properties can add visual interest, increase readability, and reflect a company's identity, in addition to making your site easier for search engines to find. You can use a predefined color for the page background, or define characteristics to create a custom color.

The **page title** displays on the title bar of a browser and should be meaningful to a visitor. If the visitor adds the page to his or her browser Favorites or Bookmarks list, the page title is often what appears in the Favorites list, depending on the browser. Search engines display the **page description** in search results, and use **keywords** to place your page in search results by matching the keywords listed in the site with the user's search criteria.

---

**Determine the page properties or settings that will apply to the page.**
You can set page properties at any time, but it is a good design strategy to set them before you enter text onto the page. These page specifications should be determined during the planning and design stage while you are making decisions about the site color scheme and layout.

When deciding on a background color or graphic, keep in mind that the text on the page should be easy to read. A dark background or busy graphic might distract from the content and could cause your site visitors to miss important information.

**Plan Ahead**

BTW **Misspellings**
If some of your keywords include common misspellings, or British and American English spelling variations (such as *colour* and *color*), be sure to include them in the Page Properties dialog box.

## To Set Page Properties

To enter or change the page description and keywords, you use the General, Formatting, and other tabs in the Page Properties dialog box. The following steps change the page properties and add a custom color background to the page.

- Click File on the menu bar to display the File menu, then click Properties to display the Page Properties dialog box (Figure 1–17).

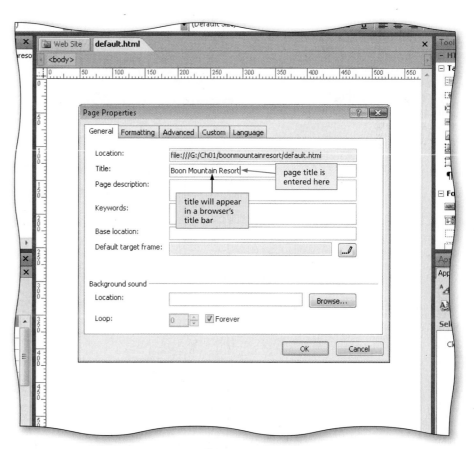

**Figure 1–17**

- On the General tab, type `Boon Mountain Resort` in the Title text box to specify the page title.

- Press the TAB key to move to the Page description text box.

- Type `Magnificent resort atop the majestic Blue Ridge Mountains.`

- Press the TAB key to move to the Keywords text box.

- Type `resort, cabins, mountains, romantic getaway, family vacation, Blue Ridge Mountains, Redhat, Georgia` (Figure 1–18).

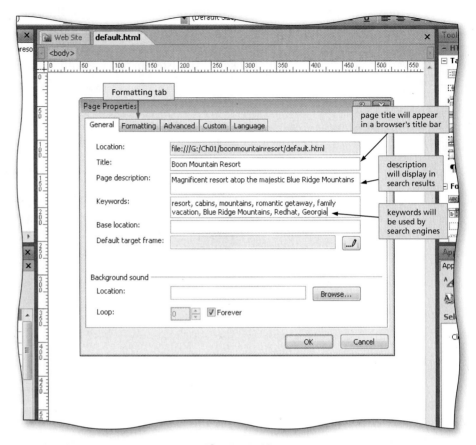

**Figure 1–18**

**3**

- Click the Formatting tab to display the background options (Figure 1–19).

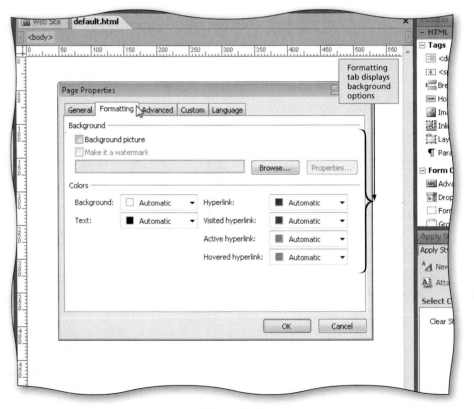

**Figure 1–19**

**4**

- In the Colors area, click the Background color button arrow to display the color palette (Figure 1–20).

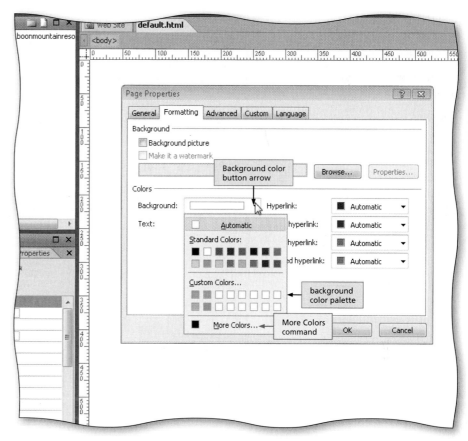

**Figure 1–20**

**5**

- Click More Colors to display the More Colors dialog box (Figure 1–21).

 What is a custom color?

A custom color is created by using numbers to define characteristics such as hue, saturation, and luminosity.

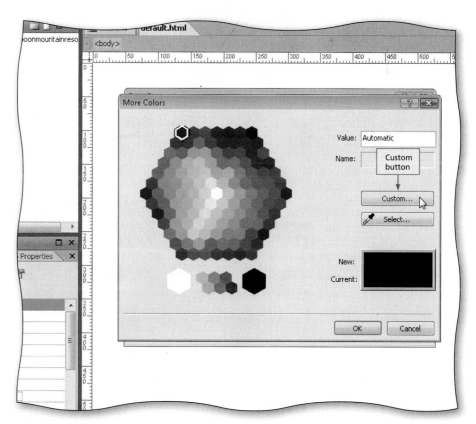

**Figure 1–21**

**6**

- Click the Custom button to open the Color dialog box.

- Click in the Hue box, then type 40.

- Click in the Sat box, then type 80.

- Click in the Lum box, then type 137 to define a light brown custom color (Figure 1–22).

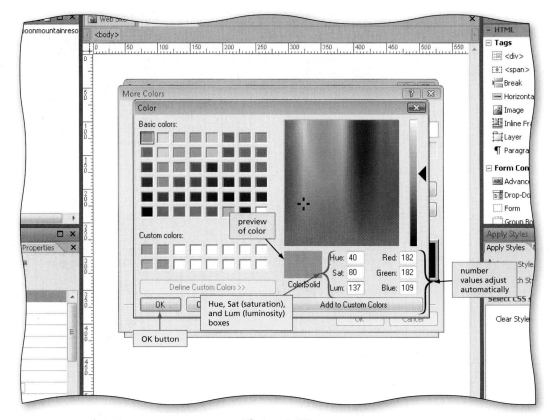

**Figure 1–22**

**7**

- Click the OK button to close the Colors dialog box (Figure 1–23).

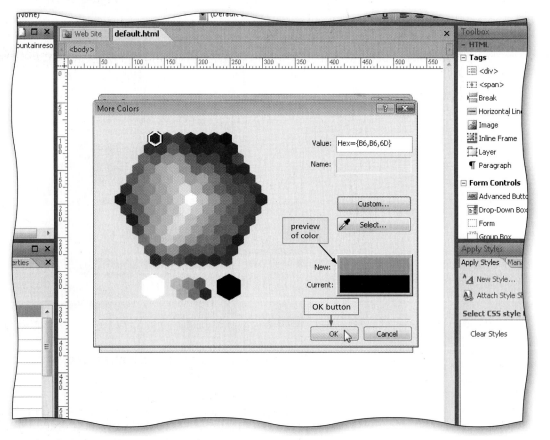

**Figure 1–23**

**8**

- Click the OK button to close the More Colors dialog box.

- Click the OK button to close the Page Properties dialog box and view the light brown page background (Figure 1–24).

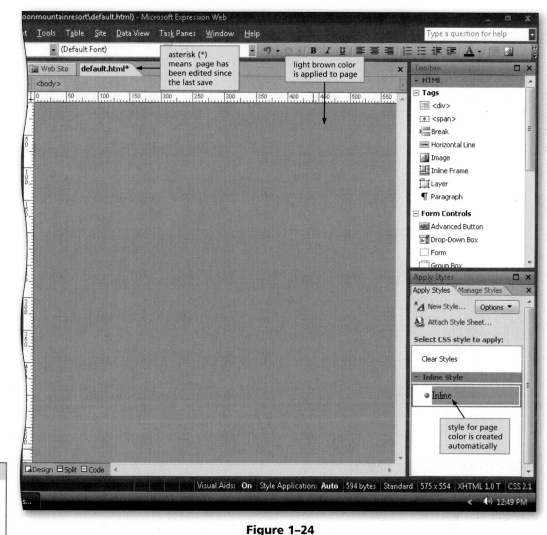

**Figure 1–24**

**Other Ways**

1. Right-click anywhere in the page to display the shortcut menu, then click Page Properties to open the Page Properties dialog box

**Plan Ahead**

**BTW**

**Web standards**
Web standards are guidelines for Web development, defined by the World Wide Web Consortium (W3C), an international organization of Web developers (www.w3c.org). Web standards ensure that viewers of a Web site who are using different browsers have a common experience.

**Decide what the page layout will look like.**
Most pages on the Internet follow similar layout rules because of the restrictions of HTML. Using a layout with which users feel comfortable allows them to focus on the content and message of your site.

- Some common elements found on each page of most professionally developed Web sites include a masthead or page banner, one or more navigational systems, a content section divided into one or more columns, and a footer area. Minor variations of page layouts throughout the site can add interest and variety to the site to enhance the visitor experience, but the overall structure should be consistent.

- A page mockup for each page, either hand drawn or computer generated, indicates what a finished page will look like.

- Select font families, color schemes or palettes to provide contrast, set the mood, and maintain consistency throughout the site.

**Determine the text content for the page.**
Avoid long paragraphs of text. Use short sentences, bulleted lists, and boldface key terms to show the main points of a page without bogging down the reader. Divide content among site pages to avoid having visitors scroll to read all information on a page.

# Entering Text

**BTW**

**Faster Downloading**
Another advantage of using a division-based layout is that it reduces the number of lines of code needed to create a page, resulting in faster downloading from the Internet.

A basic Web page layout typically contains four sections: masthead, navigation, content, and footer. These sections are enclosed within division container <div>...</div> tag elements and are called a **division-based layout**. The purpose of using <div> tags, or **divs**, is to define an area of the page that you can format using **styles**, which are collections of formatting attributes.

Using the page layout mockup shown in Figure 1–2, the home page shows the company name and tagline at the top of the page, called the **masthead**. The **navigation area** includes the names of the other site pages, each of which will contain information relating to a specific topic, and to which you will later add links. The body of the home page, called the content area, contains a bulleted list that highlights important features of the resort. The page is visually appealing and easy to read because of the varying font colors used for emphasis and the light brown page background.

Once the layout is defined, you can start entering text by clicking in a div and typing.

## To Add a <Div> Tag

As shown in Figure 1–1, the final page will include four text areas: a masthead, a navigation area, a page content area, and a footer. To define the masthead section of the page where the company name and tagline will appear, you will insert a <div> tag before typing text. You will also need to add a <div> tag, to define the navigation area of the page, into which you will type the names of the other site pages. In a later chapter, you will add links to those pages. The following steps create the first two tags and their content.

**1**
- If necessary, click at the top of the page to position the insertion point where you want the <div> tag to appear (Figure 1–25).

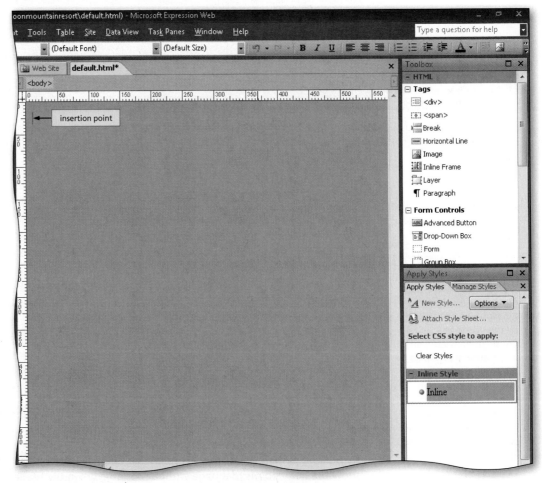

**Figure 1–25**

**2**

- Double-click the <div> tag in the Toolbox to place a <div> division container on your page at the insertion point's location (Figure 1–26).

**Q&A**

What if I double-click too many times and get more than one tag on my page?

Click the Undo button on the Common toolbar.

**Q&A**

What should I do if I cannot see the new div?

Point to Visual Aids on the View menu, and then click Show.

**Other Ways**

1. Click the <div> tag in the Toolbox, then drag the <div> tag to where you want it on the page
2. Click the <div> button on the Common toolbar

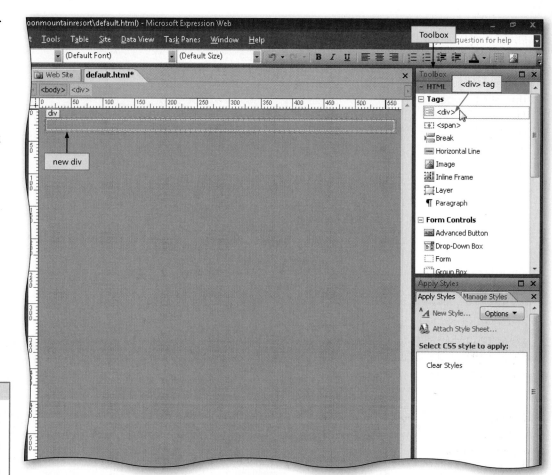

**Figure 1–26**

**3**

- Type Boon Mountain Resort, then press the ENTER key to move the insertion point to the next line (Figure 1–27).

**Q&A**

What if my insertion point is not inside the <div> container?

Click inside the <div> container.

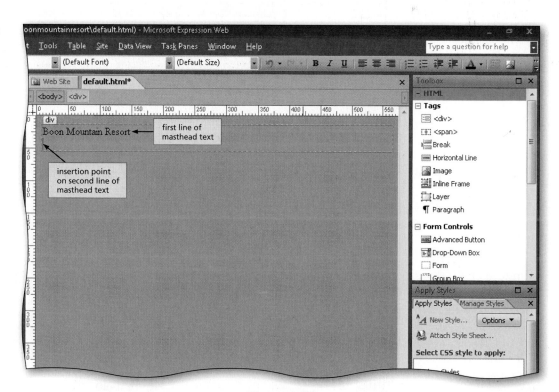

**Figure 1–27**

**4**

- Type Natural
  beauty atop
  the Blue Ridge
  Mountains, then
  click a blank spot on
  the page outside of
  the <div> tag to indi-
  cate you are finished
  entering data into it
  (Figure 1–28).

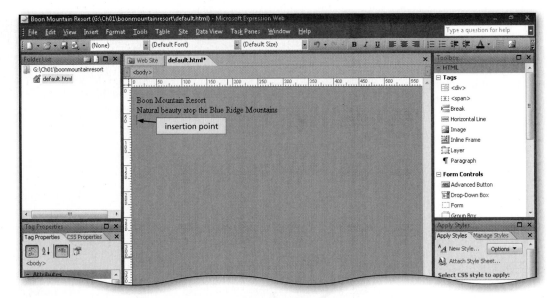

**Figure 1–28**

**5**

- Double-click the
  <div> tag in the
  Toolbox to place a
  division container at
  the insertion point's
  location (Figure 1–29).

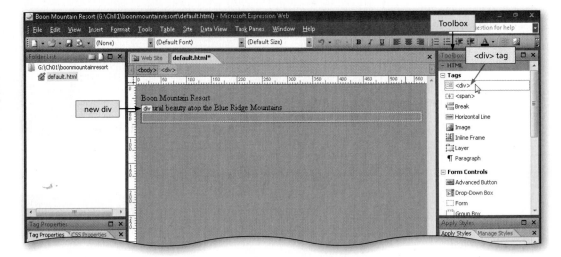

**Figure 1–29**

**6**

- Be sure the insertion
  point is inside the
  <div> tag. Type Home,
  then press TAB to
  enter the text for the
  first navigational link
  (Figure 1–30).

**Q&A** Why do I press TAB
instead of SPACEBAR?

Pressing TAB inserts
more space than
pressing SPACEBAR.
TAB is used to insert
a consistent amount
of space between
words.

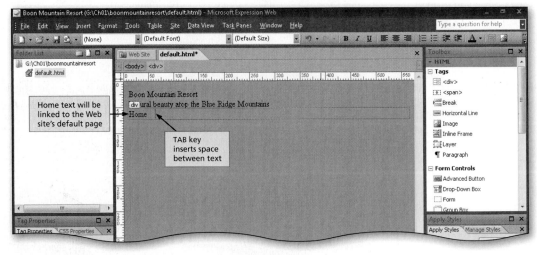

**Figure 1–30**

**7**

- Type `Accommodations` as the second link text, then press TAB.

- Type `Attractions` as the third link text, then press TAB.

- Type `Directions` as the text for the final navigational link, then click a blank spot on the page outside of the <div> to indicate you are finished entering data into it (Figure 1–31).

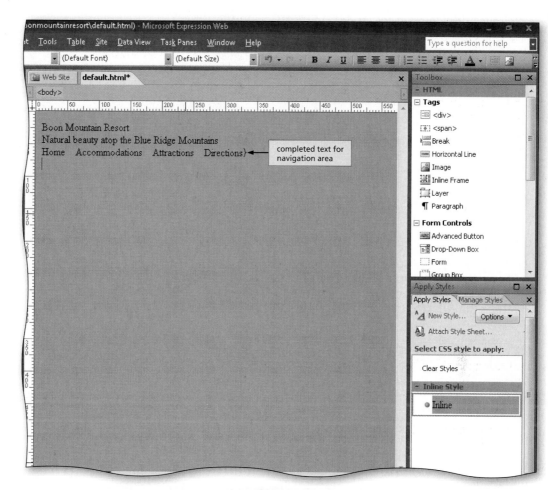

**Figure 1–31**

## To Add Paragraph Text

A paragraph is specified by using the <p> tag, and is used to contain text. When you press ENTER in a <p> tag, a new paragraph is inserted, with margin space between the two paragraphs. The following steps add space between divs on the page and add another <div> tag to contain the rest of the page content. Within the new <div> tag you will embed a paragraph <p> tag to hold the word, Experience.

- Double-click the <div> tag in the Toolbox to place a division container at the insertion point's location (Figure 1–32).

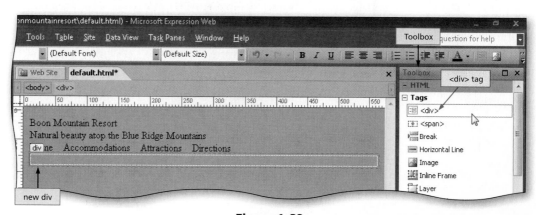

**Figure 1–32**

**2**

- With the insertion point still inside the <div> tag, press the ENTER key four times to add line spacing inside the <div> tag container (Figure 1–33).

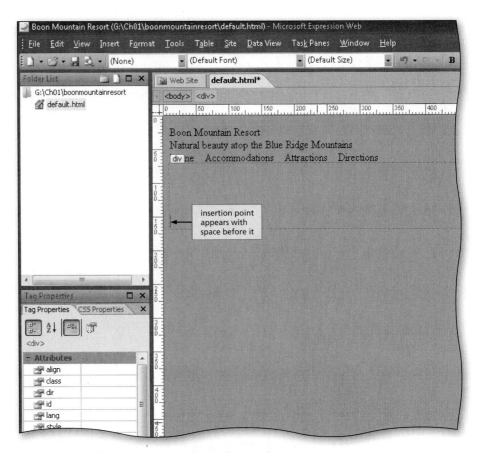

**Figure 1–33**

**3**

- Double-click the Paragraph tag in the Toolbox to place a paragraph <p> tag on the page inside of the <div> tag container (Figure 1–34).

**Q&A**

Why should I add extra lines on the page?

Using generous blank areas, or white space, helps to avoid a cluttered page.

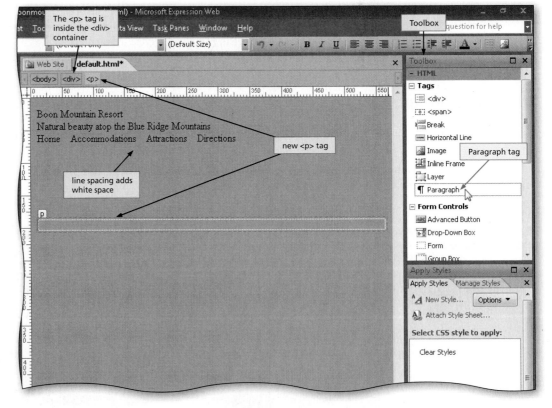

**Figure 1–34**

**4**

- With the insertion point inside the Paragraph tag, type Relaxation. Refreshment. Renewal. Experience all we have to offer at Boon Mountain Resort., then press ENTER to insert a new <p> division container (Figure 1–35).

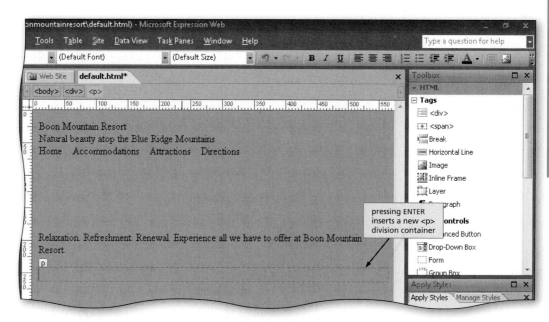

**Figure 1–35**

## To Add a Bulleted List

A **bulleted list** is used to portray several points that do not need to appear in any specific order. The following steps add features to extol the benefits of the Boon Mountain Resort by creating a bulleted list.

**1**

- Be sure the insertion point is inside the new <p> tag and then click the Bullets button on the Common toolbar to create the first bullet (Figure 1–36).

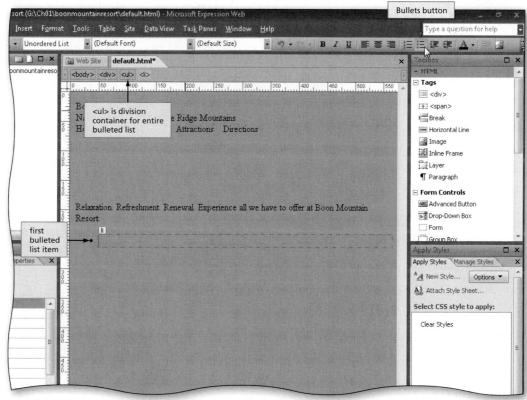

**Figure 1–36**

**2**

- **Type** Fine dining at the Arborwood Restaurant, **then press ENTER to start a new bullet (Figure 1–37).**

**Q&A**

What is the red, wavy line under Arborwood?

Expression Web underlines a word with a red, wavy line to indicate that the word is not in its dictionary. You will learn more about checking spelling later in Chapter 1.

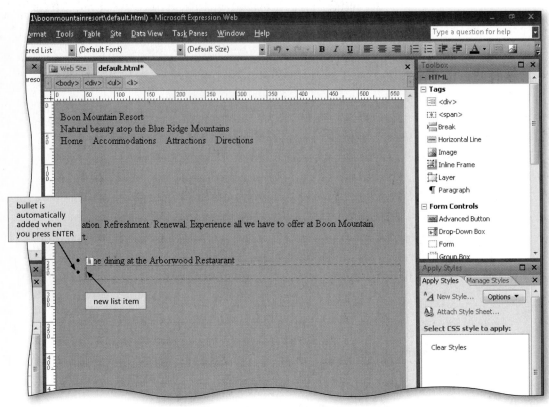

Figure 1–37

**3**

- **Type** Luxury lodge rooms **as the text for the second bullet, then press ENTER.**

- **Type** Cabins available for families or small groups **as the third list item, then press ENTER.**

- **Type** Hiking trails, water sports, and other recreation activities, **then press ENTER to start a new line (Figure 1–38).**

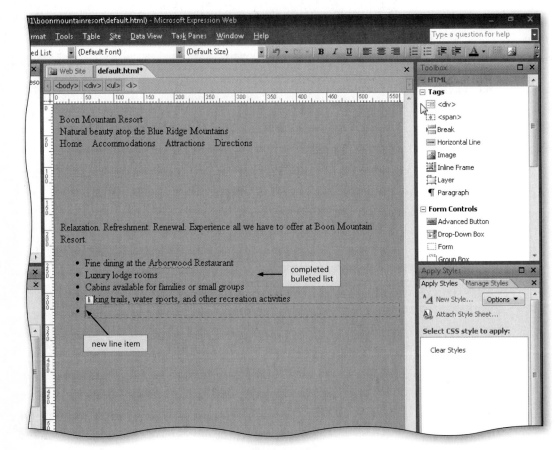

Figure 1–38

- Click the Bullets button on the Common toolbar to end the bullets and start a new paragraph by inserting a <p> tag (Figure 1–39).

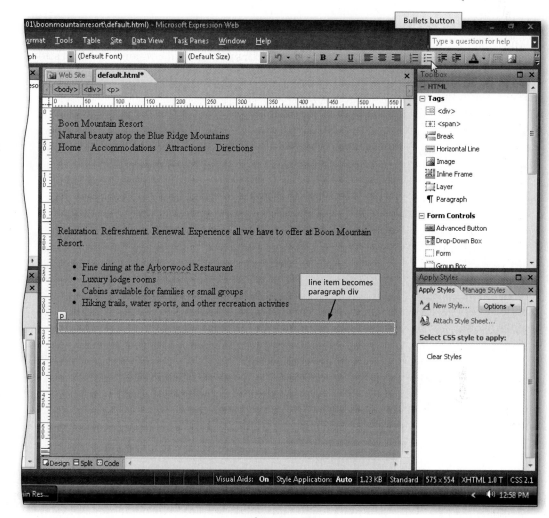

**Figure 1–39**

## To Complete Page Content

The last <p> tag in the content area on the default page will contain the resort's advertising slogan. The final <div> tag, which you add in the following steps, will be used as the footer area on the page. The following steps enter the content for the slogan and add the footer.

**1**

- With the insertion point inside the new <p> tag, type Boon Mountain is the perfect place for a family vacation or a romantic getaway. Enjoy the beauty of Boon Mountain., but do not press ENTER (Figure 1–40).

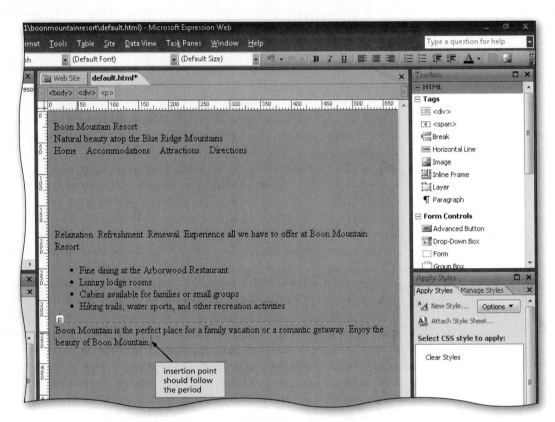

**Figure 1–40**

**2**

- Click a blank area under the <p> div, then press ENTER twice to add white space to the page (Figure 1–41).

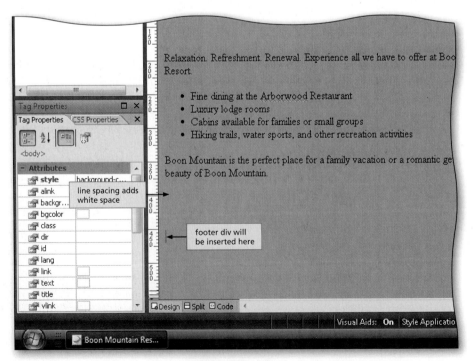

**Figure 1–41**

**3**

- Double-click the <div> tag in the Toolbox to place a division container at the insertion point's location (Figure 1–42).

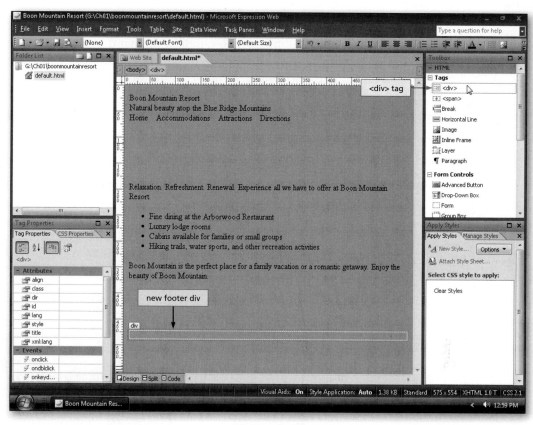

**Figure 1–42**

**4**

- Type 1275 Highway 197, Redhat, Georgia 31692, (707) 555-5397 (Figure 1–43).

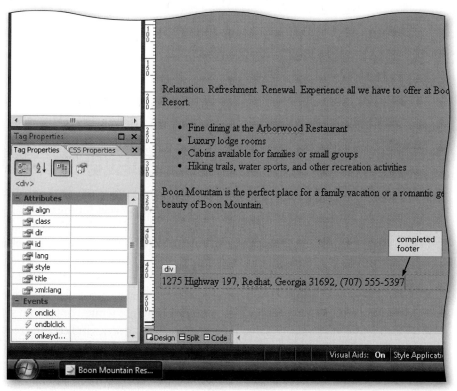

**Figure 1–43**

**AutoSave**
Depending on your system settings, Expression Web may save pages automatically as you work. If you get an error message indicating that a more recent version of the file was saved to the server, click Yes to overwrite the file.

# Saving Individual Web Pages

As you make changes to a page, an asterisk (*) appears next to the page name on the tab at the top of the editing window, indicating that it needs to be saved before your changes will be reflected in a browser. You should save your pages frequently while editing so that you do not lose any content, layout, or other work you have done on your site.

## To Save a Web Page

It is a good habit to save your page often as you are creating it. The following step saves the page you are working on.

**1**
• Click the Save button on the Common toolbar (Figure 1–44).

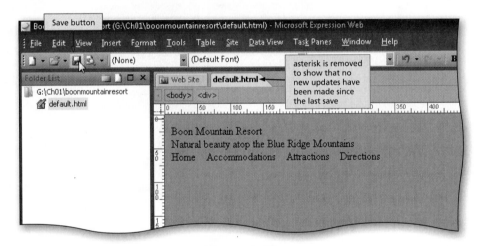

**Figure 1–44**

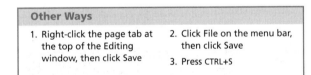

| Other Ways |
|---|
| 1. Right-click the page tab at the top of the Editing window, then click Save  2. Click File on the menu bar, then click Save  3. Press CTRL+S |

**Web Accessibility**
See Appendix B for more information about accessibility and assistive technology.

# Applying Formatting and Styles

**Formatting** is the combination of design characteristics that are applied to text, specifying a hierarchy of headings and text levels. Consistently applied formatting can guide the reader through the content on your site. Formatting techniques include changing fonts and font sizes, applying font attributes such as bold and italics, and changing the alignment and indentation of lines and paragraphs of text. To emphasize just one word or a series of words in a paragraph, you can apply the bold or italic font attribute by using formatting buttons or keyboard shortcuts.

You can apply formatting such as bold as you enter text (just as you would in a word processing program) or apply predefined or custom styles that combine a variety of attributes.

**Headings** and subheading styles indicate the relative importance of each line of text. HTML supports six levels of heading style tags, <h1>, the largest, through <h6>, the smallest. All heading styles apply the bold attribute automatically but use different font sizes to show the level. Using styles, as opposed to applying formatting directly, ensures consistency in a large site so that if you change an attribute of a style it applies automatically to other elements that share that style.

As you apply various formatting to text on the page, Expression Web creates a style in the Apply Styles task pane. The styles are given a default number as they are applied and that number becomes part of the HTML tag. You can then apply these styles to different areas of the page or site, such as for bulleted lists. You will work with the Apply Styles task pane in Chapter 3.

**Plan
Ahead**

**Design the format for the text elements on the page.**
When formatting fonts, you should select font families and assign formatting characteristics for headings, captions, and lists that help make your page attractive and easy to read.

- Readability is the first consideration for text formatting. Font size should be neither too small, which is difficult to read, or too large, which looks unprofessional and wastes screen space.

- Use headings and subheadings to emphasize important words and to draw the reader's eye to that location of the screen.

- Limit the number of fonts used in your site to two or three. Choose common fonts or font families that will be recognizable to many browsers. Avoid ornate fonts, such as handwriting or scroll fonts, because they are difficult to read and are not recognized by many browsers. If your company uses a custom or fancy font in its logo, create the logo as a graphic element rather than text to ensure that it appears the same in all browsers.

- Use font color as emphasis on important words within a paragraph or bulleted text rather than applying a color to the entire text section. Consider the background of the page and make sure that the font color you choose provides contrast.

- Avoid using underlined text, which usually represents a hyperlink.

## To Use the Quick Tag Selector

Use the Quick Tag Selector to confirm that you have selected an entire element before applying formatting or making changes to the text. The following step selects a list item and a list using the Quick Tag Selector.

- Click in the text of the third bullet to display the \<li> tag for the list item (Figure 1–45).

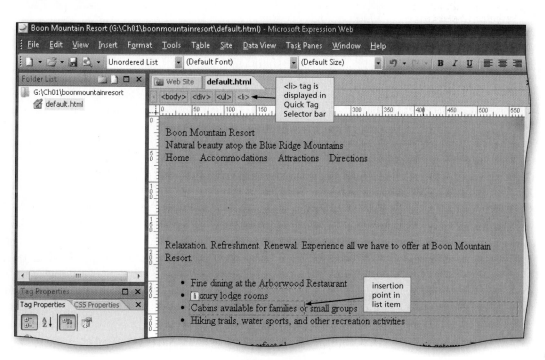

**Figure 1–45**

**2**

- Click the <li> tag on the Quick Tag Selector to select the entire bullet (Figure 1–46).

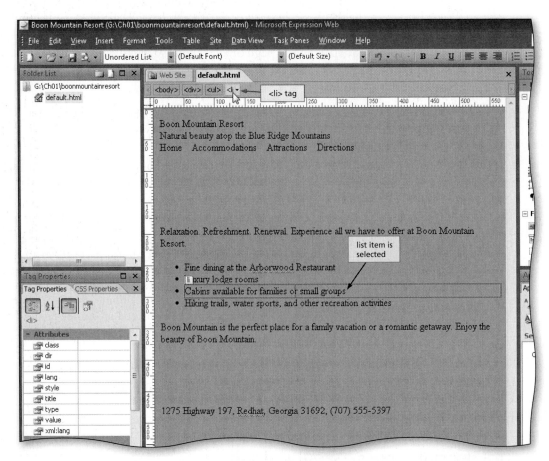

**Figure 1–46**

**3**

- Click the <ul> tag on the Quick Tag Selector to select the entire bulleted list (Figure 1–47).

**Experiment**

- Use the Quick Tag Selector bar to select other div tags, such as <body>, to see how many nested elements are selected. The farther left you click on the Quick Tag Selector, the higher you are in the hierarchy of divs on the page.

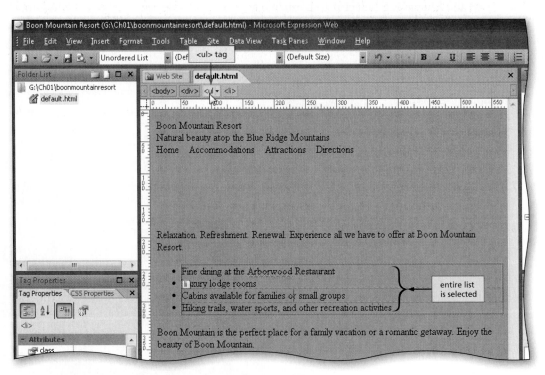

**Figure 1–47**

## To Apply a Heading Style

In addition to providing a visual cue as to a heading's relative importance, using the heading style ensures that assistive technology can distinguish how the text has been formatted, to accurately represent it to vision-impaired site visitors. The following steps use heading styles to change the font size and apply the bold attribute.

**1**

- Click after the words, Blue Ridge Mountains, at the top of the page inside the first <div> tag (Figure 1–48).

**Q&A** Can I still apply the heading style if only a few words of the div are selected?

To ensure that the heading style is applied to all of the text, click the <div> tag on the Quick Tag Selector bar to select all of the text at once.

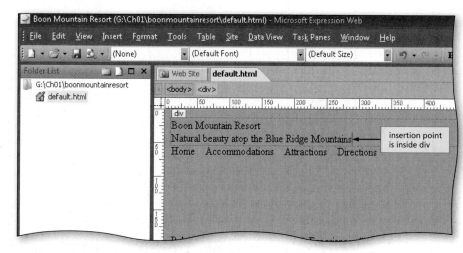

**Figure 1–48**

**2**

- With the insertion point inside the first div, click <div> on the Quick Tag Selector bar to select the entire two lines of text inside the <div> tag container (Figure 1–49).

**Q&A** Can I select the individual words rather than the entire <div> tag container?

Yes, but Expression Web will assign the code to only the selected text, which will cause problems if you later attempt to apply styles using CSS.

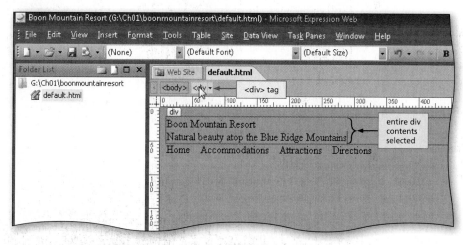

**Figure 1–49**

**3**

- Click the Style box arrow on the Common toolbar to display the Style menu (Figure 1–50).

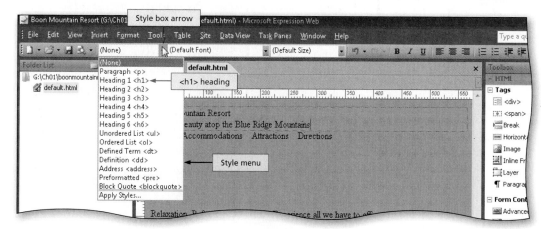

**Figure 1–50**

- Click Heading 1 <h1> to apply it (Figure 1–51).

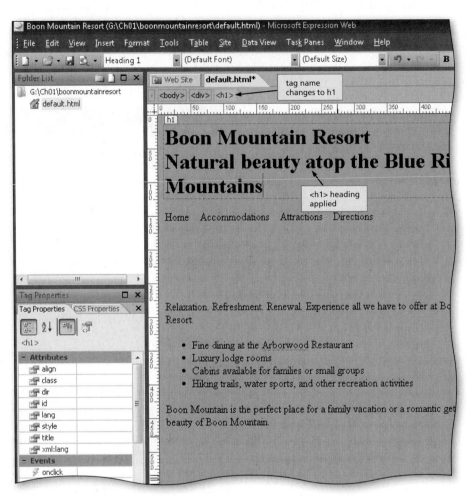

**Figure 1–51**

- Click in the word, Relaxation, to position the insertion point.

- Click the <p> tag on the Quick Tag Selector to select the div (Figure 1–52).

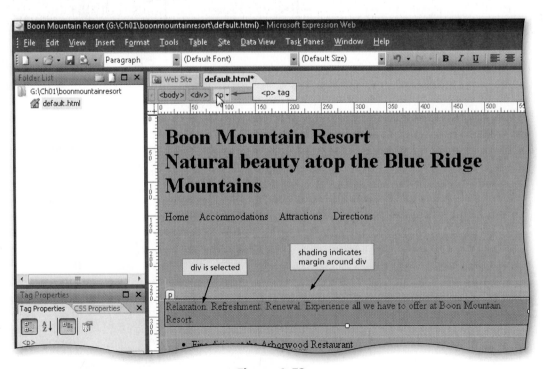

**Figure 1–52**

**6**

- Click the Style box arrow on the Common toolbar to display the menu.

- Click Heading 2 <h2> to apply it (Figure 1–53).

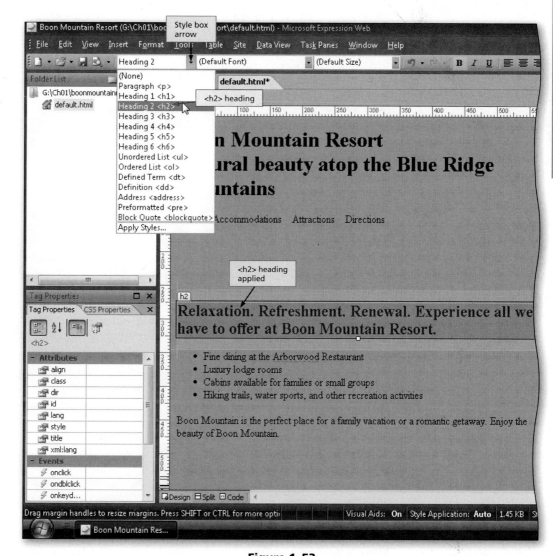

**Figure 1–53**

## To Center Text

When all of the text is aligned to the left side of a Web page, it is difficult for the visitor to scan the page. Using centered text draws the eye to certain headings and paragraphs, and improves the overall look of the page. In the following steps, you will apply center alignment to the company name and tagline.

- Click in the masthead, then click the <h1> tag on the Quick Tag Selector to select the div.

- Click the Center button on the Common toolbar to center the selected text (Figure 1–54).

- Click the Save button on the Common toolbar to save the page.

**Experiment**

- Click the Align Text Right button to see the effect. Press CTRL+Z to undo the change.

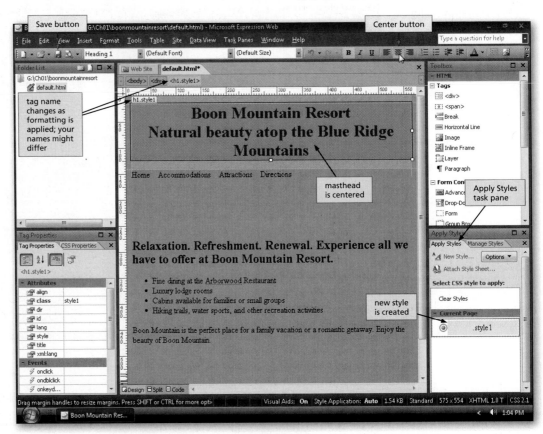

**Figure 1–54**

## Applying Font Characteristics

Text attributes can include the font family (such as Arial or Times New Roman), as well as the size, color, alignment, and other attributes of individual characters or words, such as blinking or small capital letters.

Fonts help establish the mood of the site. Clean, simple fonts convey professionalism and clarity, whereas ornate fonts can provide a feeling of excitement or creativity. Fonts with serifs (strokes at the ends of lines that make up letters) are considered easier to read in paragraphs of text. Fonts without serifs, called sans serif fonts, are often used for headings. For more information on fonts, see Special Feature 1.

Font color is also an important consideration. Most sites use a dark font on a light background, or vice versa, which provides good contrast and is easy to read. Royal blue or purple underlined text often indicates a hyperlink, so avoid using this combination of characteristics unless it is for a link.

**BTW**

**Centering Usage**
Centering, like all formatting techniques, should not be overdone. Apply centering to headings or elements such as footers. Paragraphs and lists are usually left-aligned.

# To Change Font Color

Many sites use colored fonts to distinguish headers but use black for paragraphs of text. The following steps add font colors to selected text to contrast with the light brown page background.

**1**
- With the company name and tagline text still selected, click the Font Color button arrow on the Common toolbar to display the Font Color menu (Figure 1–55).

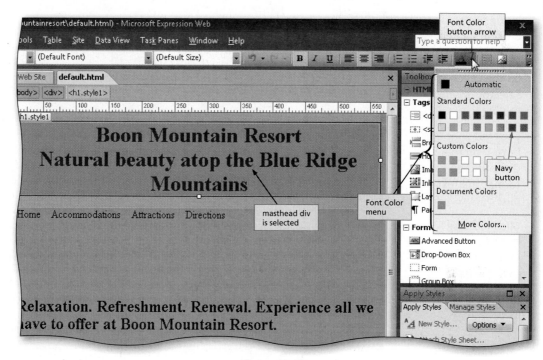

**Figure 1–55**

**2**
- Click the Navy button on the Standard Colors palette to make the masthead text navy blue (Figure 1–56).

 Why did the font color change for the first line of text only?

Click the Font Color button again to apply the font color to the second line of text.

**Experiment**
- Select a lighter font color to see how difficult it is to see a color that does not contrast with the page background. Press CTRL+Z to undo the change.

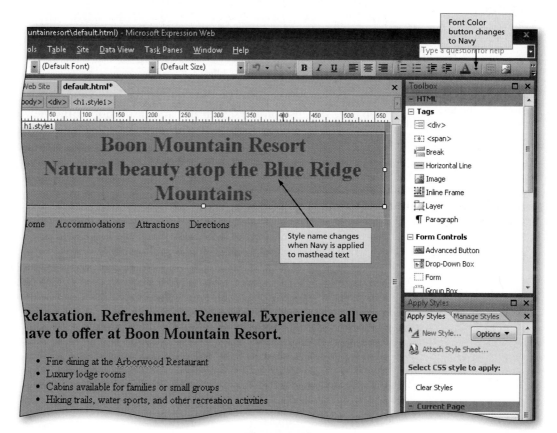

**Figure 1–56**

**3**

- Click at the end of the word, Relaxation, to place the insertion point inside the paragraph division section.

- Click the <h2> tag on the Quick Tag Selector to select the div.

- Click the Font Color button on the Common toolbar to format the text with blue (Figure 1–57).

- Click the Save button on the Common toolbar to save the page.

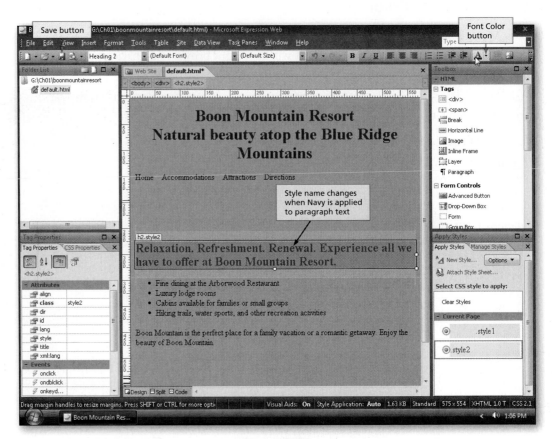

**Figure 1–57**

# Changing Font Sizes

Unlike in printed documents, the appearance of the actual point size of fonts in a Web page depends on the screen size and resolution of the viewer's computer setup and browser resolution. Using text that is too small might cause you to lose visitors with poor eyesight. Avoid text that is too large to conserve space and retain a professional look. Using all capital letters, except in a heading, is difficult to read and is the Web equivalent of SHOUTING.

Font size options use a relative system of increments, such as xx-small, which is approximately 8 points, to xx-large, which is approximately 36 points.

## To Change Font Size

The default font size for the \<h2> heading style is x-large. The default font size of plain text is medium. The following steps change the font size of the bulleted list and the paragraph above it.

**1**
- With the insertion point still in the Relaxation div, click the Font Size box arrow on the Common toolbar to display the Font Size menu (Figure 1–58).

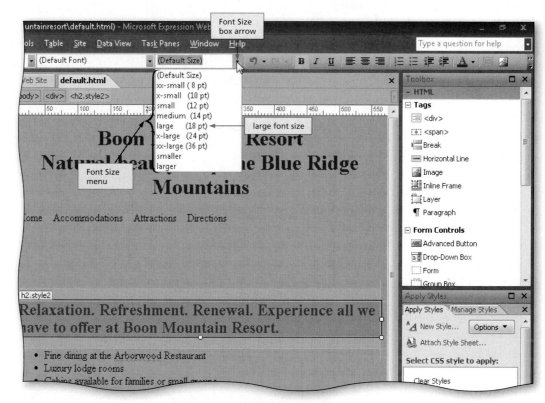

**Figure 1–58**

**2**
- Click large (18 pt) to decrease the size of the text (Figure 1–59).

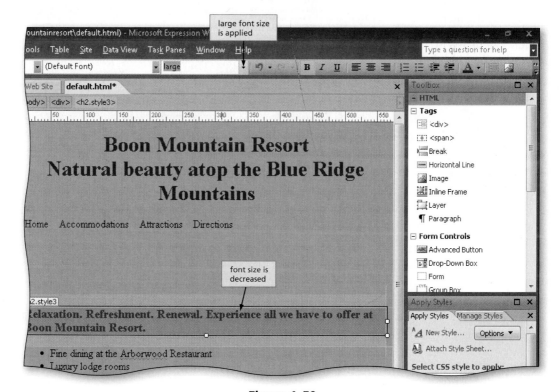

**Figure 1–59**

**3**

- Click at the end of the first bulleted item after the word, Restaurant.

- Click the <ul> tag on the Quick Tag Selector to select all four lines of the bulleted list (Figure 1–60).

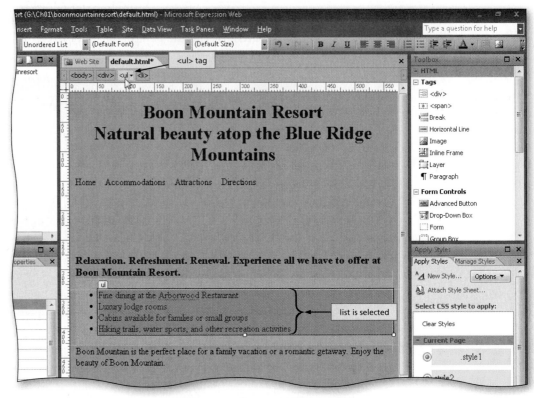

**Figure 1–60**

**4**

- Click the Font Size box arrow on the Common toolbar to display the menu.

- Click large (18 pt) to apply it (Figure 1–61).

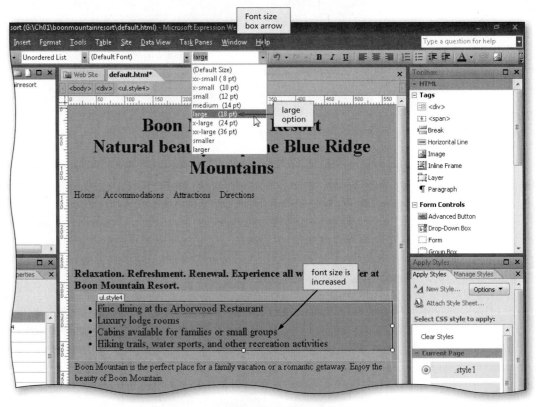

**Figure 1–61**

## To Indent Text

**Indenting** text moves it away from the margin. Usually, you will see text indented from the left margin, such as at the beginning of the first line of a paragraph of text. You can also indent multiple lines at once to nest them below a heading. The following step indents the bulleted list.

**1**

- With the bulleted list still selected, click the Increase Indent Position button on the Common toolbar to move the list to the right (Figure 1–62).

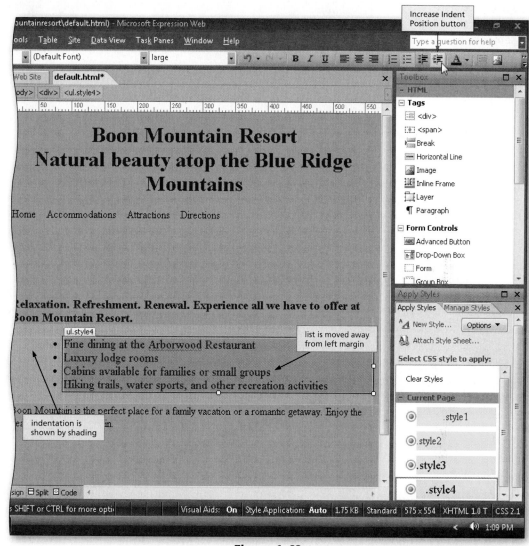

**Figure 1–62**

BTW

**Indent Size**

To indent further, click the Increase Indent Position button until you reach the desired indentation. Click the Decrease Indent Position button to move closer to the left margin. Clicking Paragraph on the Format menu opens the Paragraph dialog box, where you can specify indentation from the left and right margins, or for the first line of text only.

## To Italicize Text

Italicized text appears slanted and is another type of font attribute. The following steps italicize the text below the bulleted list.

- Click anywhere in the first sentence below the bulleted list.

- Click the <p> tag on the Quick Tag Selector bar to select both sentences in the div (Figure 1–63).

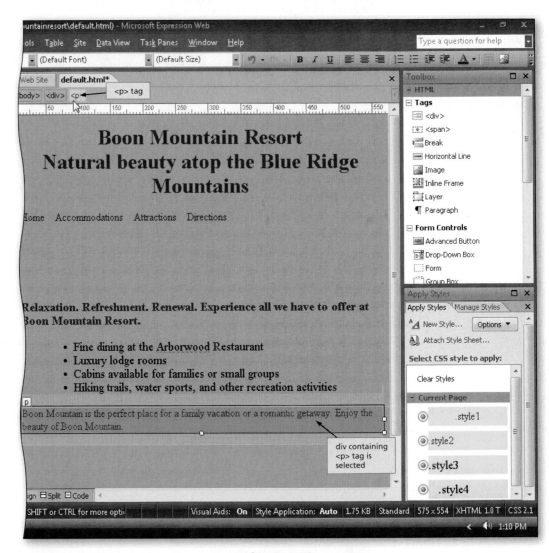

**Figure 1–63**

**2**

- Click the Italic button on the Common toolbar to apply the italic attribute to the selected text (Figure 1–64).

- Click the Save button on the Common toolbar to save the page.

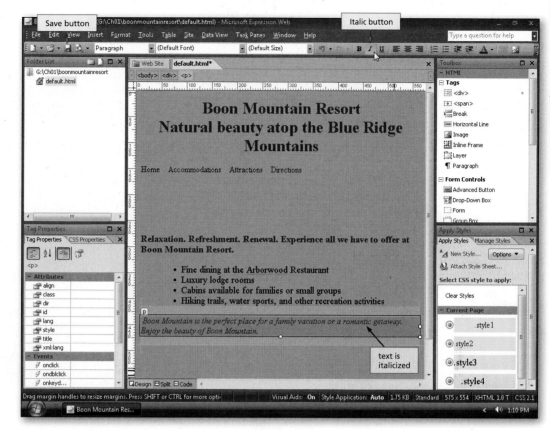

**Figure 1–64**

## Choosing a Font

The fonts that appear on a Web page in the visitor's browser depend on the fonts installed on his or her computer. Expression Web provides font families (groups of similar fonts) to control how your pages appear. If your pages use font families, the page will default to the next available font in the family if the first font choice is not available to your visitor's browser.

BTW

**Expression Web Help**
The best way to become familiar with Expression Web Help is to use it. Appendix A includes detailed information about Expression Web Help and exercises that will help you gain confidence in using it.

## To Change a Font

The following steps change the font family from the default to a sans serif font family.

**1**

- Click the <body> tag on the Quick Tag Selector bar to select all of the page content (Figure 1–65).

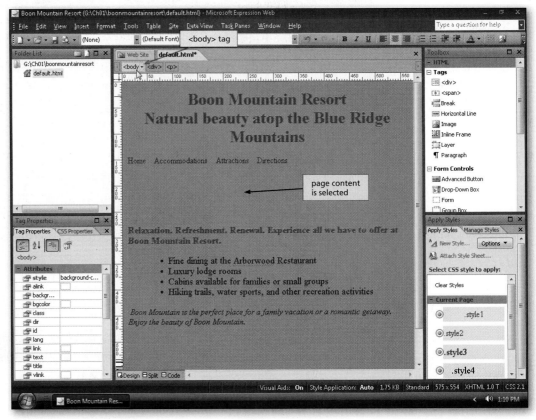

**Figure 1–65**

**2**

- Click the Font box arrow to display the Font gallery (Figure 1–66).

**Experiment**

- Scroll in the list of fonts to view the various fonts and font families available.

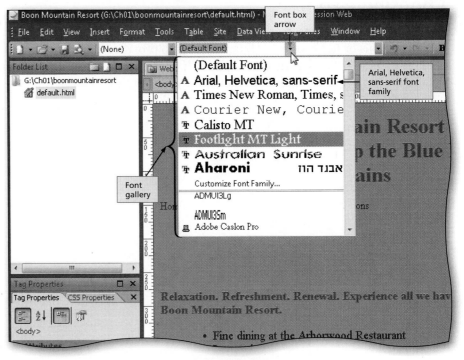

**Figure 1–66**

**3**

- Click the Arial, Helvetica, sans-serif font family to apply it (Figure 1–67).

- Click the Save button on the Common toolbar to save the page.

**Q&A** What if my list of fonts differs?

Depending on your installation, you may have different fonts and font families available to you. Choose a similar font family or one that appeals to you.

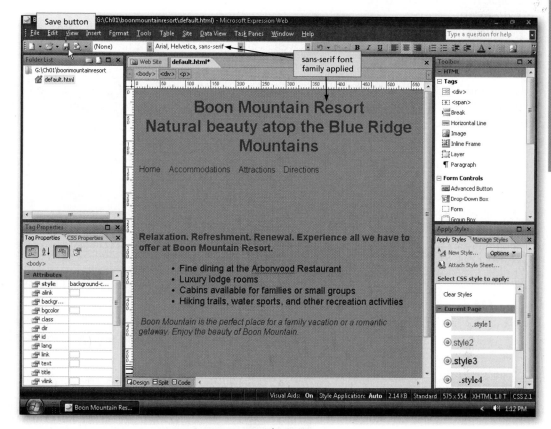

Figure 1–67

# Spell Checking Pages

Spelling and grammar errors can distract a reader and make your site look unprofessional. Expression Web has a built-in **spell checker** that displays a red wavy line below words that are not included in the Expression Web dictionary. Words that Expression Web flags as being misspelled are not necessarily incorrect; for example, Expression Web's spell checker does not recognize some proper nouns. Using the spell checker, you can correct misspelled words and choose to ignore words that are proper nouns, or that are otherwise acceptable.

## To Spell Check a Page

It is a good idea to check for spelling errors when you are finished entering text. The following steps introduce a spelling error, then correct that error as well as any others you might have made while entering text.

• Select the word, groups, in the third line of the bulleted list.

• Type gourps, then press the SPACEBAR to make the word appear with a red wavy line below it (Figure 1–68).

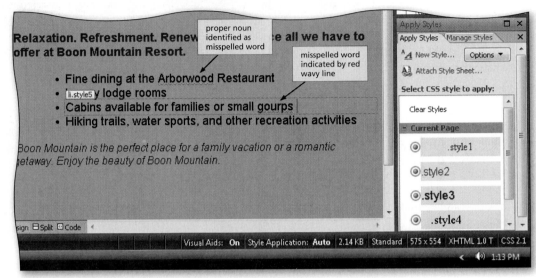

**Figure 1–68**

• Click a blank area of the page to deselect all text.

• Click Tools on the menu bar to open the Tools menu and then point to Spelling to display the Spelling submenu (Figure 1–69).

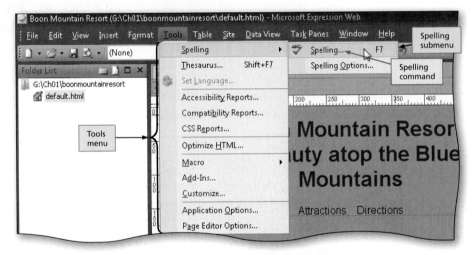

**Figure 1–69**

**3**

• Click the Spelling command to start the spell checker and open the Spelling dialog box.

• Click the Ignore button to skip the name of the restaurant, Arborwood, because it is correct (Figure 1–70).

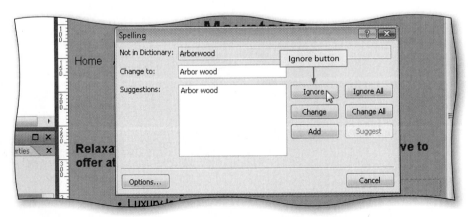

**Figure 1–70**

**4**

- Click groups in the Suggestions box.

- Click the Change button to correct the word (Figure 1–71).

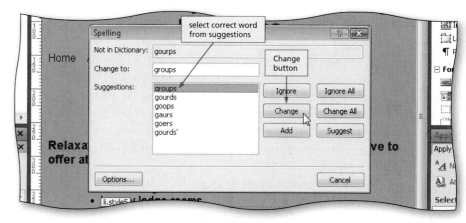

**Figure 1–71**

**5**

- Click the Ignore button to skip the name of the town, Redhat (Figure 1–72).

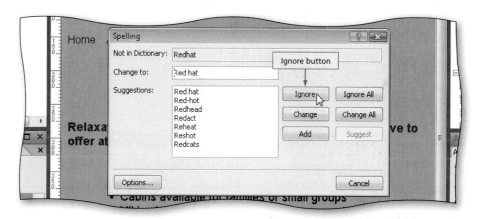

**Figure 1–72**

**6**

- Click the OK button to close the message box indicating that spell checking is complete (Figure 1–73).

- Click the Save button on the Common toolbar to save the page.

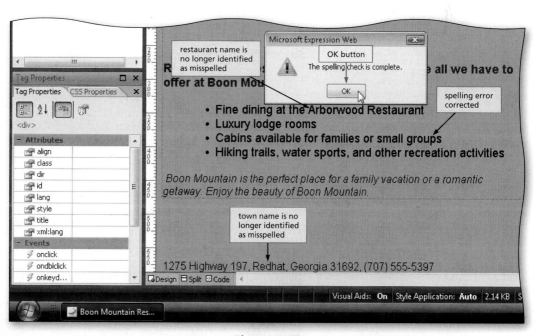

**Figure 1–73**

---

**Other Ways**

1. As you are typing, right-click a flagged word to display a short-cut menu that includes a list of suggested spelling corrections

2. Press the F7 key to start the spell checker

# Switching Views

A Web page is created using **Hypertext Markup Language (HTML)** and **Extensible Hypertext Markup Language (XHTML)** tags. HTML and XHTML tags consist of the code within a Web page that instructs a browser where formatting is to be applied, how the layout should appear, and where images should be placed. A **browser** is software that is used to display Web pages. HTML and XHTML are the markup languages used to create Web documents. You do not need to know how to write or use HTML/XHTML codes to create Web pages in Expression Web, because as you enter and format content onto your page, Expression Web inserts the appropriate **HTML tags** to define position and formatting attributes.

Expression Web provides three views for working with Web pages. Thus far in this chapter, you have used **Design view**, which gives you a general idea of what your page will look like when viewed in a browser. **Code view** displays the underlying HTML code, which is the data that the browser will use to interpret the content, formatting, and layout when displaying your site on the Internet. In **Split view**, you can see the underlying HTML code in the top half of the Editing window and your page in the bottom half of the editing window.

Looking at the code generated by Expression Web will help you become more familiar with how HTML tags are applied to your page. Figure 1–74 shows part of the code for the Boon Mountain Resort home page.

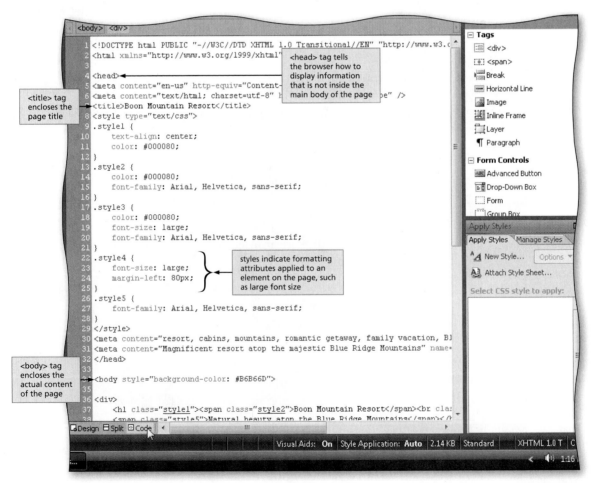

**Figure 1–74**

## To Show Code and Split Views

Now that you have added content to the page, the following steps use the various view buttons to display the HTML code Expression Web has generated.

- Click the Show Code View button at the bottom of the editing window to see the HTML tags (Figure 1–75).

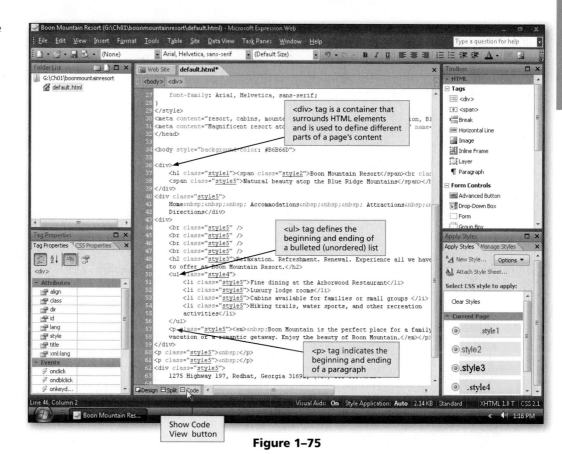

**Figure 1–75**

**2**

- Click the Show Split View button at the bottom of the Editing window to show both Code and Design views simultaneously (Figure 1–76).

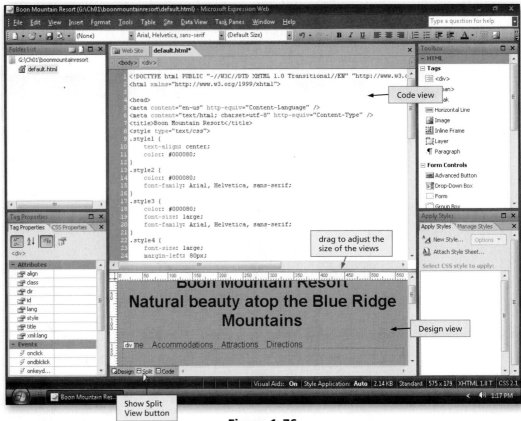

**Figure 1–76**

**3**

- Drag the separator that divides the two sections up to display more of the Design view editing window Figure (1–77).

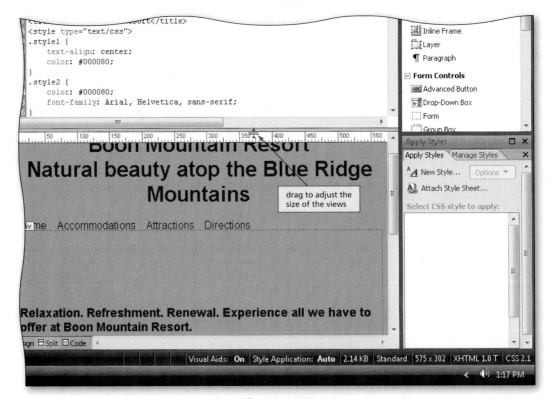

**Figure 1–77**

**4**

- Select the words, Natural beauty, in the Design window to select them in the Code view (Figure 1–78).

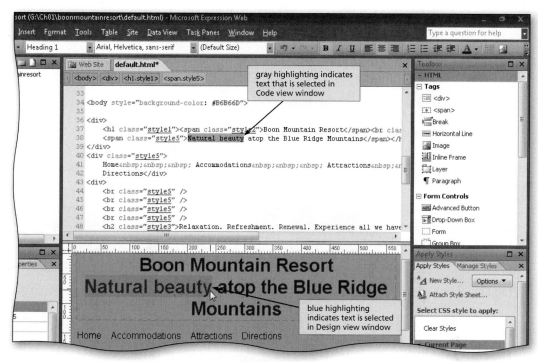

**Figure 1–78**

**5**

- Click the Show Design View button to close Code view (Figure 1–79).

 **Q&A**

Why would I want to learn HTML if Expression Web generates the code for me?

As you become a more experienced Web designer, you will find it easier to make changes and troubleshoot errors by editing the HTML code directly.

**Figure 1–79**

# Visual Aids and Quick Tags

Expression Web uses visual aids to make it easier to work with page elements, such as layers, borders, and padding while in Design View. **Visual aids** are onscreen labels that do not appear on the actual Web page, but in Expression Web, they allow you to see the HTML tags and sizing information for elements in order to better work with them. Visual aids can also help make sure that you are selecting an entire div, or container, before applying formatting or making other changes. By default, visual aids are turned on. You can turn them off to have a better sense of how your final page will look, then turn them back on to fine-tune elements.

**Quick tags** are a type of visual aid that display labels for the HTML elements on a Web page, such as paragraphs, tables, and headers. When a page element is selected, a box with a label appears around the element; this box is the selected element's visual aid. The tag for the item also appears on the Quick Tag Selector. With some page elements, such

**BTW**

**Toggle commands**
Visual Aids are a toggle command, meaning that you click the same command to both turn them on and off.

as an item in a bulleted list, you can select just one line (the tag <li> for line item), or click the tag to the left of it (the tag <ul> for unordered list) to select the entire list. Use the Quick Tag Selector to make sure that you have selected the correct item before applying formatting or making other changes.

## To Hide and Display Visual Aids

You can choose to show only certain types of visual aids, such as margins or padding, or choose to show or hide all types. The visual aid settings are shown as On or Off on the status bar. The following step uses the View menu to turn off all visual aids to view the page as it would appear when finished, then turns them back on.

**1**

- Click in the first line of the bulleted list to select the first item, and notice that the <li.style5> tag appears above the element (Figure 1–80).

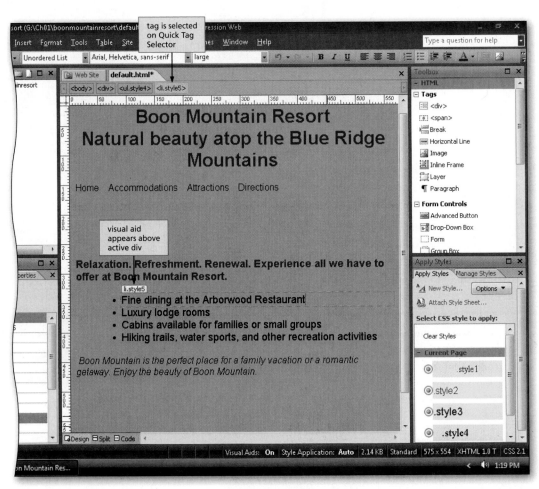

**Figure 1–80**

**2**

- Click View on the menu bar to open the View menu, point to Visual Aids to display the Visual Aids submenu, and then click Show to turn off visual aids.

- Click the second line of the bulleted list, and notice that no tag appears above the line (Figure 1–81).

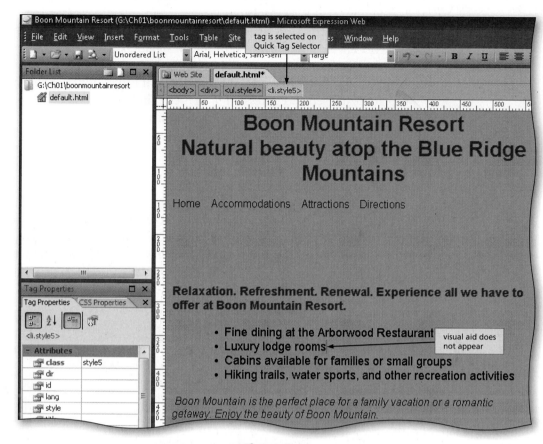

**Figure 1–81**

**3**

- Click View on the menu bar to open the View menu, point to Visual Aids to display the Visual Aids menu, then click Show to display visual aids.

- Click the first line of the bulleted list, and notice that the <li> tag appears above the line (Figure 1–82).

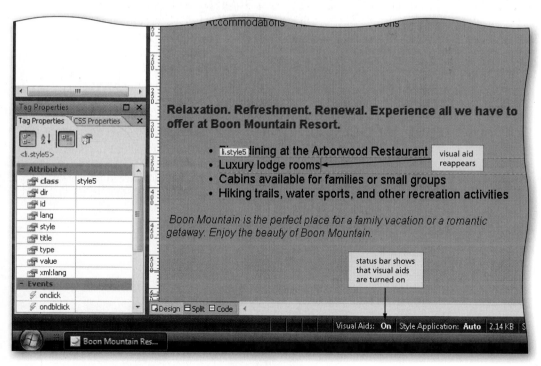

| Other Ways |
| --- |
| 1. Double-click the Visual Aids button on the status bar to turn visual aids off and on |
| 2. Press CTRL + / to turn visual aids off and on |

**Figure 1–82**

**BTW**

**Publishing a Site**
See Appendix C for more information about publishing to the Web.

# Previewing in Browsers

Web surfers use a variety of browsers. The most popular are Windows Internet Explorer, Mozilla Firefox, Opera, Netscape Navigator, and Apple Safari. Variations among browsers can cause your pages to appear slightly differently from browser to browser, so it is important to test your pages in as many different browsers as possible before publishing your site to a Web server. Expression Web uses Windows Internet Explorer as the default browser, but you can add others to the browser list.

## To Preview in a Browser

Although the WYSIWYG interface of Expression Web gives a reasonable sense of how the page will look in a browser, it is still a good idea to preview the page from within the browser program to check for any obvious errors. You can also simulate various page sizes that represent a range of screen resolutions to get a better idea of how the visitor's browser will render your page. The following steps preview the site in Internet Explorer using various resolutions.

- Click the Preview in Windows Internet Explorer 7.0 button arrow to display the browser list (Figure 1–83).

 **Experiment**

- Choose different browser programs and resolutions to view any differences in how the site appears.

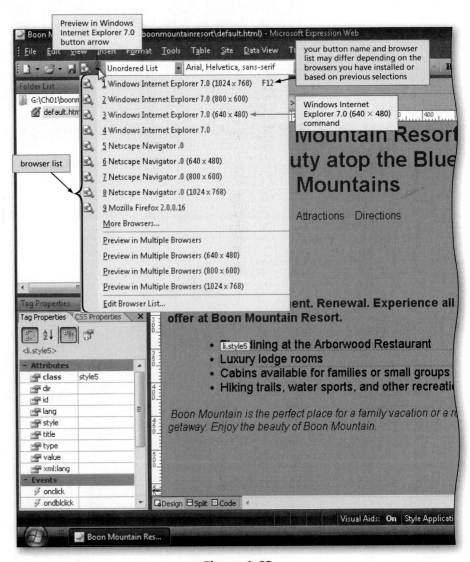

**Figure 1–83**

**2**

- Click Windows Internet Explorer 7.0 (640 × 480) in the menu to view the page in a browser (Figure 1–84).

- If the Maximize button appears, click it to view the browser window maximized.

**3**

- When you are finished looking at your page in the browser, click the Close button on the browser's title bar to return to Expression Web.

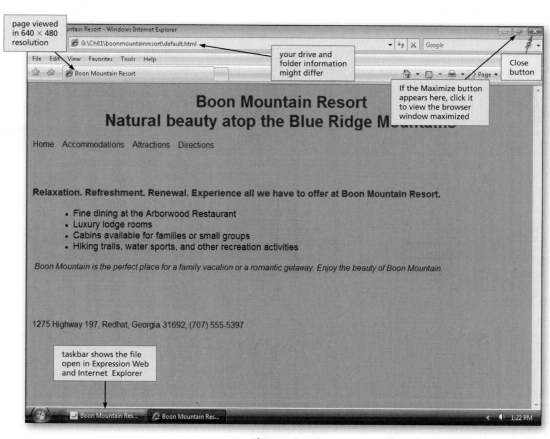

**Figure 1–84**

| Other Ways |
|---|
| 1. Press the F12 key to preview the site using the most recently used browser |
| 2. Click the Preview button on the Common toolbar |

# Printing a Web Page

Expression Web allows you to print a page that looks just like it will appear in a browser. You might want a printout or hard copy of your site pages for proofreading or design markup. Printouts can also be used as archive copies and for distributing to clients.

**BTW**

**Conserving Ink and Toner**
You can print a Web page in black-and-white to conserve ink or toner by clicking the Properties button in the Print dialog box to open the Properties dialog box. Click the Color tab, click the Print in grayscale check box, click the Black ink only option button, then click OK to close the Properties dialog box.

## To Print a Web Page

To save ink and paper, use the Print Preview feature before printing a page to make sure that it fits on a reasonable number of pages. Expression Web adds the page title and a page number to the printed page. Web page background images or colors do not appear on the printed output. The following steps preview and then print the Boon Mountain Resort home page.

**1**

- Click File on the menu bar to open the File menu, and then point to Print to display the Print submenu.

- Click Print Preview on the Print submenu to see what the page will look like before printing it (Figure 1–85).

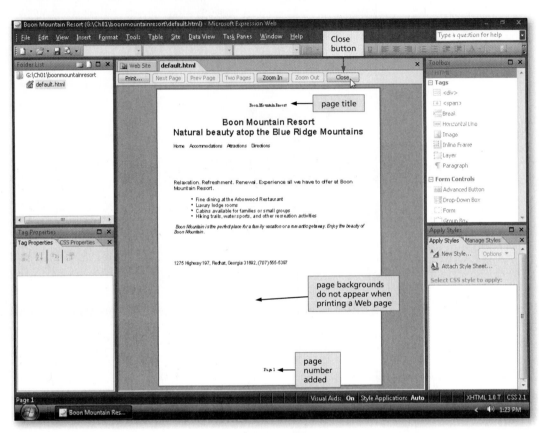

**Figure 1–85**

**2**

- Click the Close button at the top of the Print Preview window to close Print Preview.

- Click File on the menu bar to open the File menu, and then point to Print to display the Print submenu.

- Click Print to open the Print dialog box (Figure 1–86).

- Click the OK button in the Print dialog box to begin printing.

**Q&A** What if I do not want to print at this time?

Click the Cancel button to close the Print dialog box.

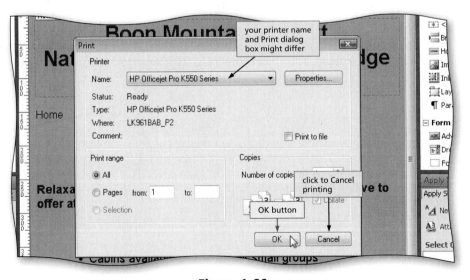

**Figure 1–86**

**Other Ways**

1. Press CTRL+P, then press the ENTER key

# Closing Expression Web

If you quit Expression Web without closing the Web page, Expression Web will attempt to open the page when the program is restarted. If you are not the next user of the program, others might have access to your work. If you are storing your Web page files on a portable device such as a flash drive, Expression Web will display an error message if the portable device is not connected. To avoid these pitfalls, it is a good policy to save and close your files before you exit the Expression Web program.

**BTW**

**Saving Before Closing**
If you have made changes since the last time a page was saved, you will be prompted to save the page before closing the site.

## To Close a Web Page

Now that you are finished working on the Boon Mountain home page, the following steps close the page, then close the site.

- Right-click the default.html tab at the top of the editing window (Figure 1–87).

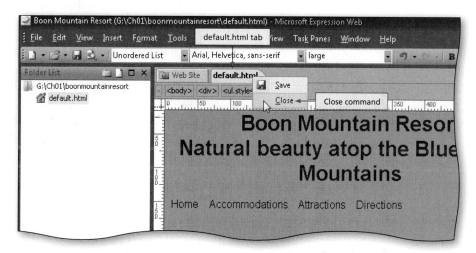

**Figure 1–87**

**2**

- Click Close on the shortcut menu.

- Click File on the menu bar to open the File menu, then click the Close Site command (Figure 1–88).

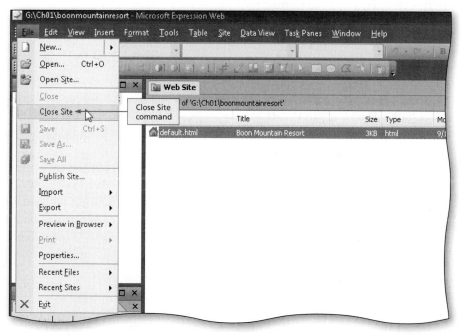

**Other Ways**

1. Click the Close button in the upper-right corner of the Editing window

**Figure 1–88**

## To Quit Expression Web

You have finished the initial text design and formatting for the Boon Mountain Resort Web site. The following step closes Expression Web.

- Click File on the menu bar to open the File menu (Figure 1–89).

- Click the Exit command to quit Expression Web.

**Figure 1–89**

**Other Ways**

1. Click the Close button on the Expression Web title bar to close the program

## Chapter Summary

In this chapter, you have learned how to use Expression Web to open a Web site, enter text, modify text, apply styles, and preview and print a Web page. The items listed below include all the new Expression Web skills you have learned in this chapter.

1. Start Expression Web (EW 6)
2. Reset Workspace Layout (EW 9)
3. Create a Web Site (EW 10)
4. Open a Web Page (EW 14)
5. Set Page Properties (EW 15)
6. Add a <Div> Tag (EW 20)
7. Add Paragraph Text (EW 23)
8. Add a Bulleted List (EW 25)
9. Complete Page Content (EW 28)
10. Save a Web Page (EW 30)
11. Use the Quick Tag Selector (EW 31)
12. Apply a Heading Style (EW 33)
13. Center Text (EW 36)
14. Change Font Color (EW 37)
15. Change Font Size (EW 39)
16. Indent Text (EW 41)
17. Italicize Text (EW 42)
18. Change a Font (EW 44)
19. Spell Check a Page (EW 46)
20. Show Code and Split Views (EW 49)
21. Hide and Display Visual Aids (EW 52)
22. Preview in a Browser (EW 54)
23. Print a Web Page (EW 56)
24. Close a Web Page (EW 57)
25. Quit Expression Web (EW 58)

If you have a SAM user profile, you may have access to hands-on instruction, practice, and assessment. Log in to your SAM account (http://sam2007.course.com) to launch any assigned training activities or exams that relate to the skills covered in this chapter.

## Learn It Online

Test your knowledge of chapter content and key terms.

*Instructions:* To complete the Learn It Online exercises, start your browser, click the Address bar, and then enter the Web address scsite.com/ew2/learn. When the Expression Web Learn It Online page is displayed, click the link for the exercise you want to complete and then read the instructions.

### Chapter Reinforcement TF, MC, and SA
A series of true/false, multiple choice, and short answer questions that test your knowledge of the chapter content.

### Flash Cards
An interactive learning environment where you identify chapter key terms associated with displayed definitions.

### Practice Test
A series of multiple choice questions that test your knowledge of chapter content and key terms.

### Who Wants To Be a Computer Genius?
An interactive game that challenges your knowledge of chapter content in the style of a television quiz show.

### Wheel of Terms
An interactive game that challenges your knowledge of chapter key terms in the style of the television show *Wheel of Fortune.*

### Crossword Puzzle Challenge
A crossword puzzle that challenges your knowledge of key terms presented in the chapter.

## Apply Your Knowledge

Reinforce the skills and apply the concepts you learned in this chapter.

### Modifying Text and Formatting a Web Site
*Instructions:* Start Expression Web. Open the Web site, Apply 1-1 Jessica's Jewels, from the Data Files for Students. See the inside back cover of this book for instructions for downloading the Data Files for Students, or see your instructor for information about accessing the required files.

The Web site you open contains an unformatted home page. You are to open the default.html file and modify and format the text so it looks like Figure 1–90.

*Continued >*

**Apply Your Knowledge** *continued*

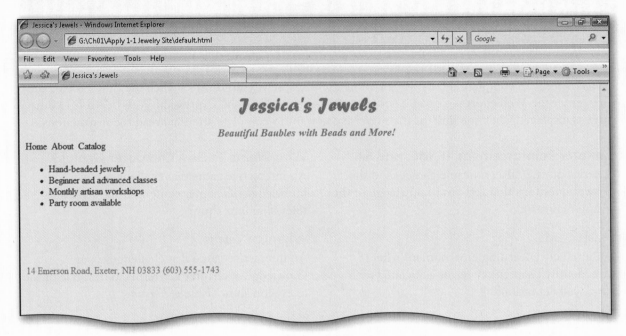

**Figure 1–90**

*Perform the following tasks:*

1. Add the text, Jessica's Jewels, as the page title.

2. Add a page description: Beautiful Baubles with Beads and More!

3. Add the following as keywords: beads, bauble, jewels, jewelry, necklace, bracelet.

4. Change the page background to light blue.

5. Select the div containing the company name Jessica's Jewels, then apply the Heading 1 <h1> style.

6. Change the font for the company name to Forte (or another font of your choice).

7. Change the font color for the company name to a teal color using the More Colors option on the Font Color palette.

8. Center-align the company name.

9. Select the div containing the slogan.

10. Change the slogan font color to the same teal as the company name.

11. Center-align the slogan.

12. Change the font size of the slogan to Large.

13. Apply bold and italics to the slogan.

14. Select the div containing the navigation area and change the font color to plum.

15. Add a paragraph div under the div containing the navigation area.

16. Apply bullets to the new paragraph.

17. Type the following bulleted list, pressing ENTER after each line:

    • Hand-beaded jewelry

    • Beginner and advanced classes

    • Monthly artisan workshops

    • Party room available

18. Press ENTER again after the last line to end the bulleted list.

19. Select the div containing the bulleted list and change the font color of the list text to plum.

20. Add a div at the bottom of the page for the footer.

21. Press ENTER twice at the beginning of the div to add some space.

22. Type the company address in the div: 14 Emerson Road, Exeter, NH, 03833 (603) 555-1743.

23. Change the font color of the address to teal.

24. Save the default.html Web page.

25. Spell check the Web page.

26. Preview the site in two different browsers or resolutions.

27. Use Print Preview to view the site.

28. Print the site.

29. Change the site properties, as specified by your instructor. Save the site using the filename, Apply 1-1 Jewelry Site.

30. Submit the revised site in the format specified by your instructor.

31. Close the default.html Web page.

32. Close the site.

## Extend Your Knowledge

Extend the skills you learned in this chapter and experiment with new skills. You may need to use Help to complete the assignment.

### Formatting a Web Site

*Instructions:* Start Expression Web. Open the Web site, Extend 1-1 Music Festival, from the Data Files for Students. See the inside back cover of this book for instructions for downloading the Data Files for Students, or see your instructor for information about accessing the required files.

You will enhance the Web page to match the one shown in Figure 1–91.

*Perform the following tasks:*

1. Use Help to learn about changing the default font color and how to insert a horizontal line.

2. Print the default.html page.

3. Make notes on the hard copy as to how you will change the Web page to more closely match Figure 1–91.

4. Use the Page Properties dialog box to change the page background to orange and the default font color to blue.

5. Change the font of the masthead to Alba (or another font of your choice) and the font color to red.

6. Deselect all text and divs, double-click the horizontal line div in the Toolbox, and drag to position it under the masthead.

7. Change the font of both the bulleted list and the paragraph to Arial.

8. Increase the font size of the bulleted list text to large and apply the bold attribute.

9. Select the text, Incoming Flight, then click the Italic button on the Common toolbar.

*Continued >*

STUDENT ASSIGNMENTS

**Extend Your Knowledge** *continued*

10. On a separate piece of paper, draw a mock-up of the final page, identifying each part of the page. Make two suggestions for changes based on your own design preferences.

11. Change the site properties, as specified by your instructor.

12. Save the presentation using the filename, Extend 1-1 Music Site.

13. Submit the revised site in the format specified by your instructor.

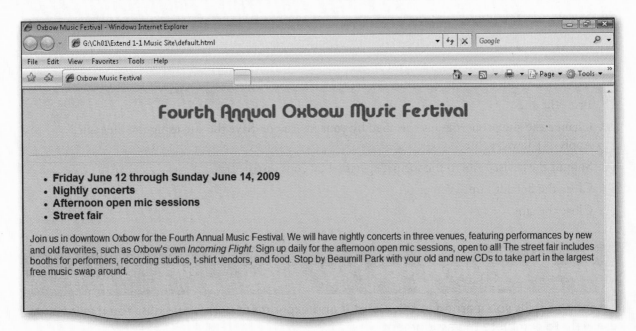

**Figure 1–91**

## Make It Right

Analyze a site and correct all errors and/or improve the design.

### Increasing Readability and Correcting Spelling Errors

*Instructions:*   Start Expression Web. Open the Web site, Make It Right 1-1 Swim Club, from the Data Files for Students. See the inside back cover of this book for instructions for downloading the Data Files for Students, or see your instructor for information about accessing the required files.

The site's font colors and sizes do not provide enough contrast to be easily readable from the screen, and the Expression Web dictionary has flagged several words as being erroneous, as shown in Figure 1–92. You are to change the background, indent, and change text alignment, and change the font sizes and colors to make the text more readable and to show a hierarchy of information. Correct each spelling error by right-clicking the flagged text and clicking the appropriate correction or option on the shortcut menu. Change the page title in the Page Properties dialog box to Macon Waves Swim Club.

Change the site properties, as specified by your instructor. Save the site using the file name, Make it Right 1-1 Swim Club Site. Submit the revised site in the format specified by your instructor.

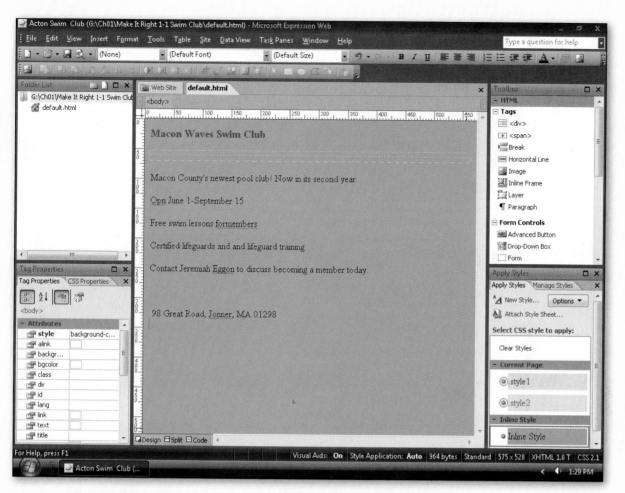

**Figure 1–92**

# In the Lab

Design and/or format a Web site using the guidelines, concepts, and skills presented in this chapter. Labs are listed in order of increasing difficulty.

### Lab 1: Creating a New Home Page

*Problem:* You work part-time at a small bike repair shop. Your boss, Jonas Wolfowitz, has asked you to create a home page for the shop to which he will later add more pages. You create the one-page Web site shown in Figure 1–93 based on Jonas's plan.

*Continued >*

**In the Lab** *continued*

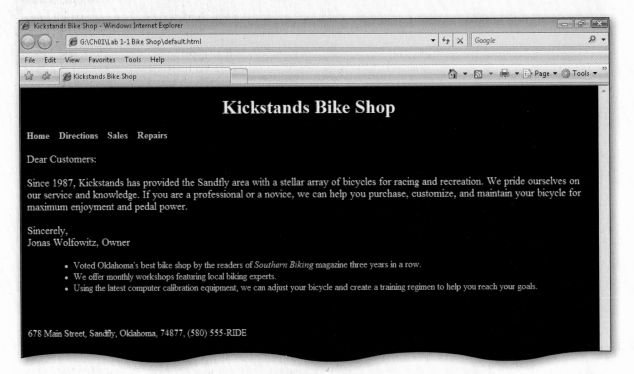

**Figure 1–93**

*Instructions:*

1. Start Expression Web.

2. Create a new one-page Web site named Lab 1-1 Bike Shop and save it on a USB flash drive.

3. Open the default.html page.

4. Enter `Kickstands Bike Shop` as the page title, `Bike Sales and Repairs` as the description, and the following keywords: `bike, bicycle, repair, Sandfly, Oklahoma`.

5. Change the page background to black and the default font color to white.

6. Add a masthead that includes the company name, Kickstands Bike Shop. Assign it the h1 style and center-align the masthead text.

7. Add a div that will include a navigation area for future pages in the site. Type `Home`, `Directions`, `Sales`, and `Repairs`, pressing TAB between each word.

8. Apply bold to the navigation area and change the font color to bright yellow.

9. Add a new div, press ENTER twice, then type the following text. *Hint:* Press ENTER twice in between each paragraph to add line spacing.

`Dear Customers:`

`Since 1987, Kickstands has provided the Sandfly area with a stellar array of bicycles for racing and recreation. We pride ourselves on our service and knowledge. If you are a professional or a novice, we can help you purchase, customize, and maintain your bicycle for maximum enjoyment and pedal power.`

`Sincerely,`

`Jonas Wolfowitz, Owner`

10. Add a new div, then create a new bulleted list with yellow font color. Indent the list from the left margin. Type the following list:

- `Voted Oklahoma's best bike shop by the readers of Southern Biking magazine three years in a row.`
- `We offer monthly workshops featuring local biking experts.`
- `Using the latest computer calibration equipment, we can adjust your bicycle and create a training regimen to help you reach your goals.`

11. Create a new div for the footer. Type the following text:

`678 Main Street, Sandfly, Oklahoma, 74877, (580) 555-RIDE`

12. Instruct the spell checker to ignore Wolfowitz and Sandfly.

13. View the HTML code using Split view.

14. Practice selecting text in the Code window, but do not make any changes to the HTML code.

15. Switch back to Design view.

16. Save the changes you have made to default.html, then preview the page in a browser.

17. Change the site properties, as specified by your instructor.

18. Submit the site in the format specified by your instructor, then close the site.

# In the Lab

## Lab 2: Formatting Fonts and Images

*Problem:* You own a baking business and want to enhance your home page. You finish formatting the site to create the one-page Web site shown in Figure 1–94.

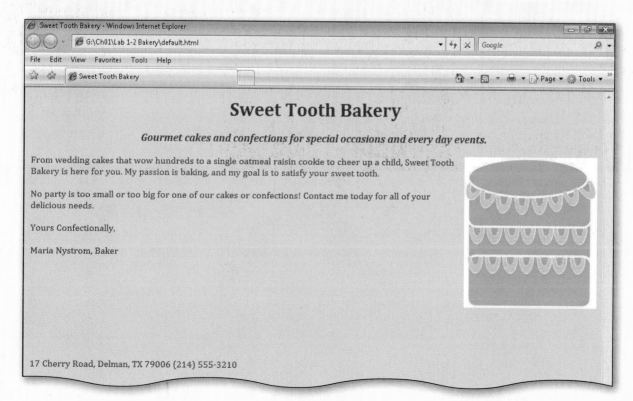

**Figure 1–94**

*Continued >*

**In the Lab** *continued*

*Instructions:*

1. Start Expression Web.
2. Open the Web site Lab 1-2 Bakery.
3. Open the default.html page.
4. Add `Sweet Tooth Bakery` as the title, `Gourmet confections for all of your events` as the page description, and the following keywords: `cake`, `bakery`, `caterer`, `baking`, `cookies`.
5. Change the page background to light pink and the default text color to dark brown.
6. Select the <body> tag on the Quick Selector, then change the default font to Cambria or another font of your choice.
7. Select the tagline div, then apply italics and increase the font size to Large.
8. Deselect all text and divs, then right-click the image of the cake to open the shortcut menu for the image.
9. Click Picture Properties on the shortcut menu.
10. Click the Appearance tab in the Picture Properties dialog box, click Right under Wrapping style, then close the dialog box.
11. Run the spell checker and ignore all of the flagged words. Save the changes you have made to default.html, then preview the page in a browser.
12. Change the site properties, as specified by your instructor.
13. Submit the site in the format specified by your instructor, then close the site.

## In the Lab

### Lab 3: Creating a New Web Site

*Problem:*   Your school's drama club has asked you to prepare a Web page for its upcoming performance. You create the one-page Web site shown in Figure 1–95.

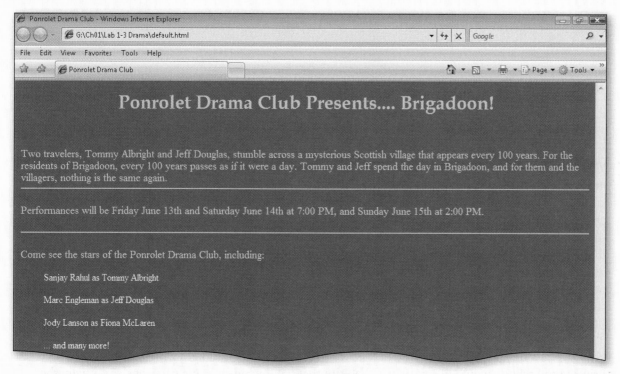

**Figure 1–95**

*Instructions:*   Perform the following tasks.

1. Start Expression Web.

2. Create a new one-page Web site called Lab 1-3 Drama.

3. Open the default.html page.

4. Add Ponrolet Drama Club as the title, Presenting Brigadoon! as the page description, and the following keywords: drama, Ponrolet, acting, Brigadoon.

5. Change the page background to dark green and the default text color to yellow.

6. Change the default body font to Book Antiqua (or another font of your choice).

7. Enter the text and apply heading, indents, and formatting as shown in Figure 1–95.

8. Add and position two horizontal lines using the Toolbox.

9. Save the changes you have made to default.html, then preview the page in a browser. Change the site properties, as specified by your instructor.

10. Submit the site in the format specified by your instructor, then close the site.

# Cases and Places

Apply your creative thinking and problem-solving skills to design and implement a solution.

• Easier    •• More Difficult

## • 1: Work with the Expression Web Window

You want to practice working with the Expression Web window. Open any site that you created in Chapter 1, then open that site's default.html page. Use the Page Properties dialog box to add a keyword. Switch to Code view, then split the view. Select text in Code view, but do not make any changes to the HTML code. Switch to Design view. Insert a new paragraph div using the Toolbox. In the paragraph, create a numbered list with three items, and include one misspelled word and one name that Expression Web identifies as a misspelling. Check the spelling on the page; correct the misspelled word and ignore the name. Select one item using the Quick Tag Selector, then use the Quick Tag Selector to select the entire list. Close the default.html page without saving any changes, close the Web site, then quit Expression Web.

## • 2: Design and Plan a School Web Site

You have just finished a class on Web design. The school administration of Pinkham Academy, a private high school, would like to plan a Web site that will include a home page, and eventually they will add other pages. Sketch a plan on a piece of paper for the home page of the Web site that you can present to the administration and use to gather their feedback. Include a masthead that lists the school name and a navigation area with links to the library, administration, and calendar. The administration wants to include the school logo on the home page. Include an area for a letter from the principal and a footer for the address. The school's colors are blue and white; indicate on the Web site sketch how you will incorporate the school's colors.

## •• 3: Format a One-Page Alumni Web Site

You have recently joined the Connecticut branch of your college alumni association. You have been working on a home page that can tell other local graduates of Gulliver College about upcoming alumni events. You have already entered the text for the home page. Open the site Cases and Places 3 Alumni, then open the page default.html. Use the page properties to add a title, description, and four appropriate keywords. Use the heading style and other formatting techniques to apply italics, bold, center alignment, and indentations to make the home page easy to read.

## •• 4: Create a Job Search Home Page

**Make It Personal**

When you are looking for a job, it is helpful to have a resume or list of your skills that you can share with potential employers. What is your dream job? Imagine yourself a decade from now—what amazing skills and job experiences have you collected? Have you won any awards, made a scientific discovery, learned a foreign language, or gone to art school? Create a one-page Web site that you can use to show potential employers all of the things that you have learned and done over the past ten years that would qualify you for your dream job. Include a masthead, bulleted list, footer, and any other information you think is relevant. Format the Web site attractively, including adding a background color, changing the fonts, and applying effects such as bold and italics. Add a page title, description, and keywords.

• • 5: Create a Home Page for a Sports Team

**Working Together**

One of your local sports teams wants to create a multi-page Web site for its fans. The site will include a home page, the calendar for the upcoming season, and biographies of the players and coaches. The home page should include a masthead, navigation area, bulleted list with highlights from the previous season, and a footer with contact information. Working as a team with several of your classmates, you are to design a Web site and create the home page. As a group, decide on the type of sport, the name of the team, and the team colors. Each team member should plan on paper the three pages (home, calendar, biographies) that will eventually be included in the site and present their plan to the group. As a group, decide on elements of each plan that you will incorporate into creating the home page, and start creating the home page using Expression Web. Add a page title, description, and keywords. Format the Web site attractively, including incorporating the team colors into the background and fonts, changing the fonts, and applying effects such as bold and italics. Run the spelling checker, use Print Preview, then print the site. Make notes as a group about any changes you need to make, then preview the site in multiple browsers and resolutions.

# 2 | Working with Images and Links

## Objectives

You will have mastered the material in this chapter when you can:

- Insert and align an image
- Change the workspace
- Add borders and margins to an image
- Copy page elements to the Clipboard
- Edit an image
- Create an image thumbnail

- Create a folder for images
- Add internal links
- Add external links
- Add a bookmark
- Add an e-mail link
- Add a ScreenTip

# 2 | Working with Images and Links

## Introduction

Text is an important part of Web site content — it describes the purpose of the site and conveys valuable details related to the site's subject matter. No matter how well written the text is, however, a site without images or that is difficult to navigate will not hold a visitor's attention for long. **Graphics** or **images** in Web pages serve a practical purpose by illustrating a product or service described in the text, displaying a company's logo, or serving as links to further information. Images also help make a site more attractive and effective by providing visual interest and continuity. **Hyperlinks**, or simply **links**, are text or graphics used to jump to another location in the same Web page, elsewhere in the site, or to another Web site. A link can also open the visitor's e-mail program that allows the visitor to send an e-mail to the site owner or other recipient. Links, in either text or graphic format, help to organize a site by providing navigation to other areas of the World Wide Web.

## Project — Enhancing the Boon Mountain Resort Web Site

A Web site for a business, such as the Boon Mountain Resort, needs to inform and attract current and potential customers. Visitors to a Web site want to get an impression of the product or service very quickly. Sites that feature eye-catching images and that are easy to navigate and informative, can help build a customer base, leading to increased success of the business.

A navigation area that includes links to each of the main pages on a site usually appears on the left side or below the masthead on each page of a site. The navigation area also might appear in both locations.

The project for this chapter uses Expression Web to add images and links to the home page for the Boon Mountain Resort, as shown in Figure 2–1. Additional pages and content have been added to the Web site that you created in Chapter 1, based on the site plan and feedback from site visitors and Boon Mountain Resort staff. Now you will add a logo and images so that visitors to the site can see images of the resort's various accommodations. You will also create a navigational structure, add links to other attractions near the resort, create a bookmark for a long page, and add a link that visitors can use to send an e-mail to the resort.

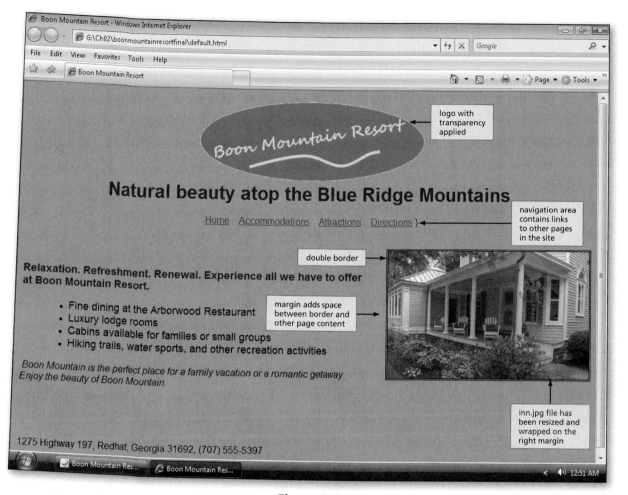

**Figure 2–1**

## Overview

As you read this chapter, you will learn how to add images and links to the Web site shown in Figure 2–1 by performing these general tasks:

- Choose and insert images.
- Adjust the workspace layout.
- Position images in relation to text and page margins.
- Distinguish an image by modifying margins and borders.
- Make changes to the appearance and format of an image.
- Add links to other pages in the site, to other sites, and to an e-mail address.

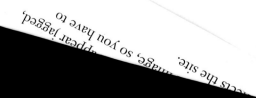

Plan
Ahead

**General Project Guidelines**

When adding images and links to a Web site, you should keep in mind the goals of the site. Any images that you add should not only be attractive but should also serve a purpose. Links should assist a reader in finding information quickly. A navigation area is essential, but additional links to pages, page areas, or external locations can enhance a visitor's experience and allow them to find the information they need quickly. As you add text and images to a Web site, such as the project shown in Figure 2–1, you should follow these general guidelines:

1. **Properly use images that enhance the message of your site.** Adding too many images or using poor quality ones will detract from the message you are trying to deliver. Consider having a professional photographer take the pictures to ensure their quality. Always make sure that you have the proper permission to use an image before you add it to your site and that you give credit to your source. You should plan for borders, image placement, and spacing around your image to guide the reader's eye and distinguish your image.

2. **Identify changes to make to the images.** Removing unnecessary background areas by **cropping** will emphasize the portion of the image that is relevant. Physically resizing an image takes up more or less space on the screen. You can give visitors the option of seeing a larger version of an image by providing them with a thumbnail that, when clicked, enlarges the image. Including thumbnails can make the site quicker to download, increasing the usability of your site. You should also organize the image files into a folder or series of folders.

3. **Determine the necessary internal and external links.** A navigation area includes links to the main pages in a site. A large site can have thousands of Web pages, but the designers of the site generally organize the pages into categories and subcategories to help visitors quickly find the information they are seeking. Linking to external sites can enhance the information on a site. For example, providing links to area attractions helps visitors learn more about the Boon Mountain Resort vicinity. Providing an e-mail link allows visitors to interact with the site by requesting additional information or by adding their address to a mailing list. Text is often used as a link, but images, such as photos and graphic logos, can also be used as links as well.

Specific details about these guidelines are presented at appropriate points in the chapter. The chapter will also identify what tasks will be performed and how decisions are made during the creation of the Web site shown in Figure 2–1.

BTW
**Sources for Images**
You can insert images installed on a disk or network folder to which you have access, use images saved to your Web site folder, or insert images directly from a digital camera or electronic scanner.

BTW
**File Sizes**
A higher file resolution delivers a better quality of image, but higher file sizes take longer to download. You can usually reduce file sizes using compression software without visibly diminishing the quality of the image as displayed on the page.

## Choosing Images and File Types

Web page images are digital files that you can acquire as stock photography from a CD or downloaded file, or you can use images that are imported from a device such as a digital camera. Regardless of the origins of your image files, all images included in your site need to be **embedded**, or saved as a part of the Web site so that when you publish your site, all of the files are accessible.

## Technical Considerations for Image Files

Adding images to a Web site increases the site's attractiveness but adds complexity in terms of increased page file sizes and variations in graphic resolution. Image files that exceed 100 kilobytes in size can download slowly in a visitor's browser, a situation you should avoid. Image files are composed of dots, or **pixels**, which are the smallest amount of visible data in an image. An image's **resolution** is the concentration of dots that make up the image. High-quality images typically require larger file sizes, because higher-quality images are **high resolution** (high res), containing a high concentration of dots per inch (dpi). If an image file has a low resolution (low res), the image can a or **pixilated**. A high-resolution file provides a better quality of i balance the quality of an image with how its size aff

A **file format** is the way the file is encoded and stored electronically. An image's file format differs depending on the type of image, the program that created it, or how it was saved. To appear in a browser, your site's images must be saved in a format supported by most browsers. The most common image file formats used on the Web are .gif (Graphics Interface Format, pronounced "jiff"), .jpg (Joint Photographic Experts Group, pronounced "jaypeg"), and .png (Portable Network Graphics, pronounced "ping").

The .gif, .jpg, and .png file formats differ in how they **compress**, or reduce the size of image files by removing extraneous file data. **Lossy** compression means that a certain amount of quality is lost when the image is compressed. For an image that uses broad swatches of uniform colors, this is not usually visible. For photographs, you should use **lossless** compression, where the image retains its quality. Photos that have lost considerable quality appear pixilated and display blocks of color (Figure 2–2).

**BTW**

**Images from External Devices**
If you have images stored on a digital camera or captured electronically using a scanner, insert the device or storage media as directed by the device manufacturer, then use the From Scanner or Camera submenu on the Insert | Picture menu to insert the image.

squares indicate lossyness

**Figure 2–2**

Table 2–1 describes common image formats.

| Table 2–1 Image File Types | | | |
|---|---|---|---|
| **File Format** | **Extension(s)** | **Compression** | **About** |
| Graphics Interface Format (GIF) | .gif | Lossless | Introduced by CompuServe in 1987. Best for drawn graphics or logos. Supports animations. Uses data compression for large files. Limited to 256 colors. |
| Joint Photographic Experts Group (JPEG) | .jpg, .jpeg | Lossy | A compression method and file format used for photographs. |
| Portable Network Graphics (PNG) | .png | Lossless | Developed as a non-proprietary file format to be used without restrictions. Best for drawn graphics or logos. Does not support animations. Uses data compression for large files. |

## Accessibility Properties

Because some visitors to your site might have a vision impairment that requires them to use a screen reader program or other adaptive technology, you should complete the information in the Accessibility Properties dialog box that opens when you insert an image. Depending on a visitor's browser and settings, this information, called **alternate text**, appears next to an image while it downloads and provides information to those who use devices to assist with visual impairments.

Write your alternate text to describe the image that it is associated with so that users of visual assistance software will get a complete description of the image and how it differs from other pictures on your site. For instance, on a Web site for a band that features all of the album covers from the past 20 years, the alternate text for each image should have the complete album name, year of publication, and a brief description of the images used on the cover, instead of "album cover."

<table>
<tr><td>

**Plan Ahead**

</td><td>

**Properly use images that enhance the message of your site.**
When deciding on how to enhance your site with images, consider both the aesthetic value of each image and whether the image conveys the necessary information or message to visitors to your site. Choose only images that are necessary to enhance the site and inform visitors, and make sure to seek permission where necessary.

- **Determine the type of images you will need.** You can enhance your Web page with many types of images.
  - Company logos are graphics created by a designer, usually incorporate the company name, and use color and shapes to create an easily recognizable image that can be used on letterhead, Web pages, and other communications to identify the company. On a Web page, a company logo often appears on the masthead.
  - Photographs taken with a digital camera or scanned into an electronic format are valuable for depicting a location or product.
  - Use a graphic design program to create images that look drawn, such as logos or cartoons, or to decrease the file size or make other enhancements to photographs or other images.
  - **Animated graphics** use a series of motions and sounds to make an image appear to be moving.
- **Store the images in a central folder location, and make sure that you have the proper permissions to use them.**
  - You can create a folder within the Web site to manage your digital assets, such as image files.
  - Acquire permission to use non-original images, give credit to the source, and make sure that you are using the image according to the agreement with the source and any guidelines that may have been set.
  - It is the responsibility of the person using the image to gain permission. Even if an image does not have a copyright notice with it, it is still not free for public use unless express permission has been given.

</td></tr>
</table>

The following pages show you how to insert, place, and format images after you have started Expression Web.

**BTW**

**Placeholders**
A **placeholder** is a container to which you add text or images. The Image icon in the Toolbox is used to insert a placeholder to which you will later add an image. This is helpful if you do not have the image at the time. You can resize the placeholder to determine the spacing and layout of your page until you insert the image.

# Inserting an Image

When you insert an image into a Web page, Expression Web automatically creates a div to contain the image. To wrap text around an image, insert the image into the div that contains the text. If you want to align and position the image separately from surrounding text, insert it into its own div.

## To Start Expression Web

If you are using a computer to step through the project in this chapter, and you want your screens to match the figures in this book, you should change your computer's resolution to 1024 × 768. For information about how to change a computer's resolution, read Appendix F. If you are using a lab computer or have changed the workspace layout, reset the workspace to the default settings to match the screens in this book.

The following steps, which assume you are running Windows Vista, start Expression Web based on a typical installation and reset the workspace layout. You may need to ask your instructor how to start Expression Web for your computer.

**Note:** If you are using Window XP, see Appendix E for alternate steps.

**1**

- Click the Start button on the Windows Vista taskbar to display the Start menu.

- Click All Programs at the bottom of the left pane on the Start menu to display the All Programs list.

- Click Microsoft Expression on the All Programs list to display the Microsoft Expression list.

**2**

- Click Microsoft Expression Web 2 to start Expression Web.

**3**

- Click Task Panes on the menu bar to open the Task Panes men, then click Reset Workspace Layout.

## To Open a Web Site

An Expression Web site consists of at least one folder and file; most sites include multiple files and folders. When you open a site, all of the files and folders appear in the Folder List and can be individually opened and accessed. Always open all of the site's files at once using Expression Web. If you use a Windows Explorer window to open one page or file of a site at a time, you can create errors of inconsistency and broken links. The following steps open the Boon Mountain Resort Web site and the default.html page.

**1**

- With your USB flash drive connected to one of the computer's USB ports, click File on the menu bar to open the File menu (Figure 2–3).

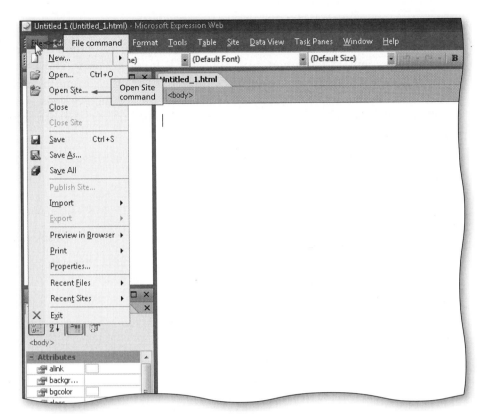

**Figure 2–3**

**2**

- Click Open Site on the File menu to open the Open Site dialog box.

- Click Computer in the Favorite Links section to display a list of available drives.

- If necessary, scroll until USB (G:) appears in the list of available drives (Figure 2–4).

**Q&A**
My dialog box is different.

If your dialog box shows a Folders List below the Folders button, click the Folders button. If Computer is not displayed in the Favorite Links, drag the top or bottom edge of the Save As dialog box until Computer is displayed.

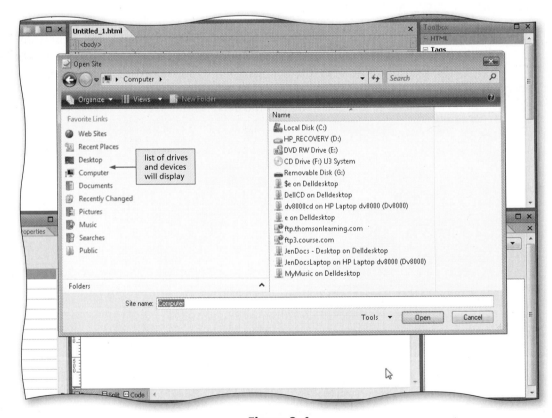

**Figure 2–4**

**3**

- Double-click USB (G:) to display the contents of the drive.

- Double-click the Ch02 folder to display its contents.

- Click the boonmountain-resortfinal Web site folder to select it (Figure 2–5).

**Figure 2–5**

**4**

- Click the Open button to open the site (Figure 2–6).

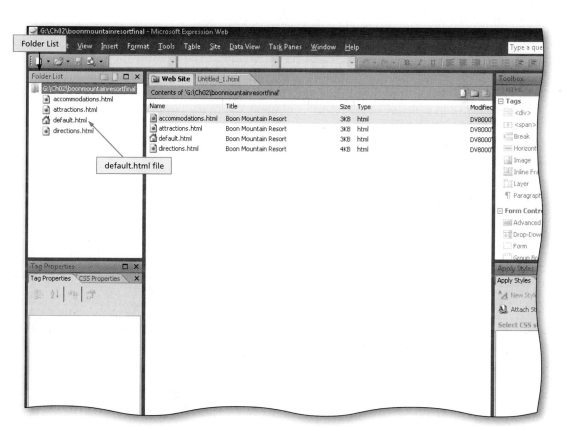

**Figure 2–6**

- Double-click the default.html page in the Folder List to open it (Figure 2–7).

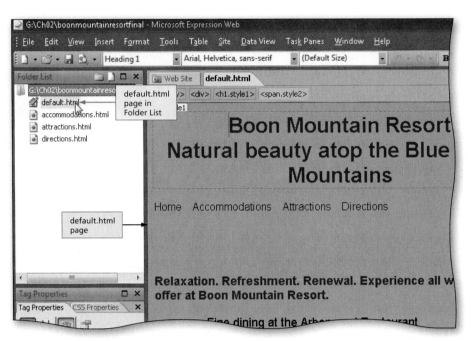

**Figure 2–7**

## To Insert an Image

All images that you insert into a page need to be embedded into your site to make them available when your page is viewed in a browser. When you make changes to an image, you will be prompted to resave the embedded file. In the Save Embedded Files dialog box there are options to rename the image, save the image in a folder, assign an action, and change the file type.

All images used in the Boon Mountain Resort site were taken by the owner, so no credits are necessary. The following steps add a picture of the resort's main building to the home page from an external folder, assign accessibility properties, and embed the image into your site.

- In the Expression Web editing window, click above the line beginning with the word, Relaxation, to place the insertion point in the div (Figure 2–8).

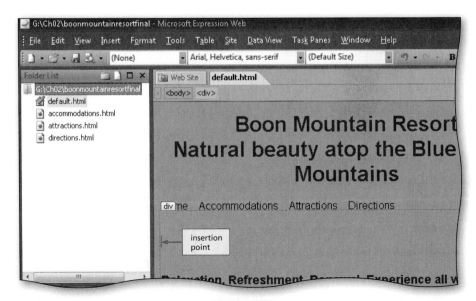

**Figure 2–8**

**2**

• Click Insert on the menu bar to open the Insert menu (Figure 2–9).

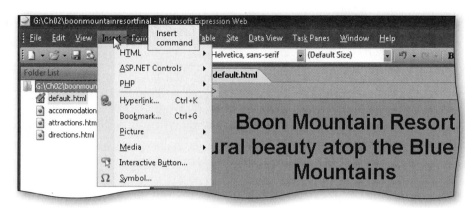

**Figure 2–9**

**3**

• Point to Picture on the Insert menu, then point to From File (Figure 2–10).

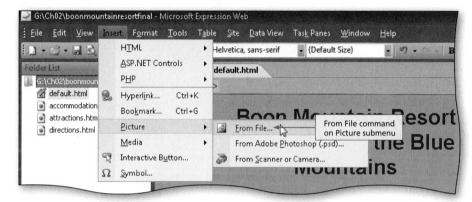

**Figure 2–10**

**4**

• Click From File to open the Picture dialog box.

• Navigate to the USB G: drive, if necessary, then double-click the folder that contains your data files (Figure 2–11).

**Figure 2–11**

**5**

- Double-click the folder boon-mountainresort_ images to open it.

- Click the file inn.jpg to select it (Figure 2–12).

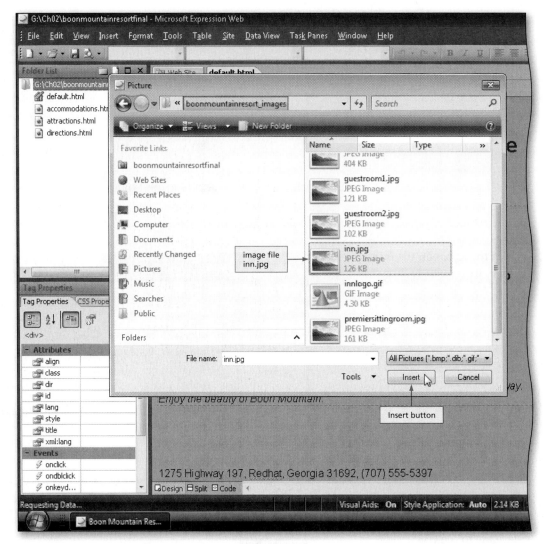

**Figure 2–12**

**6**

- Click the Insert button to open the Accessibility Properties dialog box.

- In the Accessibility Properties dialog box, type Front porch of inn in the Alternate text text box (Figure 2–13).

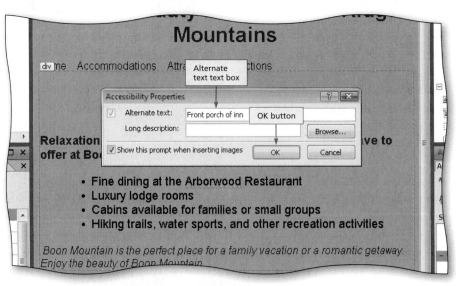

**Figure 2–13**

Expression Web Chapter 2

**7**

- Click the OK button to close the dialog box and see the inserted image on the page (Figure 2–14).

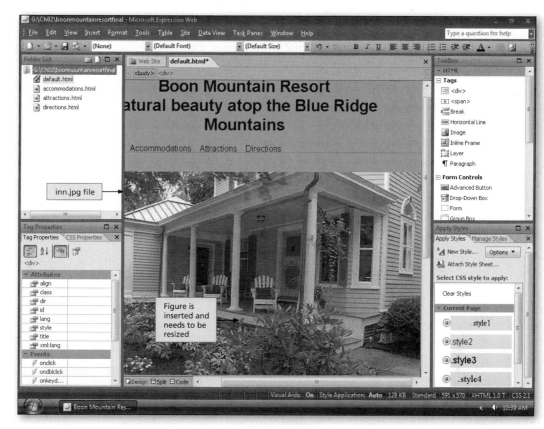

**Figure 2–14**

**8**

- Press CTRL+S to save the default.html page.

- Click the OK button in the Save Embedded Files dialog box (Figure 2–15).

**Experiment**

- Click the Change Folder, Set Action, and Picture File Type buttons in the Save Embedded Files dialog box to see the options available in the dialog boxes that open. Click the Cancel button in each dialog box to close it without making any changes.

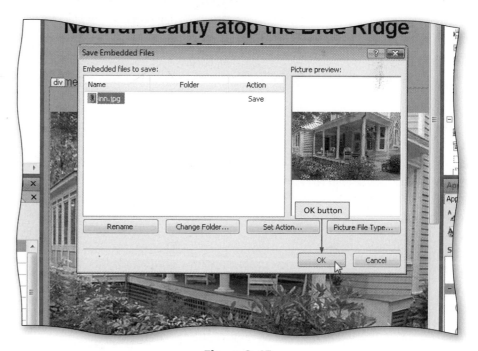

**Figure 2–15**

**Other Ways**

1. Click the Insert Picture from File button on the Common toolbar

# Adjusting the Workspace Layout

As you work with Web pages, you may want to adjust the layout of the workspace by opening, moving, maximizing, minimizing, or closing task panes. You can open, close, or rearrange task panes to best fit your preferences or to access specific tools. You should only open the task panes that you need; having too many task panes open makes your workspace cluttered and leaves you less room for editing. Expression Web saves the arrangement and uses it as the default the next time you start the program.

As you work with images, it is helpful to display the rulers as a guide for cropping and resizing. Images often are inserted into a Web page at a size that is too large, so you might need to close task panes in order to view more of the editing window on the screen and display rulers so that you can accurately size, position, and crop images.

## Task Panes

Expression Web contains 18 task panes; the four default task panes (Folder List, Tag Properties, Apply Styles, and Toolbox) are docked on the left and right sides of the editing window. Table 2–2 lists different ways you can adjust the workspace using the task panes. Examples are shown in Figure 2–16 (a and b).

| Table 2–2 Task Pane Actions | | |
| --- | --- | --- |
| **Skill** | **Method** | **Effect** |
| Undocking | Hold the insertion point over the task pane title bar until the insertion point changes to a four-headed arrow, then drag the task pane to the center of the editing window | Allows you to move it to a new location or have it float anywhere in the Expression Web window (see Figure 2–16 a) |
| Docking | Hold the insertion point over the task pane title bar until the insertion point changes to a four-headed arrow, then drag the task pane to the left or right of the editing window until it docks | Allows you to move it to a fixed location on a side of the Expression Web window (see Figure 2–16 a) |
| Maximizing | Click the Maximize button on the task pane title bar | Enlarges a task pane so that you can see more of its content (see Figure 2–16 a) |
| Minimizing | Click the Restore Window button on the task pane title bar | Minimize a task pane to view more of another task pane in the same column (see Figure 2–16 a) |
| Opening | Click Task Panes on the menu bar, then click a task pane | Displays a task pane in order to access its tools (see Figure 2–16 b) |
| Closing | Click the Close button on the task pane title bar | Closes a task pane to see more of another task pane or more of the editing window (see Figure 2–16 a) |

Figure 2–16 (b) shows the task panes menu, which can be accessed through the Task Panes command on the menu bar. A check mark next to the task pane name in the Task Pane menu indicates it is visible. To show a task pane, click the task pane name in the menu to add a check mark. To hide a task pane, click the name that contains the check mark to remove the check mark.

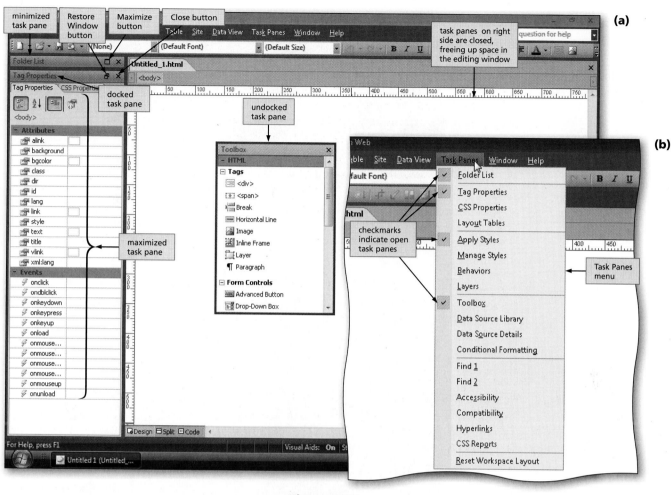

**Figure 2–16**

## To Close a Task Pane

The following step closes the two task panes on the right side of the window, giving you more space in the editing window to format the images.

**1**

- Point to the Close Window button on the Apply Styles task pane title bar (Figure 2–17).

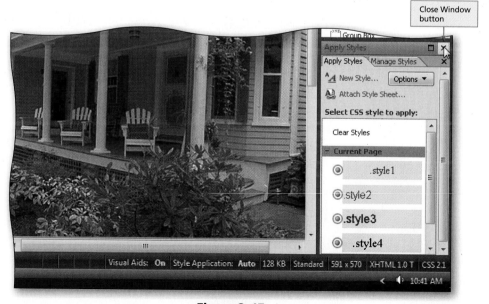

**Figure 2–17**

**2**

- Click the Close Window button on the Apply Styles task pane title bar to close the Apply Styles task pane (Figure 2–18).

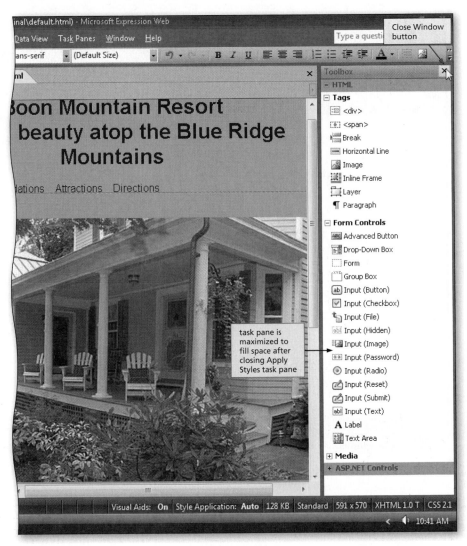

**Figure 2–18**

**3**

- Click the Close Window button on the Toolbox title bar to close the Toolbox (Figure 2–19).

both task panes closed; entire image can be viewed

**Figure 2–19**

## To Display the Ruler

The image file you just inserted is too large and you will need to resize it. The Expression Web workspace can include rulers to assist you with adjusting page layout. When you display the rulers, they appear along the left (vertical) and top (horizontal) edges of the window and use pixels as measurement. In the following steps, you will display the rulers so that you can position and size the images and margins.

**1**

- Click View on the menu bar to open the View menu, then point to Ruler and Grid to display the submenu (Figure 2–20).

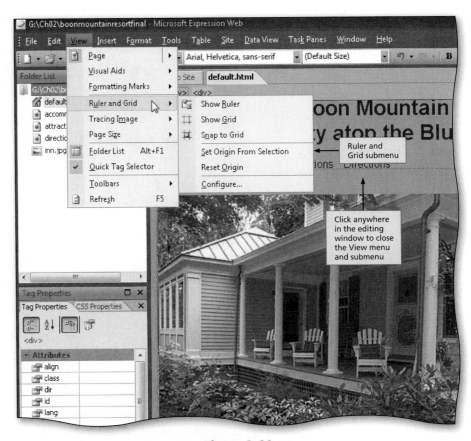

**Figure 2–20**

**2**

- Click Show Ruler on the submenu to display the rulers.

- Click the image to select it and to close the menu (Figure 2–21).

**Q&A**

What should I do if my rulers are already displayed?

Show Ruler is a toggle command, meaning that the same steps are used to turn the rulers on and off. If your rulers were already displayed, either skip these steps or repeat them to display the rulers.

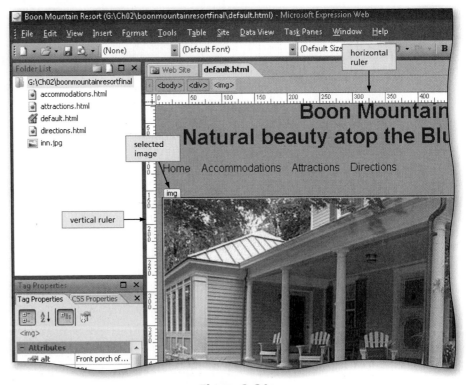

**Figure 2–21**

# Adjusting Proportions

The relationship between an image's height and width is an image's **proportions**, or **aspect ratio**. If an image's proportions are changed, it can distort the image like a carnival funhouse mirror. To maintain the aspect ratio when resizing an image manually, drag a corner sizing handle to adjust the height and width at the same time. When you change the height of an image in the Picture Properties dialog box, click the Keep aspect ratio check box so that the width automatically adjusts proportionately, and vice versa. After you have resized an image, you should **resample** it to improve the image quality by adjusting the resolution of pixels to the new image size.

**BTW**

**Changing image size**
Resizing an image can make your layout more attractive but does not change the file size of the image. When you make an image larger, you risk decreasing the image quality because as you increase the size on the page, you are spreading out the existing pixels in the file. Testing your site in a browser can identify problems with resized images.

## To Resize an Image

Expression Web uses the actual pixel width and height of the picture as the size when it inserts the image. You can resize the physical space that the picture takes up by dragging the image using the sizing handles or by specifying the height and width in pixels in the Picture Properties dialog box. In the following steps, you will resize the image, then resample it.

- Click Format on the menu bar to open the Format menu, then point to Properties (Figure 2–22).

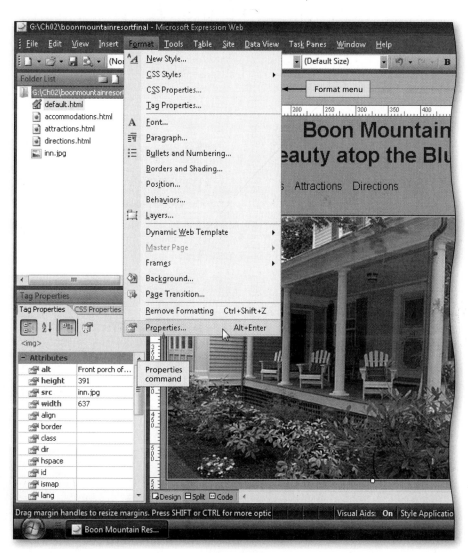

**Figure 2–22**

**2**

- Click Properties to open the Picture Properties dialog box.

- Click the Appearance tab (Figure 2–23).

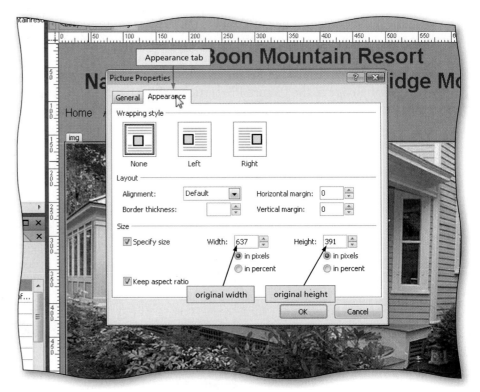

**Figure 2–23**

**3**

- If necessary, click the Keep aspect ratio check box to select it.

- Type 400 in the Width box to decrease the figure's size (Figure 2–24).

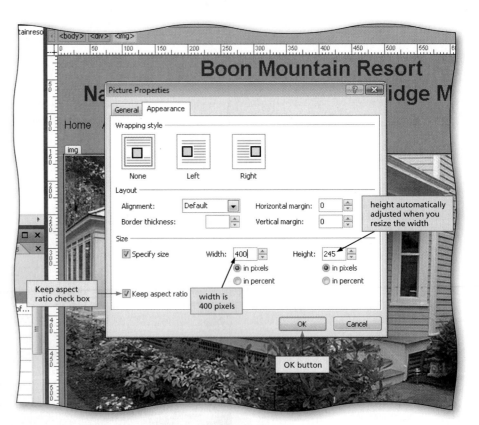

**Figure 2–24**

- Click the OK button to close the Picture Properties dialog box.

- If necessary, click the picture to select it and make sizing handles appear around the perimeter (Figure 2–25).

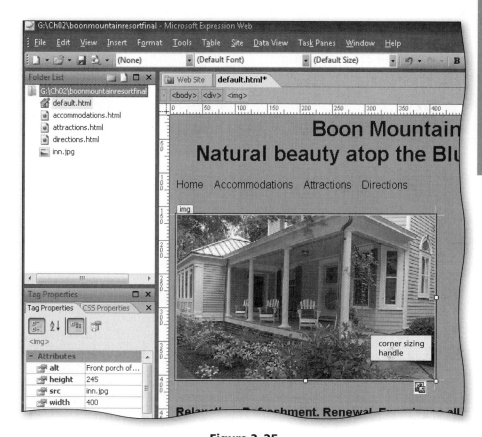

**Figure 2–25**

- Position the pointer over the lower-right handle so that it changes to a double-headed arrow (Figure 2–26).

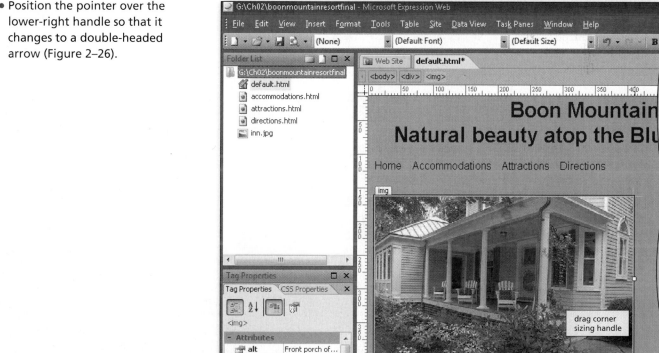

**Figure 2–26**

**6**

- Drag the sizing handle up and to the left so that the width is approximately 350 and the height is approximately 216 pixels, according to the ScreenTip (Figure 2–27).

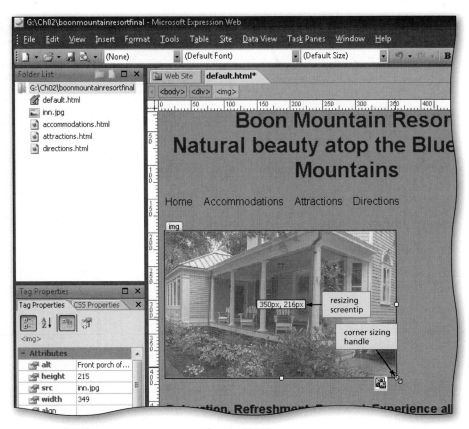

**Figure 2–27**

**7**

- Click the Picture Actions button below the resized image to open the menu (Figure 2–28).

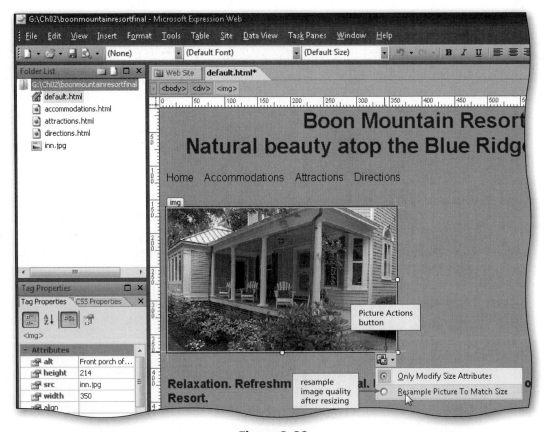

**Figure 2–28**

**8**
- Click the Resample Picture To Match Size option button to resample the image.

- Press CTRL+S to save the page (Figure 2–29).

- Click the OK button to save the embedded file.

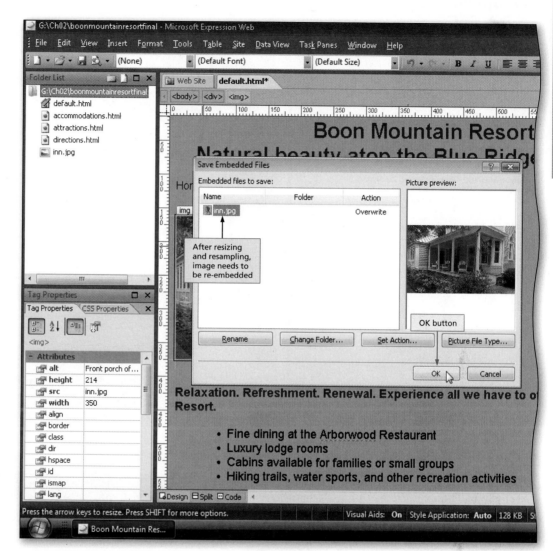

After resizing and resampling, image needs to be re-embedded

OK button

**Figure 2–29**

**Other Ways**

1. Double-click the picture to open the Picture Properties dialog box

2. Right-click the picture, then click Picture Properties to open the Picture Properties dialog box

## Positioning an Image

Changing the alignment and spacing of text and images allows you to create a flow to your page that is visually interesting and guides the reader's eye down the page. You can choose to align to the left or right margin, or to the center of the page. When you align an image that is surrounded by text, you should position the image in relation to the text. When positioning text around an image, use the **text wrapping** feature to guide how the text flows around the image. This method is preferable to using the alignment buttons on the Common toolbar, which would adjust the image and text alignment at the same time.

## To Align an Image

In the following steps, you will align the image to the right margin and wrap the text around it.

- Double-click the image to open the Picture Properties dialog box.

- Click the Appearance tab.

- Click the Right button in the Wrapping style section of the Appearance tab (Figure 2–30).

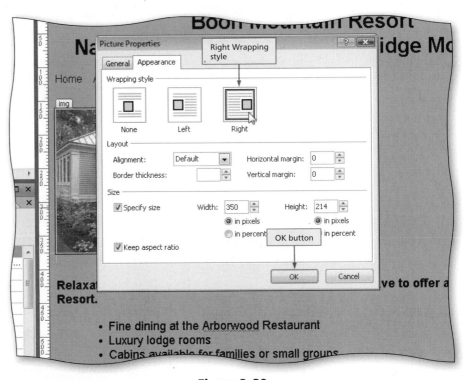

**Figure 2–30**

- Click the OK button to close the dialog box. Click anywhere outside of the figure to deselect it (Figure 2–31).

- Press CTRL+S to save the page.

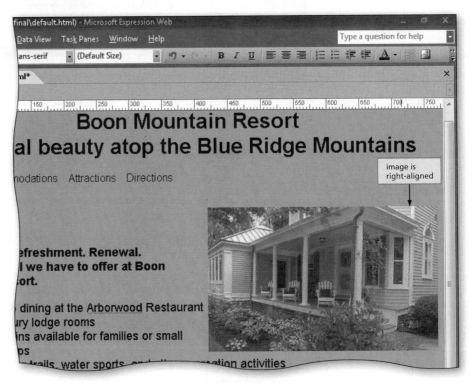

**Figure 2–31**

# Adding Borders and Spacing

There are many different **borders** available from the Borders tab of the Borders and Shading dialog box that you can use to surround your image with lines, graphics, or effects. You can also create a custom border, or use the Borders button on the Common toolbar to add a basic border.

Image **margins** surround the top, bottom, left, and right edges of an image and separate it from adjacent text or images. Adding a margin to an image ensures that the image has sufficient spacing around it. Margins are measured in pixels.

**Padding**

**Padding** is space between the image and its border. When an image has been padded, you can see the page background between the edge of the image and the border. Including padding is different from adding a margin.

## To Add a Border to an Image

A border around an image can give it definition and distinction. As you click an option in the Style list of the Borders and Shading dialog box, the Preview pane of the dialog box changes to show you what the border will look like. The following steps add the double border style to the image.

- Click the image to select it.

- Click Format on the menu bar to open the Format menu, then point to Borders and Shading (Figure 2–32)

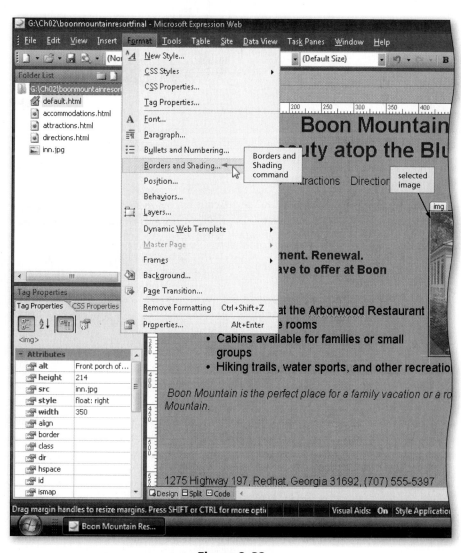

**Figure 2–32**

**2**

- Click Borders and Shading on the Format menu to open the Borders and Shading dialog box.

- Click double in the Style list to select it (Figure 2–33).

🔎 **Experiment**

- Click other options in the Style list to view them in the Preview box, then click double to select it.

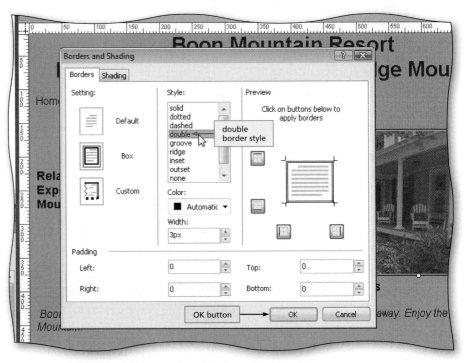

**Figure 2–33**

**3**

- Click the OK button to close the dialog box and apply the border.

 How can I reverse a change to the page?

To undo the last change you have made to a page, press CTRL+Z or click the Undo button on the Common toolbar. Repeat this step to undo multiple changes that have occurred since your last save. After you save a page, you cannot undo the changes.

- Click outside the image to deselect it (Figure 2–34).

- Press CTRL+S to save the page.

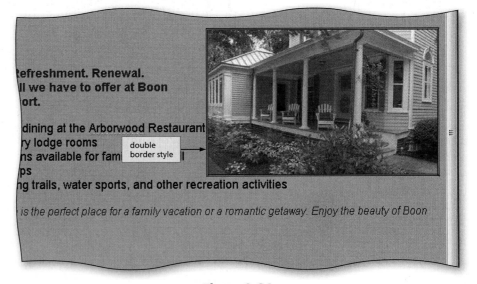

**Figure 2–34**

**Other Ways**

1. Select the image, click the Borders button arrow on the Common toolbar, then click an option from the gallery to apply it

## To Modify Image Margins

Adding a margin to an image increases the space between the image and the surrounding text and helps the image to stand out. The following steps manually adjust the left and bottom image margins of the image using ScreenTips to determine the size of the margin.

**1**

● Click the image to select it.

● Position the pointer over the left margin to view the margin ScreenTip, which should be margin-left: (0 px).

● Hold down the left mouse button and drag the left margin border to the left until the ScreenTip shows that it is 25 pixels (Figure 2–35).

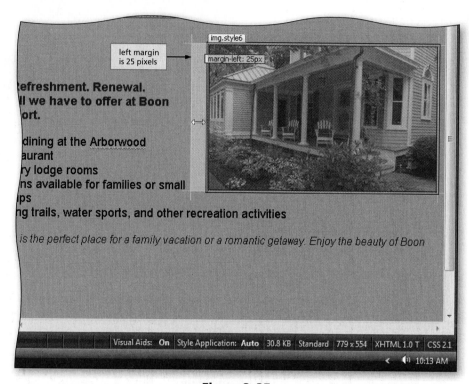

**Figure 2–35**

**2**

● Release the mouse button to set the left margin. Using the double-headed arrow pointer, click and drag the bottom margin border down until the ScreenTip shows that it is 15 pixels, then release the mouse button (Figure 2–36).

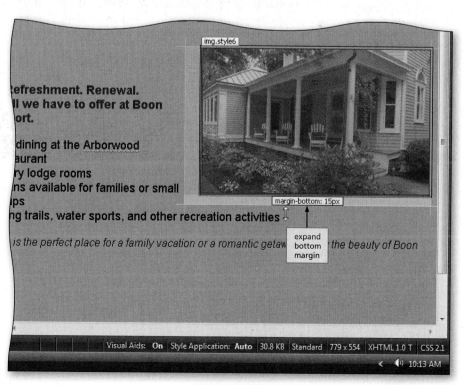

**Figure 2–36**

**3**

- Release the mouse button to view the expanded margin.

- Click outside of the image to deselect it (Figure 2–37).

- Press CTRL+S to save the page.

**Q&A**

Why did my picture resize when I dragged the margin border?

Make sure that you position the pointer over the edge of an image, but not on one of its sizing handles.

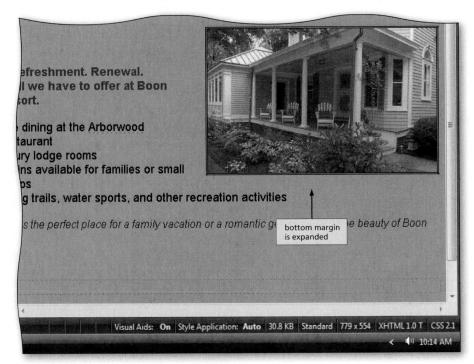

**Figure 2–37**

# Enhancing an Image

**Enhancing**, or improving, an image can be as simple as removing unnecessary parts by cropping, or it can be more involved, such as subtly changing the brightness of an image. You can use a photo editing program to perform complex image editing and manipulation, but Expression Web provides a comprehensive range of image editing tools on the Pictures toolbar. Table 2–3 lists common image formatting options available, along with other tools, on the Pictures toolbar (Figure 2–38).

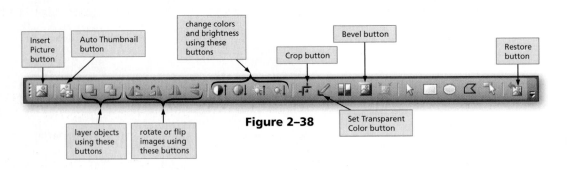

**Figure 2–38**

### Table 2–3 Image Enhancement Options

| Enhancement | Effect |
|---|---|
| Layering | Stacks images on top of each other, specifying the order in which the images appear |
| Rotating or Flipping | Rotates images 90 degrees to the left (counterclockwise) or right (clockwise), or flips the image horizontally or vertically |
| Adjusting Contrast | Changes the contrast between the dark and light colors in your image |
| Changing Brightness | Increases the brightness of the colors or decreases the brightness to make them duller and more subtle |
| Cropping | Removes unnecessary or unwanted parts of a picture |
| Beveling | Adds a bevel, using shadows, so that the edges of an image appear to form a three-dimensional frame, similar to a window pane or mirror |
| Adjusting Color | Changes an image to grayscale (black-and-white) or to color washout (fade) |
| Resampling | Changes the file size by increasing or decreasing the depth of pixel concentration after resizing an image |
| Creating Transparency | Makes a certain color in an image transparent so that the background can be seen. Good for images that have rounded edges and a square background; not possible for JPEG files |

**Identify changes to make to the images.**

**Plan Ahead**

Making changes to images can increase their relevance, appearance, and usability.

1. **Relevance.** Ensure that the image conveys the correct information. Cropping unnecessary portions helps the visitor focus on the relevant points of the picture and can increase the white space or allow you to increase the image size.

2. **Appearance.** Applying formatting can make the image stand out from the rest of the page.

3. **Usability.** Creating thumbnails that you can use in an image gallery can help compress the image into a format that will download more quickly for the visitor.

## To Add Transparency to an Image

An image that has rounded corners, like a logo, may appear with a white background when the image is inserted into a page. To make the logo rounded, you can add transparency to the image background, which removes the image background and makes the page background visible. The following steps replace the resort name in the masthead with a logo. Logos do not typically need very descriptive alternate text. You will add transparency to the logo and resize it.

- At the top of the page, select the words, Boon Mountain Resort.

- Click Insert on the menu bar to open the Insert menu.

- Point to Picture, then point to From File (Figure 2–39).

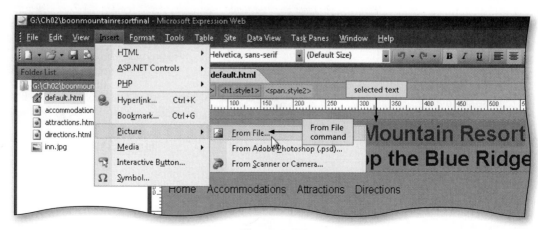

**Figure 2–39**

**2**

- Click From File to open the Picture dialog box. Navigate to the USB G: drive, then open the folder boon mountainresort_ images if necessary.

- Click the innlogo.gif file (Figure 2–40).

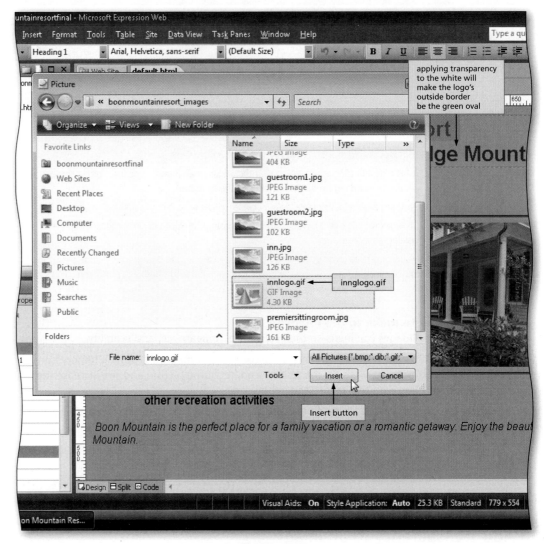

Figure 2–40

**3**

- Click the Insert button to close the Picture dialog box and open the Accessibility Properties dialog box.

- Type Boon Mountain Resort logo in the Alternate text text box , then click the OK button to close the dialog box (Figure 2–41).

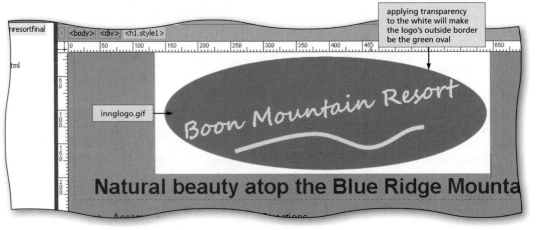

Figure 2–41

**4**

- Double-click the logo to open the Picture Properties dialog box.

- Click the Appearance tab (Figure 2–42).

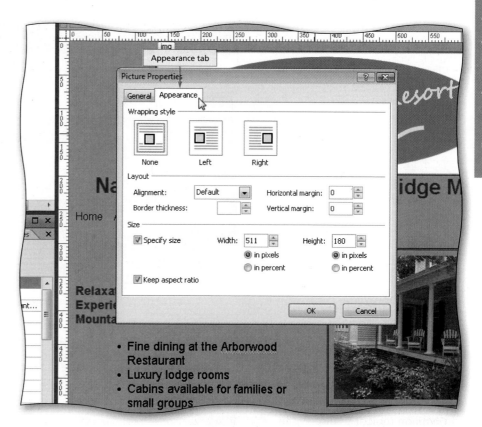

**Figure 2–42**

**5**

- Change the width to 400 pixels (Figure 2–43).

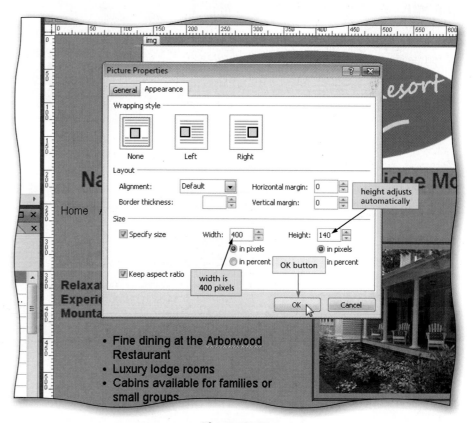

**Figure 2–43**

6

- Click the OK button to resize the logo.

- Click the Picture Actions button below the resized image (Figure 2–44).

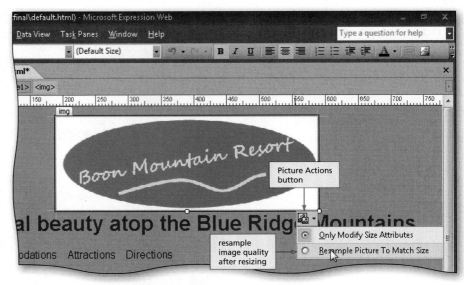

**Figure 2–44**

7

- Click the Resample Picture To Match Size option button to resample the logo.

- Right-click a blank area below the Common toolbar to display the Toolbar menu (Figure 2–45).

Q&A

What if my Pictures toolbar was already displayed?

Opening and closing a toolbar is a toggle command. If your Pictures toolbar was already displayed, either skip step 7 or repeat it to redisplay the toolbar.

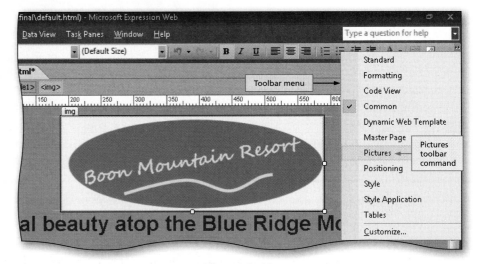

**Figure 2–45**

8

- Click Pictures to open the Pictures toolbar.

- Click the Set Transparent Color button on the Pictures toolbar (Figure 2–46).

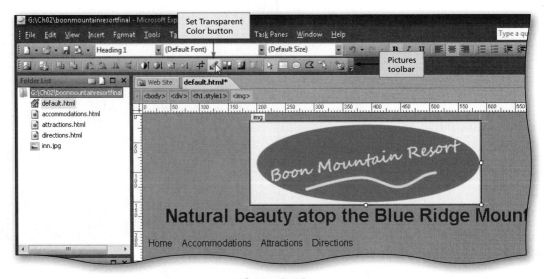

**Figure 2–46**

**9**

- Using the transparency pointer, click the white logo background to remove it.

- Click anywhere in the editing window to deselect the image (Figure 2–47).

Why is my Pictures toolbar in the middle of the screen?

Dock the toolbar to get it out of the way by dragging it beneath the Common toolbar until it docks.

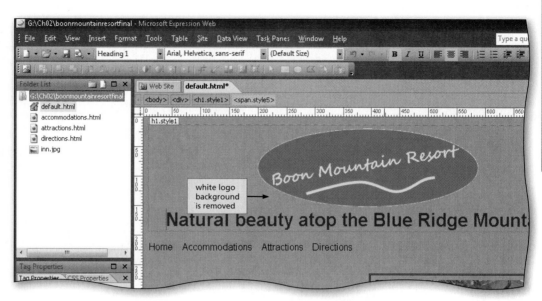

**Figure 2–47**

## The Clipboard

Instead of recreating an element, such as a navigation bar, on each page, you can copy the element to the Clipboard and paste it in other locations. The **Clipboard** temporarily stores text or page elements so that you can move or copy them to other pages or locations.

## To Copy an Image to Other Pages

When creating a Web site, you should repeat certain elements throughout the site to help reinforce the site's message. The following steps copy the modified logo on the default.html page to the Clipboard, and paste them onto the Accommodations, Attractions, and Directions pages in the Boon Mountain site.

**1**

- Click the logo to select it.

- Click Edit on the menu bar to open the Edit menu (Figure 2–48).

**Figure 2–48**

**2**

- Click Copy to copy the logo to the Clipboard.

- Double-click the accommodations. html page in the Folder List to open it (Figure 2–49).

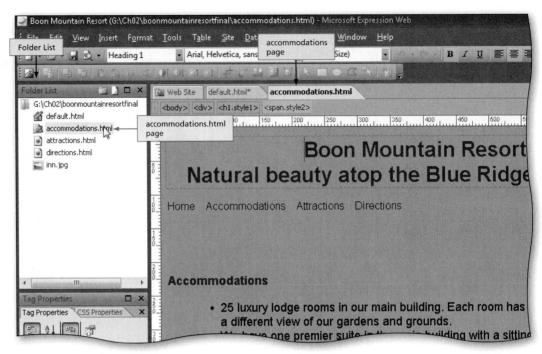

Figure 2–49

**3**

- Select the words, Boon Mountain Resort, on the Accommodations page.

- Click Edit on the menu bar to open the Edit menu (Figure 2–50).

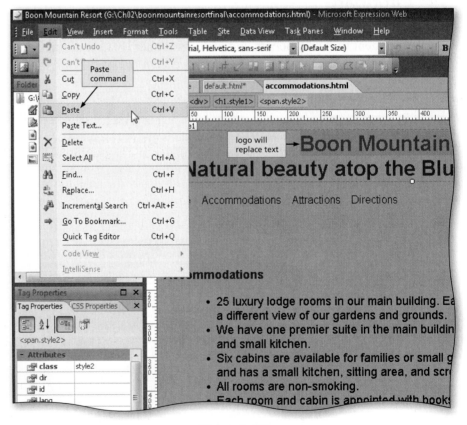

Figure 2–50

**4**

- Click Paste to insert the logo on the Accommodations page.

- Repeat Steps 2 and 3 to insert the logo on the Attractions and Directions pages (Figure 2–51).

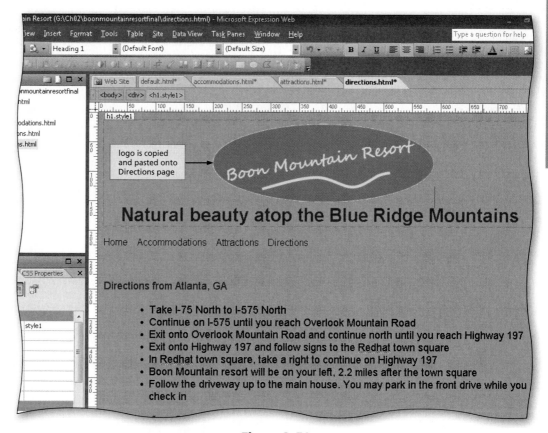

Figure 2–51

**5**

- Click File on the menu bar to open the File menu (Figure 2–52).

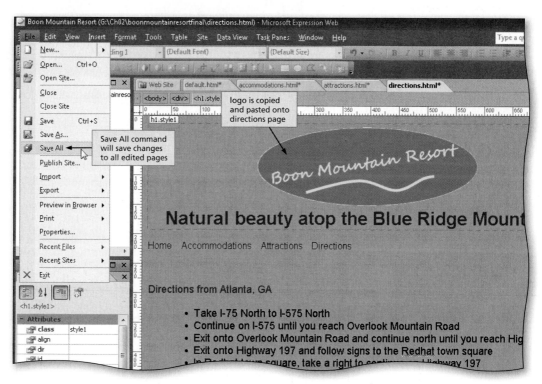

Figure 2–52

**6**

- Click Save All to save the changes you made to all the pages in the site.

- Click the OK button to save the embedded image if necessary (Figure 2–53).

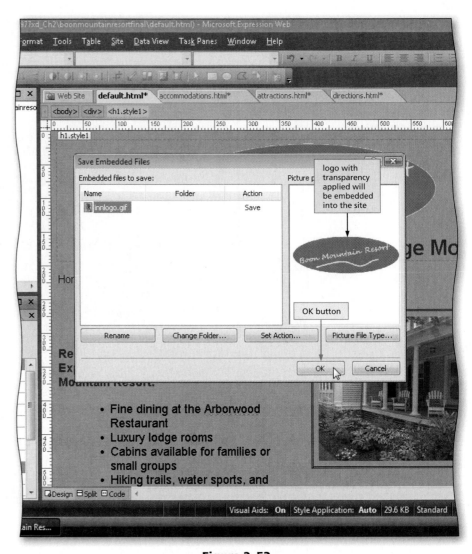

**Figure 2–53**

## To Crop an Image

Digital images can be **cropped**, or trimmed, to show only the relevant portions. Like resizing, cropping an image can be done manually or by using the Picture Properties dialog box to specify exactly how much to crop on each side. When you are cropping an image manually, a box with sizing handles indicates the area that will remain after you crop. You can adjust the cropped area by dragging the cropping handles until you are satisfied. The following steps insert an image on the accommodations page and crop it.

- Click the accommodations.html tab to make it the active Web page.

- Click between the masthead and Accommodations to place the insertion point (Figure 2–54).

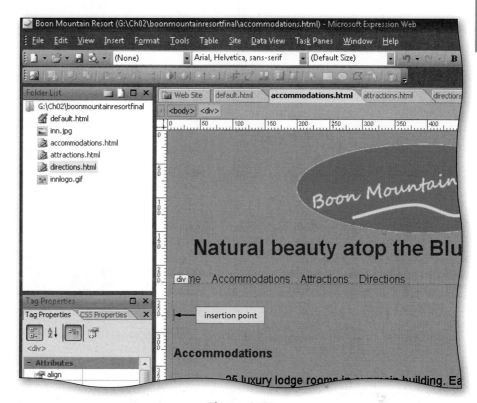

**Figure 2–54**

- Click Insert on the menu bar to open the Insert menu, then point to HTML to open the HTML submenu (Figure 2–55).

**Figure 2–55**

**3**

- Click div to insert a new div for the image.

- Click in the new div, if necessary, to place the insertion point (Figure 2–56).

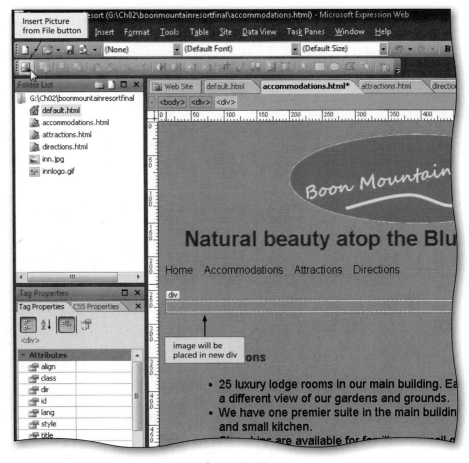

**Figure 2–56**

**4**

- Click the Insert Picture from File button on the Pictures toolbar to open the Picture dialog box.

- Click the file guestroom1.jpg to select it (Figure 2–57).

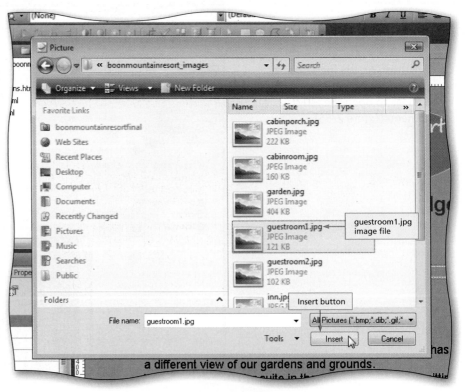

**Figure 2–57**

**5**

- Click the Insert button to open the Accessibility Properties dialog box.

- In the Alternate text text box within the Accessibility Properties dialog box, type Guest room decorated with quilts and artwork (Figure 2–58).

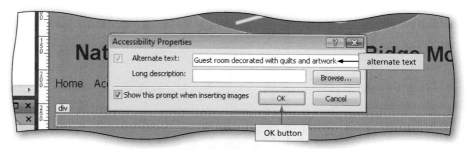

**Figure 2–58**

- Click the OK button to close the Accessibility Properties dialog box and insert the picture (Figure 2–59).

**Figure 2–59**

**6**

- Click the image to select it (Figure 2–60).

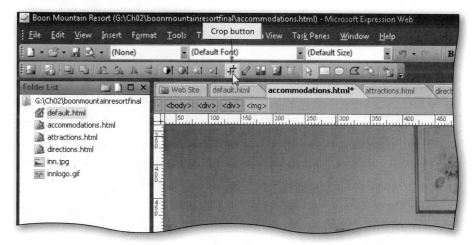

**Figure 2–60**

**7**

- Click the Crop button on the Pictures toolbar to display the cropping area.

- Using the double-headed arrow pointer, drag the cropping handles to adjust the cropping area so that it appears similar to Figure 2–61.

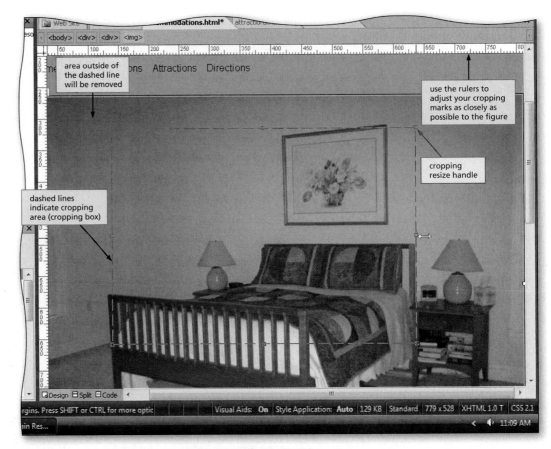

**Figure 2–61**

**8**

- Click the Crop button to accept the cropping changes you have made (Figure 2–62).

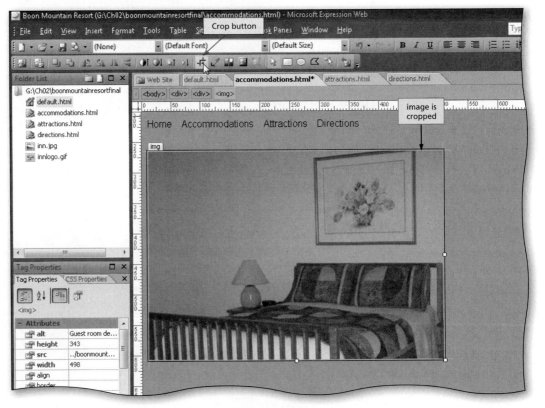

**Figure 2–62**

● Click the Center
button on the
Common toolbar
to center the image
between the Web
page margins
(Figure 2–63).

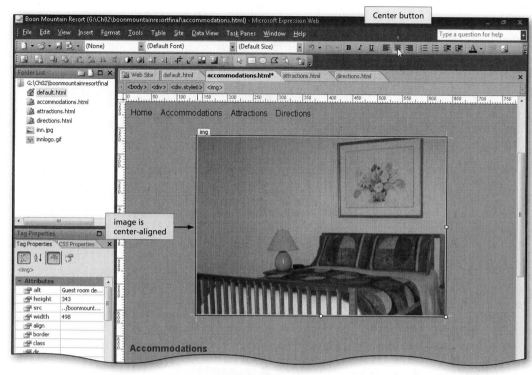

**Figure 2–63**

● Double-click the image to open
the Picture Properties dialog box.

● Click the Appearance tab.

● Type 350 in the Width text box
(Figure 2–64).

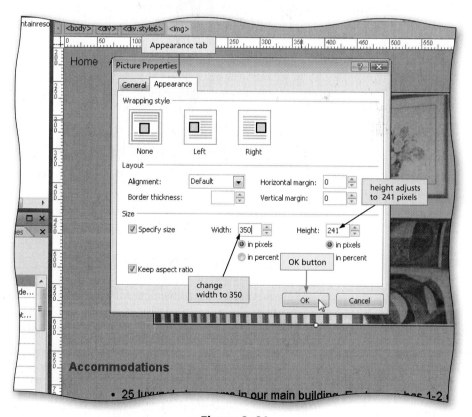

**Figure 2–64**

- Click the OK button to resize the guest room image.

- Click the Picture Actions button below the resized image (Figure 2–65).

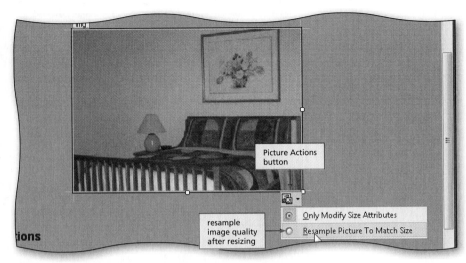

**Figure 2–65**

**12**

- Click the Resample Picture To Match Size option button to resample the image.

- Press CTRL+S to save the page (Figure 2–66).

- Click the OK button to save the embedded image.

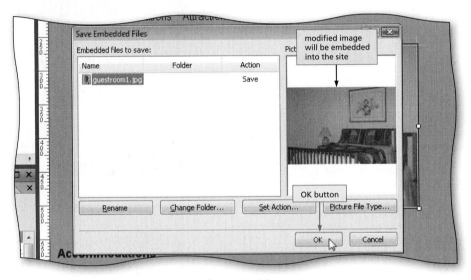

**Figure 2–66**

**BTW**

**Internet Connection Speed**
Depending on a user's Internet connection, the speed at which a site's contents download into his or her browser can vary. You should test your sites using multiple connection types, including high-speed connections such as a digital subscriber line (DSL) or cable, and slower connections such as a dial-up modem.

# Controlling Image Files

Web sites need to be convenient for visitors to use; otherwise, the users will move on to other sites. Including too many large image files in a Web page can make a page slow to download into a visitor's browser, leading to frustration. Recall that the file size in bytes is the determining factor; the visual size of the image on the page does not affect its download speed.

## Thumbnail Images

A **thumbnail** version of an image file is a small rendition that serves as a preview of the large version. Thumbnails also have smaller file sizes, which reduces download time. If the visitor clicks the thumbnail image, the larger version opens in its own window.

Thumbnail images are useful when displaying multiple pictures, such as in a product catalog.

## To Create a Thumbnail

Resizing the image or displaying a thumbnail, a smaller version of an image, frees up room on the Web page. When you use Expression Web to create an automatic thumbnail, Expression Web does three things: changes the image on the page to a smaller version; saves the new version with the filename *imagename*_small.jpg (where *imagename* is the original image's filename), and creates a new window in which the larger version of the thumbnail opens when the user clicks it. The following steps create a gallery of images for different guest rooms and resort areas.

- Click the Accommodations page tab to make it the active Web page, if necessary.

- Scroll if necessary, then position the insertion point at the end of the last line item in the bulleted list.

- Press ENTER twice to create a new paragraph div, into which you will insert a gallery of thumbnails (Figure 2–67).

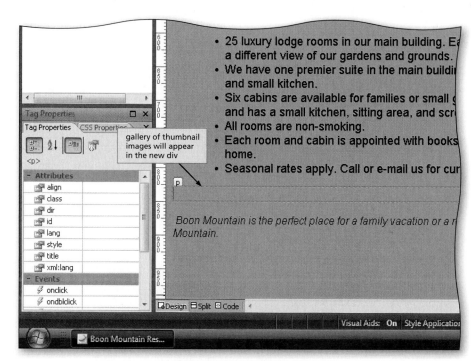

**Figure 2–67**

**2**

- Click the Insert Picture from File button on the Pictures toolbar to open the Picture dialog box (Figure 2–68).

**Figure 2–68**

- Click the guestroom2.jpg image (Figure 2–69).

**Figure 2–69**

- Click the Insert button to open the Accessibility Properties dialog box.

- In the Alternate text text box within the Accessibility Properties dialog box, type Guestroom with antique doll collection (Figure 2–70).

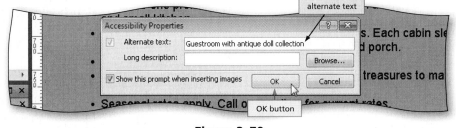

**Figure 2–70**

- Click the OK button to close the dialog box.

- In the editing window, click the image to select it.

- Click the Auto Thumbnail button on the Pictures toolbar to create a thumbnail (Figure 2–71).

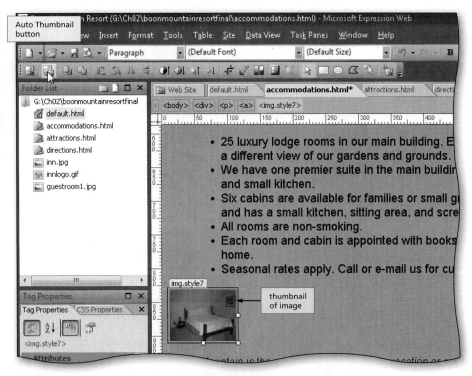

**Figure 2–71**

**6**

- Click to the right of the image to deselect it, then press TAB to insert space between the thumbnails (Figure 2–72).

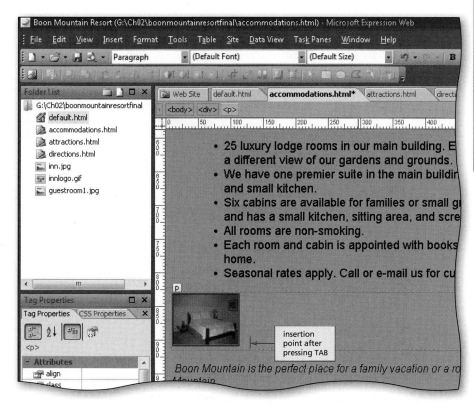

**Figure 2–72**

**7**

- Click the Insert Picture from File button on the Common toolbar to open the Picture dialog box (Figure 2–73).

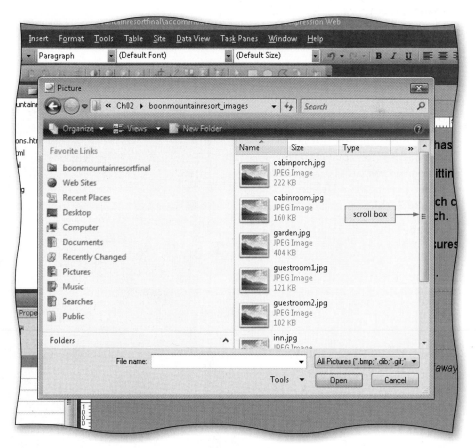

**Figure 2–73**

- If necessary, drag the scroll box down, then click the premiersittingroom.jpg image (Figure 2–74).

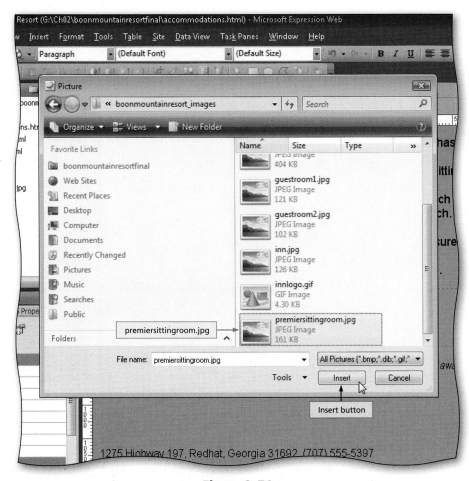

**Figure 2–74**

⑨

- Click the Insert button to close the Picture dialog box.

- In the Alternate text text box within the Accessibility Properties dialog box, type Cozy sitting area in premier suite (Figure 2–75).

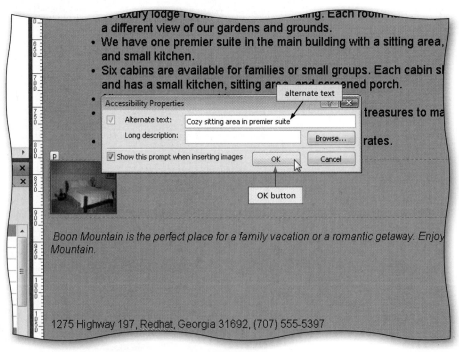

**Figure 2–75**

**10**

- Click the OK button to close the dialog box.

- Click the image in the editing window to select it, then click the Auto Thumbnail button on the Pictures toolbar to create a thumbnail (Figure 2–76).

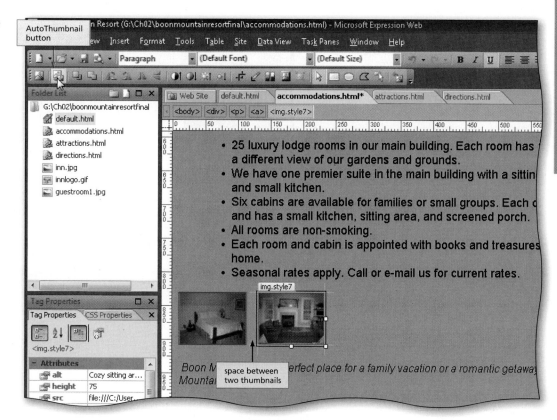

**Figure 2–76**

**11**

- Following the instructions in Steps 6–10, create thumbnails for the garden.jpg image with the alternate text Lush perennial bed, for the cabinporch. jpg image with the alternate text Each cabin has a screened porch, and for the cabinroom.jpg image with the alternate text Cabin bedroom with bookshelves, pressing TAB between the thumbnails to insert a space between each one (Figure 2–77).

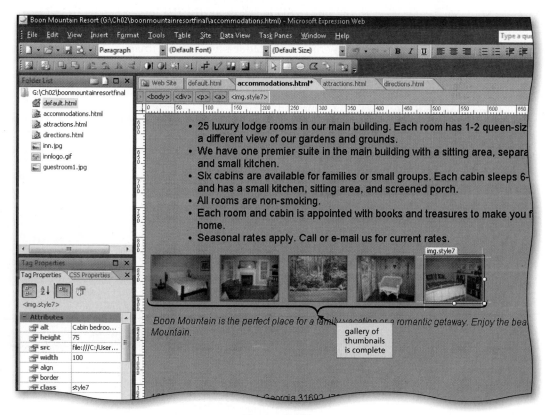

**Figure 2–77**

- Press CTRL+S to save the page.

- Click the OK button to save the embedded files (Figure 2–78).

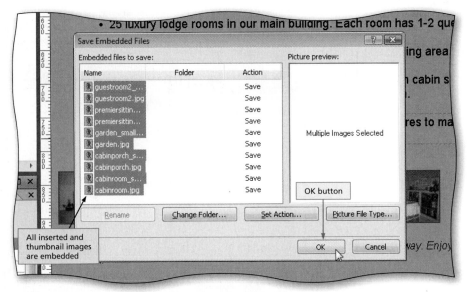

**Other Ways**

1. Press CTRL+T to convert a selected image into a thumbnail

**Figure 2–78**

## To Create a Folder for Images

To keep your site organized and help make updates easier, you should store all media files, including images and video, in a common folder. When you move an image using the Folder List, Expression Web automatically adjusts any coded references to the image file location so that the image can be found and placed appropriately on the page when viewed in a browser. You can create a separate folder for each page that includes the page and any assets, or for a smaller site, you can create one folder for all of the images. The following steps create a folder for storing files and move multiple images into it.

- Click anywhere in the Folder List to activate it.

- Click the New Folder button on the Folder List to create a new folder (Figure 2–79).

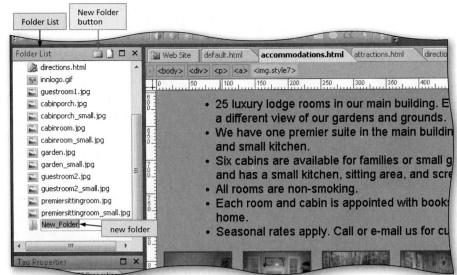

**Figure 2–79**

**2**

- Type images, then press Enter to name the folder (Figure 2–80).

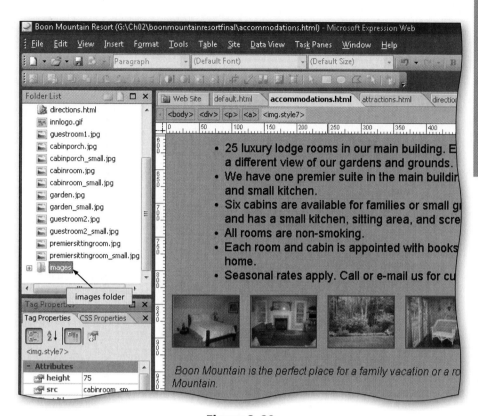

**Figure 2–80**

**3**

- Click the Web Site tab to display the site contents in the editing window (Figure 2–81).

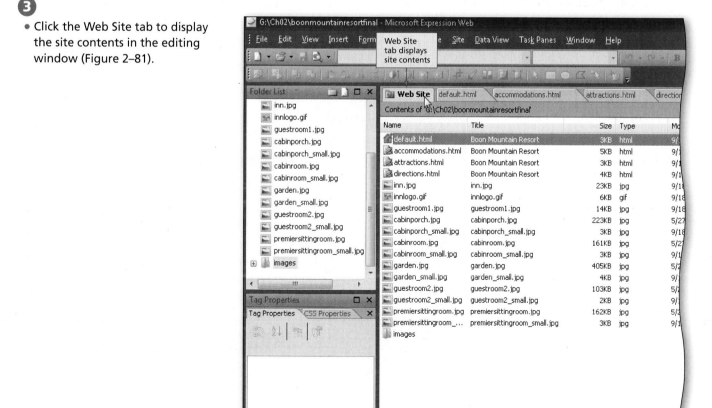

**Figure 2–81**

**4**

- Click the Type column header to sort the files and folders by type (Figure 2–82).

- Click the innlogo.gif image filename to select it.

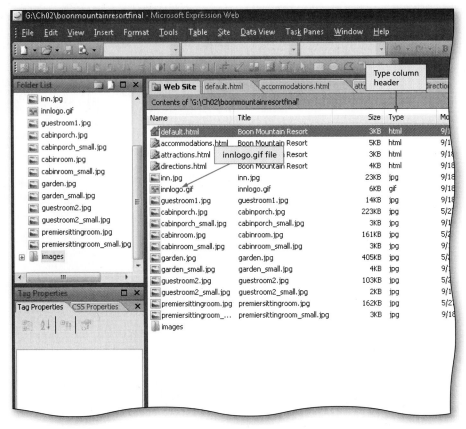

**Figure 2–82**

**5**

- Drag innlogo.gif to the images folder in the Folder List (Figure 2–83).

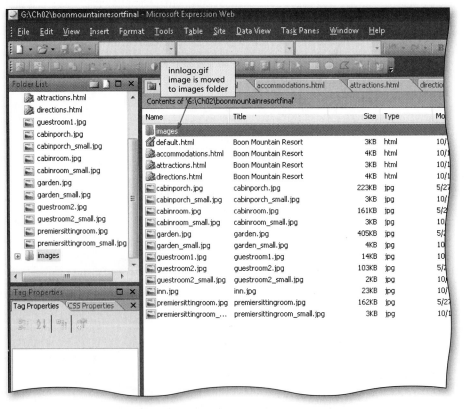

**Figure 2–83**

**6**

- Click the first jpg image, press and hold SHIFT, then click the last jpg image to select all of the image files (Figure 2–84).

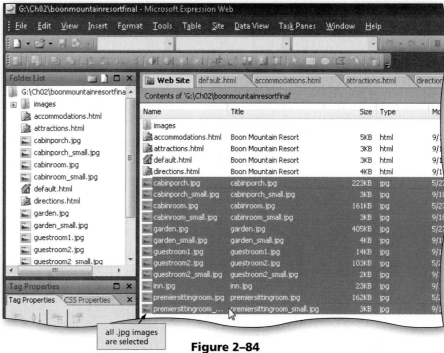

all .jpg images are selected

**Figure 2–84**

**7**

- Drag the selected images to the images folder in the Folder List (Figure 2–85).

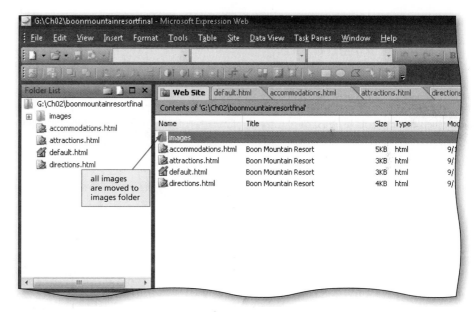

all images are moved to images folder

**Figure 2–85**

# Adding Navigational Links to a Site

The advantage of looking for information on the Web is that you can easily jump to related information with a simple mouse click. Using hyperlinked text and images, visitors to a site can view the information that is relevant to their experience, interests, and needs. Within your site, you can use internal links called **bookmarks** to let visitors move around within long pages. A bookmark is a page anchor that is attached to a specific portion of the page.

**BTW**

**Browser Bookmarks**
Expression Web calls links within a page bookmarks, but you should not confuse them with bookmarks used by browsers, which save a page to a Favorites list.

**Search Boxes**
Many large sites include search boxes in addition to navigation areas. Search boxes are forms that allow a visitor to enter keywords and find information within the site that matches the search criteria.

Every page in a site should have a navigation area that appears in the same location on the page. The navigation area usually appears vertically on the left side of the page or horizontally under the masthead. The navigation area for a small site is a group of links to every main page. In a larger site, the navigation area contains links for each information topic in the site, which takes you to a page that gives you more information and allows you to drill down further to reach the information you want.

**External links** point the visitor's browser to a site that is outside of your own Web site, but that could be useful or interesting for your site's visitors. In addition to browsing related sites of interest, you can use links to open and download files. E-mail links allow users to write and send an e-mail to the site's management or other recipients using the visitor's e-mail editing program. E-mail links are called **mailto links**.

Plan Ahead

> **Determine the necessary internal and external links.**
> Web site visitors should easily be able to find the information they seek, whether they are navigating within your site or getting information from other sources.
>
> - Add internal links to create a navigation area and include the navigation area in the same place on every page.
>
> - Add external links to sites that might be useful for your visitors.
>
> - When pages are too long to be viewed on the screen without scrolling, consider adding bookmarks so visitors can jump to locations on the same pages.
>
> - If appropriate, include e-mail links for your visitors.

## To Add an Internal Link

The following steps create the links to the navigation area.

**1**

- Click the default.html page tab to make it the active Web page.

- Select the word, Home, in the navigation area (Figure 2–86).

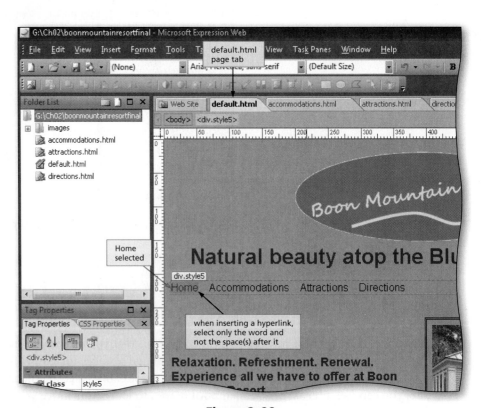

**Figure 2–86**

- Click Insert on the menu bar to open the Insert menu (Figure 2–87).

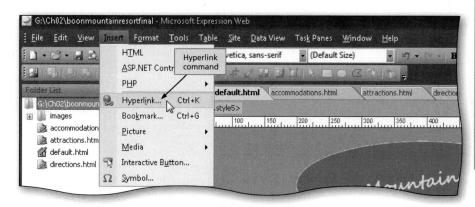

**Figure 2–87**

- Click Hyperlink to open the Insert Hyperlink dialog box.

- Click the default. html page in the list to select it as the hyperlink target (Figure 2–88).

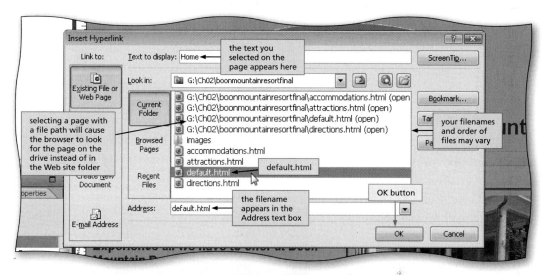

**Figure 2–88**

- Click the OK button to close the Insert Hyperlink dialog box and format the word, Home, as a hyperlink (Figure 2–89).

**Q&A**

Why doesn't the link work when I click on it in the editing window?

To test a link in the editing window, press CTRL, then click the link.

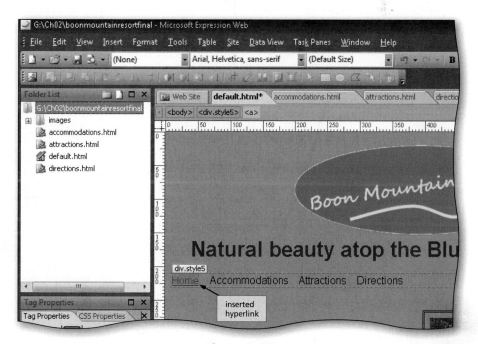

**Figure 2–89**

- Select the word, Accommodations, in the navigation area.

- Press CTRL+K to open the Insert Hyperlink dialog box.

- Click the accommodations.html page in the list to select it as the hyperlink target (Figure 2–90).

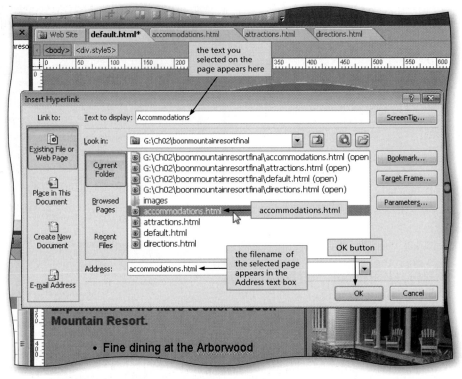

**Figure 2–90**

- Click the OK button to close the Insert Hyperlink dialog box and display the new hyperlink (Figure 2–91).

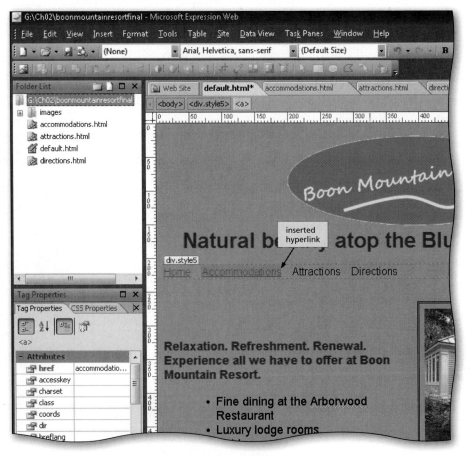

**Figure 2–91**

- Following the instructions in Steps 5 and 6, create a hyperlink from the word, Attractions, in the navigation area, to the attractions. html page.

- Following the instructions in Steps 5 and 6, create a hyperlink from the word, Directions, in the navigation area, to the directions.html page (Figure 2–92).

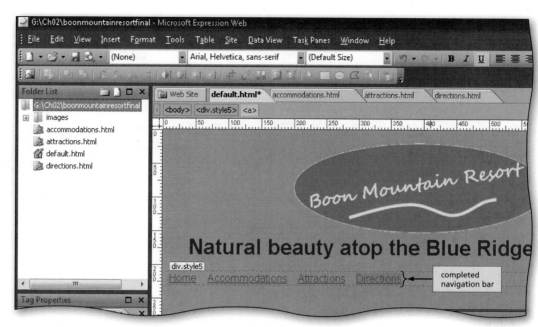

**Figure 2–92**

8

- On the Quick Tag Selector bar, click the navigation area div tag, div.style5, to select the div (Figure 2–93)

**Q&A**

Why does my div name differ?

Div names change based on the actions and order of completion. Your div names might differ slightly.

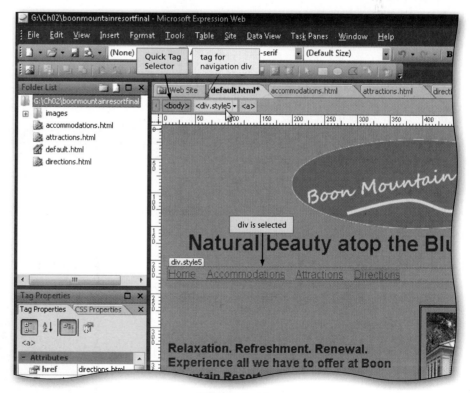

**Figure 2–93**

● Click the Center
button on the
Common toolbar to
center the navigation
area (Figure 2–94).

● Press CTRL+S to save
the default.html page.

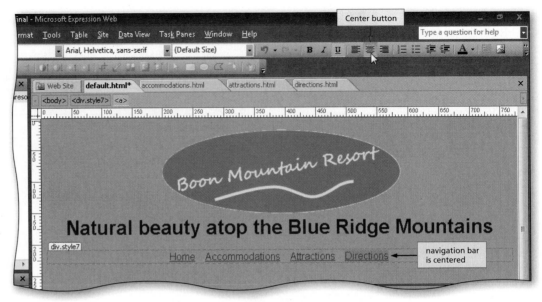

**Figure 2–94**

## To Test Internal Links

The following steps open the page in a browser window and test the links in the navigation bar. Once you
have confirmed that the links work, you can copy the navigation area to the other pages in the site.

● Point to the Preview in Browser
button (Figure 2–95).

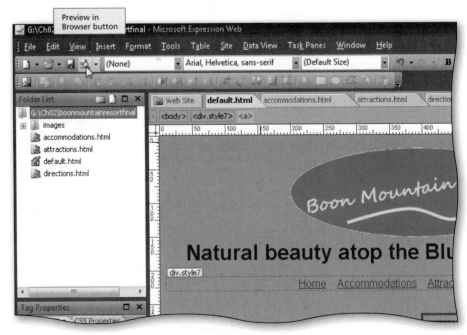

**Figure 2–95**

**2**

- Click the Preview in Browser button to display the page in the browser.

- Click the Accommodations link in the navigation area to open the Accommodations page (Figure 2–96).

**Q&A** My browser window is not maximized.

Click the Maximize button in the upperright corner of the browser window to maximize it.

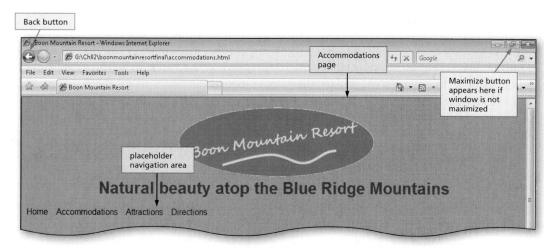

**Figure 2–96**

**3**

- Click the browser Back button to return to the default page (Figure 2–97).

**Figure 2–97**

**4**

- Repeat steps 2 and 3 to test the Attractions and Directions links (Figure 2–98).

- Click the Close button to close the browser window to return to Expression Web.

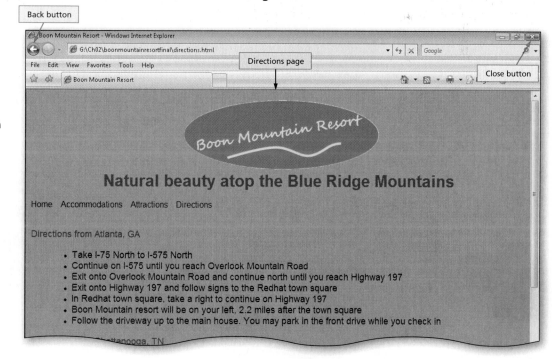

**Figure 2–98**

## To Copy and Paste Internal Links

After you have verified that the navigation bar links work, you will add it to each page in the site in the same location. For layout purposes, a placeholder navigation area appears on each page, listing the pages but without any links. The following steps replace the placeholder navigation area on the Accommodations, Attractions, and Directions pages.

- Select the navigation div, if necessary.

- Press CTRL+C to copy the entire navigation div to the Clipboard.

- Click the attractions. html tab to make it the active Web page.

- Click the placeholder navigation area to select it (Figure 2–99).

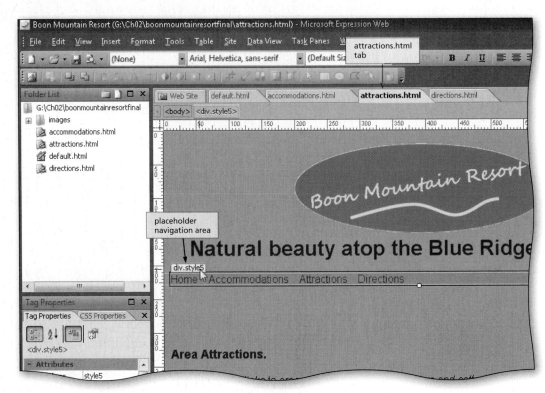

**Figure 2–99**

- Press CTRL+V to insert the navigation area on the Attractions page (Figure 2–100).

**Q&A**

Why isn't my navigation bar centered?

If the pasted navigation bar isn't centered, select the div, then click the Center button on the Common toolbar.

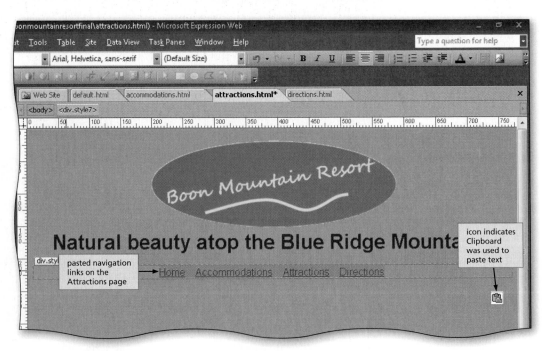

**Figure 2–100**

**3**

- Follow Steps 1 and 2 to insert the navigation area below the masthead on the accommodations. html and directions. html pages (Figure 2–101).

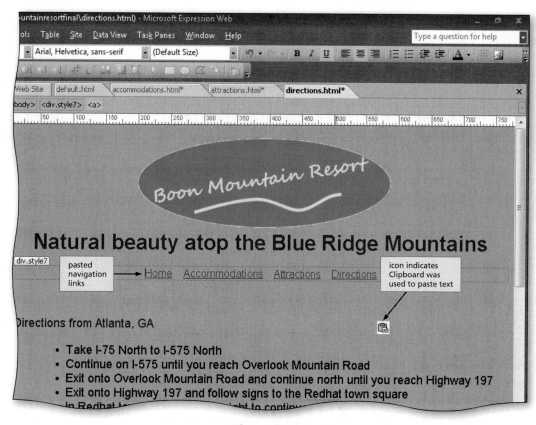

**Figure 2–101**

**4**

- Click File on the menu bar to open the File menu (Figure 2–102).

- Click Save All to save all open pages at once.

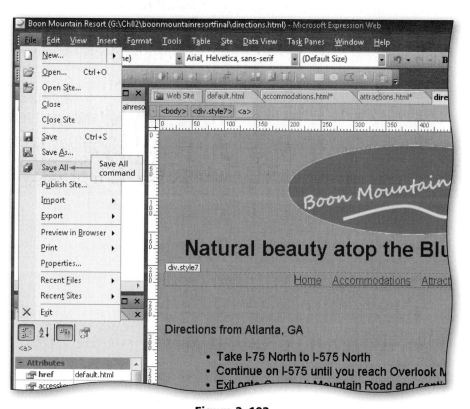

**Figure 2–102**

## To Add an External Link

Adding external links allows you to include access to resources whose sites and content you do not control. Such links can help visitors to your site gain information that might enhance their experience on your site or with your organization. When you add a hyperlink to an external site, the default is for links to open in another browser window. The following steps insert links to attractions near the Boon Mountain Resort.

- Click the attractions. html tab to display the attractions page.

- Select the text in the first bulleted list item.

- Click Insert on the menu bar to open the Insert menu (Figure 2–103).

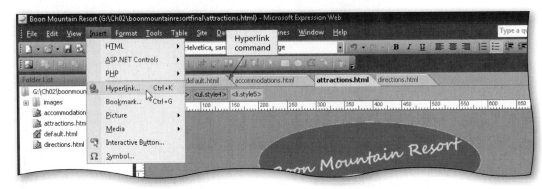

**Figure 2–103**

- Click Hyperlink to open the Insert Hyperlink dialog box.

- In the Address text box, type http://www.gastateparks. org/info/littlewhite to create a link to a page in the Georgia State Parks Web site (Figure 2–104).

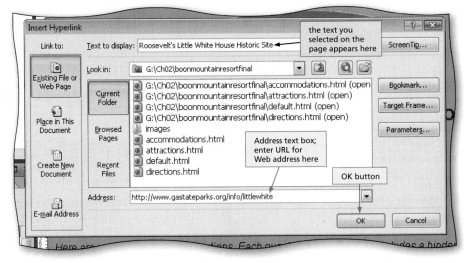

**Figure 2–104**

- Click the OK button to close the Insert Hyperlink dialog box.

- Select the text in the second bulleted list item.

- Press CTRL+K to open the Insert Hyperlink dialog box.

- In the Address text box, type http://www.gastateparks. org/info/crookriv to create a second external link (Figure 2–105).

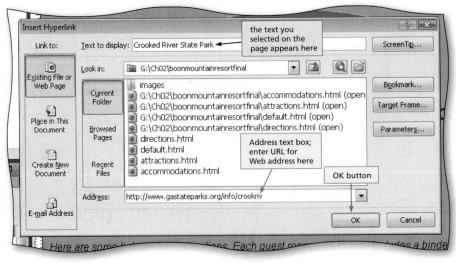

**Figure 2–105**

**4**

- Click the OK button to close the Insert Hyperlink dialog box (Figure 2–106).

**Q&A**

Why can't I add a link to the text I selected?

Make sure that you have not selected a page element, such as a line item or a div. Hyperlinks can only be added to text and images.

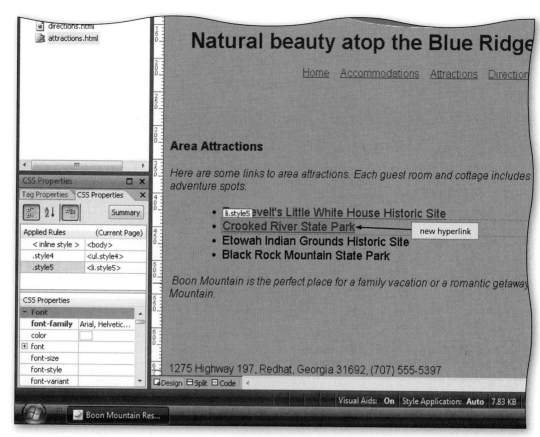

**Figure 2–106**

**5**

- Repeat Steps 3 and 4 to create a link from the third bullet to http://www.gastateparks.org/info/etowah.

- Repeat Steps 3 and 4 to create a link from the fourth bullet to http://www.gastateparks.org/info/blackrock (Figure 2–107).

- Press CTRL+S to save the page.

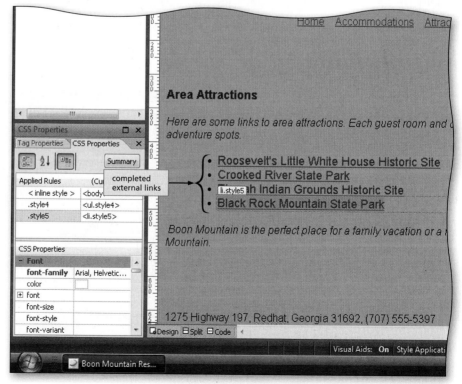

**Figure 2–107**

## To Test External Links

The following steps open the page in a browser window, and test the links in the navigation bar.

**1**

- Press F12 to display the Attractions page in the browser.

- Click the first bullet link in the list to open the Little White House Web page in a new browser window (Figure 2–108).

**Figure 2–108**

**2**

- Click the Back button or click the Close button if your browser opened the page in a new window, then repeat the second bullet in step 1 to test the other three external links (Figure 2–109).

**Figure 2–109**

- Click the Close button on the browser window (Figure 2–110).

- Click the Close Tabs button, if necessary, to close it.

- Click the Close button on any other open browser windows to return to Expression Web.

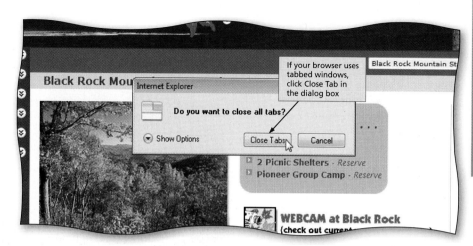

**Figure 2–110**

## To Add a Bookmark

When creating a bookmark, first you assign the bookmark text or image to which you want to jump (the link's target or destination), then you can insert the bookmark hyperlink in the desired location on the page. The following steps add a bookmark link at the bottom of the Directions page that returns to the top of the page.

- Click the directions. html tab to make it the active Web page.

- Select the words, Natural beauty atop the Blue Ridge Mountains, below the logo.

- Click Insert on the menu bar to open the Insert menu (Figure 2–111).

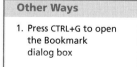

**Other Ways**

1. Press CTRL+G to open the Bookmark dialog box

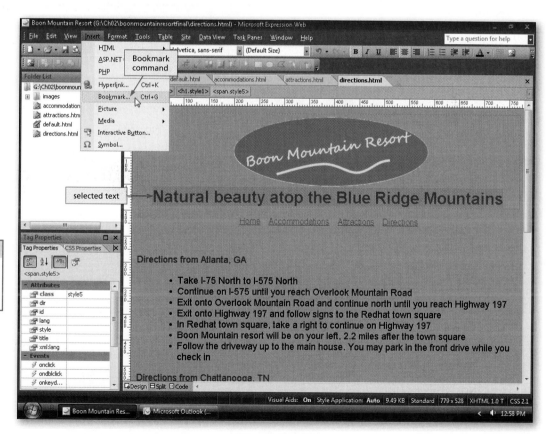

**Figure 2–111**

**2**

- Click Bookmark to open the Bookmark dialog box.

- Type `Top of Page` in the Bookmark name text box to specify the wording that will appear as the link (Figure 2–112).

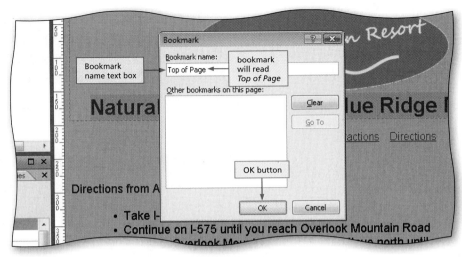

**Figure 2–112**

**3**

- Click the OK button to close the Bookmark dialog box.

- Click at the end of the last bullet list item (below Directions from Redhat County Airport), then press ENTER twice to create a new paragraph div (Figure 2–113).

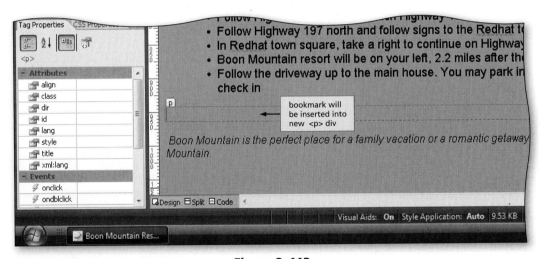

**Figure 2–113**

**4**

- Press CTRL+K to open the Insert Hyperlink dialog box.

- Click the Place in this Document button to display the list of bookmarks.

- Click Top of Page to select it as the target bookmark (Figure 2–114).

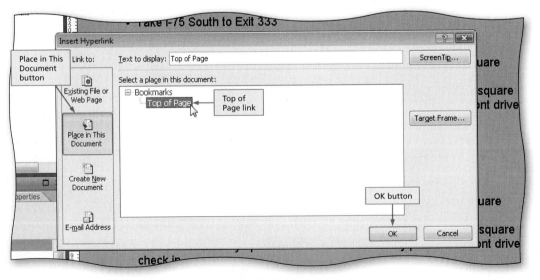

**Figure 2–114**

**5**

- Click the OK button to close the dialog box and insert the bookmark link (Figure 2–115).

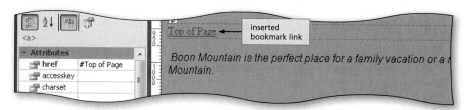

**Figure 2–115**

**6**

- Press CTRL, then click the Top of Page link to test the bookmark link (Figure 2–116).

- Click the Save button on the Common toolbar to save the page.

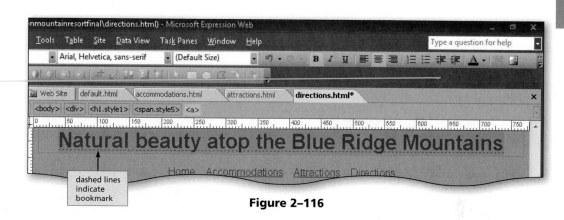

**Figure 2–116**

BTW

**Forms vs. E-Mail Links**
There are programs that search the Web collecting e-mail addresses to use them in mass e-mailings. Some sites avoid including e-mail links and instead use forms to collect user feedback and requests for this reason.

## To Add an E-Mail Link

An e-mail link opens a new, blank e-mail window using the visitor's e-mail program. In the following steps, you will add an e-mail link to your e-mail address for requests for room rates.

**1**

- Click the accommodations.html page tab so it is the active Web page tab in the editing window.

- In the last bullet item, select the word, e-mail, to make it a hyperlink.

- Press CTRL+K to open the Insert Hyperlink dialog box.

- Click the E-mail Address button (Figure 2–117).

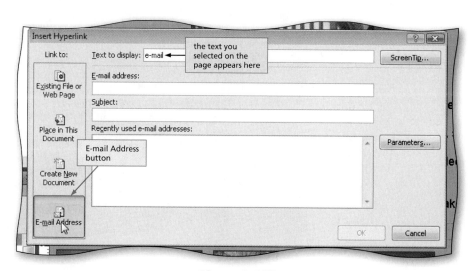

**Figure 2–117**

**2**

- In the E-mail address text box, type `mailto:` followed by your e-mail address.

- In the Subject text box, type `Rooms and Rates` (Figure 2–118).

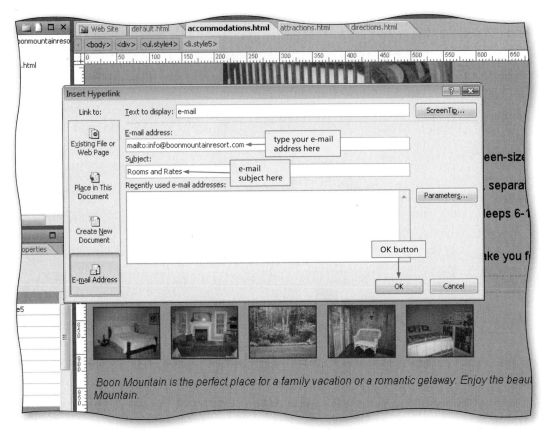

**Figure 2–118**

**3**

- Click the OK button to close the Insert Hyperlink dialog box and create the mailto link (Figure 2–119).

- Press CTRL+S to save the page.

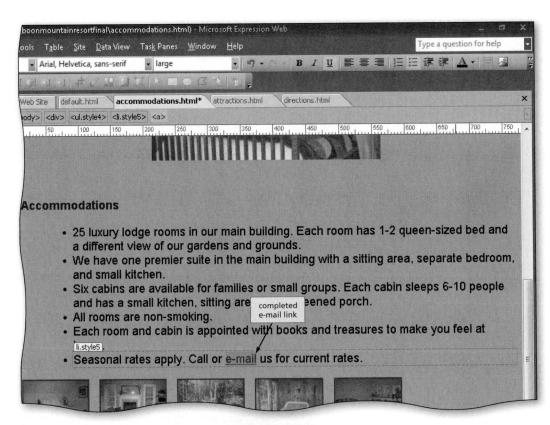

## Accommodations

- 25 luxury lodge rooms in our main building. Each room has 1-2 queen-sized bed and a different view of our gardens and grounds.
- We have one premier suite in the main building with a sitting area, separate bedroom, and small kitchen.
- Six cabins are available for families or small groups. Each cabin sleeps 6-10 people and has a small kitchen, sitting are[...] [...]eened porch.
- All rooms are non-smoking.
- Each room and cabin is appointed with books and treasures to make you feel at
- Seasonal rates apply. Call or e-mail us for current rates.

**Figure 2–119**

- Press F12 to display the page in the browser.

- Click the e-mail link to test it.

- Close the e-mail window if it opens (Figure 2–120).

- Close the browser window to return to Expression Web.

**Q&A** Why do I get an error message when I click the e-mail link?

Your e-mail program or browser might not be configured to process mailto links.

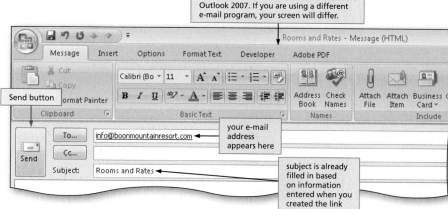

**Figure 2–120**

 **Experiment**

- If an e-mail window opens click the Send button to send the e-mail to yourself.

## To Add a ScreenTip

A **ScreenTip** is a window containing descriptive text that appears when you position the pointer over a button or link. Adding a ScreenTip to the e-mail address lets users know that they can contact you with any questions. The following steps add a ScreenTip to the mailto link.

**1**

- Select the e-mail link.

- Press CTRL+K to open the Edit Hyperlink dialog box (Figure 2–121).

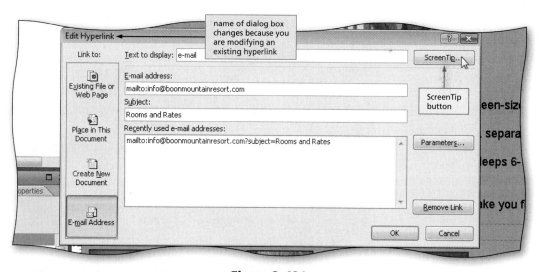

**Figure 2–121**

**2**

- Click the ScreenTip button to open the Set Hyperlink ScreenTip dialog box.

- In the ScreenTip text text box, type `Contact us by e-mail with any questions` (Figure 2–122).

**Figure 2–122**

**3**

- Click the OK button to close the Set Hyperlink ScreenTip dialog box.

- Click the OK button to close the Edit Hyperlink dialog box (Figure 2–123).

- Press CTRL+S to save the page.

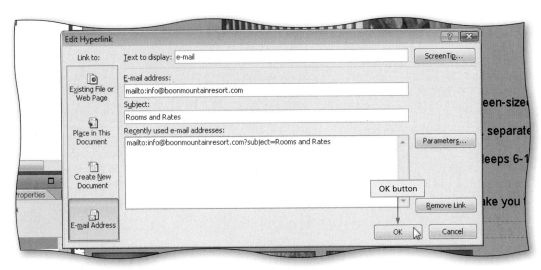

**Figure 2–123**

## To Preview the Site

In the following steps, you will preview the site in your browser to view all of the pages and view and test the ScreenTip.

**1**

- Click the default. html tab to make it the active Web page.

- Press F12 to open the page in a browser (Figure 2–124).

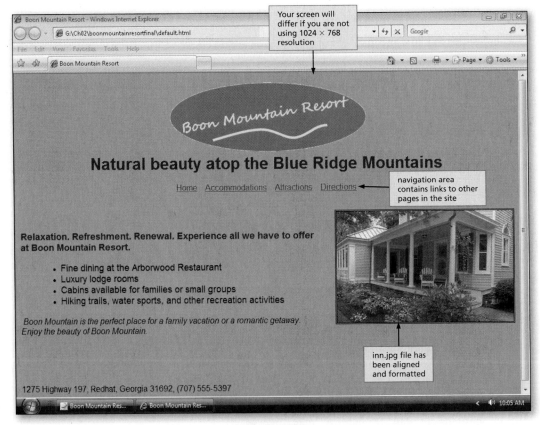

**Figure 2–124**

- Click the Accommodations link on the navigation bar.

- Position the pointer over the e-mail link to view the ScreenTip (Figure 2–125).

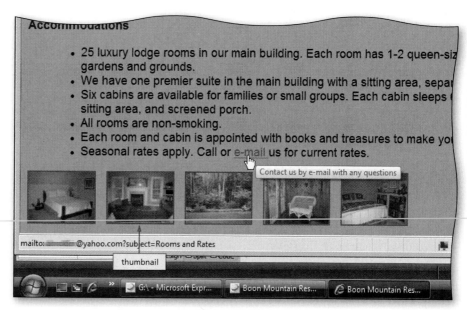

**Figure 2–125**

- Click the second thumbnail image to open the larger image (Figure 2–126).

- Click the Close button to close the browser window and return to Expression Web.

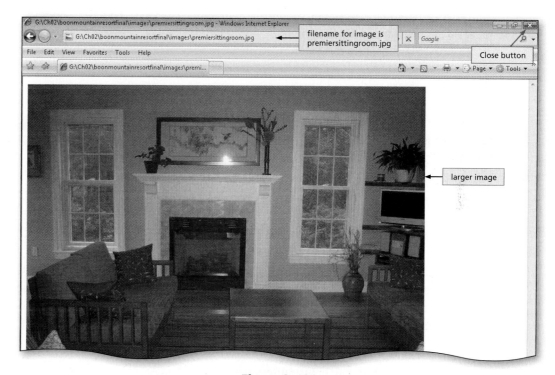

**Figure 2–126**

## To Close a Site and Quit Expression Web

- Click File on the menu bar, then click Close Site.

- Click File on the menu bar, then click Exit.

# Chapter Summary

In this chapter, you have learned how to use images to enhance and add value to Web pages. You used Expression Web to insert, align, and format images. You learned that controlling image file size and organization is accomplished through the use of thumbnail images and folders. You have also learned to add different types of links, including internal, external, and mail links, to your site. The items listed below include all the new Expression Web skills you have learned in this chapter.

1. Open a Web Site (EW 77)
2. Insert an Image (EW 80)
3. Close a Task Pane (EW 85)
4. Display the Ruler (EW 87)
5. Resize an Image (EW 89)
6. Align an Image (EW 94)
7. Add a Border to an Image (EW 95)
8. Modify Image Margins (EW 97)
9. Add Transparency to an Image (EW 99)
10. Copy an Image to Other Pages (EW 103)
11. Crop an Image (EW 107)
12. Create a Thumbnail (EW 113)
13. Create a Folder for Images (EW 118)
14. Add an Internal Link (EW 122)
15. Test Internal Links (EW 126)
16. Copy and Paste Internal Links (EW 128)
17. Add an External Link (EW 130)
18. Test External Links (EW 132)
19. Add a Bookmark (EW 133)
20. Add an E-Mail Link (EW 135)
21. Add a ScreenTip (EW 137)
22. Preview the Site (EW 138)

 If you have a SAM user profile, you may have access to hands-on instruction, practice, and assessment. Log in to your SAM account (http://sam2007.course.com) to launch any assigned training activities or exams that relate to the skills covered in this chapter.

## Learn It Online

Test your knowledge of chapter content and key terms.

*Instructions:* To complete the Learn It Online exercises, start your browser, click the Address bar, and then enter the Web address `scsite.com/ew2/learn`. When the Expression Web Learn It Online page is displayed, click the link for the exercise you want to complete and then read the instructions.

**Chapter Reinforcement TF, MC, and SA**
A series of true/false, multiple choice, and short answer questions that test your knowledge of the chapter content.

**Flash Cards**
An interactive learning environment where you identify chapter key terms associated with displayed definitions.

**Practice Test**
A series of multiple choice questions that test your knowledge of chapter content and key terms.

**Who Wants To Be a Computer Genius?**
An interactive game that challenges your knowledge of chapter content in the style of a television quiz show.

**Wheel of Terms**
An interactive game that challenges your knowledge of chapter key terms in the style of the television show *Wheel of Fortune*.

**Crossword Puzzle Challenge**
A crossword puzzle that challenges your knowledge of key terms presented in the chapter.

# Apply Your Knowledge

Reinforce the skills and apply the concepts you learned in this chapter.

### Adding Images and Links

*Instructions:* Start Expression Web. Open the Web site, Apply 2-1 Photography, from the Data Files for Students. See the inside back cover of this book for instructions for downloading the Data Files for Students, or see your instructor for information about accessing the required files.

      The Web site you open contains a home page with formatting and text. You are to open the default.html file and add and format an image, create thumbnails, and add an e-mail link with a ScreenTip so that the page looks like Figure 2–127.

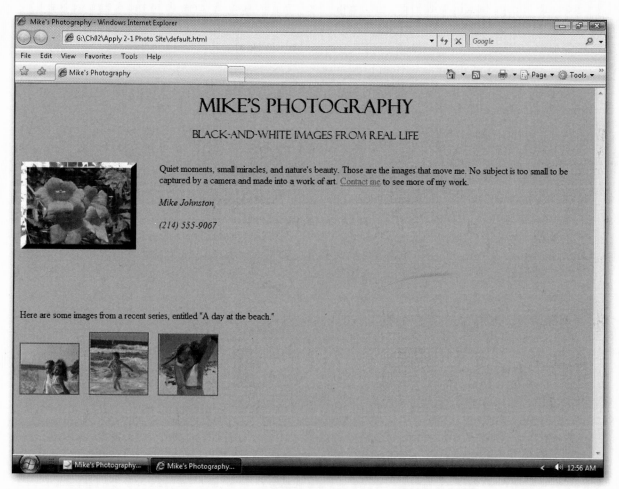

**Figure 2–127**

*Perform the following tasks:*

1. Open the default.html Web page.

2. Click before the words, Quiet moments.

3. Click the Insert Picture from File button on the Pictures toolbar.

4. Select the picture flowerphoto.jpg from the Apply 2-1 images folder, then click Insert.

5. Type `Lily on bush` in the Alternate text text box, then click OK.

6. Select the image, right-click the image, then click Picture Properties from the shortcut menu.

*Continued >*

**Apply Your Knowledge** *continued*

7. Click the Appearance tab, click the Left Wrapping style button, then click the OK button.

8. Drag the lower-right sizing handle until the picture is resized to approximately 200 × 146 pixels.

9. Drag the right margin handle to resize the right margin to 40 pixels.

10. Drag the bottom margin handle to resize the bottom margin to 30 pixels.

11. Click the Bevel button on the Pictures toolbar to add a bevel to the image.

12. Save the default.html page, then click OK to save the embedded picture.

13. Click before the words, Here are some images, then press ENTER three times.

14. Click anywhere below the line that begins, Here are some images, then double-click the div tag in the Toolbox.

15. Insert the image beachphoto1.jpg, then type `Two girls on a beach` in the Alternate text text box

16. Select the image, then click the Auto Thumbnail button on the Pictures toolbar.

17. Click to the right of the image, then press TAB.

18. Insert the image beachphoto2.jpg, type `Girl in surf` in the Alternate text text box, create a thumbnail, click next to the image, then press TAB.

19. Insert the image beachphoto3.jpg, type `Girl with towel` in the Alternate text text box, then create a thumbnail.

20. Save the default.html page, then click OK to save the embedded pictures.

21. Select the words, Contact me.

22. On the Insert menu, click Hyperlink.

23. Click the E-mail Address button, then type your e-mail address in the E-mail address text box.

24. Click the ScreenTip button, type your e-mail address in the ScreenTip text text box, then click the OK button twice to close the open dialog boxes.

25. Preview the site and test the thumbnails and links.

26. Change the site properties, as specified by your instructor. Save the site using the file name, Apply 2-1 Photo Site. Submit the revised site in the format specified by your instructor.

27. Save the page, then close the site.

## Extend Your Knowledge

Extend the skills you learned in this chapter and experiment with new skills. You may need to use Help to complete the assignment.

### Creating Links to Images and Bookmarks

*Instructions:* Start Expression Web. Open the Web site, Extend 2-1 Music Festival, from the Data Files for Students. See the inside back cover of this book for instructions for downloading the Data Files for Students, or see your instructor for information about accessing the required files.

You will enhance the Web page to match the one shown in Figure 2–128.

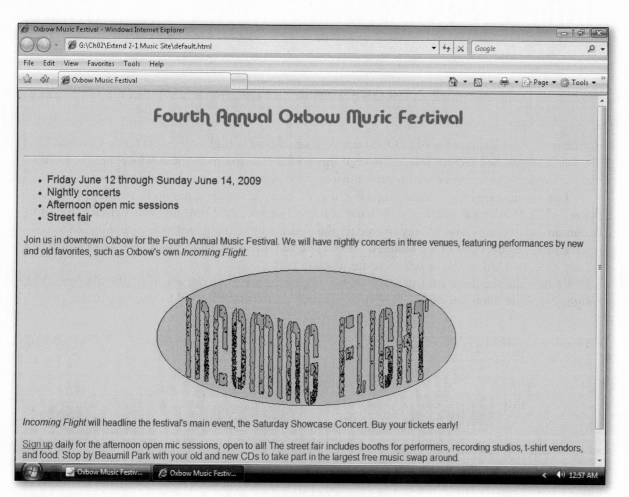

**Figure 2–128**

*Perform the following tasks:*

1. Use Help to learn about inserting a link to a file.

2. Open the default.html page, position the insertion point before the words, Incoming Flight, at the beginning of the second paragraph, then press ENTER.

3. In the new div, insert the image, bandlogo.gif from the folder Extend 2-1 images, and type `Incoming Flight band logo` as the Alternate text.

4. Center the image on the page.

5. Select the image, then open the Insert Hyperlink dialog box.

6. Click the Existing File or Web page button if necessary, type `http://www.incomingflightband.com` in the Address text box, then click the OK button. (*Note:* this Web page does not exist. You will get an error message when you test it.)

7. Select the words, Sign up, then open the Insert Hyperlink dialog box.

8. Click the Existing File or Web Page button if necessary, click signup_form.pdf, then click the OK button.

9. Save the default.html page, preview the page and test all links, then close the browser window.

10. Change the site properties, as specified by your instructor. Save the presentation using the filename, Extend 2-1 Music Site. Submit the revised site in the format specified by your instructor.

## Make It Right

Analyze a site and correct all errors and/or improve the design.

### Placing and Formatting Images

*Instructions:*   Start Expression Web. Open the Web site, Make It Right 2-1 Swim Club, from the Data Files for Students. See the inside back cover of this book for instructions for downloading the Data Files for Students, or see your instructor for information about accessing the required files.

The site has one image that is large, not aligned with the text, and has no formatting, as shown in Figure 2–129. In addition, there is no link to the second page of the Web site, which gives more information on swim lessons, and no way to contact the director by sending him an e-mail. You are to position the image to the right of the bulleted list and size and format it, add a link to the swim lesson text, and add an e-mail link to the director's name.

Change the site properties, as specified by your instructor. Save the site using the filename, Make it Right 2-1 Swim Club Site. Submit the revised site in the format specified by your instructor.

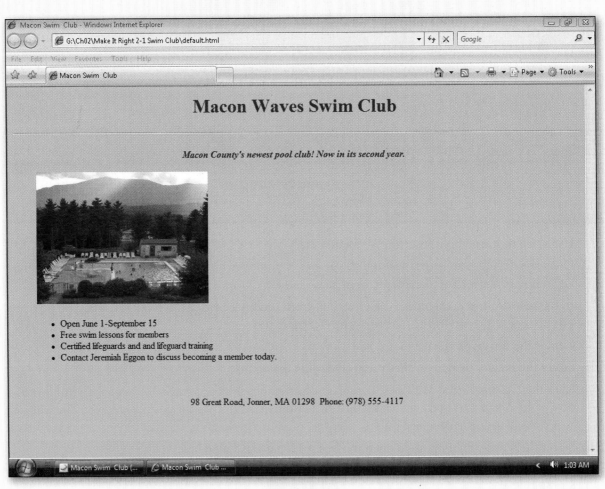

**Figure 2–129**

# In the Lab

Design and/or format a Web site using the guidelines, concepts, and skills presented in this chapter. Labs are listed in order of increasing difficulty.

## Lab 1: Creating a Navigation Area and Inserting an Image

*Problem:*   You work part-time at a small bike repair shop. Your boss has asked you to add images and create a navigation area for the shop's Web site. You add images and links to the page shown in Figure 2–130.

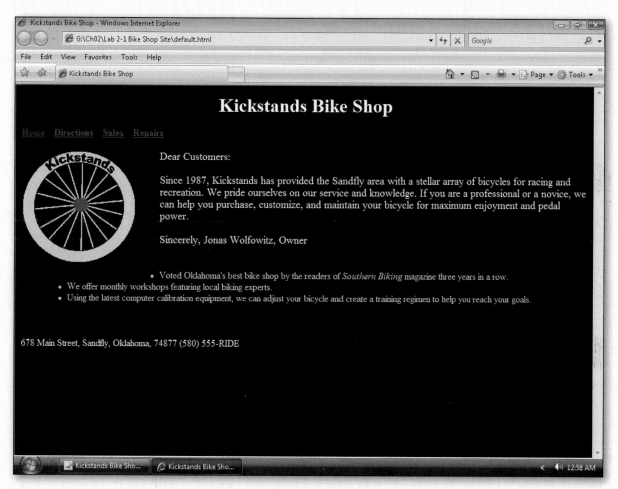

**Figure 2–130**

*Instructions:*

1. Start Expression Web.

2. Open the Web site Lab 2-1 Bike Shop.

3. Open the default.html page.

4. Position the insertion point in the line above the words, Dear Customers, then insert a new div.

5. Insert the kickstands_logo.gif image from the Lab 2-1 images folder. Do not assign alternate text.

6. Resize the logo to 200 pixels wide, keeping the image proportions the same so that the height automatically adjusts. If necessary, drag the image up to align the text as shown in Figure 2–130.

*Continued >*

**In the Lab** *continued*

7. Left-align the image around the text.

8. Insert line breaks after the words, Jonas Wolfowitz, Owner, until the bulleted list is below the logo.

9. Increase the right margin of the logo to 40 pixels and the bottom margin to 20 pixels.

10. Create a navigation area using the text below the masthead, then copy it to each page in the site.

11. Save the changes you have made to all pages at once, then preview the site in a browser.

12. Rename the site Lab 2-1 Bike Shop Site. Change the site properties, as specified by your instructor.

13. Submit the site in the format specified by your instructor, then close the site.

## In the Lab

### Lab 2: Adding a Horizontal Line, Bookmark, and Link to a File

*Problem:* You own a baking business and want to attract customers by making your site's home page easier to navigate. On the featured recipe section of the home page, you add a horizontal line at the top of the recipe and a bookmark link at the bottom to help users navigate back to the top of the page, as shown in Figure 2–131. You also add a link to an order form that users can download.

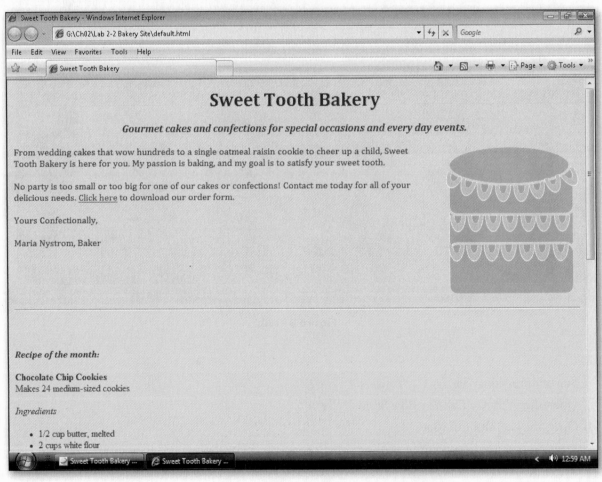

**Figure 2–131**

*Instructions:*

1. Start Expression Web.

2. Open the Web site Lab 2-2 Bakery, then open the default.html page.

3. Insert a horizontal line above the text, Recipe of the month.

4. Create a bookmark called Top of Page to the words, Sweet Tooth Bakery, in the masthead.

5. Insert the bookmark link at the bottom of the page between the directions and address.

6. Add a link from the words, Click here, to the file orderform.pdf.

7. Change the left margin of the cake image to 35 pixels.

8. Apply transparency to the white background of the cake image.

9. Preview the site in a browser and test the link and bookmark.

10. Rename the site Lab 2-2 Bakery Site, then change the site properties, as specified by your instructor.

11. Submit the site in the format specified by your instructor, then close the site.

# In the Lab

## Lab 3: Formatting an Image

*Problem:* Your school's travel club has a Web page for its upcoming trip to New York. You will insert, align, and format an image as shown in Figure 2–132.

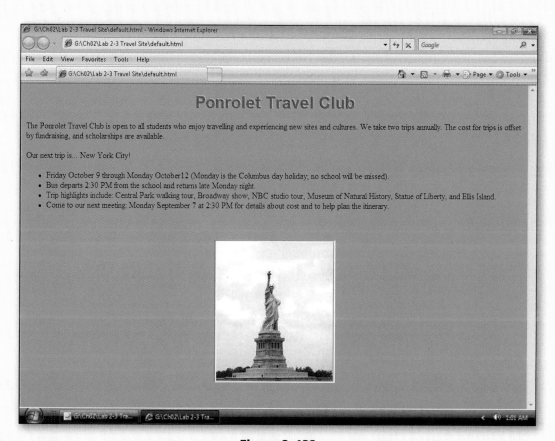

**Figure 2–132**

*Continued >*

**In the Lab** *continued*

*Instructions:* Perform the following tasks.

1. Start Expression Web.

2. Open the Web site Lab 2-3 Travel.

3. Open the default.html page.

4. Click after the last bulleted list item, press ENTER twice, then insert the image statue.jpg from the Lab 2-3 images folder.

5. Crop the top, left, and right sides so that the image appears as shown in Figure 2–132.

6. Center-align the image.

7. Use the Borders and Shading dialog box to add a groove border, and add 4 pixels of padding around all sides.

8. Click the More Brightness button twice.

9. Click the Color button arrow, then click Grayscale.

10. Click the More Contrast button twice.

11. Save the changes you have made to default.html and save the embedded image.

12. Preview the page in a browser.

13. Change the site properties, as specified by your instructor.

14. Rename the site Lab 2-3 Travel Site, submit the site in the format specified by your instructor, then close the site.

# Cases and Places

Apply your creative thinking and problem solving skills to design and implement a solution.

• Easier   •• More Difficult

### • 1: Add Internal and External Links

You want to practice adding links to a Web site. Open any site that you created in Chapter 1, then open that site's default.html page. Add a link to your school's Web page, add a link to your e-mail address, and create and insert a bookmark. Close the default.html page without saving any changes, close the Web site, then quit Expression Web.

### • 2: Add Images and Links to a School Web Site

The administration of Pinkham Academy would like to include images and links on a Web site. If you completed the Cases and Places 2 activity in Chapter 1, you can use the sketch of the Web site as a basis for this exercise. Create a one-page Web site that has a masthead, and at least one paragraph and bulleted list describing the school's features. Next to the bulleted list, insert a right-aligned image (use a photo from an exercise in this chapter or use one of your own). Add a margin and a bevel to the image. Add an e-mail link with a ScreenTip to your e-mail address.

### •• 3: Add a Gallery of Images to an Alumni Web Site

You have recently joined the Connecticut branch of your college alumni association. You have been working on a home page that can tell other local graduates of Gulliver College about upcoming alumni events. You have already entered the text for the home page. Open the site Cases and Places 2-3 Alumni, then open the page default.html. Add four images and create a gallery of thumbnails for them (use photos from an exercise in this chapter or use your own). Center-align the thumbnails and make sure to add space between each image. Save the changes to the default.html file and embed all image files, then test your thumbnails in your browser.

### •• 4: Create a Personal Home Page

**Make It Personal**

You want to create a personal home page that you can use to link to your favorite sites and allow others to e-mail you. Create a one-page Web site and include a masthead, bulleted list, footer, and any other information you think is relevant. Format the Web site attractively. Add at least one image that you crop, size, and align with text wrapping. Add a border to the image. Insert three links to sites that you like to visit. Add a ScreenTip to each of the links that displays the name of the site or what type of information the visitor will see when they click it. Insert an e-mail link to your e-mail address.

### •• 5: Enhance a Home Page for a Restaurant

**Working Together**

A local restaurant wants to create a multi-page Web site for its customers. The site will include a home page, a menu page, and a page with directions. All pages should include a masthead, navigation area with links, at least one image, one or two paragraphs or lists of information, and a footer with contact information. Working as a team with several of your classmates, you are to design and create the Web site. As a group, decide on the name of the restaurant and the menu. Each team member should plan on paper the three pages (home, menu, and directions), and present their plan to the group. As a group, decide on elements of each plan that you will incorporate into creating the home page, and start creating the home page using Expression Web. Format the Web site attractively. Add the text for each page. Add images and use text wrapping, thumbnails, and apply formatting. Create a navigation area and copy it to each page.

# 3 | Working with Templates and Styles

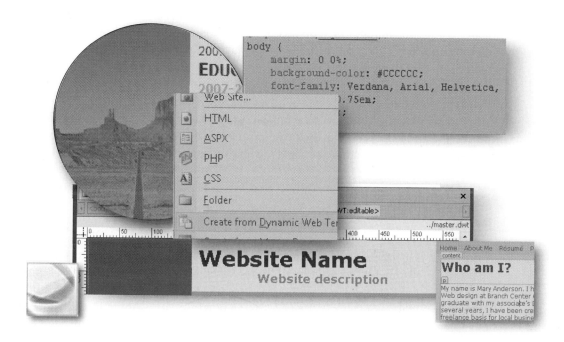

## Objectives

You will have mastered the material in this chapter when you can:

- Create an Expression Web site from a template
- Rename a page
- Rename a folder
- Add and delete pages
- Add and delete folders
- Replace content in the template
- Copy and paste text from an external document

- Edit the editable regions
- Make global changes with templates
- Define styles and style sheets
- Modify a style
- Create a style
- Apply a style

# 3 | Working with Templates and Styles

## Introduction

Creating a Web site from scratch allows you the flexibility to choose fonts, layouts, and styles that meet your needs — this is a useful approach when your needs are very specific. But, to save time and ensure consistency, you can use a wide range of pre-established content and layouts to create a Web site.

In its most general form, a template is a model document for creating a new version of an existing document, based on layout and content of the model. An Expression Web **Web template** is a site that includes sample layouts, pages, styles, fonts, text, and images. You can modify the template-based site's structure, content, and style to suit your needs.

Expression Web uses XHTML-based templates called **dynamic Web templates**. Dynamic Web templates specify a site's layout, formatting, and content, and are saved with the file extension .dwt. When you use a template, a site structure consisting of several folders and an HTML file for each page in the site is created. Each page has common elements, such as a masthead, footer, and navigation bar, which you can modify by editing the master.dwt file.

## Project — Personal Portfolio

**Securing Personal Information**
When creating a personal Web site, consider your privacy needs before entering personal information, such as your phone number or address. Only provide as much information as is needed for the site's purpose; a business will require additional contact information that a personal blog will not.

A **portfolio** is a collection of documents, images, or projects, compiled to show a variety of examples of someone's work. Portfolios are used by graphic artists, photographers, Web designers, and other creative professionals to show to potential clients the breadth of their experience or range of work. When creating a portfolio, you should include both written information about your experience in the form of a résumé or list of clients and graphic images that illustrate your work.

The project in this chapter uses Expression Web to create the home page and résumé page of an online portfolio, as shown in Figure 3–1. Mary Anderson is working on a degree in Web design and would like to create a Web site to showcase her work. She would also like to have a résumé, some general information about her objectives and experience, and graphics of Web sites she has worked on. Mary chooses an Expression Web site, the Personal 2 template, from the personal category because she likes the colors and graphics in the template. Expression Web's templates provide a quick way to build her site while ensuring consistency and sound design.

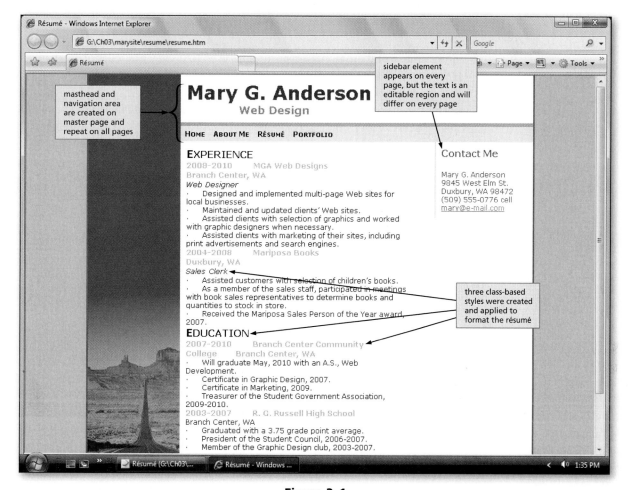

**Figure 3–1**

## Overview

As you read this chapter, you will learn how to create the portfolio Web site shown in Figure 3–1 by performing these general tasks:

- Start a new Web site using a template.
- Specify the page and folder names.
- Insert and remove pages and folders.
- Enter and edit text.
- Paste text from another source.
- Modify the dynamic Web template.
- Modify, create, and apply styles.

Plan
Ahead

**General Project Guidelines**

As you create a portfolio, such as the project shown in Figure 3–1, you should follow these general guidelines:

1. **Consider the purpose of the site.** A Web portfolio is used to display examples of creative work to potential clients, galleries, and customers. You will need to choose a template that meets your needs and reflects your personal design choices.

2. **Determine the structure of the site.** Although you can always add or delete pages, your Web site plan should provide an idea of the general number of pages before starting your site. Pages and folders should be named appropriately in order to keep the site organized.

3. **Determine, accumulate, and organize the content that you will use.** You can enter and edit text directly into the placeholders, which is good for short amounts of text. Pasting content into the site can save you time by using text you have already proofread. Gather all of the images and text files you have already created and collect them in a folder or group of folders. Make a note of any global changes you will need to make to the template to modify it to your specific needs.

4. **Distinguish the site using styles.** Use the styles task panes and CSS files to assign and modify styles to enhance the content and layout of your site. Changing the formatting using styles ensures consistency among common site elements and increases the professional look of your site.

When necessary, specific details about these guidelines are presented at appropriate points in the chapter. The chapter also will identify the tasks performed and decisions made regarding these guidelines during the creation of the portfolio shown in Figure 3–1.

BTW

**Images in Templates**
When you use a dynamic Web template, the site you create often has background images that appear on every page. These images are stored in the images folder in the main directory for the site and cannot easily be changed or replaced. Make sure that you like the image in a site template before choosing it.

# Starting a New Web Site Using a Template

Many Web sites use similar structures and contain standard elements. A site created with a template provides visitors to your site with familiar page layout and navigation tools, helping new visitors to your site to easily find the content they are looking for. After creating a site with a template, you can customize the page content.

Like the Web site you created in Chapter 1, Web sites created with templates are organized using box-like divs to define areas such as the masthead, navigation area, body content, and footer. You can nest divs within one another to apply formatting, such as centering within the browser window, to a div and any subordinate divs (Figure 3–2).

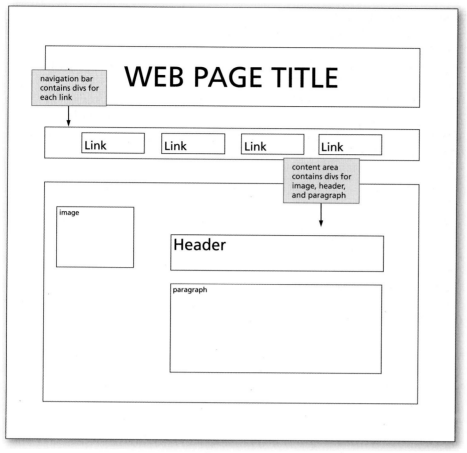

navigation bar contains divs for each link

WEB PAGE TITLE

Link   Link   Link   Link

content area contains divs for image, header, and paragraph

image

Header

paragraph

**Figure 3–2**

Expression Web includes three types of templates: page, style, and site. Page templates specify the layout of a page, including columns, navigation area, and header and footer. Style templates use CSS to define the formatting of a page or site, including fonts and colors. Site templates include multiple pages and folders in an organized site structure, and a dynamic Web template file that controls the layout and formatting of all pages. In this chapter, you will use a site template that includes multiple HTML pages that share layout and formatting and include content areas, a dynamic Web template page (master.dwt), as well as style sheets that define layout and formatting. Three types of site templates are installed automatically with your software: for personal use, for organizations, and for small businesses.

**BTW**

**Template types**
Templates can be used to create a site with a design theme or that serves a specific purpose, such as for a small business, a charitable organization, or for personal use.

**Consider the purpose of the site.**
When choosing a template, keep in mind what you would like the completed portfolio to look like and how it will be used. Choose an appropriate type and design, both of which you can modify later.

- **Site categories.** A personal Web site template will contain different content and layout options than one for a small business or organization. Select a category that most closely fits your needs.

- **Template design.** The themes and colors of the template you choose will have an effect on the mood of the site, although you can always modify these. Bright colors used in a site layout can distract from your work samples. Consider your audience. For example, if you are promoting a children's toy store, you will want to choose a very different look for your site than if you are creating a site for an insurance business.

**Plan Ahead**

## To Start Expression Web and Reset the Workspace Layout

If you are using a computer to step through the project in this chapter, and you want your screens to match the figures in this book, you should change your computer's resolution to 1024 × 768. For information about how to change a computer's resolution, read Appendix F. If you are using a lab computer or have changed the workspace layout, reset the workspace to the default to match the screens in this book.

The following steps, which assume Windows Vista is running, start Expression Web based on a typical installation and reset the task panes in the workspace. You may need to ask your instructor how to start Expression Web for your computer.

**Note:** If you are using Window XP, see Appendix E for alternate steps.

**1**
- Click the Start button on the Windows Vista taskbar to display the Start menu.
- Click All Programs at the bottom of the left pane on the Start menu to display the All Programs list.
- Click Microsoft Expression on the All Programs list to display the Microsoft Expression list.

**2**
- Click Microsoft Expression Web 2 to start Expression Web.

**3**
- Click Task Panes on the menu bar to open the Task Panes menu, then click Reset Workspace Layout.

---

**BTW**

**Naming files and folders**
The site name, which is the folder that contains the site contents, can include spaces. Within the site, folders and filenames cannot contain uppercase letters, spaces, or certain characters, such as # (the pound sign) or * (an asterisk). You can separate words in a filename by using an underscore (_), such as in the folder name assets_images or the filename web_page2.html.

## Placeholders

In a page created using an Expression Web template, a **placeholder** is a div that is used to specify the placement of headers, images, and text on pages. Placeholders, including those for sidebars and a main content area, contain sample text that you replace with your own content. If a placeholder is not needed on your page, delete the placeholder content; when your site is viewed in a browser, the placeholder is not visible.

## To Create a New Web Site from a Template

You use the New dialog box to create a new Web site using a template. The New dialog box contains options for creating blank Web pages and Web sites and options for using templates. Select a template type to view a thumbnail of it. After you specify the folder location of your new site, you should also specify the site name.

After selecting a template and closing the New dialog box, the site is open for editing and contains placeholder text, folders, and pages. In the following steps, you create a new Web site from a template.

**1**

- Click File on the menu bar to open the File menu, point to New, then point to Web Site (Figure 3–3).

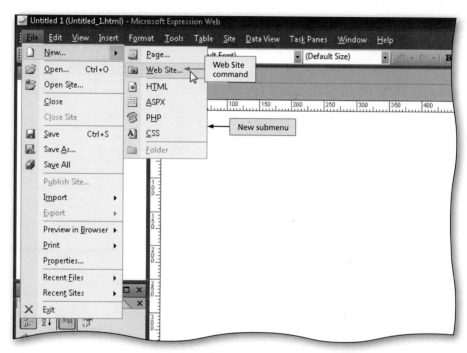

**Figure 3–3**

**2**

- Click Web Site to open the New dialog box.

- Click Templates in the left pane of the Web Site tab to display template options (Figure 3–4).

 **Experiment**

- Click other options in the list of templates to view thumbnails in the Preview window.

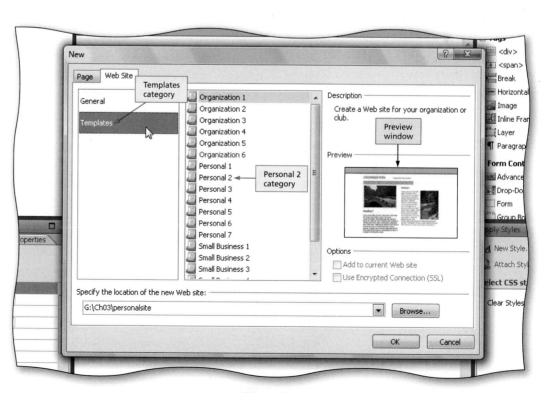

**Figure 3–4**

**3**

- Click Personal 2 from the list of templates to view a thumbnail of it (Figure 3–5).

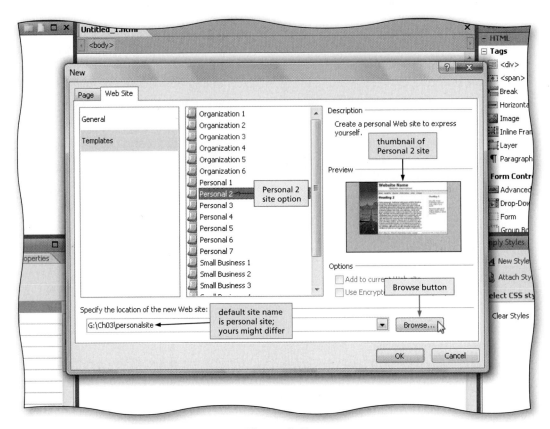

**Figure 3–5**

**4**

- Click the Browse button to open the New Web Site Location dialog box.

- Navigate to the location where you store your data files in the New Web Site Location dialog box (Figure 3–6).

**Figure 3–6**

**5**

- Click the Open button to select your location.

- Click after the folder name in the Specify the location of the new Web site text box.

- Type marysite (Figure 3–7).

**Q&A**

Why do I have a default site name?

When you create a site in a folder you have used before, or if you are working in a lab setting and your port and file path match that of previous users, Expression Web may assign a default site name, such as personalsite or mysite2, depending on the last site that was created.

To select the default site name, select the word(s) that appear after the last backslash (\) in the Specify the location of the new Web site text box.

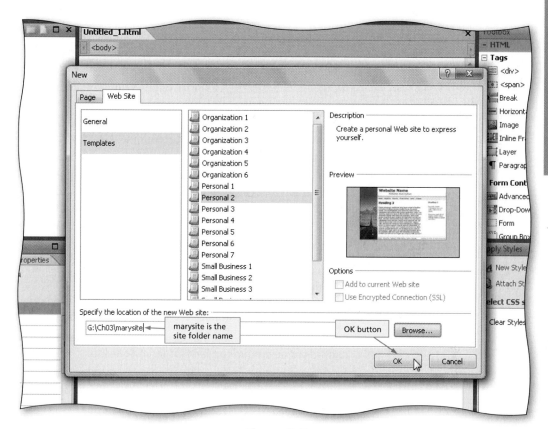

Figure 3–7

**6**

- Click the OK button to close the New dialog box and open a new site that contains multiple pages and folders in Design view.

- Double-click the default.html filename in the Folder List to open it (Figure 3–8).

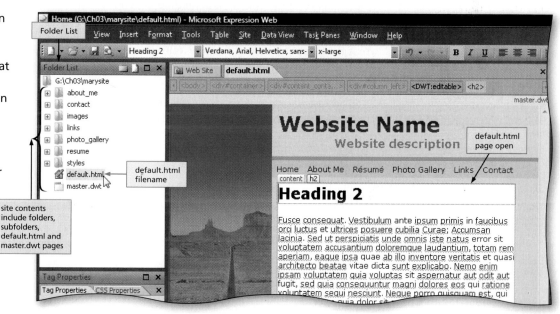

Figure 3–8

**BTW**

**Subfolders**
A folder within a folder is called a subfolder.

**BTW**

**Metadata**
Metadata is information about styles and structure that is created as part of a Web site. Metadata is stored in hidden files and folders that do not appear in the Folder List, but it will be visible if you view a site's folder contents in Windows Explorer; it should not be deleted, moved, or edited.

# Specifying the Structure of the Site

As you learned in previous chapters, a Web site can include folders to organize and store files. A template provides a folder for each page; each page folder includes the HTML file for the page and any embedded placeholder images or files for that page, such as the landscape image included in Mary's portfolio. When you create a new site from a template, you will see the folders for all pages except the default.html page, which is the home page. Because templates use style sheets to specify the formatting of the site, you will also see a folder for the style sheets. A separate folder exists for the common site images, such as the one on the left side of the page, which appears on all pages. A site created with a template includes many pages, including ones that you might not need or whose names you may want to change. You might also need to add pages to your site. Keeping a site organized includes adding new files and folders, placing newly created files or images that you embed on a page into the correct folder so that you know where to look for them when you need them, and deleting files and folders that are not needed.

**Plan Ahead**

> **Determine the folder structure of the site.**
> In addition to renaming files and folders generated by a template, adding and deleting pages can help you to customize a template-based site to your needs.
>
> - **Change the file and folder names.** File and folder names should be meaningful to you, and should be unique for each folder in your site.
>
> - **Remove extraneous pages.** Including too many pages can make your Web site difficult to navigate. Each page that a user can access should provide relevant information; if a template includes a page for which you have no need, remove it to keep your site streamlined.
>
> - **Remove extraneous folders.** Having extra folders can make managing your Web site unnecessarily complicated. Keep the folder structure as simple as possible. If you add pages and folders to the site, a logical and easy-to-follow folder structure will help you manage the site as it grows.
>
> - **Add necessary pages.** Sometimes templates don't provide all the pages you need. You can add a new blank page or create one based on an existing page or dynamic Web template. Choosing the appropriate method depends on the content of the new page. If you are displaying photographic images of a tree and want a separate page for each season of the year, it would make sense to create four pages that are based on the same page so that the layout for spring, summer, fall, and winter is the same, and your reader can focus on the changes in the images of the tree rather than the changes in the page layout or formatting.
>
> - **Add necessary folders.** Adding a new folder, such as one in which to store a newly created page, can help to keep the HTML file and embedded image files for that page in one location.

## To Rename a Folder

You can rename any folder or Web page within the Folder List. Folder and file names should be lowercase and not contain spaces. Expression Web prompts you to instruct the program to update all links and references to the page or folder you are renaming so that your site contains no broken links. The following steps rename a folder.

**1**

- Click the about_me folder name in the Folder List, then click the folder name again to select it (Figure 3–9).

**Q&A** Why did the folder's contents display in the Folder List?

Clicking a selected folder or file should select the name for editing. However, if you click it again too fast, it is double-clicked and its contents open. Click the folder name again, and it should select the folder name.

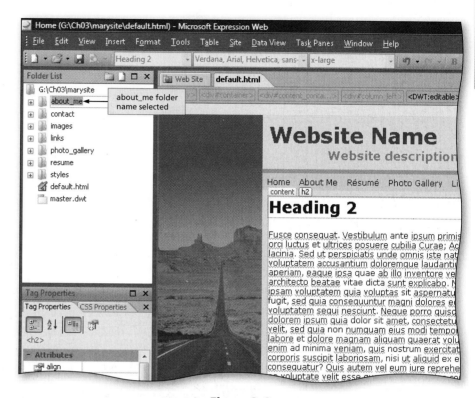

**Figure 3–9**

**2**

- Type about_mary, being sure to type the underscore between the two words, as the new name (Figure 3–10).

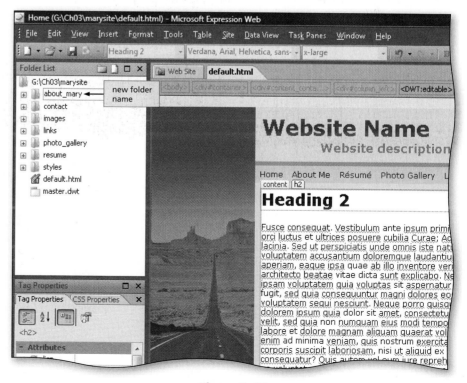

**Figure 3–10**

**3**

- Press ENTER to change the folder name (Figure 3–11).

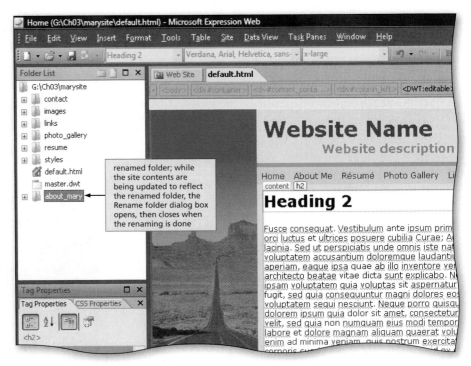

renamed folder; while the site contents are being updated to reflect the renamed folder, the Rename folder dialog box opens, then closes when the renaming is done

**Figure 3–11**

**Other Ways**

1. Right-click the page or folder name in the Folder List, then click Rename on the shortcut menu to select the name

## To Rename a Web Page

Renaming a Web page is done using the same steps as renaming a folder. Be sure to add the file extension to the page name. You can use either .htm or .html as the file extension, as they are both used to represent HTML files. The following steps rename the Web page.

**1**

- Click the about_mary plus sign in the Folder List to expand the folder and view its contents (Figure 3–12).

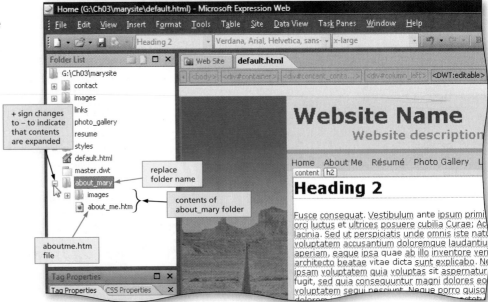

+ sign changes to – to indicate that contents are expanded

replace folder name

contents of about_mary folder

aboutme.htm file

**Figure 3–12**

- Click the about_me filename in the Folder List, then click the filename again to select it.

- Type `about_mary.htm`, including the underscore (Figure 3–13).

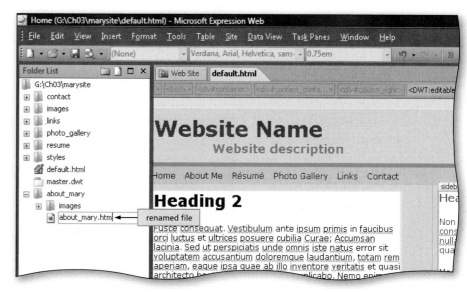

**Figure 3–13**

❸

- Press ENTER to open the Rename dialog box (Figure 3–14).

- In the Rename dialog box, click the Yes button to update references to the page.

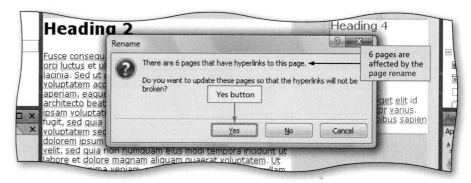

**Figure 3–14**

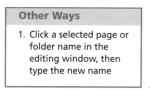

**Other Ways**

1. Click a selected page or folder name in the editing window, then type the new name

# Modifying the Structure of a Web Site

After determining the site's purpose, objectives, and goals, the next step in planning a site is to determine the number of pages that you will need. In Mary's case, she needs a home page, a résumé page, and portfolio page. A site created with a template comes with a sample structure, which might not reflect the pages required for your planned site. By deleting, adding, and renaming pages, Mary can organize the structure of her site to reflect her needs, then start customizing or creating the content by adding text and images.

Even though each Web page is stored on your computer as a separate file, you should avoid deleting, renaming, or moving Web site pages or image files using Windows Explorer. When deleting or renaming pages and images with Expression Web, the software prompts you to update all relevant links and make changes within the site that reflect the page deletion. If you use Windows Explorer or another file management program, you risk creating errors, such as broken links, in your site.

**BTW**

**Updating the Navigation Bar**
When revising your site structure, you must update the navigation bar to reflect the changes by editing the master.dwt file. You will do so later in this lesson.

## To Delete a Web Page

Deleting a page only deletes the HTML file; any folders and embedded files are kept in the site. Removing extra Web pages from your site also helps to reduce the file size of the entire site, increasing its usability. You cannot undo a page or folder deletion, so make sure that you do not need it before you delete it. The following steps delete a Web page, the contact.htm page, that Mary does not need according to her site plan.

- Click the contact folder plus sign in the Folder List to expand the folder and view its contents (Figure 3–15).

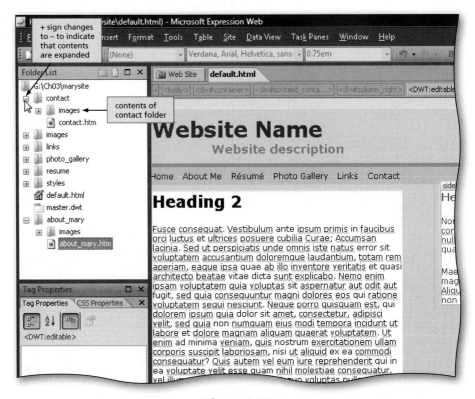

**Figure 3–15**

- Click the contact.htm filename in the Folder List to select it (Figure 3–16).

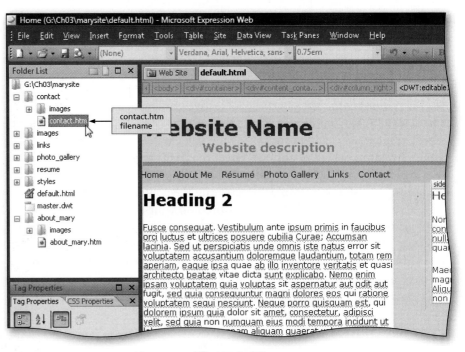

**Figure 3–16**

• Click Edit on the menu bar to open the Edit menu, then click Delete to open the Confirm Delete dialog box (Figure 3–17).

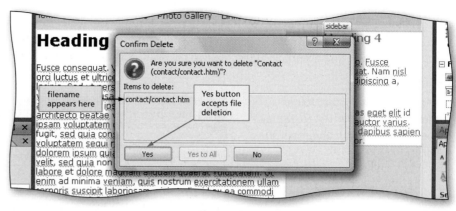

**Figure 3–17**

**4**

• In the Confirm Delete dialog box, click the Yes button to delete the file (Figure 3–18).

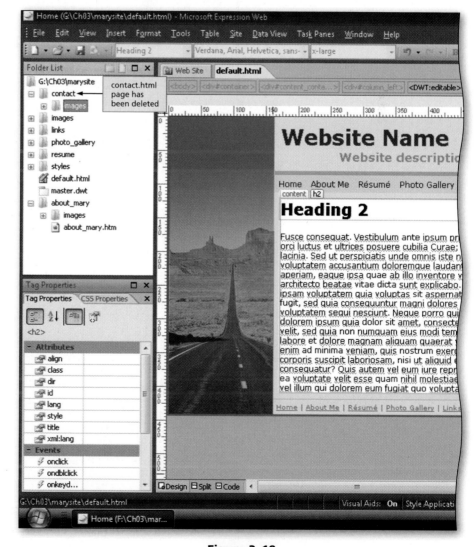

**Figure 3–18**

| Other Ways |
| --- |
| 1. Right-click the page name in the Folder List, then click Delete on the shortcut menu to open the Confirm Delete dialog box | 2. Click the page name in the Folder List, then press DELETE to open the Confirm Delete dialog box |

## To Delete a Folder

When you delete a folder, all of its contents are removed. Make sure that any files within the folder are not being used by other pages before you delete a folder and its contents. In the following steps, you will delete folders for contacts, links, and a photo gallery, that Mary does not need according to her site plan.

- Right-click the contact folder name in the Folder List to display the shortcut menu, and point to Delete (Figure 3–19).

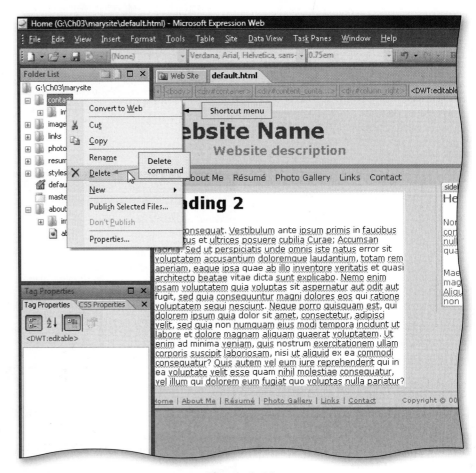

**Figure 3–19**

- Click Delete to open the Confirm Delete dialog box.

- In the Confirm Delete dialog box, click the Yes button to delete the contact folder (Figure 3–20).

- Repeat Steps 1-2 to delete the links and photo_gallery folders.

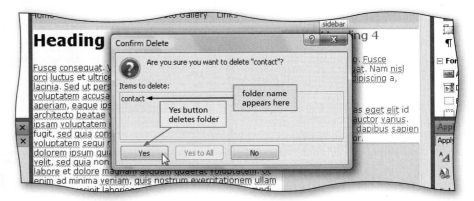

**Figure 3–20**

---

**Other Ways**

1. Right-click the folder name in the Folder List, then click Delete on the shortcut menu to open the Confirm Delete dialog box

2. Click the folder name in the Folder List, then press DELETE to open the Confirm Delete dialog box

## To Add a Folder

When adding folders to a site, it is important to insert them in the appropriate location. New folders often belong in the site's top-level folder, which stores all of the Web site files. To add a folder in this main folder, select the top folder name in the Folder List. Otherwise, your new folder might be created as a subfolder of another folder, which can be confusing and might not function as intended. The following steps add a new folder to Mary's Web site, to which she will add a newly created Web page in accordance with her site plan.

**1**

• Click the marysite folder name, which is the top folder name in the Folder List (Figure 3–21).

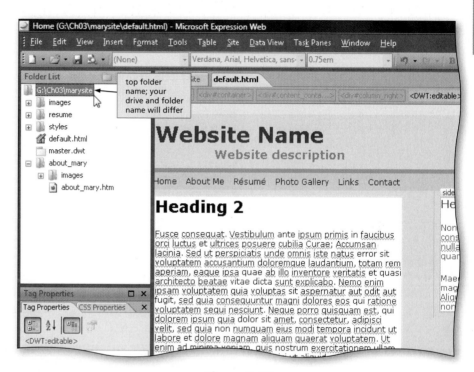

**Figure 3–21**

**2**

• Click the New Folder button on the Folder List to create a new folder in the Folder List (Figure 3–22).

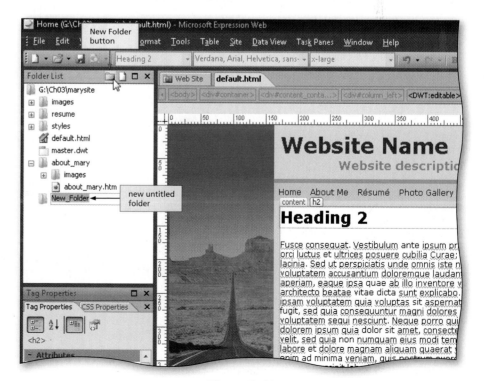

**Figure 3–22**

- Type `portfolio` as the new folder name (Figure 3–23).

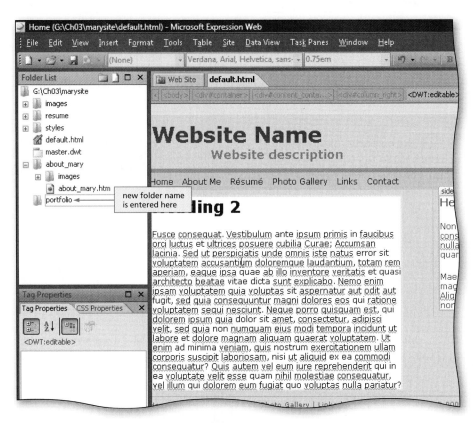

**Figure 3–23**

- Press ENTER to rename the folder (Figure 3–24).

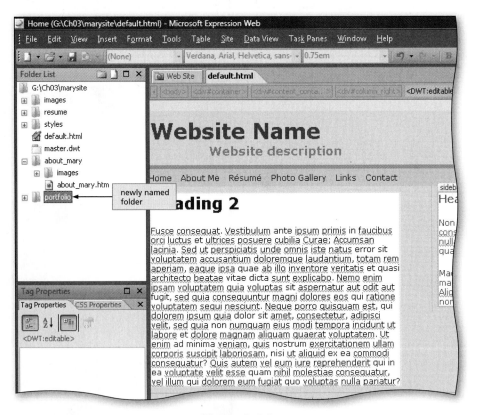

**Figure 3–24**

## To Add a Web Page

When you add a page in a site created with a template, you must attach the dynamic Web template to it; otherwise, the page will be blank. You can copy and paste pages in the Folder List to create pages that have similar content and layout and determine whether you need to create a folder in which to store the page, or whether it fits logically into an existing folder. The following steps create the new page Mary needs for a new portfolio, saves the page in the portfolio folder, and attaches the dynamic Web template to the page so that it matches the other pages in the site.

- Click File on the menu bar to open the File menu, point to New, then point to Create from Dynamic Web Template (Figure 3–25).

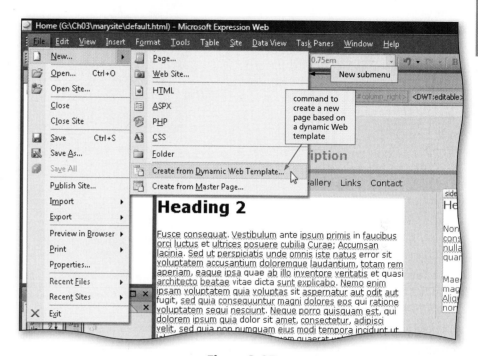

**Figure 3–25**

❷

- Click Create from Dynamic Web Template to open the Attach Dynamic Web Template dialog box.

- Scroll down, if necessary, then click master.dwt to attach it to the new page (Figure 3–26).

**Figure 3–26**

- Click the Open button to create a new, untitled Web page.

- Click the Close button to close the alert box.

- Right-click the Untitled_1.html page tab (Figure 3–27).

**Figure 3–27**

4

- Click Save to open the Save As dialog box.

- Double-click the portfolio folder in the right pane of the dialog box to open it.

- Select any text in the File name text box, then type `portfolio.html` to name the page (Figure 3–28).

**Figure 3–28**

**5**

- Click the Save button to name the new page and save it in the portfolio folder (Figure 3–29).

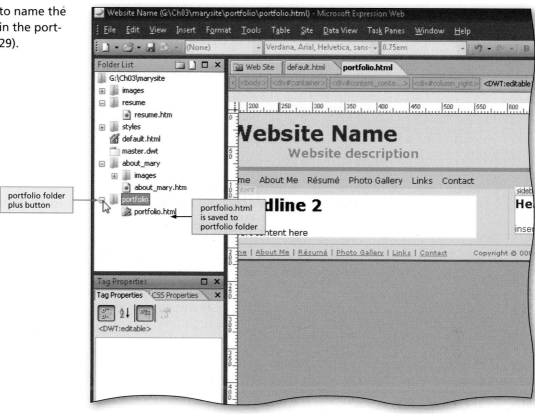

portfolio folder plus button

portfolio.html is saved to portfolio folder

**Figure 3–29**

**6**

- Right-click the portfolio page tab (Figure 3–30).

- Click Close to close the page.

Close command

**Figure 3–30**

# Entering and Editing Text

All Web pages contain content areas, called **editable regions**, including sidebars, headings, and main content areas. The editable regions are where you include the content and images specific to each page. There are two types of editable regions: headers and body text. Headers are indicated by the header level or description of the content that you should replace it with (such as Heading 1 or About Company). Body text is indicated by Latin text (such as Fusce consequat). Both headers and body text have styles attached to them, but you can modify the formatting to suit your needs.

To enter header or body content, click the area you want to edit, select the div to select all of the placeholder content, then type or paste the new text.

Plan
Ahead

> **Determine, accumulate, and organize the content you will use.**
>
> * Each page should have a header that states its purpose and has appropriate text and graphic content. Make sure to proofread your text before inserting or after typing it into the page. Reusing text from other Web pages or text files will make your work easier and reduces errors.
>
> * Modify the dynamic Web template content on the master.dwt page that is the same for every page: the page title, footer, and navigation area.

## To Replace Template Placeholder Text

Mary's portfolio site needs customized headings. The following steps replace heading placeholder text on the home page.

* If necessary, click the default.html page tab.

* Click in the words, Heading 2, to select the h2 div (Figure 3–31).

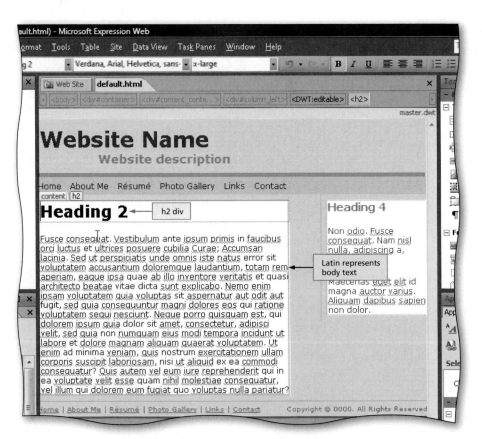

**Figure 3–31**

• Click the h2 tag on the Quick Tag Selector bar to select all of the placeholder text within the heading (Figure 3–32).

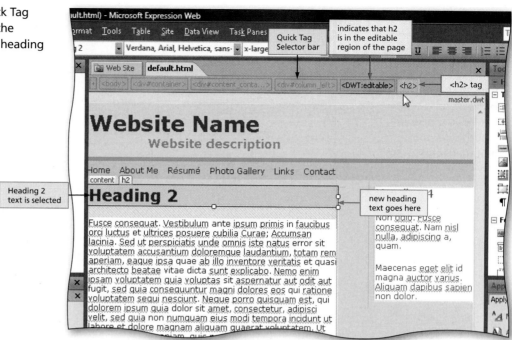

**Figure 3–32**

• Type Who am I? to customize the placeholder (Figure 3–33).

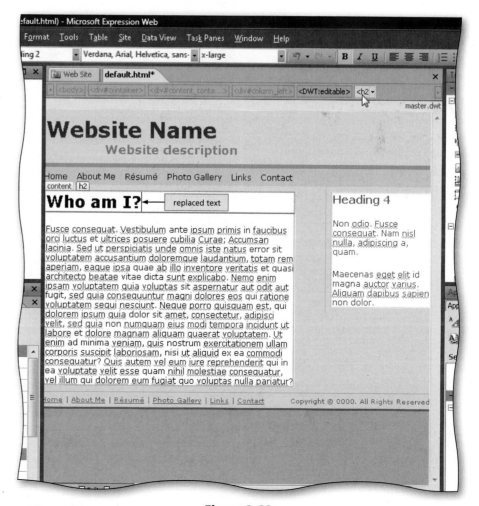

**Figure 3–33**

4

- If necessary, use the horizontal scroll bar to move the page view to the right.

- Click in the words, Heading 4, to select the sidebar heading placeholder for editing (Figure 3–34).

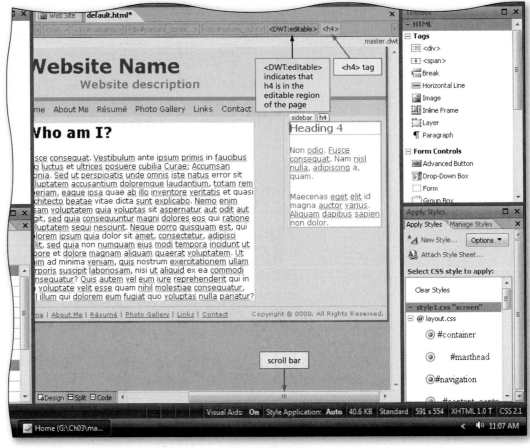

**Figure 3–34**

5

- Click the h4 tag on the Quick Tag Selector bar to select all of the placeholder text within the heading (Figure 3–35).

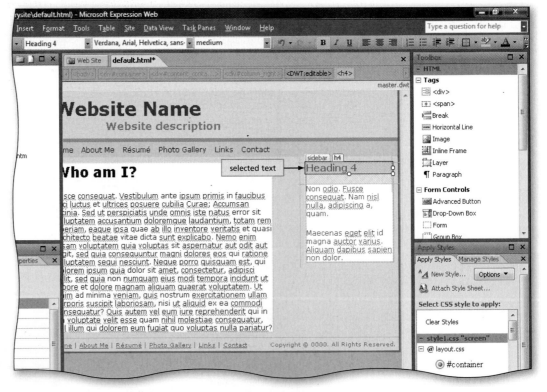

**Figure 3–35**

**6**

- Type `Objective` to customize the placeholder (Figure 3–36).

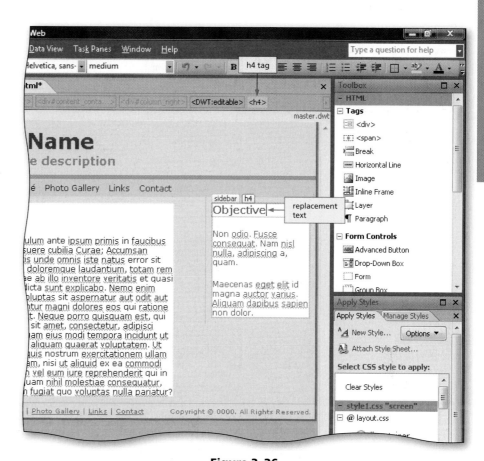

**Figure 3–36**

**7**

- Click in the paragraph below the word, Objective.

- Click the <p> tag on the Quick Tag Selector bar to select all of the place-holder text within the paragraph (Figure 3–37).

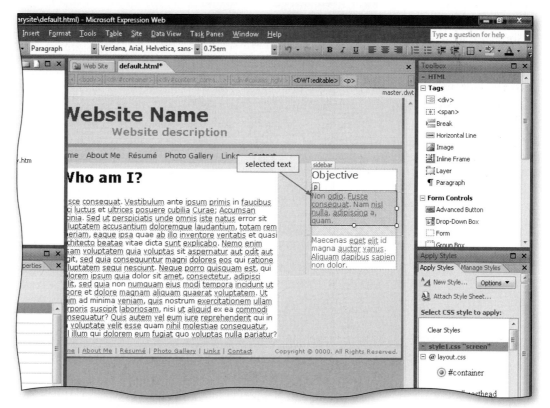

**Figure 3–37**

- Type To obtain a job as a Web designer in which I can combine my technical background and business knowledge to create Web sites that are attractive, easy-to-use, and meet the needs of my clients. (Figure 3–38).

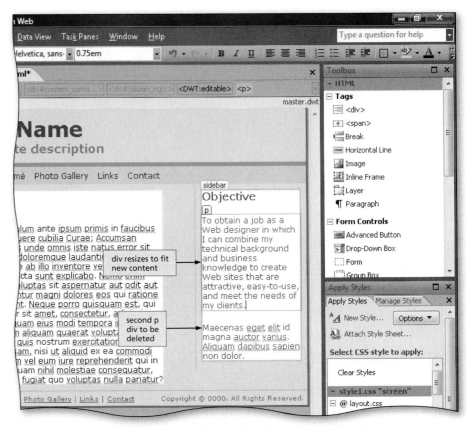

**Figure 3–38**

- Click the <p> tag below the text you just typed to select the second paragraph in the sidebar, then press DELETE to delete it (Figure 3–39).

- Press CTRL+S to save the page.

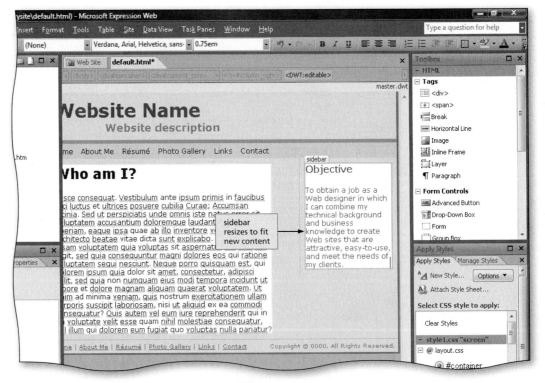

**Figure 3–39**

# Pasting Text

To use content, including text, images, or a table, that is saved in another file or Web page, copy it to the Clipboard, then paste it into the placeholder. The Clipboard, which you used in Chapter 2 to paste text between pages in your site, is shared by other Windows programs and can be used to paste text from other programs, such as Microsoft Word, into Expression Web.

When pasting text into a Web page, it is important to remove any formatting so that it does not clash with the site's formatting. Using the Paste Text command on the Edit menu, you can choose to insert the text with or without line breaks and other paragraph formatting. All character formatting, such as boldface and italics, is removed when using the Paste Text command.

**BTW**

**Removing Formatting**
To remove formatting from text, select the text, then click Remove Formatting on the Format menu. Alternatively, you can paste the text and then use the Paste Options button that appears at the bottom of the div containing the pasted text to remove the formatting.

**BTW**

**Extra Line Breaks**
Make sure to remove all extra line breaks at the end of a document that you are selecting, or they will appear when pasted into the Web site.

## To Paste Text

To insert text from another source, such as a Word document or text file, you first need to open the file in its native program and copy the text to the Clipboard. Mary needs to add her résumé to her Web site. The following steps open Microsoft Word, open two files, copy the text, then paste it in without formatting into the résumé page.

**1**

- Click the Start button on the Windows Vista taskbar to display the Start menu.

- Click All Programs at the bottom of the left pane on the Start menu to display the All Programs list.

- Click the Microsoft Office folder on the All Programs list to display the Microsoft Office list.

- Click Microsoft Office Word 2007 to start Word and open a blank document (Figure 3–40).

 **Q&A**

What if I don't have Word 2007?

If you have another version of Word you can use that, or use any text editor, such as Notepad or WordPad.

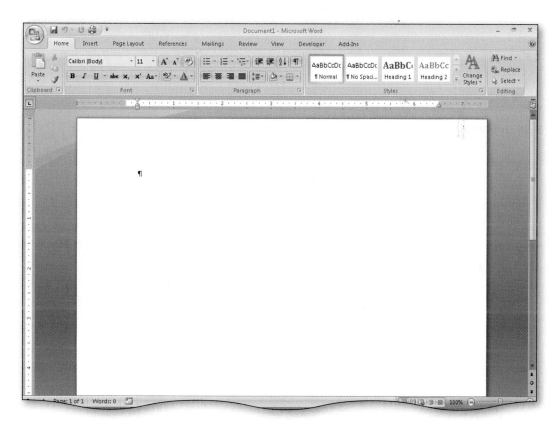

**Figure 3–40**

● Press CTRL+O to open the Open dialog box.

● If necessary, navigate to your Data Files, open the mary_ documents folder, and then select the hometext.doc file (Figure 3–41).

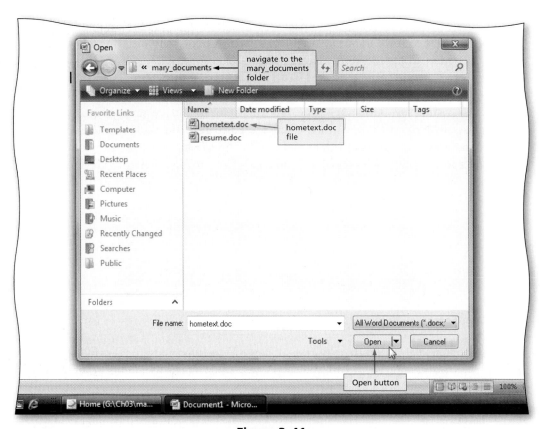

**Figure 3–41**

● Click the Open button to open the file in Word.

● Press CTRL+A to select all of the text in the document.

● Click the Copy button in the Clipboard group on the Ribbon to copy the selection to the Clipboard (Figure 3–42).

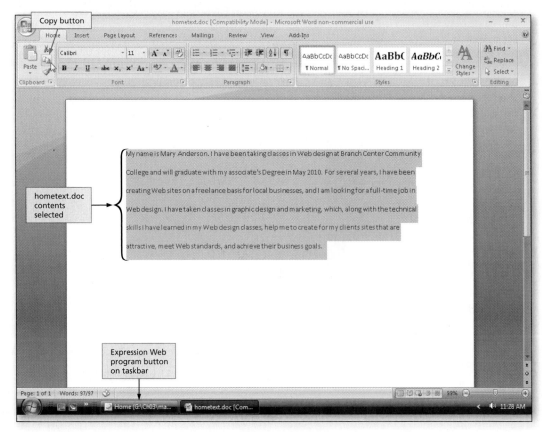

**Figure 3–42**

- Click the Expression Web button on the taskbar to return to Expression Web.

- Click in the div below Who am I?, then click the <p> tag on the Quick Tag Selector bar to select the placeholder text (Figure 3–43).

**Figure 3–43**

- Click Edit on the menu bar to open the Edit menu (Figure 3–44).

**Figure 3–44**

**6**

- Click Paste Text to open the Paste Text dialog box.

- Click Normal paragraphs with line breaks (Figure 3–45).

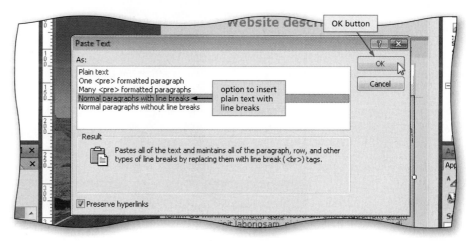

**Figure 3–45**

**7**

- Click the OK button to close the dialog box and insert the pasted text.

- Press CTRL+S to save the default.html page.

- Click the hometext. doc Word program button on the taskbar to return to Word.

- Repeat steps 2–6 to open the resume. doc file and copy its contents to the Clipboard and then return to Expression Web.

- Click the resume folder plus button in the Folder List to view its contents (Figure 3–46).

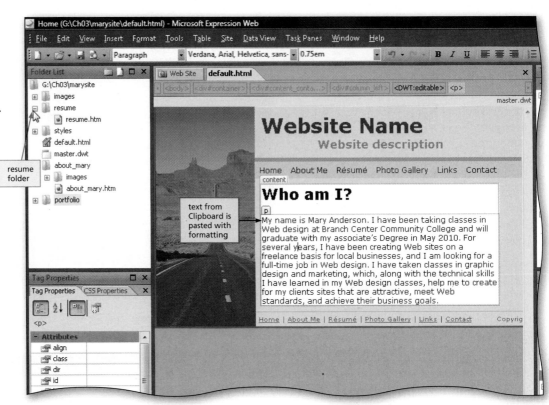

**Figure 3–46**

**8**

- Double-click the resume.htm page in the Folder List to open it.

- Click the content div to select the text (Figure 3–47).

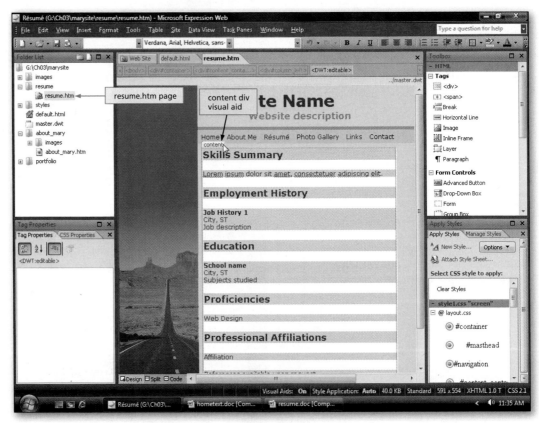

**Figure 3–47**

● Press DELETE to remove the
placeholder text from the
content div.

● Click Edit on the menu bar to
open the Edit menu, then click
Paste Text to open the Paste Text
dialog box.

● If necessary, click Normal
paragraphs with line breaks
(Figure 3–48).

 **Experiment**

● Try pasting text with the other
options in the Paste Text dialog
box to see the effect.

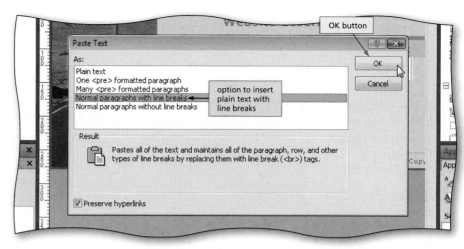

**Figure 3–48**

● Click the OK button to paste the
text (Figure 3–49).

● Click CTRL+S to save the resume.
htm page.

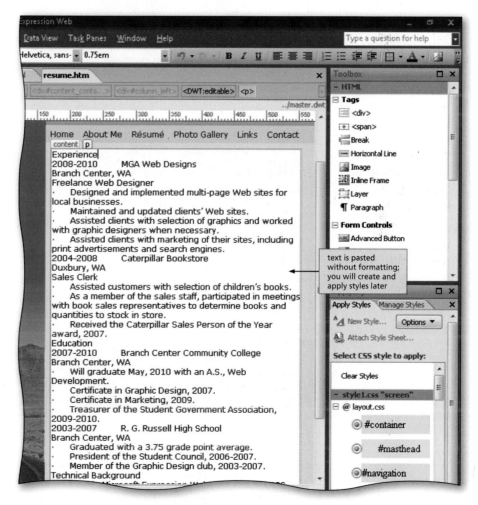

**Figure 3–49**

**Other Ways**

1. Press CTRL+C to copy
   selected text or images to
   the Clipboard.

2. Press CTRL+V to paste
   selected text or images
   from the Clipboard.

## To Close Microsoft Word

Closing files and quitting programs after you are done working with them frees up computer resources for other tasks and prevents data loss. The following steps close both Microsoft Word windows and the two files, hometext.doc and resume.doc.

 **1**

- Click the hometext.doc Word program button on the task-bar to return to Word (Figure 3–50).

- Click the Close button to close the file and the program.

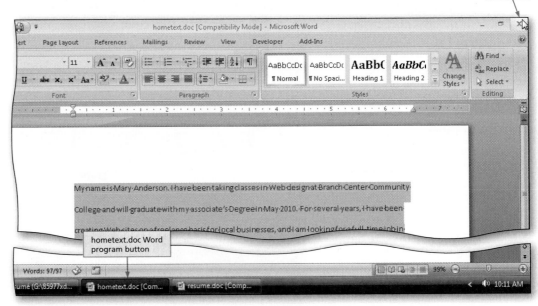

**Figure 3–50**

 **2**

- Click the resume.doc Word program button on the taskbar to return to Word (Figure 3–51).

- Click the Close button to close the file and the program and return to Expression Web.

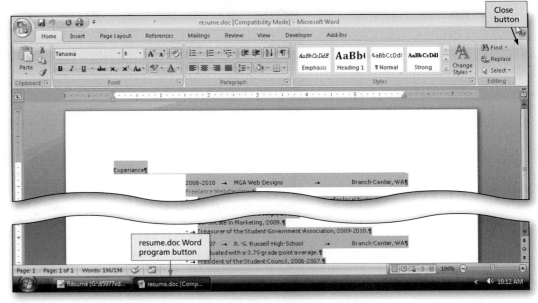

**Figure 3–51**

## Editing Text

When you edit text, you change its content by rewording, removing, adding, or moving words. Sometimes editing requires that you change all occurrences of a word or phrase. Editing can be done directly on the Web page using skills you have likely used in a word processing program such as Microsoft Word. To edit text by typing additional text or by using keys such as

DELETE or BACKSPACE, you must first position the insertion point (click) where your edits will take place. To delete more than one word or sentence, you must first select the text you want to remove, then delete it by pressing the DELETE or BACKSPACE key, or replace it by typing new text. Table 3–1 outlines different editing commands and shortcuts.

**Table 3–1: Editing Commands and Shortcuts**

| Action | Effect |
|---|---|
| Double-click a word | Selects the word and the space after it |
| Triple-click in a paragraph | Selects the paragraph |
| Press BACKSPACE | Deletes text one character at a time to the left of the insertion point |
| Press DELETE | Deletes text one character at a time to the right of the insertion point |
| Press SHIFT, then the left or right ARROW on the keyboard | Selects text one character at a time to the left or right of the insertion point |
| Press SHIFT and CTRL, then press the left or right arrow on the keyboard | Selects text one word at a time from the left or right of the insertion point |

**BTW**

**Quick Reference**
For a table that lists how to complete the tasks covered in this book using the mouse, shortcut menu, and keyboard, see the Quick Reference Summary at the back of this book, or visit the Expression Web 2 Quick Reference Web page (scsite.com/ew2/qr).

You can also find and change all instances of a word or phrase using the Find and Replace tools. For instance, to change a person or company's name, you use the Find tool to locate each instance of the name, then replace or ignore each instance individually, or replace all at once.

## To Edit Text

The title of the sidebar is, by default, the page name, résumé. The sidebar text and title on the résumé page need to be revised to reflect Mary's contact information. When entering lines of text into a paragraph (p) div, pressing ENTER automatically inserts a new p div for the next line and adds space between the divs. To create multiple lines of text within one paragraph div, press SHIFT+ENTER instead of ENTER to insert a line break that moves the insertion point to the next line but keeps it in the div. The following steps edit text using the keyboard to delete and type text and using the mouse to select text.

- Use the vertical and horizontal scroll bars, if necessary, to view the sidebar.

- Drag to select the sidebar title, Résumé, then type `Contact Me` to replace the placeholder text (Figure 3–52)

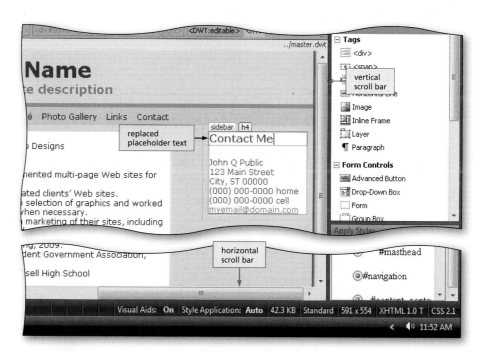

**Figure 3–52**

**2**

- Drag to select the sidebar text (Figure 3–53).

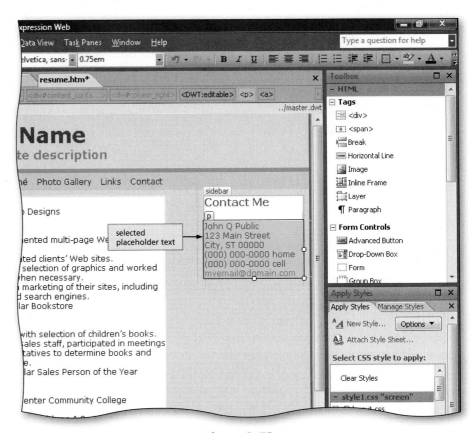

**Figure 3–53**

**3**

- Press DELETE to delete the placeholder text.

- Type Mary G. Anderson, then press SHIFT+ENTER to start a new line in the p div (Figure 3–54).

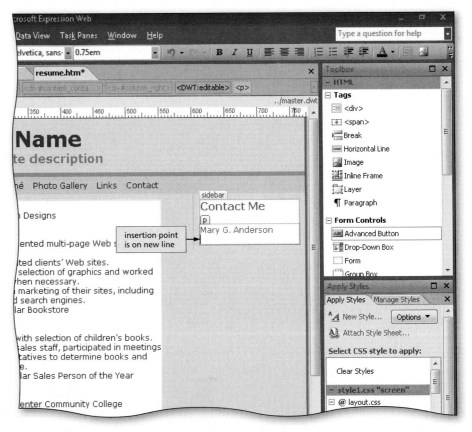

**Figure 3–54**

**4**

- Type `9845 West Elm St.`, then press SHIFT+ENTER.

- Type `Duxbury, WA 98472`, then press SHIFT+ENTER.

- Type `(509) 555-0776 cell`, then press SHIFT+ENTER.

- Type `mary@e-mail.com`, then press the spacebar to create the e-mail hyperlink (Figure 3–55).

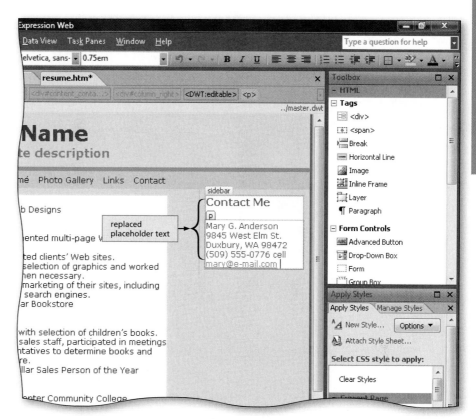

**Figure 3–55**

**5**

- Click after the word, Bookstore, in the div that contains the résumé (about one-third of the way down the document).

- Press BACKSPACE four times to change the word to Books (Figure 3–56).

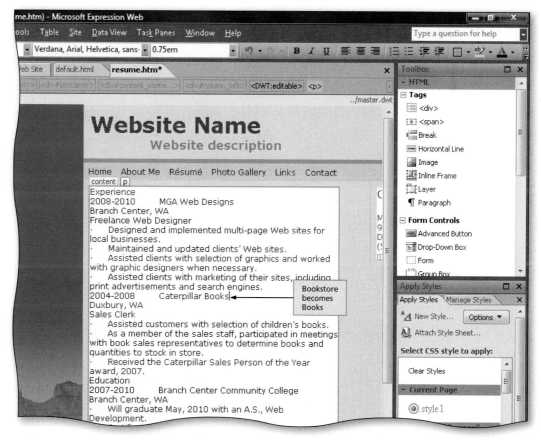

**Figure 3–56**

● Double-click the word, Freelance, which is the first word on the fourth line of the content div, to select it.

● Press BACKSPACE to delete the word (Figure 3–57).

● Press CTRL+S to save the page.

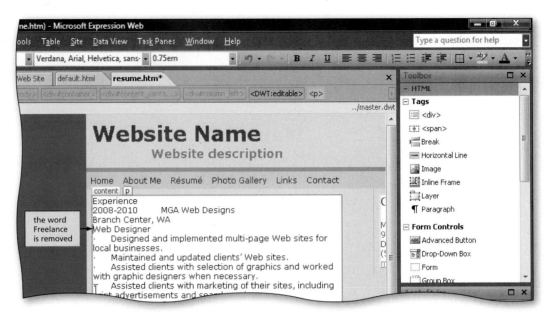

**Figure 3–57**

## To Find and Replace Text

You can use the Find and Replace commands to locate and change single instances or all occurrences of a word or phrase, or use the Replace command on its own to replace words or phrases without first using the Find command. The bookstore where Mary has been working has recently changed its name from Caterpillar to Mariposa. Mary is not sure whether the name change occurred before or after she last saved her résumé, so she will first use the Find command, then the Replace command. The following steps find all instances of the word, Caterpillar, and replace them with Mariposa.

● Click Edit on the menu bar to open the Edit menu, then point to Find (Figure 3–58).

**Figure 3–58**

- Click Find to open the Find and Replace dialog box.

- If necessary, select any text in the Find what text box and type `Caterpillar` (Figure 3–59).

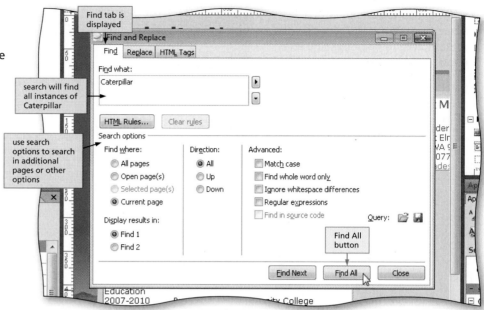

**Figure 3–59**

- Click the Find All button to display the search results in the Find pane at the bottom of the editing window (Figure 3–60).

**Figure 3–60**

- Click Edit on the menu bar to open the Edit menu, and then click Replace to open the Find and Replace dialog box.

- If necessary, select any text in the Replace with text box and type Mariposa (Figure 3–61).

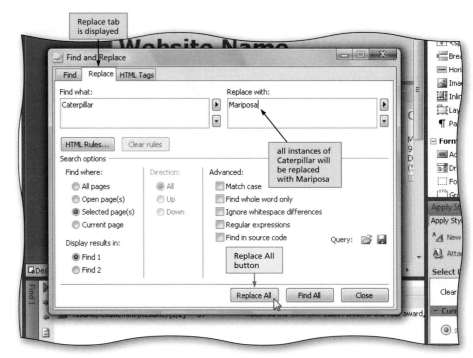

**Figure 3–61**

- Click the Replace All button to replace the text (Figure 3–62).

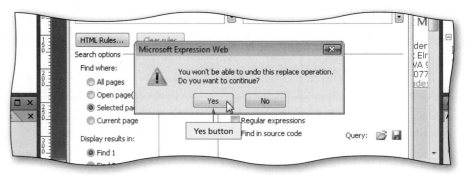

**Figure 3–62**

- Click the Yes button in the alert box to proceed with the replacement (Figure 3–63).

**Experiment**

- Open the Find and Replace dialog box, click the HTML Tags tab, and try searching for tags such as div and p.

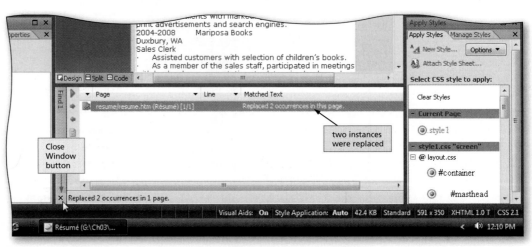

**Figure 3–63**

**7**

- Click the Close Window button on the Find task pane to complete the find and replace operation.

- Press CTRL+S to save the résumé page.

- Right-click the résumé page tab to open the shortcut menu (Figure 3–64).

- Click Close to close the page.

What if I get an alert box?

If you get an alert box telling you that you will not be able to undo the Replace command, click Yes or OK, depending on the type of alert you receive. You are still able to undo the replace if necessary.

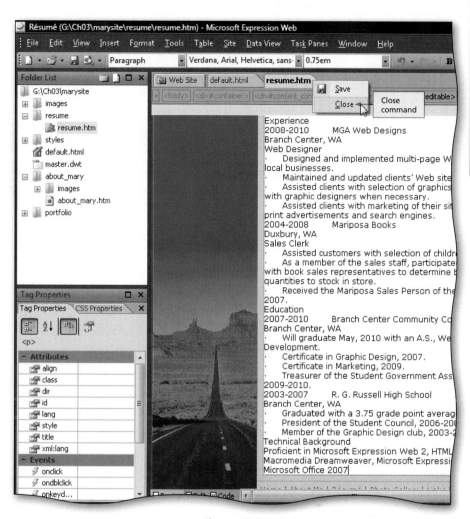

**Figure 3–64**

# Dynamic Web Page Template Pages

**Creating Templates**
You can also create a dynamic Web template from an existing page to create additional pages that share the same formatting and layout. To do so, you need to remove all text and define the editable regions.

Each page in a site contains common text or image elements that relate general information about the site. This information can include a masthead with a company name or logo, a footer with copyright information or the company's address, and a navigation bar with links to the main pages of the site. The dynamic Web template uses placeholders for this information; these placeholders can only be edited from the master.dwt page. Placeholders on the master.dwt page describe the type of information that you need to add, such as Web Site name or Web Site description.

To edit master page information, such as the Web site title or description, you must edit the dynamic Web page master file, master.dwt. You should save and close all open pages prior to opening the master.dwt page. When you make edits to the master page, you must save the master page before the changes are applied to the affected pages. You will be prompted to accept the changes for all pages, or you can accept them individually.

## To Make Global Changes to a Template

All of Mary's Web pages should include a name for her Web site (in this case, her name), a description, and copyright information. The following steps edit the master.dwt page to add text to the masthead and footer. You will also edit the navigation bar on the master.dwt page to reflect the pages you have added and deleted by deleting, renaming, and reassigning the hyperlinks. These changes will be made to all pages that are attached to the template.

**1**

- Right-click the default.html page tab, then click Close to close the page.

- Double-click the master.dwt page in the Folder List to open it in the editing window.

- Select the text in the Website Name div (Figure 3–65).

**Figure 3–65**

**2**

- Type Mary G. Anderson to customize the site name.

- Select the text in the Website description div, then type Web Design to reflect the site's purpose.

- Scroll right if necessary, click in the Copyright div, select the year, then type 2010 to update the year (Figure 3–66).

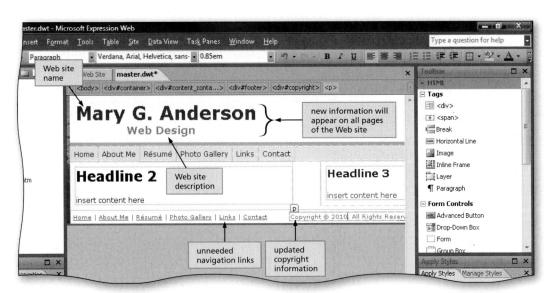

**Figure 3–66**

- In the footer, click after the word, Contact, and then select the word, Contact.

- Press DELETE to remove the link.

- Select the word, Links, and the vertical lines before and after it, then press DELETE to remove the link.

- Select the words, Photo Gallery, then type `Portfolio` to change the link name (Figure 3–67).

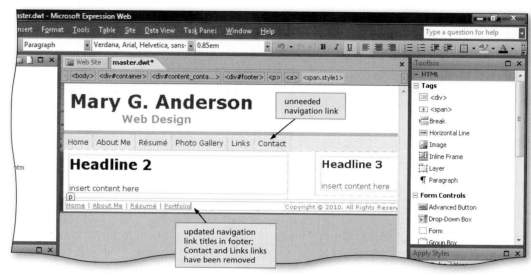

**Figure 3–67**

- In the navigation bar below the Web Design div, click in the word, Contact.

- Click the <a> tag on the Quick Tag Selector bar to select the div (Figure 3–68).

**Figure 3–68**

- Press DELETE to remove the contact link.

- Select the Links div, then press DELETE to remove the link.

- Select the words, Photo Gallery, then type `Portfolio` to change the link name (Figure 3–69).

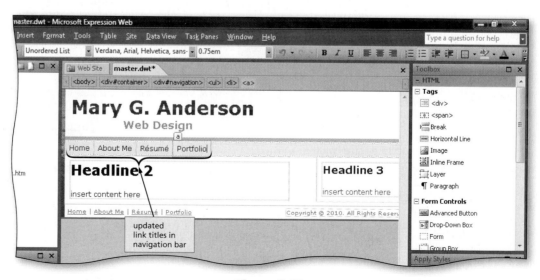

**Figure 3–69**

- Drag to select the word, Portfolio.

- Click Insert on the menu bar to open the Insert menu, then click Hyperlink to open the Edit Hyperlink dialog box (Figure 3–70).

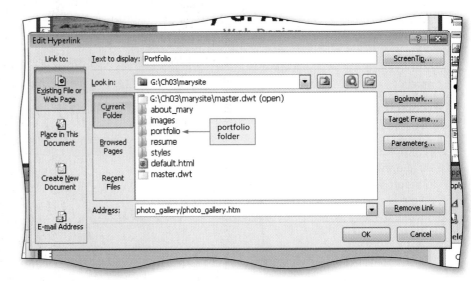

**Figure 3–70**

- Double-click the portfolio folder to open it.

- Click the portfolio.html file to select it (Figure 3–71).

- Click the OK button to update the hyperlink.

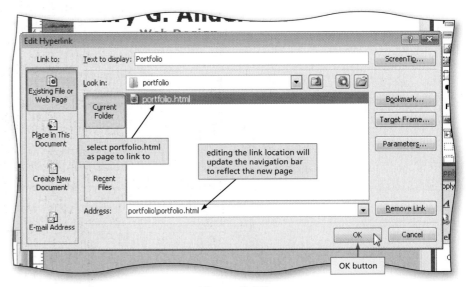

**Figure 3–71**

- Repeat steps 6 and 7 to update the portfolio link in the bottom navigation bar.

- Press CTRL+S to save the master.dwt page and open an alert box confirming that the changes will be made to all site pages (Figure 3–72).

**Figure 3–72**

• Click the Yes button in the alert box to update the four attached files (Figure 3–73).

**Figure 3–73**

⑩
 • Click the Close button to close the alert box.

 • Right-click the master.dwt page tab, then click Close to close the master template.

 • Double-click default. html in the Folder List to open the default.html page and see the changes you made on the master.dwt page (Figure 3–74).

 • Right-click the default.html page tab, then click Close.

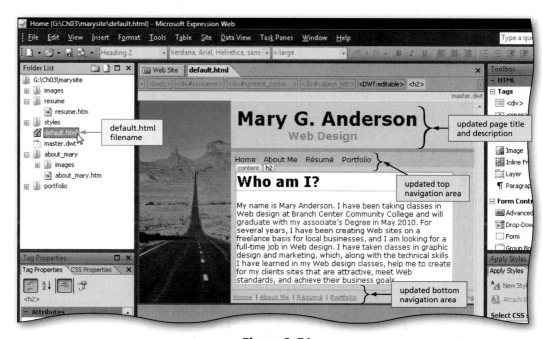

**Figure 3–74**

# Defining Styles and Style Sheets

In a Web page created using an Expression Web template, the layout and formatting are saved to cascading style sheet (CSS) files. You can customize the look of your site by creating, modifying, and applying styles that use a combination of formatting attributes, and that can be used to create consistency across all pages.

A style is a formatting attribute or group of attributes applied to a single character, a word, a section, or an entire Web site. A **style sheet** is a collection of style rules that are applied to specific elements. CSS is a type of style sheet. The style rules list the properties, such as formatting and layout, that apply to an element. Using style sheets ensures consistency of styles among elements. For instance, to change all bulleted lists from round to square bullets, you can simply change the style in the style sheet, and the change is applied to all bulleted lists in your site. Style sheets separate the content of a page (written in HTML) from the formatting. **Cascading** refers to the weighting, or prioritizing, of potential style conflicts. Priority is determined by **specificity**, which generally means that the rule that is higher in the priority is used if there is a conflict. A site can have several style sheets, each of which controls different aspects of formatting and layout. Expression Web templates come with embedded styles saved to style sheets, which are stored in the styles folder.

## Style Sheet Types

Style sheets can be internal, which means they are associated with a page or site, or external, which means they are saved as a separate file that can be applied to multiple pages or sites. By storing styles in a separate file, called an **external style sheet**, you can control the formatting of a site and also apply that style sheet to other pages or sites. Styles can also be saved as an **internal style sheet** by embedding them into the header of an XHTML page; an internal style sheet can only be used on the page in which it is embedded, however. An **inline style** is used to format a section of text and is defined by including a tag in the body of the document. An inline style only applies to the exact section of text or element to which you apply it and cannot be reused for other elements or pages. When style conflicts arise, inline styles have first priority and are applied first, followed by internal styles, then external styles.

**BTW**

**CSS Versions**
All browsers support slightly different features of CSS. It is important to test your site using various browsers before publishing it to make sure that the formatting appears the same on all browsers.

## Style Rule Syntax

In general, syntax refers to a set of rules, for instance to specify wording and punctuation in HTML or CSS code. A style rule's syntax has three parts: a **selector** (the element to which the rule applies, such as h1), a **property** (how the element will be changed, such as font style or font size), and a **value** (the specific change or degree of change, such as bold or large). Selectors can refer to a specific element, a class of element, or a single instance of an element.

As with HTML, you do not need to know how to code a style when creating it, but it is important to understand the **syntax**, or the order of the rules. The first part of a style is the selector, followed by the property and value, which together make up the **declaration** (Figure 3–75). Proper use of punctuation, such as braces, semicolons, and colons, ensures that your styles are interpreted correctly by a browser. Make sure to enter a semicolon to separate each style rule, and do not move or delete braces or other punctuation marks, unless you are sure that they are unnecessary.

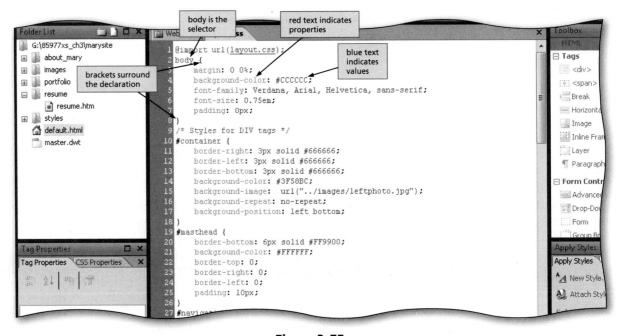

**Figure 3–75**

> **Distinguish the site using styles.**
> When deciding on the styles to use in your site, note that you can modify an existing style, create element-based styles that can apply to all instances of an element, or format a specific element or text area by creating a class-based style rule.

**Plan Ahead**

## To Modify a Style

To apply, create, and modify styles and style sheets, you can use the Apply Styles and Manage Styles task panes, located below the Toolbox. When you add or edit a style, the style sheet file opens and needs to be saved along with the page that you are modifying.

Mary would like to modify the look of her site by revising the appearance of the links. The following steps change the style of the navigation bar.

- Double-click the master.dwt page in the Folder List to open it.

- In the Apply Styles task pane, point to the #navigation style, then click the arrow to open the menu (Figure 3–76).

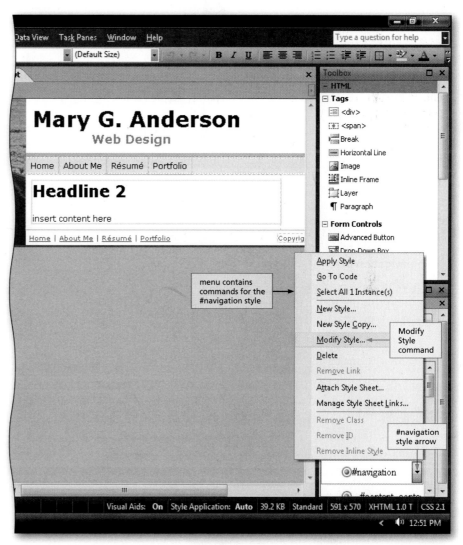

**Figure 3–76**

● Click Modify Style on the menu to open the Modify Style dialog box (Figure 3–77).

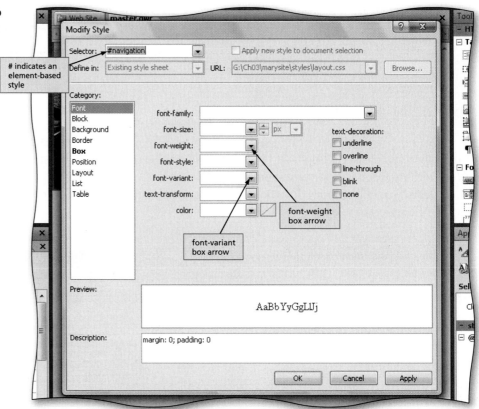

**Figure 3–77**

● Click the font-weight box arrow, then click bold to apply bold to the navigation bar.

● Click the font-variant box arrow, then click small-caps to change the lettering style (Figure 3–78).

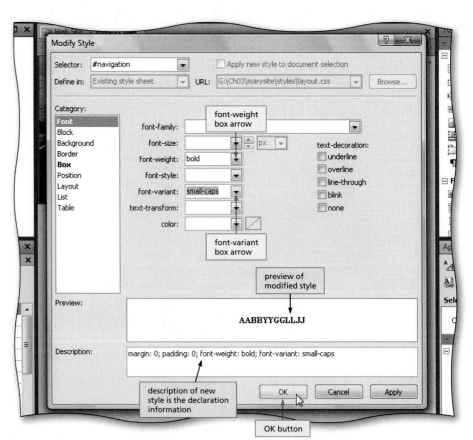

**Figure 3–78**

**4**

- Click the OK button to close the Modify Style dialog box.

- Save and close the master.dwt file.

- Press CTRL+S to save the layout.css file.

- Right-click the layout.css page tab to display the menu (Figure 3–79).

**Q&A**

What is the layout.css file and why did it open?

When you edit a style, the style sheet where it is stored opens and must be saved in order to save the updated styles.

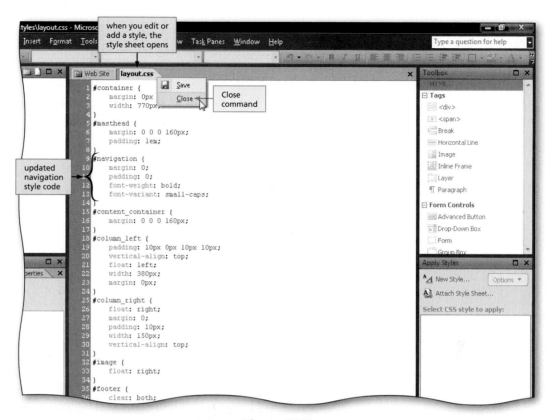

**Figure 3–79**

**5**

- Click Close on the menu to close the layout.css file.

- Open the default.html page to view the modified navigation bar (Figure 3–80).

- Close the default.html page.

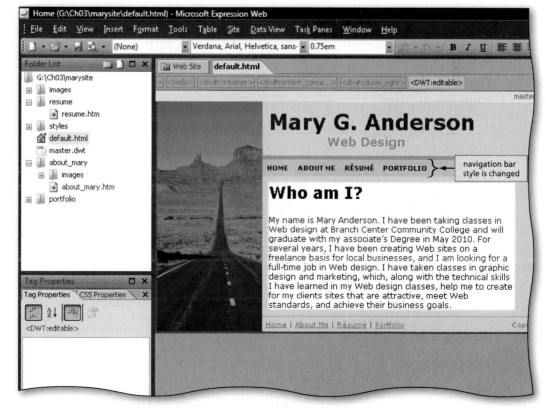

**Figure 3–80**

## To Create a Style

You create styles in the New Style dialog box and save them to the current page, a new style sheet, or an existing style sheet. When you create multiple styles, you only have to specify the saved location once; subsequent styles are by default saved to the location you choose when defining the first style. When naming a class-based style, you must include a period before the name, such as .category. Within the New Style dialog box, Expression Web inserts a period before the default style name. Do not delete this period. The following steps create three styles for Mary's résumé to an existing style sheet, which you will apply to sections of the résumé, formatting it to be readable.

- Right-click the layout.css page tab, then click Close.

- Double-click the resume.htm page in the Folder List to open it (Figure 3–81).

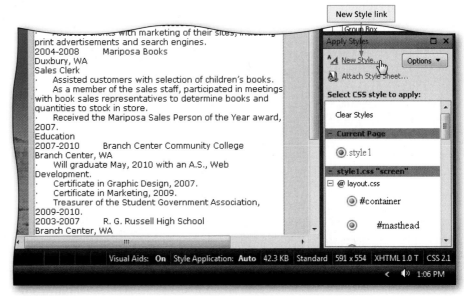

**Figure 3–81**

2

- Click the New Style link on the Apply Styles task pane to open the New Style dialog box.

- In the Selector text box, type category to name the new style for the general headings in Mary's resume.

- Click the Define in list arrow, then click Existing style sheet to add the new style to a pre-existing style sheet.

- Click the URL box arrow, then click styles/style1.css to specify style1. css as the style sheet to which the new .category style will be added (Figure 3–82).

**Q&A**  Why does the style sheet name include "styles/"?

Styles is the folder name where the style sheet is stored.

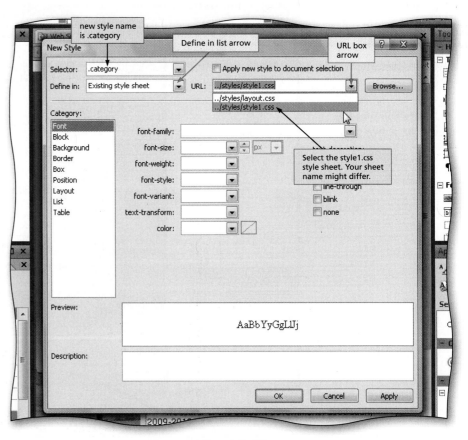

**Figure 3–82**

- Click the font-size box arrow, then click large to make the new style large.

- Click the font-weight box arrow, then click bold to make the new style bold.

- Click the font-variant box arrow, then click small-caps to change the new style to small caps (Figure 3–83).

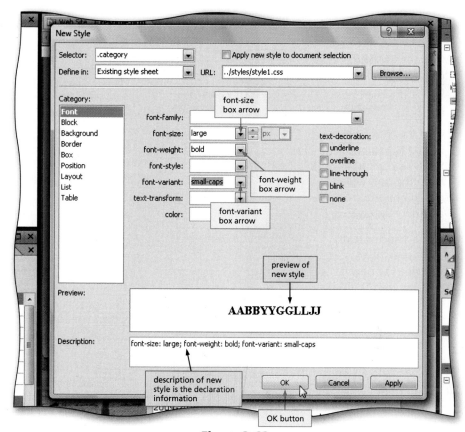

**Figure 3–83**

- Click the OK button in the New Style dialog box to save the new style rules.

- Click the New Style link on the Apply Styles task pane to open the New Style dialog box and create another new style.

- In the Selector text box, type dates to name the new style for the dates that appear in Mary's resume.

- Click the font-size box arrow, then click small.

- Click the font-weight box arrow, then click bold.

- Click the color box arrow to display the color palette (Figure 3–84).

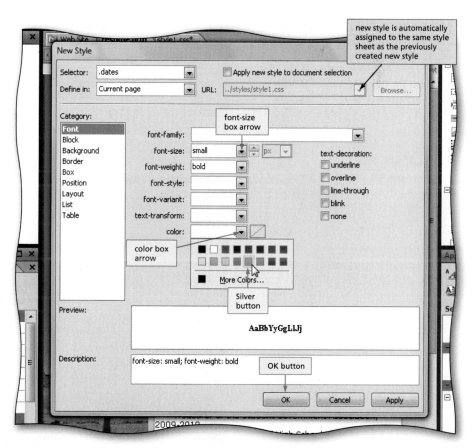

**Figure 3–84**

**5**

- Click Silver on the color palette.

- Click the OK button in the New Style dialog box to save the new .dates style.

- Click the New Style link on the Apply Styles task pane to open the New Style dialog box and create another new style.

- In the Selector text box, type jobtitle to name the new style for the job titles in Mary's resume.

- Click the font-size box arrow, then click small.

- Click the font-style box arrow, then click italic (Figure 3–85).

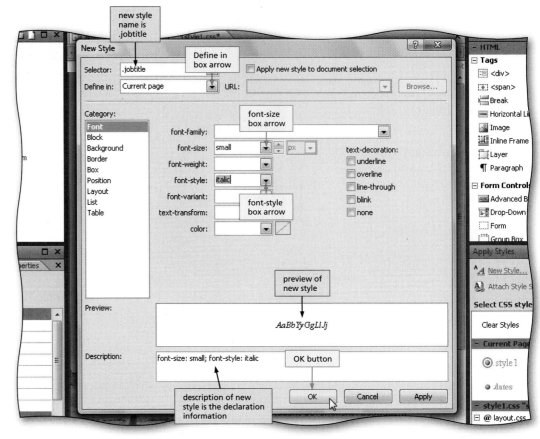

**Figure 3–85**

**6**

- Click the OK button to close the New Style dialog box.

- Scroll in the Apply Styles task pane to see the new styles in the task pane (Figure 3–86).

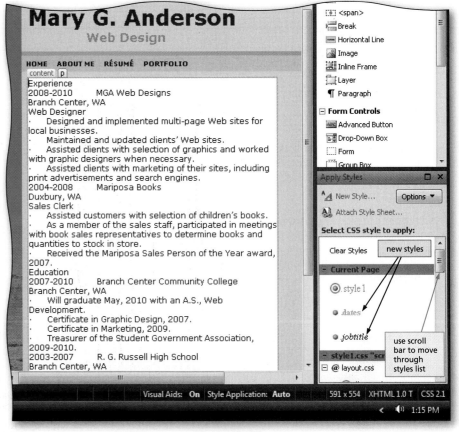

**Figure 3–86**

**7**

- Press CTRL+S to save the style1.css file.

- Right-click the style1.css page tab, then click Close to close the style sheet (Figure 3–87).

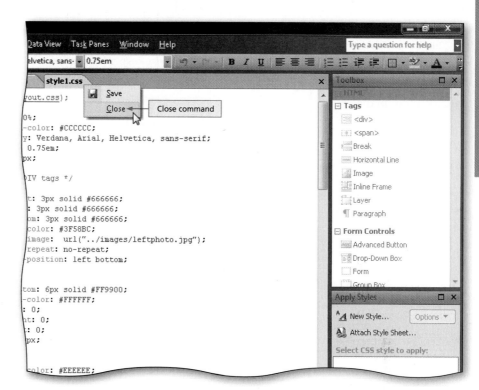

**Figure 3–87**

## To Apply a Style

The following steps apply the styles you created to format the résumé attractively.

**1**

- Select the word, Experience, at the top of the résumé.

- Click .category in the Apply Styles task pane to apply the .category style.

- Apply the .category style to the words, Education and Technical Background (Figure 3–88).

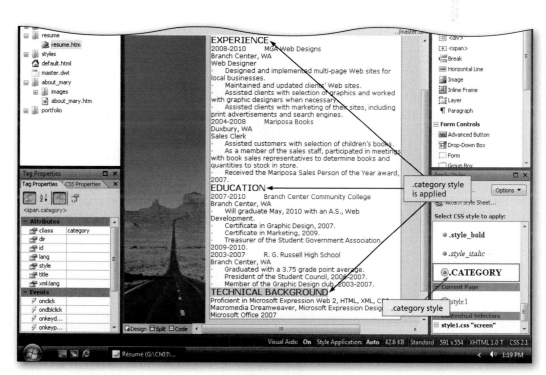

**Figure 3–88**

- Select the words, 2008-2010 MGA Web Designs Branch Center, WA.

- Click .dates in the Apply Styles task pane to apply the dates style.

- Apply the .dates style to the words, 2004-2008 Mariposa Books Duxbury, WA

- Apply the .dates style to the words, 2007-2010 Branch Center Community College Branch Center, WA.

- Apply the .dates style to the words, 2003-2007 R. G. Russell High School Branch Center, WA (Figure 3–89).

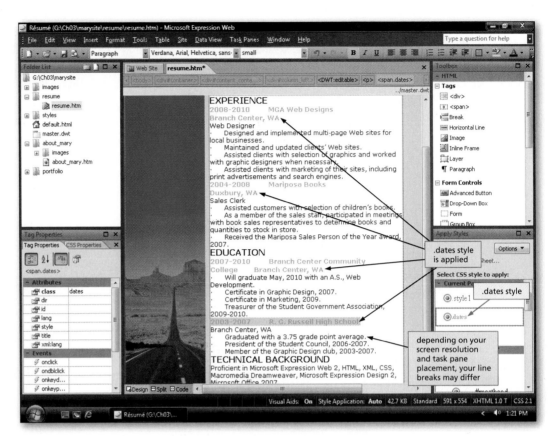

**Figure 3–89**

**3**

- Select the words, Web Designer.

- Click .jobtitle in the Apply Styles task pane to apply the job title style.

- Select the words, Sales Clerk.

- Click .jobtitle in the Apply Styles task pane to apply the job title style (Figure 3–90).

- Press CTRL+S to save the resume.htm page.

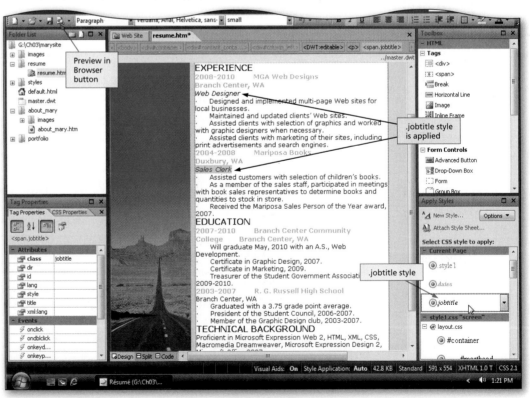

**Figure 3–90**

## To Preview the Site

The following steps preview the site in a browser window and test a link.

**1**

- Click the Preview in Browser button arrow on the Common toolbar, then click Windows Internet Explorer 7.0 (1024 × 768) to open the Resume page in Internet Explorer (Figure 3–91).

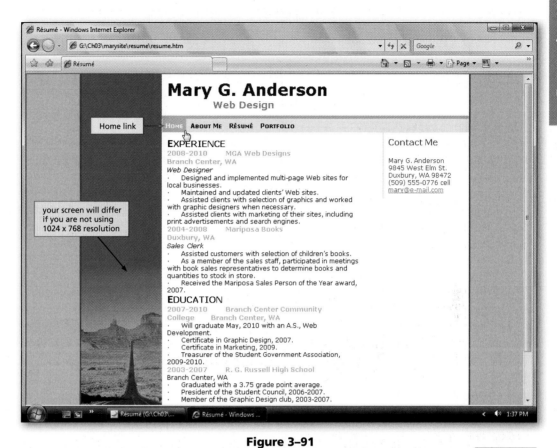

Home link

your screen will differ if you are not using 1024 x 768 resolution

**Figure 3–91**

**2**

- Click the Home link on the navigation bar to test the link and open the Home page (Figure 3–92).

- Click the Close button on the browser window title bar to close Internet Explorer.

Close button

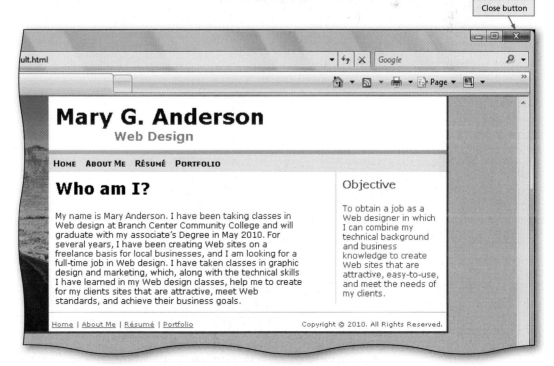

**Figure 3–92**

## To Close a Site and Quit Expression Web

**1**

- Click File on the menu bar to open the File menu, then click Close Site.

- Click File on the menu bar to open the File menu, then click Exit.

## Chapter Summary

In this chapter, you learned how to create a new site from a template and modify the structure of the template by adding, deleting, and renaming files and folders and attaching the template to a new Web page. You learned how to replace template text by typing or pasting text, and you edited the text. By making changes in the master.dwt page, you learned how to make changes to all pages in the Web site at once. You created, modified, and applied styles using CSS. The items listed below include all the new Expression Web skills you have learned in this chapter.

1. Create a New Web Site from a Template (EW 157)
2. Rename a Folder (EW 161)
3. Rename a Web Page (EW 162)
4. Delete a Web Page (EW 164)
5. Delete a Folder (EW 166)
6. Add a Folder (EW 167)
7. Add a Web Page (EW 169)
8. Replace Template PlaceholderText (EW 172)
9. Paste Text (EW 177)
10. Close Microsoft Word (EW 182)
11. Edit Text (EW 183)
12. Find and Replace Text (EW 186)
13. Make Global Changes to a Template (EW 190)
14. Modify a Style (EW 195)
15. Create a Style (EW 198)
16. Apply a Style (EW 201)
17. Preview the Site (EW 203)

 If you have a SAM user profile, you may have access to hands-on instruction, practice, and assessment. Log in to your SAM account (http://sam2007.course.com) to launch any assigned training activities or exams that relate to the skills covered in this chapter.

# Learn It Online

Test your knowledge of chapter content and key terms.

*Instructions:* To complete the Learn It Online exercises, start your browser, click the Address bar, and then enter the Web address `scsite.com/ew2/learn`. When the Expression Web Learn It Online page is displayed, click the link for the exercise you want to complete and then read the instructions.

### Chapter Reinforcement TF, MC, and SA
A series of true/false, multiple choice, and short answer questions that test your knowledge of the chapter content.

### Flash Cards
An interactive learning environment where you identify chapter key terms associated with displayed definitions.

### Practice Test
A series of multiple choice questions that test your knowledge of chapter content and key terms.

### Who Wants To Be a Computer Genius?
An interactive game that challenges your knowledge of chapter content in the style of a television quiz show.

### Wheel of Terms
An interactive game that challenges your knowledge of chapter key terms in the style of the television show *Wheel of Fortune*.

### Crossword Puzzle Challenge
A crossword puzzle that challenges your knowledge of key terms presented in the chapter.

# Apply Your Knowledge

Reinforce the skills and apply the concepts you learned in this chapter.

### Creating a Site from a Template
*Instructions:* Start Expression Web. You are to create a new Web site from a template, replace template text, delete and add folders and files, paste text from a Word document, and apply and modify styles so that the page looks like Figure 3–93.

*Continued >*

**Apply Your Knowledge** *continued*

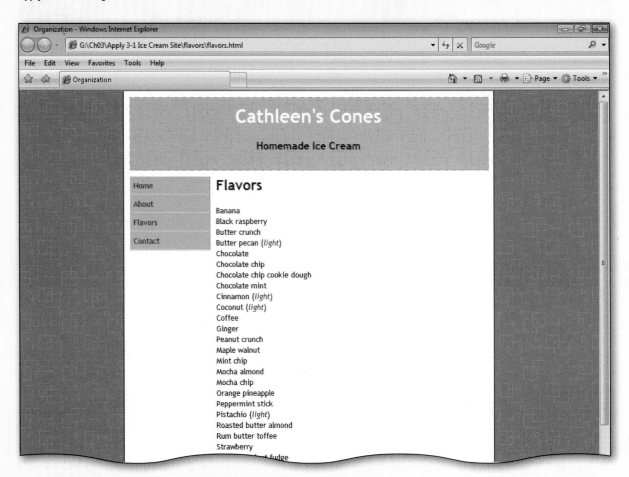

**Figure 3–93**

*Perform the following tasks:*

1. Create a new site called Apply 3-1 Ice Cream Site using the Organization 4 site template.

2. Open the faq folder.

3. Delete the faq.htm file.

4. Delete the faq, information_links, news, photo_gallery, and calendar folders.

5. Add a new folder named menu to the top folder in the site (the one that lists the drive and folder name).

6. Insert a new page into the menu folder and attach the master.dwt file to it.

7. Save the new page as flavors.html in the menu folder.

8. Change the name of the menu folder to flavors.

9. Open the flavors.html page.

10. Open Microsoft Word 2007.

11. Open the document flavors.doc from the Apply 3-1 documents folder in your Data Files.

12. Select the list and copy the text to the Clipboard.

13. Return to Expression Web.

14. Select the text in the paragraph div below Headline 2.

15. Click Edit on the menu bar, then click Paste Text.

16. Click the Normal paragraphs with line breaks option, then click OK.

17. Replace all instances of lowfat with light.

18. Select the Heading 2 div, then type Flavors.

19. Save the flavors page, then close it.

20. Open the master.dwt page.

21. Change the left navigation bar to have four links: Home, About, Flavors, and Contact.

22. Change the hyperlink of the Flavors link to link to flavors.html.

23. Change the title to Cathleen's Cones and the description to Homemade Ice Cream, then save and close the master.dwt page.

24. Create a new class-based style called .light in the style1.css file.

25. Assign the Purple font color and the italic font style to the .light style.

26. Open the flavors.html page, then apply the .light style to the four instances of the word, light.

27. Save the style1.css style sheet and the flavors.html page.

28. Preview the site and test the thumbnails and links.

29. Change the site properties, as specified by your instructor. Submit the revised site in the format specified by your instructor.

30. Save all pages, then close the site.

## Extend Your Knowledge

Extend the skills you learned in this chapter and experiment with new skills. You may need to use Help to complete the assignment.

### Modifying a Template

*Instructions:* Start Expression Web. You will create a new site based on a template, and then modify the text and styles in the master.dwt file to make the default.html page match the one shown in Figure 3–94.

*Continued >*

**Extend Your Knowledge** *continued*

**Figure 3–94**

*Perform the following tasks:*

1. Use Help to learn about adding an editable region to a dynamic Web template.

2. Use the Organization 2 template to create a Web site named Extend 3-1 Softball Site, then open the master.dwt page.

3. Click in a blank area above the footer, then press ENTER.

4. Point to Dynamic Web Template on the Format menu, then click Manage Editable Regions.

5. In the Editable Regions dialog box, type fact in the Region name text box.

6. Click the Add button, then click the Close button.

7. Create a new style named .fact.

8. Choose the medium font size, the italics font style, and the Maroon color, then click the OK button.

9. Apply the .fact style to the fact div.

10. Replace Organization with The LaSalle Sharks, then replace Organization Description with Girls' Softball.

11. Save and close the master.dwt page, update all attached pages, then open the default.html page.

12. Replace the contents of the Heading 2 div with The 2010 Season is here!.

13. Replace the contents of the paragraph div under the heading with Players, parents, and fans... Get ready for another great year of Sharks softball.

14. Change the sidebar title to 2009 League Champions.

15. Change the sidebar caption to `Congratulations to the 2009 Sharks, who won the Tri-County League Champion game 10-8.`

16. Delete the sidebar photo.

17. Replace the contents of the fact div with `Shortstop Katie Yang has a 3.9 GPA and plays the viola.`

18. Save the default.html page, preview the page, then close the browser window.

19. Change the site properties, as specified by your instructor. Submit the revised site in the format specified by your instructor.

## Make It Right

Analyze a site and correct all errors and/or improve the design.

### Placing and Formatting Images

*Instructions:*   Start Expression Web. Open the Web site, Make It Right 3-1 Tools, from the Data Files for Students. Additional files needed for this activity are located in the Make It Right 3-1 Files folder. See the inside back cover of this book for instructions for downloading the Data Files for Students, or contact your instructor for information about accessing the required files.

The site needs to be changed by removing the Calendar link from the two navigation areas and changing the copyright information in the footer. You will also need to insert and apply the tool_logo.gif to the master.dwt page and apply transparency (*Hint*: right-click the Logo placeholder, then click Picture Properties on the shortcut menu). Change the headline, description, and subheading as shown in Figure 3–95. Insert the tool_sales.doc file on the default.html page. Create a new style called .highlight that uses bold, italics, Navy font color, and small font size and apply it as shown in Figure 3–95.

Change the site properties, as specified by your instructor. Save the site using the filename, Make it Right 3-1 Tools Site. Submit the revised site in the format specified by your instructor.

*Continued >*

**Make It Right** *continued*

**Figure 3–95**

## In the Lab

Design and/or format a Web site using the guidelines, concepts, and skills presented in this chapter. Labs are listed in order of increasing difficulty.

### Lab 1: Creating a New Site from a Template

*Problem:* You have been hired to create a Web site for a local park. As part of creating the site, you are to add and edit page content. You use a template to create the new site and insert and edit text to create the site shown in Figure 3–96.

**Figure 3–96**

*Instructions:*

1. Start Expression Web.

2. Create a new Web site called Lab 3-1 Park Site using the Organization 1 template.

3. Open the master.dwt page. Replace the word, Organization, with `Forest Edge Park`. Replace the words, Organization Description, with `Mitcheltown, Delaware`.

4. Save and close the master.dwt page, and update all associated pages.

5. Open the about.htm page. Change the Heading 2 to About Forest Ridge Park.

6. Start Word and open the about_park.doc file from the Lab 3-1 documents folder. Select and copy the text, then close the file and Word.

7. Paste the text as normal paragraphs without line breaks into the paragraph under About Forest Ridge Park.

8. Use the Replace command to replace all instances of the word Ridge with `Edge`. Close the Find and Replace dialog box.

9. In the right sidebar, replace the words, Additional Resources, with `Natural Beauty`. In the paragraph below Natural beauty, type `Forest Edge Park was created to preserve the area as an open space for Mitcheltown residents and to protect the wildlife and plant life that call it home.`

10. Save the changes to the about.htm page, close the page, then preview the site in a browser.

11. Submit the site in the format specified by your instructor, then close the site.

# In the Lab

## Lab 2: Replacing Template Text and Modifying the Dynamic Web Template

*Problem:* You are the owner of an interior design company. You want to create a Web site you can use to attract new clients. Use a template to create a new site, modify the site contents, and modify styles to create the site shown in Figure 3–97.

**Figure 3–97**

*Instructions:*

1. Start Expression Web.

2. Create a new Web site called Lab 3-2 Interior Design Site using the Personal 7 template.

3. Change the contact folder name to clients, and change the contact.htm filename to clients.htm.

4. Open the master.dwt page. Change the link name in the navigation bars from contact to clients. Verify that the hyperlinks for both link to the clients.html page and edit if necessary.

5. Replace the words, My Website, with `Beachfront Design`. Replace the words, Website description, with `by Maggie Waterson`.

6. Modify the following styles, using Table 3–2 for instruction.

| Table 3–2 | | |
| --- | --- | --- |
| **Style Name** | **Affects** | **Change To** |
| #masthead h1 | Beachfront Design | Navy; bold; Times New Roman, Times, Serif; xx-large |
| h3 | Maggie Waterson | Black; italic; Times New Roman, Times, Serif; large |
| #navigation a | Top navigation bar | Navy; bold; Times New Roman, Times, Serif |
| h2 | Headline 2 | Navy; bold; Times New Roman, Times, Serif; x-large |
| a | Bottom navigation bar | Navy; Times New Roman, Times, Serif |

7. Save and close the master.dwt page, and update all associated pages. Save and close the style3.css file.

8. Open the about_me.htm page. Change the Heading 2 to About Me.

9. Start Word, and open the aboutme.doc file from the Lab 3-2 documents folder. Select and copy the text, then close the file and Word.

10. Paste the text into the paragraph under About Me. Do not include formatting but keep the line breaks.

11. Delete the bottom sidebar. In the right sidebar, type "Our beach cottage is a fun, casual retreat." (Sarah M., Nantucket).

12. Save the changes to the about_me.htm page, then preview the site in a browser.

13. Change the site properties, as specified by your instructor.

14. Submit the site in the format specified by your instructor, then close the site.

## In the Lab

### Lab 3: Creating and Applying Styles

*Problem:* Your client owns a coffee shop and has asked you to add a page with a menu to a site he has created using a template. You will create a new page, add links to it, and create and apply styles to format the page as shown in Figure 3–98.

**Figure 3–98**

*Continued >*

**In the Lab** *continued*

*Instructions:* Start Expression Web. Open the Web site, Lab 3-3 Coffee, from the Data Files for Students. An additional file needed for this activity is located in the Lab 3-3 documents folder of the Data Files for Students. See the inside back cover of this book for instructions for downloading the Data Files for Students, or see your instructor for information about accessing the required files.

*Perform the following tasks.*

1. Create a new folder in the main directory called menu.

2. Create a new page from a dynamic Web template, using the master.dwt page from the site. Save the page as menu.html in the menu folder.

3. Select the words, Headline 2, then type Menu.

4. Open Word. Open the file menu.doc from the Lab 3-3 documents folder. Select all of the text, then copy it to the Clipboard. Close the document and quit Word.

5. Use the Paste Text command to insert the copied text into the paragraph under the Menu headline using normal text without line breaks.

6. Create a new style called .category and define it in the style0.css style sheet. Format the style with the large font size, bold font weight, and small caps font variant. Click the underline and overline check boxes in the text-decoration section, then click OK to complete the new style.

7. Create a new style called .item and define it in the style0.css style sheet. Format the style with the medium font size, italic font style, and Silver color. Click OK to complete the new style.

8. Apply the .category style to the following lines: JUST FOR BREAKFAST, MUFFINS, SCONES/ BISCUITS/CROISSANTS, FOR THE YOUNG AT HEART, and DRINKS.

9. Apply the .item style to the following lines: Sandwich, Parfait, Morning Glory, Blueberry Bran, Corn, Lowfat Raspberry, White Chocolate Ginger, Cheddar Chive Biscuit, Croissant, Strawberry Tart, Blueberry Turnover, and Cinnamon Twist.

10. Save and close the menu.html page and the style sheet.

11. Open the master.dwt page and create a link in both navigation areas from the word, Menu, to the menu.htm page. Save and close the master.dwt page.

12. Preview the page in a browser.

13. Change the site properties, as specified by your instructor.

14. Rename the site Lab 3-3 Coffee Site, submit the site in the format specified by your instructor, then close the site.

# Cases and Places

Apply your creative thinking and problem solving skills to design and implement a solution.

● EASIER    ●●MORE DIFFICULT

## ● 1: Changing a Site Structure

Practice adding and removing pages and folders to a Web site by first creating a site using any template. Delete a folder and its contents. Open a folder that contains a page and delete the page, then delete the folder. Rename a file and folder. Add a new folder to the main directory, then add a new page based on the master.dwt page to the new folder. Close the site without saving any changes, then quit Expression Web.

## ● 2: Make Global Changes to a Web Site

Create a new site for your book club using a template. Delete at least one page and its folder. Open the master.dwt page, and add a title and description for your site. Update the navigation area by deleting references to the pages you deleted. Change other information, such as copyright or logo, as necessary. Save and close the master.dwt page. Open the default.html page and view the changes you made.

## ●● 3: Paste and Edit Text

Using one of the Small Business templates, create a site for a travel agency. Use Word to create an itinerary for a trip you have taken or would like to take. Include a word that you will later replace with another after you have pasted the text into your Web site. Copy and paste the text into a page in your Web site. Use the Replace command to find and replace at least one word in the text. Practice selecting words and characters and deleting text. Enter text into the other editable regions on the page, then save and close the page. Open the master.dwt page, then edit the placeholder text. Save and close the master.dwt page, then close the site.

## ●● 4: Create a Personal Home Page

**Make it Personal**

You want to create a site that includes your résumé and information about you. Create a new site using one of the Personal templates. Enter information on the master.dwt page and the default.html page, then save and close the pages. Use Word to create a résumé, open a previously created résumé, or open the résumé file from the project in this chapter. Copy the résumé to the Clipboard. Open the résumé page, then paste the résumé from the Clipboard. Create at least two styles and apply them to the résumé page to format it. Save the pages and style sheets, then close the site.

## ●● 5: Enhance Text using Styles

**Working Together**

Your local pizzeria wants to create a site for its business with three pages: home, menu, and directions. Working as a team with several of your classmates, you are to plan and create the Web site. As a group, decide on the name of the restaurant and the menu. Each team member should create the text for the three pages in Word. As a group, decide on an Expression Web template for the pizzeria site. Add, delete, and rename pages as necessary so that your site contains the appropriate pages. Edit the text and navigation area(s) on the master.dwt page as necessary. Modify two of the existing styles in the style sheet. On each of the three pages, edit the placeholder text and insert the Word files you have created. On the menu and directions page, create and apply at least two styles. Preview the site, test the navigation bar, and make sure that your site is readable and attractive. Save and close the pages and style sheet, then close the site.

**Expression Web Design Feature**

# Web Design Basics

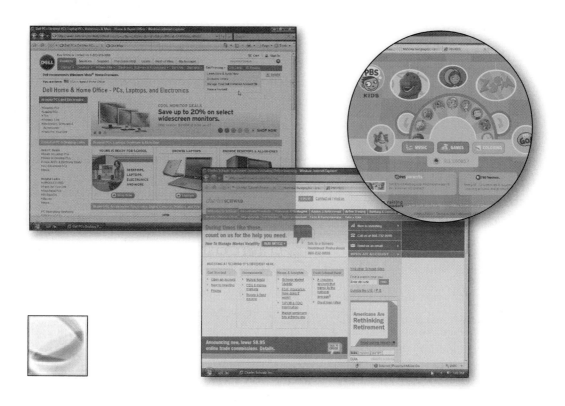

## Objectives

You will have mastered the material in this special feature when you can describe how to:

- Identify a Web site's purpose, target audience, and structure

- Plan a site's navigation system

- Use color and page layout to unify the look and feel of a Web site

- Write and format effective Web page text

- Select and format appropriate Web page images, animation, and multimedia elements

- Perform pre- and post-publishing testing

# Introduction

A successful Web site is one that winningly communicates its overriding message — learn something new, have fun, share ideas, make a purchase, and so forth — while, at the same time, satisfying site visitors' expectations. Creating a successful Web site begins with developing a solid design plan that provides answers to a variety of Why? What? How? and Who? questions:

- Why will the site exist?
- Who is likely to visit the site and why will they do so?
- What types of Web pages will be included?
- How will the site's structure, color scheme, and page layout support its overall message?
- How will visitors navigate among the site's pages?
- What content will appear on the site's individual pages?
- How can I make certain that the site's features continue to work correctly and its content remains up-to-date and accurate?

Incorporating the answers to these and similar questions into a formal design plan enables you to apply the elements of good basic Web design to your site: a consistent color scheme; effective content positioning; easy-to-understand linking relationships; easy-to-read, accurate, and up-to-date text; and attractive, useful images.

To learn more about Web site planning, visit **scsite.com/ew2/websources** and click a link under Special Feature 1, Planning a Web Site.

# Web Site Purpose, Target Audience, and Structure

Your first step in developing a Web site should be to establish the site's goals and objectives in order to clarify the site's overall purpose. Next, you should identify its potential visitors. Once the site's purpose is established and its potential visitors are identified, you are ready to identify the types of Web pages to be included at the site and the site's overall structure.

# Establishing Your Site's Purpose

The planning process for successful Web sites of all types — from personal sites to small business sites to large commercial enterprise sites — begins with establishing one or more goals for the site. A **Web site goal** is a time-bounded and measurable result of a Web-based activity. The individuals and organizations that own Web sites often identify a single **primary goal** for their sites, augmented by several **secondary goals**. For example, the primary goal for an e-commerce Web site might be to increase the sales of products or services by 10 percent over 12 months; the secondary goals might include improving customer support by cutting support response time by 8 percent over 24 months and providing daily updated information about the company's stock price and other relevant information for investors.

A **Web site objective** is the method you choose to accomplish your Web site's goals. In our previous example, the Web site's sales goal might be accomplished by a variety of design objectives, such as creating an attractive product catalog that includes images, adding a site search feature to help visitors quickly find a specific product or service, or adding an easy-to-use shopping cart system. Summarizing a Web site's goals and the objectives necessary to accomplish those goals into a formal statement of purpose (Figure SF 1–1) for the site can help set the stage for its development.

---

**Web Site Design Plan**
**Statement of Purpose**

The Web site's primary goal is to increase sales of products and services by 10 percent over the first 12 months after the site is published. The site's secondary goals are to improve customer support by cutting support response time by 8 percent over 24 months and provide up-to-date stock prices and other relevant information for investors on a daily basis.

To accomplish these goals, the company will develop an attractive, easy-to-use Web site that includes a(n):
- product catalog with images,
- site search feature,
- easy-to-use shopping cart system,
- live chat customer support feature, and
- 'From the President' page with current information about the company.

---

**Figure SF 1–1**

## Identifying Your Site's Target Audience

Potential visitors to a site are called its **target audience**. A site might have more than one target audience. Identifying the target audience requires developing a general profile for audience members. While the target audience for a small personal site might be well known to the site's owner, a small business owner or the management of a large commercial enterprise will likely find it necessary to research the demographic characteristics (age, gender, educational level, income, and so forth) and psychographic characteristics (social group affiliations, purchasing preferences, political affiliations, and so forth) that define their sites' target audience in order to build a satisfactory profile.

Good sources of material for developing a target audience profile include the U.S. Department of Labor, the Census Bureau, and the Small Business Administration Web sites and publications. After creating a target audience profile to identify who will likely visit your site, you should determine the types of pages to be featured at your site and each page's general content.

## Types of Web Pages

Your site will have a starting page, called its home page. Because the home page is generally the primary page at a site — and often a visitor's entry point to the site — it is important that the home page content answers three important questions:

- *Who* owns and publishes the site?
- *What* information is available at the site?
- *Where* is specific information located at the site?

Figure SF 1–2, the Harry & David site home page, illustrates content that adequately answers visitors' Who?, What?, and Where? questions. The owner's name, graphic logo, and similar identifying content elements on the home page identifies the site's owner. Text and images on the home page tell visitors what information or features can be found at the site, while links tell visitors where the information or features are located at the site.

**Figure SF 1–2**

The type and number of additional pages, called **subsidiary pages**, varies depending on a site's purpose. While a personal Web site might include only a home page and one or two subsidiary pages, a commercial Web site is likely to have a much more complex set of subsidiary pages. For example, Figure SF 1–3 illustrates just three subsidiary pages of the many pages at the Harry & David site: a product catalog page, a shopping cart page, and an About Us page. Each of these subsidiary pages can be quickly viewed by clicking a link on the Harry & David home page.

**Figure SF 1–3**

A **splash** or **entry page** is generally used to introduce a site and, where used, appears before the home page appears. The use of entry or splash pages is not universally supported by Web designers. Many designers think that splash or entry pages are a distraction that unnecessarily comes between the site visitor and the information he or she wants to find at a Web site. Additionally, many Web visitors do not like dealing with splash or entry pages.

Organizing your site's pages in a logical way will determine how well visitors can move from page to page at the site and how quickly they can find what they need.

## Site Structure

The way in which you organize the pages at your site creates their linking relationships and is called the site's **structure**. Common Web site structures include the:

- **linear structure**, in which pages are organized and linked in sequential order; for example, in a step-by-step presentation of information

- **hierarchical structure**, in which pages are organized by level of detail; links flow from the home page, which provides summary information, to the first level of detail pages, then from first level detail pages to a second level of detail pages, and so forth. Each subsequent level provides pages with an increasing amount of detailed information

- **webbed structure**, in which pages are not organized or linked in any specific order; visitors can jump from page to page, depending on their interests

More complex Web sites are typically organized using some effective combination of these basic structures, as shown in Figure SF 1–4. The goal of any site's structure is to create logical linking relationships that enable visitors to find what they are looking for by clicking a minimum number of links; the structure you choose for your site should help you best achieve this goal. You can manually draw a flowchart of your site's structure or use a variety of software tools, such as the Microsoft Office drawing tools, to draw your site's structure.

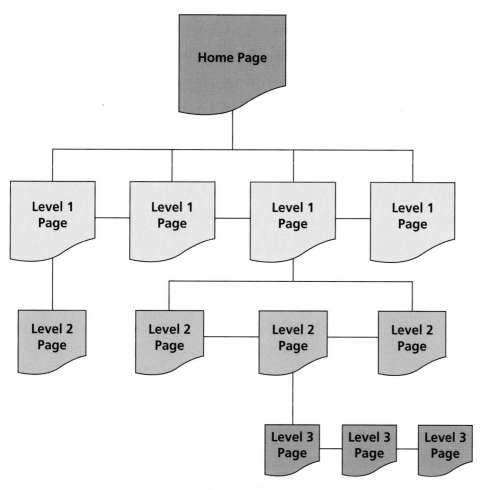

**Figure SF 1–4**

Now that you have planned your site's pages and structure, you are ready to design its navigation system.

# Site Navigation System

Your site's **navigation system** should combine different types of links from the home page to subsidiary pages and from subsidiary page to subsidiary page, as necessary. When designing your site's navigation system, your first consideration should be your target audience's needs and expectations for moving from page to page at your site. Site visitors should be able to easily identify your site's navigational elements, quickly determine the logic behind the linking relationships at your site, and comfortably move from page to page based on their interests.

Depending on the complexity of your site, you will likely use a combination of different navigational elements, including text links, navigation menus, bars, tabs, image links, a site map, a breadcrumb trail, and, for a large complex site, a site search feature.

- **Text link** — a commonly used navigational element generally presented as underlined, often colored, text
- **Navigation menu** — a list of related text links
- **Navigation bar** — related links presented as a series of graphic buttons
- **Navigation tabs** — a series of tabs, similar to folder tabs, that often present alternate views of similar content
- **Image links** — an image to which a link has been added
- **Site map** — a summary list of all major links at a site
- **Breadcrumb trail** — a horizontal list of followed links
- **Site search feature** — keyword search capability for the site's pages

Figures SF 1–5 and SF 1–6 illustrate these various types of navigational elements at the Dell Web site.

**Figure SF 1–5**

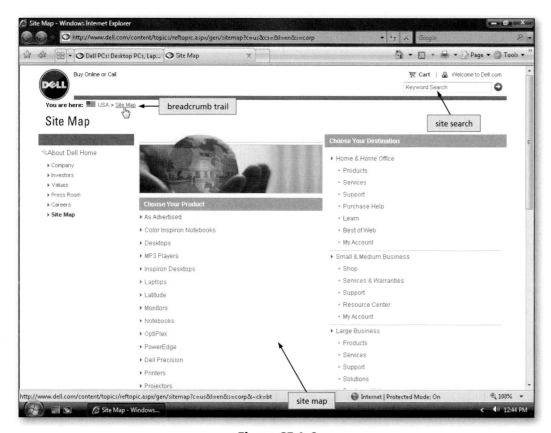

**Figure SF 1–6**

To help ensure a positive visitor experience at your site, follow these basic Web design guidelines when creating and positioning your site's links.

- Be consistent in the style and placement of navigational elements on all pages at your site. Using the same formatting for text links and the same style for navigation bars and menus and then positioning the navigational elements in the same location on every page helps visitors quickly identify links as they move from page to page.

- Place the most important navigational elements at the top and/or down the left side of your pages. Studies indicate a typical visitor first looks at the top of a page and then down the page's left side before focusing on the content at the center of the page.

- Clearly identify a link's target (destination) page. For example, use Contact Us or similar short, clearly worded text for a link to a subsidiary page containing contact information.

- Never use color alone to identify a link, and provide a text equivalent for a graphic link, such as a clickable hot spot on an image map.

- Place a Home Page link on all subsidiary pages to help visitors quickly jump back to your site's home page. If using a linear structure with pages to be visited in sequential order, add Next Page or Previous Page links.

- Provide a site map and a site search feature for a complex site with many subsidiary pages.

- Add a breadcrumb trail, if desired, to provide visitors with a visual guide of the links they have followed; however, a breadcrumb trail should only be used *in addition to* other navigational elements, such as navigation menus and bars.

Avoid rollover links — a link that appears only when the mouse pointer hovers over it — or other hidden navigational elements that might hinder your visitors' ability to quickly and easily find what they want and need at your site. Remember that your site's design, including its navigational elements and other content, should focus on communicating your site's message and satisfying your visitors' expectations, not on displaying your technical skills.

A good way to ensure that your site's navigation system will be easy to use is to perform **usability testing** of the system during its development and design phase. Participants in a usability testing team should include representative members of your site's target audience in addition to other interested parties, such as development team members, friends, family, and so forth.

The color scheme you choose and the way you position content elements on your site's pages directly affect the pages' attractiveness and usability.

# Color Schemes and Page Layout

An important part of designing your Web site is to unify its look and feel through the consistent application of color and by repeating content elements, such as logos and navigational elements, across all the pages at your site. Figure SF 1–7 illustrates the unified look and feel of the Rackspace Web site's pages achieved by applying a distinct white/black/red color scheme and by repeating content elements, such as the logo and critical links, on all pages at the site.

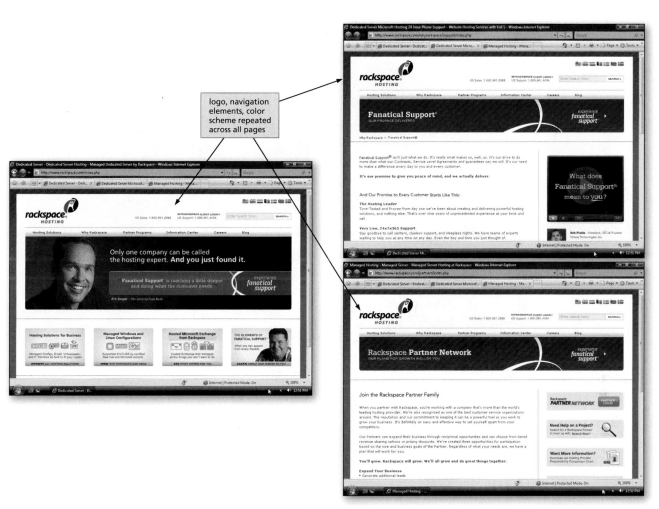

logo, navigation elements, color scheme repeated across all pages

**Figure SF 1–7**

**BTW**

**Web Templates**
A template is a model document. Web templates are models that contain consistent formatting, element placement, and color scheme used to give Web pages a unified look and feel. For more information about Expression Web templates, see Chapter 3.

## Color Schemes

Color is an important design tool that you can use to ensure the unity and overall look and feel of your Web site's pages. To create an attractive and appropriate color scheme, you can choose three or four colors; for example, from the primary or secondary colors on the traditional color wheel (Figure SF 1–8). Choose colors that both set the mood — energetic and fun, competent and trustworthy, or crisp and businesslike — for your site and also help communicate its message. Figures SF 1–9 and SF 1–10 illustrate the different color schemes that support the very different Web site messages at the Charles Schwab and PBS Kids sites.

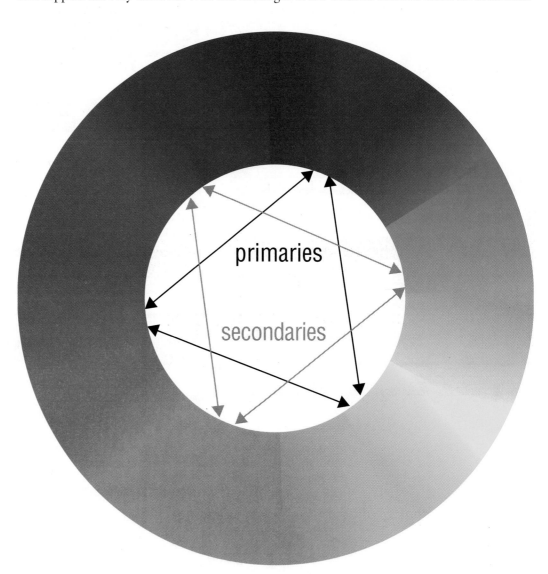

**Figure SF 1–8**

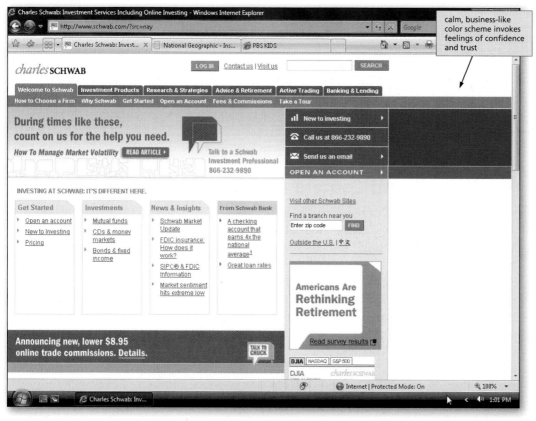

**Figure SF 1–9**

**Figure SF 1–10**

**BTW**

**Web-Safe Palette**
The Web-safe palette consists of 216 of the 256 colors that can be displayed by an 8-bit computer screen. Because most Web site visitors today use computer screens that can display millions of colors, many Web designers no longer adhere to the Web-safe palette.

Additionally, you should choose background and foreground colors that provide adequate contrast. For example, the light-colored background, dark text, and complementary accent colors in the Charles Schwab site's color scheme provide an appropriate background and foreground contrast, as do the more vibrant colors in the PBS Kids site color scheme.

Colors have significant psychological and cultural traits that you must consider when choosing your Web site's color scheme. To learn more about color traits and designing with color, visit **scsite.com/ew2/websources** and click a link under Special Feature 1, Designing with Color.

## Page Length and Content Positioning

Web site visitors characteristically dislike scrolling Web pages either vertically or horizontally, so you should create a logical layout for each of your site's pages that keeps page length as close to a single screen's viewing area as possible while also positioning the most important content elements so that visitors can easily see and access them. For example, consider positioning identifying information, such as a logo or name, in the upper-left corner of each page, major navigational elements near the top and/or on the left side of the each page, and important text and image content in one or two columns in the center of the page below and to the right of the identifying and navigational elements — all within a single viewing screen, if possible.

The Taco Bell Web site (Figure SF 1–11) successfully limits page length to a single screen (when viewed at the common 1024 × 768 screen resolution). Additionally, critical navigational and identification content are effectively positioned at the top of each page.

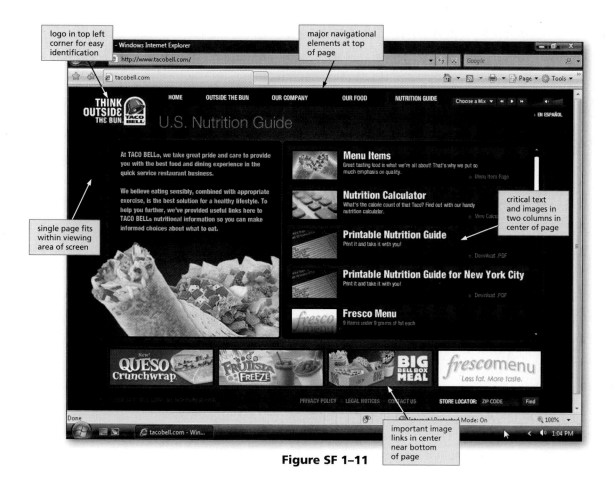

logo in top left corner for easy identification

major navigational elements at top of page

single page fits within viewing area of screen

critical text and images in two columns in center of page

important image links in center near bottom of page

**Figure SF 1–11**

The screen resolution at which visitors view your Web pages will vary and can affect their need to scroll pages either vertically or horizontally (or both) to view the pages' content. To learn more about designing Web sites to accommodate different screen resolutions, visit **scsite.com/ew2/websources** and click a link under Special Feature 1, Screen Resolution.

Arranging individual elements on a page so that the page conveys the correct message and evokes the desired mood requires that you combine the basic design concepts of balance, proximity, alignment, and focus in positioning page content elements.

BTW

**Legal and Privacy Issues**
Certain types of content related to legal and privacy issues, such as a copyright statement or links to pages that contain the site owner's privacy policy statement or its disclaimer of liability statement, is generally positioned at the bottom of a site's pages.

## Balance, Proximity, Alignment, and Focus

**Balance** refers to the symmetric (in balance) or asymmetric (out of balance) arrangement of elements in relationship to each other. Like color, balance can set the mood of a Web site. For example, the Web site of a prestigious organization, such as Guggenheim.org (Figure SF 1–12), can use a symmetric arrangement of content elements to evoke a calm, conservative mood. On the other hand, an educational site directed at children, such as the Discovery Kids site (Figure SF 1–13), can effectively use an asymmetric arrangement of elements to create a mood of excitement, enthusiasm, and fun.

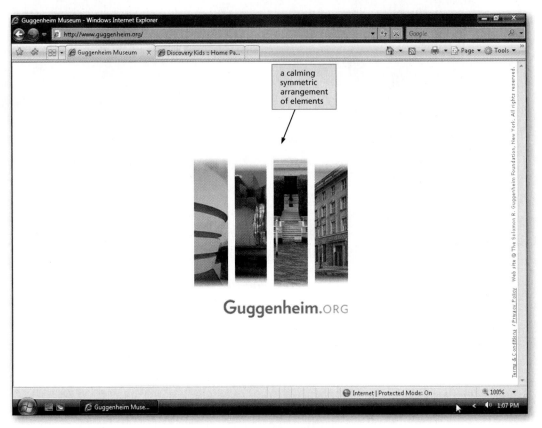

**Figure SF 1–12**

**Figure SF 1–13**

Placing related content elements near each other — for example, an image and its caption — uses **proximity** to visually link the related elements. **Alignment** of page elements either horizontally and/or vertically gives a page a well-organized, professional look. The most dominant element, or **focal point**, on a page is the element upon which visitors concentrate their attention when they view a page. Photographs or other striking images, such as those in Figure SF 1–12, are commonly used as a page's focal point. The Guggenheim.org entry page illustrates the effective use of balance, proximity, alignment, and focus to grab visitors' attention and reinforce the site's message: Check out the Guggenheim.org exhibits and collections!

One of the most important content elements at your site is the text you use to convey accurate and current information. How you write and organize your site's textual content plays an important role in enhancing your site's usability.

**BTW**

**Layout Tables and Frames**
Although Web standards support using CSS to control element positioning and page layout, most modern WYSIWYG editors, including Expression Web, also provide tools for using layout tables to control element positioning. Using frames to display multiple Web pages on the same screen is, like layout tables, considered to be an outdated layout approach.

# Writing Web Page Text

When composing the text for your Web pages, remember that visitors typically scan Web page text for useful information instead of reading the text word for word. Unless a page's textual content is intended to be printed and read offline, your pages' text should be easily scannable.

You can write scannable text by:

- using simple, modern language
- avoiding slang or industry jargon
- structuring your topic paragraphs in a chunked text style composed of a short sentence or two followed by a bulleted or numbered list that summarizes the paragraph's essential information
- organizing your text so that the main point or masthead appears on the home or major level page in the site's structure and relevant details appear on subsidiary pages
- avoiding text formatting that implies a link, such as the traditional colors of blue or purple or underlining the text, and using bold or italic formatting sparingly
- avoiding excessive use of uppercase characters that are more difficult to scan

Figure SF 1–14 compares a densely worded topic paragraph written for the printed page and then a portion of the paragraph summarized as scannable text for a Web page.

Identifying the potential visitors to a site, called its **target audience**, requires developing a general profile for audience members. While the target audience(s) for a small personal site might be well known to the owner, a small business owner or the management of a large commercial enterprise will likely find it necessary to research the demographic characteristics (age, gender, educational level, income, and so forth) and psychographic characteristics (social group affiliations, purchasing preferences, political affiliations, and so forth) that define their sites' targeted audiences in order to build a satisfactory profile.

densely worded paragraph for printed page

scannable text for Web page

**Target Audience Profile**
- Demographic Characteristics
  age
  gender
  educational level
  income
- Psychographic Characteristics
  social group affiliation
  purchasing preferences
  political affiliations

**Figure SF 1–14**

A **font** is a combination of typeface, size, and style used to create text characters. You are likely familiar with selecting a font, such as Times New Roman or Arial, when creating a word processing document. A **serif** is a small line added to the top and bottom edges of a character. Readability studies conducted in the early days of the Web suggested that certain fonts designed specifically to enhance readability of printed characters, called serif fonts, decreased the scannability of online text and should be avoided. Modern studies suggest that the readability of online text is more likely to be affected by other issues, such as character size and spacing, the length of the text line, and the amount of surrounding white space.

Today, both serif and sans serif fonts are widely used on Web pages, and Web designers are more likely to make their font selection based on the availability of fonts on the typical visitor's computer system and the way in which the site's fonts help establish the look and feel of the site to convey the site's message.

Selecting the right serif or sans serif font for your Web page text can enhance the pages' readability. For more information about selecting fonts and Web page readability, visit **scsite.com/ew2/websources** and click a link under Special Feature 1, Fonts and Readability.

Web page images, animation, and multimedia elements, like text, are also used to communicate with visitors and enhance their experiences at your site.

# Web-Ready Images and Multimedia

Web page images — drawings, photographs, animated characters — and multimedia elements that combine images with audio and video, such as Flash movies or interactive games, are powerful tools for attracting visitors to your site, communicating with those visitors, and then encouraging them to take some type of action at your site.

For example, the Dell e-commerce site, illustrated previously in Figures SF 1–5 and SF 1–6, emphasizes unity by identifying pages with a graphic logo while converting shoppers into buyers by including attractive product photographs. The Taco Bell site, illustrated previously in Figure SF 1–11, successfully uses multimedia elements to help keep page content to a single viewing screen and interest visitors in menu items. Cable news sites use multimedia to tell today's interesting stories and encourage visitors to upload their own newsworthy audio and video for sharing with other site visitors. At social networking sites, member networking is enhanced by the inclusion of members' photographs in their profiles.

While Web page images can add impact to your site, poorly chosen or sloppily edited images can detract from your site's message and discourage return visitors. Consider the following guidelines when choosing images and multimedia elements for your site.

- Include only those images and multimedia elements that are in context with and support the other content at your site; never include images or multimedia elements just because they look great or to show off your technical skills.

- Use animated images and multimedia — including animated GIFs, gadgets, avatars, audio, video, and Flash movies — sparingly, and then only in context.

- Select images whose colors harmonize with your site's color scheme.

- Prepare Web-ready images by using image creation and editing software, such as Expression Design, to crop and clean up photographs, convert drawings into bitmap images, and optimize saved bitmap files for size and quality.

- Add alternate text to each image that appears when browser images are turned off.

- Never use images alone to convey information; include a text equivalent for every image so that visitors using assistive technologies, such as screen readers, can access your site's content.

For more information about selecting, editing, and optimizing images for the Web, visit **scsite.com/ew2/websources** and click a link under Special Feature 1, Web-ready Images. To learn about current design standards and guidelines for Web page images, visit **scsite.com/ew2/websources** and click a link under Special Feature 1, Design Standards and Guidelines.

Testing your site's features and content during development, before you publish it, and on an ongoing basis after it is published is a critical part of your Web site planning and design.

# Pre- and Post-Publishing Testing

Earlier in this feature, you learned about the importance of performing usability testing of your site's navigational system during the site's developmental phase. After your site is completely developed, but before you publish it to a live server, you should personally test all of the site's features and content by:

- reviewing the site's pages in various browsers and browser versions running under different operating systems
- verifying that all link text clearly indicates the link's target and that navigational elements work as designed
- ensuring that all images appear in the correct position on each page, that text equivalents are available for each image, and that alternate text is provided if browser images are turned off
- establishing that all textual content is accurate and current

Additionally, you should gather a team of testers, including representative members of your target audience and other interested parties, to test and critique your site's usability. Testing team members should review the site's structure, navigation system, color and page layout, and content, including the use of text and images.

After making revisions and corrections to your site based on the results of the pre-publishing testing, you are ready to publish your site to a live Web server. Once your site goes live, you should schedule periodic testing of the site's features and content to make certain content is up to date and features continue to work properly.

For a closer look at the Web site examples used in this feature, visit **scsite.com/ ew2/websources** and click a link under Special Feature 1, Web Design Examples.

# Feature Summary

In this feature, you have learned how important it is to first identify a Web site's purpose, target audience, and structure before you begin creating its pages. You should also carefully plan the site's navigation system, color scheme, and individual page layout to give the site a unified look and feel. You also learned how to use the design concepts of balance, proximity, alignment, and focus to lay out attractive Web pages.

You learned how to write scannable text for your pages and the importance of including only those Web-ready images, animations, and multimedia elements that support a site's message. Finally, you learned about the significance of pre- and post-publishing testing of the site and all its features.

# In the Lab

Use the Web design concepts discussed in this special feature to evaluate the design of existing Web sites, create your own Web sites with a unified look and feel, and edit existing text to be scannable Web page text.

## Lab 1: Evaluating Web Site Design

*Problem:*   You are the administrative assistant to the manager of a Web design firm. Your manager is putting together a seminar for new employees that will review Web design basics. She asks you to find three examples of existing sites she can use during the seminar to illustrate Web design issues.

*Instructions:*   Use the search tool of your choice to locate three Web sites: a personal site, an educational site, and a site that sells products or services directly to consumers.

1. Evaluate each of the three sites based on the following questions.

   a. What is the site's overall purpose or message?

   b. Who is the site's target audience?

   c. How well do the site's design elements (structure and navigational system, fonts, color scheme, and page layout) and content elements (text, images, and other content) support the site's message, satisfy target audience expectations, and contribute to the overall look and feel of the site? Be specific by discussing the effectiveness of each design or content element.

   d. Are the design concepts of balance, proximity, alignment, and focus evident in the site's design? If yes, where? If no, what changes would you suggest to incorporate these design concepts?

   e. Does the home page adequately provide answers to visitors' Who?, What?, and Where? questions? If yes, how? If no, what suggestions can you make to design or content that will adequately answer these basic home page questions?

2. Summarize your evaluation in a word processing document.

3. Save the document using the filename, Lab SF1-1 Evaluation.

4. Print the document at the direction of your instructor.

# In the Lab

## Lab 2: Designing for a Unified Look and Feel

*Problem:*   Two family friends, who know about your experience using Expression Web, ask for your help in designing a unified look and feel for their proposed Web sites. The sites have very different messages and target audiences. You create two sample multipage Web sites that illustrate the use of color, fonts, and navigational elements to create a unified look and feel appropriate for each site.

*Instructions:*
1. Start Expression Web.

2. Create a multipage Web site named Lab SF1-2 Design Consulting. The site should include, at minimum, a home page and two subsidiary pages. *Do not use a Web site template.*

3. Apply a unifying color scheme of your choice to the pages. The color scheme should be appropriate for a small business that will sell consulting services to other businesses through its new Web site.

4. Add sample content of your choice, including text, images, and navigational elements, to each page. Make certain that your choices, such as font selection or images, are consistent with the color scheme and are appropriate for the consulting business site.

5. Change the site properties, as specified by your instructor.

6. Save the site and submit it in the format specified by your instructor, and then close the site.

7. Create a multipage Web site named Lab SF1-2 Design Sports. The site should include, at minimum, a home page and two subsidiary pages. *Do not use a Web site template.*

8. Apply a unifying color scheme of your choice to the pages. The color scheme should be appropriate for a Web site that promotes extreme sports and provides information on extreme sports events.

9. Add sample content of your choice, including text, images, and navigational elements, to each page. Make certain that your choices, such as font selection or images, are consistent with the color scheme and are appropriate for the extreme sports site.

10. Change the site properties, as specified by your instructor.

11. Save the site and submit it in the format specified by your instructor, and then close the site.

## In the Lab

### Lab 3: Writing Scannable Text

*Problem:*   You need to convert text written for a document to be printed and read offline into scannable text for a Web page.

*Instructions:*

1. Open the data file Lab SF1-3 Text in Microsoft Word and save it as Lab SF1-3 Web Text.

2. Revise the dense paragraph text into scannable text using short introductory paragraphs and bulleted lists.

3. Resave the edited document.

4. Print the edited document at the direction of your instructor.

# 4 | Creating Styles and Layouts with CSS

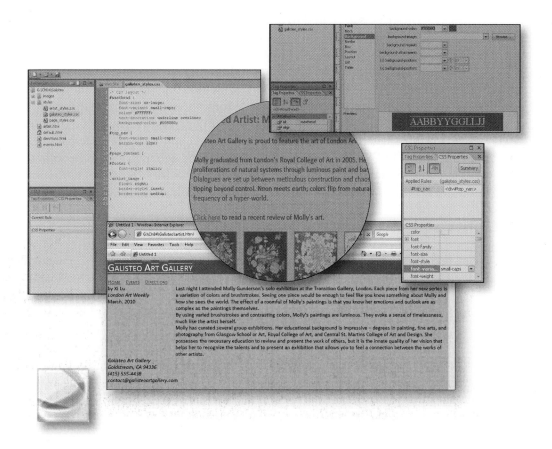

## Objectives

You will have mastered the material in this chapter when you can:

- Create ID-based styles
- Position content with CSS
- Format text with CSS
- Identify CSS syntax
- Use the CSS Properties task pane
- Create a font family
- Create an external style sheet

- Modify a style sheet using code
- Attach a style sheet
- Add a Web page using CSS layouts
- Copy and paste elements among pages
- Organize style sheets
- Create a CSS report

# 4 | Creating Styles and Layouts with CSS

## Introduction

Styles are rules used to control the formatting and layout of pages as well as individual elements and text in a Web page. The goal of using styles is to create consistently formatted pages that can be easily updated. You can apply styles directly to text or an element to format it individually, or you can save groupings of styles to a file called a **style sheet**. When a style sheet is **attached** to a Web page or pages, or to all pages in a Web site, it formats all like elements the same way. You can apply multiple style sheets to a single Web page: one for layout and one for text formatting, for instance.

Expression Web uses **Cascading Style Sheets (CSS)**, a style sheet language, to store style rules. CSS is the W3C preferred method for page layout and font. Expression Web is a great tool for using CSS to define formatting and layout. Expression Web will even create styles for you based on changes that you make to your page content, and uses task panes and dialog boxes to create, modify, and apply styles. The actual styles are saved to style sheets as CSS files, which can be viewed and edited by using the style language to enter and modify the style code.

## Project — Gallery Web Site

Galisteo Art Gallery in Goldstream, California, has a Web site that is in need of enhancing. The site currently consists of a few pages of simple text and images. The owner would like the site to look more professional and have the page elements consistent within the site. She also wants to add a new page that has a different layout and use CSS to make the new page's formatting consistent with the other site pages.

The project in this chapter uses Expression Web to create, modify, and apply formatting and layout guidelines using CSS to enhance the content and images of the unformatted Web site. The consistently formatted elements will appear on each page. You will create a new style sheet and define style rules while viewing the style sheet code. You will also add a page that uses CSS to define its layout and run a report to check for unused or incorrect CSS codes. The enhanced site is shown in Figure 4–1.

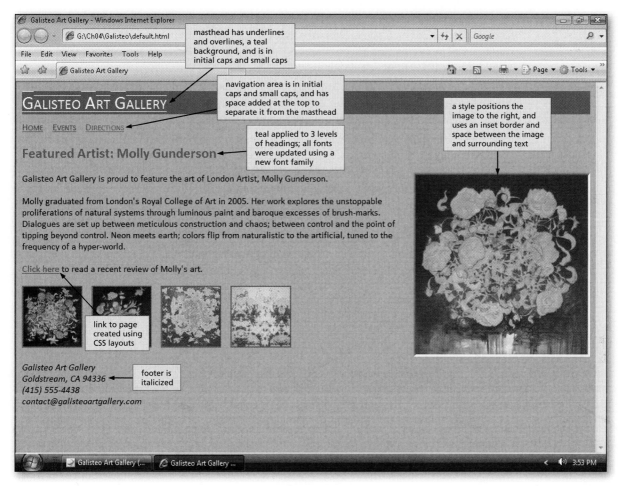

**Figure 4–1**

## Overview

As you read this chapter, you will learn how to create the Web site shown in Figure 4–1 by performing these general tasks:

- Use CSS to format and layout Web pages
- Create and modify styles
- Create a new font family
- Create an external style sheet
- Modify style sheet codes
- Attach a style sheet to pages in a Web site
- Add a Web page using CSS layouts
- Create a CSS report

**Plan Ahead**

**BTW**

**Web Accessibility**
See Appendix B for more information about Web standards and accessibility and assistive technology.

**General Project Guidelines**

When formatting a Web site with CSS, you should keep in mind the purpose of using styles: to create consistent, accessible Web sites that are easy to maintain.

As you plan to enhance a Web site using styles, such as the one shown in Figure 4–1, you should follow these general guidelines:

1. **Define formatting and layout using styles.** Formatting and layout are two ways to enhance and organize your site. With CSS, you can use and create style rules that define the appearance (formatting) and position (layout) for each element on your Web site.

2. **Create your own styles and style sheets.** Saving the styles you create in Expression Web to a style sheet allows you to edit the style sheet(s) to make modifications to your site by rewriting the code or using task panes and dialog boxes. When saving styles, you must specify whether the styles are part of an inline style that is used for only one instance of one element, as an embedded or internal style sheet that is applied only to the current page, or as an external style sheet that you can apply to other Web pages. Viewing the CSS style rules in Expression Web's Code view allows you to see text-based code that you can modify, copy, and reprioritize. Attaching the same style sheet to multiple pages ensures style consistency.

3. **Evaluate style sheets.** You can test the compatibility of your site with its associated style sheet(s) by running a CSS report. A CSS report alerts you to areas that you may need to fix, such as unused or conflicting style rules.

**BTW**

**Removing Formatting**
You can remove all associated styles to selected text or an element by clicking Remove Formatting from the Format menu.

# Using CSS to Control Formatting and Layout

A style sheet is a file that stores style rules using a coded stylesheet language. CSS is the type of stylesheet language used with Expression Web. There are three ways to save styles using CSS: external, internal, and inline. Table 4–1 defines and distinguishes the three ways to save styles.

**Table 4–1 CSS Style Saving Options**

| Storage option | Stored in | Used for |
|---|---|---|
| External style sheet | A file that contains only the CSS code and that is saved with the extension .css | Applying styles to a page, site, or multiple site pages |
| Internal style sheet | The Head section of the XHTML file for the page | Formatting the document in which it is created |
| Inline style | The Body section of the XHTML file for the page | Applying formatting to a single instance of an element or selection |

**BTW**

**Extensible Stylesheet Language (XSL)**
XSL is another stylesheet language supported by the W3C. Unlike CSS, it has the capability to transform already-created documents into HTML files with supporting CSS. CSS is considered easier to use.

## CSS Syntax

A CSS rule has three parts: a selector (the "what," such as h1), a property (the "how," such as font-size), and a value (the "how much," such as xx-large). There are three main types of selectors: a specific element, a class of element, or an ID selector, which affects a single instance of an element. You can even assign a style rule to multiple selectors. There are also three selectors that are used when creating internal and external CSS styles: element, class, and ID. A selector defines the target to which a style rule is applied; an inline style only applies to one instance, which is the selector. When viewing the style rules in a CSS file, the selector appears before the bracketed information.

Figure 4–2 shows a style sheet from the Galisteo Web site. Expression Web uses color coding to distinguish the different parts of the style rules. Gray is used to show comments or headings that give information about the styles or style sheets, but that do not contain code. Line breaks and indentations help differentiate rules and parts of rules. Braces are used to show beginnings and endings of rules.

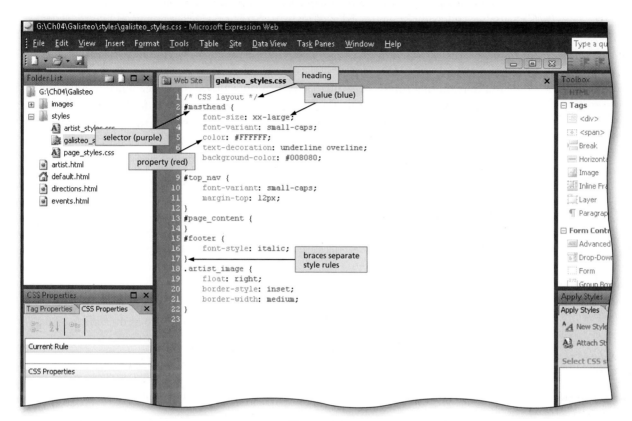

**Figure 4–2**

An **element-based style rule** affects an HTML page element, such as paragraphs, lists, or body text, and applies that rule to all instances of that element. When you create an element-based style rule, it uses **inheritance**, which means that it affects not only the element to which you apply the rule but also any elements contained within that element — for instance, the body element, which can contain paragraphs, lists, and so on. A **class-based style rule** is used to format a specific instance of an element or a part of an element. When you create a class-based style rule, you must manually apply it to page content, as opposed to an element-based style rule, which automatically is applied to all instances of that element. An **ID-based style rule** is used to format a specific element that only appears once per page, such as the footer. An ID-based style rule must be applied directly to the element for it to take effect. Table 4–2 defines and distinguishes the three CSS types.

| Table 4–2 CSS Style Types | | |
|---|---|---|
| **Style type** | **Used for** | **Example** |
| Element | A rule that you want applied for every instance of an HTML element, such as defining the margins that surround every p div | h1 {font-size: xx-large} |
| Class | A rule that you want to repeat several times in a page or site, such as to format headings within a block of text that contains a résumé | .jobtitle {color: red; font-size: large} |
| ID | A rule that you want applied to a single instance that will appear only once per page, such as a footer or masthead | #footer {color: blue; font-variant: italic} |

# Using CSS to Prioritize Rules

Because a single page might have multiple CSS rules and style sheets associated with it, CSS applies styles in a specific order of priority. Style rules are prioritized by their specificity or locality. Inline styles take precedence over internal styles, and internal styles take precedence over external styles. ID style rules are applied over conflicting class or element style rules.

If a portion of a rule is overruled, such as font size, by the precedence of a higher priority rule, any other non-conflicting portions of the rule, such as font color, will still be applied. For example, an inline style that formats header fonts as extra-large will take precedence over an internal style sheet that formats header fonts as large and navy blue. The navy blue font color is still applied. Within a style sheet, conflicts are resolved by giving precedence over whichever rule is furthest down in the list of rules.

**Plan Ahead**

**Define formatting and layout using styles.**
When enhancing a Web page, you should consider the types of elements you need to format and the type of CSS rule that best fits each element. Keep in mind the goal of achieving consistency within the site.

- Use direct formatting sparingly, doing so only to emphasize certain words or phrases that are not repeated.

- Create ID-based style rules to easily update like page elements, such as the masthead or footer on all pages at once.

- Create class-based style rules to change the style of headings or paragraphs, or to reposition or add a border to an image.

- Use a combination of task panes, dialog boxes, and Code view to create and modify styles.

**BTW**

**Storing Color Information**
Although Expression Web prompts you to select colors by their names, the specification for colors is shown using letters that indicate the exact color specification to the browser.

## To Start Expression Web and Reset the Workspace Layout

If you are using a computer to step through the project in this chapter, and you want your screens to match the figures in this book, you should change your computer's resolution to 1024 × 768. For information about how to change a computer's resolution, read Appendix F.

You may need to ask your instructor how to start Expression Web for your computer. The following steps, which assume Windows Vista is running, start Expression Web based on a typical installation and reset the task panes in the workspace to the default.

**Note:** If you are using Window XP, see Appendix E for alternate steps.

**1** Click the Start button on the Windows Vista taskbar to display the Start menu.

**2** Click All Programs at the bottom of the left pane on the Start menu to display the All Programs list.

**3** Click Microsoft Expression on the All Programs list to display the Microsoft Expression list.

**4** Click Microsoft Expression Web 2 to start Expression Web.

**5** Open the Task Panes menu, and then click Reset Workspace Layout.

## To Open a Web Site and Web Page

The following steps open the Galisteo Web site and the default.html page.

- Click File on the menu bar to open the File menu (Figure 4–3).

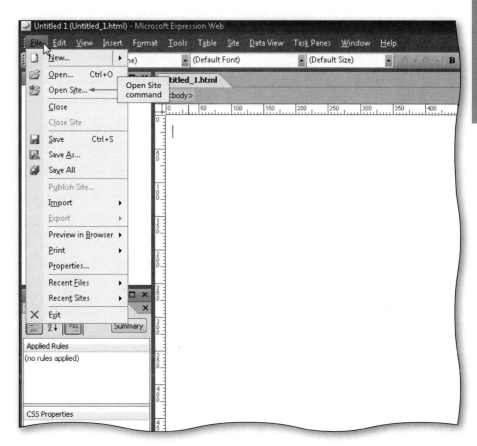

**Figure 4–3**

- Click Open Site to open the Open Site dialog box.

- Navigate to the data files and double-click the Ch04 folder to display its contents (Figure 4–4).

**Figure 4–4**

- Click the Galisteo folder, then click the Open button to open the site in Expression Web (Figure 4–5).

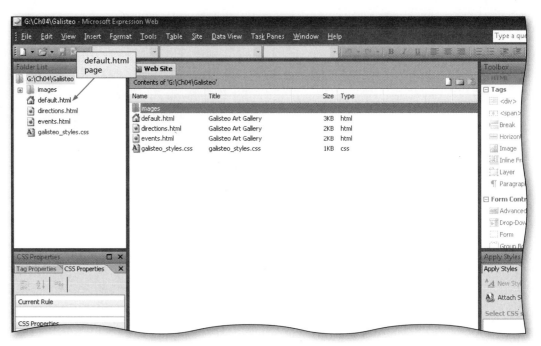

**Figure 4–5**

- Double-click the default.html page from the Folder List to open it (Figure 4–6).

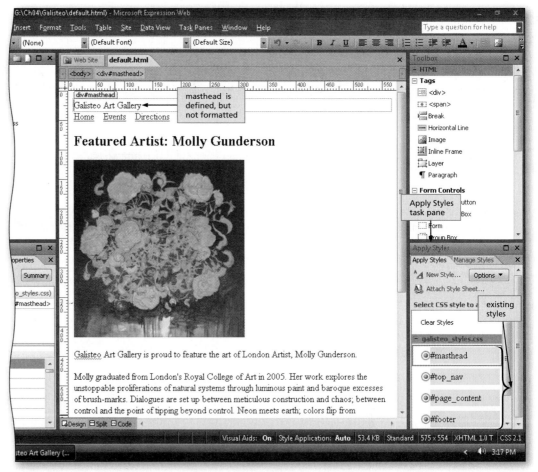

**Figure 4–6**

## To Define an ID-Based Style

When creating an ID-based style, you must define the element to which it will apply, such as the masthead or the footer. The Galisteo Web pages were created using a CSS layout, which means that ID-based styles for the four page elements were created when the page was created. These styles appear in the Apply Styles task pane, but no formatting has been assigned, so the elements look very plain. Using the Modify Styles dialog box, the following steps modify the ID-based styles to format the masthead and footer elements for all pages.

- Click the arrow next to #masthead in the Apply Styles task pane to view the menu (Figure 4–7).

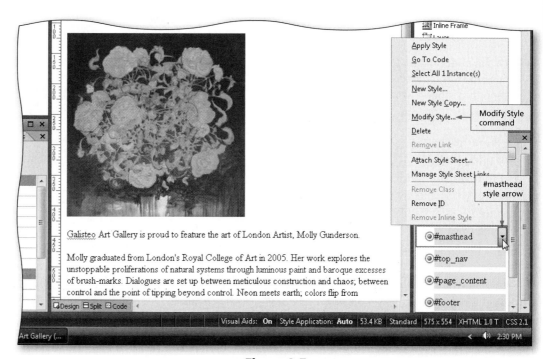

**Figure 4–7**

- Click Modify Style to open the Modify Style dialog box.

- Click the font-size box arrow to display the font size options (Figure 4–8).

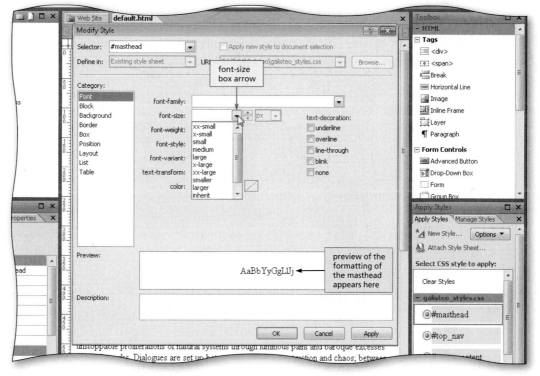

**Figure 4–8**

• Click xx-large to change the masthead text size.

• Click the font-variant box arrow, then click small-caps to change the masthead text style.

• Click the color box arrow, then click White to change the masthead text color.

• Click the underline and overline check boxes in the text-decoration section to further customize the masthead (Figure 4–9).

🔍 **Experiment**

• Select other font-color, font-size, and font-variant options to view the effect in the Preview box. Change your dialog box selections back to match Figure 4–9.

**Q&A** Why is the Preview box blank?

The white font color cannot be seen on a white background. Steps 4 and 5 change the background color of the masthead to contrast with the white font color.

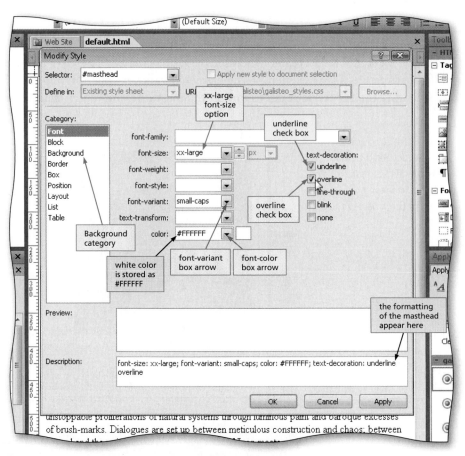

**Figure 4–9**

• Click Background in the Category list to display background formatting options.

• Click the background-color box arrow to display the color palette (Figure 4–10).

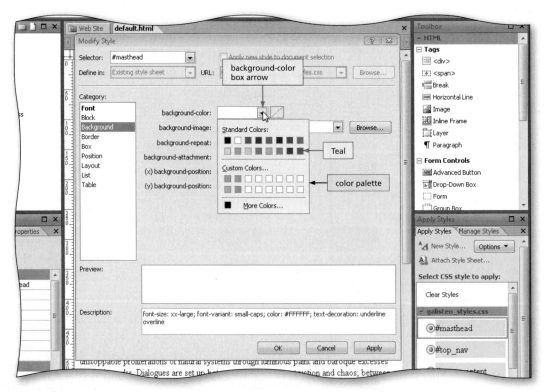

**Figure 4–10**

**⑤**

• Click Teal to make the masthead background teal (Figure 4–11).

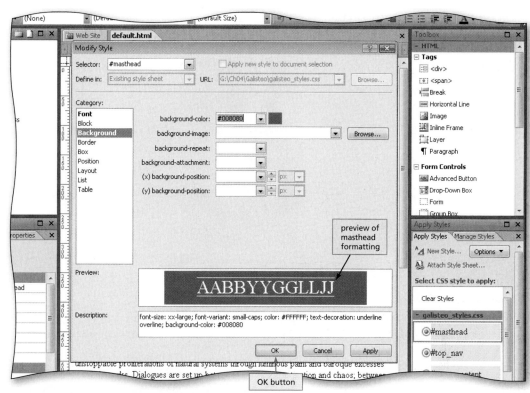

**Figure 4–11**

• Click the OK button to close the Modify Style dialog box (Figure 4–12).

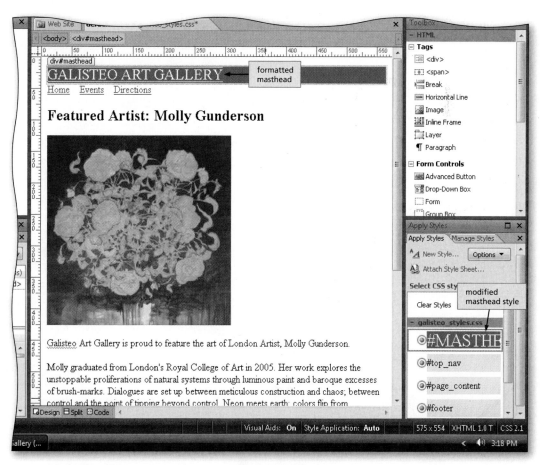

**Figure 4–12**

● Click the #footer style arrow in the
Apply Styles task pane to view the
menu, then point to Modify Style
(Figure 4–13).

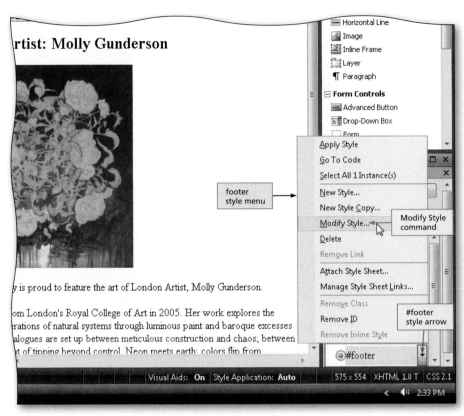

**Figure 4–13**

**7**

● Click Modify Style to open the
Modify Style dialog box.

● Click the font-style box arrow,
then click italic to change the
footer font style (Figure 4–14).

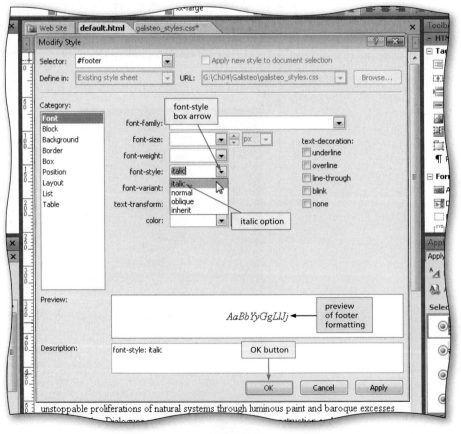

**Figure 4–14**

**8**

- Click the OK button to close the Modify Style dialog box.

- Drag the vertical scroll box to scroll down the page and view the changes in the footer if necessary (Figure 4–15).

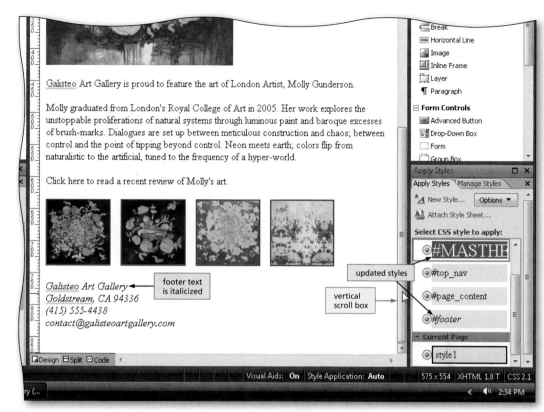

**Figure 4–15**

**9**

- Click File on the menu bar, then click Save All to save changes to all open pages (Figure 4–16).

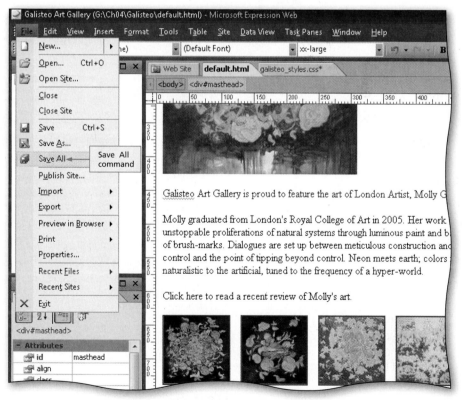

**Figure 4–16**

## To Position Content Using a Class-Based Style

Using CSS, you can specify the position of elements such as images. The following steps create a class-based style for the main image on the home page by specifying its position and defining a margin.

• Click the New Style link on the Apply Styles task pane to open the New Style dialog box (Figure 4–17).

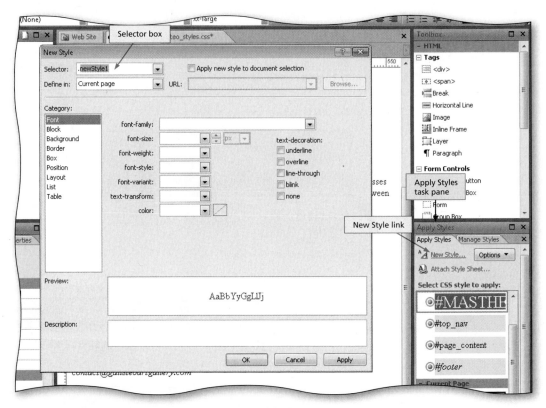

**Figure 4–17**

• In the Selector box, type .artist_ image to name the new style.

• Click the Define in box arrow, then click Existing style sheet to activate the URL box.

• Click the URL box arrow to display a list of existing style sheets.

• Click galisteo_styles. css to select the location where the new style will be saved (Figure 4–18).

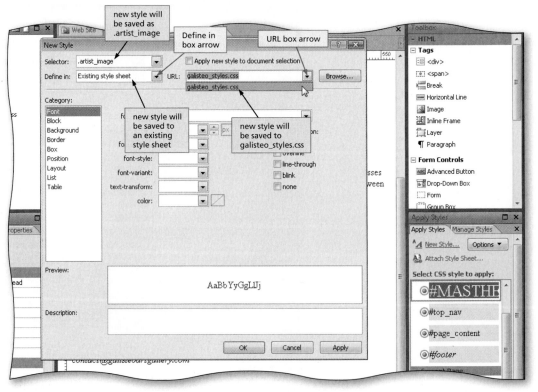

**Figure 4–18**

**3**

- Click Layout in the Category list to display layout formatting options.

- Click the float box arrow, then click right to align the element to which the style will be applied with the right page margin (Figure 4–19).

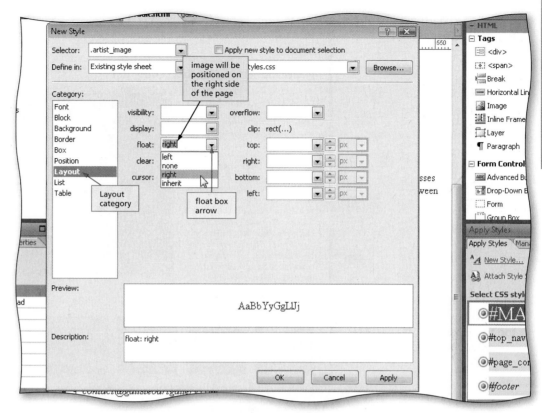

Figure 4–19

**4**

- Click Border in the Category list to display border formatting options.

- Click the top border-style box arrow to display the menu, then click inset from the menu.

- Click the top border-width box arrow, then click medium to add a medium-width border to the element to which the style will be applied (Figure 4–20).

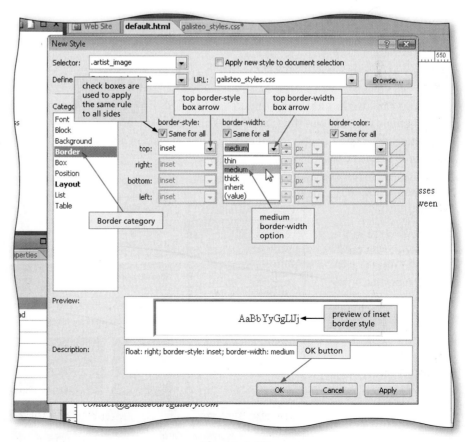

Figure 4–20

**5**

- Click the OK button to close the New Style dialog box.

- If necessary, drag the vertical scroll box up to view the image at the top of the page.

- Click the image at the top of the page to select it.

- Click .artist_image in the Apply Styles task pane to apply the new style to the image (Figure 4–21).

- Save all open files and click the OK button to embed files, if necessary.

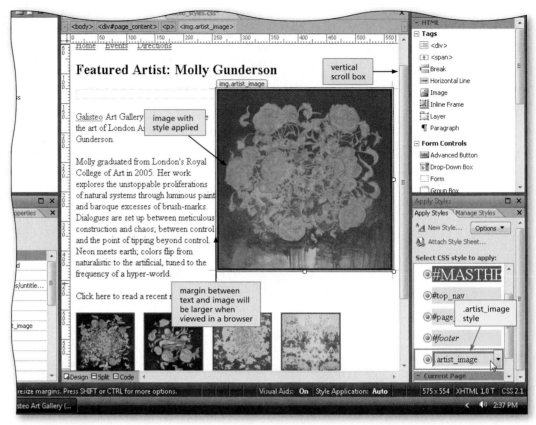

**Figure 4–21**

## To Use the CSS Properties Task Pane

You can also modify styles directly in the CSS Properties task pane instead of opening the Modify Styles dialog box. Changes you make in the CSS Properties task pane are applied automatically. The following steps use the CSS Properties task pane to apply small caps to the navigation area and to add a space at the top of the navigation area to separate it from the masthead.

**1**

- Click the CSS Properties tab in the Tag Properties task pane to display the CSS Properties task pane (Figure 4–22).

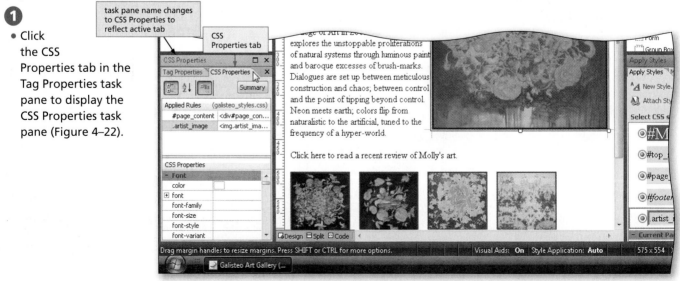

**Figure 4–22**

**2**

- Scroll up in the editing window, if necessary, and click in the navigation area to display the style properties in the CSS Properties task pane (Figure 4–23).

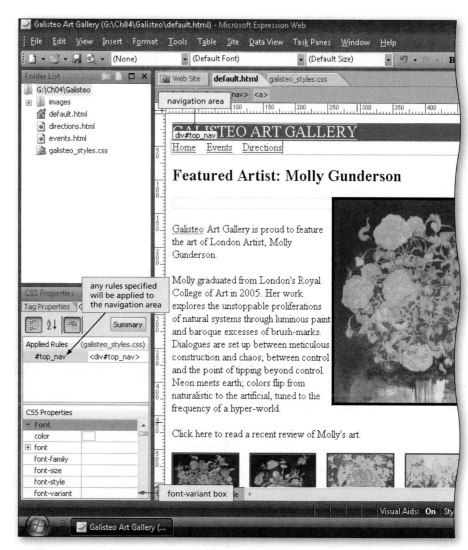

**Figure 4–23**

**3**

- Click in the font-variant box to display the arrow.

- Click the font-variant box arrow, then click small-caps to apply small caps to the navigation area (Figure 4–24).

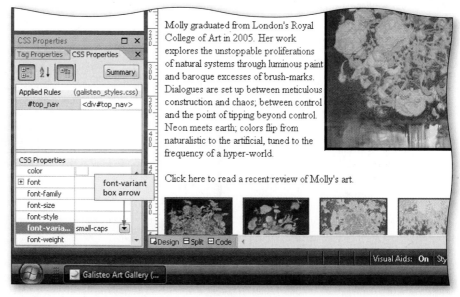

**Figure 4–24**

**4**

- In the CSS Properties list, scroll to the Box section, then click in the margin-top box to display the arrow.

- Click the margin-top box arrow to display the margin-top list (Figure 4–25).

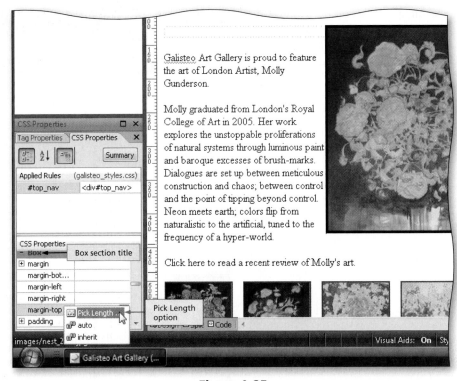

**Figure 4–25**

**5**

- Click Pick Length to open the Length dialog box, where you will specify how much space to add between the masthead and the navigation area.

- Type 12 in the Length value box to specify 12 pixels of space between the top of the navigation bar and the masthead (Figure 4–26).

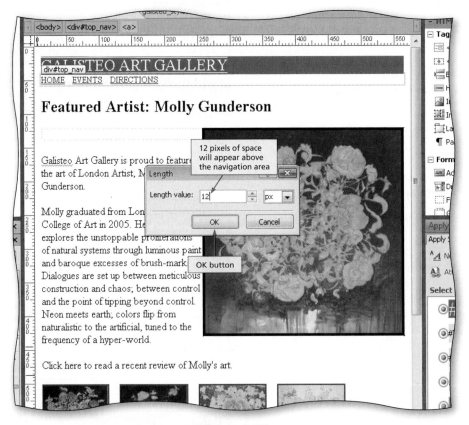

**Figure 4–26**

**6**

- Click the OK button to close the Length dialog box (Figure 4–27).

- Save changes to all open and embedded files.

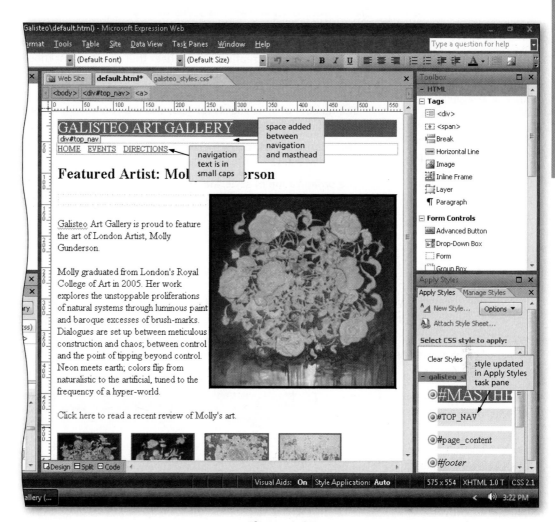

Figure 4–27

# Creating and Attaching Style Sheets

Before CSS, formatting was specified within the individual HTML pages of a site, requiring that the formatting and layout for each element be specified at each occurrence. CSS allows you to store the style rules for an element in a CSS file and the content in the HTML files. This separation allows for greater flexibility when making changes.

You can create style sheets that separate styles for a certain purpose, such as all of the layout guidelines, or all of the general page guidelines. Style rules for a new style sheet can be defined either by using the New Style dialog box to name, define, and save a style, or by entering style code directly in the style sheet. A style sheet can be attached to the active Web page, to all open pages, or to all pages in the site.

**BTW**

**Speed**
Pages styled using CSS are usually faster to download because the HTML page is smaller as it doesn't contain formatting. The first visited page may take longer as the browser has to download both the CSS and the HTML file; for subsequent site pages, the CSS will already be in the browser's cache, so only the HTML file will need to be downloaded.

**Plan**
**Ahead**

**Create your own styles and style sheets.**
A style sheet can be used to group certain styles so that they can be applied to Web sites as a collection of specific formats. For example, you can apply styles for the font family and page background by creating a style sheet that specifies just those elements. You can then apply the style sheet to pages that may use different layouts.

When creating style sheets, plan for the following:

- **The number of style sheets for your site.** Do you need one for layout and one for formatting? Are there pages that require their own style sheets?

- **The priority of styles.** Are there styles that may be conflicting? How will you ensure the priority of rules?

- **The organization of style sheets.** How will you name the sheets to ensure that you know what each includes? Will you store your style sheets in a folder or series of folders?

**BTW**

**User-Defined**
**Style Sheets**
Another accessibility feature of CSS is that a user can instruct his or her browser to override a site's CSS styles and apply a local CSS file, which will present the Web site in a format that fits the user's needs.

## To Create an External Style Sheet

A style sheet that you create in Expression Web is a blank file with the extension .css. To specify styles, you must enter code by typing in the file or assign styles to the CSS file in the New Style dialog box. The following steps create a new, blank style sheet in the Galisteo Web site. You will later enter code into the style sheet for all of the general page specifications, then attach it to all site pages.

**1**

- Open the File menu, then point to New to open the New submenu (Figure 4–28).

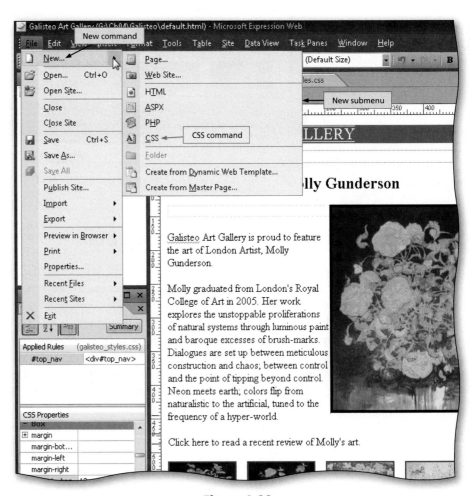

**Figure 4–28**

**2**

- Click CSS to open a new, untitled CSS file (Figure 4–29).

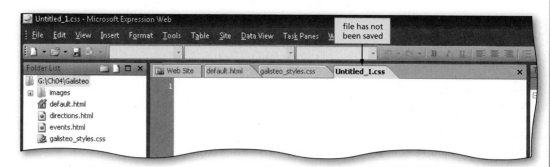

**Figure 4–29**

**3**

- Press CTRL+S to open the Save As dialog box.

- Type page_styles.css in the File name box (Figure 4–30).

**Q&A**

Do I have to type .css at the end of the filename?

Yes. The default file type for new Expression Web files is HTML, so you must specify that the file is a style sheet by including the file extension .css.

**Figure 4–30**

- Click the Save button to name the new CSS file (Figure 4–31).

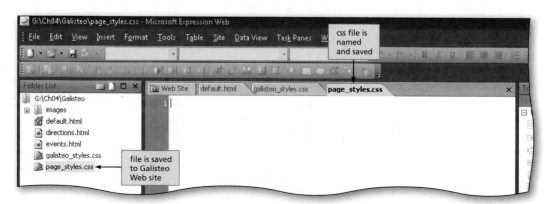

**Figure 4–31**

# Font Families

Using a consistent font family in your site provides visitors with a common experience, regardless of the fonts they have installed on their computer. A **font family**, or font set, is a collection of similar font styles that a browser applies to text on a Web page. Expression Web includes three default font families, and you can also create your own. Specifying font families increases the usability of your site by providing a default font, then providing alternative fonts and font styles in case the font you specify isn't available on the Web page visitor's system. Font families, like other formatting characteristics, can be applied as a style. You can specify the default font or font family for a Web page by including it in the body section of a style sheet.

There are three types of fonts that are preferred according to CSS specifications, due to availability on users' systems and also readability on the screen: serif, sans serif, and monospace. Serifs refer to the strokes at the ends of a letter's lines; serif fonts have strokes, and **sans serif** fonts do not. **Monospace** fonts resemble old-style computer fonts, and are not as commonly used as serif and sans serif fonts. Two other types of fonts, cursive (or script), and fantasy fonts, should be avoided as they are difficult to read and are not considered Web-safe as they are difficult to read online and not widely available on all users' systems.

When creating a font family, first decide whether to use all serif or all sans serif fonts, then choose two or three fonts of that type that are generally available in most browsers. Lastly, include a generic font type, such as serif, sans serif, or monospace, in your font family. Including a generic font type as part of your font family ensures that a browser can display a substitute font type in the event that your site's specific fonts are not available on the site visitor's system.

## To Create a Font Family

The following steps create a font family using two sans serif fonts and the generic sans-serif font type. You will later use this font family to define the body font in a style sheet, then apply the style sheet to all of the pages in the Galisteo site.

**1**
- Click Tools on the menu bar to open the Tools menu (Figure 4–32).

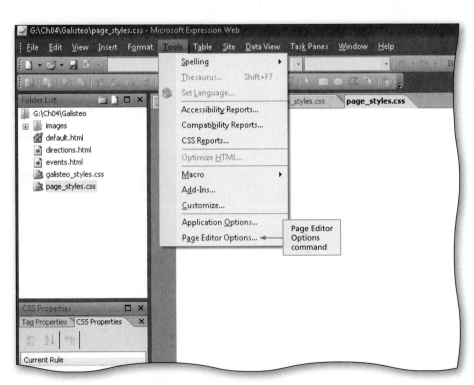

**Figure 4–32**

**2**

- Click Page Editor Options to open the Page Editor Options dialog box (Figure 4–33).

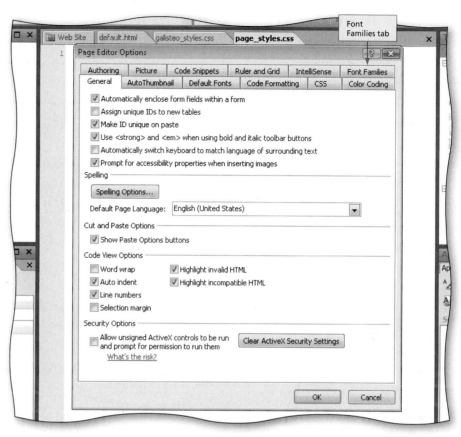

**Figure 4–33**

**3**

- Click the Font Families tab to display font family options.

- Click (New Font Family) in the Select font family list to start creating a new font family, if necessary (Figure 4–34).

 **Q&A**

How do I know what fonts look like and what type they are?

If you don't have a specific font in mind or are not sure what font type a font is, click the Font list arrow in the Expression Web window to view fonts available on your system and see a preview of each font. Make a list of the fonts you would like to use, then do an Internet search for Web-safe fonts and see if yours comply.

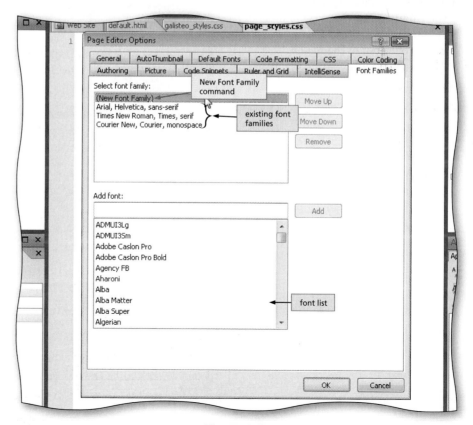

**Figure 4–34**

**4**

- Scroll to and click Calibri in the Add font list

**Q&A**

What if Calibri isn't available?

Your list of fonts may differ. Find another sans serif font to include, such as Verdana.

- Click the Add button to create a new font family with Calibri as the main font (Figure 4–35).

**Experiment**

- Scroll through the list of available fonts to view all of the possible options.

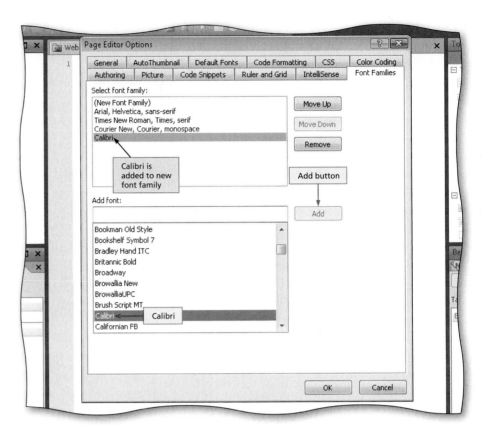

**Figure 4–35**

**5**

- Scroll to and click Gill Sans MT in the Add font list, then click the Add button to add Gill Sans MT as the second font in the new font family (Figure 4–36).

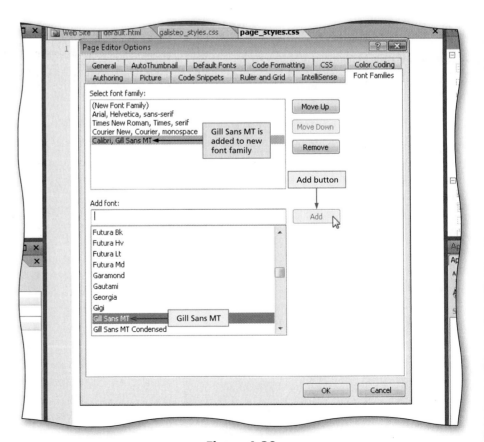

**Figure 4–36**

- Scroll to and click sans-serif in the Add font list, then click the Add button to include a generic sans serif font to the font family (Figure 4–37).

- Click the OK button to close the Page Editor Options dialog box.

**Q&A** Will the font family I create be available for me when I am working with other Web sites?

Yes. Font families that you create are stored on your computer and are available when you are using your version of Expression Web.

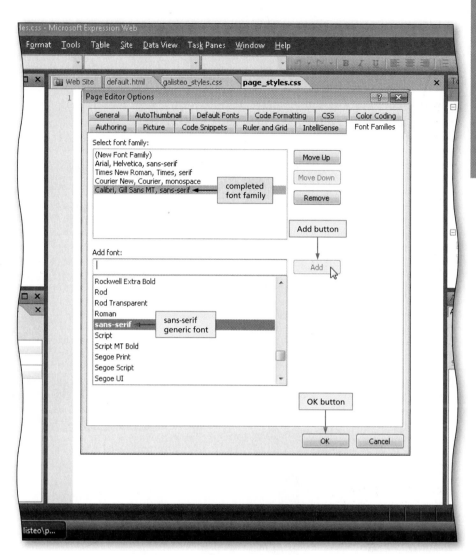

**Figure 4–37**

# Entering CSS Code

When entering code into a style sheet, it is good design practice to include headings and comments that explain the background of the sheet and its rules. As you enter CSS code in an style sheet, Expression Web uses a feature called **Intellisense** to prompt you by displaying shortcut menus of suggested selectors and options based on what you type. When a shortcut menu appears, double-click an option, press ENTER to accept the highlighted option, or continue typing to narrow your choices.

**BTW**

**Comments in a CSS File**
Comments are added to a document using the /*comment text*/ syntax. Adding comments to a CSS file can help you and others to understand the development of the CSS, by pointing out formatting for a specific section of the page, or by noting changes that you have made to the file.

## To Modify a Page in Code View

When creating an element-based style rule, you can use multiple selectors, such as different heading levels, to apply the same rule, such as font-color, to each of them by separating them with commas.

Remember to enter code very carefully, as your styles will not be properly applied if the code contains typing errors. Using the Intellisense shortcut menus can help to eliminate errors. The following steps use Code view to enter a heading and define style rules for the Galisteo Web site body font and page background color, then enter code to change three levels of headings to teal.

- In the new CSS file, type /*External Style Sheet to define page content by Your Name */ (type your own name) to add a title to the page_styles.css page, then press ENTER twice (Figure 4–38).

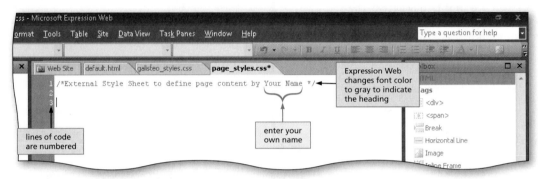

**Figure 4–38**

- Type bo to display the shortcut menu (Figure 4–39).

**Figure 4–39**

- Double-click body on the shortcut menu to start defining the styles for the body of the page.

- Press the Spacebar, then type { to start a declaration block for the body content.

- Type f to display the shortcut menu, then drag the scroll box down to view the font-family option (Figure 4–40).

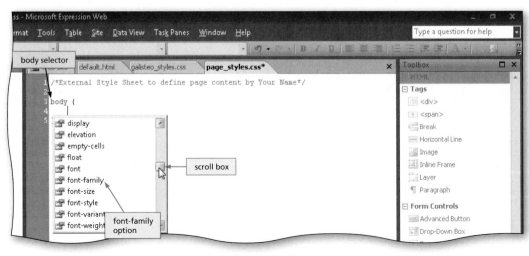

**Figure 4–40**

- Double-click font-family to select it and open the font-family shortcut menu (Figure 4–41).

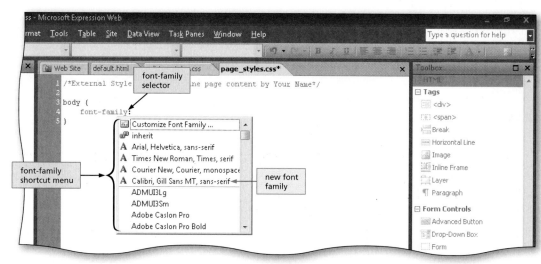

**Figure 4–41**

- Double-click Calibri, Gill Sans MT, sans-serif to specify this font family (Figure 4–42).

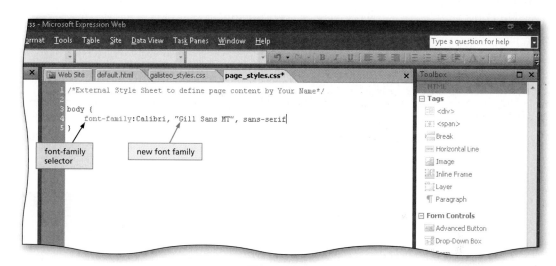

**Figure 4–42**

- Type ; then press ENTER to start a new line of code.

- Use the shortcut menus to select background-color.

- Use the shortcut menus to select silver; to specify the color for the page background, then press ENTER.

- Type } to finish entering styles for the body, then press ENTER to start a new line of code (Figure 4–43)

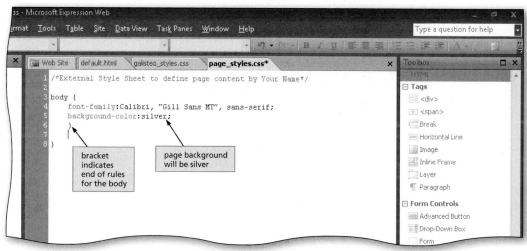

**Figure 4–43**

- Type `h1,h2,h3 {` to start a new rule that will be applied to three heading levels.

- Use the shortcut menus to select color as the value.

- Use the shortcut menus to select teal as the property.

- Press ENTER, then type `}` (Figure 4–44).

- Press CTRL+S to save the style sheet.

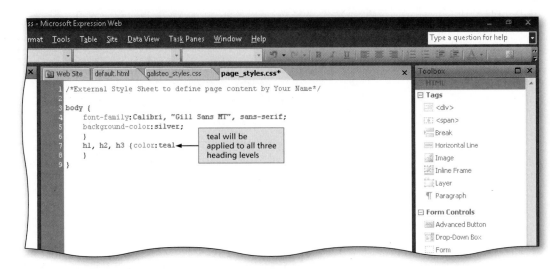

**Figure 4–44**

## To Attach a Style Sheet

When attaching a style sheet, you can attach it to a single page or to all pages in the site. The following steps open the events.html page, attach the page_styles.css style sheet to all pages in the Galisteo Web site at once, and view the changes.

- Double-click events.html in the Folder List to open the page (Figure 4–45).

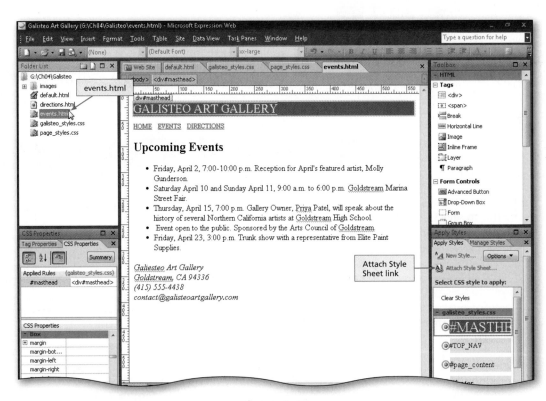

**Figure 4–45**

**2**

- Click the Attach Style Sheet link in the Apply Styles task pane to open the Attach Style Sheet dialog box.

- Click the All HTML pages option button to select it (Figure 4–46).

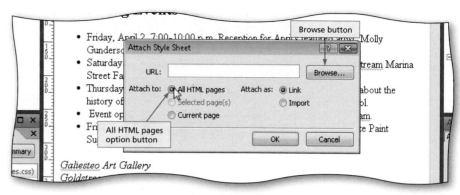

**Figure 4–46**

**3**

- Click the Browse button to open the Select Style Sheet dialog box.

- Click page_styles.css to select it (Figure 4–47).

**Figure 4–47**

- Click the Open button to close the Select Style Sheet dialog box (Figure 4–48).

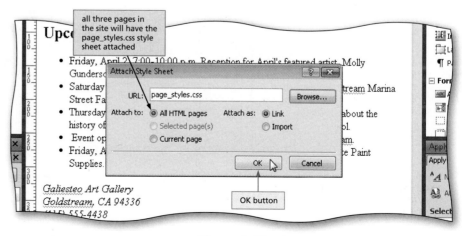

**Figure 4–48**

- Click the OK button to close the Attach Style Sheet dialog box (Figure 4–49).

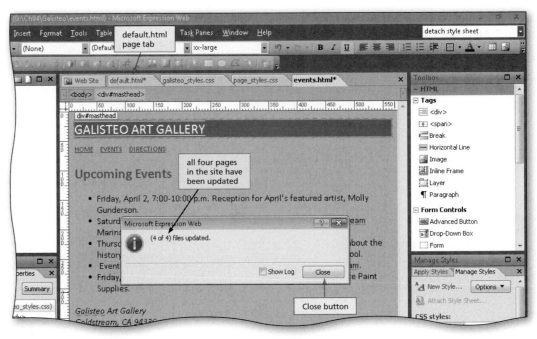

**Figure 4–49**

- Click the Close button to close the alert box.

- Click the default. html page tab to view the changes (Figure 4–50).

- Save changes to all open and embedded files.

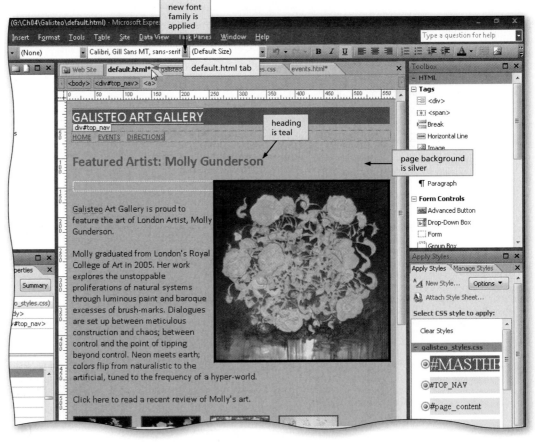

**Figure 4–50**

# Pre-Built CSS Layouts

Expression Web provides blank pages that use a CSS layout that includes divs for all of the page elements (masthead, content area, footer, columns, and so on) that are defined by using ID-based styles. When you use a CSS layout to create a new page, two files will open: an HTML page and a style sheet that includes the ID-based styles, which are blank. You can attach additional style sheets to the new Web page to apply consistent formatting with other pages in your site.

## To Use Pre-Built CSS Layouts

The Galisteo Web site needs to add a new page with a different layout. The following steps create and save the new page and the style sheet.

**1**
- Open the File menu, point to New, then click Page to open the New dialog box (Figure 4–51).

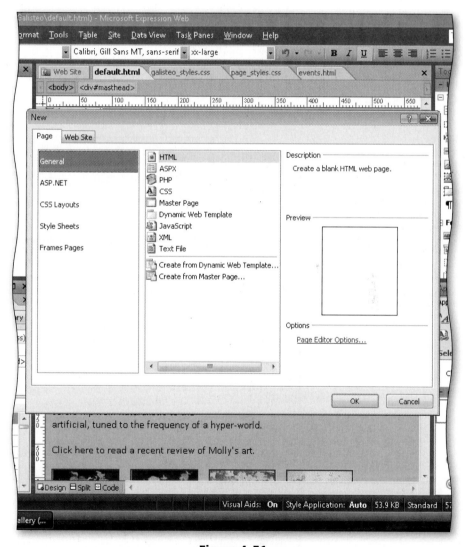

**Figure 4–51**

- Click CSS Layouts in the left pane to display CSS layout options.

- Click Header, nav, 2 columns, footer in the middle pane to select it as the new page layout and view the page preview thumbnail (Figure 4–52).

🔎 **Experiment**

- Click the other CSS layout options to view them in the Preview box, then click Header, nav, 2 columns, footer.

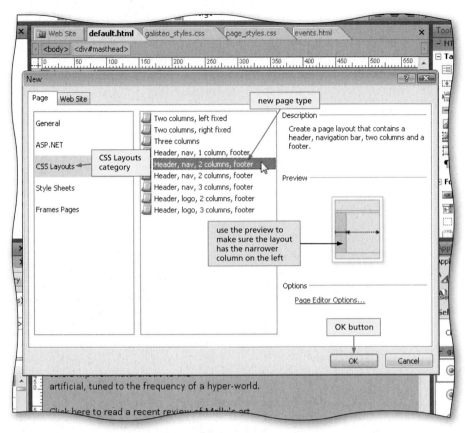

**Figure 4–52**

- Click the OK button to close the New dialog box and open the page (Figure 4–53).

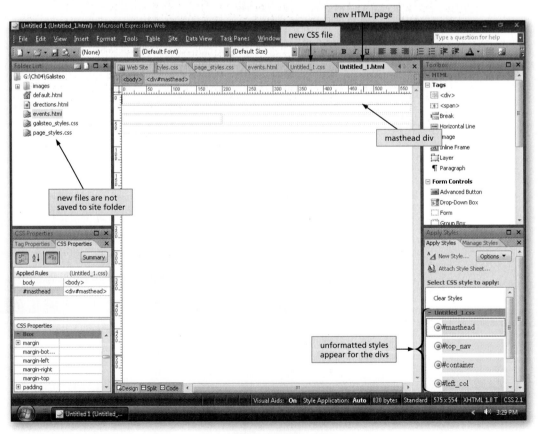

**Figure 4–53**

**4**

- Press CTRL+S to open the Save As dialog box.

- Type `artist.html` in the File name text box (Figure 4–54).

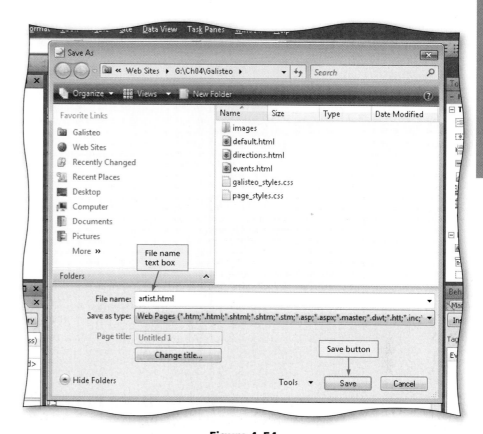

**Figure 4–54**

**5**

- Click the Save button to open the Save As dialog box for the CSS file.

- Type `artist_styles.css` in the File name text box (Figure 4–55).

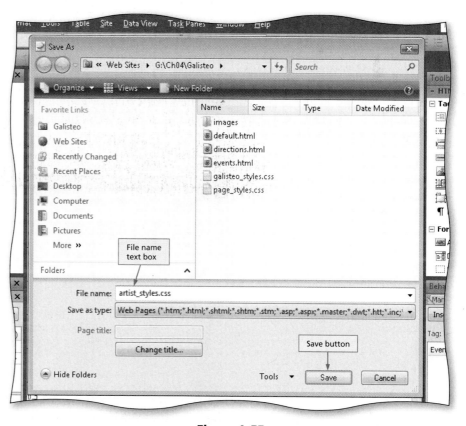

**Figure 4–55**

**6**
- Click the Save button to save the CSS file to the site folder (Figure 4–56).

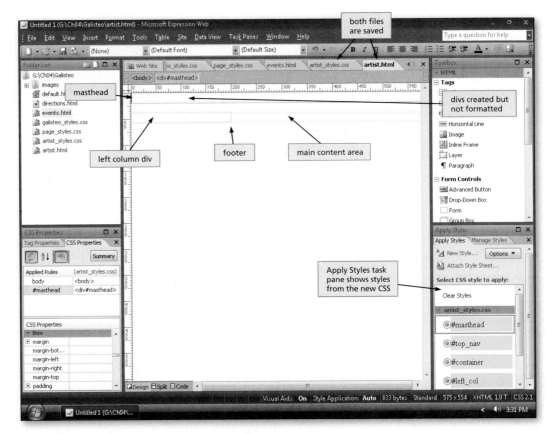

**Figure 4–56**

## To Copy and Paste Elements

The following steps add content to the new artist page by copying and pasting text from other pages. Later in this chapter you will attach style sheets to the artist.html page to make the formatting consistent with the other site pages.

**1**

- If necessary, click in the masthead, then type Galisteo Art Gallery as the masthead text (Figure 4–57).

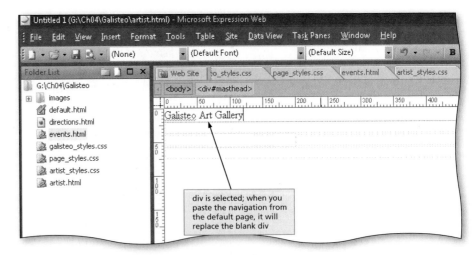

**Figure 4–57**

**2**

- Click the default.html page tab to display the default.html page.

- Click in the navigation area, then click div#top_ nav on the Quick Tag Selector bar to select the entire div (Figure 4–58).

**Figure 4–58**

**3**

- Press CTRL+C to copy the navigation div to the Clipboard.

- Click the artist.html page tab to display the artist.html page, then select the #top_nav div (Figure 4–59).

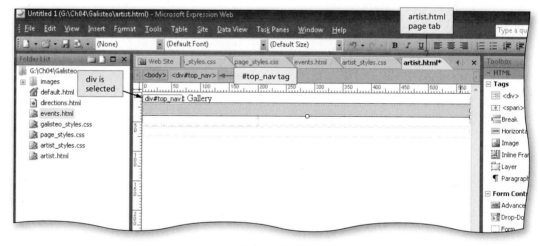

**Figure 4–59**

**4**

- Press CTRL+V to replace the existing div with the copied navigation area (Figure 4–60).

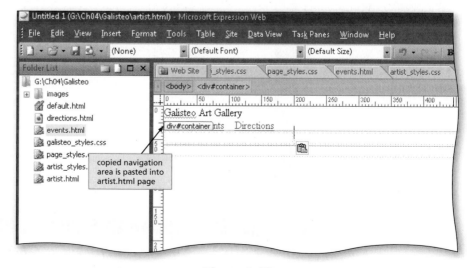

**Figure 4–60**

- Repeat Steps 3 and 4 to copy and paste the footer from the default.html page to the artist.html page (Figure 4–61).

- Press CTRL+S to save the artist.html page.

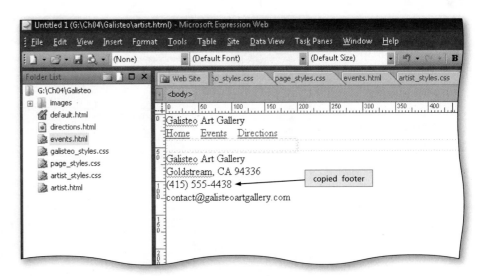

Figure 4–61

## To Complete Page Content

The following steps add content and a link to the new artist page by copying and pasting text from a Word file, and typing directly into divs.

- Click the Start button on the task bar, point to All Programs, click Microsoft Office, then click Microsoft Office Word 2007 to start Microsoft Word (Figure 4–62).

**Q&A**

What if I don't have Word 2007?

If you have another version of Word you can use that, or use any text editor, such as Notepad or WordPad.

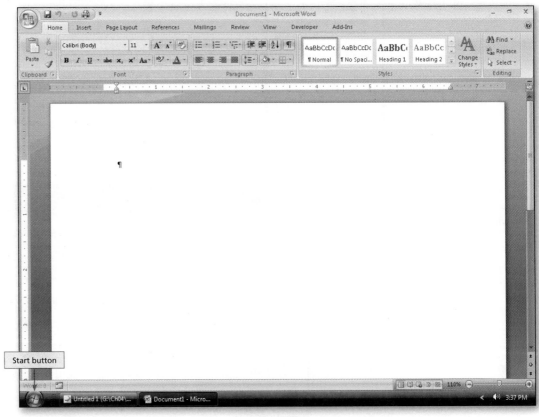

Figure 4–62

- Press CTRL+O to open the Open dialog box.

- Navigate to the location where your data files are stored.

- Double-click the galisteo_documents folder to open it.

- Click the about_ artist.doc file (Figure 4–63).

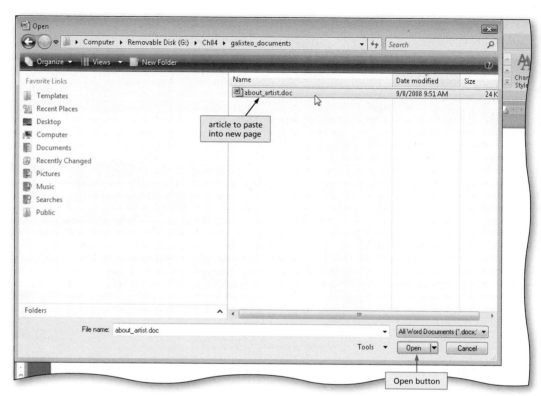

**Figure 4–63**

**3**

- Click the Open button to open the file in Word (Figure 4–64).

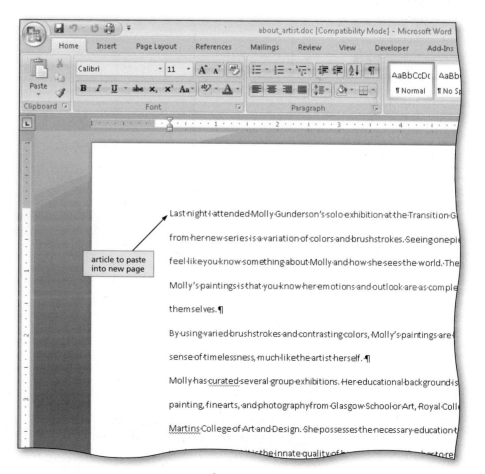

**Figure 4–64**

- Press CTRL+A to select all of the content.

- Press CTRL+C to copy the content to the Clipboard (Figure 4–65).

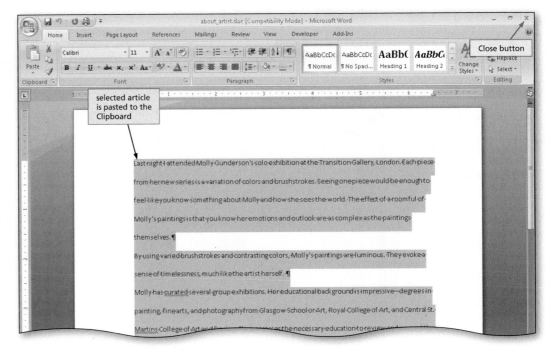

**Figure 4–65**

- Click the Close button to close the file and quit Microsoft Word.

- Click in the #page_content div to position the insertion point (Figure 4–66).

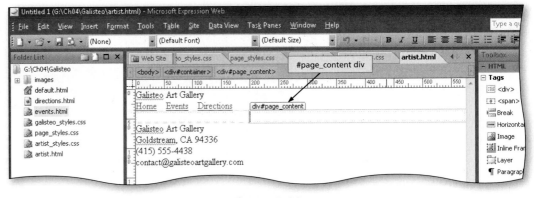

**Figure 4–66**

6

- Click Edit on the menu bar and then point to Paste Text (Figure 4–67).

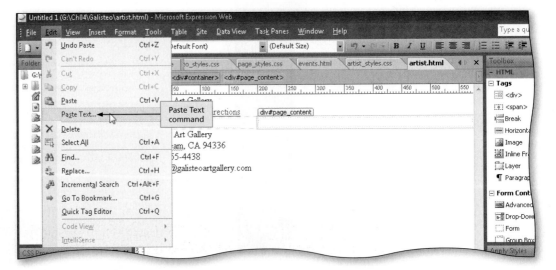

**Figure 4–67**

**7**

- Click Paste Text to open the Paste Text dialog box.

- Click Normal paragraphs with line breaks (Figure 4–68).

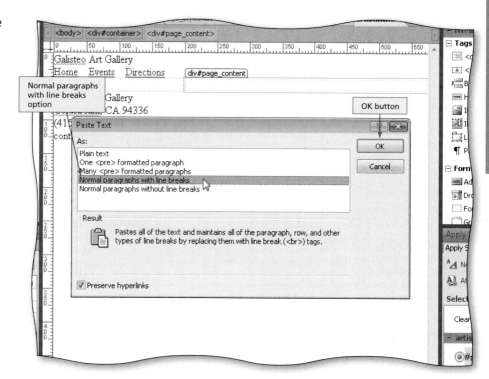

**Figure 4–68**

**8**

- Click the OK button to insert the text.

- Click in the #left_col div to position the insertion point.

- Type by Xi Lu, then press ENTER.

- Type London Art Weekly, then press ENTER.

- Type March, 2010 (Figure 4–69).

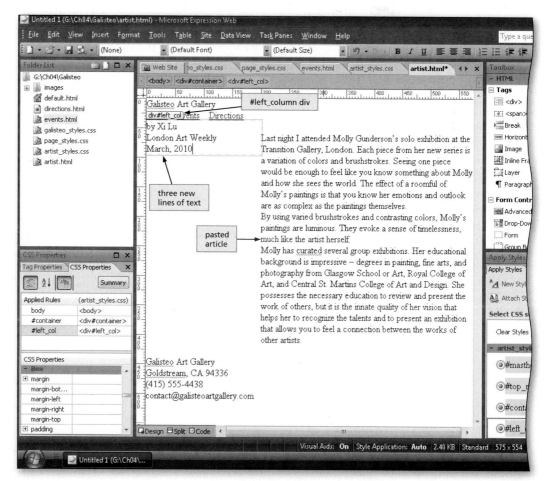

**Figure 4–69**

- Select the words, London Art Weekly, then click the Italic button on the Common toolbar to italicize the text (Figure 4–70).

- Press CTRL+S to save the artist.html page.

**Other Ways**

1. Click the Copy button on the Common toolbar (Expression Web) or the Ribbon (Word) to copy selected text or images to the Clipboard.

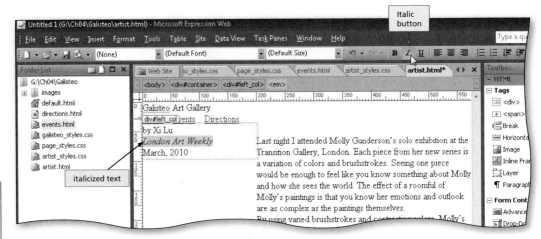

Figure 4–70

## To Attach Multiple Style Sheets

To format the artist.html page so that it is consistent with the other site pages, you will attach two style sheets to the page. The galisteo_styles.css file was created when the default.html page was created, and it contains the styles for the masthead and other page elements, which you updated earlier. You created a new style sheet, page_styles.css, to define styles for the page background and headers. The artist_styles.css file was created when the artist.html page was created. It defines the page objects, such as the masthead, navigation area, and footer, but there are no formatting style rules associated with that style sheet. When you attach the galisteo_styles.css file, the style rules for the masthead, footer, and navigation area will be applied to those objects on the artist.html page. Because no formatting is defined in the artist_styles.css, no conflicts will occur. The following steps attach the page_styles.css and the galisteo_styles.css style sheets to the new page.

- Click the Attach Style Sheet link in the Apply Styles task pane to open the Attach Style Sheet dialog box (Figure 4–71).

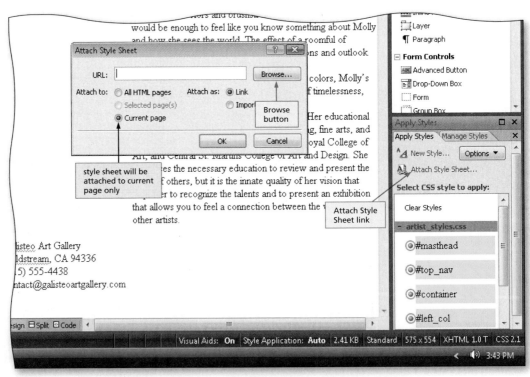

Figure 4–71

**2**

- Click the Browse button to open the Select Style Sheet dialog box.

- Click the page_styles.css file to select it (Figure 4–72).

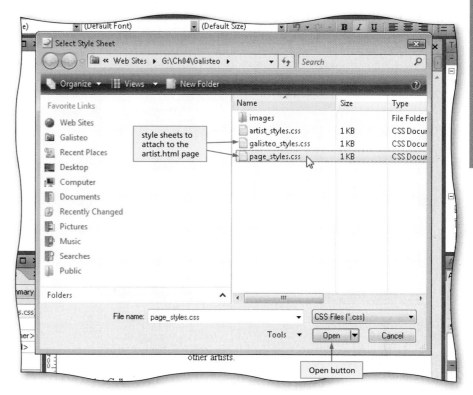

**Figure 4–72**

**3**

- Click the Open button to close the Select Style Sheet dialog box (Figure 4–73).

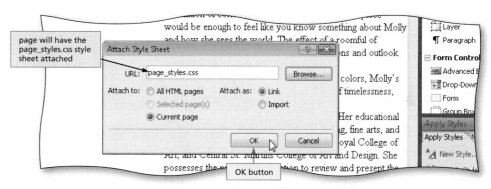

**Figure 4–73**

**4**

- Click the OK button to close the Attach Style Sheet dialog box and attach the page_styles.css style sheet to the new Web page (Figure 4–74).

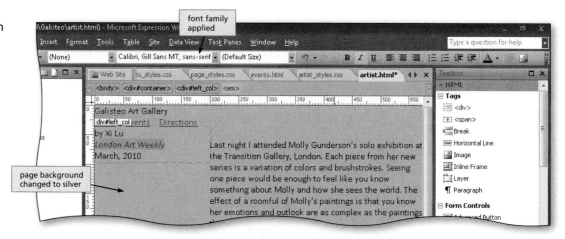

**Figure 4–74**

- Repeat Steps 1-4 to attach the galisteo_styles.css style sheet from the Galisteo site folder to the artist.html page (Figure 4–75).

- Press CTRL+S to save the page.

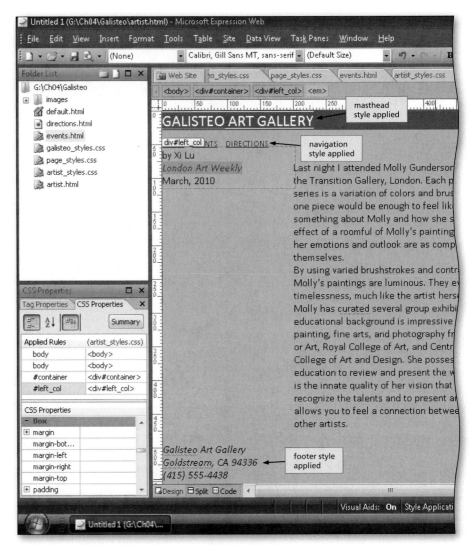

**Figure 4–75**

## To Add a Hyperlink

The following steps create a link from the default.html page to the artist.html page.

 **1**

- Click the default. html page tab to display the default. html page.

- Select the words, Click here (Figure 4–76).

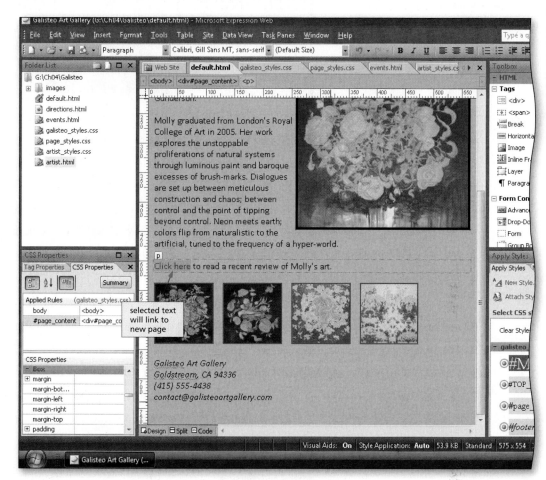

**Figure 4–76**

**2**

- Press CTRL+K to open the Insert Hyperlink dialog box.

- Click artist.html to select it as the link target (Figure 4–77).

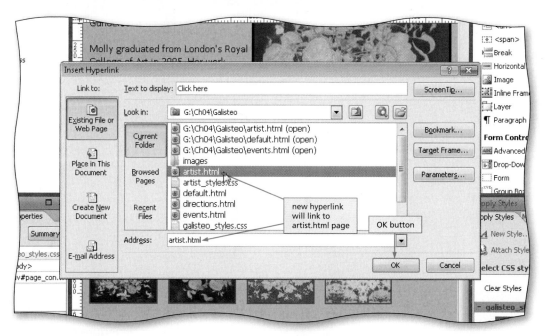

**Figure 4–77**

- Click the OK button to close the Insert Hyperlink dialog box and create the link (Figure 4–78).

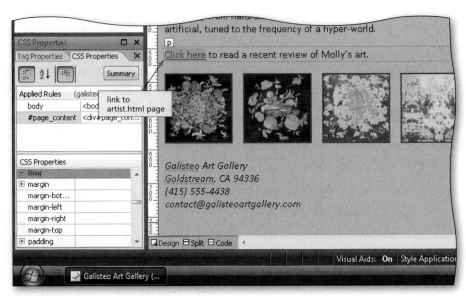

**Figure 4–78**

## To Organize Style Sheets

It is important to keep your site organized by adding folders to store related files. Keeping all of the style sheets in one folder makes them easy to locate. The following steps add a new folder and move the three style sheets into it.

- Click the Web Site tab to display the Web site contents (Figure 4–79).

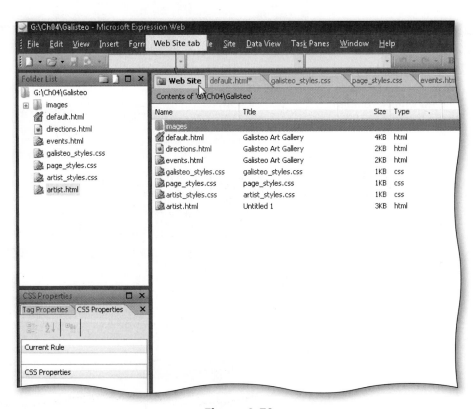

**Figure 4–79**

- Right-click a blank area of the Web Site window to open the shortcut menu.

- Point to New, then point to Folder (Figure 4–80).

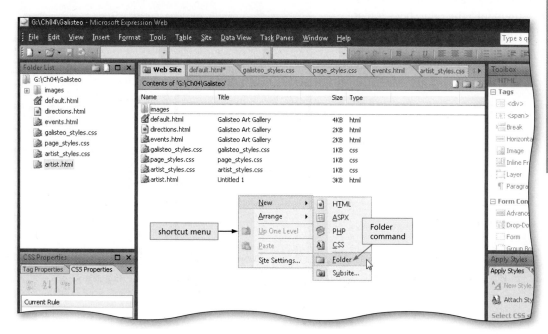

**Figure 4–80**

- Click Folder to add a new untitled folder to the Web site.

- Type styles as the new folder name, then press ENTER (Figure 4–81).

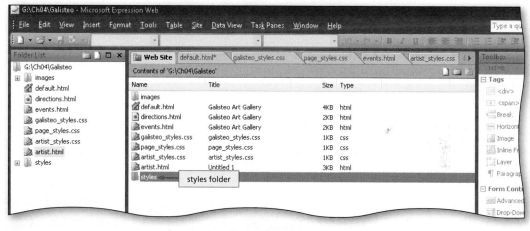

**Figure 4–81**

④

- Press and hold SHIFT, then click each of the three style sheets (the .css files) to select them (Figure 4–82).

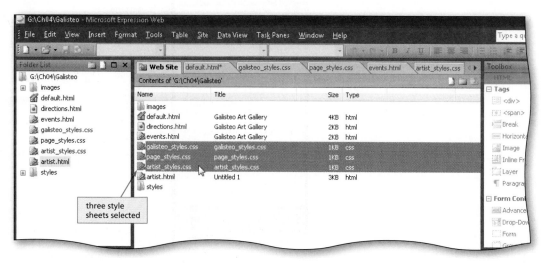

**Figure 4–82**

- Drag the selected files to move them into the new styles folder (Figure 4–83).

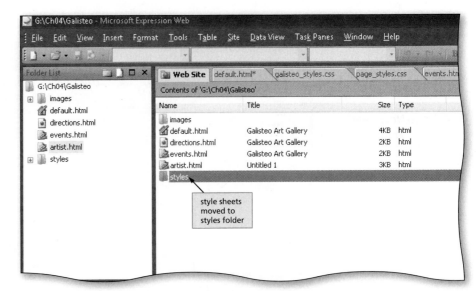

**Figure 4–83**

**Plan Ahead**

**Evaluate style sheets.**

A CSS report is a task pane that lists any possible errors, including style conflicts or unused styles. You can run a report for the entire site, for a particular page, or for a specific style. The task pane can be used to scroll through the results, open the style sheet that contains an error, or sort or filter the results.

## To Create a CSS Report

The following steps run a CSS report. You do not need to fix either of the errors, because you want to keep the unused styles for future site pages and content.

- Open the Tools menu, then point to CSS Reports (Figure 4–84).

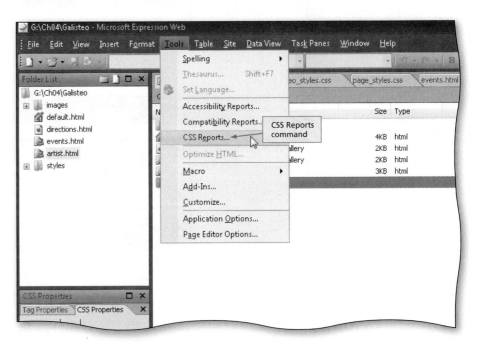

**Figure 4–84**

- Click CSS Reports to open the CSS Reports dialog box.

- Click the All pages option button to include all the Galisteo Web site pages in the report.

- Click any unselected check boxes in the Check for section to specify the report options (Figure 4–85).

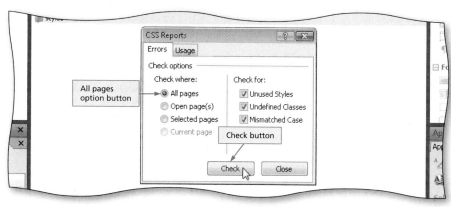

**Figure 4–85**

- Click the Check button to start the check and open the CSS Reports task pane (Figure 4–86).

- Examine the report results, then click the Close button on the CSS Reports task pane to close it.

- Save all open and embedded files.

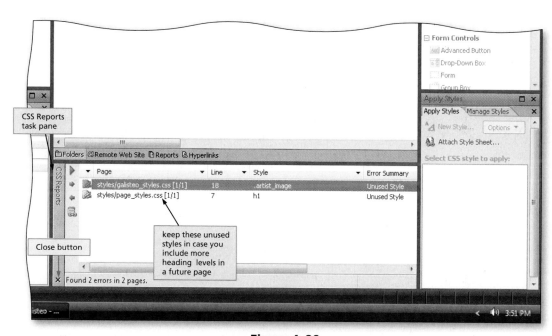

**Figure 4–86**

## To Preview the Site

The following steps preview the site and check the links.

 **1**

- Click the default.html tab to make it active.

- Click the Preview in Browser button arrow on the Common toolbar to open the browser menu. (Figure 4–87).

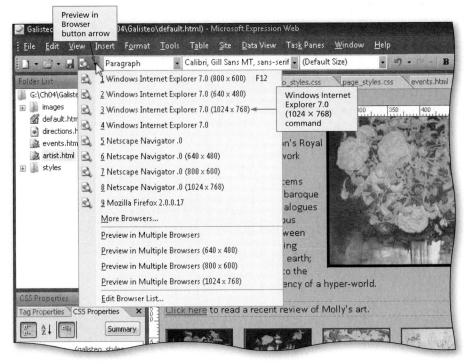

**Figure 4–87**

 **2**

- Click Windows Internet Explorer 7.0 (1024 × 768) to open the page in a browser window (Figure 4–88).

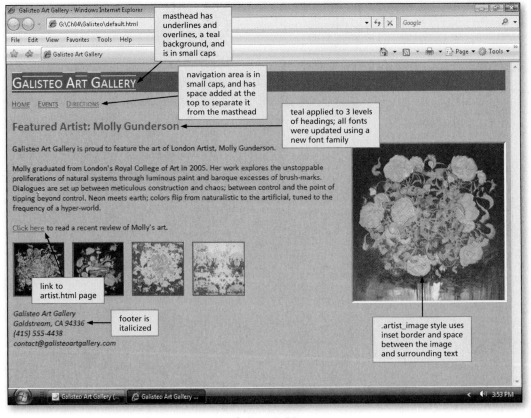

**Figure 4–88**

**3**

- Click the Click here link to display the artist.html page in the browser (Figure 4–89).

**Figure 4–89**

## To Close a Site and Quit Expression Web

**1** Click the Close button on the browser title bar to close the browser window.

**2** On the File menu, click Close Site.

**3** On the File menu, click Exit.

# Chapter Summary

In this chapter, you have learned to work with style sheets to create and modify styles that formatted and positioned text and elements. You created a style sheet using code based on Expression Web prompts. You created a new font family and a new page that included CSS layouts. You practiced attaching style sheets to individual pages and all pages in a site. The items listed below include all the new Expression Web skills you have learned in this chapter.

1. Open a Web Site and Web Page (EW 247)
2. Define an ID-Based Style (EW 249)
3. Position Content Using a Class-Based Style (EW 254)
4. Use the CSS Properties Task Pane (EW 256)
5. Create an External Style Sheet (EW 260)
6. Create a Font Family (EW 262)
7. Modify a Page in Code View (EW 266)
8. Attach a Style Sheet (EW 268)
9. Use Pre-Built CSS Layouts (EW 271)
10. Copy and Paste Elements (EW 274)
11. Complete Page Content (EW 276)
12. Attach Multiple Style Sheets (EW 280)
13. Add a Hyperlink (EW 283)
14. Organize Style Sheets (EW 284)
15. Create a CSS Report (EW 286)
16. Preview the Site (EW 288)

If you have a SAM user profile, you may have access to hands-on instruction, practice, and assessment. Log in to your SAM account (http://sam2007.course.com) to launch any assigned training activities or exams that relate to the skills covered in this chapter.

## Learn It Online

Test your knowledge of chapter content and key terms.

*Instructions:* To complete the Learn It Online exercises, start your browser, click the Address bar, and then enter the Web address `scsite.com/ew2/learn`. When the Expression Web Learn It Online page is displayed, click the link for the exercise you want to complete and then read the instructions.

**Chapter Reinforcement TF, MC, and SA**
A series of true/false, multiple choice, and short answer questions that test your knowledge of the chapter content.

**Flash Cards**
An interactive learning environment where you identify chapter key terms associated with displayed definitions.

**Practice Test**
A series of multiple choice questions that test your knowledge of chapter content and key terms.

**Who Wants To Be a Computer Genius?**
An interactive game that challenges your knowledge of chapter content in the style of a television quiz show.

**Wheel of Terms**
An interactive game that challenges your knowledge of chapter key terms in the style of the television show *Wheel of Fortune*.

**Crossword Puzzle Challenge**
A crossword puzzle that challenges your knowledge of key terms presented in the chapter.

## Apply Your Knowledge

Reinforce the skills and apply the concepts you learned in this chapter.

### Creating a Site from a Template

*Instructions:* Start Expression Web. You will create a new Web site using a CSS layout, enter text and images, and create and attach a style sheet so that the page looks like Figure 4–90.

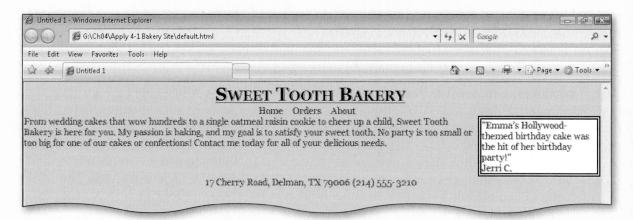

**Figure 4–90**

*Perform the following tasks:*
1. Point to New on the File menu, click Page, then click CSS Layouts.
2. Click the second instance of Header, nav, 2 columns, footer from the list, make sure that the preview shown has the narrower column on the right side, then click the OK button.

3. Open the Save As dialog box, navigate to the drive and folder where you save your Data Files, click the New Folder button, then name the new folder Apply 4-1 Bakery Site.

4. Save the page as default.html and the style sheet as bakery_styles.css to the bakery_site folder.

5. Click in the masthead div, then type Sweet Tooth Bakery.

6. Click in the navigation div, then type Home, press TAB, type Orders, press TAB, then type About.

7. Click in the footer, then type 17 Cherry Road, Delman, TX 79006 (214) 555-3210.

8. Click in the right column, then type "Emma's Hollywood-themed birthday cake was the hit of her birthday party!", press ENTER, then type Jerri C..

9. Click in the page content area, then type

   From wedding cakes that wow hundreds to a single oatmeal raisin cookie to cheer up a child, Sweet Tooth Bakery is here for you. My passion is baking, and my goal is to satisfy your sweet tooth. No party is too small or too big for one of our cakes or confections! Contact me today for all of your delicious needs.

10. Click the masthead arrow on the Apply Styles task pane, then click Modify style.

11. Modify the style so that the font is xx-large, bold, small-caps, and has an underline, and that the text is center-aligned. (*Hint*: text-align is in the Block category.)

12. Use the Modify Style dialog box to center-align the navigation area.

13. Display the CSS Properties task pane, then click in the footer.

14. Scroll to the Block heading in the CSS Properties task pane, click the text-align box arrow, then click center.

15. Display the bakery_styles.css. Click at the end of the line, float: right;.

16. Press ENTER, type background-color:white;, press ENTER, type border-style:double;, press ENTER, then type border:thick;.

17. Click Page Editor Options on the Tools menu, then click the Font Families tab.

18. Create a new font family using Georgia, Book Antiqua, and serif.

19. Point to New on the File menu, then click CSS. Save the new CSS as site_styles.

20. Type the following in the new style sheet:

    ```
    /*Style Sheet to define page content by Your Name*/
    body {
    font-family:Georgia, "Book Antiqua", serif;
    background-color:#FFCCFF;
    }
    }
    ```

21. Attach the new style sheet to the default.html page.

22. Save all pages at once.

23. Preview the site and test the links.

24. Change the site properties as specified by your instructor. Submit the revised site in the format specified by your instructor.

25. Save all pages, then close the site.

# Extend Your Knowledge

Extend the skills you learned in this chapter and experiment with new skills. You may need to use Help to complete the assignment.

## Modifying a Template

*Instructions:* Start Expression Web. You will create a new Web site with one page that uses a CSS layout and styles to make the default.html page match the one shown in Figure 4–91.

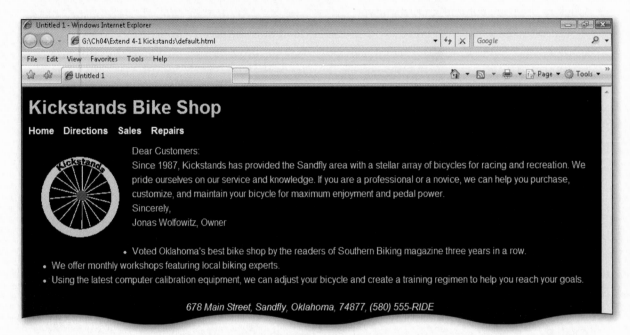

**Figure 4–91**

*Perform the following tasks:*
1. Click File on the menu bar, point to New, then click Web site.
2. Click Empty Web Site.
3. Navigate to the flash drive where you save your data files, select the default site name, type `Extend 4-1 Kickstands`, then click the OK button.
4. Click File on the menu bar, point to New, then click Page.
5. Click the CSS Layouts category, click Header, nav, 1 column, footer, then click the OK button.
6. Save the HTML page as default.html and the CSS as kickstand_styles.css.
7. Type `Kickstands Bike Shop` in the masthead div.
8. Type `Home`, `Directions`, `Sales`, and `Repairs` in the navigation div, pressing TAB between each word.
9. Click in the page content div, then type:

`Dear Customers:`

`Since 1987, Kickstands has provided the Sandfly area with a stellar array of bicycles for racing and recreation. We pride ourselves on our service and knowledge. If you are a professional or a novice, we can help you purchase, customize, and maintain your bicycle for maximum enjoyment and pedal power.`

`Sincerely,`

`Jonas Wolfowitz, Owner`

*Dbl. click on all in toolbox*

10. Press ENTER twice. Insert a paragraph div.

11. Click the Bulleted list button on the Common toolbar.

12. Type the following list, pressing ENTER after each line.

    · Voted Oklahoma's best bike shop by the readers of Southern Biking magazine three years in a row.

    · We offer monthly workshops featuring local biking experts.

    · Using the latest computer calibration equipment, we can adjust your bicycle and create a training regimen to help you reach your goals.

13. Type 678 Main Street, Sandfly, Oklahoma, 74877, (580) 555-RIDE in the footer div.

14. Save the default.html page, then display the kickstand_styles.css file.

15. Click after the heading (), then press ENTER.

16. Type the following, using the prompts as necessary:

    body {

    background:black;

    font-family:Arial, Helvetica, sans-serif;

    color:yellow

    }

17. Save the kickstand_styles.css file, then display the default.html page.

18. Click the arrow next to masthead, then click Modify Style.

19. Apply the following rules: font-size: xx-large; font-weight: bold; text-transform: capitalize. Then click the OK button.

20. Click in the top_nav div, then display the CSS Properties task pane.

21. Use the CSS Properties task pane to apply the following rules: color: white; font-weight: bold; margin-top: 12 px; margin-bottom: 12 px. Then click the OK button.

22. Click the arrow next to page_content, then click Modify Style.

23. Click the Block category, click the line-height box arrow, click (value), type 24, then click the OK button.

24. Click in the footer, then use the CSS Properties task pane to apply the following rules: color: white; font-style: italic; text-align: center; margin-top: 24.

25. Click in the page_content div after the last line, then press ENTER twice.

26. Click Insert on the menu bar, point to Picture, then click from File.

27. Insert the image kickstands_logo.gif from the Extend 4-1 Image folder. Do not enter text in the Accessiblity Properties dialog box.

28. Click the New Style link on the Apply Styles task pane.

*rules*

29. Create a new style called .image and save it to kickstand_styles.css. Apply the following rules: float: left; margin: 20px. Then click the OK button.

30. Select the image, then apply the .image style to it.

31. Preview the page, then close the browser window.

32. Change the site properties as specified by your instructor. Save the presentation using the file name, Extend 4-1 Kickstands. Submit the revised site in the format specified by your instructor.

# Make It Right

Analyze a site and correct all errors and/or improve the design.

### Placing and Formatting Images

*Instructions:* Start Expression Web. Open the Web site, Make It Right 4-1 Drama, from the Data Files for Students. See the inside back cover of this book for instructions for downloading the Data Files for Students, or see your instructor for information about accessing the required files.

Create and apply an external style sheet using task panes, dialog boxes, and Code view to format the Web page while keeping in mind the guidelines for this chapter to create the home page shown in Figure 4–92.

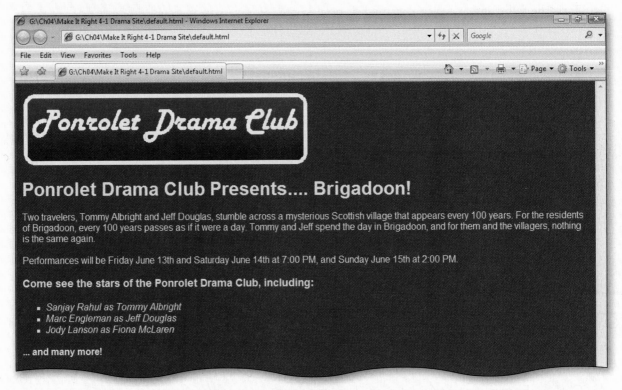

**Figure 4–92**

1. Create and save a new CSS file called drama_styles.css.
2. Add a title to the CSS page by typing /*Page Styles created by Your Name*/.
3. Define the body styles by typing:

   ```
   body
   {
       background-color:maroon;
       font-family:Arial, Helvetica, sans-serif;
       color:#FFFF99
   }
   ```

4. Save the drama_styles.css file, then attach it to the default.html page.
5. Create a new style called .cast_list and save it to the drama_styles.css page. The style should have font-style:italic and list-style-type: square.

6. Apply the .cast_list style to the bulleted list of cast members.

7. Change the site properties as specified by your instructor. Save the site using the file name, Make it Right 4-1 Drama Site. Submit the revised site in the format specified by your instructor.

## In the Lab

Design and/or format a Web site using the guidelines, concepts, and skills presented in this chapter. Labs are listed in order of increasing difficulty.

### Lab 1: Creating a New Style Sheet

*Problem:* You are a photographer, and you want to update your business's home page by creating a style sheet that you can apply to future pages. You will create styles and a style sheet to create the page shown in Figure 4–93.

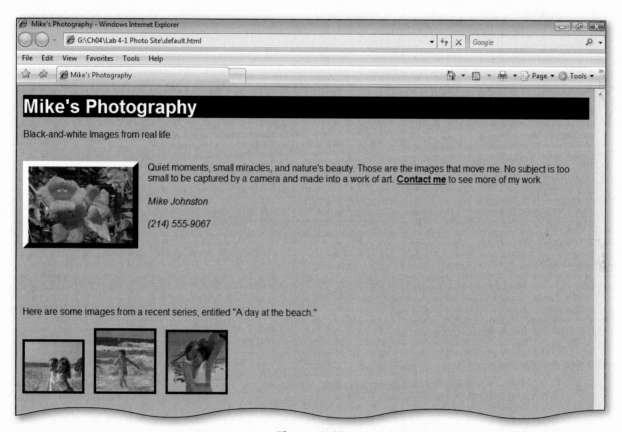

**Figure 4–93**

*Instructions:*

1. Start Expression Web.

2. Open the Web site, Lab 4-1 Photo, from the Data Files for Students.

3. Create a new CSS and save it as photo_styles.css.

4. Type page title at the top of the CSS: /*External Style Sheet to define page content by Your Name*/.

5. Use the prompts in Code view to apply to the body the Arial, Helvetica, sans-serif font-family and the silver background color to the page.

*Continued >*

**In the Lab** *continued*

6. Save the changes to the CSS, then attach it to the default.html page.

7. Select the flower image, then use the CSS Properties task pane to add a 16-pixel margin to the right of the image.

8. Create a new style called .thumbnail in the photo_styles.css style sheet. Click the Border category. Specify that the border is the same for all sides, and use the ridge style, medium width, and black color.

9. Apply the .thumbnail style to each of the three thumbnails at the bottom of the page.

10. Create a new style called .e-mail in the photo_styles.css style sheet. Specify that the font weight is bold, the color black, and apply underline.

11. Select the words, Contact me, and apply the .e-mail style.

12. Save the changes to the default.htm page, close the page, then preview the site in a browser.

13. Submit the site in the format specified by your instructor, then close the site.

## In the Lab

### Lab 2: Creating and Applying Styles

*Problem:* You have volunteered to update the Web site for the Connecticut branch of the Gulliver College Alumni Society. You will modify the styles to format the site as shown in Figure 4–94.

**Figure 4–94**

*Instructions:* Start Expression Web. Open the Web site, Lab 4-2 Alumni, from the Data Files for Students. See the inside back cover of this book for instructions for downloading the Data Files for Students, or see your instructor for information about accessing the required files.

*Perform the following tasks:*

1. Open the style sheet. Press ENTER after the header to start a new line, then type and use prompts to specify the following style rules for the body: font-family: Times New Roman, Times, serif; color:green; background-color: #CCFF66; font-size:large. (*Hint:* use the Pick Value option to choose the light green background color with the appropriate values.)

2. Modify the style rules for the masthead using the Modify Style dialog box. Specify the following formatting: background-color: silver; font-size: xx-large; font-weight: bold; text-align: center.

3. Modify the style rules for the top_nav div using the CSS Properties task pane. Specify the following formatting: margin-top: 16px; margin-bottom: 16px; text-align: center; font-size: x-large; font-variant: small-caps.

4. Use whatever method you prefer to modify the style rules for the footer. Specify the following formatting: margin-top: 10px; text-decoration: overline; font-size: medium; font-style: italic; text-align: center.

5. Save all pages at once.

6. Preview the page in a browser and use the navigation bar to view all pages.

7. Change the site properties as specified by your instructor.

8. Rename the site Lab 4-2 Alumni Site, submit the site in the format specified by your instructor, then close the site.

## In the Lab

### Lab 3: Creating a Site Using a CSS Layout

*Problem:*   Your client, a preschool, wants to create a home page that they can use to attract clients, and to which they will later add other pages. You create a Web site folder and a page using a CSS layout and format the page using styles to create the page shown in Figure 4–95.

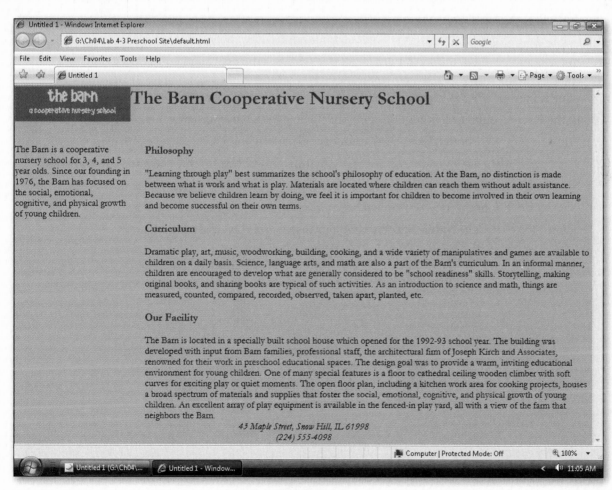

**Figure 4–95**

*Continued >*

**In the Lab** *continued*

*Instructions:*

1. Start Expression Web.

2. Create an empty Web site folder called Lab 4-3 Preschool Site.

3. Add a new page based on the Header, logo, 2 columns, footer CSS layout.

4. Save the page as default.html and the associated style sheet as preschool_styles.css.

5. In the logo div, insert the image preschool_logo.gif from the Lab 4-3 Preschool Files folder in your Data Files. Resize the logo to 200 pixels wide, then resample it.

6. In the Header div, type The Barn Cooperative Nursery School, then apply h1 to the div.

7. In the left column, type `The Barn is a cooperative nursery school for 3, 4, and 5 year olds. Since our founding in 1976, the Barn has focused on the social, emotional, cognitive, and physical growth of young children.`

8. Start Microsoft Word, open the file preschool_text.doc, select the text, copy it to the Clipboard, then close the file and Word.

9. In the right column, paste the text with line breaks.

10. Apply h3 to the lines Philosophy, Curriculum, and Our Facility.

11. In the footer, type `43 Maple Street, Snow Hill, IL 61998`, press ENTER, then type `(224) 555-4098`.

12. Create a new font family with the fonts Garamond, Century Schoolbook, and serif.

13. In the body section of the style sheet, add a rule that uses the new font family. Specify the background color by choosing Pick Value in the prompt list, then clicking the light orange square whose color value is Hex={FF,99,33}. (*Hint:* use the Value text box to verify the color).

14. In the #page_content section of the style sheet, change the margin-left value to 225px.

15. Add a new rule for both h1 and h3 that uses the blue font color.

16. Use the CSS Properties task pane to specify that the footer text is italicized and center-aligned.

17. Save both files, then preview the site in a browser.

18. Change the site properties as specified by your instructor.

19. Submit the site in the format specified by your instructor, then close the site.

# Cases and Places

Apply your creative thinking and problem solving skills to design and implement a solution.

• EASIER  •• MORE DIFFICULT

### • 1: Creating a New Page using CSS Layouts

Create a new blank Web site about a favorite vacation and add a page using the CSS layout of your choice. Enter content in all of the divs. Modify the style sheet to specify formatting for the page. Add rules for the page background, font family, and text color. Use task panes and dialog boxes to modify the styles for two content areas, such as the footer or masthead. Close the site without saving any changes, then quit Expression Web.

### • 2: Updating a Site using CSS

Create a new site using a dynamic Web template. Use a small business such as a video store or fitness center as the site's focus. Preview the site in your browser and choose at least four style rules that you would like to modify. Open the CSS (if there is more than one style sheet, choose one) in Code view and change two style rules. Save the style sheet as Cases and Places 4-2.css, close the style sheet, and view the changes. Use the CSS Properties task pane to change one style rule and use the Modify Styles dialog box to change another. Keep modifying styles until you are satisfied with your changes. Save the modified style sheet.

### •• 3: Removing Conflicting CSS rules

Open any multi-page Web site you created in Chapter 2. Create a new style sheet and add three style rules to it. Attach it to all files in the site at once. Make note of areas where inline styles are taking priority over the style sheet. See if you can remove any conflicting inline styles by deleting them in the Apply Styles task pane. Rename and save the pages and style sheets, then close the site.

### •• 4: Creating a Personal Home Page

**Make it Personal**

You want to create a one-page site that includes information about your favorite hobby. Create a new blank site and add a page using one of the two-column CSS layouts. Enter information on the default. html page, and include at least one photo and two heading styles (h1, h2, etc). Assign style rules using the style sheet that came with the CSS layout. Create a new style sheet and add a title, specifications for the page background, and font-family. Create one rule that changes the font color of all of the heading styles you have used on your default page, and another that defines borders and margins for the image. Apply the new image style and attach the new style sheet to the default.html page. Save the pages and style sheets, then close the site.

### •• 5: Enhancing Text Using Styles

**Working Together**

A tutor wants to create a site for his business with three pages: home, references, and résumé. Working as a team with several of your classmates, plan and create the Web site. Each team member should contribute to creating text for the three pages in Word. As a group, decide on a CSS layout for each page in your site (they can all be the same or all be different) and create the site folder and the pages. Create the navigation area by inserting hyperlinks to the pages. On each of the three pages, edit the placeholder text and insert the Word files you have created. Use the style sheets to define the page elements. If your site has multiple style sheets, practice copying style rules between the pages, attaching a style sheet to another page, and using other methods to ensure consistency among page elements in the site. Preview the site, test the navigation bar, and make sure that your site is readable and attractive. Save and close the pages and style sheet, then close the site.

# 5 | Working with Data Tables and Inline Frames

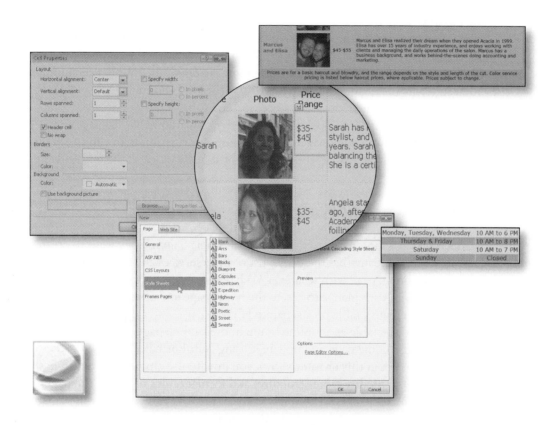

## Objectives

You will have mastered the material in this chapter when you can:

- Use a preformatted style sheet
- Insert a data table
- Change table and cell properties
- Add text and images
- Add rows and columns
- Merge and split table cells

- Format a table using CSS
- Convert text to a table
- Use table AutoFormat
- Distribute rows and columns
- Create an inline frame
- Target links in an inline frame

# 5 | Working with Data Tables and Inline Frames

## Introduction

A **data table** is used to display data in a combination of horizontal **rows** and vertical **columns**. The intersection of a row and column is called a **cell**. Cells organize the table data, such as text, values, or images. By aligning information in rows and columns and using row and column headers to identify categories of information, information can be presented in an orderly, organized way.

Table properties can be defined by specifying the width of the table as a fixed pixel width, as a percentage of a page, or by allowing the width to be manually adjusted or fit to the text. You can modify the table structure by changing the number of columns or rows. You can format data tables using styles or Expression Web tools such as AutoFormat to add borders or background colors.

An **inline frame**, or **I-frame**, is a fixed-size window that displays another HTML page. When the embedded page contains more information than can be shown in the I-frame, scroll bars appear to allow the visitor to view more of the embedded page.

## Project — Hair Salon

Marcus and Elisa Goldman are the owners of Acacia Salon. They want to create a home page for their company that includes a list of their services and prices. They have asked you to create the home page with whatever Web design tools you recommend. Based on the needs of the site, your plan is to create the home page and attach a preformatted style sheet to it. You will create a table on a separate HTML page, enter data and images, format the table, then add the table as an inline frame to their home page. You will also create a table from text on the home page and update it using AutoFormat.

The project in this chapter shows you how to use a preformatted style sheet, insert a table, add data, modify table structure, and format tables to create the pages shown in Figure 5–1. You will also learn how to convert text to a table, use AutoFormat to apply table formatting, and embed an HTML page that contains the table as an inline frame in the home page.

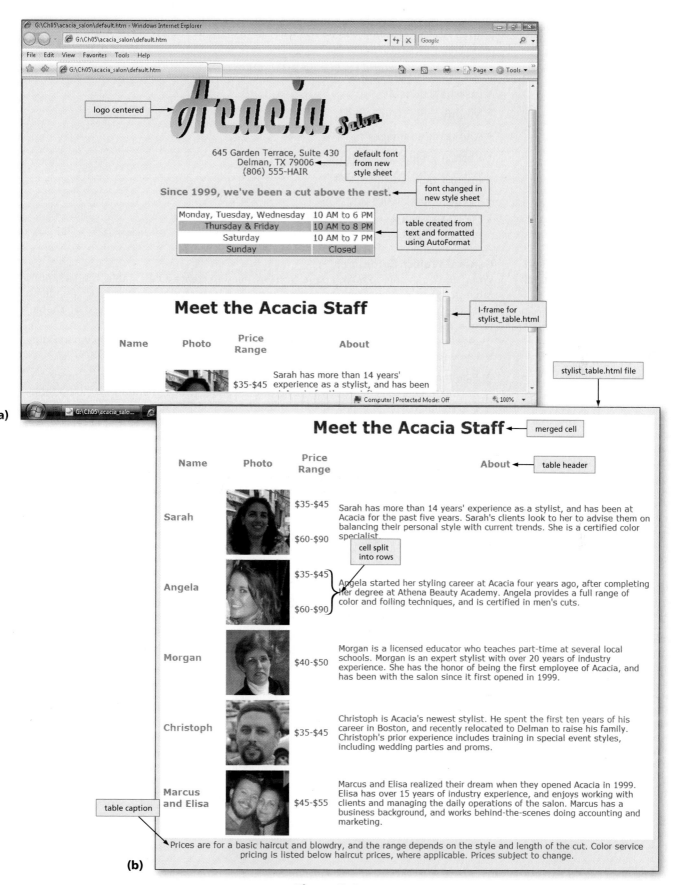

**Figure 5–1**

# Overview

As you read this chapter, you will learn how to create the Web page shown in Figure 5–1 by performing these general tasks:

- Use a preformatted style sheet
- Insert a data table
- Modify table structure
- Add text and images
- Format table text
- Format table backgrounds
- Create a table from text
- Use inline frames

**Plan Ahead**

> **General Project Guidelines**
>
> When adding a table to a Web page, you will need to create a basic table, then adapt the table structure, content, and formatting as needed by performing actions such as adding and deleting rows and columns, splitting and merging cells, and applying text and table formatting.
>
> As you plan to enhance a Web page by adding a table, such as the one shown in Figure 5–1, you should follow these general guidelines:
>
> 1. **Plan the basic table structure.** Use a style sheet to provide formatting consistency between the table content and the rest of the page. When creating a new data table, you should have some idea of the number of rows and columns that you will need before you start, by planning the content that will be displayed in the table. If necessary, sketch a plan for the table on paper, or make a list of the rows and columns you might need.
>
> 2. **Add and arrange table content.** Once your table is created, add headings as needed to help you identify where to enter data. Table cells usually contain text (words or numbers), but including images in a table can provide visual data, or make your table more attractive. Once the table's content has been entered, delete rows and columns that you do not need, or add cells for more data. Arranging the table data by combining cells that contain like data, or separating one cell into two to provide additional information within a row or column, helps organize the table.
>
> 3. **Design the table.** Determine the degree to which your table should stand out from the rest of the page. Depending on the data in your table and the information on the rest of the page, you may want your table to be a subtle tool to organize data, or it could be a bold page element that will catch a visitor's eye. Choosing the appropriate table background and border options or using AutoFormat will help your table meet the design needs. Using styles to format your table helps maintain consistency with other site pages and makes the table format easier to update.
>
> 4. **Organize existing content into the table.** Text that exists in your site can be converted from regular text into a table. The benefit of organizing data into a table is that you can align rows and columns so that the text is easier to read.
>
> 5. **Add an inline frame to display a page.** Any HTML page can be embedded into an inline frame on a Web page to provide visitors with a view of the embedded page while controlling the viewing size and not requiring an additional link. For a site that is only one page, you can keep more of the main page visible within the browser window by providing a small, scrollable window that displays additional information.

## To Start Expression Web and Reset Workspace Layout

If you are using a computer to step through the project in this chapter, and you want your screens to match the figures in this book, you should change your computer's resolution to 1024 × 768. For information about how to change a computer's resolution, read Appendix F.

The following steps, which assume Windows Vista is running, start Expression Web based on a typical installation, and reset the task panes in the workspace to the default layout. You may need to ask your instructor how to start Expression Web for your computer.

**Note:** If you are using Window XP, see Appendix E for alternate steps.

**1** Click the Start button on the Windows Vista taskbar to display the Start menu.

**2** Click All Programs at the bottom of the left pane on the Start menu to display the All Programs list.

**3** Click Microsoft Expression on the All Programs list to display the Microsoft Expression list.

**4** Click Microsoft Expression Web 2 to start Expression Web.

**5** Click Task Panes on the menu bar, then click Reset Workspace Layout.

## To Create a New Web Site and Web Page

The following steps create the Acacia Web site folder and the default.html page.

**1**

• Point to New on the File menu, then click Web Site to open the New dialog box (Figure 5–2).

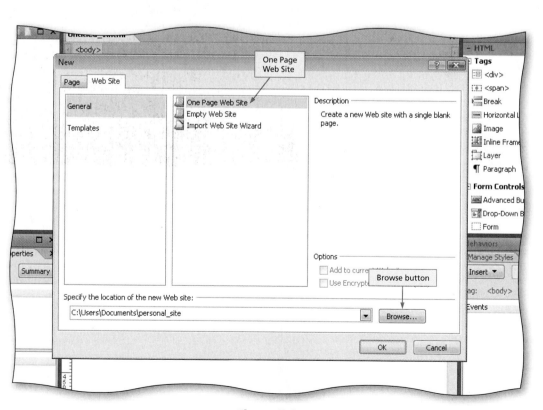

**Figure 5–2**

- Click One Page Web Site, then click the Browse button to open the New Web Site Location dialog box.

- Navigate to the flash drive where your Data Files for Students are located, then click the Open button.

- Type `acacia_salon` in the Specify the location of the new Web site text box, then click the OK button to open the site in Expression Web (Figure 5–3).

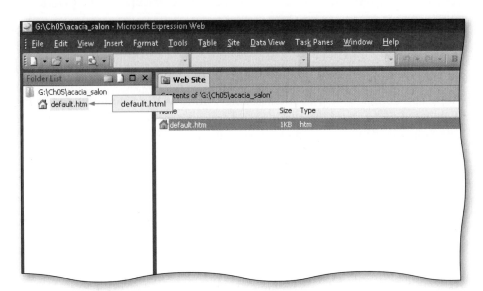

**Figure 5–3**

- Double-click the default.html page from the Folder List to open it.

- Point to Picture on the Insert menu, then click From File to open the Picture dialog box.

- Navigate to the Flash Drive where your Data Files for Students are located, and double-click the acacia_images folder to open it.

- Click acacia_logo.gif to select it (Figure 5–4).

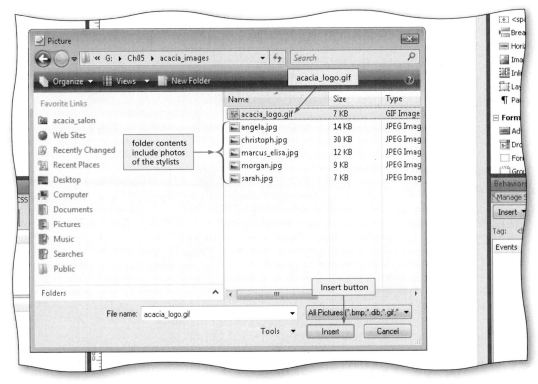

**Figure 5–4**

4

- Click the Insert button to open the Accessibility Properties dialog box.

- Type `Acacia Salon logo` in the Alternate text text box (Figure 5–5).

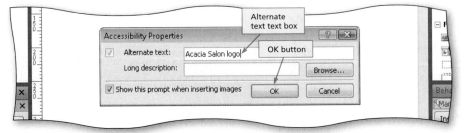

**Figure 5–5**

- Click the OK button to insert the logo at the top of the home page.

- Click the <p> div on the Quick Tag Selector bar to select the image, then click the Center button on the Common toolbar to center the image (Figure 5–6).

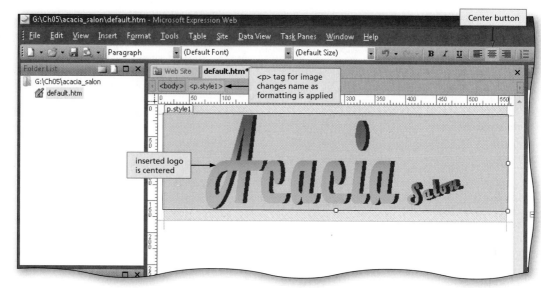

**Figure 5–6**

**6**

- Click below the logo to deselect it.

- Double-click the Paragraph div in the Toolbox to insert a new paragraph.

- Type 645 Garden Terrace, Suite 430 as the first line of the address, then press SHIFT+ENTER to start a new line in the paragraph.

- Type Delman, TX 79006, then press SHIFT+ENTER to start a new line in the paragraph.

- Type (806) 555-HAIR.

- Click the <p> div on the Quick Tag Selector bar to select the paragraph, then click the Center button on the Common toolbar to center the paragraph (Figure 5–7).

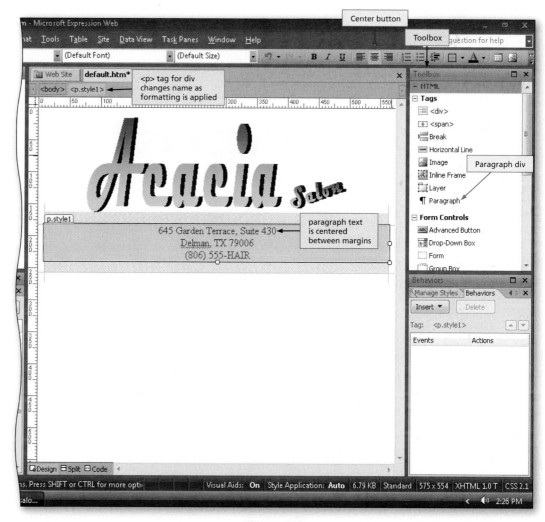

**Figure 5–7**

**7**

- Click below the paragraph to position the insertion point.

- Double-click the Paragraph div in the Toolbox to insert a new paragraph.

- Type Since 1999, we've been a cut above the rest..

- Click the <p> div on the Quick Tag Selector bar to select the paragraph.

- Click the Style box arrow on the Common toolbar to display the Style menu (Figure 5–8).

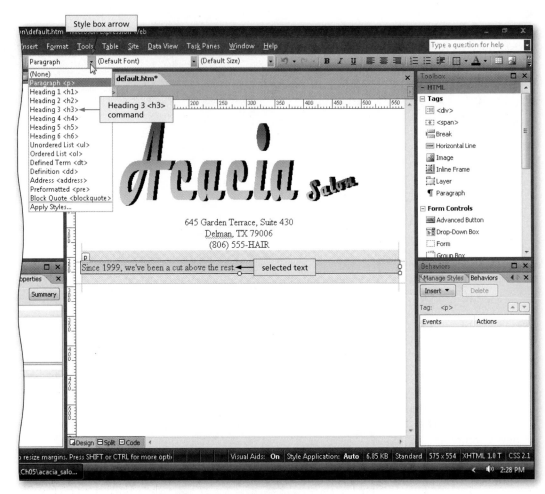

**Figure 5–8**

**8**

- Click Heading 3 <h3> to apply it to the text (Figure 5–9).

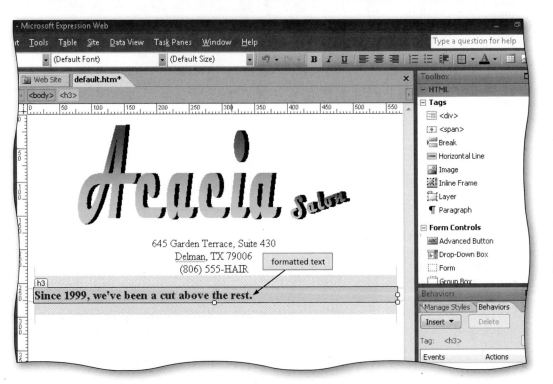

**Figure 5–9**

**9**
- Press CTRL+S to save the default.html page, and click the OK button in the Save Embedded Files dialog box to save the logo to the page (Figure 5–10).

**Figure 5–10**

# Using a Preformatted Style Sheet

Just as you can create a new Web page using a CSS layout or a new Web site using a dynamic Web template, you can create a new style sheet using a preformatted option provided by Expression Web. Using a preformatted style sheet saves you time and ensures that the code is entered correctly. Like any completed style sheet, a preformatted style sheet contains code that you can edit and modify to suit your needs.

**Plan the basic table structure.**
Plan the formatting for all pages in the site, including the page that you will embed as an I-frame. Use a preformatted style sheet as a basis, then modify it as necessary. Determine the approximate number of columns and rows that you will need to display the data, including any necessary row and column headers. If your table includes a title, consider whether to add it as a line of text above the table, or as a merged cell that spans the width of the table. A caption above or below your table describes the table contents or its purpose. You should specify table and cell properties, such as text alignment, alignment of the table relative to the page margins, and spacing between cells.

**Plan Ahead**

BTW | **Nested Table**
A nested table is a table inside another table.

## To Create a New Style Sheet

The following steps create the acacia_styles.css file using a preformatted style sheet. You want all of the fonts to be the same throughout the page, so you will delete the code that specifies different font type and color for the heading styles. Then you will attach the style sheet to the default.html page.

- Point to New on the File menu, then click Page to open the New dialog box.

- Click Style Sheets in the left pane to display the style sheet options (Figure 5–11).

🔎 **Experiment**

- Click different options in the Style Sheets list to view descriptions.

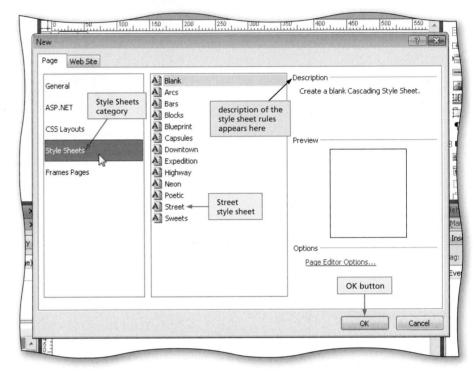

**Figure 5–11**

- Click the Street style sheet to select it.

- Click the OK button to create the new style sheet (Figure 5–12).

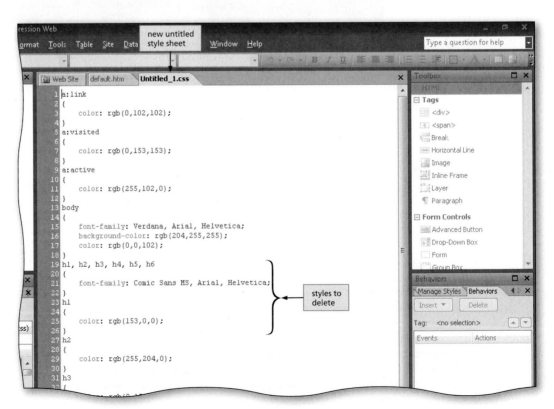

**Figure 5–12**

**3**

- Select the code and brackets in lines 19 through 25 that formats the headings in a different font and h1 in a different color (Figure 5–13).

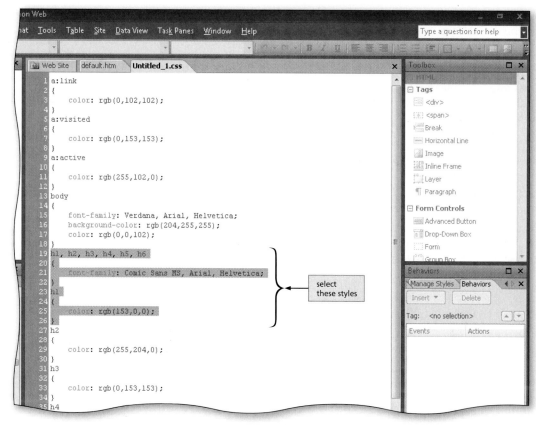

**Figure 5–13**

**4**

- Press DELETE to delete the code.

- Press CTRL+S to open the Save As dialog box.

- Type acacia_styles.css in the File name text box (Figure 5–14).

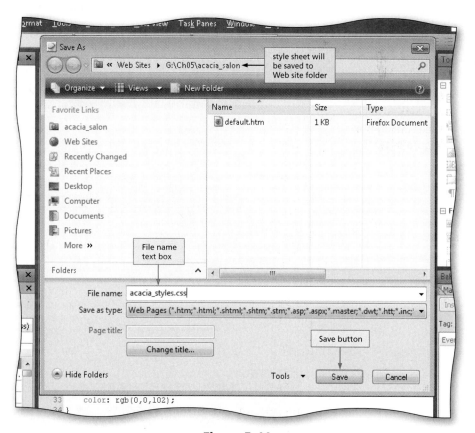

**Figure 5–14**

● Click the Save button to save the style sheet (Figure 5–15).

● Close the style sheet.

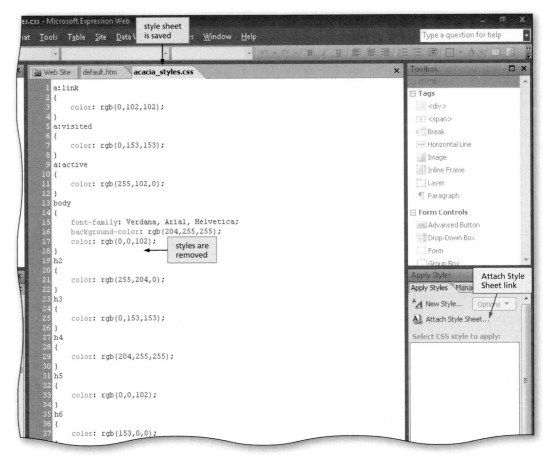

**Figure 5–15**

**6**

● Click the Attach Style Sheet link in the Apply Styles task pane to open the Attach Style Sheet dialog box (Figure 5–16).

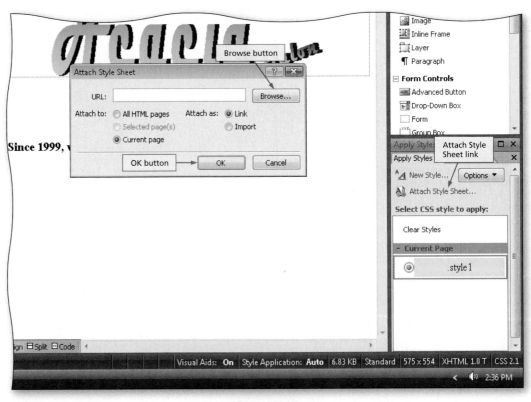

**Figure 5–16**

- Click the Browse button to open the Select Style Sheet dialog box.

- Click acacia_styles.css to select it (Figure 5–17).

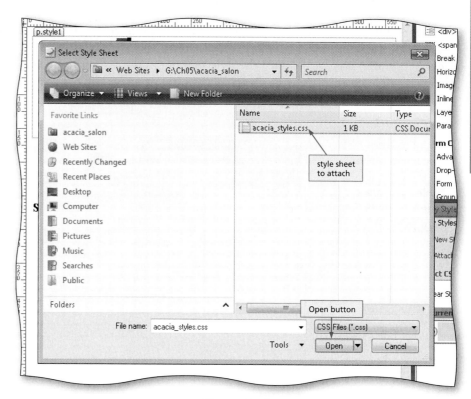

**Figure 5–17**

**8**

- Click the Open button to close the Select Style Sheet dialog box.

- Click the OK button to close the Attach Style Sheet dialog box and attach the style sheet to the page (Figure 5–18).

- Save the default. html page.

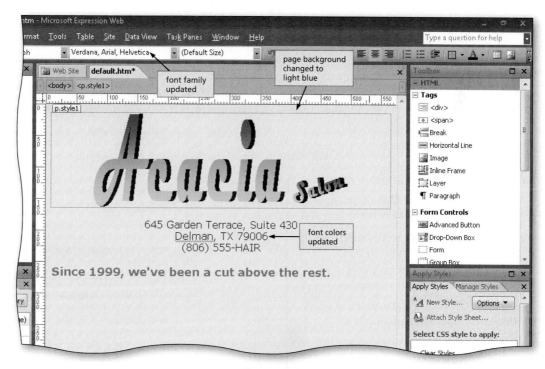

**Figure 5–18**

**Other Ways**

1. Click the New button arrow on the Common toolbar, then click Page to open the New dialog box.

2. Point to CSS Styles on the Format menu, then click Attach Style Sheet to open the Attach Style Sheet dialog box.

## To Create a New Page and Attach a Style Sheet

You must create a new page for the table so that you can embed it as an inline frame on the home page. The page background, font family, and other styles for the page containing the table should be consistent with other pages in the site, so you will attach the style sheet from the default.html page to the new page. Later in the chapter, when you apply heading styles to the table, the heading styles will use the defined heading rules of the CSS. The following steps create a new blank page and attach the acacia_styles CSS.

- Click the New Document button on the Common toolbar to insert a new blank page (Figure 5–19).

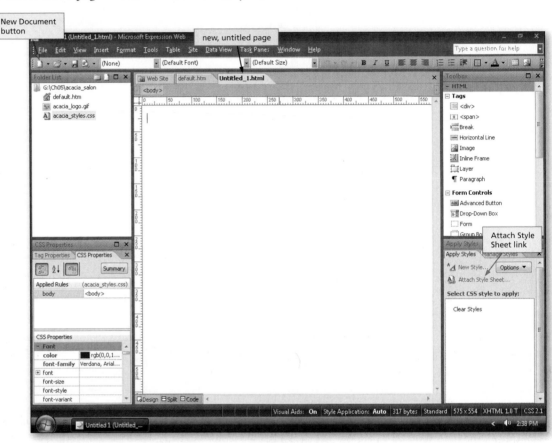

**Figure 5–19**

- Click the Attach Style Sheet link in the Apply Styles task pane to open the Attach Style Sheet dialog box.

- Click the Browse button to open the Select Style Sheet dialog box.

- Click acacia_styles.css to select it.

- Click the Open button to close the Select Style Sheet dialog box (Figure 5–20).

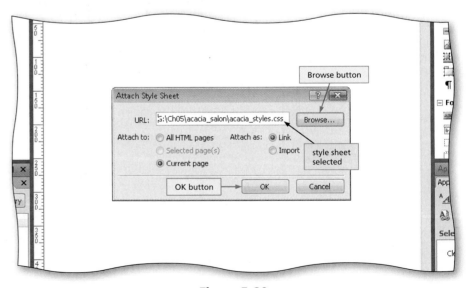

**Figure 5–20**

- Click the OK button to close the Attach Style Sheet dialog box (Figure 5–21).

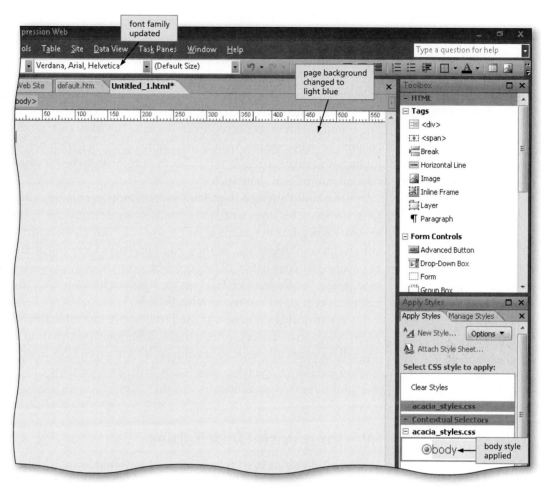

**Figure 5–21**

- Press CTRL+S to open the Save As dialog box.

- Type stylist_table.html in the File name text box, then click the Save button to save the new page (Figure 5–22).

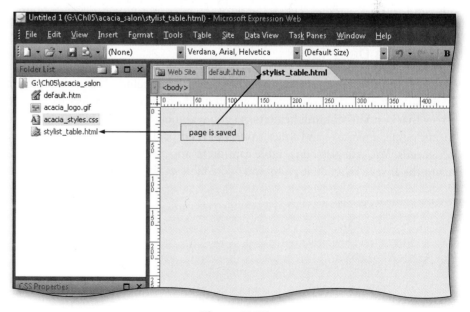

**Figure 5–22**

**Other Ways**

1. Press CTRL+N to open a new blank page.

# Creating Data Tables

**BTW**

**Table Background Image**
Another way to make your table stand out is to add a background image that appears behind the table. Only use this option when necessary, because it increases the file size (causing slower download time in a browser), and can distract from the table data.

A table used to present data is called a **data table**, or just a table. Data is entered into cells, and cells are arranged in horizontal rows and vertical columns. When creating a table, you begin by specifying numbers of rows and columns, and then you modify the table properties to customize its appearance.

Tables are often used on Web pages and other documents to list items and characteristics. For example, a list of products offered at a store can show each product on its own new row, with columns of characteristics, such as description, price, item number, and so on. Column headers for each characteristic enable the visitor to scan through the list of items and determine the relevant information about each.

You could attempt to present information in columns and rows by using the TAB key to insert space between words to simulate columns and the ENTER key to start new lines to simulate rows, but this method will cause your text to misalign when presented at different screen resolutions and is not a good practice. Creating a table enables you to use CSS to ensure that your data will be accessible, consistently presented, and easy to format and reorganize. Tables use HTML tags to define captions (<tc>), rows (<tr>), headers (<th>), cell data (<td>), and the entire table (<table>).

**BTW**

**Saving Default Table Settings**
In the Table Properties dialog box, click the Set as default for new tables check box to save your settings for future tables in your site to ensure consistency and save you time.

A **caption** is a line of text used to describe the table to visitors using screen readers or other adaptive devices, or to provide additional information about the table. A caption typically appears above or below the table. Although CSS has the option to create a caption on the side of the table, this is not widely supported by browsers, so Expression Web does not offer this capability.

## Working with Data Tables

Cell divisions in a table are shown as dotted lines, which are a type of visual aid called **tracer lines**. By default, there are no gridlines that separate table row and column borders, so it is important to have Visual Aids turned on when working with a table so that you can see where cells are divided.

### To Insert a Data Table

All of the information on the new page will be included as part of the table. The salon has three stylists, each of whom will have their own row; you will need one row for owners Marcus and Elisa, and you will need to include a row that contains column headers, so you will include a total of five rows. Each stylist will have a column for his or her name, a picture, and a description of their background and services, so you will need three columns — a total of 15 cells. You will also add a table caption to appear below the table. The following steps insert a new blank table using the Insert Table dialog box and add a table caption.

**1**

- Click Insert Table on the Table menu to open the Insert Table dialog box.

- Type 5 in the Rows box to specify a five-row table, then press TAB to move to the Columns box.

- Type 3 in the Columns box to specify a three-column table (Figure 5–23).

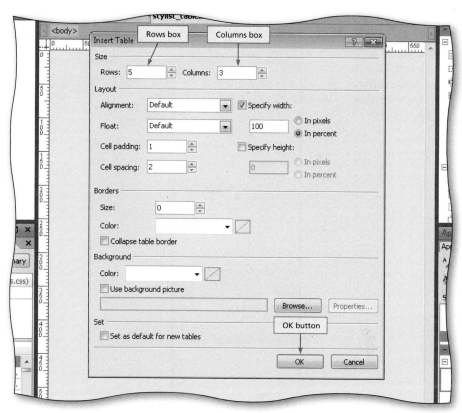

**Figure 5–23**

**2**

- Click the OK button to close the Insert Table dialog box and insert the new table (Figure 5–24).

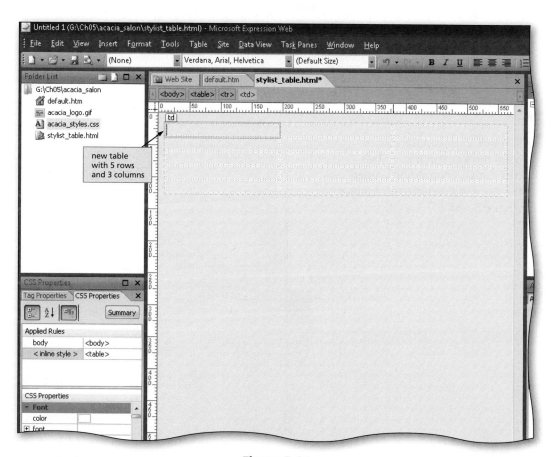

**Figure 5–24**

**3**

• Point to Insert on the Table menu, then click Caption to insert a div for the table caption above the table (Figure 5–25).

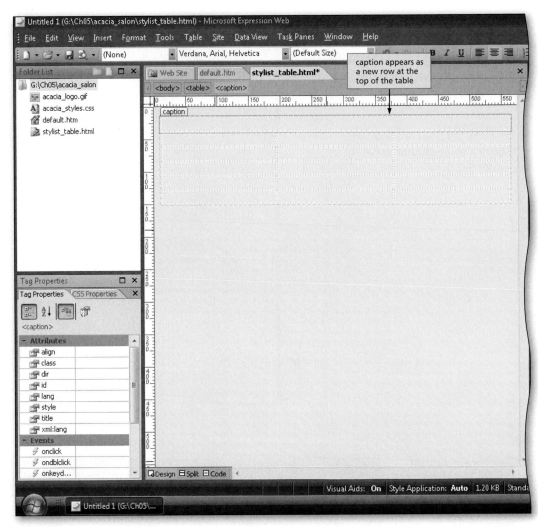

**Figure 5–25**

**4**

• Right-click the caption row to open the shortcut menu, then click Caption Properties to open the Caption Properties dialog box (Figure 5–26).

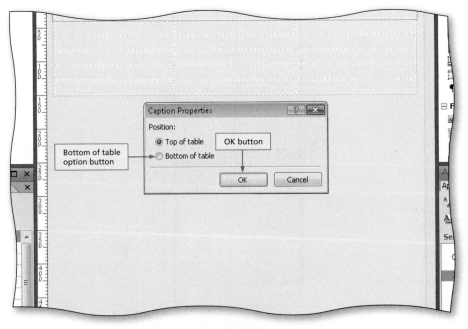

**Figure 5–26**

**5**
- Click the Bottom of table option button to select it.

- Click the OK button to close the dialog box and position the caption below the table (Figure 5–27).

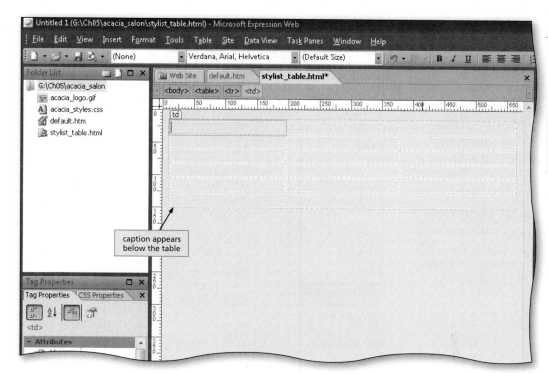

Figure 5–27

**Other Ways**

1. Point to Table Properties on the Table menu, then click Caption to open the Caption Properties dialog box.

# Table and Cell Properties

Table properties define the alignment, borders, and background of the table, and also define default cell settings, such as padding and text alignment. Table properties apply to all cells in a table. You can change the same settings (alignment, background, and so on) for a certain amount of cells by changing their cell properties. Changing the cell properties modifies the settings for the cell containing the insertion point, or for any selected cells, rows, or columns.

To select an entire row or column, position the I-beam pointer to the left of the row or the top of the column to select, then when the pointer changes to the row selector, a small black arrow, click to select the row or column.

Defining a **header** row assigns the <th> HTML tag for that row and applies bold formatting to the text in that row. Headers are often distinguished from the body of the table with different text formatting, such as a heading style or bold, or by applying a different background color. When a table is being read by a screen reader for a visitor with visual impairment, the screen reader will read the header categories when reading the data for each row. For example, in a table that lists the members of John's basketball team and includes the name, number, and position of each player, the screen reader would read Name: John; Number: 33; Position: Center.

By default, the table will span 100% of the page width. You can create a data table that does not span the entire width of the page by reducing the width percentage to less than 100% or by specifying the data table's width in pixels instead of a percentage. A data table that does not span the entire width of the page can be aligned at the left or right margin of the page or centered between the margins. By default, the height of a table is not specified when you create the table. Because the height for each row might need to expand to fit the cell contents, it is best to leave the height of the table unspecified in order to avoid truncating table data.

BTW

**Web Accessibility**
See Appendix B for more information about accessibility and assistive technology.

BTW

**Adjusting Cell Margins**
To adjust the column width or row height, drag the column divider manually. Click the Distribute Rows Evenly or Distribute Columns Evenly buttons on the Tables toolbar to make all rows and columns the same height or width. The AutoFit to Contents button on the Tables toolbar adjusts the column width based on the cell with the most content in that column.

## To Change Table and Cell Properties

The following steps use the Table Properties dialog box to add padding to increase the white space between the cell contents and cell margins. You will also add a table background color, format the cell properties of the top row to change the text alignment to center, and specify the table header.

- Point to Table Properties on the Table menu, then click Table to open the Table Properties dialog box.

- Click the Cell padding up arrow three times to change the padding to 4 pixels (Figure 5–28).

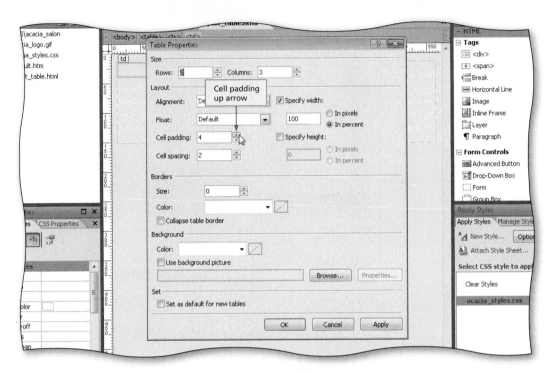

**Figure 5–28**

- Click the Color box arrow in the Background section to display the color palette (Figure 5–29).

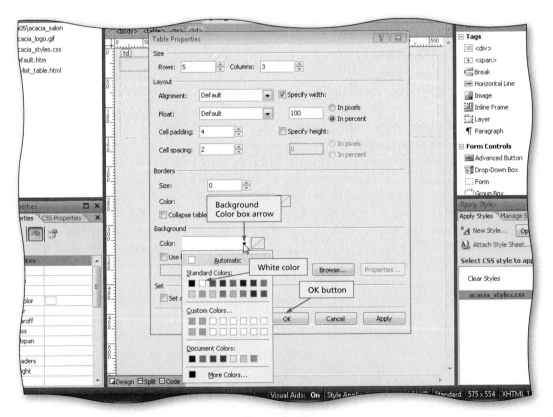

**Figure 5–29**

**3**

- Click White on the color palette to change the table background to white.

- Click the OK button to close the Table Properties dialog box (Figure 5–30).

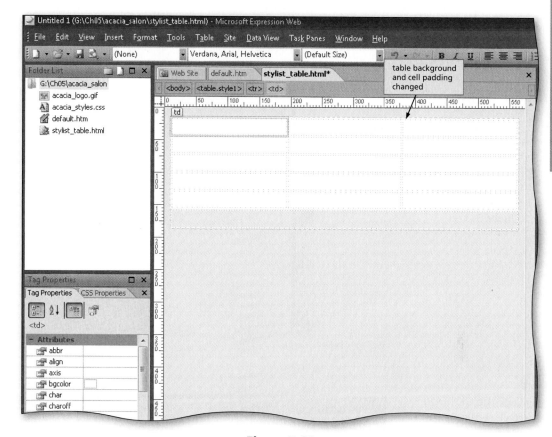

**Figure 5–30**

**4**

- Position the insertion point to the left of the top row to change the pointer to the row selector, a black, right-pointing arrow.

- Click to select the top row of the table (Figure 5–31).

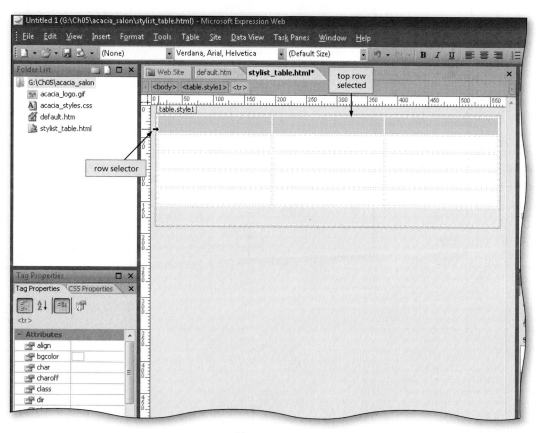

**Figure 5–31**

● Point to Table Properties on the Table menu, then click Cell to open the Cell Properties dialog box.

● Click the Horizontal alignment box arrow, then click Center to center-align the text in the top row of the table.

● Click the Header cell check box to select it and define the top row of the table as the header (Figure 5–32).

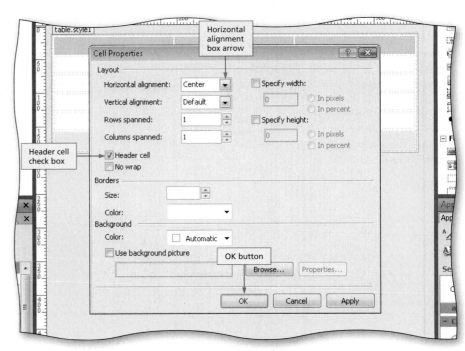

**Figure 5–32**

**6**

● Click the OK button to close the Cell Properties dialog box (Figure 5–33).

🔎 **Experiment**

● Open the Table Properties dialog box again and select different options, such as changing the table width or background. Close the dialog box, view your changes, then press CTRL+Z to undo them.

Q&A My Visual Aids are not turned on.

Point to Visual Aids on the View menu, then click Show to turn them on.

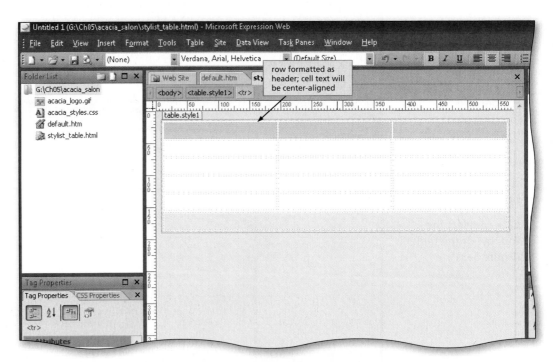

**Figure 5–33**

**Other Ways**

1. Right-click an area of the table, then click Table Properties or Cell Properties to open the Table or Cell Properties dialog box.

**Plan Ahead**

**Add and arrange table content.**

Including a table header simplifies data entry by clearly indicating where information should appear. Once the content has been added to the table, you should evaluate the table to see whether additional rows or columns are needed, and whether any cells should be combined or divided. Consulting with a colleague or your client is a good way to ensure that your table reads well to others and that no additional content is needed. Splitting and merging cells gives you flexibility when presenting data — you can combine cells to show relationships between data or to create a table header, or you can separate cells to add additional information.

BTW

**Controlling Column Width**

To control a column's width when typing the header data, position cell content onto two lines by pressing SHIFT+ENTER to insert a line break. Do not insert line breaks in non-header cells, as this will cause your table data to flow awkwardly when viewed at different screen resolutions.

# Entering Text into Cells

In a blank data table, all columns are the same width and all rows are the same height. As you enter data, the width of the current column expands and the other columns adjust.

Click the cell in which you want to enter content, then start typing. To navigate in a table, you can use the pointer to click a cell or use the keyboard shortcuts outlined in Table 5–1 to move the insertion point around the table.

**Table 5–1 Table Navigation Keyboard Shortcuts**

| Press | To go to |
|---|---|
| TAB | The next cell in the row, or when at the end of a row, to the first cell in the next row. |
| SHIFT+TAB | The previous cell in the row, or when at the beginning of a row, to the last cell in the previous row. |
| DOWN ARROW | The cell in the row below. |
| UP ARROW | The cell in the row above. |
| RIGHT ARROW | The next empty cell in the table, if there is no content in the cell. If there is content in the cell, the insertion point moves forward through the content one character at a time. |
| LEFT ARROW | The previous empty cell in the table, if there is no content in the cell. If there is content in the cell, the insertion point moves backward through the content one character at a time. |

## To Add Text to a Table

The following steps enter data in the header row, caption, and other cells in the table. You will leave the Photo column blank for now.

**1**

- Click the upper-left cell in the table to position the insertion point in the header row.

- Type Name, then press TAB to move to the next cell (Figure 5–34).

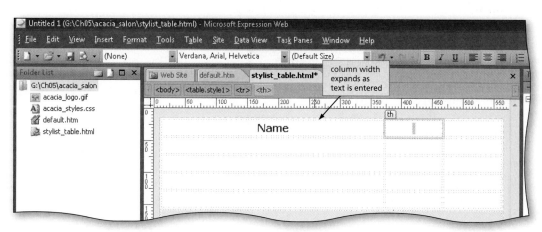

**Figure 5–34**

● Type `Photo`, then press TAB to move to the next cell.

● Type `About`, then press TAB to move to the first cell in the next row (Figure 5–35).

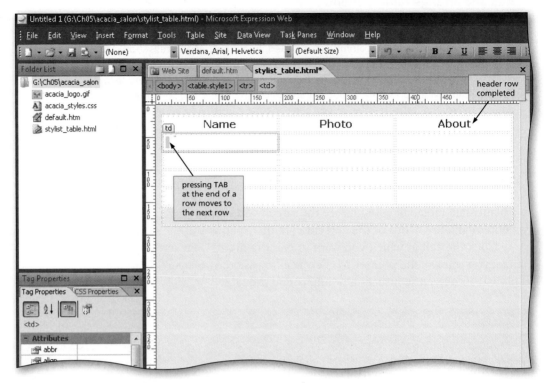

**Figure 5–35**

● Type `Sarah`, then press TAB twice to move to the About column.

● Type `Sarah has more than 14 years' experience as a stylist, and has been at Acacia for the past five years. Sarah's clients look to her to advise them on balancing their personal style with current trends. She is a certified color specialist.`, then press TAB to move to the first cell in the next row (Figure 5–36).

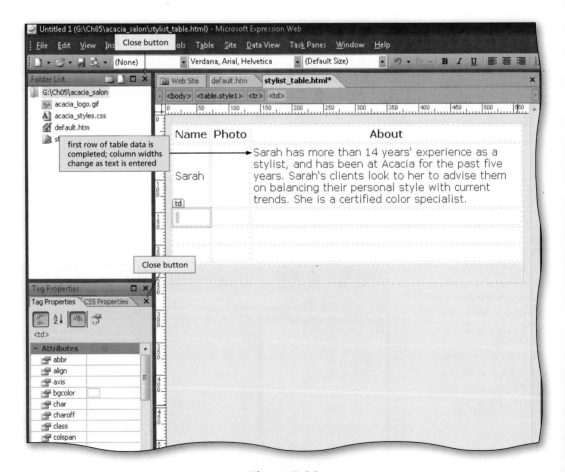

**Figure 5–36**

**4**

- Click the Close buttons on the Folder List and Tag Properties task pane to provide more space in the editing window.

- Type Angela, then press TAB twice to move to the About column.

- Type Angela started her styling career at Acacia four years ago, after completing her degree at Athena Beauty Academy. Angela provides a full range of color and foiling techniques, and is certified in men's cuts., then press TAB to move to the first cell in the next row.

- Type Morgan, then press TAB twice to move to the About column.

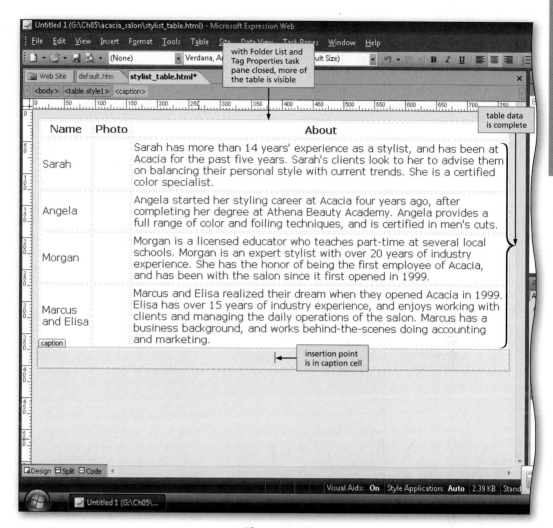

**Figure 5–37**

- Type Morgan is a licensed educator who teaches part-time at several local schools. Morgan is an expert stylist with over 20 years of industry experience. She has the honor of being the first employee of Acacia, and has been with the salon since it opened in 1999., then press TAB to move to the first cell in the next row.

- Type Marcus and Elisa, then press TAB twice to move to the About column.

- Type Marcus and Elisa realized their dream when they opened Acacia in 1999. Elisa has over 15 years of industry experience, and enjoys working with clients and managing the daily operations of the salon. Marcus has a business background, and works behind-the-scenes doing accounting and marketing.

- Click in the caption cell to position the insertion point (Figure 5–37).

**5**

- **Type** `Prices are for a basic haircut and blowdry, and the range depends on the style and length of cut. Color service pricing is listed below haircut prices, where applicable. Prices subject to change.` **as the caption text (Figure 5–38).**

- **Press CTRL+S to save the page.**

caption text is center-aligned

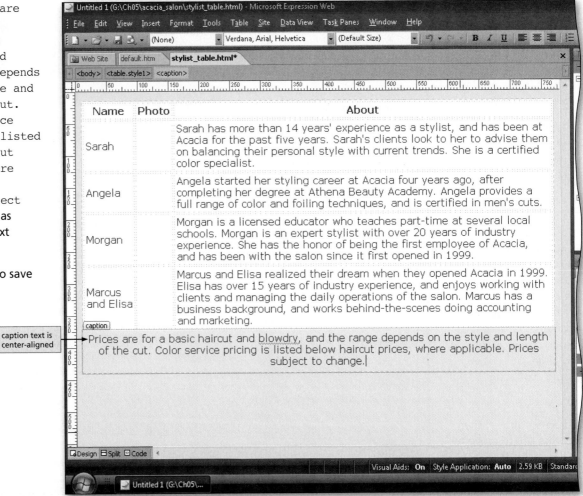

**Figure 5–38**

# Adding Images into Cells

Images will increase the file size of the page containing the table, so you should take into consideration some of the decisions and actions discussed in Chapter 2. Use images that display with the correct quality, but with a file size that does not considerably slow down the page when downloading in a browser. Only include images to enhance and illustrate table data, and make sure that the image is resized to fit the desired space.

## To Add Images to a Table

The following steps add images to the Photo column for Sarah, Angela, and Morgan.

- Click the cell to the right of the word, Sarah, to position the insertion point.

- Point to Picture on the Insert menu, then click From File to open the Picture dialog box.

- Click the file sarah.jpg to select it (Figure 5–39).

**Figure 5–39**

❷

- Click the Insert button to open the Accessibility Properties dialog box.

- Type `Sarah's photo` in the Alternate text text box, then click the OK button to insert the image (Figure 5–40).

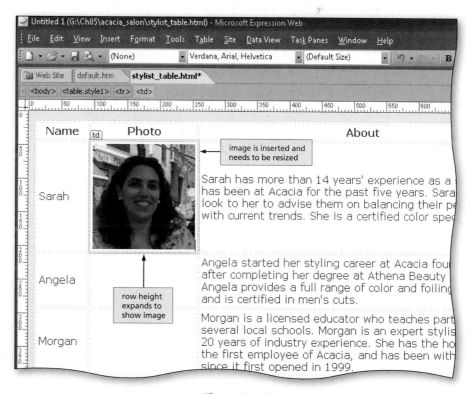

**Figure 5–40**

- Right-click the image to open the shortcut menu, then click Picture Properties to open the Picture Properties dialog box.

- Click the Appearance tab to display the sizing options.

- Type 125 in the width box to change the height and width to 125 pixels (Figure 5–41).

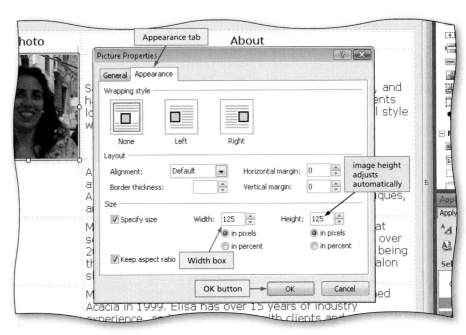

**Figure 5–41**

- Click the OK button to close the Picture Properties dialog box and insert the image.

- Click the Picture Actions button to display the menu (Figure 5–42).

- Click the Resample Picture To Match Size option button to resample the image.

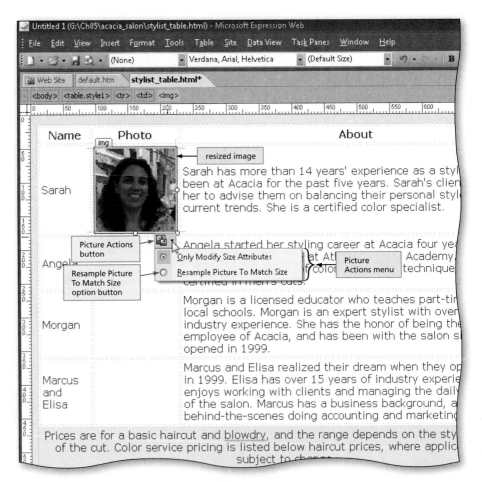

**Figure 5–42**

**5**

- Repeat Steps 1 to 4 to insert the angela.jpg, morgan.jpg, and marcus_elisa.jpg images (Figure 5–43).

- Save the page and all embedded images.

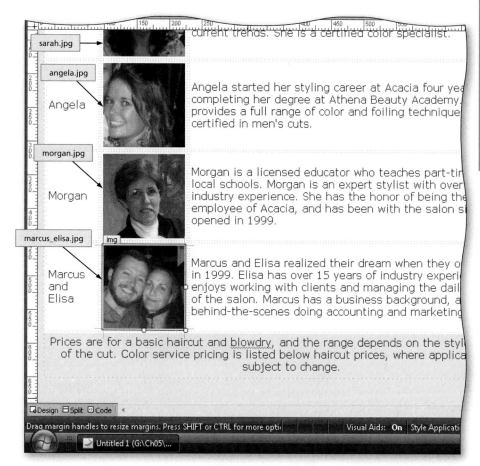

**Figure 5–43**

# Adding Rows and Columns

After creating a table, you might need to add rows and columns to it. To add a row when entering content, you can simply press TAB after entering data in the last cell in the table, and a new row is automatically added to the end of a table. You can also insert rows above or below any row in the table, or insert columns to the left or right of any column in the table.

## The Tables Toolbar

The commands for adding rows and columns are available on the Table menu, as well as on a task-specific Tables toolbar. Like the Pictures toolbar that you used in previous chapters to modify images, the Tables toolbar provides access to the necessary tools to make modifications to your table. Using buttons on the Tables toolbar, you can insert and delete rows and columns, merge and split cells, and specify table and cell properties, such as text alignment and background color.

## To Add Rows and Columns

The following steps display the Tables toolbar, add a column for the price range for each stylist, and then add a new row for a stylist who has just joined the Acacia staff and enter his data.

 **1**

• Right-click a blank area above the Common toolbar to open a shortcut menu, then click Tables to display the Tables toolbar (Figure 5–44).

**Q&A**

My Tables toolbar is not docked.

Position the insertion point over the toolbar's title bar, click, then drag the toolbar up below the Common toolbar until it docks.

**Figure 5–44**

**2**

• Click any cell in the About column to position the insertion point.

• Click the Column to the Left button on the Tables toolbar to add a new column (Figure 5–45).

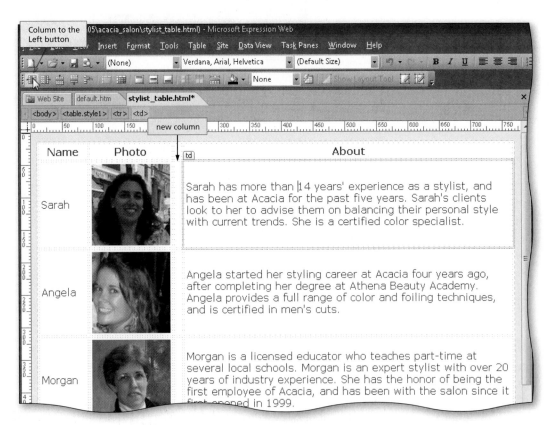

**Figure 5–45**

**3**

- Click the top cell in the new column to position the insertion point in the column header.

- Type Price Range to add a header to the new column (Figure 5–46).

**Figure 5–46**

**4**

- Click any cell in the Morgan row to position the insertion point.

- Click the Row Below button on the Tables toolbar to add a new row (Figure 5–47).

 **Experiment**

- Add another row or column, select it, then click the Delete Cells button on the Tables toolbar to practice deleting rows or columns.

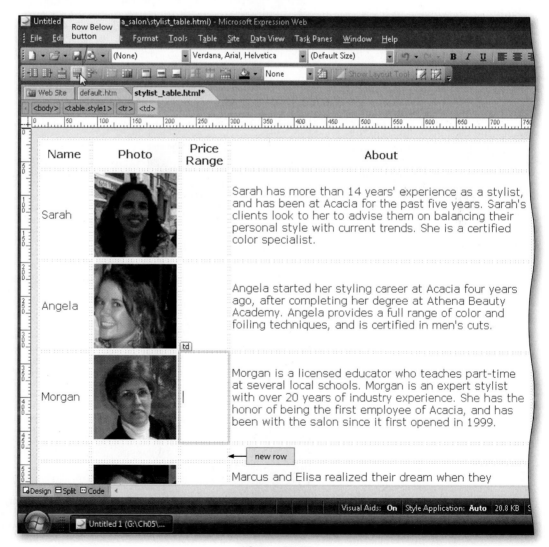

**Figure 5–47**

**5**

- Click the first cell in the new row to position the insertion point.

- Type `Christoph`, then press TAB to move to the next cell.

- Point to Picture on the Insert menu, then click From File to open the Picture dialog box.

- Click the christoph.jpg image to select it.

- Click the Insert button to open the Accessibility Properties dialog box.

- Type `Christoph's photo`, then click the OK button to close the Accessibility Properties dialog box and insert the image.

- Right-click the image to open the shortcut menu, then click Picture Properties to open the Picture Properties dialog box.

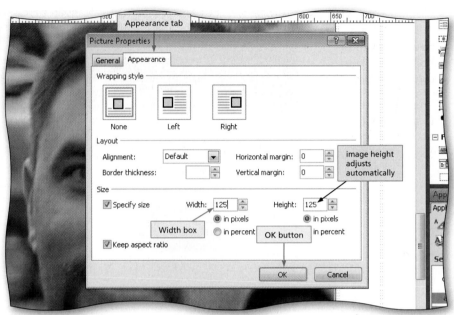

**Figure 5–48**

- Click the Appearance tab, then type `125` in the Width box to change the height and width to 125 pixels (Figure 5–48).

 **6**

- Click the OK button to close the dialog box and insert the image.

- Click the Picture Actions button to display the menu.

- Click the Resample Picture To Match Size option button to resample the image (Figure 5–49).

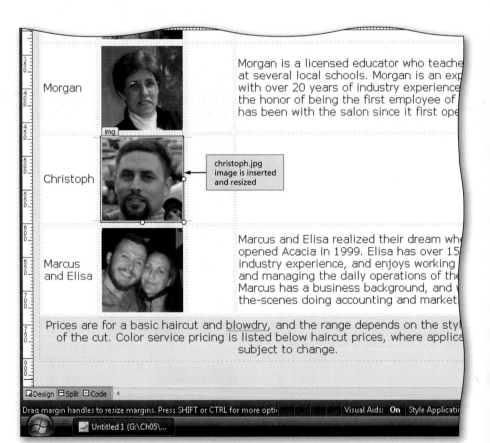

**Figure 5–49**

**7**

- If necessary, press the right arrow key to deselect the image but keep the insertion point in the cell.

- Press TAB twice to position the insertion point in the About column.

- Type Christoph is Acacia's newest stylist. He spent the first ten years of his career in Boston, and recently relocated to Delman to raise his family. Christoph's prior experience includes training in special event styles, including wedding parties and proms. to complete the new row content (Figure 5–50).

- Save the stylist_table.html page and embedded files, and close the default.html page.

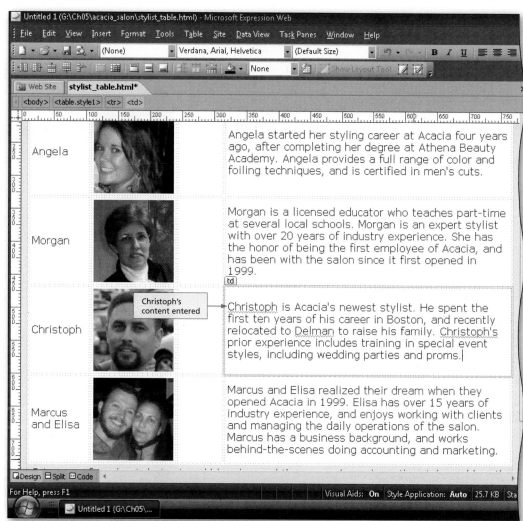

**Figure 5–50**

**Other Ways**

1. Point to Insert on the Table menu, then click an option to add or delete rows or columns.

## Table Fill

Using the **Table Fill** command, you can complete a column or row of data with the same data content to save time when entering table data. Table Fill is a useful feature when most or all of the data in a row or column is the same. For example, at the salon, many of the stylists have the same rates for services. For the cells with content that differs from the filled data, select the cells and replace the data with the correct data.

## To Use Table Fill

The following steps use Table Fill to fill the price range column. You will then edit two entries in the column.

- Click the third cell in the Sarah row to position the insertion point in the new Price Range column.

- Type $35–$45 to enter the data that will be used to fill the column (Figure 5–51).

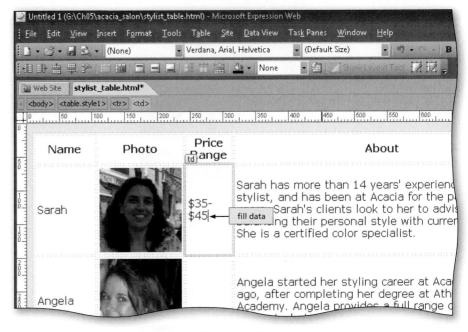

**Figure 5–51**

- Select the cell in the Sarah row in which you entered a price range and drag down to select the rows below it to specify the fill value and range (Figure 5–52).

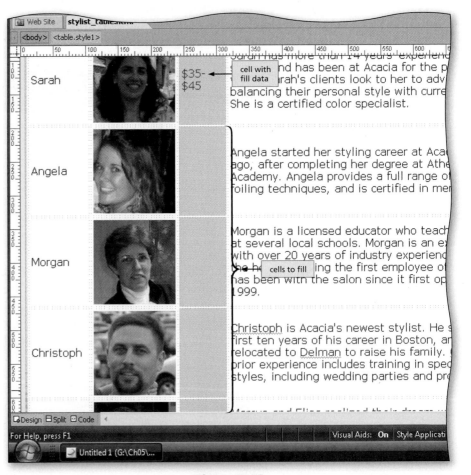

**Figure 5–52**

**3**

- Point to Fill on the Table menu (Figure 5–53).

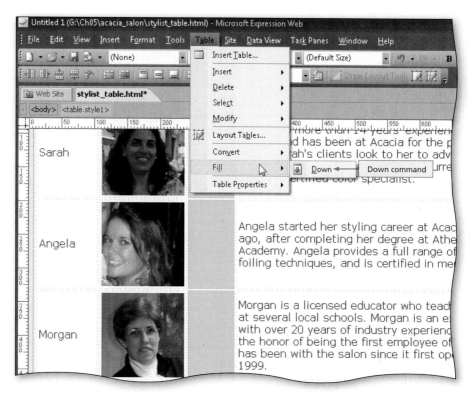

**Figure 5–53**

**4**

- Click Down to fill the value in the column (Figure 5–54).

 **Experiment**

- Add a new row, type text into the first cell, then select the row. Point to Fill on the Table menu, then click Right to practice filling a row. Delete the row.

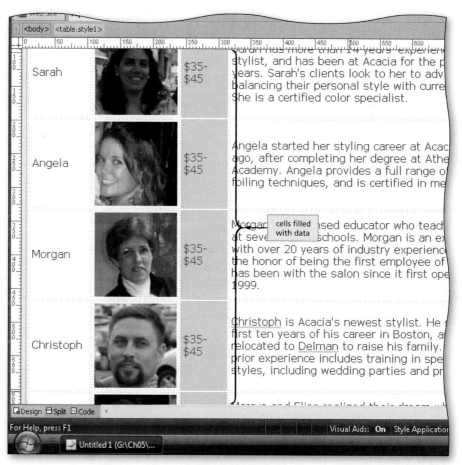

**Figure 5–54**

**5**

- Click in the cell containing Morgan's price range.

- Type $40–$50.

- Click in the cell containing Marcus and Elisa's price range.

- Type $45–$55 (Figure 5–55).

- Save the stylist_table.html page and all embedded files.

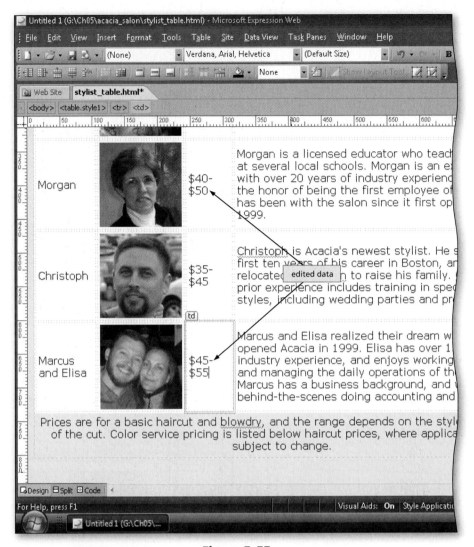

**Figure 5–55**

**BTW**

**Splitting and Merging Cells**

When you merge cells that contain data, the data from both cells is combined in the merged cell. When you split a cell that contains data, the data appears in the left or top cell, depending on whether you split into rows or columns.

# Merging and Splitting Cells

Combining two or more adjacent cells is called **merging**. **Splitting** a cell creates two or more rows or columns within a cell. Merging and splitting cells is done to combine or separate content in order to clarify table data.

Merging a row at the top of the table is often done to create a **title row** for the table; the title row has the same properties as the rest of the table. A title row differs from a caption. A caption is a description of the table contents or purpose, whereas a title row is used to name the rows in the table.

## To Merge Table Cells

The following steps add a new row for the table title, then merge the cells in the new row.

**1**
- Click anywhere in the table header row to position the insertion point.

- Click the Row Above button on the Tables toolbar to insert a new row (Figure 5–56).

**Figure 5–56**

**2**
- Position the insertion point to the left of the new row to change the pointer to the row selector.

- Click to select the top row of the table.

- Click the Merge Cells button on the Tables toolbar to merge all the cells into one (Figure 5–57).

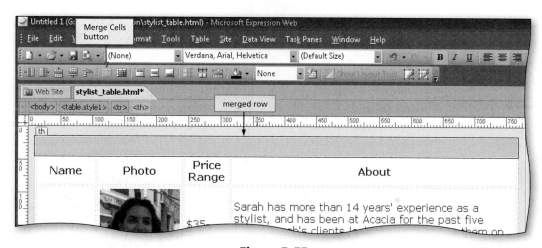

**Figure 5–57**

**3**
- Click in the merged cell to position the insertion point.

- Type Meet the Acacia Staff to enter the table title (Figure 5–58).

- Save the page.

**Q&A**

Why is the text centered in the cell?

Because the merged cells were inserted above the table header row, they are formatted as a header; in this case, with centered text.

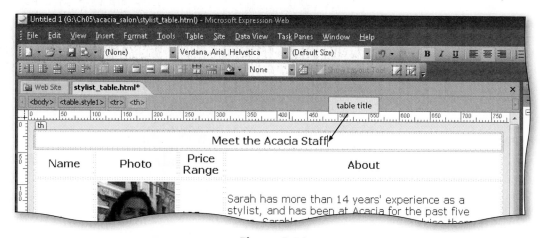

**Figure 5–58**

## To Split Table Cells

As noted in the text you typed in the table caption, some stylists have a separate price range for their haircut and coloring services. The following steps split the price range cells for Sarah and Angela into rows and enter price ranges for coloring services.

- Click in the Price Range cell in Sarah's column to position the insertion point.

- Click the Split Cells button on the Tables toolbar to open the Split Cells dialog box.

- Click the Split into rows option button to select it (Figure 5–59).

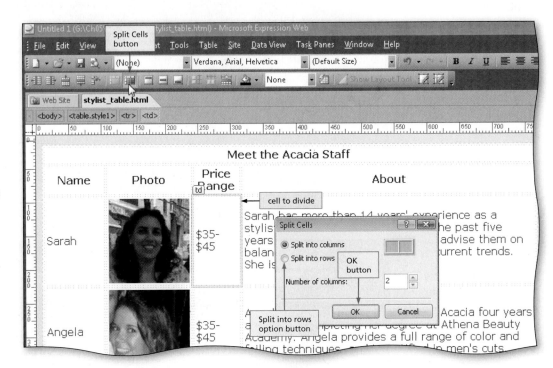

**Figure 5–59**

**2**

- Click the OK button to split the cells (Figure 5–60).

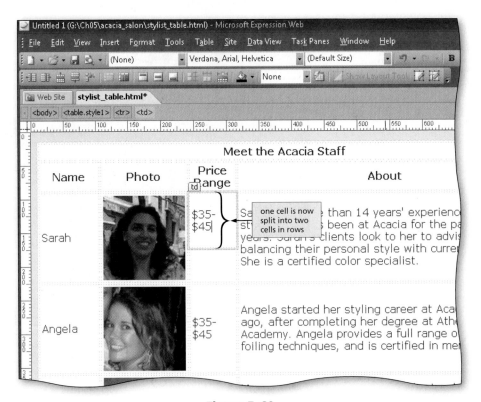

**Figure 5–60**

**3**

- Click the second row of the split cell to position the insertion point.

- Type $60-$90 to enter the cell content (Figure 5–61).

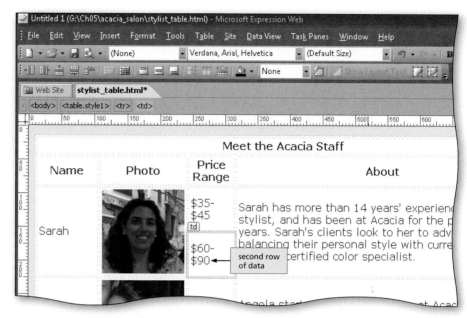

**Figure 5–61**

**4**

- Repeat Steps 1 to 3 to split Angela's price range cell into two rows and enter $60-$90 as the content for the second row of the split cell (Figure 5–62).

- Save the page.

**Experiment**

- Select any cell in the table, then click the Split Cells button. Click the Split into columns option button, type 3 in the Number of columns box, then click the OK button to close the dialog box and see the cell split into three columns. Press CTRL+Z to undo the split.

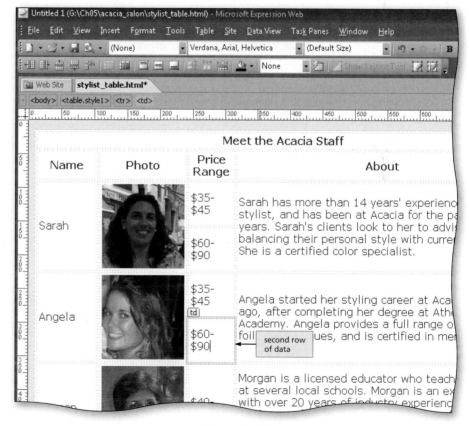

**Figure 5–62**

**Other Ways**

1. Point to Modify on the Table menu, then click an option to merge or split cells.

# Formatting Table Text

CSS text styles, such as headings, can be used to format table text so that it uses the styles defined in the attached style sheet. Using an AutoFormat allows you to apply several formatting choices at once, including font color and contrasting background colors for rows and columns (called **striping**).

| Plan Ahead | **Design the table.**<br>Determine the style of the table and how much emphasis it should have on the page: a strong emphasis, as in a different background color or with bold font color choices, or more subtle, to blend in with the existing page content. Using styles to format the table ensures consistency and enables you to update your table as changes are made to styles that affect the rest of the page or pages in your site. When choosing an AutoFormat, make sure that the look of the table matches your design plan. |
| --- | --- |

## To Apply Styles to Table Text

The following steps assign text styles to distinguish the row and column headers. The headings take on the styles defined in the associated style sheet.

- Click anywhere in the merged cell at the top of the table to position the insertion point.

- Click the <th> tag on the Quick Tag Selector to select the div.

- Click the Style box arrow on the Common toolbar, then point to Heading 1 <h1> (Figure 5–63).

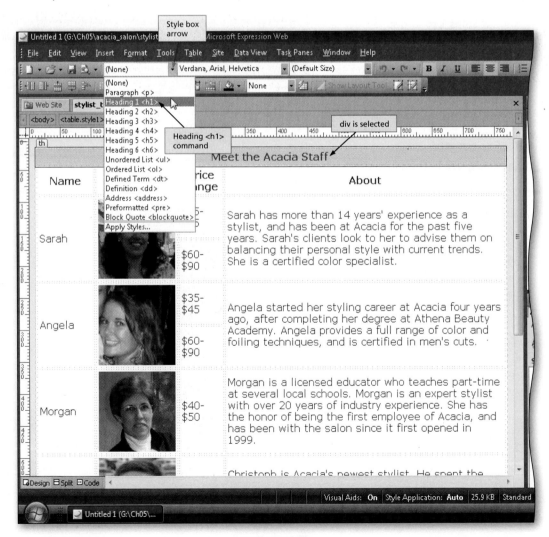

**Figure 5–63**

**2**

- Click Heading 1 <h1> to apply the h1 style to the title row.

- Position the insertion point to the left of the header row to change the pointer to the row selector.

- Click to select the header row.

- Click the Style box arrow on the Common toolbar, then point to Heading 3 <h3> (Figure 5–64).

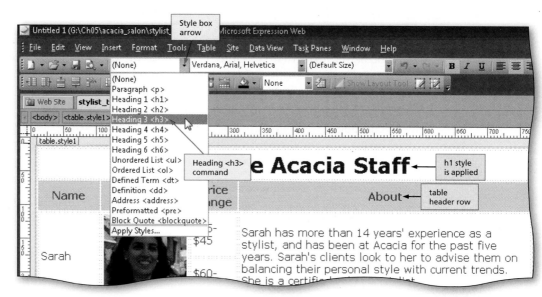

**Figure 5–64**

**3**

- Click Heading 3 <h3> to apply the h3 style to the header row.

- Select the five cells containing the stylists' names.

- Click the Style box arrow on the Common toolbar, then click Heading 3 <h3> to apply the h3 style to the selected cells (Figure 5–65).

- Save and close the stylist_table. html page.

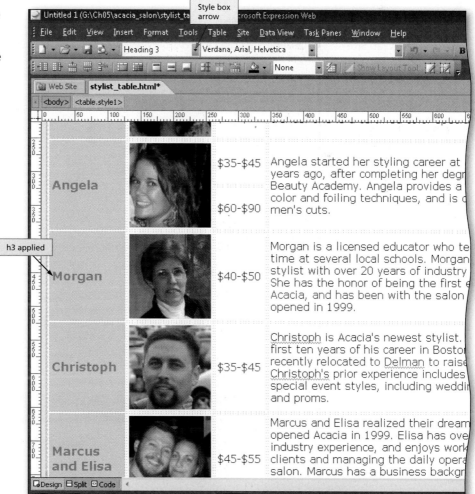

**Figure 5–65**

# Converting Text to a Table

You may encounter a situation when you realize that text you entered on a page would be better formatted as a table. When entering large amounts of text in a document, you should consider this before you start typing, but for small amounts of text it is fine to convert text to a table after it is typed. In order to convert text into a table, it needs to be properly **delineated**, or separated into groupings using commas, spaces, or tabs. When entering text, do not attempt to align it by adding extra spaces or tabs. Doing so will create cells for each extra delineation, causing your table to be misaligned.

**Plan Ahead**

**Organize existing content into the table.**
Converting text to a table allows text to be aligned in columns and rows and formatted consistently. Text in tables appears in rows and columns, and you can add headers to describe the table data.

## To Convert Text to a Table

The following steps open the default.html text, enter text in a new div, and convert it to a table.

**1**

- Double-click default.html in the Web Site tab to open the page.

- Click below the line with the words, Since 1999, to position the insertion point.

- Double-click the Paragraph div in the Toolbox to insert a new paragraph.

- Type Monday, Tuesday, Wednesday, then press TAB to insert space as the column delineator.

- Type 10 AM to 6 PM, then press ENTER to complete the first line of the table text (Figure 5–66).

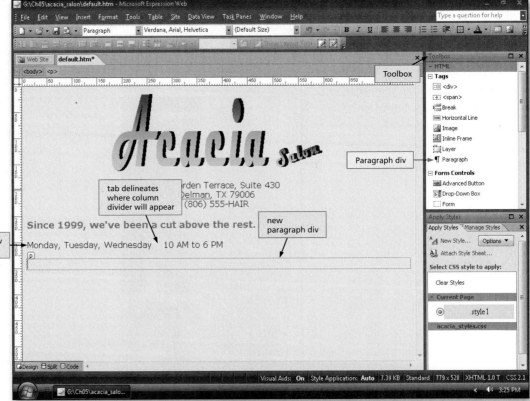

**Figure 5–66**

**2**

- Type `Thursday & Friday`, then press TAB to insert space.

- Type `10 AM to 8 PM`, then press ENTER to complete the second line of the table text.

- Type `Saturday`, then press TAB to insert space.

- Type `10 AM to 7 PM`, then press ENTER to complete the third line of the table text.

- Type `Sunday`, then press TAB to insert space.

- Type `Closed`, then press ENTER to complete the table text (Figure 5–67).

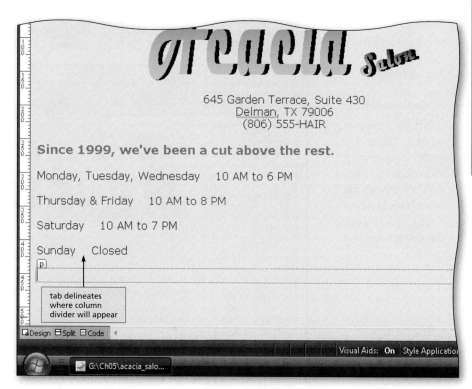

**Figure 5–67**

**3**

- Select the four lines of text.

- Point to Convert on the Table menu, then click Text to Table to open the Convert Text to Table dialog box.

- Click the Tabs option button to select it (Figure 5–68).

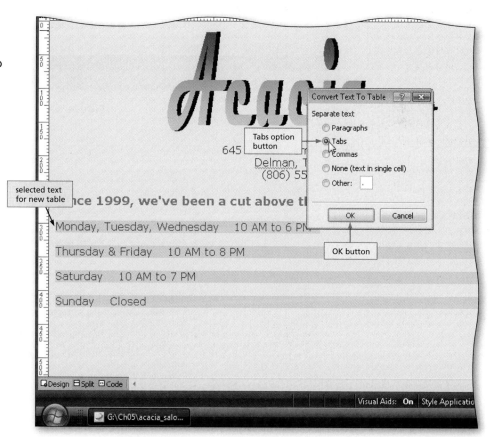

**Figure 5–68**

**4**

- Click the OK button to create a table from the text (Figure 5–69).

🔍 **Experiment**

- Select the new table, point to Convert on the Table menu, then click Table to Text to convert the table back to text. Press CTRL+Z to undo the conversion.

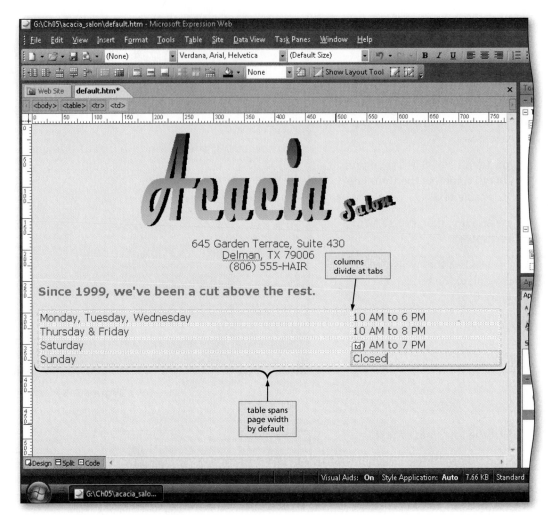

**Figure 5–69**

## To Distribute Rows and Columns

The following steps deselect the Specify width table property; doing so automatically **distributes** the columns, or resizes the width of each column to fit to the width of its content. You will then center the table on the page.

**1**

• Right-click the table to open the shortcut menu, then click Table Properties to open the Table Properties dialog box.

• Click the Specify width check box to deselect it (Figure 5–70).

**Figure 5–70**

**2**

• Click the OK button to close the Table Properties dialog box and resize the column width (Figure 5–71).

 **Experiment**

• Position the pointer between two columns until the pointer turns into a two-sided arrow, then drag left or right to manually adjust the column width. Press CTRL+Z to undo the change.

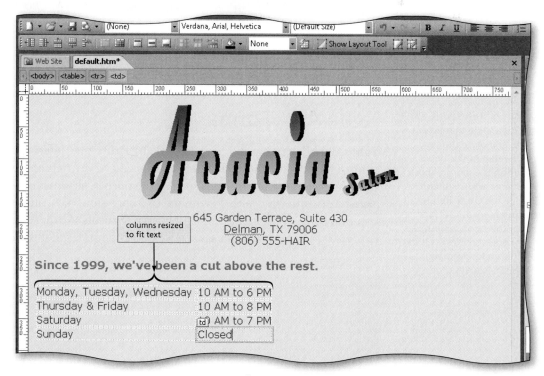

**Figure 5–71**

**3**

- Click the <table> tag on the Quick Tag Selector bar to select the table.

- Click the Center button on the Common toolbar to center the table (Figure 5–72).

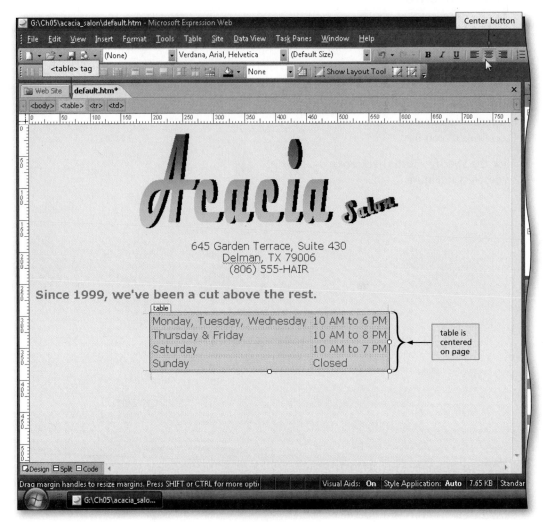

**Figure 5–72**

# Table AutoFormat

**Table AutoFormat** is an Expression Web feature that offers predetermined formatting options for tables. AutoFormat lets you specify rows or columns to differentiate as headers and whether to modify features such as the border, shading, or font. AutoFormat is a Web page formatting feature that is unique to Expression Web, although you may have used it in other Microsoft applications, such as Microsoft Word. As an AutoFormat is applied, Expression Web creates and saves styles as inline styles, not to a style sheet.

## To Use Table AutoFormat

To add visual appeal, Marcus and Elisa want to add formatting to the table on the default.html page. The following steps apply an AutoFormat to the new table. Your table does not have header or column row text, so you will not have special formatting applied to the first row or column in the table.

- Click the Table AutoFormat button on the Tables toolbar to open the Table AutoFormat dialog box (Figure 5–73).

**Experiment**

- Click options in the Formats list to view them in the Preview window.

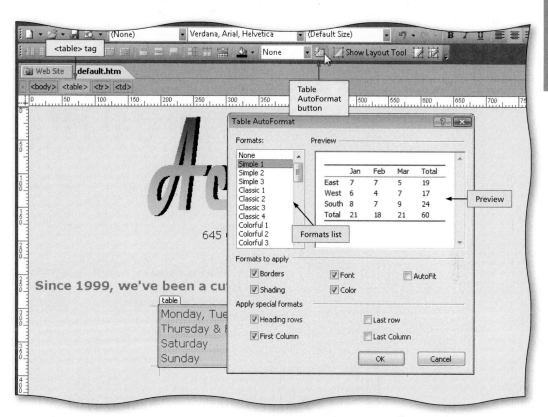

**Figure 5–73**

2

- Click the Heading rows check box to deselect it.

- Click the First Column check box to deselect it.

- Scroll down the Formats list, then click the List 1 option to select it (Figure 5–74).

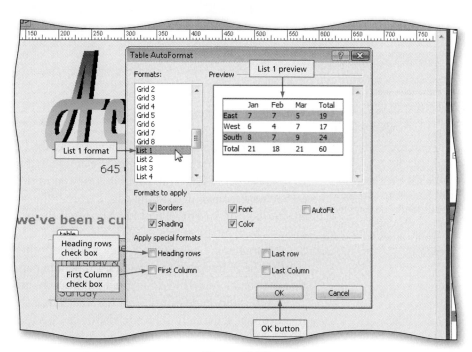

**Figure 5–74**

**3**

- Click the OK button to close the Table AutoFormat dialog box and apply the formatting to the table.

- Click outside of the table to deselect it (Figure 5–75).

- Save the page.

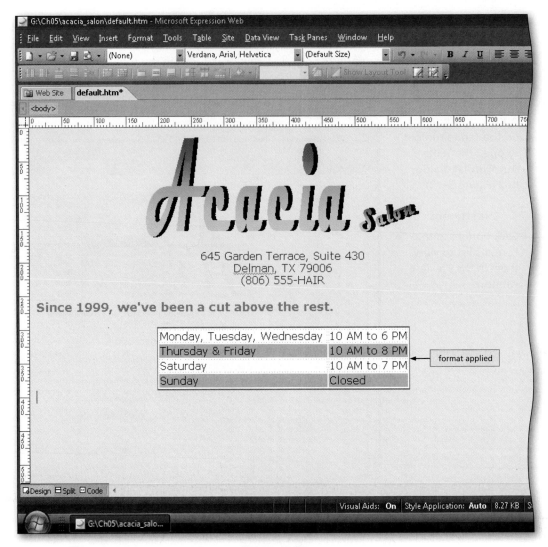

**Figure 5–75**

**BTW**

**I-frame Security**
I-frames have been used by hackers to implant malicious code onto legitimate Web sites, causing security issues for the site visitors.

# About Inline Frames

An inline frame, or an I-frame, is a way to embed one HTML file into another. Specifying the size of the frame that contains the embedded HTML page helps control the page size of the original HTML file when it is viewed in the browser. Recall that every element on a Web page contributes to the page's overall file size. Scroll bars make it possible to view the content of the embedded HTML file if the frame in which it is embedded is not large enough to view the entire HTML file.

I-frames are helpful to display a table or other pages with large amounts of data that may not be of interest to all visitors. Embedding an advertisement, or including information that may be in a sidebar of a printed publication, are other uses for I-frames.

One advantage of using an I-frame is that the main page and the embedded file load in a browser separately. The site visitor can perform various actions within the embedded file without affecting the main page. For instance, clicking an item on a navigation bar can cause a new embedded HTML page to load without the browser having to reload the original page.

**Plan
Ahead**

**Add an I-frame to display a page.**
An important consideration when adding an I-frame to a Web page is the display size of the main HTML page. Adding a frame for a table allows the visitor to see all or most of the page content without scrolling; for a table that provides additional reference information but is not the main focus of the page, having a small, scrollable window allows the visitor to peruse the information in the table if they wish, while keeping their browser window on the original page. Changes to the table do not affect the main page, and vice versa.

## To Create an I-Frame

The following steps insert and resize the I-frame that will contain the stylist table.

**1**

- Click below the table, then press ENTER to position the insertion point where you want the I-frame to appear (Figure 5–76).

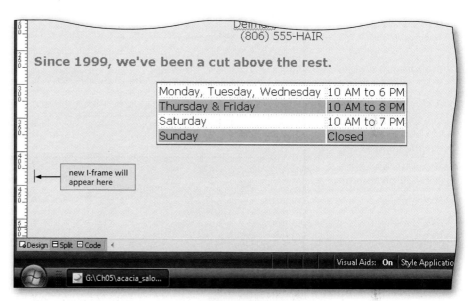

**Figure 5–76**

**2**

- Double-click Paragraph in the Toolbox to insert a new paragraph div.

- Point to HTML on the Insert menu, then click Inline Frame to insert a new I-frame (Figure 5–77).

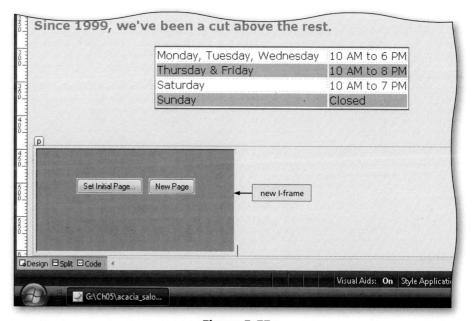

**Figure 5–77**

**3**

● Click the right edge of the frame, then drag to the right until the ScreenTip reads, width: 700px (Figure 5–78).

I cannot see the ScreenTip while resizing.

Unlike when resizing an image, the ScreenTip does not show when resizing an I-frame. Use Figure 5–78 as a guideline when dragging the edge, then position the insertion point over the edge to view the ScreenTip. Make your I-frame as close to 700 pixels wide and 325 pixels high as you can.

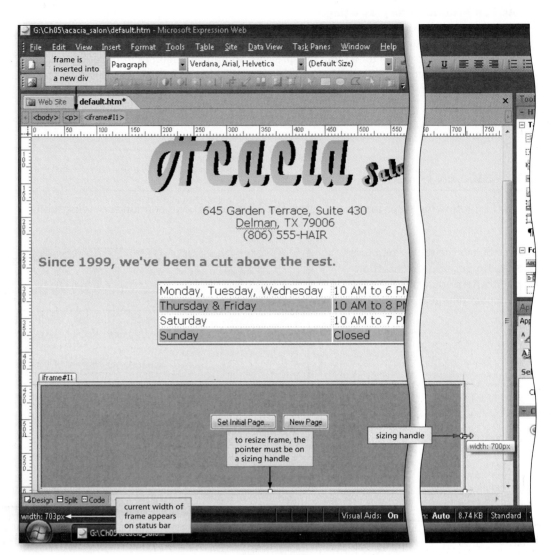

**Figure 5–78**

**4**

- Click the Center button on the Common toolbar to center the frame between the page margins.

- Click the bottom edge of the frame, then drag down until the ScreenTip reads, height: 325px (Figure 5–79).

- Save the page.

**Q&A** | I cannot drag the frame down far enough to resize the height.

Drag the vertical scroll box down to the bottom of the page to make it visible in order to resize the frame height.

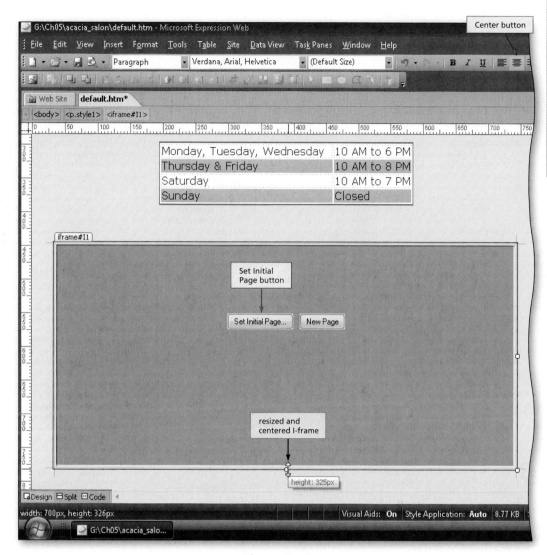

Figure 5–79

**Other Ways**

1. Double-click the Inline Frame button in the Toolbox to insert an I-frame.

## To Target Links in an I-Frame

The following steps embed the stylist_table.html file into the I-frame.

• Click the Set Initial Page button in the Frame to open the Insert Hyperlink dialog box (Figure 5–80).

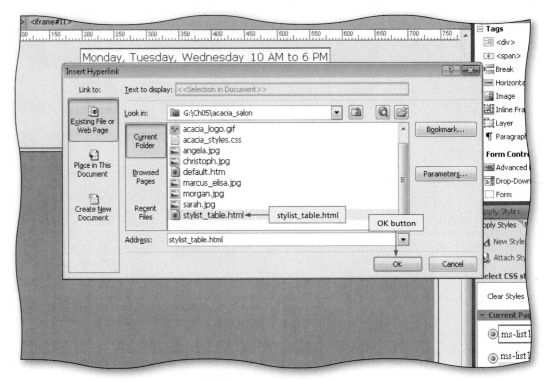

**Figure 5–80**

**2**

• Click stylist_table.html to select it as the frame link.

• Click the OK button to close the Insert Hyperlink dialog box and insert a link to the table (Figure 5–81).

• Save the page.

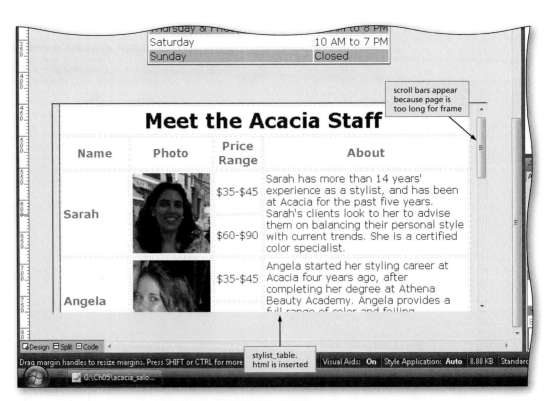

**Figure 5–81**

**3**

- Click the Preview in Browser button arrow on the Common toolbar, then click Windows Internet Explorer 7.0 (1024 × 768) to open the page in the browser (Figure 5–82).

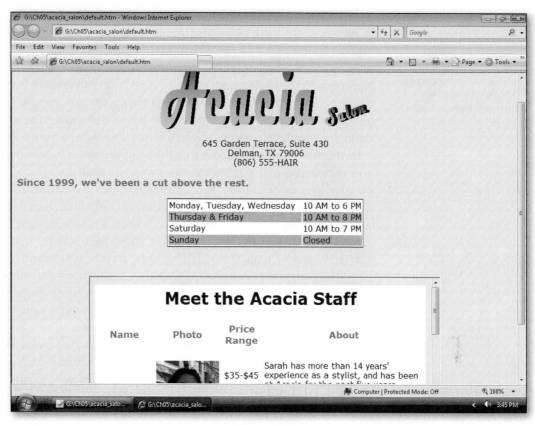

**Figure 5–82**

**4**

- Scroll through the embedded page to view the table contents (Figure 5–83).

- Click the Close button on the browser title bar to close the browser window.

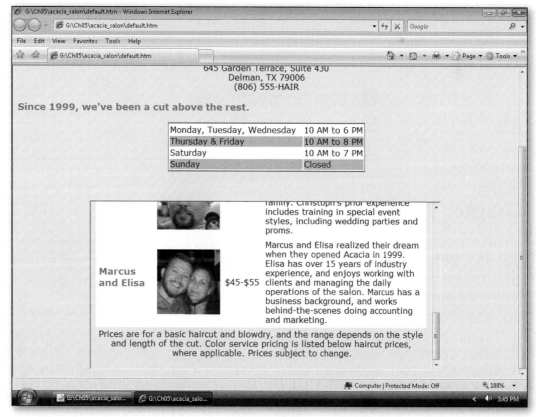

**Figure 5–83**

**BTW**

**Expression Web Help**
The best way to become familiar with Expression Web Help is to use it. Appendix B includes detailed information about Expression Web Help and exercises that will help you gain confidence in using it.

# Using Frames and Tables to Lay Out a Web Page

Framesets and HTML tables are two methods that have historically been used to lay out Web pages. A **frameset** is a single Web page constructed from multiple HTML files (the "frames"), while an HTML **layout table** controls the positioning of elements within a page by the table properties. With the development of CSS and other style sheet languages that position page elements using styles, however, frames and tables are now considered outdated, non-standards-compliant techniques. Layout frames and layout tables can cause issues with browsers, bookmarks, search engines, and printing. You may encounter existing Web pages designed using layout frames or tables, which is why these approaches are mentioned here.

Framesets define page areas by including each area (footer, content, navigation, and so on) as a separate HTML file. Frames allow certain page elements, such as the masthead and navigation area, to remain consistent and only load once in the browser, while the main page content changes from page to page. Frames also can be used to separate page content to make a page easier to update; if you only wanted to change the navigation bar, you would simply replace that HTML file, and the rest of the page would be unchanged.

To create a frames page in Expression Web, choose one of the Frames Pages options in the New dialog box. For each frame, click the Set Initial Page button, then select the page to display within that frame. You can customize the frames page by resizing, splitting, and deleting frames, or changing the page which displays.

Layout tables are another method that can be used to layout Web pages. Unlike framesets, which treat each page element as a separate file, tables include each page component within a row, column, or cell. Layout tables must be copied from page to page to maintain consistency of common elements such as navigation, which makes updating these items problematic.

To create a page using a layout table in Expression Web, click Layout Tables from the Table menu to display the Layout Tables task pane. Click an option in the Table layout section of the task pane to get started, then add, delete, resize, split, and merge cells to create the page layout you want, then enter the page content.

## To Close a Site and Quit Expression Web

**1** On the File menu, click Close Site.

**2** On the File menu, click Exit.

# Chapter Summary

In this chapter, you have learned to create and modify a new style sheet using a preformatted style sheet provided by Expression Web. You created a data table, entered text and added images, defined cell and table properties, added styles, and split and merged cells. You created a table from delineated text, then applied an AutoFormat. Lastly, you created an I-frame, resized it, and added a link to an HTML page.

The items listed below include all the new Expression Web skills you have learned in this chapter.

1. Create a New Web Site and Web Page (EW 305)
2. Create a New Style Sheet (EW 310)
3. Create a New Page and Attach a Style Sheet (EW 314)
4. Insert a Data Table (EW 316)
5. Change Table and Cell Properties (EW 320)
6. Add Text to a Table (EW 323)
7. Add Images to a Table (EW 327)
8. Add Rows and Columns (EW 330)
9. Use Table Fill (EW 334)
10. Merge Table Cells (EW 337)
11. Split Table Cells (EW 338)

12. Apply Styles to Table Text (EW 340)
13. Convert Text to a Table (EW 342)
14. Distribute Rows and Columns (EW 345)

15. Use Table AutoFormat (EW 347)
16. Create an I-Frame (EW 349)
17. Target Links in an I-Frame (EW 352)

 If you have a SAM user profile, you may have access to hands-on instruction, practice, and assessment. Log in to your SAM account (http://sam2007.course.com) to launch any assigned training activities or exams that relate to the skills covered in this chapter.

## Learn It Online

Test your knowledge of chapter content and key terms.

*Instructions:* To complete the Learn It Online exercises, start your browser, click the Address bar, and then enter the Web address scsite.com/ew2/learn. When the Expression Web Learn It Online page is displayed, click the link for the exercise you want to complete and then read the instructions.

**Chapter Reinforcement TF, MC, and SA**
A series of true/false, multiple choice, and short answer questions that test your knowledge of the chapter content.

**Flash Cards**
An interactive learning environment where you identify chapter key terms associated with displayed definitions.

**Practice Test**
A series of multiple choice questions that test your knowledge of chapter content and key terms.

**Who Wants To Be a Computer Genius?**
An interactive game that challenges your knowledge of chapter content in the style of a television quiz show.

**Wheel of Terms**
An interactive game that challenges your knowledge of chapter key terms in the style of the television show *Wheel of Fortune*.

**Crossword Puzzle Challenge**
A crossword puzzle that challenges your knowledge of key terms presented in the chapter.

## Apply Your Knowledge

Reinforce the skills and apply the concepts you learned in this chapter.

**Creating a Data Table**
*Instructions:* Start Expression Web. You will create a new Web site, add a new page, and create and attach a new style sheet to each page. You will create a data table and enter data and change the properties, then insert a new page into an I-frame so that the page looks like Figure 5–84.

*Continued >*

**Apply Your Knowledge** *continued*

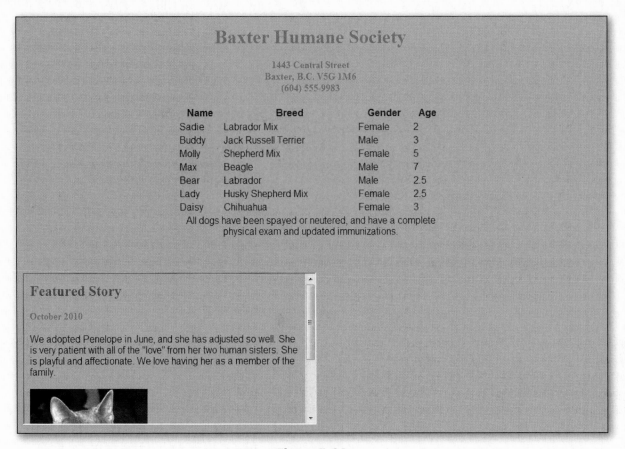

**Figure 5–84**

*Perform the following tasks:*

1. Point to New on the File menu, click Web Site, then click One Page Web Site.

2. Navigate to the drive and folder where you save your Data Files, type `baxter_humane` in the Specify the location of the new Web site text box, then click the OK button.

3. Point to New on the File menu, then click Page. Click Style Sheets, then click the Bars style sheet type and click the OK button.

4. Save the new style sheet as baxter_styles.css.

5. Open the default.html page, then attach the baxter_styles.css.

6. Insert a paragraph div for the page header, type `Baxter Humane Society`, then format the div with the header style h1 and centered.

7. Insert a new paragraph div below the header, select the h4 heading style and center the div, then type the following, pressing SHIFT+ENTER at the end of each line.

   ```
   1443 Central Street
   Baxter, B.C. V5G 1M6
   (604) 555-9983
   ```

8. Insert a new table with four columns and seven rows. Type the following data into the table.

| Name | Breed | Gender | Age |
|------|-------|--------|-----|
| Sadie | Labrador Mix | Female | 2 |
| Buddy | Jack Russell Terrier | Male | 3 |
| Molly | Shepherd Mix | Female | 5 |
| Max | Beagle | Male | 7 |
| Lady | Husky Shepherd Mix | Female | 2.5 |
| Daisy | Chihuahua | Female | 3 |

9. Right-click the table, then click Table Properties to open the Table Properties dialog box.

10. Type 450 in the Specify width box, click the In Pixels option button if necessary, center-align the table, apply a silver table background, then click the OK button to close the dialog box.

11. Select the top table row, right-click the row, then click Cell Properties to open the Cell Properties dialog box.

12. Click the Header cell check box, then click the OK button to close the dialog box.

13. Insert a new row above the row with Lady's data.

14. Type the following in the new row:

| Bear | Labrador | Male | 2.5 |
|------|----------|------|-----|

15. Right-click the table, point to Insert, then click Caption. Right-click the caption, then click Caption Properties to open the Caption Properties dialog box.

16. Click the Bottom of table option button, then click the OK button. Type the caption, All dogs have been spayed or neutered, and have a complete physical exam and updated immunizations.

17. Press CTRL+N to create a new blank page, then save it as october_feature.html.

18. Attach the baxter_styles.css style sheet to the new page.

19. Insert a paragraph div for the page header, type Featured Story, then format the div with h2.

20. Insert a paragraph div for the page header, type October 2010, then format the div with h4.

21. Type the following in a new paragraph div: We adopted Penelope in June, and she has adjusted so well. She is very patient with all of the "love" from her two human sisters. She is playful and affectionate. We love having her as a member of the family.

22. Click the Insert Picture from File button, navigate to the Data Files for Students, double-click the humane_documents folder to open it, click the penelope.jpg image, then click the Insert button to open the Accessibility Properties dialog box.

23. Type Gray cat in the Alternate text text box, then click the OK button.

24. Double-click the image to open the Picture Properties dialog box, type 200 in the Width text box, then click the OK button.

25. Click the Picture Actions button, then click the Resample Picture To Match Size option button.

26. Save the page and the embedded image, then close the page.

27. Double-click the Inline Frame button on the Toolbox to insert a new I-frame.

28. Select the I-frame, then drag the top and bottom to resize the frame to 500 pixels wide and 250 pixels high.

29. Click the Set Initial Page button, click the october_feature.html file, then click the Insert button.

*Continued >*

**Apply Your Knowledge** *continued*

30. Save the default.html page.

31. Preview the site and test the thumbnails and links.

32. Change the site properties, as specified by your instructor. Submit the revised site in the format specified by your instructor.

33. Save all pages, then close the site.

## Extend Your Knowledge

Extend the skills you learned in this chapter and experiment with new skills. You may need to use Help to complete the assignment.

### Converting Text to a Table

*Instructions:* Start Expression Web. You will open a Web site and insert a text file with delineated data, then convert the data to a table. Change the table properties to add a background image, and manually adjust the column width. You will add a new I-frame to make the default.html page match the one shown in Figure 5–85.

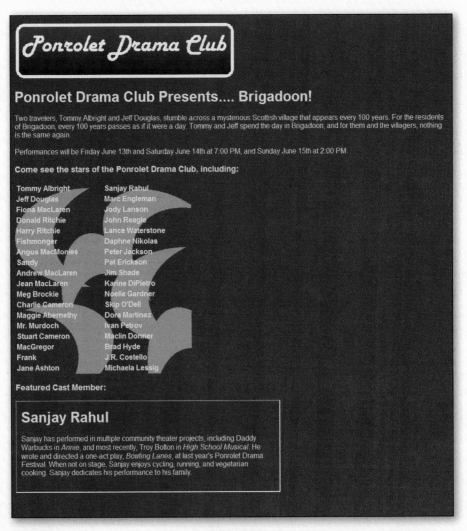

**Figure 5–85**

*Perform the following tasks:*

1. Click File on the menu bar, then click Open.

2. Navigate to the flash drive where you save your data files, click the Extend 5-1 Drama folder to select it, then click the Open button.

3. Open the default.html page, then position the insertion point in the paragraph div below the line, Come see the stars...

4. Open Microsoft Word and open the file brigadoon_cast.doc from the drama_documents folder from the Data Files for Students.

5. Select the text, copy it to the Clipboard, then quit Microsoft Word.

6. Click Paste Text on the Edit menu, click the Normal paragraphs with line breaks option, then click the OK button.

7. Select the pasted text.

8. Point to Convert on the Table menu, then click Text to Table.

9. Click the Commas option button, then click the OK button.

10. Open the Table Properties dialog box, then specify that the table width is 400 pixels.

11. Add a background image, using the file background_image.gif from the drama_documents folder, then close the Table Properties dialog box.

12. Drag the divider between the two columns until the first column is 260 pixels wide.

13. Select the table, then click the Bold button.

14. Select the right column, then click the AutoFit to Contents button on the Table toolbar.

15. Click in the last cell in the table, then press TAB to insert a new row.

16. Type Jane Ashton, press TAB, then type Michaela Lessig.

17. Insert a new parargraph div below the table, type Featured Cast Member:, then format the paragraph as h3.

18. Press ENTER, then insert a new I-frame. Resize the frame to 600 pixels wide and 200 pixels high.

19. Insert the sanjay_feature.html page from the Web Site folder.

20. Save the default.html page. Preview the page, then close the browser window.

21. Change the site properties as specified by your instructor. Save the presentation using the file name, Extend 5-1 Drama Site. Submit the revised site in the format specified by your instructor.

## Make It Right

Analyze a site and correct all errors and/or improve the design.

### Creating and fixing a data table

*Instructions:* Start Expression Web. Open the Web site, Make It Right 5-1 Fitness, from the Data Files for Students. See the inside back cover of this book for instructions for downloading the Data Files for Students, or see your instructor for information about accessing the required files.

Create a new data table on the default.html page by converting the lines of delineated text into a table and fixing the error that occurs. Add a new row in the middle of the table, define the header row, add a caption, and apply a Table AutoFormat to create the home page shown in Figure 5–86.

*Continued >*

**STUDENT ASSIGNMENTS**

**Make It Right** *continued*

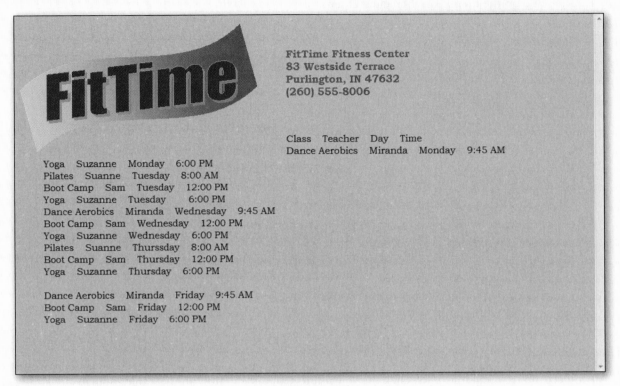

**Figure 5–86**

1. Open the default.html page.
2. Select the lines of delineated text (from Class to Friday 6:00 PM).
3. Convert the text to a table.
4. Fix the errors by moving the data in the extra column and deleting the extra column and row.
5. Add a new row between the second and third rows and enter the following data: Boot Camp, press TAB, Sam, press TAB, Monday, press TAB, 12:00 PM.
6. Define the top row as a table header.
7. Add a caption to the top of the table, and type All classes are 50 minutes long. Instructors can change without notice.
8. Apply the List 7 Table AutoFormat to the table.
9. Change the site properties as specified by your instructor. Save the site using the file name, Make It Right 5-1 Fitness Site. Submit the revised site in the format specified by your instructor.

# In the Lab

Design and/or format a Web site using the guidelines, concepts, and skills presented in this chapter. Labs are listed in order of increasing difficulty.

## Lab 1: Creating a New Table

*Problem:*   You are a photographer and want to update your home page by creating a list of prices for printed photos. You will insert a table, specify the table and cell properties, and enter table data to create the page shown in Figure 5–87.

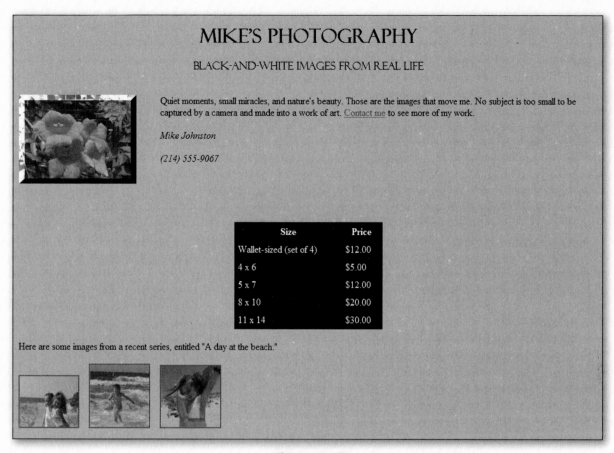

**Figure 5–87**

*Instructions:*

1. Start Expression Web.

2. Open the Web site, Lab 5-1 Photo, from the Data Files for Students, and open the default.html page.

3. Create a new table with two columns and five rows above the line, Here are some images...

4. Enter the following data into the table, pressing ENTER at the end of the last row in the table in order to create a new row for the rest of the data.

| Size | Price |
|---|---|
| Wallet-sized (set of 4) | $12.00 |
| 4 x 6 | $5.00 |
| 5 x 7 | $12.00 |
| 8 x 10 | $20.00 |
| 11 x 14 | $30.00 |

5. Define the top row as the header by setting the cell properties.

6. Specify the following table properties: black background, 250 pixels wide, and 4 pixels of cell padding.

7. Change the font color of the table text to white and center the table on the page.

8. Save the changes to the default.htm page, close the page, then preview the site in a browser.

9. Submit the site in the format specified by your instructor, then close the site.

# In the Lab

## Lab 2: Creating an I-Frame

*Problem:* You have volunteered to update the Web site for the Connecticut branch of the Gulliver College Alumni Society. You will create a new page with a table and insert it as an I-frame onto the default.html page, as shown in Figure 5–88.

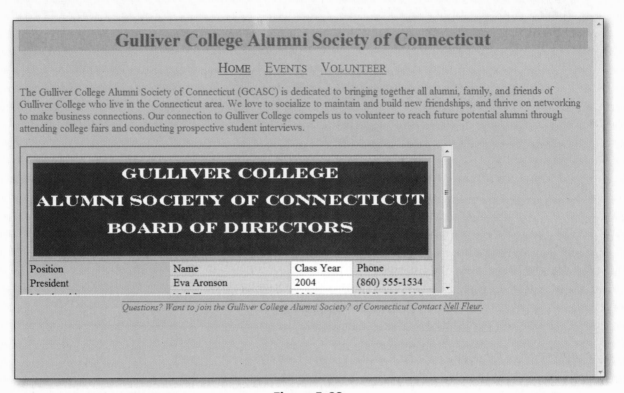

**Figure 5–88**

*Instructions:* Start Expression Web. Open the Web site, Lab 5-2 Alumni, from the Data Files for Students. See the inside back cover of this book for instructions for downloading the Data Files for Students, or see your instructor for information about accessing the required files.

*Perform the following tasks.*

1. Create a new, blank page. Save it as alumni_board.html and attach the alumni_styles.css style sheet.

2. Open Microsoft Word and open the board.doc file from the Lab 5-2 Documents folder. Copy and paste the contents of the Word document into Expression Web as normal paragraphs with line breaks. Quit Microsoft Word.

3. Convert the pasted text into a table.

4. Use the Table Properties dialog box to set the table at a fixed width of 700 pixels.

5. Create a new row above the table and merge the cells into one.

6. Insert the board_logo.gif file from the Lab 5-2 Documents folder into the merged cell.

7. Apply the Column 5 Table AutoFormat, keeping the Heading row and First Column check boxes selected.

8. Modify the .ms-column5-left style that is created from the AutoFormat using the Modify Styles dialog box to have normal font-weight instead of bold.

9. Save and close the alumni_board.html page, then open the default.html page.

10. Click after the words, student interviews., then press ENTER twice.

11. Insert a new I-frame using the Toolbox.

12. Drag to resize the I-frame so that it is 750 pixels wide and 250 pixels high.

13. Set the page to link to the alumni_board.html page.

14. Save the default.html page.

15. Preview the page in a browser and scroll through the table.

16. Rename the site Lab 5-2 Alumni Site, submit the site in the format specified by your instructor, then close the site.

## In the Lab

### Lab 3: Creating a New Web Page as an I-frame

*Problem:*   Your client, a tutor, wants to create a home page that he can use to attract clients. You create a one-page Web site and a new style sheet using a preformatted style sheet, and add another page in an I-frame to the home page shown in Figure 5–89.

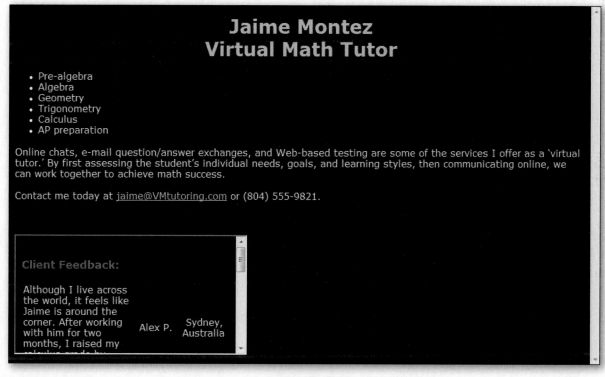

**Figure 5–89**

*Instructions:*

1. Start Expression Web.

2. Create a one-page Web site called Lab 5-3 Tutor Site, then open the default.html page.

3. Create a new style sheet based on the Highway style sheet, save it as tutor_styles.css, then attach it to the default.html page.

4. Insert a new blank div, then in the div, insert a paragraph.

*Continued >*

**In the Lab** *continued*

5. Type `Jaime Montez`, press SHIFT+ENTER, then type `Virtual Math Tutor`.

6. Format the paragraph div as h1, then center it.

7. Click below the paragraph, then insert a new paragraph div. Start a bulleted list.

8. Type the following as the bulleted list text, pressing ENTER after each line and ENTER twice at the end of the last line.

   - `Pre-algebra`
   - `Algebra`
   - `Geometry`
   - `Trigonometry`
   - `Calculus`
   - `AP preparation`

9. In the new paragraph div, type the following: `Online chats, e-mail question/answer exchanges, and Web-based testing are some of the services I offer as a 'virtual tutor.' By first assessing the student's individual needs, goals, and learning styles, then communicating online, we can work together to achieve math success.`

10. Press ENTER to start a new paragraph, then type `Contact me today at jaime@VMtutoring.com or (804) 555-9821.`

11. Click below the paragraph, then insert a new I-frame.

12. Resize the I-frame to 400 pixels wide and 200 pixels high.

13. Click the New Page button in the I-frame to create a new blank HTML page within the frame.

14. Right-click the I-frame, then click Open Page in New Window.

15. Attach the tutor_styles.css style sheet and save the new page as client_feedback.html.

16. Insert a new paragraph div, type `Client Feedback:`, then format the text as h3.

17. Create a new table with three columns and four rows, then type the following data into the table:

| | | |
|---|---|---|
| Although I live across the world, it feels like Jaime is around the corner. After working with him for two months, I raised my calculus grade by 10%! | Alex P. | Sydney, Australia |
| The extra online exams I took helped increase my confidence in test taking, and allowed me to see my progress. | Sarah J. | Ithaca, NY |
| Our weekly online chats gave me the personal, real-time instruction that I needed to fully understand the concepts being taught in my geometry class. | Wilhelm C. | Enid, OK |
| I recommend Jaime to all of my AP math students. He will work with them individually to offer extra one-on-one assistance as well as test-taking skills. | Bailey W. | Strayer, WI |

18. Save both files, then preview the site in a browser.

19. Change the site properties as specified by your instructor.

20. Submit the site in the format specified by your instructor, then close the site.

# Cases and Places

Apply your creative thinking and problem solving skills to design and implement a solution.

• EASIER   ••MORE DIFFICULT

## • 1: Creating a New Table

Create a new blank Web site that contains information about your favorite musician or musical group, and add a page using the CSS layout of your choice. Enter content in all of the divs. Create a new style sheet based on a preformatted style sheet and attach it to the page. Modify at least one of the styles, such as the page background or font family. Create a table listing the musician's albums and songs and format it using headings. Merge the top row of the table to create a table title. Enter a caption at the bottom of the table. Define and enter content for a header row. Delete a row from the middle of the table, and add a row at the end of the table by pressing TAB. Save and close all pages, then quit Expression Web.

## • 2: Creating an I-Frame

Create a new one-page Web site dedicated to your favorite professional athlete. Add a new blank HTML page to the site. Create a style sheet using a preformatted option, and attach it to both pages. Enter data into both pages, featuring career highlights on the default.html page. On the second page, include at least one table of statistics to which you add an image, apply an AutoFormat, and merge and split cells. Create an I-frame on the home page for the second page. Resize the frame so that when the home page is previewed in the browser, the entire home page is visible.

## •• 3: Troubleshooting Tables

Create a new blank HTML page for your current class schedule. Enter information that you will convert to a table and delineate the data using commas or tabs. In at least one row, add an extra delineator, and add a blank line in the middle of the table. Convert the text to a table, then move data, and delete rows and columns. Select the table, then convert it back to text. Select the data and convert it back to a table and fix any table errors. Change the table properties and formatting of the table. Save the page, then close it.

## •• 4: Creating a Research Home Page

**Make It Personal**

You want to create a one-page site that includes information from a paper or research project you have done for another class. Create a new one-page site and a style sheet from a preformatted style sheet and attach the style sheet. Enter information on the default.html page, including a table with a caption and header row. Create an I-frame and a page to link to it that includes information relevant to the topic. Save the pages and style sheets, then close the site.

## •• 5: Creating a Web Page with an I-Frame

**Working Together**

A video store wants to display a list of new releases in an I-frame on its home page. Working as a team with several of your classmates, you are to plan and create the home page and table page. Each team member should contribute to supplying titles, ratings, descriptions, or other information for the list. As a group, decide on the information you need for the table, including the number of columns of information and the number of rows you need to list all of the titles you have come up with. Create a site folder with a blank page and attach a style sheet that you create using a preformatted style sheet. Make at least one modification to the styles in the style sheet. Enter information on the page, such as a

*Continued >*

**Cases and Places** *continued*

logo or masthead, address, and other relevant information. Create a new blank page and attach the style sheet to it. Create a table using the planned data, and make sure to merge and split some cells. Format the site using table and cell properties, headings, and other formatting techniques. Insert and resize an I-frame on the home page, and link the table page to it. Preview the site, test the navigation bar, and make sure that your site is readable and attractive. Save and close the pages and style sheet, then close the site.

# 6 | Adding Interactivity

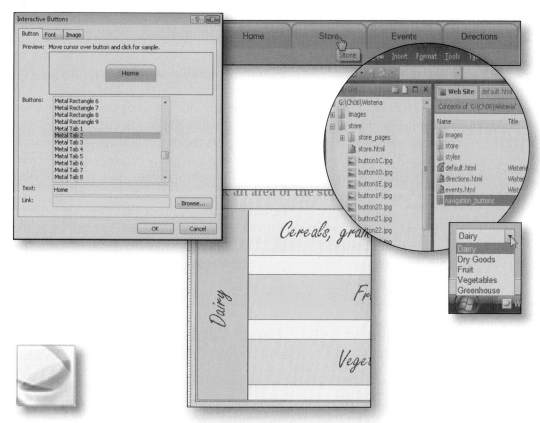

## Objectives

You will have mastered the material in this chapter when you can:

- Create an interactive button
- Duplicate an interactive button
- Edit an interactive button
- Test an interactive button
- Define how behaviors work
- Use the Behaviors task pane

- Add a jump menu behavior
- Add a status message behavior
- Add a swap image behavior
- Modify a behavior
- Test a behavior
- Create an image map

# 6 | Adding Interactivity

## Introduction

**Interactivity** is the term used to describe the connection that occurs between a Web site and a site visitor through actions such as clicking a button, list item, or part of an image. Interactivity goes beyond simple site navigation through hyperlinks; users can trigger an event, such as opening a new Web page or e-mail, zooming on an image, or launching a chat window by performing actions such as clicking or hovering the mouse pointer over an element. Interactive tools are commonly used in site navigation, but can also provide additional information to site visitors by changing an image or displaying a message in a new window or in the status bar.

Elements that are interactive have behaviors attached to them. **Behaviors** are the embedded functions that occur as a result of site events, such as a page opening in a browser window, or user interaction, such as clicking or hovering the mouse. Expression Web tools create behaviors using code from a scripting language called **JavaScript**. As with HTML and CSS, you do not need to know JavaScript to create and modify behaviors in Expression Web.

There are many ways to add interactivity to your Web page, including **interactive buttons**, also called **rollover buttons**, that look different when they are inactive, have a mouse pointer hovering over them, and are clicked. **Jump menus** are lists that contain links. **Image maps** are graphics that have links, called **hotspots**, associated with different areas of the graphic.

## Project — Farm Stand Web Site

Wisteria Farms, a farm stand and grocery store in Dilton, New Hampshire, currently has a Web site that needs more interactivity. The site has four main pages for the home page, store, events, and directions, but no method for navigating between them. You will create a navigation area for the main site pages by adding interactive buttons to each page. The owners want it to be easy to view descriptions of the store's main areas. You will create a jump menu on the home page as well as an image map on the store page that allows users to view pages about the different store departments.

The project in this chapter shows you how to use Expression Web to add interactivity to create the site shown in Figure 6–1. You will create a navigation bar using interactive buttons that you will copy to each main page of the site. You will create a jump menu and an image map and place them appropriately to link to each of the store pages. You will create behaviors for an image swap and a status bar message. Although Expression Web provides tools for creating many types of interactivity, you will add only these five types of behaviors so that your site is not overwhelmed by interactivity.

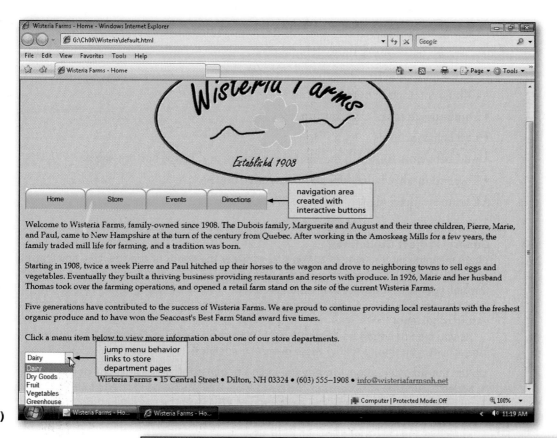

(a)

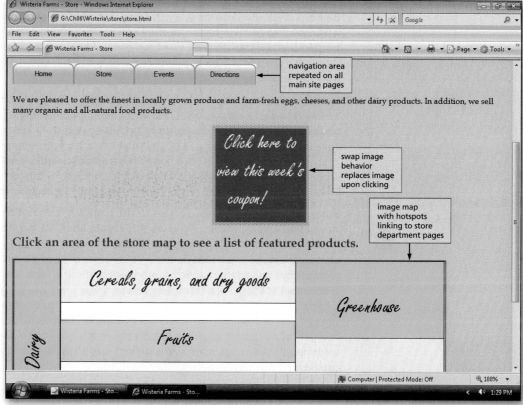

(b)

**Figure 6–1**

# Overview

As you read this chapter, you will learn how to create the Web page shown in Figure 6–1 by performing these general tasks:

- Create an interactive button
- Edit an interactive button
- Duplicate an interactive button
- Use behavior tools
- Add behaviors for jump menus, image swaps, and status bar messages
- Test and modify behaviors and interactive buttons
- Create an image map

**Plan Ahead**

**BTW**

**Adding Interactivity**
See Special Feature 1
for alternatives and con-
cerns regarding adding
interactive elements.

**General Project Guidelines**

When planning interactivity in a Web site, consider the needs of the site. Like any feature, only add what makes sense for your site plan and what will help site visitors to navigate through your site easily. Use Expression Web tools instead of typing complicated code. Reuse elements by copying and pasting them, then modifying as necessary, to save time and ensure consistency.

As you plan to enhance a Web site, such as the one shown in Figure 6–1, by adding interactivity, you should follow these general guidelines:

1. **Plan the site navigation.** Identify the main site pages for which links will need to be added to all pages of your site. The navigation area should be located on the same place on each page to make your site easier to use. What will the site navigation look like? Interactive buttons are often stacked vertically or horizontally (or both) to make an attractive and user-friendly navigation area.

2. **Determine which elements you can reuse and copy to save time and ensure consistency.** After creating one interactive button, you can copy it to create the others. Interactive buttons are editable, so once you have created one, you will only need to change the text on the button and the page to which it is linked. After you have created the navigation area, you can copy and paste it to each site page.

3. **Identify behaviors that will help site visitors' experiences.** Avoid adding behaviors such as sound and pop-up messages that visitors could find annoying or distracting. Consider adding behaviors that assist a user by providing necessary access to other site elements. Take into account the file size of the page when adding behaviors; the code used to program interactivity adds to your page's file size, which will increase the download time in a visitor's browser. Balance the value of the interactivity against the increase in file size. Test all behaviors and buttons to confirm that they work as intended.

4. **Assess how you will provide access to site pages that do not have links in the primary navigation area.** Sometimes you want to create an HTML page to provide additional information that is not appropriate to add to the primary navigation area, which should contain the most important page names or categories of pages. A **secondary navigation element** can link to more specific information about a topic. For example, in a site for an elementary school, there could be a link in the primary navigation area for the school's curriculum, then on the curriculum page, a secondary navigation element could provide links to grade-specific curriculum information. A jump menu is an example of a secondary navigation element that allows visitors to use a list to link to pages for specific additional information. An image map is an excellent way to present information visually, while providing a way to navigate by clicking hotspots.

## To Start Expression Web and Reset Workspace Layout

If you are using a computer to step through the project in this chapter, and you want your screens to match the figures in this book, you should change your computer's resolution to 1024 × 768. For information about how to change a computer's resolution, read Appendix F.

The following steps, which assume Windows Vista is running, start Expression Web based on a typical installation, and reset the task panes in the workspace to the default layout. You may need to ask your instructor how to start Expression Web for your computer.

> **Note:** If you are using Window XP, see Appendix E for alternate steps.

**1** Click the Start button on the Windows Vista taskbar to display the Start menu.

**2** Click All Programs at the bottom of the left pane on the Start menu to display the All Programs list.

**3** Click Microsoft Expression on the All Programs list to display the Microsoft Expression list.

**4** Click Microsoft Expression Web 2 to start Expression Web.

**5** Click Task Panes on the menu bar, then click Reset Workspace Layout.

## To Open a Web Site and Web Page

The following steps open the Wisteria Farms Web site and the default.html page.

**1** Click File on the menu bar to open the File menu, then click Open Site to display the Open Site dialog box.

**2** Navigate to the Data Files and double-click the Ch06 folder to display its contents.

**3** Click the Wisteria folder, then click the Open button to open the site in Expression Web.

**4** Double-click the default.html page from the Folder List to open it (Figure 6–2).

| Other Ways |
| --- |
| 1. Double-click the default.html page in the Web Site pane to open it. |

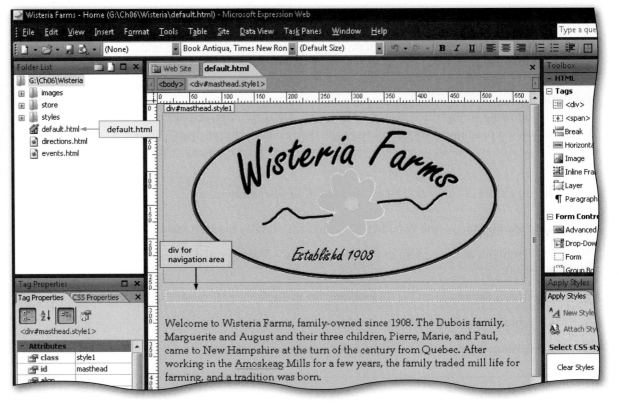

**Figure 6–2**

# Creating an Interactive Navigation Area

BTW

**Dynamic Web Templates**
Interactive buttons were a part of the dynamic Web templates you used in Chapter 3.

As you have seen in previous chapters, a navigation area, at minimum, contains text-based hyperlinks for each of the main site pages. To make your navigation area more attractive and professional looking, add interactive buttons. Several of the button options are to be used for columns or rows of buttons, and are identified as such in the Interactive Button dialog box.

When you create an interactive button using Expression Web, you are actually creating image files for each state of the button. At any given time, a button is in one of three states:

- Being pressed
- Hover, where the visitor's pointer is hovering over the button
- Inactive, where the visitor's pointer is elsewhere on the page

BTW

**Fonts on Interactive Buttons**
Because interactive buttons are saved as image files, you can use any font for the text, not just those that are considered Web-safe.

You can use interactivity to visually depict these three different states. To add interactivity to a button, Expression Web creates three interchangeable images that replace each other depending on the state of the button. Setting your page to download all three images into the visitor's browser when the page downloads is called **preloading** and increases the speed of interactivity.

## Interactivity and Web Browsers

Expression Web embeds the interactive functions you add to your page as **ActiveX controls**, which are Microsoft-developed small programs used to enhance functionality in a program or Web page.

For security purposes, many Web browsers automatically block interactive site features to protect you from potentially harmful scripts that could infect your computer with a virus or that look for personal information on your computer.

When a browser loads a page, it looks for ActiveX controls and other scripted code, and displays a message letting you know that content has been blocked. These messages may differ depending on your browser or the type of script detected, but they most often appear as dialog boxes or alert messages at the top of the page.

Because the site you are viewing in this chapter is one that you have created yourself, you know that the scripts and controls on the pages you view are safe, and therefore you can temporarily allow them. You will most likely have to enable them each time you load a new page in your browser. Although you could change your browser security settings to allow these types of controls to display automatically, that is not a recommended setting. If you cannot enable the interactive content because of your security settings (for instance, if you are on a shared or lab computer), ask your instructor or technical support person for assistance.

**BTW**

**Expression Web Help**
The best way to become familiar with Expression Web Help is to use it. Appendix B includes detailed information about Expression Web Help and exercises that will help you gain confidence in using it.

---

**Plan the site navigation.**

As with any feature you add to your site pages, consider the desired look of the button, including colors, shape, font, and size. These attributes are set in the Interactive Buttons dialog box. Keep the button text simple, preferably one word, and make sure that the button's label clearly indicates where the button will take the site visitor. A navigation area should be located on the same place on each page of the site, and should include a button to return to the site's home page.

**Plan
Ahead**

---

## To Create an Interactive Button

The following steps create and test an interactive button for the home page and set a different text color for the hovered state. It is important to test a button before duplicating it; otherwise, you will have to change each copied instance. By default, when you create one interactive button, three images will be created: for inactive, hovering, and pressing states. You can create fewer button images by changing the settings on the Image tab.

**1**

• Click in the top navigation div (div#top_nav) below the logo to position the insertion point (Figure 6–3).

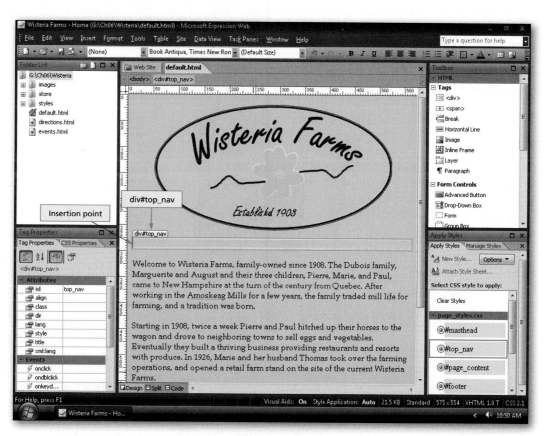

**Figure 6–3**

**2**

- Click Interactive Button on the Insert menu to open the Interactive Buttons dialog box (Figure 6–4).

 **Experiment**

- Click options in the Buttons list to view a description and available preview of various button types.

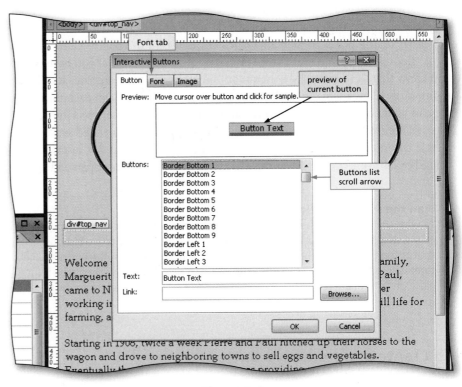

**Figure 6–4**

**3**

- Drag the scroll box in the Buttons list down, then click the Metal Tab 2 option.

- Select the words, Button Text, in the Text text box, then type Home (Figure 6–5).

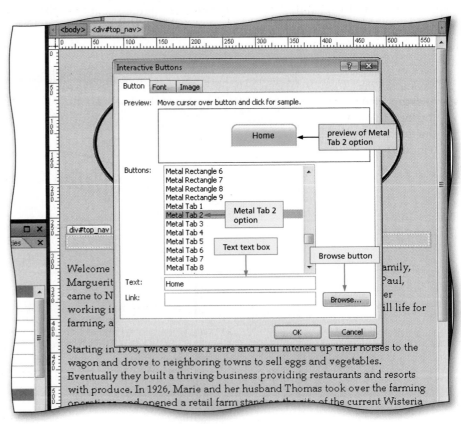

**Figure 6–5**

**4**

- Click the Browse button to open the Edit Hyperlink dialog box (Figure 6–6).

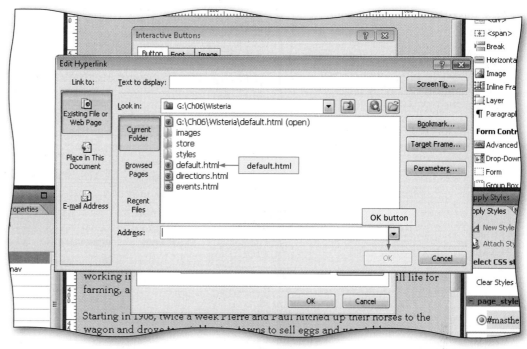

**Figure 6–6**

**5**

- Click the default.html page, then click the OK button to close the Edit Hyperlink dialog box (Figure 6–7).

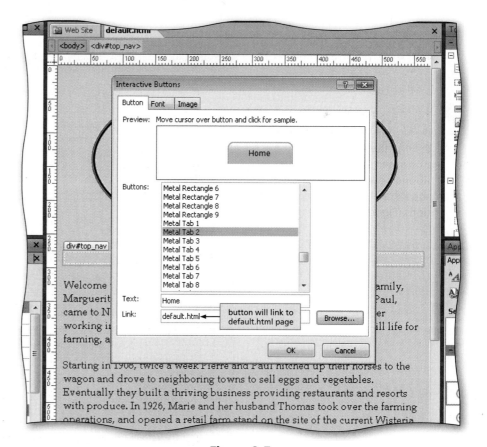

**Figure 6–7**

**6**

- Click the Font tab to display Font choices.

- Drag the scroll bar down, then click the Times New Roman option in the Font box to change the font for the buttons.

- Click the Hovered Font Color box arrow to display the color palette (Figure 6–8).

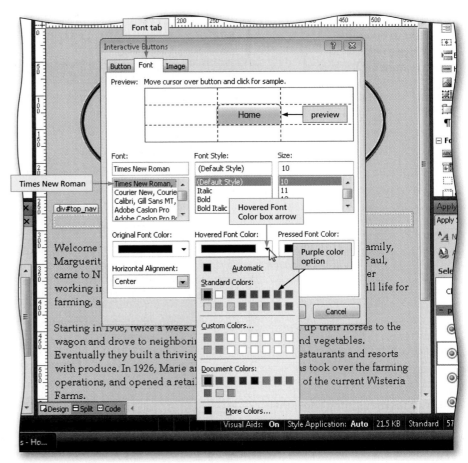

**Figure 6–8**

**7**

- Click Purple in the color palette to change the font color for the button when the mouse pointer is positioned over it, then click the Image tab to display the image options (Figure 6–9).

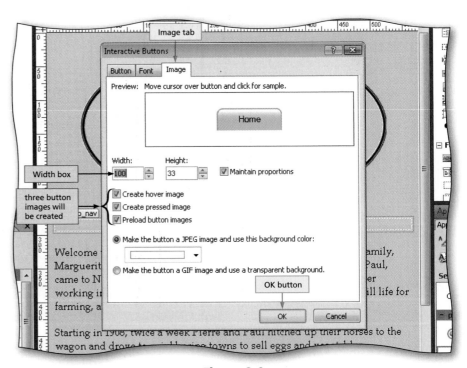

**Figure 6–9**

● Type 120 in the Width text box, then click the OK button to close the Interactive Buttons dialog box and insert the button (Figure 6–10).

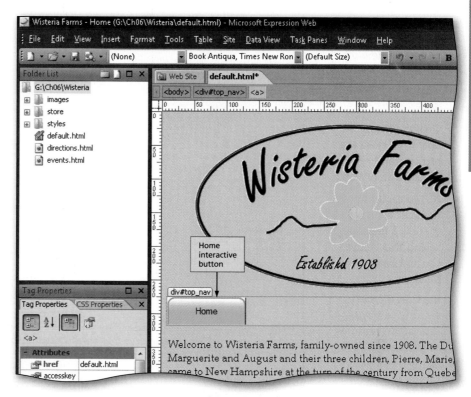

**Figure 6–10**

● Press CTRL+S to save the page, then click OK in the Save Embedded Files dialog box.

● Click the Preview in Windows Internet Explorer 7.0 button arrow, then click Windows Internet Explorer 7.0 to open the default.html page in a browser window (Figure 6–11).

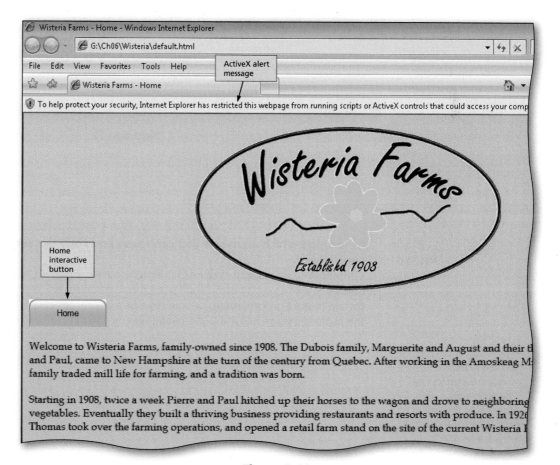

**Figure 6–11**

**10**

- Position the pointer over the Home button to view the change in button text color in hovered state (Figure 6–12).

- Click the Close button to close the browser and return to Expression Web.

**Q&A**

At the top of my browser window, there is a message saying that ActiveX content has been blocked.

Because of your security settings, interactive features might be blocked automatically. Click the message at the top of the browser window, click Allow Blocked Content, then click the Yes button in the alert box to allow ActiveX controls for this site, or ask your instructor or technical support person for permission and assistance. You will have to perform this step every time you view a new page in a browser.

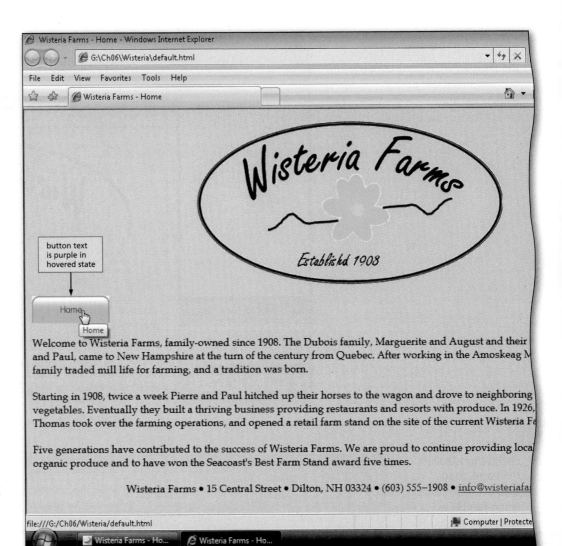

**Figure 6–12**

---

**Plan Ahead**

**Determine which elements you can reuse and copy to save time and ensure consistency.**

Efficient Web page creators reuse elements by copying, pasting, and modifying them as needed. Creating each button from scratch can introduce errors if you forget to include a certain feature or formatting, or enter text or a link incorrectly. After you copy and paste the buttons, you should move the image files into folders to keep your site organized.

**BTW**

**Other Uses for Interactive Buttons**
You can place an interactive button anywhere on a page. For example, at the end of a form page for user input, include a button to submit the form data.

## To Duplicate an Interactive Button

The following steps copy the button image from the home page to the Clipboard and paste the button three times to create a total of four links — one for each of the main pages — inserting space between each link.

**1**

- Right-click the Home button to display the shortcut menu, then click Copy to copy the button and its properties to the Clipboard.

- Click to the right of the button to position the insertion point next to it.

- Press CTRL+V to paste a copy of the Home button.

- Press CTRL+V to paste another copy of the Home button.

- Press CTRL+V to paste the final copy of the Home button (Figure 6–13).

**Q&A**

My button names are different.

Your button file names might differ depending on past usage. This is fine.

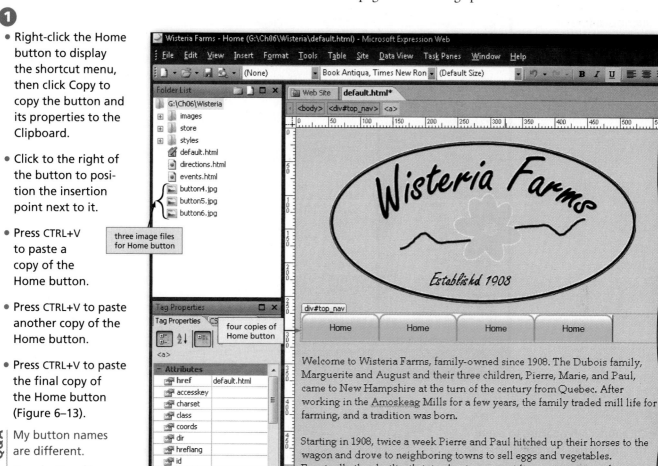

**Figure 6–13**

| Other Ways |
| --- |
| 1. Click Copy on the Edit menu to copy a selection to the Clipboard. 2. Click Paste on the Edit menu to paste a selection from the Clipboard. |

# Editing and Organizing Interactive Buttons

When you edit a copied interactive button, you should only change the specifications that are necessary to distinguish each button: the target link and the button text. Unless your site design can support other changes, such as different colors for each button or a pattern of button colors, keep everything else the same.

Once your navigation area is complete, you should test it before copying it and pasting it to other site pages. That way, if you choose the wrong target or mistype the button text, you will only have to correct it once, instead of in each pasted location.

# To Edit an Interactive Button

The following steps edit each interactive button by changing the text and link.

- Right-click the second button from the left to display the shortcut menu (Figure 6–14).

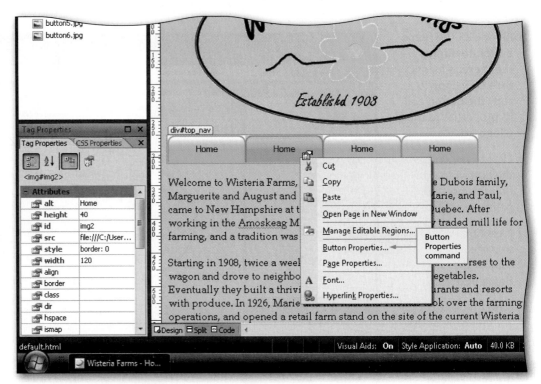

**Figure 6–14**

- Click Button Properties to open the Interactive Buttons dialog box.

- Select the word, Home, in the Text text box, then type Store (Figure 6–15).

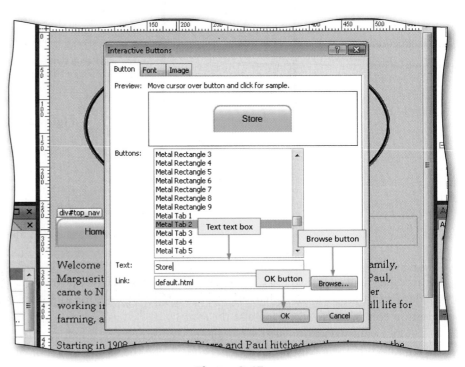

**Figure 6–15**

**3**

- Press TAB to move the insertion point to the Link text box and select the text box contents, then click the Browse button to open the Edit Hyperlink dialog box.

- Double-click the store folder to open it.

- Click the store.html page to select it (Figure 6–16).

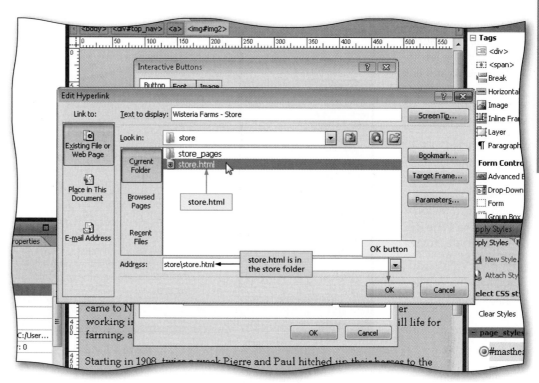

**Figure 6–16**

**4**

- Click the OK button to close the Edit Hyperlink dialog box.

- Click the OK button to close the Interactive Buttons dialog box and accept the edits to the button text and link (Figure 6–17).

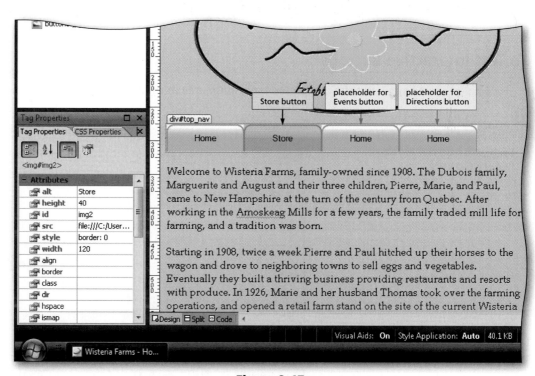

**Figure 6–17**

- Follow Steps 1–4 to edit the third button from the left to read Events and link to the events.html page in the main site folder.

- Follow Steps 1–4 to edit the fourth button from the left to read Directions and link to the directions.html page in the main site folder (Figure 6–18).

- Save the page and all embedded files.

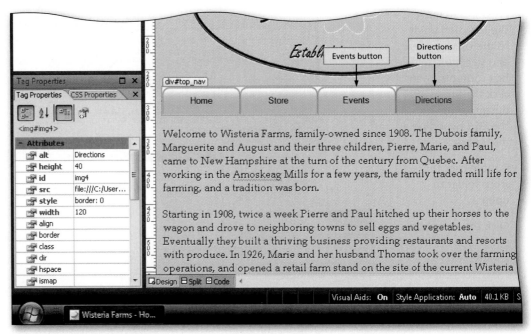

**Figure 6–18**

**Other Ways**

1. Double-click a button to open the Interactive Buttons dialog box.

## To Test Interactive Buttons

The following steps test the completed navigation area in the browser.

- Press **F12** to open the default.html page in a browser window (Figure 6–19).

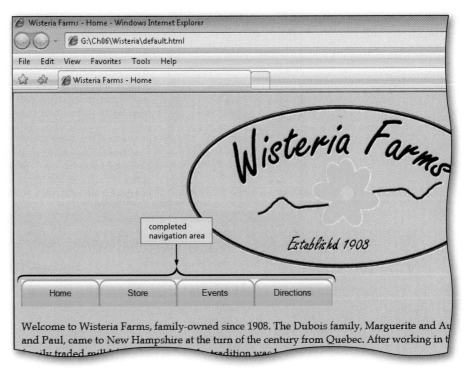

**Figure 6–19**

**2**

- Position the mouse pointer over the Store button to view the hover image (Figure 6–20).

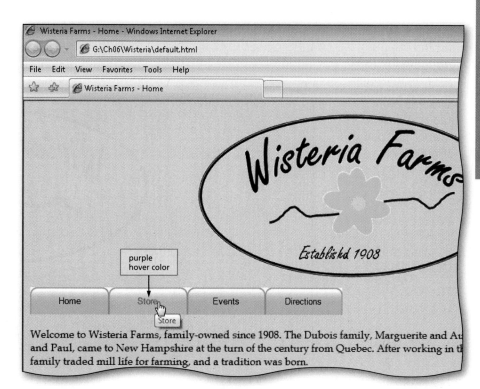

**Figure 6–20**

**3**

- Click the Store button to display the store.html page (Figure 6–21).

**Figure 6–21**

● Click the Back button to return to the default.html page.

● Click the Events tab to display the events.html page (Figure 6–22).

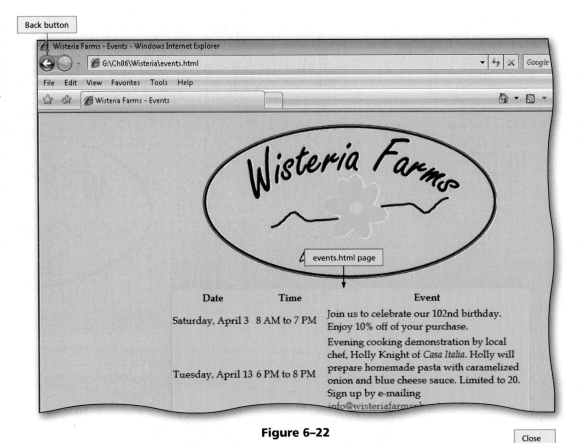

Figure 6–22

● Click the Back button to return to the default.html page.

● Click the Directions tab to display the directions.html page (Figure 6–23).

● Click the Close button to close the browser and return to Expression Web.

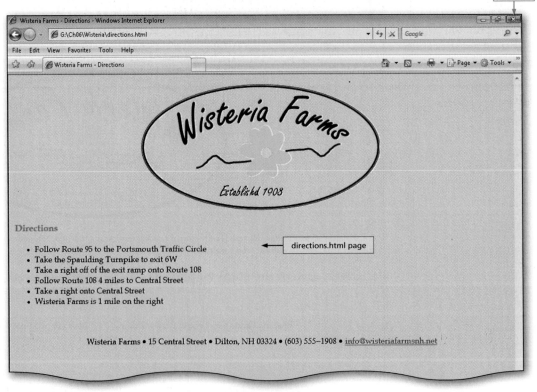

Figure 6–23

## To Copy and Paste the Navigation Area

The following steps open the three other main site pages: store.html, events.html, and directions.html; and copy the navigation area from the default.html page and paste it into the navigation div for each page to create a consistent and functional navigation area.

**1**

- Click the div#top_nav visual aid to select the navigation area (Figure 6–24).

- Press CTRL+C to copy the navigation area to the Clipboard.

**Q&A** Can I just select the buttons?

Make sure to select the entire navigation div both when copying and pasting the navigation area.

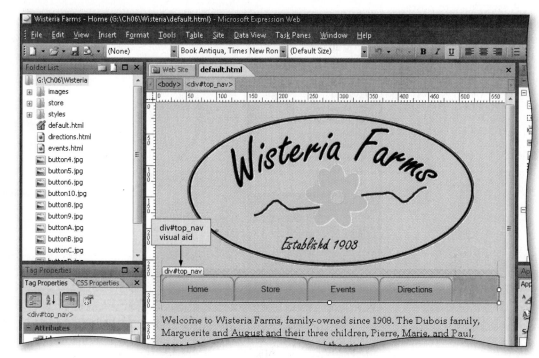

**Figure 6–24**

**2**

- Click the Store folder plus sign in the Folder List to display the contents of the folder.

- Double-click the store.html page in the Folder List to open it (Figure 6–25).

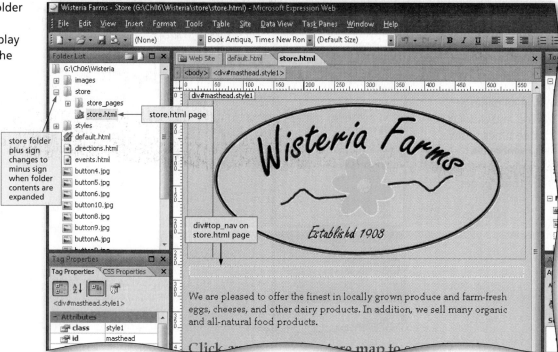

**Figure 6–25**

**3**

- Click the div#top_nav visual aid to select the empty navigation div.

- Press CTRL+V to paste the navigation area from the Clipboard to the store.html page (Figure 6–26).

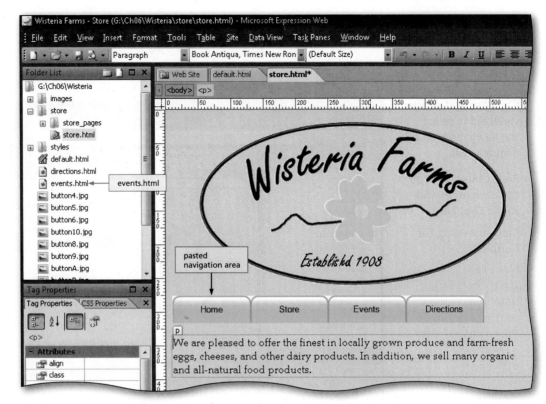

**Figure 6–26**

**4**

- Repeat Steps 2–3 to open the events.html and directions.html pages from the Folder List and paste the navigation area onto both pages (Figure 6–27).

- Save all pages at once, and click OK three times to save the embedded images you added to the three pages.

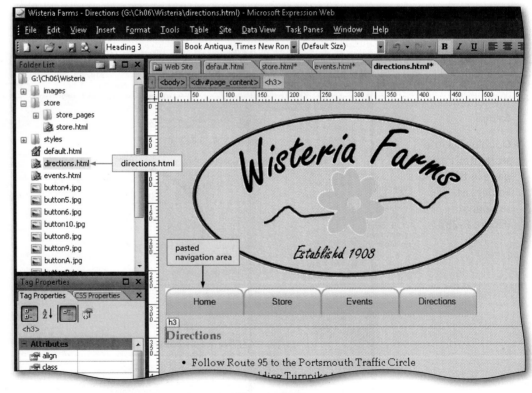

**Figure 6–27**

## To Organize the Button Images into Folders

Every interactive button on every page has three image files associated with it, which creates a lot of image files in the site folder (which contains all of the button images for the default, events, and directions pages) and the store page's subfolder (which only contains the images for the store page). When you move the buttons to a folder, Expression Web updates the links. The following steps create folders for the button images, and move the button images into the folder.

- Click the Web Site tab to display the contents of the site folder (Figure 6–28).

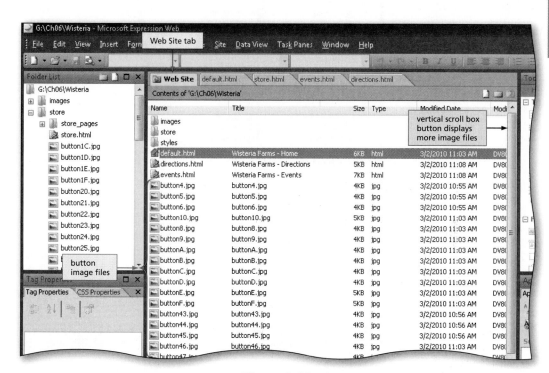

**Figure 6–28**

- Point to New on the File menu, then click Folder to insert a new folder (Figure 6–29).

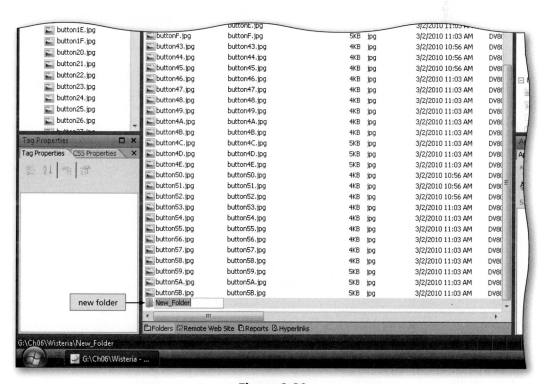

**Figure 6–29**

- Type navigation_
  buttons, then press
  ENTER to name the
  folder (Figure 6–30).

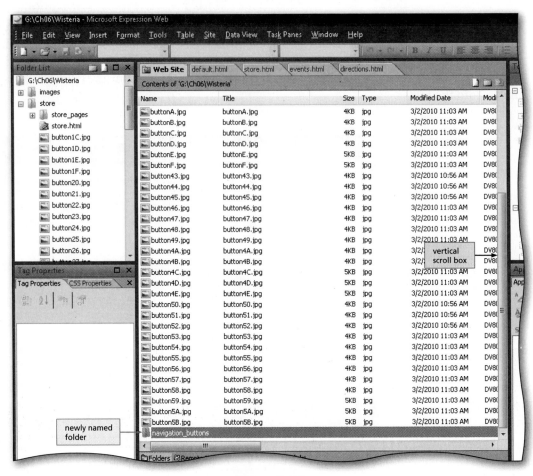

**Figure 6–30**

- Click the JPEG image file above the
  folder, press and hold SHIFT, scroll,
  then click the top JPEG image file
  in the site folder to select all of the
  navigation button image files.

- Drag the selected files to the
  navigation_buttons folder to
  move them (Figure 6–31).

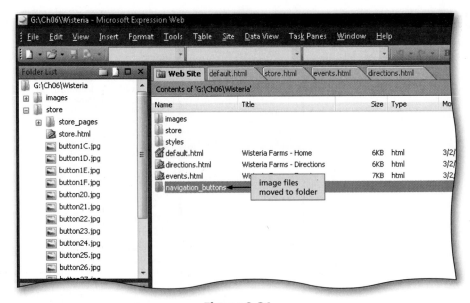

**Figure 6–31**

- Double-click the store folder to open it.

- Point to New on the File menu, then click Folder to insert a new folder.

- Type navigation_buttons, then press ENTER to name the folder (Figure 6–32).

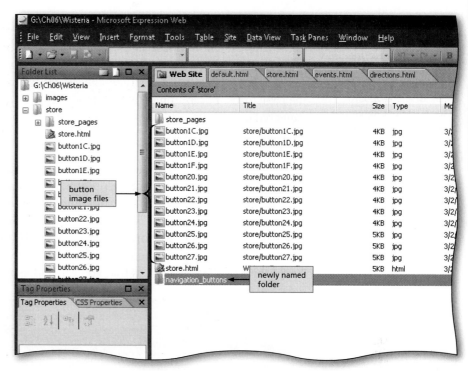

**Figure 6–32**

- Click the JPEG image file above the folder, press and hold SHIFT, then click the top JPEG image file in the site folder to select all of the navigation button image files.

- Drag the selected files to the navigation_button folder to move them (Figure 6–33).

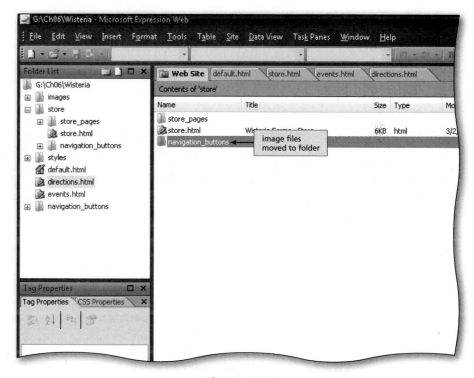

**Figure 6–33**

**Other Ways**

1. Click the New Folder button on the Folder List to insert a new folder.

2. Right-click a blank area of the Web Site pane, point to New on the shortcut menu, then click Folder to insert a new folder.

# Defining Behaviors

**BTW**

**Quick Reference**
For a table that lists how to complete the tasks covered in this book using the mouse, shortcut menu, and keyboard, see the Quick Reference Summary at the back of this book, or visit the Expression Web 2 Quick Reference Web page (scsite.com/ew2/qr).

Behaviors are actions triggered by events. They include changes in page appearance, such as the replacement of one image with another or a change in font size. Behaviors can also include functions such as an alert message displaying or a new browser window opening. They occur as a result of activity by the site visitor or are automated occurrences when the page loads. For example, moving a pointer over a specific area of the page (a visitor-triggered event) can result in a behavior such as a change in button appearance. Behaviors are generally used to increase the interactivity and utility of a given page without requiring much additional code.

Some behaviors are one-step occurrences, such as when a site checks the visitor's computer for a browser version or plug-in, or displays text in the status bar. Others, such as swapping one image for another upon mousing over or clicking an image, or changing the properties of an element, can require an additional step to restore an element to its original state using the Restore command. The Restore command is available after the original behavior is established.

Table 6–1 lists behaviors that you can add using Expression Web.

| Table 6–1: Interactive Behaviors in Expression Web | |
|---|---|
| **Behavior** | **Used To** |
| Call Script | Insert JavaScript without switching to Code View. Used to add JavaScript code to create a behavior that does not exist in Expression Web. You must know JavaScript to use this behavior. |
| Change Property/Restore | Change the font, position, borders and shading, and visibility of an element. Change Property Restore returns the element to its original state. |
| Check Browser | Determine whether the visitor's browser is the correct type and version necessary to view all of the site features. |
| Check Plug-in | Determine whether the visitor's browser has a browser plug-in, such as a video player, necessary to view a site feature. |
| Go To URL | Open a Web page in a browser upon an event, such as mousing over or double-clicking. |
| Jump Menu/Go | Create a list box with a menu that contains hyperlinks. |
| Open Browser Window | Open a new browser window as a pop-up window, such as to display an advertisement. |
| Play Sound | Play sound files, such as MP3 files. |
| Popup Message | Open an alert window that the user has to close. |
| Preload Images | Load the images on a Web page before the rest of the page's content. This is a default option when creating interactive buttons, as they require three image files per button. |
| Set Text | Add a message to a frame or layer, or more commonly, to the status bar. |
| Swap Image/Restore | Change from one image to another upon clicking or hovering. Swap Image Restore returns the image to its original state. |

**Plan Ahead**

**Identify behaviors that will help site visitors' experiences.**
The goal of a behavior is to enhance visitors' experiences with your site by providing them with additional information. Add behaviors that allow for additional navigation or that provide an attractive or interesting way to interact with your site, but avoid including behaviors that visitors might find annoying, such as background sound and pop-up messages. Behaviors add to the file size of your page. Incorporate testing of behaviors into your page creation process and consider file size implications of interactive behaviors to ensure visitors have good experiences and do not encounter any problems on your site.

# Creating a Jump Menu

A jump menu is a secondary navigation device. Unlike button-based navigation areas, a jump menu most likely only appears in one location on the site.

When creating a jump menu, you must create text for each link. Like adding text for an interactive button, the text for each menu item should describe the page to which it links in as few words as possible. You can reorder the items in the list by moving them up and down in the order to show the most commonly used ones at the top, or group like items together. Each menu item is assigned a target page to which the browser will navigate when the menu item is clicked.

## To Add a Jump Menu Behavior

The following steps add a jump menu to the store departments on the home page.

**1**

- Click the default.html tab to display the default.html page.

- Click at the end of the third paragraph of text, then press ENTER to insert a new paragraph.

- Type Click a menu item below to view more information about one of our store departments., then press ENTER (Figure 6–34).

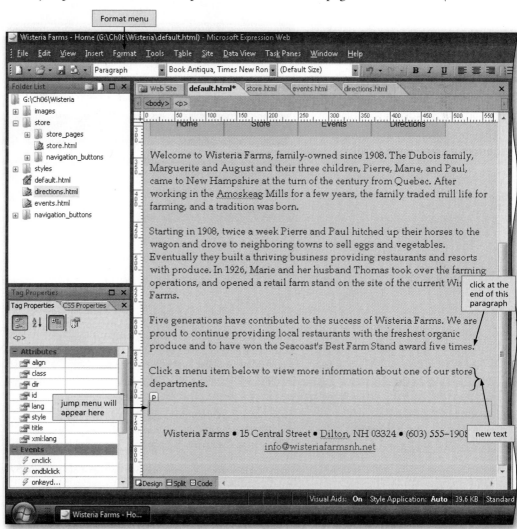

Figure 6–34

**2**

- Click Behaviors on the Format menu to open the Behaviors task pane (Figure 6–35).

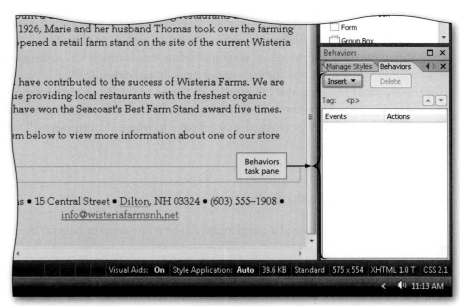

**Figure 6–35**

**3**

- Click the Insert button on the Behaviors task pane to display the shortcut menu (Figure 6–36).

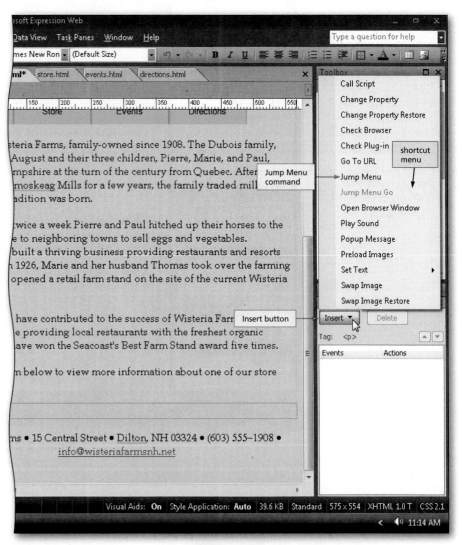

**Figure 6–36**

- Click Jump Menu on the shortcut menu to open the Jump Menu dialog box (Figure 6–37).

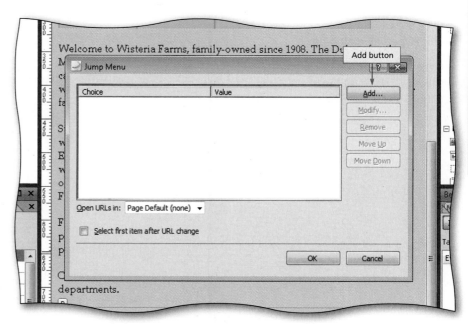

**Figure 6–37**

- Click the Add button to open the Add Choice dialog box (Figure 6–38).

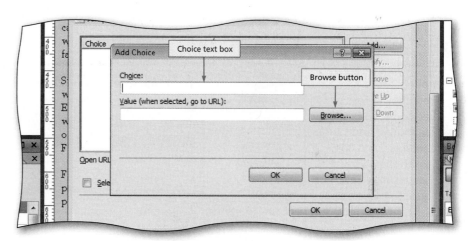

**Figure 6–38**

6

- Type Dairy in the Choice text box, then click the Browse button to open the Edit Hyperlink dialog box.

- Double-click the store folder to open it if necessary.

- Double-click the store_pages folder to open it, then click dairy.html to select it as the link target (Figure 6–39).

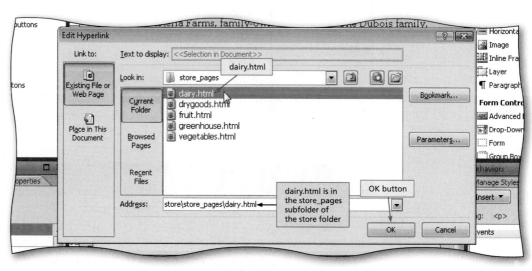

**Figure 6–39**

**7**
- Click the OK button to close the Edit Hyperlink dialog box.
- Click the OK button to close the Add Choice dialog box (Figure 6–40).

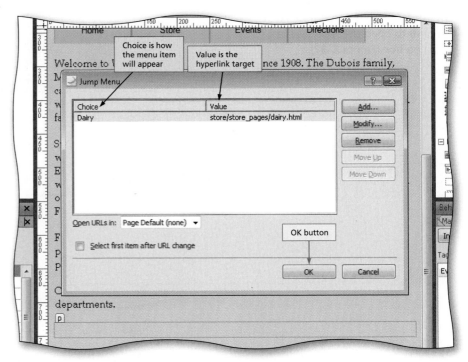

**Figure 6–40**

**8**

- Repeat Steps 5 through 7 to insert choices for Dry Goods, Fruit, Greenhouse, and Vegetables, and link them to the appropriate HTML files (Figure 6–41).

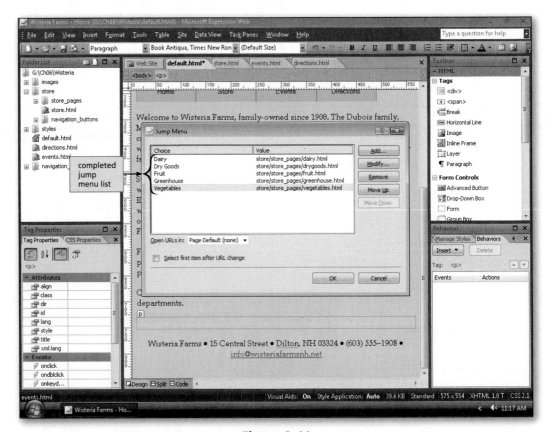

**Figure 6–41**

**9**

• Click Vegetables to select it, then click the Move Up button to move it up in the list so that it is below the Fruit menu item (Figure 6–42).

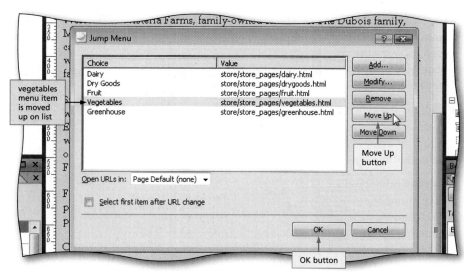

**Figure 6–42**

 **10**

• Click the OK button to close the Jump Menu dialog box and insert the jump menu (Figure 6–43).

• Press CTRL+S to save the page.

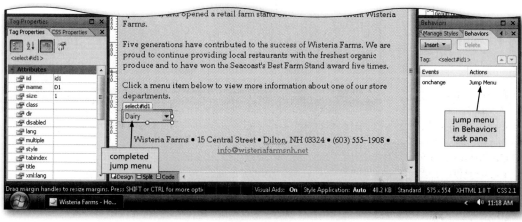

**Figure 6–43**

**11**

• Press F12 to open the page in a browser window.

• Click the jump menu box arrow to display the menu (Figure 6–44).

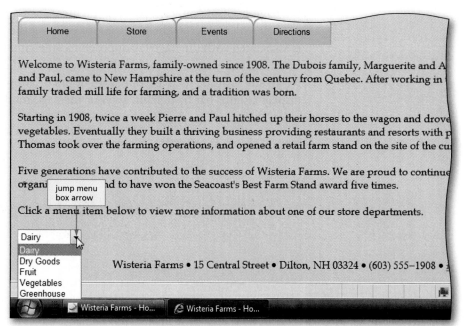

**Figure 6–44**

⑫
- Click Vegetables from the jump menu to view the vegetables.html page (Figure 6–45).

- Click the Back button to return to the default.html page.

- Test the other links in the jump menu box, then click the Close button to close the browser and return to Expression Web.

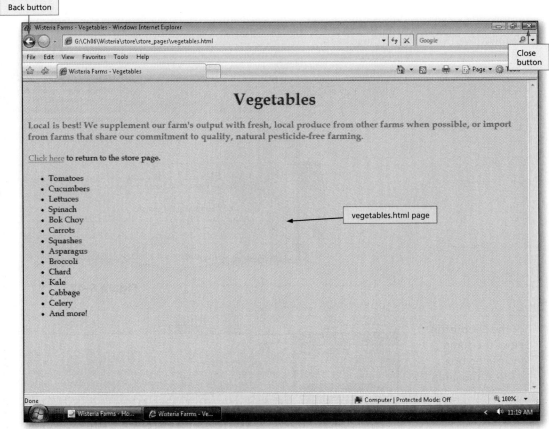

**Figure 6–45**

**Other Ways**

1. Click Behaviors on the Task Panes menu to open the Behaviors task pane.

## Creating a Status Bar Behavior

Adding text that appears in the status bar lets you deliver a message to your site visitors. A **status bar behavior** can be assigned to a particular element on the page or to the page itself. If you want to have the message associated with the page itself, you need to click a blank area of the page before creating the behavior. When a status bar behavior is associated with the page (as opposed to an element on the page), by default it appears when the page loads. Do not include status bar behaviors for information that is important for all site visitors, such as your store hours or announcing a sale, as not all browsers will display a status bar by default, so your message might not reach all visitors.

## To Add a Status Bar Behavior

The following steps add a message on the status bar for the home page, welcoming users to the site.

- Click a blank area of the default. html page to make sure only the body tag appears on the Quick Tag Selector.

- Click the Insert button on the Behaviors task pane to display the shortcut menu, point to Set Text, then click Set Text of Status Bar to open the Set Text of Status Bar dialog box.

- Type Welcome to Wisteria Farms in the Message text box (Figure 6–46).

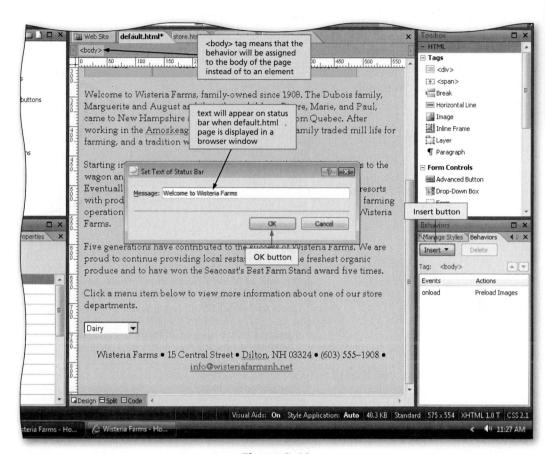

**Figure 6–46**

- Click the OK button to close the Set Text of Status Bar dialog box (Figure 6–47).

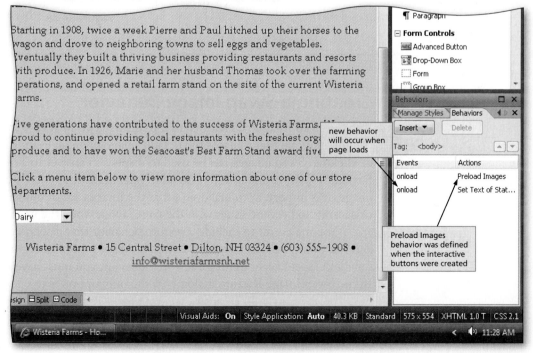

**Figure 6–47**

**3**

- Press CTRL+S to save the default. html page, then press F12 to open the page in a browser window (Figure 6–48).

- View the message in the status bar.

- Click the Close button to close the browser window and return to Expression Web.

**Q&A** I cannot see the status bar on my browser window.

Click View on the menu bar, then click Status Bar to display the status bar if necessary.

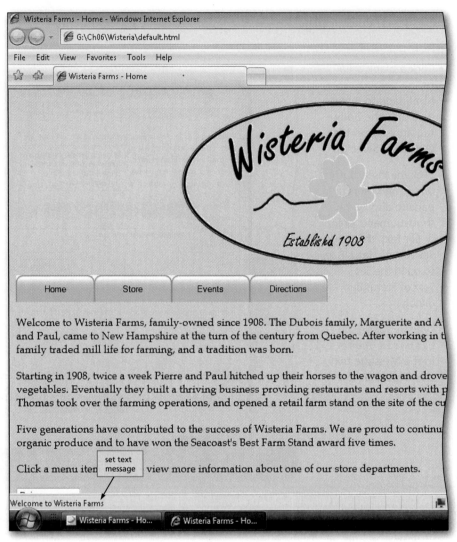

**Figure 6–48**

## Creating a Swap Image Behavior

**BTW**

**Web Accessibility**
See Appendix B for more information about accessibility and assistive technology.

A **swap image** behavior is used to display two images — one that displays by default, and one that replaces the default image upon an event such as hovering the mouse or clicking. Swap images can be used to display an answer to a question, show a transformation (before and after), or to add visual interest to your site. When adding a swap image, it is important to make sure that the images are of the same dimensional size (or close to it) to prevent issues with the page layout when the images are swapped.

You may want to include a restore behavior that displays the original image upon another event, such as moving the mouse away (onmouseout) or clicking the image again (onclick). To add a swap image restore behavior, you must have first created a swap image. In the Swap Image Restore dialog box, the only option is to click OK; Expression Web will use the information about the original image from the swap image behavior to create the restore behavior.

## To Add a Swap Image Behavior

The following steps insert an image on the store page and add a swap image behavior that displays a coupon when the mouse pointer is hovering over the image (called mouseover; this is the default event for the swap image behavior).

 **1**

- Click the store.html tab to display the store.html page.

- Click at the end of the paragraph of text that starts, We are pleased, then press ENTER to insert a new paragraph (Figure 6–49).

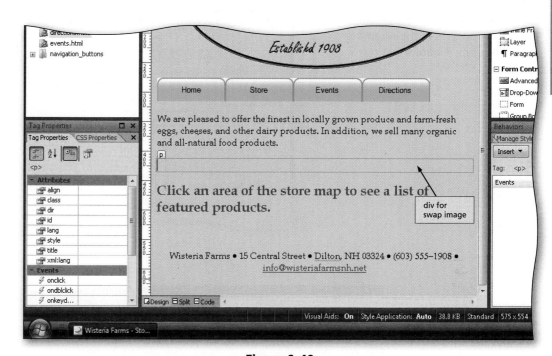

**Figure 6–49**

 **2**

- Point to Picture on the Insert menu, then click From File to open the Picture dialog box.

- Navigate to the data files and double-click the wisteria_images folder (Figure 6–50).

**Figure 6–50**

- Click the swap_image1.gif file to select it, then click the Insert button to open the Accessibility Properties dialog box.

- Type Click here to see this week's coupon in the Alternate text text box (Figure 6–51).

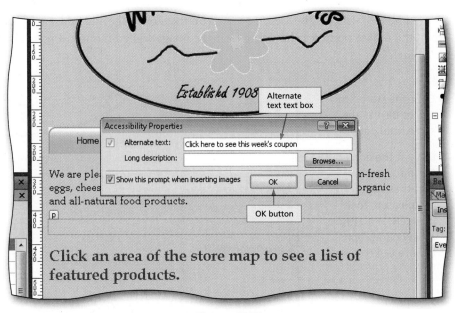

**Figure 6–51**

- Click the OK button to close the Accessibility Properties dialog box and insert the image.

- Click the image to select it, then click the Center button on the Common toolbar to center the image on the page (Figure 6–52).

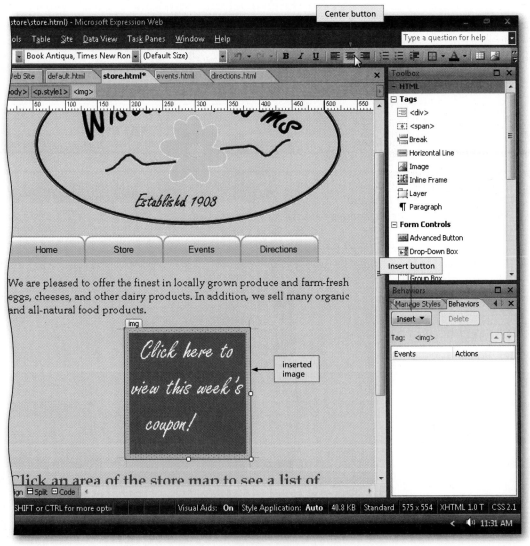

**Figure 6–52**

**5**
- Click the Insert button on the Behaviors task pane to display the shortcut menu, then click Swap Image to open the Swap Images dialog box (Figure 6–53).

**Q&A**  My list of images in the Swap Images dialog box is different.

Expression Web suggests images based on recently created or used images from your work session. Clicking the Browse button allows you access to all images in your site or on a computer, drive, or network folder.

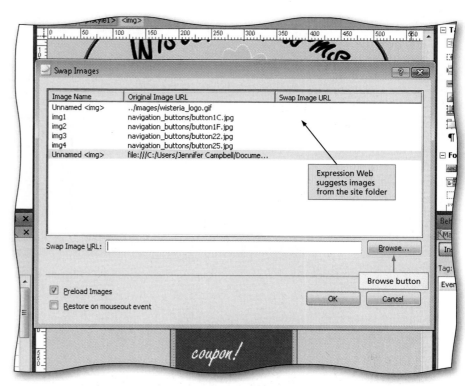

**Figure 6–53**

**6**
- Click the Browse button to open the Browse dialog box.

- Navigate to the data files, then double-click the wisteria_images folder if necessary.

- Click the swap_image2.gif file to select it, then click the OK button to close the Browse dialog box.

- Click the OK button to close the Swap Images dialog box.

- Save the page and embedded files.

- Press F12 to open the page in a browser window (Figure 6–54).

**Figure 6–54**

**7**

- Position the mouse pointer over the image to swap it (Figure 6–55).

- Click the Expression Web program button on the taskbar to return to Expression Web and leave the browser window open.

**Q&A** Why does the image text say to click it, but the image changes when I position the mouse over it?

The default event for a swap image is mouseover. In the next set of steps you will change the event to onclick to match the text on the image.

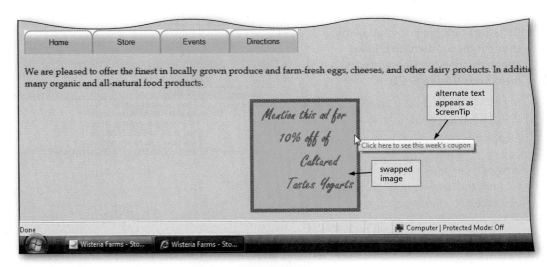

**Figure 6–55**

## To Modify a Swap Image Behavior

The previous set of steps set the image to swap when the user mouses over the image; however, the text on the image specifies that the user should click to see the coupon. The following steps add a restore behavior and change the swap image event so that the user must click the original image to see the second image. The restore behavior event is onmouseout, which means that the original image will reappear when the visitor removes the pointer from the image.

**1**

- Click the swap_image1.gif file (the image you just added) to select it if necessary.

- Click the Insert button on the Behaviors task pane to display the short-cut menu, then click Swap Image Restore to open the Swap Image Restore dialog box (Figure 6–56).

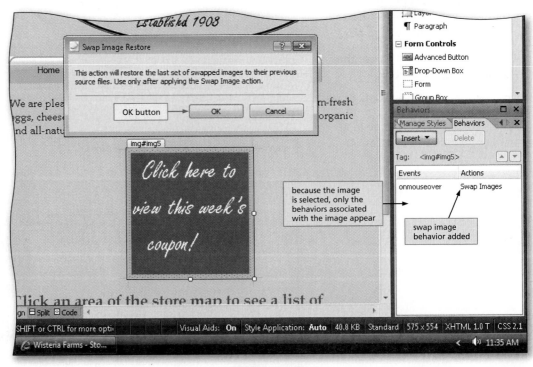

**Figure 6–56**

**2**

- Click the OK button to close the Swap Image Restore dialog box and add the swap image restore behavior to the image (Figure 6–57).

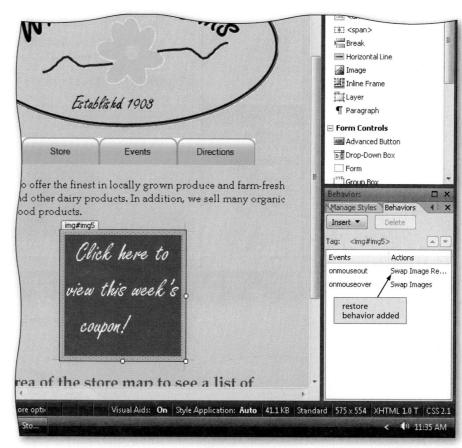

**Figure 6–57**

**3**

- Position the mouse pointer over the Swap Images behavior to display the list arrow, then click the Swap Images event list arrow to open the shortcut menu (Figure 6–58).

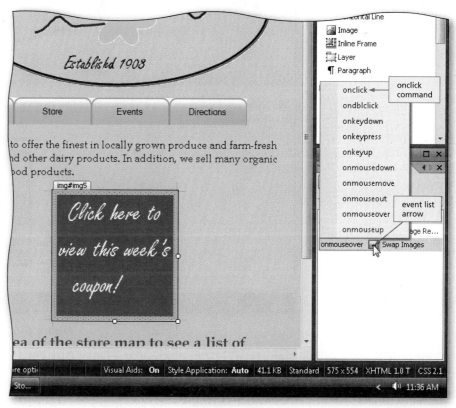

**Figure 6–58**

**4**

- Click onclick on the shortcut menu to make the swap image occur when the user clicks the image (Figure 6–59).

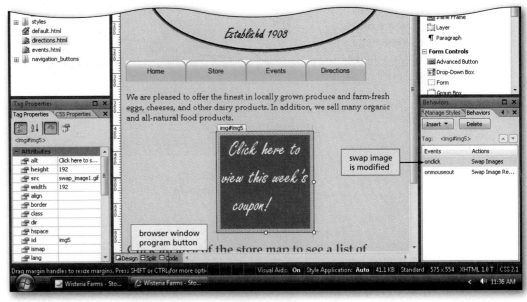

**Figure 6–59**

**5**

- Press CTRL+S to save the store.html page.

- Click the browser window program button to return to the browser.

- Press F5 to refresh the page in a browser window.

- Click the image to initiate the swap image behavior (Figure 6–60).

- Click the Close button to close the browser window.

 **Experiment**

- Select other events for the swap image and restore behaviors and test them in a browser window.

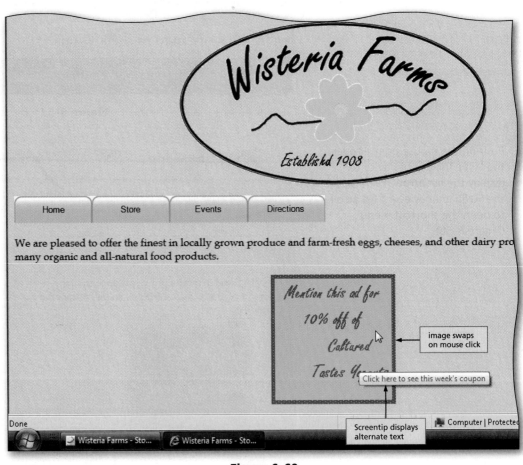

**Figure 6–60**

**Other Ways**

1. Double-click a behavior in the Behaviors task pane to open the behavior's dialog box.

Plan
Ahead

**Assess how you will provide access to site pages that do not have links in the primary navigation area.**
In addition to jump menus, such as the one you previously added in this chapter, image maps are another way to provide links to multiple, related pages. Choose a jump menu to create a list, and an image map to add interactivity and links to a graphical representation of the category of linked pages.

# Creating Image Maps

Image maps are graphics that are divided into sections. Each section is its own clickable area called a hotspot. Image maps are often used for geographical maps. On a map of Canada, for example, each province can be its own hotspot that, when clicked, displays information such as population, capital, government, or other relevant data for that province. Use image maps when the information you are conveying lends itself to a graphic representation; you would not use an image map to present stock reports, for example.

When creating an image map, you first insert the large image, then use a shape tool to define each area and assign it a link. Not every space on the image needs to be a hotspot; visitors to your site will be able to tell what is clickable by positioning the mouse pointer over the image and waiting until the hand pointer changes to indicate a hyperlink.

A hotspot, like any linked text or element, displays the address of its target page in the status bar when you position the pointer over it. Checking the status bar is another way to test links to be sure of the accuracy of the content of the linked page and to confirm that the linked page contains a method for returning to the current page.

**BTW**

**Changing Dimensions of a Graphic**
You can change aspects of a graphic, such as physical dimensions, using a graphic design program or by changing the formatting of an image in Expression Web.

## To Add an Image Map

The following steps insert the image of the store layout and create horizontal hotspots linking each store department to a page listing its featured products. You will not create a hotspot for the blank areas or the checkout area, as no additional information is required in those areas. You will close task panes so that you can view more of the editing window. You will test the links by viewing the text in the status bar, as you have already viewed these pages when testing the jump menu, so you can be sure of their content and that they contain a navigation element to return to the page.

**1**
- Click at the end of the paragraph of text that starts, Click an area, then press ENTER to insert a new paragraph (Figure 6–61).

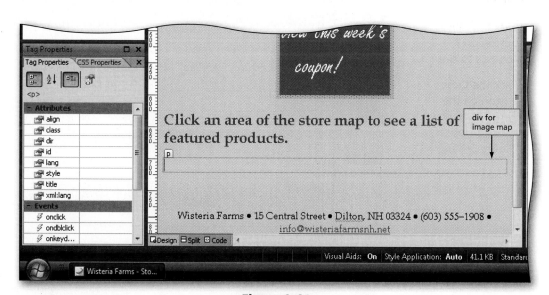

**Figure 6–61**

- Point to Picture on the Insert menu, then click From File to open the Picture dialog box.

- Navigate to the data files and double-click the wisteria_images folder if necessary.

- Click the site_map.gif file to select it, then click the Insert button to open the Accessibility Properties dialog box.

- Type `Map displays dairy; dry goods, fruit, vegetables, and greenhouse departments` in the Alternate text text box (Figure 6–62).

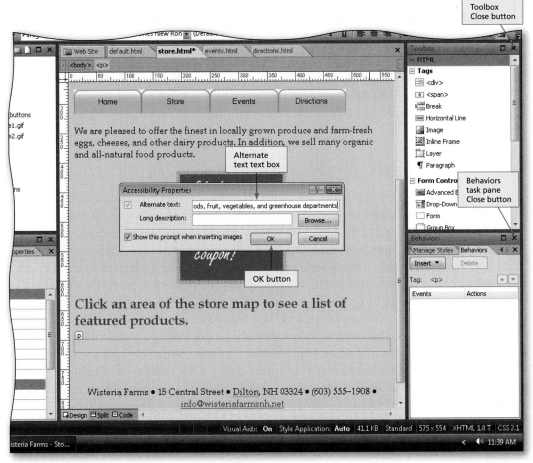

**Figure 6–62**

3

- Click the OK button to close the Accessibility Properties dialog box and insert the image.

- Click the Close button on the Toolbox to close it.

- Click the Close button on the Behaviors task pane to close it (Figure 6–63).

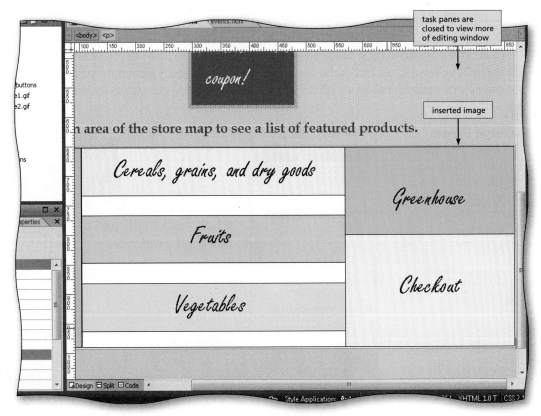

**Figure 6–63**

**4**

- Right-click the Common toolbar to display the Toolbar shortcut menu, then click Pictures to open the Pictures toolbar (Figure 6–64).

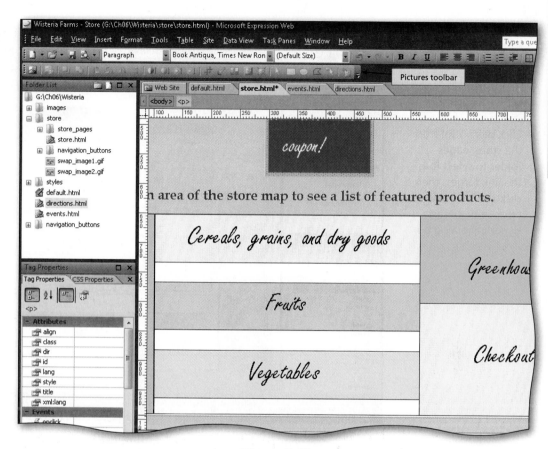

**Figure 6–64**

**5**

- Click the image to select it.

- Click Rectangular Hotspot button on the Pictures toolbar to change the pointer to a pencil (Figure 6–65).

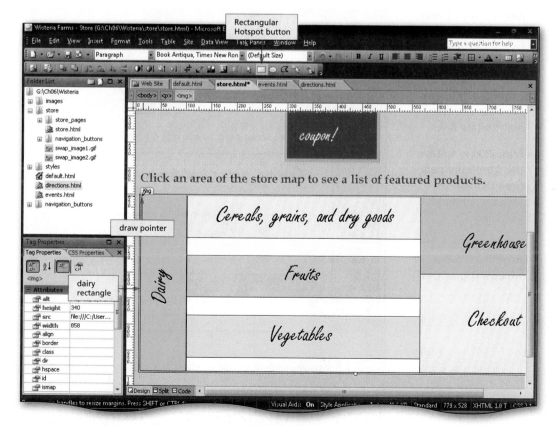

**Figure 6–65**

**6**

• Drag the pencil to select the green Dairy rectangle and open the Insert Hyperlink dialog box (Figure 6–66).

• Click dairy.html from the store_pages folder to select it as the link target, then click the OK button to close the Insert Hyperlink dialog box.

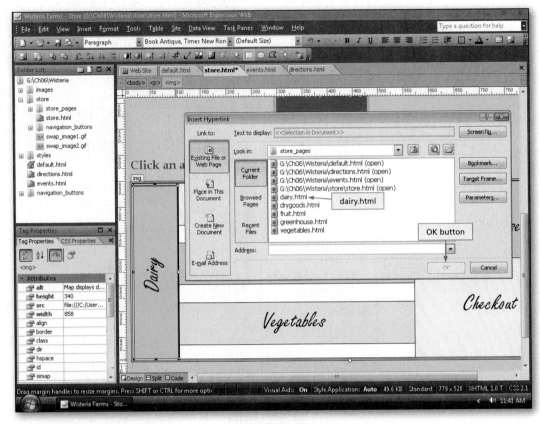

**Figure 6–66**

**7**

• Repeat Steps 5 and 6 to create hotspots for the dry goods, fruits, vegetables, and greenhouse sections of the site map with the appropriate links.

• Press CTRL+S to save the store.html page then click OK to save the embedded site images.

• Press F12 to open the page in a browser window (Figure 6–67).

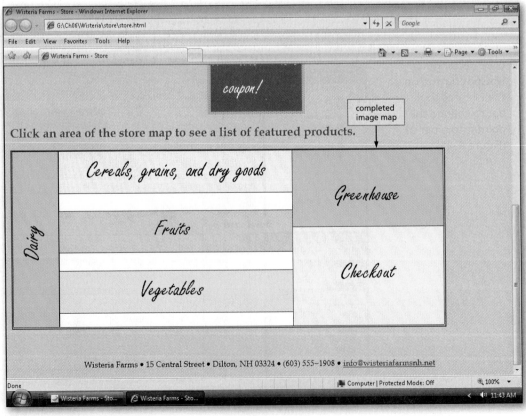

**Figure 6–67**

**8**
- Position the pointer over the image map to view the status bar and test the hotspots by viewing the address in the status bar to verify that it has the correct link (Figure 6–68).

- Click the Close button on the browser title bar to close the browser window.

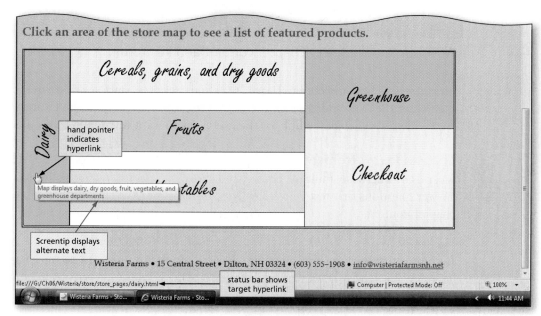

**Figure 6–68**

## To Close a Site and Quit Expression Web

**1** On the File menu, click Close Site.

**2** On the File menu, click Exit.

# Chapter Summary

In this chapter, you have learned to create, edit, and test interactive buttons to create a navigation area that you could paste onto every page. You organized your site by creating folders and moving the button images into them. You learned about behaviors, and created behaviors for a jump menu, a status bar message, and a swap image. You modified the swap image behavior, and also created an image map.

The items listed below include all the new Expression Web skills you have learned in this chapter.

1. Open a Web Site and Web Page (EW 371)
2. Create an Interactive Button (EW 373)
3. Duplicate an Interactive Button (EW 379)
4. Edit an Interactive Button (EW 380)
5. Test Interactive Buttons (EW 382)
6. Copy and Paste the Navigation Area (EW 385)
7. Organize the Button Images into Folders (EW 387)
8. Add a Jump Menu Behavior (EW 391)
9. Add a Status Bar Behavior (EW 397)
10. Add a Swap Image Behavior (EW 399)
11. Modify a Swap Image Behavior (EW 402)
12. Add an Image Map (EW 405)

 If you have a SAM user profile, you may have access to hands-on instruction, practice, and assessment. Log in to your SAM account (http://sam2007.course.com) to launch any assigned training activities or exams that relate to the skills covered in this chapter.

## Learn It Online

Test your knowledge of chapter content and key terms.

*Instructions:*  To complete the Learn It Online exercises, start your browser, click the Address bar, and then enter the Web address scsite.com/ew2/learn. When the Expression Web Learn It Online page is displayed, click the link for the exercise you want to complete and then read the instructions.

**Chapter Reinforcement TF, MC, and SA**
A series of true/false, multiple choice, and short answer questions that test your knowledge of the chapter content.

**Flash Cards**
An interactive learning environment where you identify chapter key terms associated with displayed definitions.

**Practice Test**
A series of multiple choice questions that test your knowledge of chapter content and key terms.

**Who Wants To Be a Computer Genius?**
An interactive game that challenges your knowledge of chapter content in the style of a television quiz show.

**Wheel of Terms**
An interactive game that challenges your knowledge of chapter key terms in the style of the television show *Wheel of Fortune*.

**Crossword Puzzle Challenge**
A crossword puzzle that challenges your knowledge of key terms presented in the chapter.

## Apply Your Knowledge

Reinforce the skills and apply the concepts you learned in this chapter.

**Creating an Interactive Navigation Area and Adding a Behavior**
*Instructions:*  Start Expression Web. You will create a new one-page Web site, create and attach a new style sheet, then copy the default.html page to create the other site pages as shown in Figure 6–69. You will create a navigation area using interactive buttons. You will also create a swap image behavior. You will leave most of the site content blank at this point, but you will add folders and move the pages and interactive buttons into them.

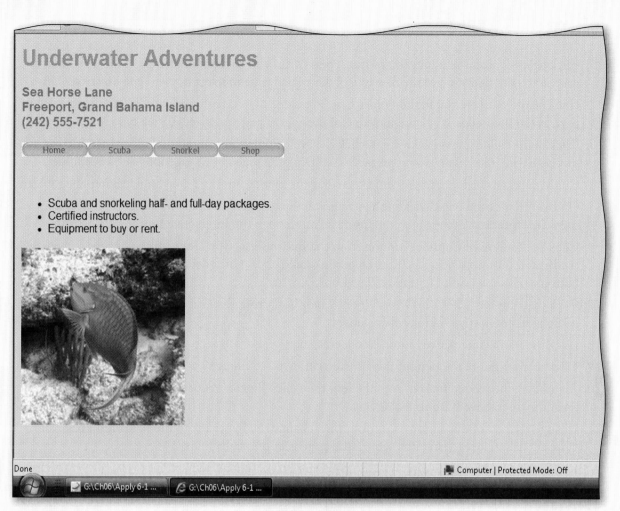

**Figure 6–69**

*Perform the following tasks:*

1. Point to New on the File menu, click Web Site, then click One Page Web Site.

2. Navigate to the drive and folder where you save your Data Files, type `Apply 6-1 Underwater` in the Specify the location of the new Web site text box, then click the OK button.

3. Point to New on the File menu, then click Page. Click Style Sheets, then click the Capsules style sheet type and click the OK button.

4. Save the new style sheet as underwater_styles.css.

5. Open the default.html page, then attach the underwater_styles.css.

6. Insert a paragraph div for the page header, type `Underwater Adventures`, then format the div with the h1 heading style.

7. Insert a new paragraph div below the header, select the h3 heading style, then type the following, pressing SHIFT+ENTER at the end of each line.

   `Sea Horse Lane`

   `Freeport, Grand Bahama Island`

   `(242) 555-7521`

8. Press ENTER after the last line to create a new paragraph div, then save the page.

9. Click the default.html filename in the Folder List to select it, then press CTRL+C to copy it to the Clipboard.

10. Press CTRL+V to paste a copy of the default.html page in the site folder. Select the filename of the copied page to select it, then type `scuba.html`.

*Continued >*

**Apply Your Knowledge** *continued*

11. Click below scuba.html in the Folder List. Press CTRL+V to paste another copy of the default.html page in the site folder. Click the filename of the copied page to select it, then type `snorkel.html`.

12. Click below snorkel.html in the Folder List. Press CTRL+V to paste a third copy of the default.html page in the site folder. Click the filename of the copied page to select it, then type `shop.html`.

13. Click in the Folder List to activate it, click the New Folder button on the Folder List title bar, type `scuba` as the folder name, then press ENTER. Drag the scuba.html page into the scuba folder.

14. Create folders named snorkel and shop, then drag the snorkel.html and shop.html files into their folders.

15. On the default.html page, click in the paragraph div below the contact information if necessary, then click Interactive Button on the Insert menu to open the Interactive Buttons dialog box.

16. Click the Embossed Capsule 3 option from the Buttons list, type Home in the Text box, then click the Browse button to open the Edit Hyperlink dialog box. Click default.html, then click the OK button to close the Edit Hyperlink dialog box.

17. Click the Font tab. Click the Original Font Color box arrow, then click Olive. Click the OK button to close the Interactive Buttons dialog box.

18. Click the Home interactive button to select it, then press CTRL+C to copy it to the Clipboard.

19. Click to the right of the button, then press CTRL+V three times to paste three copies of the button.

20. Right-click the second button from the left, then click Button Properties on the shortcut menu to open the Interactive Buttons dialog box.

21. Change the text of the button to `Scuba`, then change the hyperlink to the scuba.html page and close all dialog boxes. (*Hint:* the scuba.html page is in the scuba folder.)

22. Rename the third and fourth buttons `Snorkel` and `Shop`, and link the buttons to the appropriate pages.

23. Save all of the image files.

24. In the Folder List, create a new folder called navigation_images, then drag all of the button images into the folder.

25. Click below the navigation area on the default.html page, then insert a new paragraph div. Click the Bullets button on the Common toolbar, then type:

    - `Scuba and snorkeling half- and full-day packages.`
    - `Certified instructors.`
    - `Equipment to buy or rent.`

26. Press ENTER twice after the last list item, then click the Insert Picture from File button on the Pictures toolbar to open the Picture dialog box. Navigate to the underwater_images folder, select the parrot_fish.jpg image, then click the Insert button. Type `Rainbow Parrot Fish and Trumpet Fish` in the Accessibility Properties dialog box, then click the OK button.

27. Click the image to select it, then click Behaviors on the Task Panes menu to open the Behaviors task pane if necessary.

28. Click the Insert button arrow, then click Swap Image from the shortcut menu to open the Swap Image dialog box.

29. Navigate to the data files, click the trumpet_fish.jpg image from the underwater_images folder, click the Restore on mouseout event check box, then click the OK button.

30. Preview the site in a browser and test the thumbnails and links.

31. Change the site properties, as specified by your instructor. Submit the revised site in the format specified by your instructor.

32. Save all pages, then close the site.

# Extend Your Knowledge

Extend the skills you learned in this chapter and experiment with new skills. You may need to use Help to complete the assignment.

## Converting Text to a Table

*Instructions:*   Start Expression Web. Open the site, Extend 6-1 Preschool, from the Data Files for Students. See the inside back cover of this book for instructions for downloading the Data Files for Students, or see your instructor for information about accessing the required files.

You will create a navigation area using a column of interactive buttons to make the default.html page match the one shown in Figure 6–70.

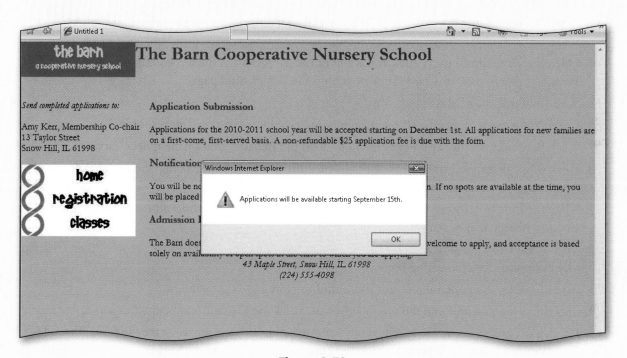

**Figure 6–70**

*Perform the following tasks:*

1. Open the default.html page, position the insertion point at the end of the paragraph in the left column, press ENTER, then double-click Paragraph in the Toolbox to insert a new paragraph div.

2. Click Interactive Button on the Insert menu to open the Interactive Buttons dialog box.

3. Click the Braided Column 3 option in the Buttons list, type home in the Button Text box, then click the Browse button to open the Edit Hyperlink dialog box.

4. Click the default.html filename, then click the OK button to close the Edit Hyperlink dialog box.

5. Click the Font tab, click in the Font box, then type Poornut to select the font. Click Bold in the Font Style box, then click 20 in the Size box. Click the Hovered Font Color box arrow, then click Navy from the color palette.

6. Click the Image tab, click in the Width box, then type 200. Click the OK button to close the Interactive Buttons dialog box.

7. Click the Home interactive button to select it, then press CTRL+C to copy it to the Clipboard.

8. Click to the right of the button, then press CTRL+V twice to paste two copies of the button.

*Continued >*

**Extend Your Knowledge** *continued*

9. Right-click the second button from the top, then click Button Properties on the shortcut menu to open the Interactive Buttons dialog box.

10. Change the text of the button to registration, then change the hyperlink to the registration. html page and close all dialog boxes.

11. Rename the third button to classes and link the button to the appropriate page.

12. Save all of the image files.

13. In the Folder List, create a new folder called navigation_images, then drag all of the button images into the folder.

14. Select the paragraph div that contains the navigation area, then press CTRL+C to copy it to the Clipboard.

15. Open the registration.html page, click at the end of the paragraph in the left column, then press ENTER. Press CTRL+V to paste the navigation area onto the registration.html page.

16. Open the classes.html page, click at the end of the paragraph in the left column, then press ENTER. Press CTRL+V to paste the navigation area onto the classes.html page.

17. Save all of the image files.

18. In the Folder List, drag all of the button images into the navigation_images folder.

19. Click Behaviors on the Task Panes menu to open the Behaviors task pane if necessary.

20. Click the registration.html tab. Select the word, Applications, in the paragraph under the Application Submission heading.

21. Click the Insert button arrow, then click Popup Message from the shortcut menu to open the Popup Message dialog box.

22. Type Applications will be available starting September 15th., then click the OK button to close the dialog box.

23. Save all pages, then open the registration.html page in a browser window.

24. Test the navigation area and the pop-up message. Click the OK button to close the pop-up message.

25. Change the site properties, as specified by your instructor. Save the site using the file name, Extend 6-1 Preschool Site. Submit the revised site in the format specified by your instructor.

## Make It Right

Analyze a site and correct all errors and/or improve the design.

### Replacing a Text-Based Navigation Area with Interactive Buttons

*Instructions:* Start Expression Web. Open the Web site, Make It Right 6-1 Drama, from the Data Files for Students. See the inside back cover of this book for instructions for downloading the Data Files for Students, or see your instructor for information about accessing the required files.

Create a new navigation area on the default.html page by replacing the text-based hyperlinks with interactive buttons. Copy and paste the navigation area to the main site pages, and create folders to store the button images to create the home page shown in Figure 6–71.

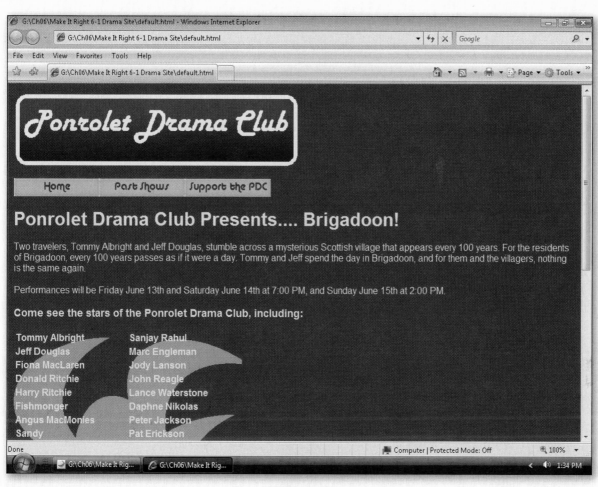

**Figure 6–71**

1. Open the default.html page.

2. Click in the div that contains the hyperlinks, select all of the content in the div, then press DELETE to remove the content.

3. Click Interactive Button on the Insert menu to open the Interactive Buttons dialog box.

4. Create a button using the Soft Rectangle 3 button, with Home as the text, linking to the default.html page, with Alba as the font, 14-point font size, Maroon as the original font color, and 150 pixels wide.

5. Copy the button, then paste two copies in the navigation area.

6. Edit the second button so that its label is Past Shows and that it links to the past_shows.html page. (*Hint*: the past_shows.html page is in the past_shows folder.)

7. Edit the third button so that its label is Support the PDC and that it links to the support.html page. (*Hint*: the support.html page is in the support folder.)

8. Save the page and all embedded files.

9. Select the div with the navigation area and replace the text-based navigation areas on the support.html and past_shows.html pages with the interactive buttons.

10. Save all pages and all embedded files.

11. Create folders for the navigation images in the main site folder, the support folder, and the past_shows folder, and move the button image files into them.

12. Change the site properties, as specified by your instructor. Save the site using the file name, Make It Right 6-1 Drama Site. Submit the revised site in the format specified by your instructor.

# In the Lab

Design and/or format a Web site using the guidelines, concepts, and skills presented in this chapter. Labs are listed in order of increasing difficulty.

## Lab 1: Adding Interactive Buttons

*Problem:* Your client, a senior center, has asked you to create a new multi-page Web site and add an interactive navigation area. You will create a new one-page site, add a preformatted style sheet, then copy the page twice. You will add interactive buttons to create a navigation area that includes links to the three site pages, copy it to each page, then create a folder for the buttons to create the page shown in Figure 6–72.

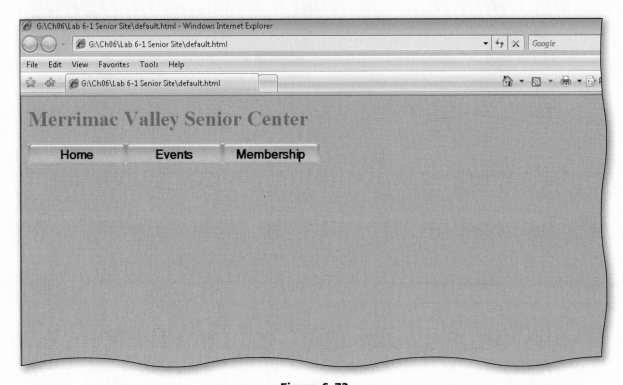

**Figure 6–72**

*Instructions:*

1. Start Expression Web.

2. Create a one-page Web site called Lab 6-1 Senior Site, then open the default.html page.

3. Create a new style sheet based on the Bars style sheet, save it as senior_styles.css, then attach it to the default.html page.

4. Insert a new paragraph div at the top of the page, type `Merrimac Valley Senior Center`, format it with h1, then press ENTER to insert a new paragraph div.

5. Save the default.html page.

6. In the Folder List, click the default.html page, press CTRL+C, then press CTRL+V twice.

7. Rename the two copies of the default.html page so that you have two new pages: events.html and membership.html.

8. With the insertion point in the new paragraph div on the default.html page, click Interactive Button on the Insert menu.

9. Create a button using the Embossed Rectangle 3 button with the text Home that links to the default.html page. Make the button text bold, 14-point, and 150 pixels wide.

10. Copy the button and paste it twice. Edit the two pasted buttons to refer and link to the two other site pages (events and membership), then select the div containing the buttons and copy it to the Clipboard.

11. Open the events.html and membership.html pages and paste the navigation area onto each page.

12. Save all pages at once and click OK three times to save the embedded images.

13. Create a new folder in the Folder List called navigation_images. Using the Web Site pane, move all button images into the folder.

14. Preview the default.html page in a browser.

15. Submit the site in the format specified by your instructor, then close the site.

## In the Lab

### Lab 2: Adding a Jump Menu

*Problem:* You want to create a menu of sample worksheets for your math tutoring business. You will add a jump menu and reorder the menu items to create the default.html page, as shown in Figure 6–73.

**Figure 6–73**

*Continued >*

**In the Lab** *continued*

*Instructions:* Start Expression Web. Open the Web site, Lab 6-2 Tutor, from the Data Files for Students. See the inside back cover of this book for instructions for downloading the Data Files for Students, or see your instructor for information about accessing the required files.

*Perform the following tasks.*

1. Open the default.html page.

2. Create a new paragraph div above the div that starts, Contact me. Type `Here are some sample worksheets:`, then press ENTER.

3. Open the Behaviors task pane if necessary, then open the Jump Menu dialog box.

4. Use the table below to create menu items. All of the pages are in the sample_worksheets folder within the main site folder.

| Choice | Value |
|---|---|
| Algebra | algebra_sample.html |
| AP preparation | AP_preparation_sample.html |
| Calculus | calculus_sample.html |
| Geometry | geometry_sample.html |
| Pre-algebra | prealgebra_sample.html |
| Trigonometry | trigonometry_sample.html |

5. Use the Move Up and Move Down buttons to change the order to: Pre-algebra, Algebra, Geometry, Trigonometry, Calculus, AP preparation.

6. Preview the site and test the jump menu.

7. Change the site properties, as specified by your instructor.

8. Rename the site Lab 6-2 Tutor Site, submit the site in the format specified by your instructor, then close the site.

## In the Lab

### Lab 3: Creating an Image Map

*Problem:* You are on your school's fundraising committee. You create a one-page Web site folder and a new style sheet using a preformatted style sheet, and add content and pages. You then insert an image and create an image map to link to the pages to create the page shown in Figure 6–74.

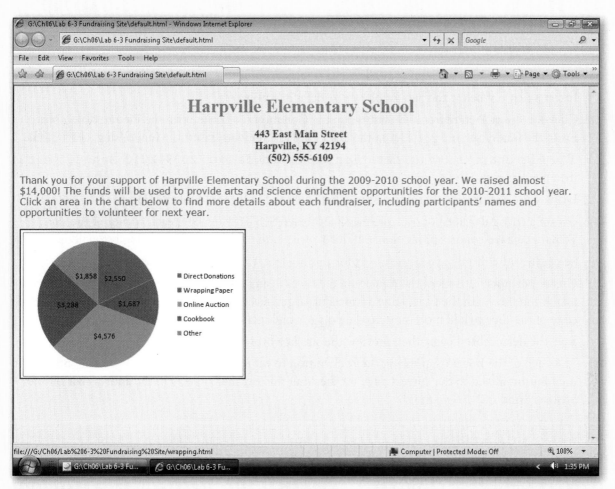

**Figure 6–74**

*Instructions:*

1. Start Expression Web.

2. Create a one-page Web site called Lab 6-3 Fundraising Site, then open the default.html page.

3. Create a new style sheet based on the Arcs style sheet, save it as fundraising_styles.css, then attach it to the default.html page.

4. Insert a new paragraph div, type `Harpville Elementary School`, format the div with the h1 heading, and center it.

5. Insert a new paragraph div, then type the following, pressing SHIFT+ENTER after each line.

   `443 East Main Street`

   `Harpville, KY 42194`

   `(502) 555-6109`

6. Format the paragraph div as h3, then center it.

7. Click below the paragraph, then insert a new paragraph div. Type

   `Thank you for your support of Harpville Elementary School during the 2009-2010 school year. We raised almost $14,000! The funds will be used to provide arts and science enrichment opportunities for the 2010-2011 school year. Click an area in the chart below to find more details about each fundraiser, including participants' names and opportunities to volunteer for next year.`

*Continued >*

**STUDENT ASSIGNMENTS**

**In the Lab** *continued*

8. Save the default.html page. Copy and paste the default.html page in the Folder List five times. Rename the copied pages to: direct.html, wrapping.html, auction.html, cookbook.html, and other.html.

9. Insert a new div below the paragraph on the default.html page.

10. Click the Insert Picture from File button on the Common toolbar to open the Picture dialog box. From the fundraiser_image folder in the Data Files for Students, insert the fundraising_chart.gif file.

11. Type `Pie chart showing donation percentages for 2009-2010 school year` as the alternate text.

12. Display the Pictures toolbar if necessary, then click the Polygonal Hotspot button.

13. Create a triangular hotspot over the pie slice labeled $1858 by clicking each corner of the slice. When you have connected the first and third corners, the Edit Hyperlink dialog box will open.

14. Select the other.html page as the target for this hotspot, then close the dialog box.

15. Create hotspots for each of the remaining pie slices, using the legend to the right of the chart to match the slice with the page name. (*Hint*: For larger slices, click multiple times along the rounded edge of the slice to add more sides to the polygon and include more of the slice in the hotspot.)

16. Save the default.html page, then preview the site in a browser.

17. Test each of the hotspots, pressing the back button to return to the default.html page. Confirm that each button linked to the correct page by checking the text that appears in the address bar on the browser window.

18. Change the site properties, as specified by your instructor.

19. Submit the site in the format specified by your instructor, then close the site.

## Cases and Places

Apply your creative thinking and problem solving skills to design and implement a solution.

● EASIER    ●●MORE DIFFICULT

### ● 1: Creating a Navigation Area using Interactive Buttons

Create a new one-page Web site for a car wash. Create a new style sheet based on a preformatted style sheet and attach it to the page. Add a header and div into which you will add a navigation area. Copy the page using the Folder List to create three other pages, and rename them. Create and test a navigation area on the default.html page for the home page using the interactive button of your choice. Specify different font colors for original, hovered, and pressed states, then change the vertical or horizontal alignment. Specify the height and width of the button. Copy and paste the button, then modify the text and hyperlink to create navigation for all pages in your site. Save the page and embedded images, then create a folder to store the images. Test the navigation area in the browser, then copy it to all site pages. Create folders as necessary to store the button images for the navigation areas. Save and close all pages, then quit Expression Web.

• **2: Creating and Modifying a Swap Image**

Create a new one-page Web site for a florist. Insert an image using a file from this chapter, a previous chapter, or using an image file of your own. Add a swap image behavior using another image of similar size. Accept the defaults in the Swap Image dialog box, then save the page and preview the image in the browser. Return to the default.html page, then modify the swap image behavior to add a restore behavior and change the event to onclick. Save the page, and refresh the browser window. Test the modified behavior. Return to the default.html page, then modify the restore image behavior to an event of your choice. Save the page, and refresh the browser window. Test the modified behavior, then save and close the site and the browser window.

•• **3: Adding Behaviors to a Dynamic Web Template**

Create a new site for a computer repair shop using a dynamic Web template. Open the default.html page and preview it in a browser window to see the interactive buttons for the navigation area. Open the master.dwt page, and set a status bar message. Add a jump menu to the default.html page that links to at least two site pages. Save all open pages, then refresh your browser to view the status bar message on the default.html page. Test the jump menu to go to another page and view the status bar message on that page. Close the browser window and the site.

•• **4: Creating a Travel Site**

**Make It Personal**

You want to create a Web site that includes information about a travel spot you have visited or would like to visit. Create a site with at least three pages, using blank pages or a CSS layout and a preformatted style sheet. Enter information on the pages, and create a navigation area for the site pages using interactive buttons. Create an image swap using two photos from your trip or that you find for public use on the Internet or from the projects in this book. Save the pages and style sheets, then close the site.

•• **5: Planning Navigation for Other Site Pages**

**Working Together**

A department store wants to create a site that has four main site pages: a home page, directions, contact information, and products. Working as a team with several of your classmates, you are to plan and create the four site pages, and at least four other site pages for store departments. You will focus on creating the pages and navigation, not on creating elaborate content for each page. Each team member should contribute to planning the layout, formatting, and navigation for the site. As a group, decide on the departments for which you will include pages, and decide the best way to include that information on your site. Start by creating a site folder, and add page using a CSS layout. Create and attach a style sheet using a preformatted style sheet. Copy that page to create additional site pages, and name each of them appropriately. Create a navigation area using either a column or row format, and add it to each of the main site pages. Create an interactive behavior such as an image map or jump menu to link to the other site pages. Create folders as necessary to keep your site organized. Preview the site, and test the navigation bar and behavior. Save and close the pages and style sheet, then close the site.

# E-Commerce Feature
# E-Commerce

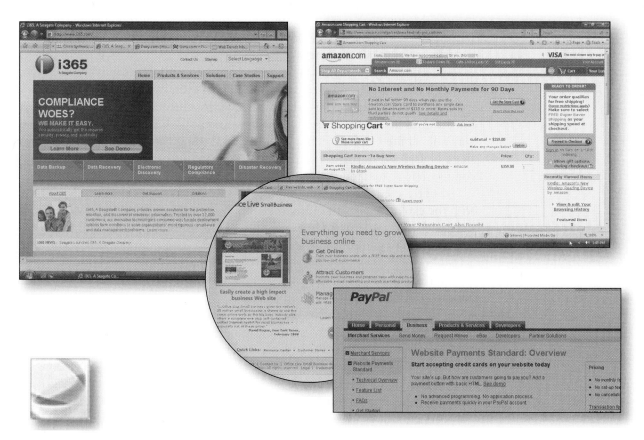

## Objectives

You will have mastered the material in this special feature when you can:

- Define e-commerce and describe the role of e-commerce in today's business environment

- Identify e-commerce business models

- List elements necessary to add e-commerce capability to a Web site

- Describe how to add e-commerce capability to a Web site using third-party payment processing or an all-in-one e-commerce solution

# The Role of E-Commerce in Today's Business Environment

**Electronic commerce** or **e-commerce** (sometimes called **e-business**) encompasses a wide variety of business transactions conducted electronically using the electronic funds transfer (EFT) and electronic data interchange (EDI) systems, corporate **intranets** (private internal networks) and **extranets** (private intranets connected using the Internet), the Internet, and the World Wide Web (Web). For example, e-commerce transactions can include the buying and selling of products and services, customer support activities after the sale, the exchange of data or funds between business partners, and so forth, using electronic communication networks.

E-commerce actually began many years ago with the advent of the EFT system, in which funds are transferred electronically between banks, and EDI systems, in which purchase orders, invoices, and other business documents are exchanged over private communications networks connecting business partners. Access to EFT and EDI systems was generally limited to the banking industry and to large corporations; smaller organizations shared business information and processed payments using traditional mail and telephone connections — methods that were slow, inconvenient, and sometimes costly.

The e-commerce revolution that touches many aspects of our daily lives started with the explosive growth of Internet and Web technologies in the 1990s and continues to be fueled by the expanding availability of high-speed, broadband Internet access to both businesses and consumers around the world. Using high-speed, broadband Internet access, today's individual or business consumer can go online and, in a matter of seconds, shop for and purchase virtually any type of product or service from a business located anywhere in the world.

While individual and business consumers benefit from increased access to products and services, businesses involved in e-commerce enjoy the opportunity to reach more customers, improve customer support, and reduce operating costs by conducting their business transactions online. To learn more about the volume of e-commerce transactions and the overall importance of e-commerce to the United States and global economy, visit **scsite.com/ew2/websources** and click a link under Special Feature 2, E-Commerce Stats.

A helpful way to look more closely at the types of businesses involved in e-commerce is to identify how the businesses generate their revenues.

# E-Commerce Business Models

A **business model** defines how a business generates its revenues. An **e-commerce business model** identifies the revenue-generation processes for a business involved in e-commerce. E-commerce business models can be defined in a number of ways. For example, a business that provides free informational content or services to visitors and generates its revenues by selling advertising space at its site can be defined as following an *advertising business model*. A retailer that sells its products online in addition to or instead of at a physical store can be defined as following a *virtual storefront business model*. An online business that offers information or services to members who pay a monthly or annual subscription fee can be defined as following a *subscription business model*. Many businesses involved in e-commerce combine multiple e-commerce models to generate revenues. For example, a small business retailer might combine business models such as advertising and virtual storefront to generate revenues by selling products directly to consumers and by selling advertising space at its site to other online businesses.

One of the most commonly used ways to broadly categorize businesses involved in e-commerce is to define the seller/buyer relationship in the revenue-generation process.

## Business-to-Consumer (B2C)

Online businesses (sellers) that sell products and services — for example, books, tickets to movies and sports events, food items, travel services, and diet and exercise plans — directly to consumers (buyers) are following the general **business-to-consumer** or **B2C** e-commerce business model. Examples of B2C e-commerce sites include:

- Prestogeorge — coffee, tea, specialty gifts (Figure SF 2–1)
- Amazon.com — books and other consumer items
- MyFoodDiary — subscription-based diet and fitness services
- Expedia — travel services

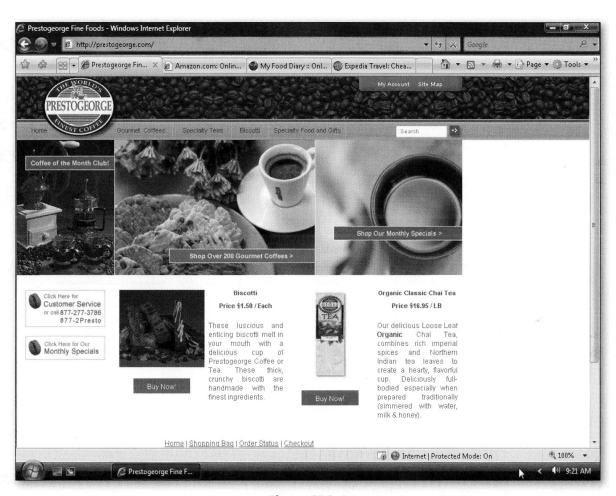

**Figure SF 2–1**

## Business-to-Business (B2B)

Businesses that sell their products or services to other businesses can be described as following the general **business-to-business** or **B2B** e-commerce business model. While you may be more familiar with B2C e-commerce, B2B e-commerce transactions actually dominate the online marketplace. Businesses that sell information technology hardware and software online, virtual stores that sell office supplies coupled with inventory management services, online data backup services, online marketplaces that attract multiple business sellers and buyers in a particular industry, online marketplaces that match suppliers with buyers, and Web site performance analysis and marketing services for online businesses are just a few examples of the wide variety of seller/buyer relationships covered by B2B e-commerce. Real-world B2B e-commerce examples that illustrate these types of seller/buyer relationships include:

- Cisco — IT products and services
- i365 — online data backup services
- Dairy.com — marketplace for the dairy industry
- Guru.com — marketplace for freelancers and employers
- WebTrends — Web site performance analysis and marketing services

An extranet is a portion of a company's internal computer network that can be accessed by outsiders, such as business partners, by using an Internet connection. The exchange of business documents, such as requests for quotes (RFQs), purchase orders, receiving reports, and bills of lading, between business partners over Internet-connected extranets is also considered B2B e-commerce.

## Consumer-to-Consumer (C2C)

The **consumer-to-consumer** or **C2C** e-commerce business model is being followed when consumers sell items or services directly to other consumers. For example, Web sites that offer online auctions in which consumers bid on items offered for sale by other consumers, online classified ads, and online entertainment or sports venue ticket resale are following the C2C e-commerce business model. eBay, TraderOnline, and StubHub! (Figure SF 2–2) are examples of sites that bring consumers together to sell and buy items to/from each other.

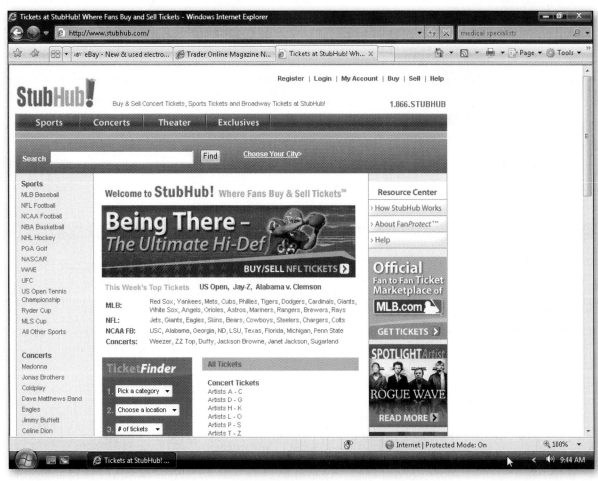

**Figure SF 2–2**

## Consumer-to-Business (C2B)

The **consumer-to-business** or **C2B** e-commerce business model uses a reverse auction process that allows consumers to make binding bids or offers for a product or service, such as airline tickets, hotel rooms, or rental cars. Participating businesses can then choose to accept or decline the consumers' bids. Priceline (Figure SF 2–3) is the e-commerce business most often associated with the C2B e-commerce business model.

**Figure SF 2–3**

## Business-to-Government (B2G)

Some e-commerce sites create an online marketplace in which businesses with products and services to sell are matched with government agencies that have procurement needs. These online marketplaces are following the general **business-to-government** or **B2G** e-commerce business model. Onvia (Figure SF 2–4), B2GMarket, and Bidmain are three examples of businesses following the B2G e-commerce business model.

**Figure SF 2–4**

## Business-to-Employee (B2E)

In addition to these general categories based on the seller/buyer relationship, many businesses exploit Internet and Web technologies to connect management and employees over the company intranet. For example, on a company intranet you often find a Web site supported by the company's human resources department (the "seller") that can be accessed by employees (the "buyers"). In this scenario, the human resources department uses its Web site to provide employees with access to important information about employment rules and guidelines, insurance benefits, 401(k) investment management, and more. This electronic connection between management and employees is often called **business-to-employee** or **B2E** e-commerce.

Some online business sites customize their offerings by engaging in multiple types of seller/buyer relationships. For example, Office Depot and Dell offer products and services directly to consumers (B2C) as well as to other businesses (B2B). The Wall Street Journal Online offers subscription services to both individual (B2C) and to business (B2B) customers.

To learn more about e-commerce business models, visit **scsite.com/ew2/websources** and click a link under Special Feature 2, E-Commerce Business Models. For a closer look at the Web site examples discussed in this section, visit **scsite.com/ew2/websources** and click a link under Special Feature 2, Business Model Examples.

# Web Site E-Commerce Elements

All e-commerce Web sites — regardless of which e-commerce business model or combination of models a business follows — must have in place certain basic elements to support e-commerce transactions, such as:

- a product catalog or information about services offered
- technologies to accept and summarize product orders, including taxes and shipping, if applicable
- technologies to respond to potential customer inquiries about services offered, such as e-mail responses to inquiries or appointment scheduling
- technologies to process orders and payments
- a method for delivering products or services and, for physical products, a method for handling product returns
- a process for providing customer support before and after the sale
- online transaction security policies and procedures

The specific elements required to add e-commerce capability to a business site depend on the needs of the business and its customers. For example, a B2B or B2C company that sells services might require only a catalog of services offered, hours of operation, contact information, and other customer service information at its Web site. However, a B2B or B2C company that sells products will require most, if not all, of the basic elements listed above to add e-commerce capability to its business site.

To illustrate how a combination of basic e-commerce elements can come together to add e-commerce capability to a Web site, assume that you are a small business owner who sells products from a brick-and-mortar store. You now want to add e-commerce capability to your existing Web site.

You will need to add to your site the technologies that allow a customer to select items for purchase, summarize the individual selections into a complete order, and then process the customer's payment for the order. Additionally, you must add to your site options for handling customer questions, complaints, and other feedback. You must also have in place a process for ensuring security of your site's online transactions and the customer information they generate.

In addition to modifying your Web site, you must also consider the modifications to your **back office operations**—the related internal business activities that take place outside your Web site, such as the process for fulfilling and shipping the customer's order.

## Product Catalog

Businesses selling products online must include pages in their Web sites that detail the products site visitors can purchase. These product pages, also called a **product catalog**, should provide the relevant information about each product — a description, a product image, sale price, benefits to the buyer, and so forth. Each item in the product catalog should have an option button or box that a visitor can click to select the product for purchase. Figure SF 2–5 illustrates a product page at the WonderBrains.com B2C site.

**Figure SF 2–5**

## Shopping Cart

A virtual **shopping cart** is software that records each individual item purchased and then summarizes the purchased items into a single order that includes total item cost, applicable sales tax, applicable coupons or discounts, and shipping costs. You can purchase shopping cart software from a wide variety of vendors and then integrate the software with your product catalog. Virtual shopping carts also generally provide a method for a customer to add or remove items from the cart before he or she finalizes the purchase through the **checkout process**. Figure SF 2–6 illustrates a pre-checkout shopping cart at the Amazon.com site.

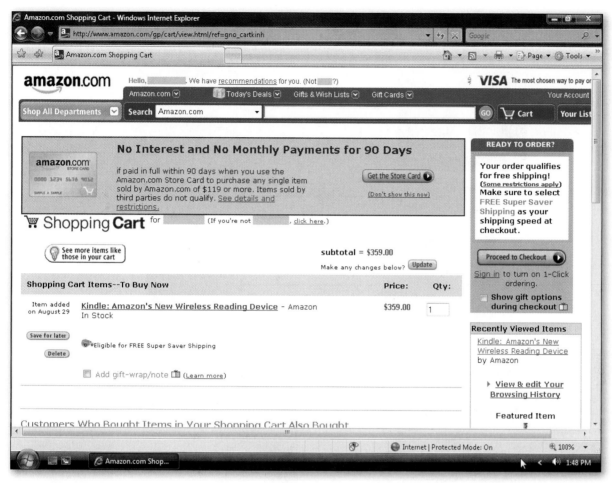

**Figure SF 2–6**

Completing an online sales order also includes the processing and approval of your customer's payment as well as your shipment of the customer's order. Figure SF 2–7 illustrates the online purchase and payment process from selection to shipment.

**BTW**

**Express Checkout**
PayPal Express Checkout and Google Checkout are add-on features to existing shopping cart software used at an e-commerce site. Express checkout features allow online customers to store their name, address, and payment information in a PayPal or Google account, then access that information during the checkout process by clicking a button in a shopping cart.

**Figure SF 2–7**

## Payment Processors, Payment Gateways, and Merchant Accounts

During the checkout process, your customer must enter applicable name, address, and payment information. Almost all online purchases in the United States are paid by credit card; to accept credit card payments, an e-commerce site must have in place a method to process and approve credit card payments and receive payment funds from credit card companies. One way to do this is to connect your site to a payment processor and a payment gateway for payment verification and approval. In addition, you must also open a merchant account into which your credit card payment funds can be deposited.

The electronic verification process for an online credit card purchase is performed by a payment processor. An e-commerce **payment processor** is a business that verifies, authorizes, and processes secure credit card transactions in real time over a network, called a **payment gateway,** that connects online stores with credit card companies and financial institutions. Figure SF 2–8 illustrates the verification, authorization, and processing of credit card transactions over a payment gateway.

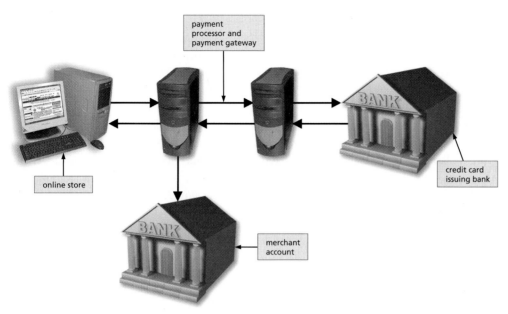

**Figure SF 2–8**

A **merchant account** is a business account at a financial institution into which proceeds from credit card payments are automatically deposited. You can apply for a merchant account at a financial institution that specializes in e-commerce transactions by providing information about your online business; for example, business overview, length of time in business, your credit history, and the type of credit cards you will accept. The fees involved with a merchant account can include:

- a one-time setup fee
- a monthly access fee
- a per-transaction fee
- a percentage of each transaction, called the **discount rate**

The financial institution providing the merchant account typically assesses its fees based on an analysis of the business risks associated with the account and its own experience with similar accounts.

A **chargeback** occurs when a financial institution must return funds to a credit card company, because the card holder refuses to pay a disputed charge. While the financial institution will deduct the chargeback from the merchant account, there is a risk that the bank might not be able to recover the chargeback if the business owner has already withdrawn the original funds from the account. The chargeback history for similar accounts to the one you open is one factor the financial institution takes into consideration when establishing its fees. The types of products or services you plan to sell at your site can also affect the financial institution's assessment of the chargeback risk on your merchant account because certain products or services historically generate more chargebacks.

An online credit card payment also increases the risk of a chargeback because, unlike a credit card transaction at a brick-and-mortar store, the credit card and the card holder are not physically present during the verification process. This is called the **card not present/card holder not present risk** and typically results in a higher discount rate for e-commerce merchant accounts.

For more information about merchant accounts, payment processors, and payment gateways, visit **scsite.com/ew2/websources** and click a link under Special Feature 2, Credit Card Processing. While most online purchases are paid by credit card, some online sellers also accept person-to-person payment methods, electronic checks, smart cards, or micropayments. For more information about online payment methods, visit **scsite.com/ew2/websources** and click a link under Special Feature 2, Online Payment Methods.

## Order Fulfillment

After a customer has made and paid for a purchase at your online store, the item or items purchased must then be delivered to the customer. The process of picking sold items from an inventory, packaging the items, and shipping them to the customer is called **order fulfillment**. A very large online business with a huge volume of product sales might choose to build and staff its own warehouses and manage its own inventory and order fulfillment processes. For your small or medium-sized online store, a more cost-effective choice might be either a virtual inventory system or outsourcing the fulfillment process.

A **virtual inventory** is an online catalog of products that actually are owned and warehoused by third-party manufacturers or wholesalers. An online store that sells from a virtual inventory sends an order and payment for that order to the manufacturer or wholesaler only after the online store's customer has paid for the order. The order fulfillment process is handled by the manufacturer or wholesaler who, upon receipt of payment from the online store, picks the ordered items from its inventory, packages the order for delivery, and ships the order directly to the online store's customer. Selling from a virtual inventory of products is called **drop ship**. Drop ship is one e-commerce choice for small businesses that do not want to tie up cash in an inventory of products or incur additional expenses for order fulfillment.

Before considering a drop ship arrangement, however, do your homework to identify legitimate drop ship opportunities. Some Web sites that advertise drop ship business opportunities or offer to sell lists of manufacturers and wholesalers that participate in drop ship might be business scams. To learn more about drop ship scams, visit **scsite.com/ew2/websources** and click a link under Special Feature 2, Drop Ship Scams.

Another alternative for a small or medium-sized online store is to own your product inventory but outsource the warehousing, inventory management, and order fulfillment processes to a third-party logistics provider. A **third-party logistics provider**, also called a **fulfillment house**, provides inventory management, order picking and packaging, and shipping services. Outsourcing the order fulfillment and inventory control functions gives you much less control over these processes; however, it can substantially reduce the expenses associated with managing an inventory and fulfilling orders. Some third-party logistics providers, such as Shipwire and Webgistix (Figure SF 2–9), focus on e-commerce.

**Figure SF 2–9**

To learn more about order fulfillment, visit **scsite.com/ew2/websources** and click a link under Special Feature 2, Order Fulfillment.

## Customer Support

Quick and efficient communication between buyer and seller is one of the prime advantages of conducting business transactions online. An online store can exploit this communication advantage to both increase sales and increase customer satisfaction by providing online customer support. At minimum, your e-commerce Web site must provide a page with contact information including physical address, phone numbers, and e-mail addresses necessary for customers to contact your business with their questions, comments, complaints, and other feedback. Adding a Frequently Asked Questions (FAQ) page containing answers to commonly asked customer questions can be helpful. Other types of online customer support, such as links to downloadable product user manuals or notifying customers by e-mail of upcoming special sales deals, should be considered depending on customers' needs and expectations.

## Transaction Security

Transaction security is also very important for the success of your online store. You must take care to ensure that your customers' personally identifiable and payment information is transmitted securely across a payment gateway and is secure from hackers who might breach your Web site. Additionally, you must look to your own business's financial security by reducing chargebacks and protecting against credit card fraud. For more information on e-commerce security issues for both consumers and your online store, visit **scsite.com/ew2/websources** and click a link under Special Feature 2, E-Commerce Security Issues.

One key to operating a successful online business is to make certain that your site's product catalog, shopping cart, payment approval and processing, and order fulfillment systems are compatible and integrate smoothly. You can choose from a wide variety of e-commerce software and services solutions to make that happen.

## Adding E-Commerce Capability to a Web Site

Some businesses involved in e-commerce have all the resources — time, money, accounting and technical staffs, and so forth — necessary to:

- create an online product or services catalog
- get approved for and open a merchant account
- design and develop in-house shopping cart software or purchase existing shopping cart software, customize it, and then integrate it with the Web site
- identify and connect to a payment processor and payment gateway system that is also compatible with the shopping cart software and the merchant account
- tie sales and payment transactions to the business's back office systems, such as order fulfillment and customer support systems

Unfortunately, many owners of small or medium-sized businesses — like the small online store scenario described in this feature — that want to move into e-commerce are likely to find that attempting to identify, purchase or arrange for, and then combine individual e-commerce elements — especially the payment verification, approval, and funding process — into a seamless whole for their Web site can be overwhelming. For many of these businesses, choosing either a third-party payment processor solution or an all-in-one e-commerce solution is a good approach.

## Third-Party Payment Processor Solution

In some instances, getting approved for a merchant account might be difficult. For example, a startup online business with an inadequate credit history or a small online store with a low sales volume could have trouble finding an institution willing to establish a merchant account. If you have a limited number of products for sale, you might find opening and maintaining a merchant account is too expensive. Additionally, you might lack the expertise to confidently research and evaluate compatible shopping carts, payment processors, and payment gateways that work with your merchant account. Contracting with a third-party payment processor is one way to resolve these issues.

Using a **third-party payment processor**, such as PayPal Website Payments Standard, 2checkout.com, and CCNow, allows your customers to shop at your online store and then pay for their purchases at the third-party payment processor's site. A third-party payment processor provides tools for creating a product catalog at your site, including links to the processor's shopping cart. When a customer clicks a product purchase link, such as a Buy Now button, in a product catalog, his or her browser is directed to a shopping cart at the processor's site where the order is summarized and payment information is entered.

The third-party processor handles the payment verification and approval and receives the payment funds, which it then passes back to your online store in a number of ways, including:

- check
- wire transfer
- direct bank account deposit
- account credit with the processor

Fees for a third-party payment processor's services might include a startup fee, transaction fees, a discount rate, and additional fees for accepting other types of payments, such as checks. Figure SF 2–10 illustrates the third-party payment processing option.

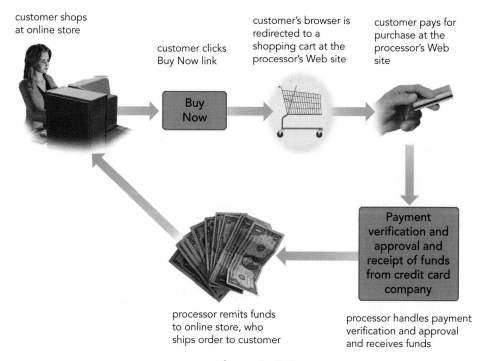

customer shops at online store

customer clicks Buy Now link

customer's browser is redirected to a shopping cart at the processor's Web site

customer pays for purchase at the processor's Web site

**Buy Now**

Payment verification and approval and receipt of funds from credit card company

processor remits funds to online store, who ships order to customer

processor handles payment verification and approval and receives funds

**Figure SF 2–10**

The primary advantage of an arrangement with a third-party payment processor is simplicity: it is easy for you to get started and offer your customers credit card payment options without the necessity of adding a shopping cart to your online store site, getting approval for a merchant account, and connecting to a payment processor and payment gateway system. The disadvantages include possible higher or unexpected fees, design limitations for your product catalog, and risking unpleasant customer experiences at your site by having your customers leave the site in order to finalize and pay for their order. To learn more about third-party payment processors, visit **scsite.com/ew2/websources** and click a link under Special Feature 2, Third-Party Payment Processors.

Alternatively, you might choose an all-in-one e-commerce package that combines all the essential elements for processing transactions at your online store.

## All-in-One E-Commerce Solution

An all-in-one e-commerce solution allows your customers to both shop at your site and then remain at your site to pay for their order. An **all-in-one e-commerce solution** generally includes, at minimum, Web page templates you can use to quickly create your site complete with a product catalog, a shopping cart, and access to the elements needed to verify, approve, and fund payments — a payment processor, access to a payment gateway system, and an account in which to receive funds.

Some all-in-one solutions go further by providing a variety of other features, such as:

- domain name registration
- an option to replace template pages with your own Web pages created in a Web authoring tool, such as Expression Web
- Web site customization and design services
- access to e-commerce Web hosting services
- Web site marketing and promotion services
- an interface to a business's back office operations, such as order fulfillment
- various levels of customer support

Fees associated with all-in-one solutions vary widely by vendor but can include a one-time setup fee, a monthly account fee based on the volume of transactions, and a per-transaction fee. Yahoo! Small Business, Microsoft Office Live Small Business (Figure SF 2–11), Volusion, and Network Solutions are examples of vendors that offer all-in-one e-commerce solutions.

**BTW**

**E-Commerce Web Hosting**
Most ISPs that offer Web hosting and companies that specialize in Web hosting offer a different range of services for hosting a Web site involved in e-commerce and charge various fees for those services. Check out Appendix C, Publishing to the Web, for more information about selecting a Web hosting alternative.

**Figure SF 2–11**

To learn more about all-in-one e-commerce solutions, visit **scsite.com/ew2/ websources** and click a link under Special Feature 2, All-in-One E-Commerce Solutions.

# Feature Summary

In this special feature, you learned how to define e-commerce and to discuss the important role e-commerce plays in today's business environment. You also learned how to classify different types of e-commerce business models based on the relationship between seller and buyer. You learned about the different elements necessary to add e-commerce capability to a Web site, including product or services catalog pages, shopping cart technologies, access to payment approval and processing services, a process for fulfilling orders, a method for providing customer support, and the importance of securing online transactions and customer information.

Finally, you learned about adding e-commerce capability to a site using either a third-party payment processor or an all-in-one e-commerce solution.

## In the Lab

Use Live Search, Google, or another search tool of your choice to locate relevant Web sites as you work through the following exercises.

### Lab 1: Planning for an E-Commerce Site

*Problem:*   You are intrigued by the idea of starting an online business based on your family's long-established coffee roasting business, but are unsure about all the ways that the site could generate revenues. You would like to explore how similar e-commerce sites are generating their revenues.

*Instructions:*   Search the Web for three e-commerce sites offering small-batch roasted coffee beans. Identify, if possible, the ways in which the real-world sites generate their revenues. Then, using what you have learned about similar real-world sites, identify the ways your site might generate revenues.

1. Using word processing or presentation software, create a presentation that summarizes your new e-commerce site, including the products and/or services it will sell. Explain all the ways your site will generate revenues. Note the e-commerce business model or combination of models your online business will follow.

2. Save your presentation as Lab SF 2-1 Planning an E-Commerce Site. At the direction of your instructor, print your presentation and give the presentation to your class.

## In the Lab

### Lab 2: Evaluating Third-Party E-Commerce Solutions

*Problem:*   Your cousin Chris runs a popular surf shop in Venice Beach. Even non-surfers make a special trip to the shop for Chris's unique T-shirt offerings. Chris would like to sell the shirts from his Web site, which currently only provides information on store hours, directions, and surf classes. You need a way to add a product catalog and shopping cart software to his site. You also know that most online payments are made using credit cards; therefore, you need a way to handle online credit card payment and processing. To save time and get Chris's online store up and running, you decide that a third-party payment processor solution would work best for Chris's online store.

*Instructions:*   Search the Web to identify and then review the services and fees provided by at least three third-party payment processors. Then select the processor that you think offers the best combination of cost and services for Chris's new online store.

1. Write a report that summarizes the services provided and costs for those services for each reviewed third-party payment processor. Choose the processor that best meets the needs of the new online store and discuss the reasons for your choice.

*Continued >*

**In the Lab** *continued*

2. Include in your report a list of the steps necessary to integrate Chris's existing Web site with the chosen third-party processor. You find this information at the processor's Web site.

3. Save your report as Lab SF 2-2 Third-party Payment Processor. At the direction of your instructor, print the report.

## In the Lab

### Lab 3: Selecting an All-in-One E-Commerce Solution

*Problem:* Refer to the Web site you created in Chapter 5 for the Acacia Salon. Salon owners Marcus and Elisa have developed their own brand of custom hair care products. Customers are buying the shampoos, conditioners, and specialty treatments as fast as the salon can stock the shelves. To exploit the popularity of their new products to increase sales, Marcus and Elisa want you to add a product sales component to their existing Web site. You know that you need a way to add a product catalog and shopping cart software to the Web site. You also know that most online payments are made using credit cards; therefore, you need a way to handle online credit card payment and processing. To save time and get the Web site's e-commerce capability up and running, you decide that an all-in-one e-commerce solution would work best for the Acacia Salon.

*Instructions:* Search the Web to identify and then review at least three all-in-one e-commerce solution vendors. Take advantage of any vendor tutorials or demos. Then select the solution that you think offers the best combination of cost and services for the salon's online store.

1. Write a report that summarizes the services provided and costs for those services for each reviewed all-in-one e-commerce solution. Choose the all-in-one e-commerce solution that best meets the Acacia Salon Web site's online store and discuss the reasons for your choice.

2. Include in your report a list of the steps necessary to integrate the salon's existing Web site with the chosen all-in-one e-commerce solution. You find this information at the vendor's Web site.

3. Save your report as Lab SF 2-3 All-in-one E-commerce Solution. At the direction of your instructor, print the report.

# 7|Working with Forms

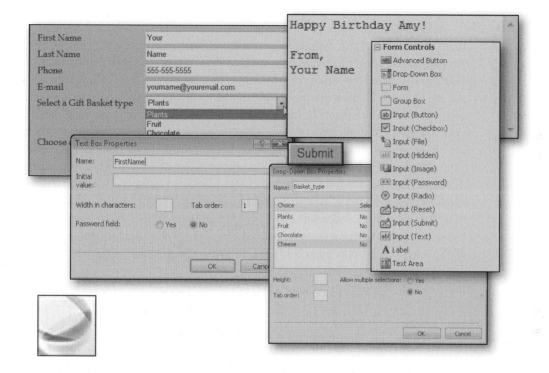

## Objectives

You will have mastered the material in this chapter when you can:

- Define HTML forms
- Add a form area
- Insert a table for form layout
- Add text boxes
- Add a drop-down list
- Add a group box
- Add check boxes
- Add radio buttons
- Add a text area
- Add a Submit button
- Format with CSS
- Test the form
- Define data collection

# 7 | Working with Forms

## Introduction

**Forms** are documents that are used to collect data. On the Web, people can use forms to fill out a survey, conduct a search, create a profile for a site, or purchase items. Forms that collect data from site visitors send the data to a database on the site server, and that data is then used to generate an event, such as displaying specific page content based on the visitor's selections, or sending a confirmation page indicating that an order was received and is being processed.

In Expression Web, forms must be created within a **form area**, which is a div that contains all of the elements for the form. Form elements include questions called **prompting text** that indicate the required data and **form controls**, or simply controls, that the visitor selects or enters text into to generate responses. Each form that you create should have a unique name to distinguish it from other forms on your site. Types of controls, also called **form fields**, include text boxes and text areas for typed data; elements that allow you to make one or more selections, including option buttons, check boxes, and list boxes; and a **Submit button** that that the visitor clicks when the data is complete.

The collected data is sent to the site server using a scripted file called a **form handler**. The form handler is activated when the visitor clicks the Submit button, and contains instructions for adding the form data to a database or other software that collects, stores, and processes data. A **database** is a collection of data organized in a manner that allows access, retrieval, and use of that data. A **database management system**, such as Microsoft Access, is software that allows you to create a database and use the stored data to generate reports, tables, and queries. Your Expression Web forms must use control names that correspond to the field names in the database. Most often, you would create the database first and then create the form.

BTW

**Option Buttons and Radio Buttons**
Radio and option buttons are the same thing. Within the Expression Web authoring tools, they are referred to as radio buttons. In this chapter, the term radio button is used to refer to the item you are adding to your form; within a dialog box, however, the term option button is used.

## Project — Farm Stand Web Site

The management of Wisteria Farms, a farm stand and grocery store in Dilton, New Hampshire, would like to add an order form to its Web site for its new line of gift baskets. The staff has asked you to create a form page on which a visitor can select and customize a gift basket order.

The project in this chapter shows you how to use Expression Web to create and add a form to a page, as shown in Figure 7–1. You will create a form area and insert a table in which to enter the form fields. The form will include text boxes, option buttons, drop-down lists, check boxes, and text areas. You will make decisions about how to collect the data and where to send it or store it, then add a link on the store.html page to the new form page.

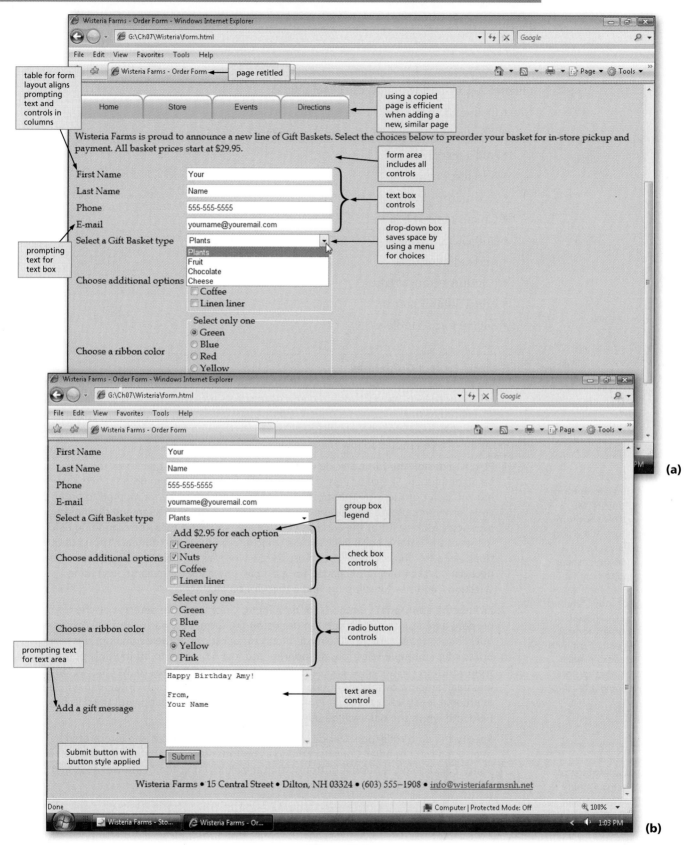

**Figure 7–1**

# Overview

As you read this chapter, you will learn how to add a form to the Web site shown in Figure 7–1 by performing these general tasks:

- Define the form field
- Use a table structure to lay out form controls
- Add a text area
- Add text boxes
- Add a drop-down list
- Create a group box
- Add check boxes
- Add radio buttons
- Edit form control labels
- Add a Submit button
- Define form handlers

**Plan Ahead**

**General Project Guidelines**

When planning a form, you must first decide its purpose, then determine the information you want to collect, the appropriate methods to collect data, and finally how the data will be submitted to the database. Forms should be easy to navigate, contain clear instructions and proper field labels, and be concise. As you plan to create a form, such as the one shown in Figure 7–1, you should follow these general guidelines:

1. **Plan and design the form.** Decide what data you want to collect and how this can best be accomplished. Sketch or type a layout plan for your form, then determine the wording and order of the form questions. Choose an appropriate layout method to organize your form data: use a table, or use spacing and indentations to align and distinguish form questions. Make a list of the controls you will add and what their corresponding field names in the database will be. Use clear, concise prompting text for each group of questions, keep the choices specific, and use as few words as possible. Consider dividing the necessary data into multiple pages; for example, one page for making purchasing selections, another for shipping, and a third for billing.

2. **Include the appropriate methods for data input.** Once you have determined the form's purpose and desired results, you can decide on the format for each question. Group like questions together, and put the most important questions at the beginning. Use check boxes when multiple selections are appropriate, radio buttons to list multiple options from which the visitor must choose only one, or a drop-down box to list multiple options in a small amount of space. Consider adding a text area into which visitors can type any additional feedback or information. Name each field to correspond with the database field into which the data will be sent.

3. **Specify the data collection.** Decide how the data will be collected and interpreted by selecting a form handler. Consider adding a confirmation page that displays after the visitor has clicked the Submit button so that they know that their data was sent, and what, if any, response they will receive.

**BTW**

**Dividing Forms**
Separating a long form into multiple HTML tables makes your form easier to use. If a visitor makes a mistake on a form page, he or she is prompted to fix it when the page is submitted instead of much later in the process. An example of a multi-part form is an order entry form with one page for product selection, another for shipping, and a third for payment.

**BTW**

**Rearranging Forms Using Tables**
Another advantage of using tables to create a form is that you can resize, insert, move, and delete rows and columns to modify the order, layout, and content of the form controls.

# Defining Forms and Form Controls

Whether paper or electronic, some of the uses of forms are to collect data as feedback for a survey, to enroll in a class or service, or to purchase items. With paper forms, a person must interpret and accumulate data from each form individually, which is time consuming and can cause errors in data entry. An electronic form collects the same data, but uses technology to receive, analyze, and process the data.

Although the terms *data* and *information* are often used interchangeably, they are not the same thing. **Data** refers to the facts and answers, known as **field values**, that are entered in a form using the form controls. For example, in a survey form for customer service, each visitor rates the service they received using a numeric scale from 1–5; those numbers are data. **Information** is the interpretation, or result of analysis, of data. In the previous example, the information might be that 40 percent of respondents rated their service 5.

## Understanding Databases

Most businesses store customer, purchasing, and inventory data in large database files. Information about a customer or product is stored in multiple fields (such as firstname, lastname, address, phone, e-mail). The collection of fields related to each customer (or product, or order, and so on) is called a **record**. Each record needs one field that uniquely identifies it. This field is called the **primary key**. For example, if you are creating a profile for yourself on a Web site and are assigned or asked to enter a username, then that username is the primary key for your record. For a product, the primary key is typically the product name or number.

When you shop online, the product information you see on the Web page, such as the product name, color, size, and price, is pulled from the company's database. Your purchase data is sent back to the company's database and is used to generate your sale, update the company's inventory by determining the number of items sold, and enter the purchase into the company's sales records.

When planning a form, you need to make a correlation between the form and the database so that you can assign the necessary properties to the form, groups, and controls. The form handler, which is the script that enters the form data into the database, will use the form name to determine a table or group of records into which the form data will be entered.

Within the records, each field name must correspond with the name assigned to a control in the *control* Properties dialog box. As database field names do not include spaces or some characters, such as hyphens, you may have to assign a field in which someone enters their first name as FirstName or their e-mail as Email. Some controls also have an option to assign a **value**; the value is the data that is entered into the corresponding field in the database, such as Yes or No or a numeric or text-based value.

Figure 7–2 shows a planning document for the Wisteria Farms form. You will use a table to align the form questions. Each control or group will be in its own cell, with prompting text in the left column. Within each group there are multiple controls.

**BTW**

**Encrypting Information**
On forms that ask visitors to provide sensitive information, such as credit cards or Social Security numbers, companies will use security protocols, such as HTTPS or SSL, to encrypt the data before it is transferred over the Internet.

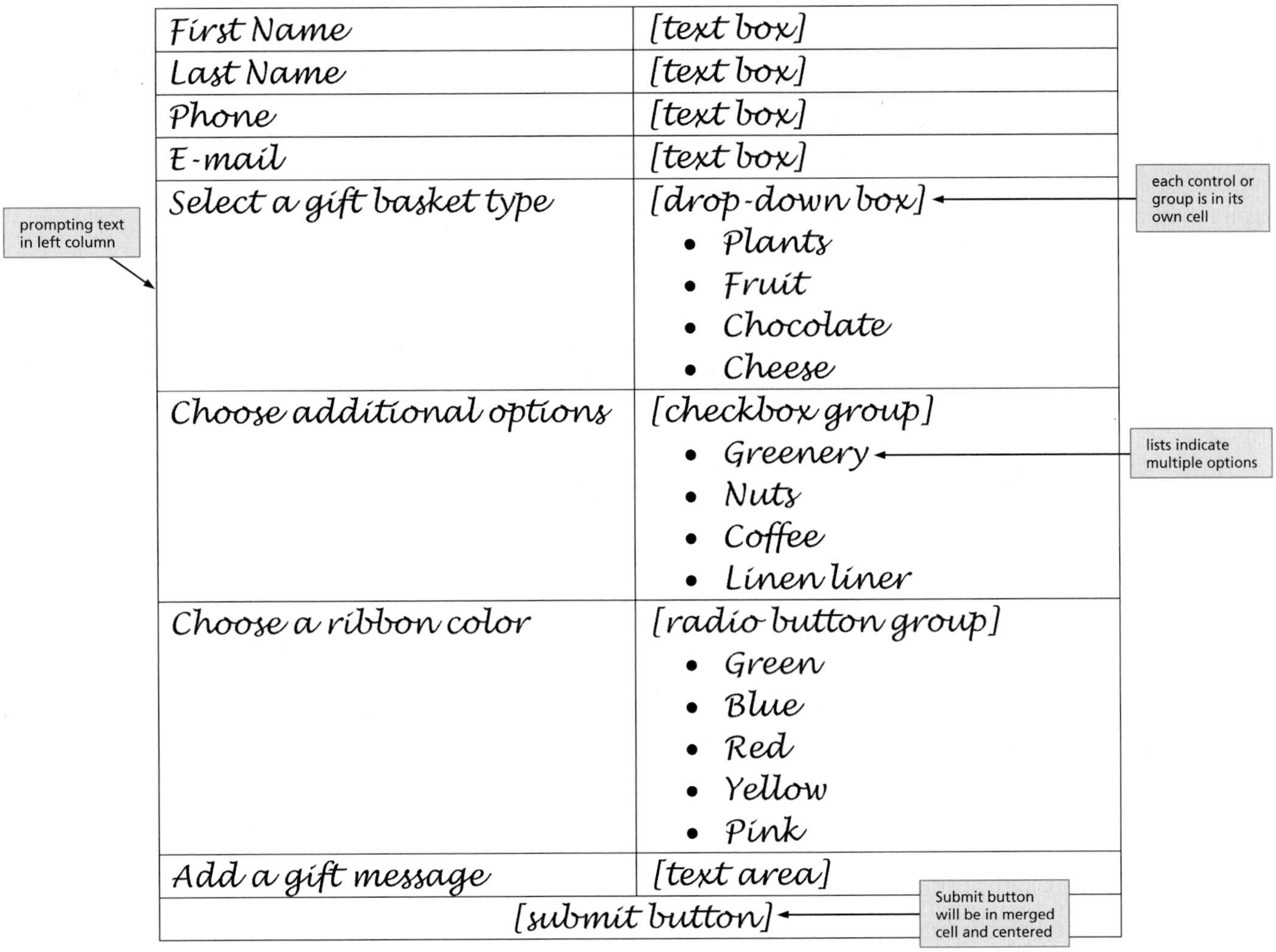

| | |
|---|---|
| First Name | [text box] |
| Last Name | [text box] |
| Phone | [text box] |
| E-mail | [text box] |
| Select a gift basket type | [drop-down box] ◄───── each control or group is in its own cell <br> • Plants <br> • Fruit <br> • Chocolate <br> • Cheese |
| Choose additional options | [checkbox group] <br> • Greenery ◄───── lists indicate multiple options <br> • Nuts <br> • Coffee <br> • Linen liner |
| Choose a ribbon color | [radio button group] <br> • Green <br> • Blue <br> • Red <br> • Yellow <br> • Pink |
| Add a gift message | [text area] |
| [submit button] ◄───── Submit button will be in merged cell and centered | |

prompting text in left column

**Figure 7–2**

**Setting Tab Order**
Some visitors, such as those without pointing devices or with certain disabilities, will need to navigate through your form using the TAB key instead of a mouse or pointing device. If you do not specify a tab order, pressing TAB will navigate in order through the form controls on the page. If you want to change the navigation to go in a different order, specify the tab order for all form controls on the page.

# Defining Form Controls

When planning a form in Expression Web, it is important to understand how the form is structured on the Web page. The form area, the div that contains the entire form, is the first item that you create on the form. The commands for adding form areas, group boxes, form controls, and labels are all located in the Toolbox.

Within the form area, you can create **group boxes** that group similar options together. A group box usually includes prompting text that indicates a question with more than one possible response, such as "What is your favorite season?" and an optional **legend**, which is descriptive or instructional text for the group name. Within the group box are the form controls the visitor will use to reply to the prompting text, such as a group of four radio buttons for Winter, Spring, Summer, and Fall. Each form control within the group box is identified with a **label**, which is text that distinguishes it from other controls in the box.

**Plan Ahead**

**Plan and design the form.**
The form purpose establishes the form's required length, questions, and input methods. When planning a form, you need to know the results you expect to achieve, and who your audience will be. If you are targeting current customers about an existing product or service, less explanation will be required. If you are looking to get input about a brand new product or service or to enroll new customers in your service, your form might need to include fields to collect additional information.

*(continued)*

**Plan Ahead**

*(continued)*
     You can use a table to organize your form and align, distribute, and group questions, or use a combination of styles, indentations, and line breaks. If you use a table, you can use one column to display the prompting text, and another for the related form controls. Prompting text and field labels should appear either above or next to the field.

## To Start Expression Web and Open a Site and Page

If you are using a computer to step through the project in this chapter, and you want your screens to match the figures in this book, you should change your computer's resolution to 1024 × 768. For information about how to change a computer's resolution, read Appendix F.

The following steps, which assume Windows Vista is running, start Expression Web based on a typical installation, and open the site folder and a page. You may need to ask your instructor how to start Expression Web for your computer.

Note: If you are using Window XP, see Appendix E for alternate steps.

**1** Click the Start button on the Windows Vista taskbar to display the Start menu.

**2** Click All Programs at the bottom of the left pane on the Start menu to display the All Programs list.

**3** Click Microsoft Expression on the All Programs list to display the Microsoft Expression list.

**4** Click Microsoft Expression Web 2 to start Expression Web.

**5** Click File on the menu bar to open the File menu, then click Open Site to display the Open Site dialog box.

**6** Navigate to the data files.

**7** Click the Wisteria folder, then click the Open button to open the site in Expression Web (Figure 7–3).

**8** Click Task Panes on the menu bar, then click Reset Workspace Layout.

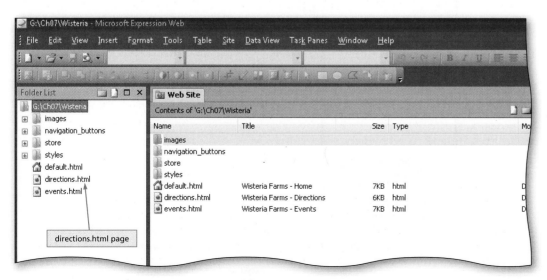

**Figure 7–3**

## To Create a Page from Another Page

Using copy and paste functions to create a new Web page from a page that you already created can save time. The new page will have the same style sheet, navigation area, footer, and other important page elements as the original, but you will customize the content, layout, and other aspects as needed. You will need to edit the page properties to rename the new page. The following steps add a new page for the form by copying the farm stand's directions page, then deleting the text and modifying the page title.

- Click the directions.html page in the Folder List, then press CTRL+C to copy it to the Clipboard.

- Press CTRL+V to insert a copy of the directions.html page into the site folder (Figure 7–4).

**Q&A**

Why is the copied page filename different?

Because there can only be one file with the same name in a directory, Expression Web adds _copy(1) to the filename. Any additional copies would be *filename*_copy(2) and so on.

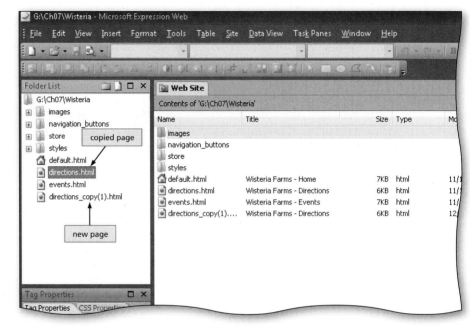

**Figure 7–4**

- Right-click the copied filename in the Folder List to display the shortcut menu, then click Rename.

- Type `form.html`, then press ENTER to rename the file (Figure 7–5).

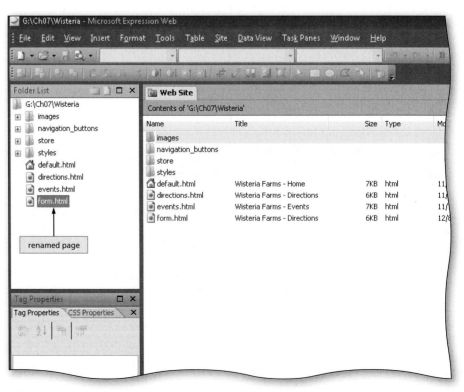

**Figure 7–5**

**3**

- Double-click the form.html page in the Folder List to open it (Figure 7–6).

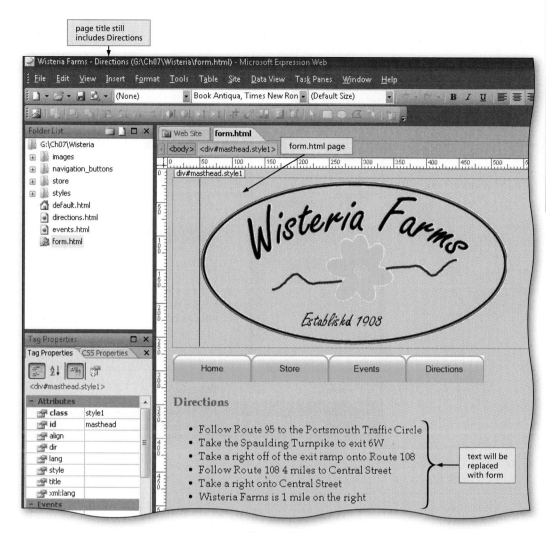

**Figure 7–6**

**4**

- Right-click a blank area of the page to display the shortcut menu, then click Page Properties to open the Page Properties dialog box (Figure 7–7).

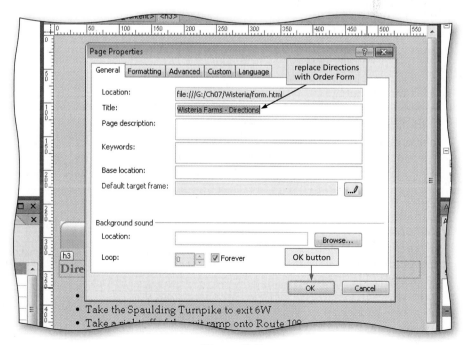

**Figure 7–7**

- Select the word, Directions, in the Title text box, then type `Order Form`.

- Click the OK button to close the dialog box and rename the page (Figure 7–8).

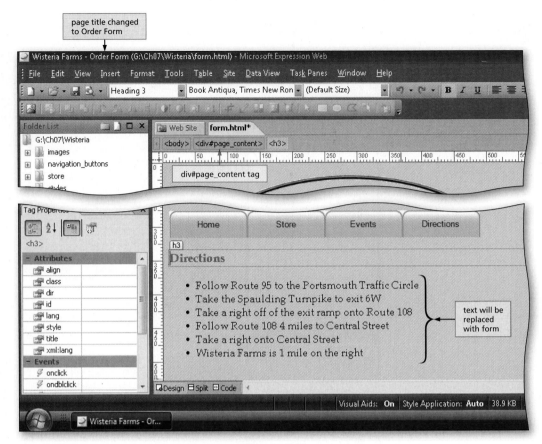

**Figure 7–8**

## To Create a Form Area

You can insert a form into a blank area of the page if that area contains no other page content, or you can convert an existing div into a form area. You cannot create a form area within a paragraph div, however. The following steps create a form area by converting the p div you just created into a form, then name the form.

- Select the div#page_content tag on the Quick Tag Selector, then press DELETE to delete it.

- Type `Wisteria Farms is proud to announce a new line of Gift Baskets. Select the choices below to preorder your basket for in-store pickup and payment. All basket prices start at $29.95.`, then press ENTER to insert a new paragraph div (Figure 7–9).

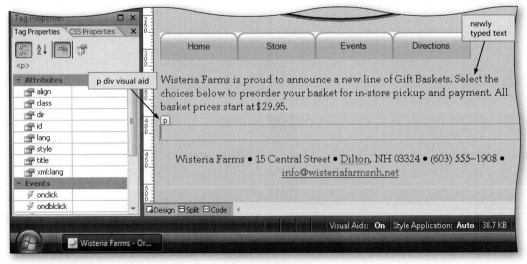

**Figure 7–9**

**2**

- Click the p div visual aid to select the new div.

- Double-click Form in the Toolbox to convert the div into a form area (Figure 7–10).

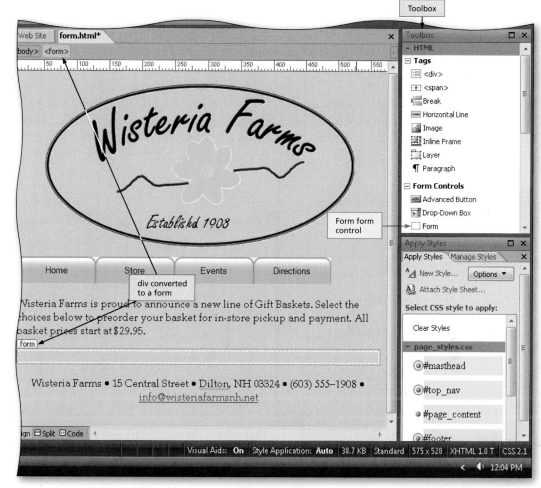

**Figure 7–10**

**3**

- Right-click anywhere in the form to display the shortcut menu.

- Click Form Properties on the shortcut menu to open the Form Properties dialog box.

- Click in the Form name text box and type `basket_order` to name the form (Figure 7–11).

- Click the OK button to close the Form Properties dialog box and name the form.

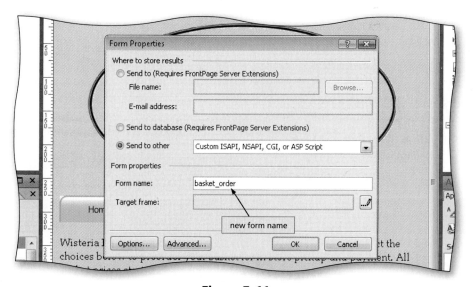

**Figure 7–11**

**Other Ways**

1. Click a blank area of the page, then double-click Form in the Toolbox to insert a new form area.

## To Create a Table

The following steps create a table to align the controls for the Wisteria Farms gift basket order form. Tables are not a part of the form data but are a very helpful layout tool when creating forms. The table will include a total of nine rows: four rows for the text boxes for First Name, Last Name, Phone, and E-mail; and one row each for the Select a Gift Basket type drop-down box, the additional options check box group, the ribbon color radio button group, the text area for the gift message, and the Submit button. The prompting text will be in the left column, and the group boxes and form controls will be in the right column, so the table will need two columns. You want the width of the columns to adjust to fit the text, so you edit the table properties to deselect the Specify width check box. You also close the Apply Styles task pane to enable you to see more of the Toolbox, which contains the form controls you will add.

- Click Insert Table on the Table menu to open the Insert Table dialog box.

- Type 9 in the Rows box.

- Click the Specify width check box to deselect it (Figure 7–12).

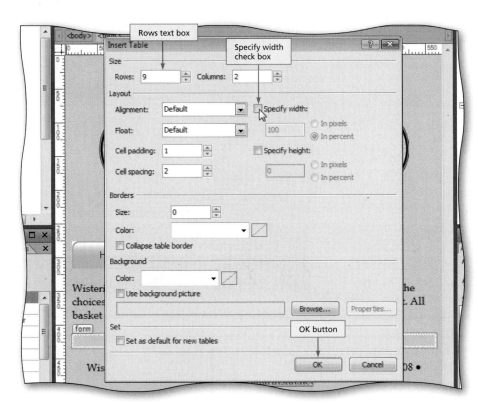

**Figure 7–12**

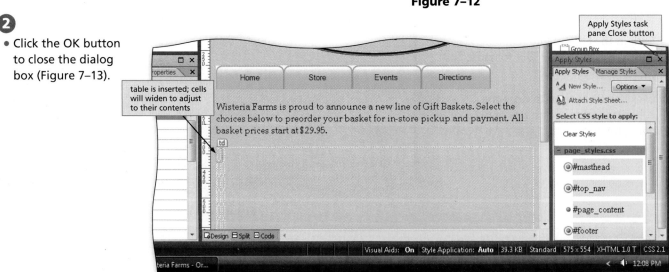

- Click the OK button to close the dialog box (Figure 7–13).

**Figure 7–13**

**3**

- Click the Close button on the Apply Styles task pane to close the task pane and expand the Toolbox (Figure 7–14).

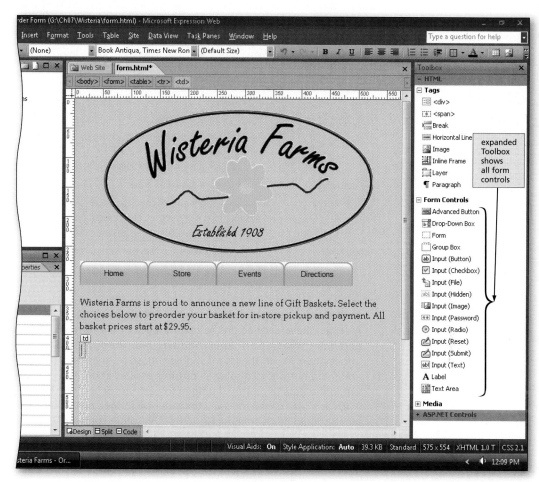

**Figure 7–14**

# Adding Form Controls

You have interacted with different types of form controls in previous chapters of this book when working with dialog boxes to make selections, so you should be familiar with how they are used. Table 7–1 describes some of the more commonly used form controls and their usages.

| Table 7–1 Form Control Types | | |
| --- | --- | --- |
| **Form Control** | **Used To** | **Example** |
| Drop-down box | Display a list of menu choices, from which the visitor can typically choose one. Also known as list boxes. | State |
| Checkbox | Provide multiple choice options, from which the visitor can choose several. | Preferred classes |

BTW

**Allowing for Multiple List Selections**
Click the Yes option button in the Allow multiple selections section of the Drop-Down Box Properties dialog box to enable visitors to choose more than one item. To select multiple list items, the visitor will have to press and hold CTRL while clicking items on the list.

BTW

**Setting a Password Text Box Control**

A text box can also be used to ask a visitor to enter or create a password. For security purposes, text entered into a password text box should be obscured by replacing the display characters with asterisks (*) or dots. You can specify that a text box be a password control in the Text Box Properties dialog box.

**Table 7–1 Form Control Types (*continued*)**

| Form Control | Used To | Example |
|---|---|---|
| Radio button | Provide multiple choice options, of which the visitor can choose only one. Also called option buttons. | Year in school |
| Text box | Collect one- to two- word responses that will be unique to a visitor. | First Name or Last Name |
| Text area | Allow a visitor to add feedback in the form of sentences or words; text area results must be analyzed by a person and are usually included at the end of a form to allow for any additional feedback not specified by the form. | Other comments? |
| File upload | Allow a visitor to upload a file. | Photo for an online profile |
| Control button | Complete the form and send the results (Submit) or clear all input to end the form without submitting results or to start the form over again. | Submit, Cancel, or Reset |
| Group box | Insert an outline around several related controls and allow you to add a name to the group. | Color choices |

**Plan Ahead**

**Include the appropriate methods for data input.**

After you have decided on the text for each of the form's questions (the prompting text), determine what type of form control is most likely to enable the visitor to enter the proper information. When the visitor should choose from among multiple choices, use check boxes and radio buttons to display all possible choices at once, or a drop-down box to save space. When the data requested is unique to each visitor, use text boxes for short amounts of data (such as a user name), or use a text area for longer, memo-type data. The prompting text or labels should be clear and ensure that the values correspond with the fields in your database.

BTW

**Setting a Character Length**

When creating a text box, you can specify the character width of the text box. This does not restrict the number of characters a visitor can enter into the box; to do that, you must edit the code.

## Text Box Controls and Text Areas

A **text box control** is ideal for when a visitor needs to enter one or more words of text, but no more than one line. Although it is called a *text* box control, visitors can use the text box to enter numbers, text, or a combination, such as their addresses. When deciding whether to include a text box field or a **text area**, ask yourself what will be done with the collected data. Data entered in a text box field is used to generate a mailing address or other useful information about a visitor. A text area is for entering memos or multiple lines of text. Examples of text area uses are to enter a gift card message or delivery instructions.

When defining the properties of a **text box control**, in addition to assigning a name that corresponds with the field name in the database, you can make other specifications. You can assign an initial value that a visitor can type over, set a character limit, specify a different tab order, or make it a password field. If you define the text box as a password field, when a visitor types their password in the form, the data they type appears as asterisks or other characters for security reasons.

## To Add a Text Box Control

The following steps create text box fields into which a visitor will enter his or her first name, last name, phone number, and e-mail address. You will insert and resize one text box, then copy it to other cells.

**1**

- Click in the first cell in the table to position the insertion point if necessary.

- Type `First Name`, then press TAB to move to the first cell in the right column (Figure 7–15).

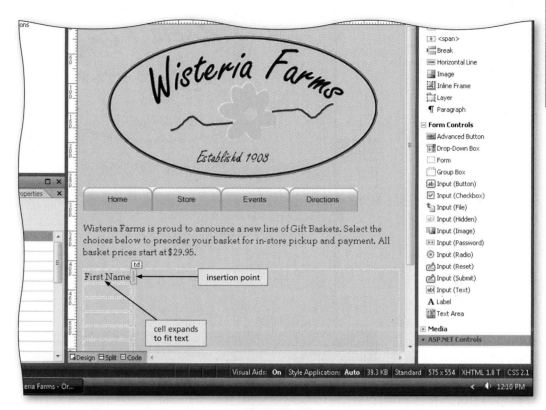

**Figure 7–15**

**2**

- Double-click Input (Text) in the Toolbox to insert a text box (Figure 7–16).

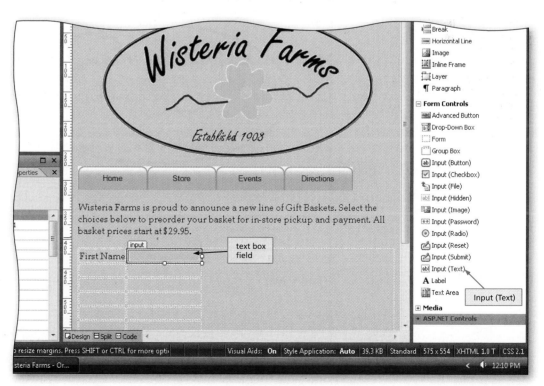

**Figure 7–16**

- In the text box, position the insertion point over the right resize handle until it turns into a two-headed arrow, click, then drag until the ScreenTip reads 250 pixels (Figure 7–17).

- Press CTRL+C to copy the resized text box to the Clipboard.

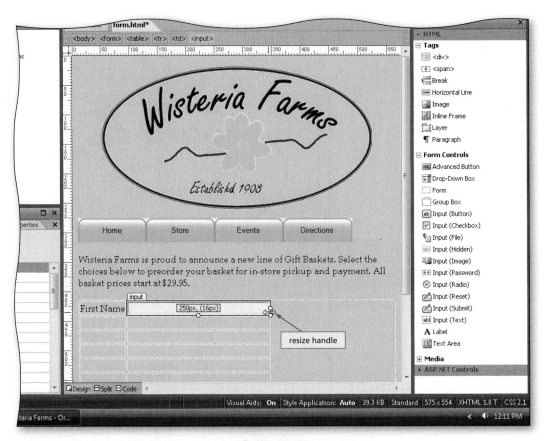

**Figure 7–17**

- Click to the right of the text box to position the insertion point.

- Press TAB to move the insertion point to the first cell in the second row.

- Type Last Name, then press TAB to move to the next cell.

- Press CTRL+V to paste the text box into the cell (Figure 7–18).

**Figure 7–18**

**5**

- Repeat Step 4 to add text fields for Phone and E-mail (Figure 7–19).

- Press CTRL+S to save the page.

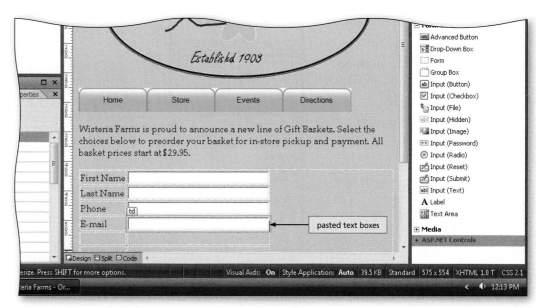

**Figure 7–19**

## To Assign Properties to a Text Box Control

The following steps use the Text Box Properties dialog box to set the control name of each text box to correspond with its field name in the Wisteria Farms sales database. Because the field names in the database cannot contain hyphens or spaces, you will type FirstName, LastName, and Email for the control names. The Phone control will have the same name as its prompting text, since it contains no spaces, hyphens, or other reserved characters, such as & or *.

**1**

- Right-click the text box for the First Name to display the short-cut menu, then click Form Field Properties to open the Text Box Properties dialog box.

- Type `FirstName` in the Name text box (Figure 7–20).

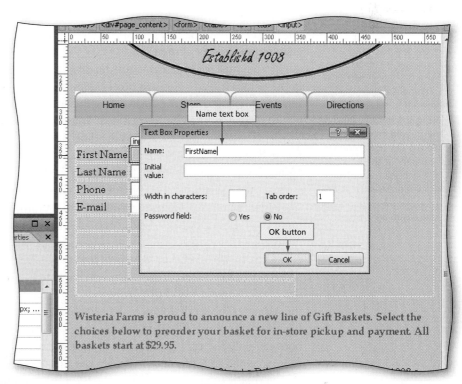

**Figure 7–20**

**2**

- Click the OK button to close the dialog box.

- Repeat Step 1 to set the following names: LastName, Phone, and Email (Figure 7–21).

- Press CTRL+S to save the page.

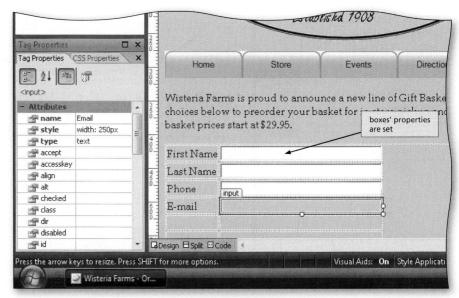

**Figure 7–21**

## Drop-Down Boxes

At first look, a **drop-down box** looks like the jump menus you created in Chapter 6. Unlike jump menus, clicking a drop-down box list item does not take you to a new page, but rather specifies a choice. As when you created a jump box, you will create a menu that has several choices, each of which should be clearly distinguished using as few words as possible. You can allow visitors to select more than one option, if necessary.

By default, a drop-down box displays only one menu item until the visitor clicks the box arrow. You can adjust the height of the box to show more options if necessary, but keep in mind the physical space the list takes up on your page. Keeping the box small enables you to save screen space.

You must assign a name for the drop-down box that corresponds with the field name in the database. A drop-down box has multiple choices, each of which needs to be added separately using the Drop-Down Box Properties dialog box. For each choice, you assign the text to display in the Choice text box. You can also assign a value for each list item, which is the data that will be entered into the database when the selection is made. The default value for each choice is the choice name. You can assign a different value by selecting the Specify Value check box and entering the value in the Specify Value check box.

You can also include a list item that does not contain a value, usually at the top of the list, which describes the list values. For example, if you are asking customers to determine the number of periodicals they subscribe to, the prompting text may read, "How many magazines or periodicals do you receive?" The top list item could read "Number of periodicals," followed by the valued list items, 1, 2, 3, etc.

A newly created drop-down box has one list item already created. You can modify this choice (and any additional choices you create) by clicking the Modify button to open the Modify Choice dialog box. To add a new choice, click the Add button to open the Add Choice dialog box. The Add Choice and Modify Choice dialog boxes contain the same options; only the title is different. Within these dialog boxes, you can assign one choice to be selected initially. If the visitor does not make a different selection, the value for the choice that is defined as initially selected is entered into the database.

# To Add a Drop-Down Box Control

The following steps create a drop-down box that includes five choices. The first choice is created by modifying the default choice created when the drop-down box is inserted, and the other four are added using the Add button and Add Choice dialog boxes. You do not need to specify a value for the choices, as the value entered in the database will be the choice name by default.

**1**

- Click in the cell below E-mail to position the insertion point.

- Type `Select a Gift Basket type`, then press TAB to move the insertion point to the next cell.

- Double-click Drop-Down Box from the Toolbox to insert a new drop-down box (Figure 7–22).

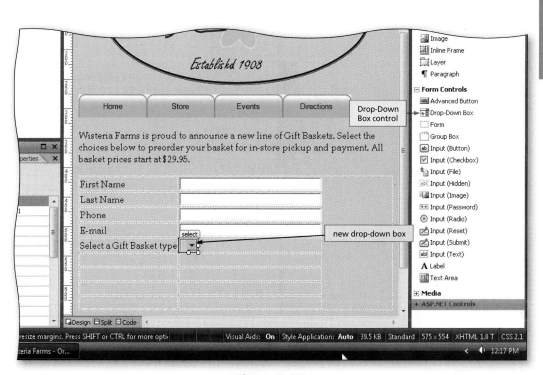

**Figure 7–22**

**2**

- In the drop-down box, position the insertion point over the right resize handle until it turns into a two-headed arrow, click, then drag until the ScreenTip reads 250 pixels (Figure 7–23).

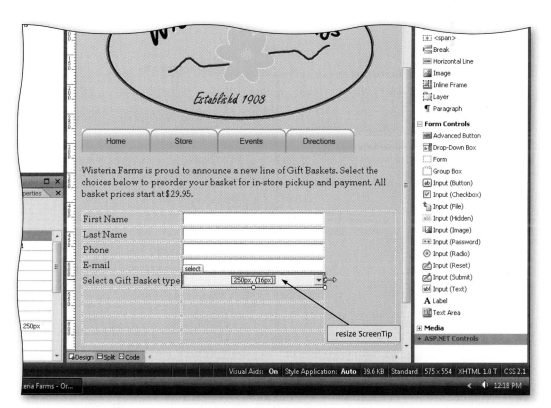

**Figure 7–23**

- Double-click the drop-down box to open the Drop-Down Box Properties dialog box.

- Select the word, Select1, in the Name box, then type `Basket_type` (Figure 7–24).

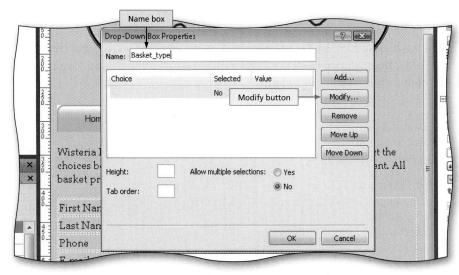

**Figure 7–24**

- Click the Modify button to open the Modify Choice dialog box (Figure 7–25).

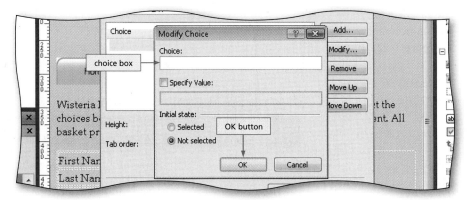

**Figure 7–25**

- Type `Plants` in the Choice box to specify the first gift basket type option.

- Click the OK button to close the Modify Choice dialog box (Figure 7–26).

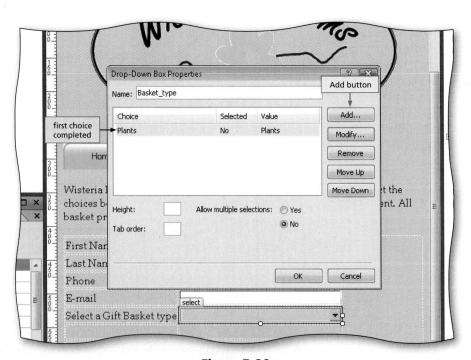

**Figure 7–26**

**6**

- Click the Add button to open the Add Choice dialog box.

- Type `Fruit` in the Choice text box to enter the second gift basket type option (Figure 7–27).

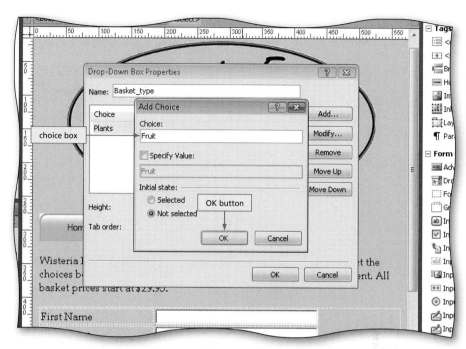

**Figure 7–27**

**7**

- Click the OK button to close the Add Choice dialog box (Figure 7–28).

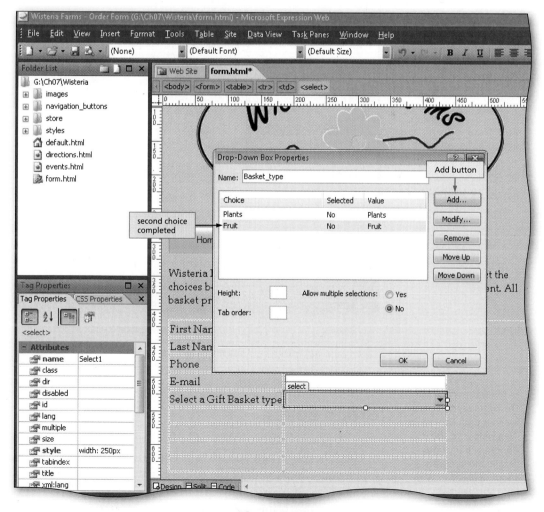

**Figure 7–28**

**8**
- Repeat Steps 6 and 7 to add choices for Chocolate and Cheese (Figure 7–29).

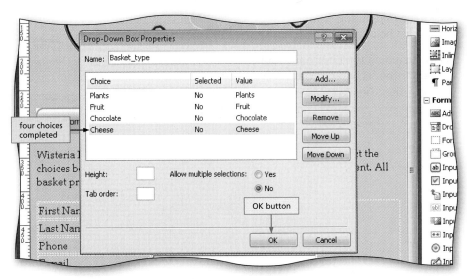

**Figure 7–29**

**9**
- Click the OK button to close the Drop-Down Box Properties dialog box and complete the field (Figure 7–30).

- Save the page.

**Q&A** Why doesn't the list display when I click the box arrow?

To test the drop-down box, you must view the page in a browser window.

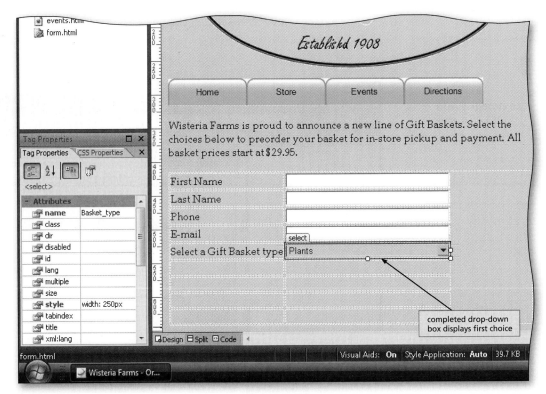

**Figure 7–30**

**BTW**

**Expression Web Help**
The best way to become familiar with Expression Web Help is to use it. Appendix B includes detailed information about Expression Web Help and exercises that will help you gain confidence in using it.

## Group Boxes

A **group box** is used to add a border around related controls, such as radio buttons or check boxes. When you add a group box, Expression Web inserts a **fieldset tag**, within which you will place all of the controls for the group. A new group box has text, called a legend, with the words, Group Box, at the top of the box. You can select the legend and type text that explains the contents of, or instructions relating to, the group box.

# To Create a Group Box Control

The following steps enter in the left column the prompting text for the additional gift basket type check boxes. You will then create a group box for the check boxes in the right column and add a legend at the top of the group box to describe its contents. You will create the check boxes in the next set of steps.

- Click in the cell below the words, Select a Gift Basket type, to position the insertion point in the sixth row of the left column of the table.

- Type Choose additional options as the prompting text for the check boxes.

- Press TAB to move to the right column.

- Double-click Group Box in the Toolbox to insert a new group box (Figure 7–31).

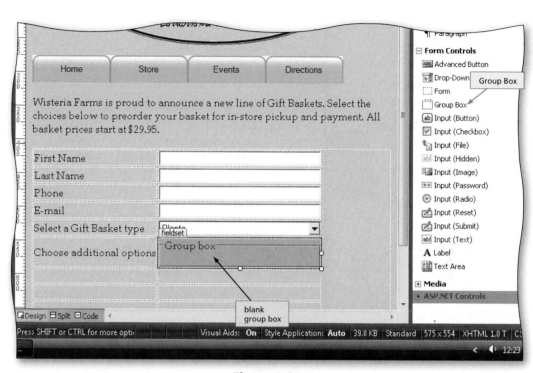

**Figure 7–31**

- Click the words, Group box, to position the insertion point in the legend (Figure 7–32).

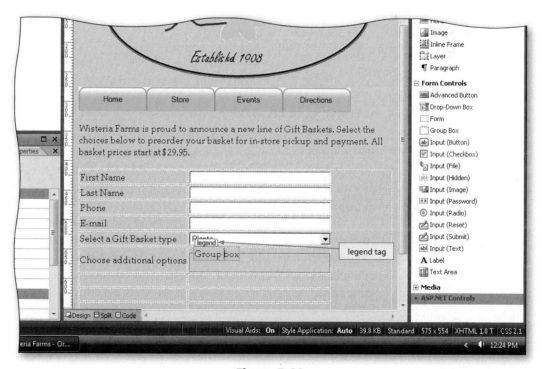

**Figure 7–32**

**3**

- In the legend, drag to select the words, Group box, then type Add $2.95 for each option.

- Click below the completed legend to position the insertion point in the group box (Figure 7–33).

- Press CTRL+S to save the page.

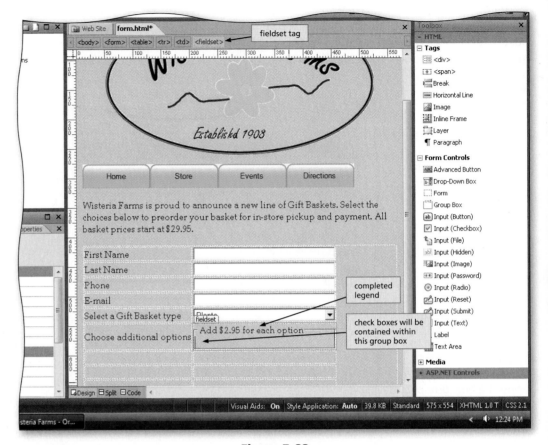

**Figure 7–33**

## Using Check Boxes and Radio Buttons

Check boxes and **radio buttons** are helpful when you want the visitor to be able to choose multiple options. If there are more than four to six options, you should consider using a drop-down box to save space on the page. Unlike check boxes and radio buttons, a drop-down box control can be set to allow a visitor to choose only one option or allow for multiple selections.

In addition to prompting text, a **label** can be assigned to each control. A control's label describes for the visitor the choice associated with the specific control. A control's label can differ from its value, which is the the data that is sent to and stored in the database. For example, a check box control could have the label Greenery. However, the corresponding value might be a code such as GR-2, which is the information required by the database. Labels make the form accessible for visitors with disabilities, because the label is read using assistive technologies and associated with the data to be entered.

When setting the properties for check boxes and radio buttons, you need to define both a control name and a value. The name indicates the field name into which the data will be entered. Since each database field can contain multiple radio buttons or check boxes, the value for each control must be different. For example, in a form that asks visitors to rate their experience on a scale from 1–5 by clicking a radio button, the name for each radio button would be rating, and each radio button would have a distinct value (1, 2, 3, 4, or 5).

It can be helpful to have one option selected by default. Typically, you would specify one option as the default selection if that option is the most likely choice, and a choice is required. If a visitor wants to choose another option, he or she can deselect the check box, then select any other(s), or simply click another radio button to change the selection.

BTW | **Web Accessibility**
See Appendix B for more information about accessibility and assistive technology.

## To Add Checkbox Controls

The following steps create check boxes for additional gift basket options and define the properties (name and value) for each check box. You will enter Options as the name for each.

**1**

- With the insertion point in the group box, double-click Input (Checkbox) in the Toolbox to insert a new check box (Figure 7–34).

- Click to the right of the check box to deselect it, then press ENTER to start a new line.

**Figure 7–34**

- Repeat Step 1 three times to insert three more check boxes (Figure 7–35).

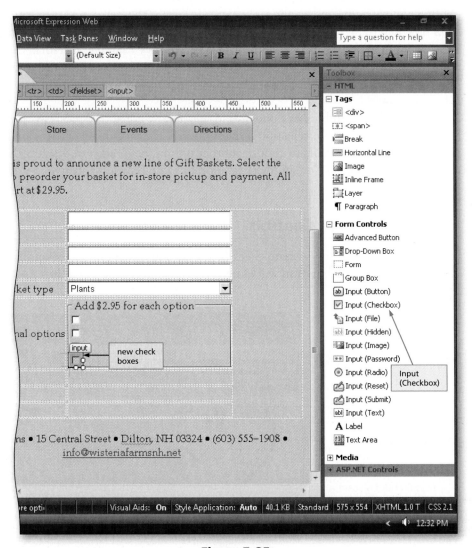

**Figure 7–35**

❸

- Double-click the first check box to open the Check Box Properties dialog box.

- Type Options in the Name text box.

- Press TAB to position the insertion point in the Value text box, then type Greenery (Figure 7–36).

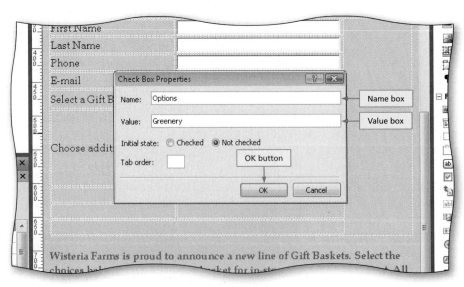

**Figure 7–36**

- Click the OK button to close the Check Box Properties dialog box.

- Format the check box properties for the remaining three check boxes: Nuts, Coffee, and Linen liner and type `Options` in the Name box for each.

- Click to the right of the first check box to position the insertion point.

- Double-click Label in the Toolbox to create the check box label.

- Type `Greenery` to add a label (Figure 7–37).

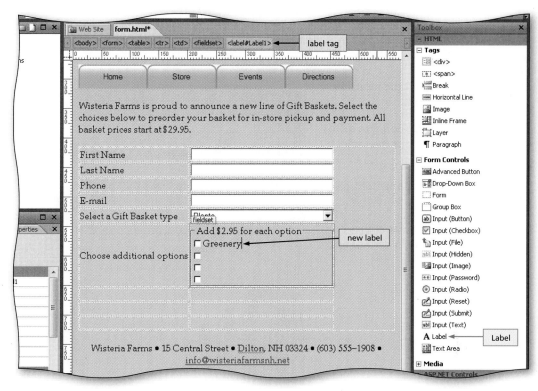

**Figure 7–37**

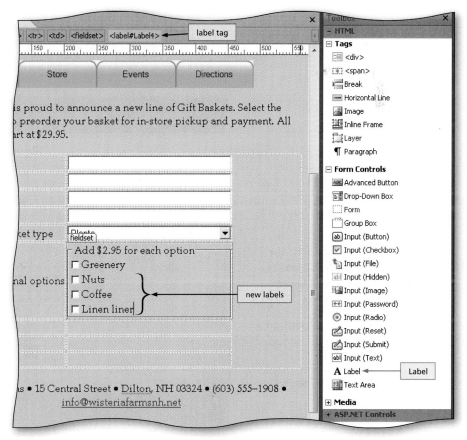

- Repeat Step 4 to add labels for Nuts, Coffee, and Linen liner.

- Press CTRL+S to save the page (Figure 7–38).

**Figure 7–38**

## To Add a Radio Button Group Box Control

The following steps enter the prompting text for radio buttons in the left column. You will then create a group box for the radio buttons in the right column and add a legend.

- Press TAB to position the insertion point in the next cell.

- Type Choose a ribbon color as the prompting text for the radio button options.

- Press TAB to move to the right column.

- Double-click Group Box in the Toolbox to insert a new group box (Figure 7–39).

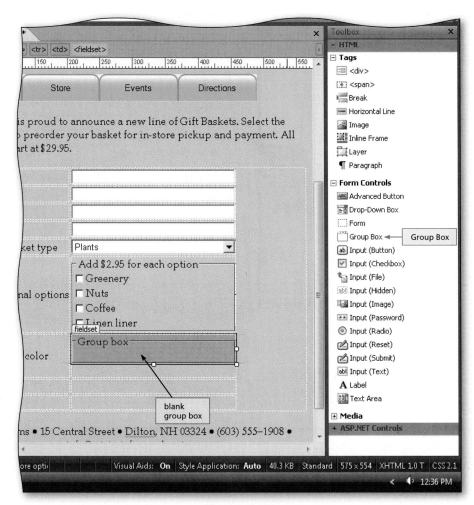

**Figure 7–39**

- Click the words, Group box, to position the insertion point in the legend.

- In the legend, drag to select the words, Group box, then type Select only one as the new legend for the group box.

- Click below the label to position the insertion point in the group box (Figure 7–40).

- Press CTRL+S to save the page.

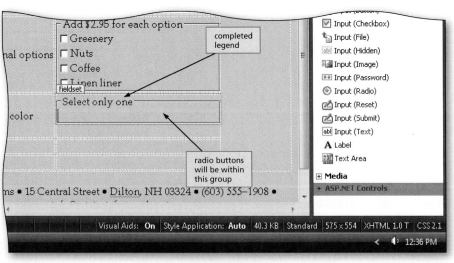

**Figure 7–40**

# To Add Radio Button Controls

The following steps create radio buttons for choosing the ribbon color. In the Option Button Properties dialog box, you will enter Ribbon as the group name for each button and different colors for the values. You will then create the label text that identifies each button.

 **1**

- If necessary, press TAB to position the insertion point in the next cell.

- Double-click Input (Radio) to insert a new radio button (Figure 7–41).

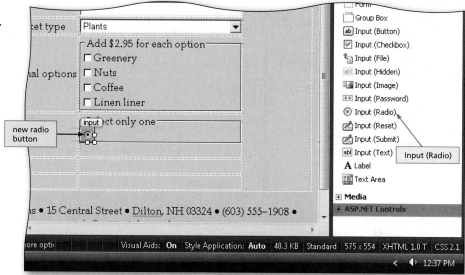

**Figure 7–41**

 **2**

- Double-click the radio button to open the Option Button Properties dialog box.

- Type Ribbon in the Group name box.

- Press TAB to position the insertion point in the Value text box, then type Green (Figure 7–42).

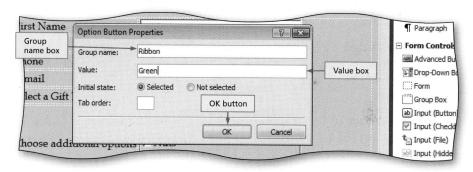

**Figure 7–42**

 **3**

- Click the OK button to close the Option Button Properties dialog box.

- Click to the right of the radio button to position the insertion point (Figure 7–43).

- Press ENTER to start a new line.

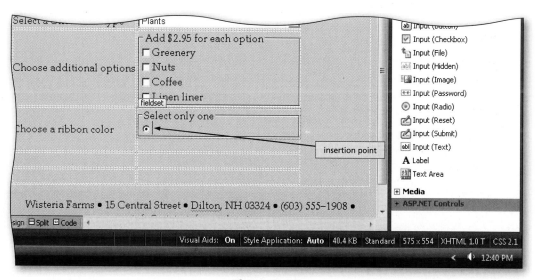

**Figure 7–43**

● Repeat Steps 1–3 to add four more radio buttons with Ribbon as the group name, and assign values of Blue, Red, Yellow, and Pink (Figure 7–44).

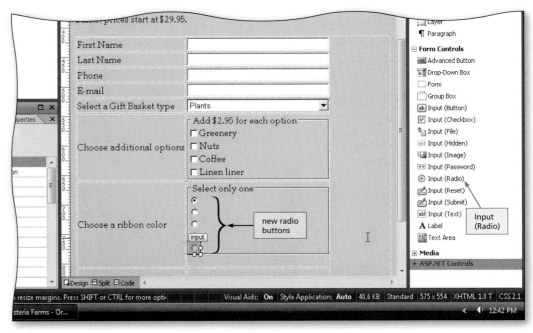

**Figure 7–44**

● Click to the right of the first radio button to position the insertion point.

● Double-click Label in the Toolbox to insert the first button label.

● Type Green to add a label to the first radio button (Figure 7–45).

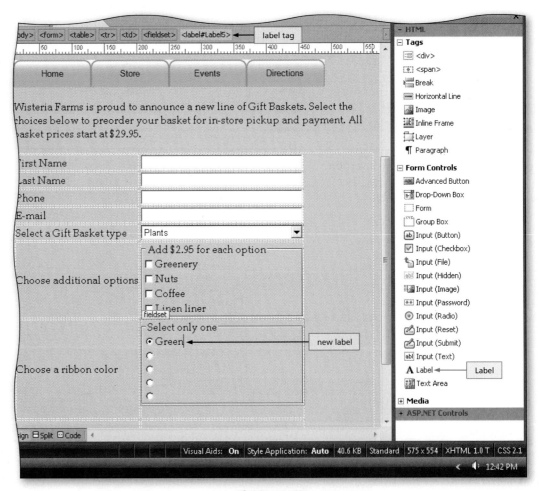

**Figure 7–45**

- Repeat Step 5 to add labels for Blue, Red, Yellow, and Pink.

- Press CTRL+S to save the page (Figure 7–46).

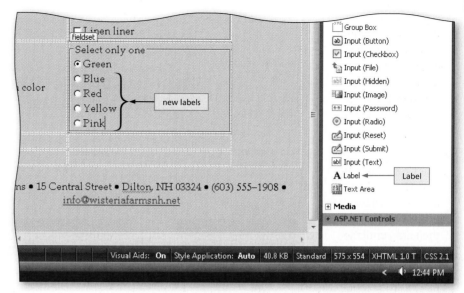

**Figure 7–46**

## To Add a Text Area Control

Many of the customers purchasing gift baskets from Wisteria Farms wish to include a gift message in the basket. Gathering the message data as part of the order process is convenient for customers and the staff. The following steps add a text area in which the visitor can add a gift message for the basket.

- Click to the right of the Pink label if necessary, then press TAB to position the insertion point in the next cell.

- Type Add a gift message as the prompting text for the text area.

- Press TAB to move to the right column.

- Double-click Text Area in the Toolbox to insert a new text area (Figure 7–47).

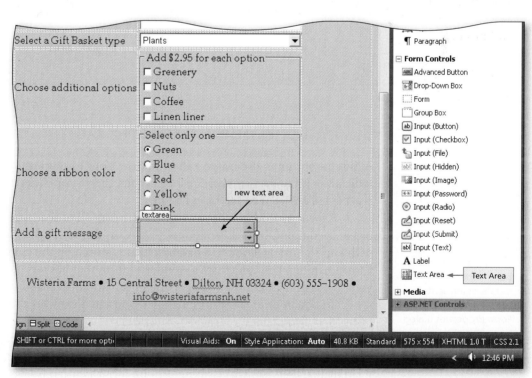

**Figure 7–47**

**2**

- Position the insertion point over the right resize handle until it turns into a two-headed arrow, click, then drag until the ScreenTip reads 250 pixels.

- Position the insertion point over the bottom resize handle until it turns into a two-headed arrow, click, then drag until the ScreenTip reads 125 pixels (Figure 7–48).

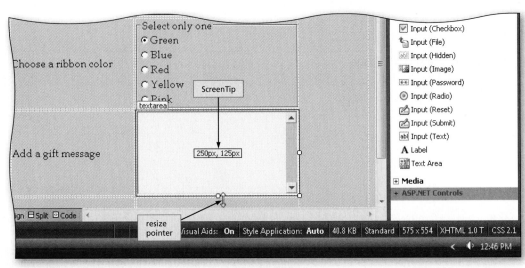

**Figure 7–48**

**3**

- Double-click the text area to open the TextArea Box Properties dialog box (Figure 7–49).

- Type Message in the Name box to assign a name to the control.

- Click the OK button to close the dialog box.

- Press CTRL+S to save the page.

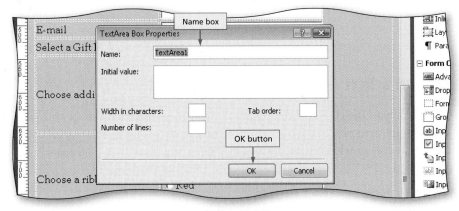

**Figure 7–49**

---

# Submitting and Collecting Data

**BTW**

**Specifying the Form Handler**
To specify a form handler in Expression Web, you must have FrontPage Server Extensions installed and know the e-mail address or database filename where the data is being sent. To add this information in the Form Properties dialog box, right-click anywhere in the form, then click Form Properties.

A Submit button is also called a Push button. Your form must include a Submit button to indicate that the data entry is finished. When the visitor clicks the Submit button, the data is accepted and sent to the form handler.

A form handler can be as simple as sending all of the form data to an e-mail address, or more complex, such the example in this chapter, where the form handler must interact with and add information to a database that is stored on the company's server. Without a form handler, you can create a wonderful form that has lots of important questions for your site visitors, but no way to get any information back from the form.

To obtain or create a form handler, you can download a scripted file or create your own. Most form handlers available for download contain simple instructions, such as to send form data to an e-mail address. You can create your own form handler or hire someone to create one that works specifically with your database. Many companies also have form handler services that you can sign up for, which can process the data and send a response, such as a confirmation e-mail, to the site visitor.

**Specify the data collection.**
Add a Submit button at the end of your form, or for each page of a multi-page form. For large forms, it is common practice to separate questions into a few smaller forms, so that if a visitor makes incorrect selections or neglects to enter or select necessary information, they can correct it before moving onto the next form section. Depending on the action you want after the Submit button is clicked, you should download, create, or hire someone to create a form handler, or sign up for a form handler service.

## To Add a Submit Button

You will not be able to specify a form handler in a lab setting, so although you can add a Submit button, there will be no action taken when the form is tested. The following steps add a Submit button and modify its properties.

- Select the bottom row of the table.

- Point to Modify on the Table menu, then click Merge Cells to merge the cells (Figure 7–50).

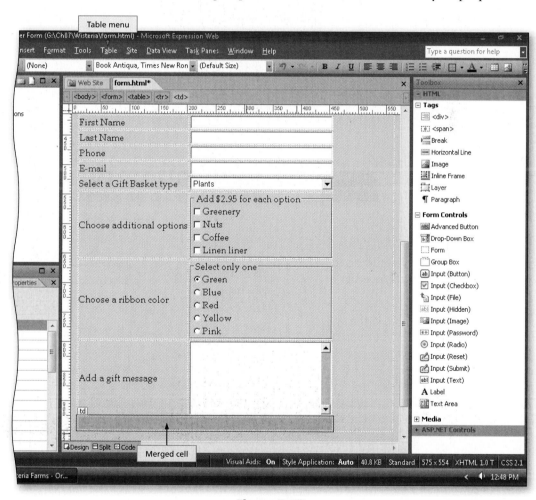

**Figure 7–50**

**2**

- Double-click Input (Submit) in the Toolbox to insert a Submit button (Figure 7–51).

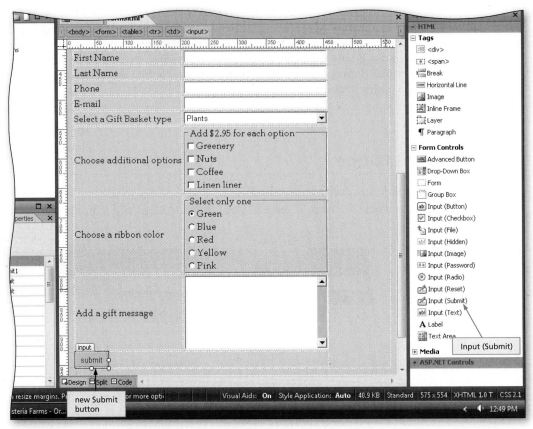

**Figure 7–51**

**3**

- Double-click the Submit button to open the Push Button Properties dialog box.

- Select the word, submit, in the Value/label box, then type Submit (Figure 7–52).

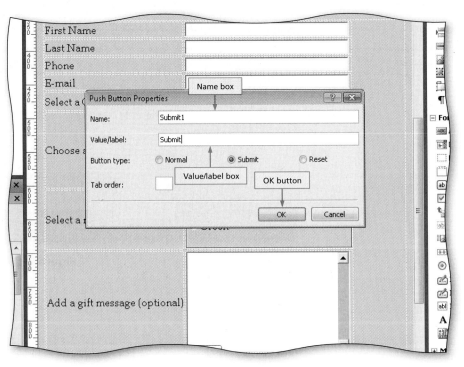

**Figure 7–52**

**4**

- Click the OK button to close the dialog box.

- Click the Center button on the Common toolbar to center the button (Figure 7–53).

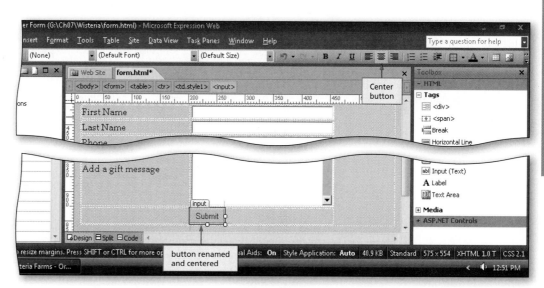

**Figure 7–53**

## To Create and Apply a New Style

The following steps create a new style for the button to make it look more like the Wisteria Farms Web site's navigation area.

**1**

- Click New Style on the Format menu to open the New Style dialog box.

- Type button in the Selector text box.

- Click the Define in box arrow, then click Existing style sheet.

- Click the URL box arrow, then click wisteria_styles.css.

- Click the font-family box arrow, then click Arial (Figure 7–54).

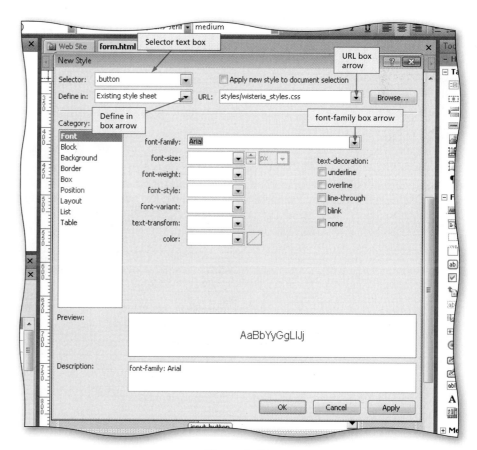

**Figure 7–54**

• Click Background in the Category list to display background formatting options.

• Click the background-color box arrow to display the palette (Figure 7–55).

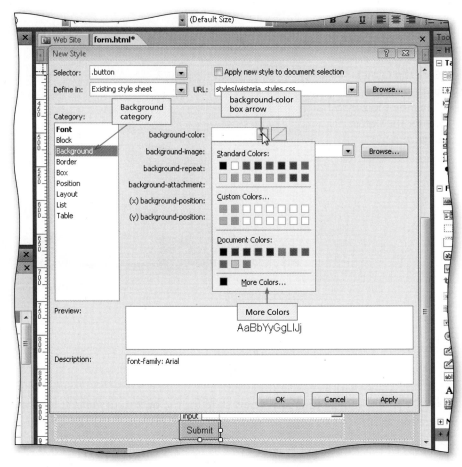

**Figure 7–55**

• Click More Colors to open the More Colors dialog box (Figure 7–56).

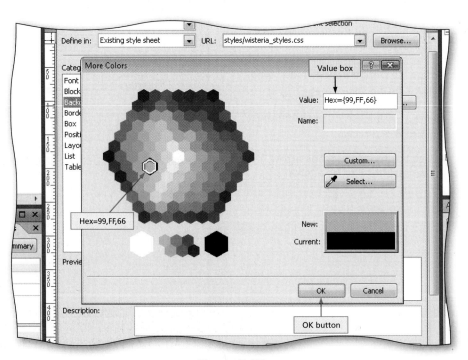

**Figure 7–56**

**4**

- Click the light green color box with the value Hex=99,FF,66 to select it.

- Click the OK button to close the More Colors dialog box and apply light green as the button's background color (Figure 7–57).

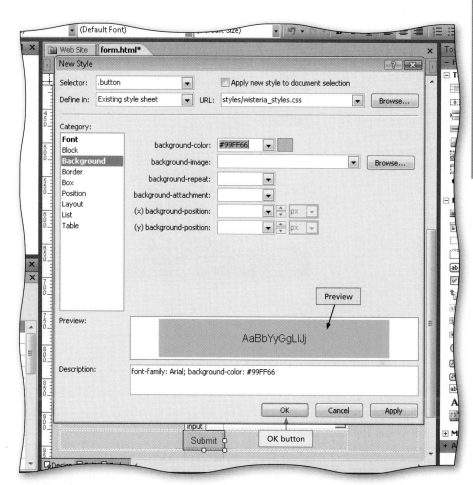

**Figure 7–57**

**5**

- Click the OK button to close the New Style dialog box.

- Point to CSS Styles on the Format menu, then click Apply Styles to open the Apply Styles task pane, and scroll if necessary to see the new .button style (Figure 7–58).

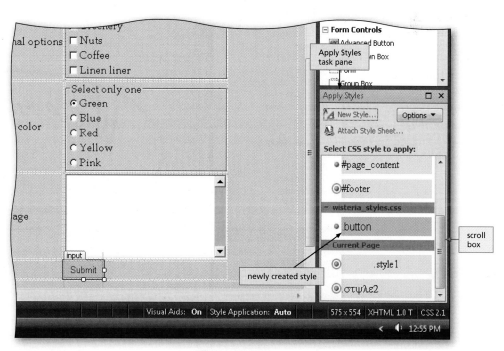

**Figure 7–58**

- Click .button in the Apply Styles task pane to change the style for the Submit button (Figure 7–59).

- Save and close the page and the embedded style sheet.

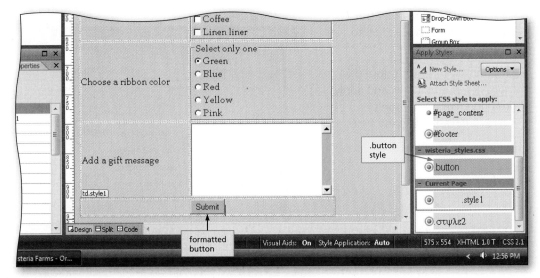

**Figure 7–59**

## To Add a Link to a Page

The following steps add a link from the store.html page to the form.html page, then preview the site in the browser to test the page link.

- In the Folder List, click the store folder plus sign to display its contents.

- Double-click store.html in the Folder List to open the page (Figure 7–60).

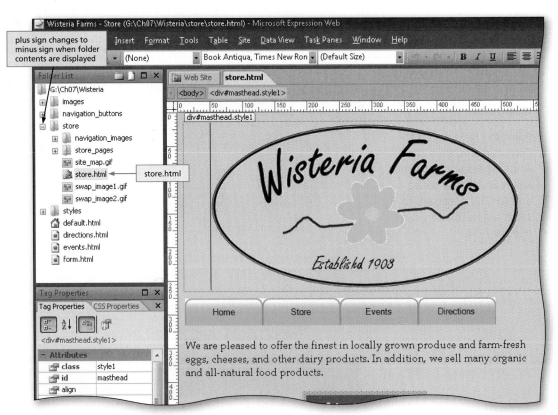

**Figure 7–60**

**2**

- Click to the right of the words, all-natural food products, to position the insertion point.

- Press ENTER to insert a new paragraph div (Figure 7–61).

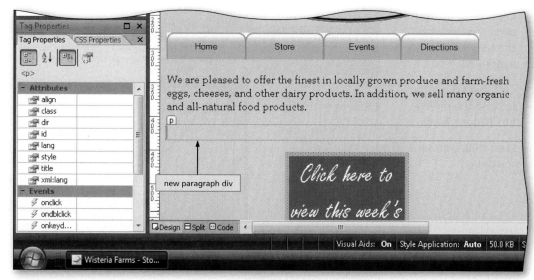

**Figure 7–61**

**3**

- Type Wisteria Farms is proud to announce a new line of customizable gift baskets. (Figure 7–62).

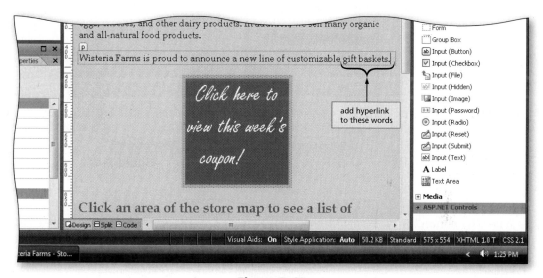

**Figure 7–62**

**4**

- Select the words, gift baskets, then press CTRL+K to open the Insert Hyperlink dialog box (Figure 7–63).

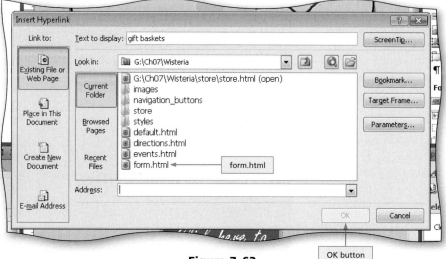

**Figure 7–63**

**5**

- Click the form.html page to select it as the target of the hyperlink.

- Click the OK button to close the dialog box (Figure 7–64).

- Press CTRL+S to save the page.

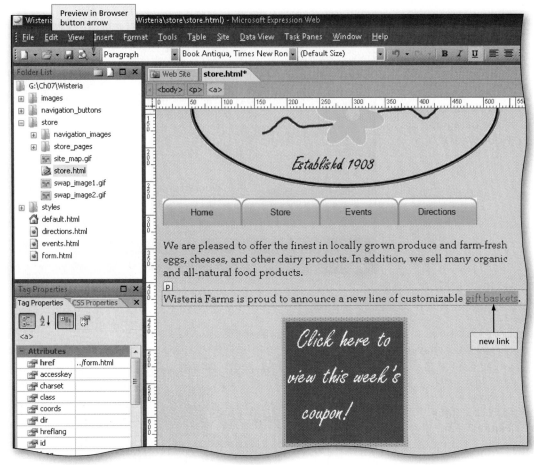

**Figure 7–64**

**6**

- Click the Preview in Browser button arrow, then click Windows Internet Explorer 7.0 (800×600) to open the page in the browser (Figure 7–65).

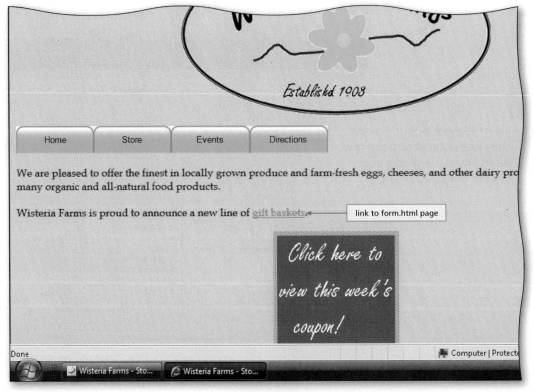

**Figure 7–65**

**7**

- Click the gift baskets hyperlink to go to the form.html page, then scroll to view more of the form (Figure 7–66).

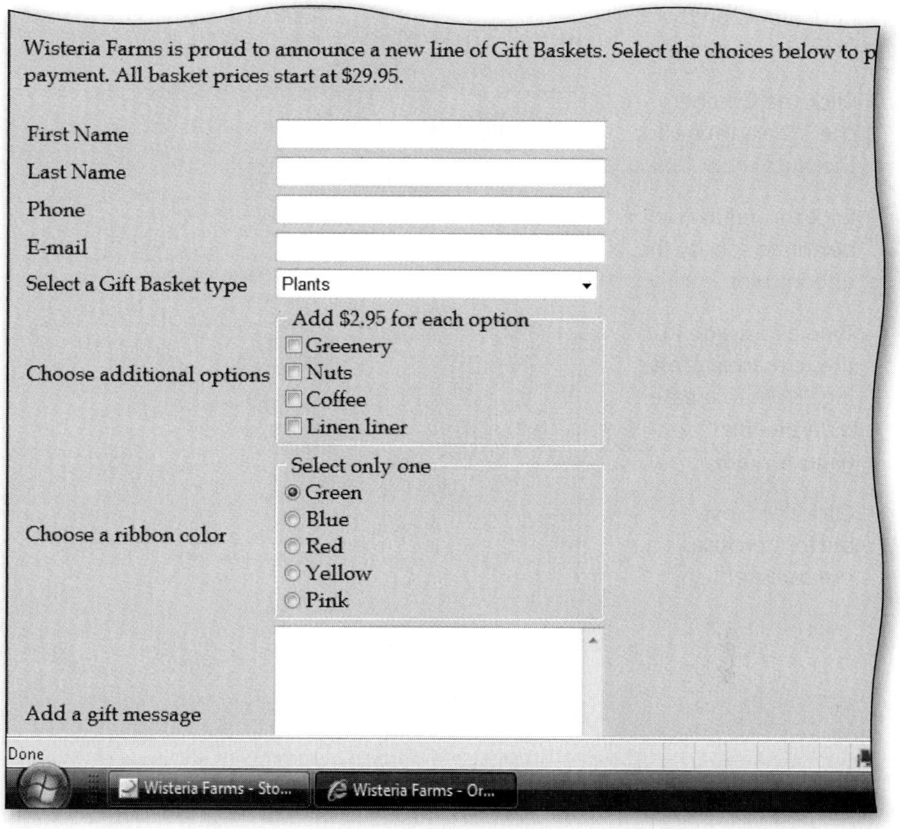

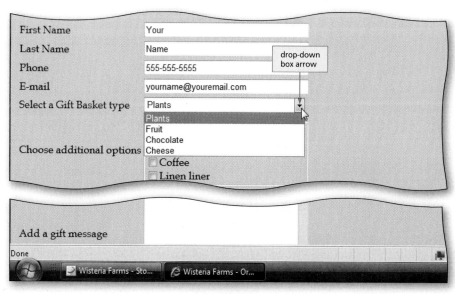

Wisteria Farms is proud to announce a new line of Gift Baskets. Select the choices below to p
payment. All basket prices start at $29.95.

First Name

Last Name

Phone

E-mail

Select a Gift Basket type     Plants

Add $2.95 for each option
☐ Greenery
Choose additional options  ☐ Nuts
☐ Coffee
☐ Linen liner

Select only one
◉ Green
◯ Blue
Choose a ribbon color     ◯ Red
◯ Yellow
◯ Pink

Add a gift message

Done

Wisteria Farms - Sto...     Wisteria Farms - Or...

**Figure 7–66**

## To Test the Form

The following steps test the form. Because no data collection method (through a form handler) has been specified, nothing will happen if you click the Submit button.

**1**

- Type your own information into the text boxes, pressing TAB to move between the boxes.

- Click the Select a Gift Basket type drop-down box arrow to display the menu (Figure 7–67).

First Name     Your

Last Name     Name

drop-down box arrow

Phone     555-555-5555

E-mail     yourname@youremail.com

Select a Gift Basket type     Plants

Plants
Fruit
Chocolate
Choose additional options  Cheese
☐ Coffee
☐ Linen liner

Add a gift message

Done

Wisteria Farms - Sto...     Wisteria Farms - Or...

**Figure 7–67**

- Click Plants on the drop-down menu.

- Click the Greenery check box, then click the Nuts check box.

- Click the Yellow radio button to specify the ribbon color.

- Type a message in the text area, pressing ENTER to create multiple lines (Figure 7–68).

- Click the Close button to close the browser.

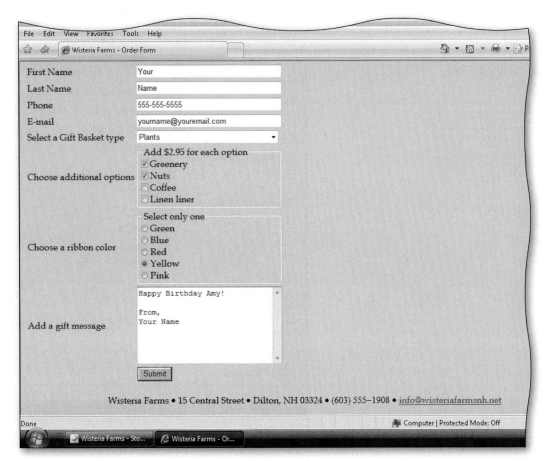

**Figure 7–68**

## To Close a Site and Quit Expression Web

**1** On the File menu, click Close Site.

**2** On the File menu, click Exit.

# Chapter Summary

In this chapter, you learned about forms and controls, and the relationship between an HTML form and a database. You were introduced to the concept of a form handler, which processes the form data, and you learned the difference between data and information. You learned how to create form areas, form controls, group boxes and legends, and how to set the properties and values for the form elements. You also learned how to set up a table to structure form fields.

The items listed below include all the new Expression Web skills you have learned in this chapter.

1. Start Expression Web and Open a Site and Page (EW 447)
2. Create a Page from Another Page (EW 448)
3. Create a Form Area (EW 450)
4. Create a Table (EW 452)
5. Add a Text Box Control (EW 455)
6. Assign Properties to a Text Box Control (EW 457)
7. Add a Drop-Down Box Control (EW 459)
8. Create a Group Box Control (EW 463)
9. Add Checkbox Controls (EW 465)
10. Add a Radio Button Group Box Control (EW 468)
11. Add Radio Button Controls (EW 469)
12. Add a Text Area Control (EW 471)
13. Add a Submit Button (EW 473)
14. Create and Apply a New Style (EW 475)
15. Add a Link to a Page (EW 478)
16. Test the Form (EW 481)

 If you have a SAM user profile, you may have access to hands-on instruction, practice, and assessment. Log in to your SAM account (http://sam2007.course.com) to launch any assigned training activities or exams that relate to the skills covered in this chapter.

# Learn It Online

## Test your knowledge of chapter content and key terms.

*Instructions:* To complete the Learn It Online exercises, start your browser, click the Address bar, and then enter the Web address `scsite.com/ew2/learn`. When the Expression Web Learn It Online page is displayed, click the link for the exercise you want to complete and then read the instructions.

### Chapter Reinforcement TF, MC, and SA
A series of true/false, multiple choice, and short answer questions that test your knowledge of the chapter content.

### Flash Cards
An interactive learning environment where you identify chapter key terms associated with displayed definitions.

### Practice Test
A series of multiple choice questions that test your knowledge of chapter content and key terms.

### Who Wants To Be a Computer Genius?
An interactive game that challenges your knowledge of chapter content in the style of a television quiz show.

### Wheel of Terms
An interactive game that challenges your knowledge of chapter key terms in the style of the television show *Wheel of Fortune*.

### Crossword Puzzle Challenge
A crossword puzzle that challenges your knowledge of key terms presented in the chapter.

# Apply Your Knowledge

Reinforce the skills and apply the concepts you learned in this chapter.

### Creating an Interactive Navigation Area and Adding a Behavior

*Instructions:* Start Expression Web. You will create a new one-page Web site, create and attach a new style sheet, then add a form area to create the signup form shown in Figure 7–69. You will add text boxes and drop-down boxes. You will add group boxes for radio buttons and check boxes. You will then add a text area and a Submit button.

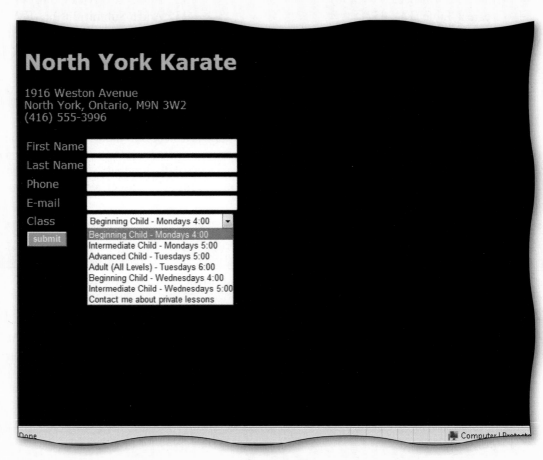

**Figure 7–69**

*Perform the following steps:*

1. Point to New on the File menu, click Web Site, then click One Page Web Site.
2. Navigate to the drive and folder where you save your Data Files, type `Apply 7-1 Karate Site` in the Specify the location of the new Web site text box, then click the OK button.
3. Point to New on the File menu, then click Page. Click Style Sheets, then click the Neon style sheet type and click the OK button.
4. Save the new style sheet as karate_styles.css.
5. Open the default.html page, then attach the karate_styles.css style sheet.
6. Insert a paragraph div for the page header, type `North York Karate`, then format the div with h1.

7. Insert a new paragraph div below the header, select the h3 heading style, then type the following, pressing SHIFT+ENTER at the end of each line.

   1916 Weston Avenue

   North York, Ontario, M9N 3W2

   (416) 555-3996

8. Press ENTER after the last line to create a new paragraph div, then save the page.

9. Click the p tag for the new paragraph div on the Quick Tag Selector, then double-click Form in the Toolbox.

10. Right-click the form area, then click Form Properties. Name the form Enroll, then click the OK button to close the dialog box.

11. Create a table with six rows and two columns, and deselect the Specify width check box.

12. In the first cell in the table, type First Name, press TAB, then double-click Input (Text) in the Toolbox to insert a new text box.

13. Drag the resize handle for the text box until it is 225 pixels wide. Select the text box, then copy it to the Clipboard.

14. Paste the copied text box into the three cells below it. Enter the following names in the cells in the left column: Last Name, Phone, and E-mail.

15. Right-click the text box in the First Name row, then click Form Field Properties. Type FirstName in the Name text box, then click the OK button. Name the next three text boxes LastName, Phone, and Email.

16. Click the first cell in the fifth row, then type Class. Press TAB to move to the next cell.

17. Double-click Drop-Down Box in the Toolbox. Drag the resize handle for the drop-down box until it is 225 pixels wide.

18. Double-click the drop-down box. Type Class in the Name text box, then click the Modify button.

19. Type Beginning Child - Mondays 4:00 in the Choice text box, then click the Specify Value check box to select it.

20. Add choices for the following: Intermediate Child - Mondays 5:00; Advanced Child - Tuesdays 5:00; Adult (All Levels) - Tuesdays 6:00; Beginning Child - Wednesdays 4:00; Intermediate Child - Wednesdays 5:00; and Contact me about private lessons. Specify the value for each.

21. Select the last row in the table. Point to Modify on the Table menu, then click Merge Cells to merge the last row of the table.

22. Double-click Input (Submit) in the Toolbox to insert a Submit button.

23. Create a new style for the button with the Lime background and White font color and save the new style to the karate_styles.css style sheet. Apply it to the button.

24. Preview the site in a browser and test the form fields by entering text and making selections.

25. Change the site properties, as specified by your instructor. Submit the revised site in the format specified by your instructor.

26. Save all pages, then close the site.

# Extend Your Knowledge

Extend the skills you learned in this chapter and experiment with new skills. You may need to use Help to complete the assignment.

### Use Styles to Align a Form

*Instructions:* Start Expression Web. Open the site Extend 7-1 Alumni from the Data Files for Students. See the inside back cover of this book for instructions for downloading the Data Files for Students, or see your instructor for information about accessing the required files.

You will create a form and align the fields to match the one shown in Figure 7–70.

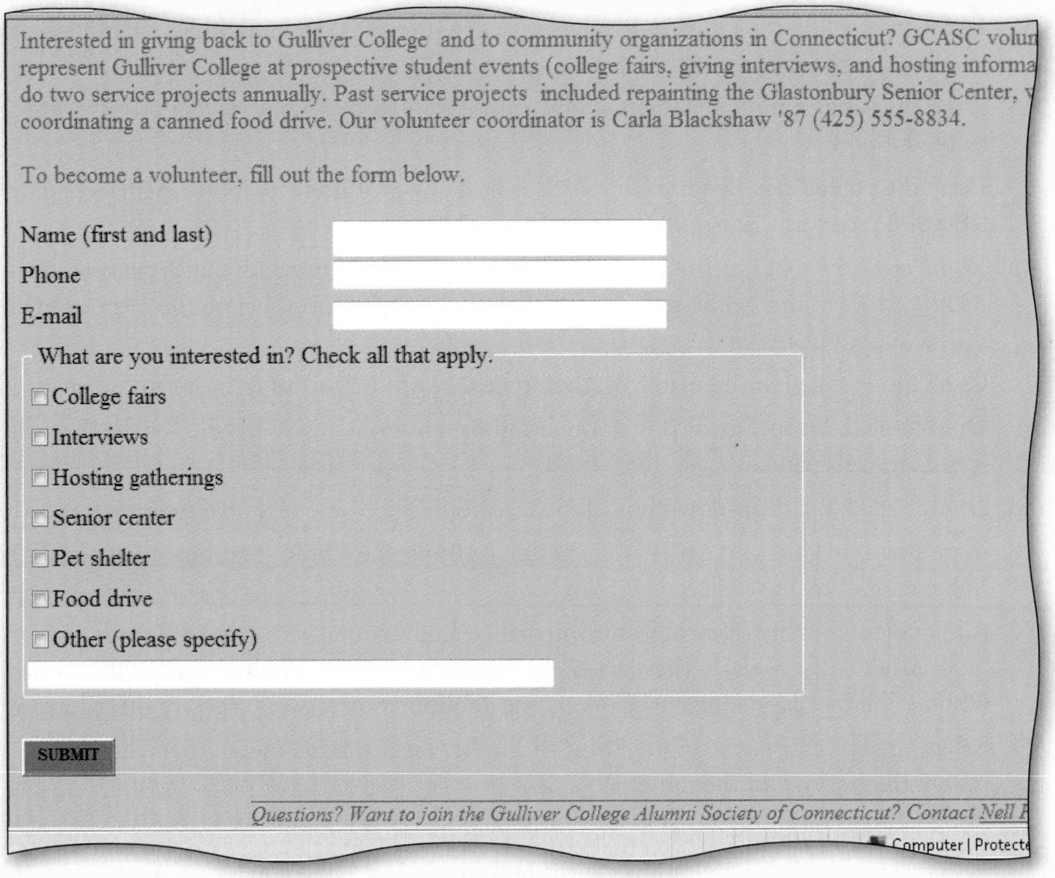

Interested in giving back to Gulliver College and to community organizations in Connecticut? GCASC volun represent Gulliver College at prospective student events (college fairs, giving interviews, and hosting informa do two service projects annually. Past service projects included repainting the Glastonbury Senior Center, coordinating a canned food drive. Our volunteer coordinator is Carla Blackshaw '87 (425) 555-8834.

To become a volunteer, fill out the form below.

Name (first and last)
Phone
E-mail

What are you interested in? Check all that apply.
☐ College fairs
☐ Interviews
☐ Hosting gatherings
☐ Senior center
☐ Pet shelter
☐ Food drive
☐ Other (please specify)

**SUBMIT**

*Questions? Want to join the Gulliver College Alumni Society of Connecticut? Contact Nell*

**Figure 7–70**

*Perform the following tasks:*

1. Open the volunteer.html page, position the insertion point at the end of the paragraph above the footer, then press ENTER.

2. Type `To become a volunteer, fill out the form below.`, then press ENTER.

3. Double-click Form in the Toolbox to insert a form area.

4. Type `Name (first and last)`, press SPACEBAR, then double-click Input (Text) to insert a text box. Drag the sizing handles to resize the text box to 250 pixels wide.

5. Double-click the text box. Type `Name` in the Name text box, then click the OK button.

6. Click to the right of the text box, then press ENTER. Type Phone, press SPACEBAR, then double-click Input (Text) to insert a text box. Drag the sizing handles to resize the text box to 250 pixels wide.

7. Double-click the text box. Type Phone in the Name text box, then click the OK button.

8. Add a new line, type E-mail, press SPACEBAR, then insert a new text box, 250 pixels wide, with the name Email.

9. Press ENTER to start a new line, then double-click Group Box in the Toolbox. Type What are you interested in? Check all that apply. as the legend.

10. Add seven check boxes, pressing ENTER after each one.

11. Double-click the first check box, then type Fairs as both the name and value. Double-click Label in the Toolbox, then type College Fairs.

12. Add the remaining names, values, and labels as follows:

| Name/Value | Label |
| --- | --- |
| Interviews | Interviews |
| Host | Hosting gatherings |
| Senior | Senior center |
| Pets | Pet shelter |
| Food | Food drive |
| Other | Other (please specify) |

13. Press ENTER after the last check box, then insert a new text box. Drag the sizing handles to resize it to 400 pixels and assign it the name Other.

14. Click below the group box but still in the form. (*Hint*: the Quick Tag Selector should display <form> instead of <fieldset>.)

15. Double-click Input (Submit) in the Toolbox.

16. Position the pointer over the right sizing handle of the form, then drag to the left until the form is 600 pixels wide.

17. Create a new style called .formtext, and save it to the alumni_styles.css style sheet. Set the font color as black. Click the Block category, and set the line-height value as 30 pixels.

18. Create a new style called .textbox, and save it to the alumni_styles.css style sheet. Click the Position category. Set the position value as absolute and the left value as 250 pixels.

19. Create a new style called .button, and save it to the alumni_styles.css style sheet. Set the font-family as Times New Roman, Times, serif. Set the font-size as medium, the font-variant as small-caps, and the font-weight as bold. Use the More Colors dialog to change the background-color to the green color with the Hex value of 00,99,00.

20. Click the form tag on the Quick Tag Selector, then click the .formtext style in the Apply Styles task pane.

21. Click the Name text box, then click .textbox in the Apply Styles task pane. Apply the .textbox style to the two text boxes below the Name text box. Do not apply it to the Other text box.

22. Apply the .button style to the Submit button.

23. Save the page and the style sheet, then open the volunteer.html page in a browser window.

24. Test the form fields by entering text and making selections.

25. Change the site properties, as specified by your instructor. Save the site using the file name, Extend 7-1 Alumni Site. Submit the revised site in the format specified by your instructor.

# Make It Right

Analyze a site and correct all errors and/or improve the design.

### Replacing a Text-Based Navigation Area with Interactive Buttons

*Instructions:* Start Expression Web. Open the Web site, Make It Right 7-1 Humane, from the Data Files for Students. See the inside back cover of this book for instructions for downloading the Data Files for Students, or see your instructor for information about accessing the required files.

Assign values and group similar fields to complete the form on the form.html page. Apply styles to format the text and create links to and from the default.html page as shown in Figure 7–71.

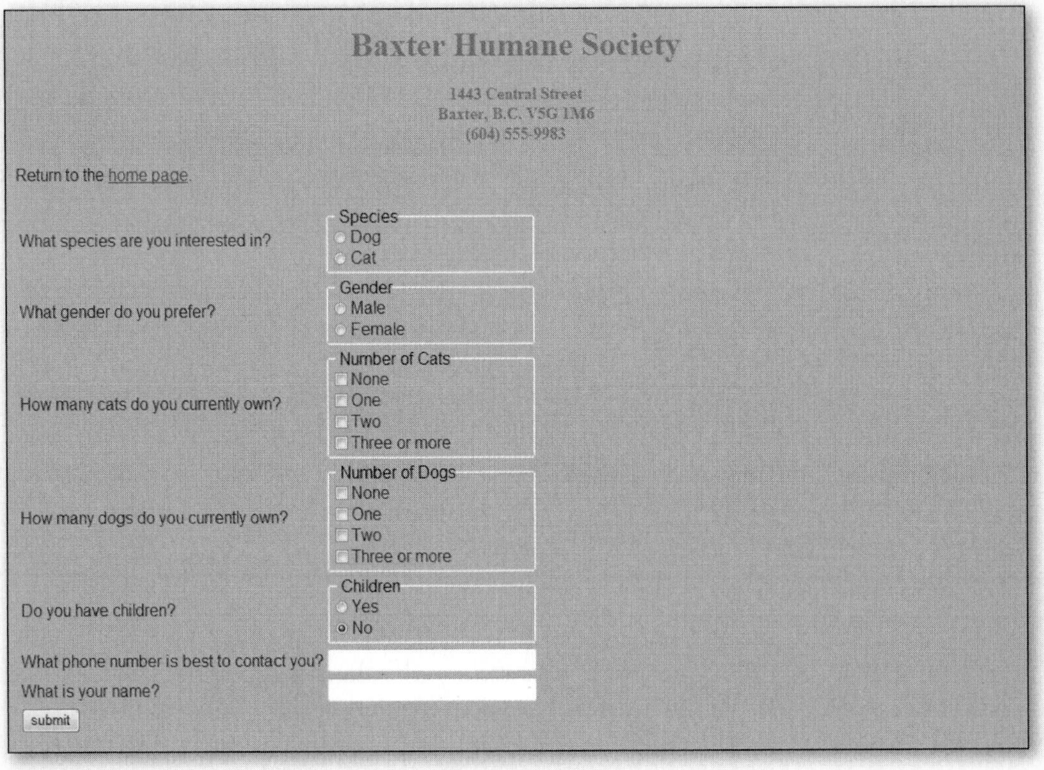

**Baxter Humane Society**

1443 Central Street
Baxter, B.C. V5G 1M6
(604) 555-9983

Return to the home page.

What species are you interested in?

Species
○ Dog
○ Cat

What gender do you prefer?

Gender
○ Male
○ Female

How many cats do you currently own?

Number of Cats
☐ None
☐ One
☐ Two
☐ Three or more

How many dogs do you currently own?

Number of Dogs
☐ None
☐ One
☐ Two
☐ Three or more

Do you have children?

Children
○ Yes
◉ No

What phone number is best to contact you?

What is your name?

submit

**Figure 7–71**

1. Open the form.html page.

2. Click in the blank paragraph div above the form. Type `Return to the home page.`.

3. Select the words, home page, then press CTRL+K to open the Insert Hyperlink dialog box. Click default.html, then click the OK button.

4. Open the default.html page. Click in the paragraph div above the I-frame. Type `Interested in adopting? Fill out this form.`.

5. Select the word, form, then open the Insert Hyperlink dialog box. Click form.html, then click the OK button. Save and close the default.html page.

6. In the first row of the form, select the words, Group box, then type `Species`.

7. Double-click the first radio button, then type `Dog` in the Group name text box and `Yes` in the Value text box. Position the insertion point to the right of the radio button, double-click Label in the Toolbox, then type `Dog`.

8. Double-click the second radio button, then type Cat in the Group name text box and Yes in the Value text box. Position the insertion point to the right of the radio button, double-click Label in the Toolbox, then type Cat.

9. In the next row, change the legend to Gender. For the first radio button, change the Group Name to Male and the Value to Yes, then add a label for Male. For the second radio button, change the Group Name to Female and the Value to Yes, then add a label for Female.

10. In the next row, change the legend to Number of Cats. Add the following Group Names, Values, and Labels to the check boxes:

| Group Name | Value | Label |
|---|---|---|
| zero_cats | 0 | None |
| one_cat | 1 | One |
| two_cats | 2 | Two |
| three_cats | 3 | Three or more |

11. Select the row you just edited, press CTRL+C to copy it to the Clipboard. Click anywhere in the cats row, then press CTRL+V to paste a copy of the cats row into the table.

12. Edit the text, values, and group names in the pasted row to replace the word, cat, with dog.

13. In the next row, change the legend to Children. Double-click the first radio button, change the Group Name to Children and the Value to Yes, set its default as deselected, then add a label for Yes. Double-click the second radio button, change the Group Name to Children and the Value to No, set its default as selected, then add a label for No.

14. In the next row, drag the sizing handle to resize the textbox to 200 pixels wide. Double-click the text box, then type Phone in the Name text box.

15. In the next row, drag the sizing handle to resize the textbox to 200 pixels wide. Double-click the text box, then type Name in the Name text box.

16. Change the site properties, as specified by your instructor. Save the site using the file name, Make It Right 7-1 Humane Site. Submit the revised site in the format specified by your instructor.

## In the Lab

Design and/or format a Web site using the guidelines, concepts, and skills presented in this chapter. Labs are listed in order of increasing difficulty.

### Lab 1: Family Reunion Form

*Problem:*   You are hosting a family reunion, and want to create a new Web page and add a form. You will create a new one-page site, add a preformatted style sheet, then add a text and a form area. You will add fields and assign values and labels to create the page shown in Figure 7–72.

*Continued >*

**In the Lab** *continued*

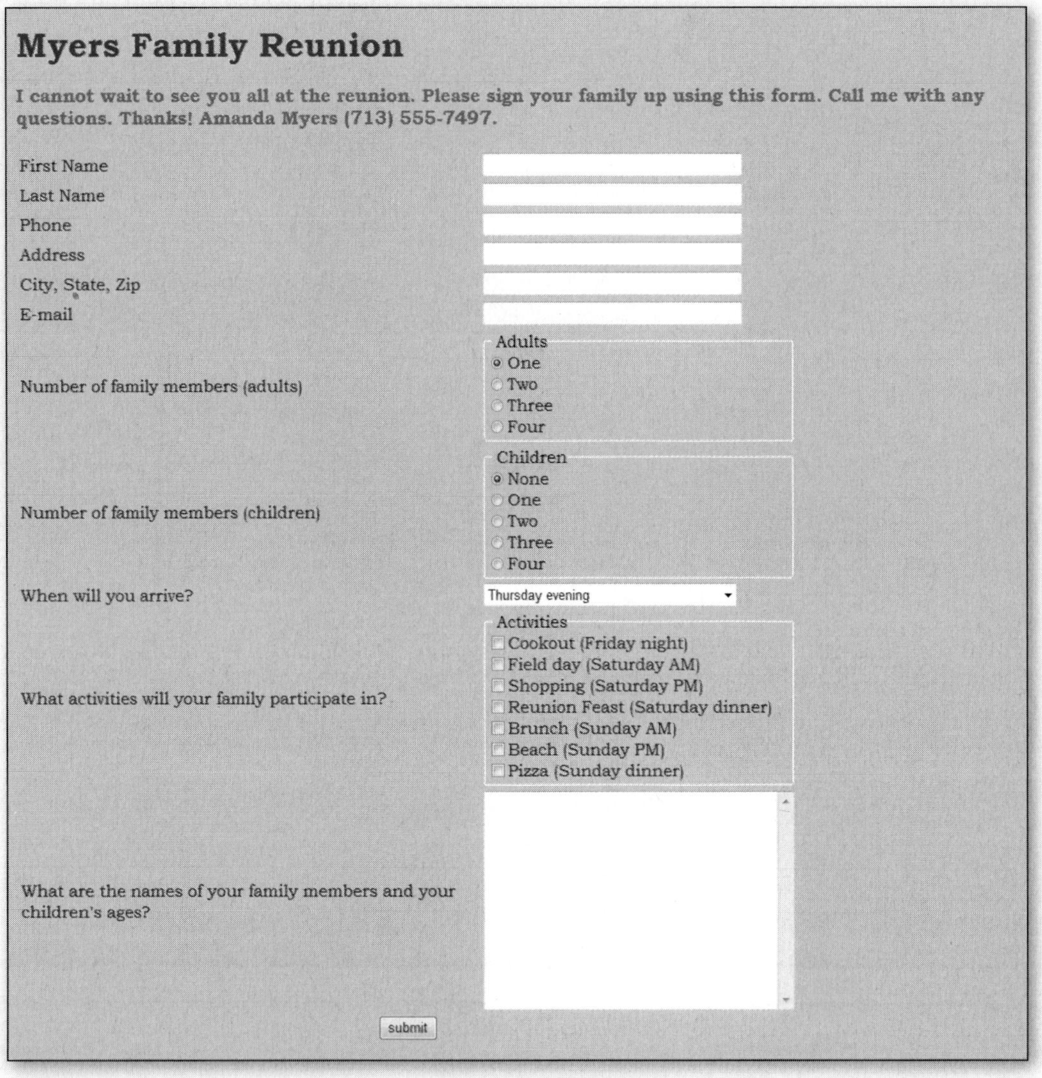

# Myers Family Reunion

**I cannot wait to see you all at the reunion. Please sign your family up using this form. Call me with any questions. Thanks! Amanda Myers (713) 555-7497.**

First Name

Last Name

Phone

Address

City, State, Zip

E-mail

Number of family members (adults)

Adults
- One
- Two
- Three
- Four

Number of family members (children)

Children
- None
- One
- Two
- Three
- Four

When will you arrive?    Thursday evening

What activities will your family participate in?

Activities
- Cookout (Friday night)
- Field day (Saturday AM)
- Shopping (Saturday PM)
- Reunion Feast (Saturday dinner)
- Brunch (Sunday AM)
- Beach (Sunday PM)
- Pizza (Sunday dinner)

What are the names of your family members and your children's ages?

submit

**Figure 7–72**

*Instructions:*

1. Start Expression Web.

2. Create a new one-page Web site called Lab 7-1 Reunion Site. Open the default.html page. Add a new style sheet based on the Block preformatted style sheet, save it as reunion_styles.css, then apply it to the default.html page.

3. Add a new paragraph div, type `Myers Family Reunion`, then format the paragraph with Heading 1.

4. Add a new paragraph div, type `I cannot wait to see you all at the reunion. Please sign your family up using this form. Call me with any questions. Thanks! Amanda Myers (713) 555-7497.`. Format the paragraph with Heading 3.

5. Click in the blank area below the paragraph, add a new form div, then name the form Reunion. Add a 12-row, two-column table in the form div and deselect the Specify width check box.

6. Add text boxes for First Name; Last Name; Phone; Address; City, State, Zip; and E-mail. Type prompting text, and assign values for the text boxes. Resize each text box to 250 pixels wide.

7. In the next empty row, type `Number of family members (adults)` in the left column, then press TAB. Add a group box with the legend Adults. Add radio buttons for One, Two, Three, and Four. Specify the value, and add labels.

8. In the next empty row, type `Number of family members (children)` in the left column, then press TAB. Add a group box with the legend Children. Add radio buttons for None, One, Two, Three, and Four. Specify the value, and add labels.

9. In the next empty row, type `When will you arrive?` Press TAB. Add a drop-down box with the name Arrival, and the following choices: Thursday evening, Friday morning, Friday evening, and Saturday morning. Make Thursday evening selected, and do not specify a separate value.

10. In the next empty row, type `What activities will you participate in?` Press TAB. Add check boxes with the choices: Cookout (Friday night), Field day (Saturday AM), Shopping (Saturday PM), Reunion Feast (Saturday dinner), Brunch (Sunday AM), Beach (Sunday PM), Pizza (Sunday dinner). Give each a numeric value from 1–7.

11. In the next empty row, type `What are the names of your family members and your children's ages?`. Press TAB. Add a text area, then resize it to 300 × 200 pixels.

12. Drag the column divider to resize the first column to 450 pixels wide.

13. In the next empty row, merge the cells. Add a Submit button and center it.

14. Preview the default.html page in a browser.

15. Submit the site in the format specified by your instructor, then close the site.

## In the Lab

### Lab 2: Using a Table to Lay Out a Form

*Problem:* Your client, an employment agency, wants to create a new Web site using a template. The first page they want you to work on is the form for new job candidates. You create a preformatted multipage Web site and add a form to one of the pages using a table to lay out the form fields. You add group boxes and fields, and set the field properties and values to create the page shown in Figure 7–73.

*Continued >*

**In the Lab** *continued*

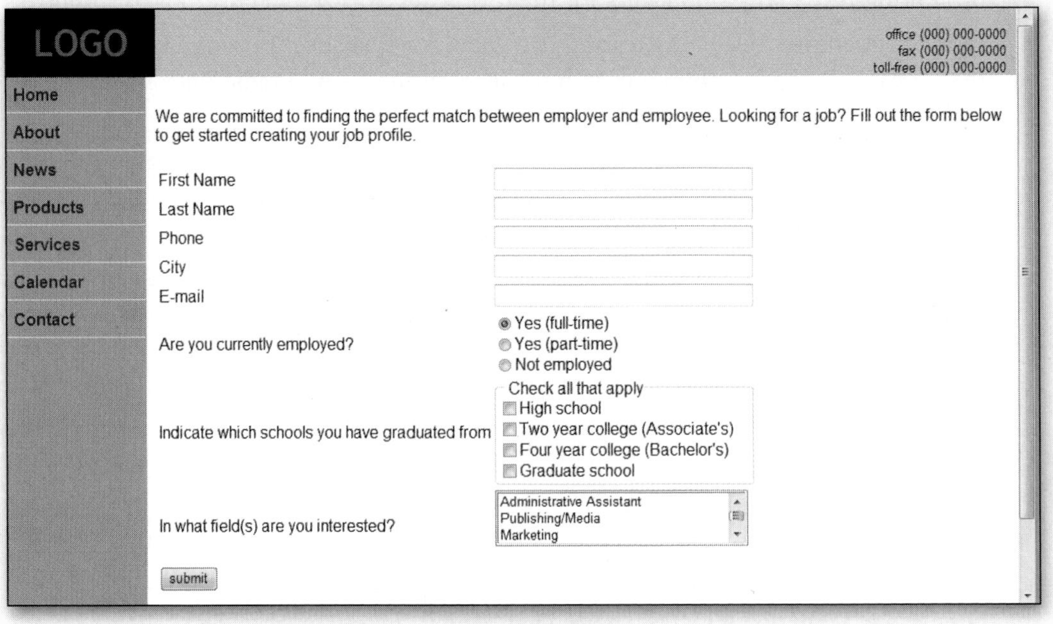

**Figure 7–73**

*Instructions:*

1. Start Expression Web.

2. Point to New on the File menu, then click Web Site. Click the Templates category, then click the Small Business 5 template.

3. Navigate to the Data Files if necessary, name the site Lab 7-2 Employment, then click the OK button.

4. In the Folder List, rename the Calendar folder Form. Click the Form folder plus button, rename the calendar.htm page form.htm, then double-click the form.htm page to open it.

5. Click the DWT: editable tag on the Quick Tag Selector to select all of the text, then click DELETE.

6. Insert a new paragraph div, then type We are committed to finding the perfect match between employer and employee. Looking for a job? Fill out the form below to get started creating your job profile.

7. Press ENTER. Click the p tag on the Quick Tag Selector to select the new paragraph.

8. Convert the paragraph to a form div, then name the form New_Client. Add a nine-row, two-column table in the form div, and deselect the Specify width check box.

9. Add text boxes for First Name, Last Name, Phone, City, and E-mail. Type prompting text, and assign values for the text boxes.

10. In the next blank row, type Are you currently employed?. Add three radio buttons: Yes (full-time), Yes (part-time), Not employed.

11. In the next blank row, type Indicate which schools you have graduated from. Add a group box with the legend, Check all that apply.

12. In the group box, add check boxes for High school, Two year college (Associate's), Four year college (Bachelor's) and Graduate school.

13. In the next blank row, type `In what field(s) are you interested?`. Add a drop-down box and resize it to 250 pixels wide by 69 pixels high.

14. Double-click the drop-down box, and click the Allow multiple selections option button. Add choices for Administrative Assistant, Publishing/Media, Marketing, Sales, Accounting, and Manufacturing. Specify the value for each.

15. In the next blank row, add a Submit button.

16. Save the form.html page, then preview the site in a browser.

17. Change the site properties, as specified by your instructor.

18. Submit the site in the format specified by your instructor, then close the site.

## In the Lab

### Lab 3: Format a Form with Styles

*Problem:*   You want to add a form for new clients for your math tutoring business. You will add a form to the form.html page, and use styles to format and layout the fields, as shown in Figure 7–74.

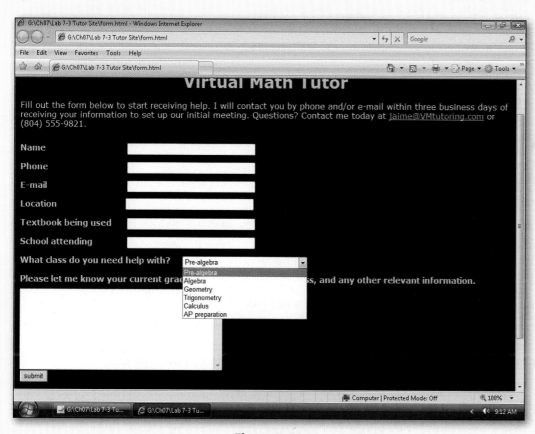

**Figure 7–74**

*Continued >*

**In the Lab** *continued*

*Instructions:*   Start Expression Web. Open the Web site, Lab 7-3 Tutor, from the Data Files for Students. See the inside back cover of this book for instructions for downloading the Data Files for Students, or see your instructor for information about accessing the required files.

*Perform the following tasks.*

1. Open the form.html page.

2. Select the paragraph div below the phone number, then double-click Form in the Toolbox to convert the div to a form.

3. Type Name, press SPACEBAR, then double-click Input (Text) to insert a text box. Double-click the text box to open the Text Box Properties dialog box, type Name in the Name text box, then click the OK button.

4. Repeat Step 3 to insert the following text boxes:

| Text to type | Name in Text Box Properties dialog box |
| --- | --- |
| Phone | Phone |
| E-mail | Email |
| Location | Location |
| Textbook being used | Textbook |
| School attending | School |

5. Type What class do you need help with?, press SPACEBAR, then double-click Drop-Down Box in the Toolbox to insert a new drop-down box. Resize the text box to 250 pixels wide.

6. Double-click the drop-down box to open the Drop-Down Box Properties dialog box, then type Class in the Name text box.

7. Click the Modify button, type Pre-algebra in the Choice text box, click the Specify Value check box to select it, then click the OK button.

8. Click the Add button, type Algebra in the Choice text box, click the Specify Value check box to select it, then click the OK button.

9. Repeat Step 8 to add choices for Geometry, Trigonometry, Calculus, and AP preparation.

10. Click to the right of the drop-down box, then press ENTER. Type Please let me know your current grade, goals, progress in the class, and any other relevant information., then press ENTER.

11. Double-click Text Area in the Toolbox to insert a text area.

12. Double-click the Text Area to open the TextArea Box Properties dialog box, type Grade_goals in the Name text box, then click the OK button.

13. Drag the resize handles to resize the text area to 400 pixels wide by 150 pixels high.

14. Click to the right of the text area, then press ENTER to move to a new line. Double-click Input (Submit) in the Toolbox to insert a new Submit button.

15. Click the New Style link in the Apply Styles task pane. Create a new style called .form_label and save it to the tutor_styles.css style sheet. Add the following style rules to the new style: font-weight: bold; color: Yellow; line-height: 36 pixels. (*Hint*: line-height is located in the Block category.)

16. Click the New Style link in the Apply Styles task pane. Create a new style called .textbox and save it to the tutor_styles.css style sheet. Add the following style rules to the new style in the Position category: position: absolute; width: 250px; left: 225px.

17. Click the New Style link in the Apply Styles task pane. Create a new style called .button and save it to the tutor_styles.css style sheet. Add a style rule that changes the background color to Yellow.

18. Click the form tag on the Quick Tag Selector bar, then click the .form_label style to apply it to all of the text in the form.

19. Click each text box, then apply the .textbox style to it. Apply the .button style to the Submit button.

20. Preview the site and test the form buttons.

21. Change the site properties, as specified by your instructor.

22. Rename the site Lab 7-3 Tutor Site, submit the site in the format specified by your instructor, then close the site.

# Cases and Places

Apply your creative thinking and problem solving skills to design and implement a solution.

• Easier  ••More Difficult

## • 1: Creating a Feedback Form for a Car Wash

Create a new one-page Web site for a car wash. Create a new style sheet based on a preformatted style sheet and attach it to the page. Add a header and other necessary text. Create a form area and a table in which you will create the form. Use radio buttons and check boxes to ask at least five questions. Include control buttons to reset and submit the form. Preview the page. Save and close the site and the browser window.

## • 2: Creating an Enrollment Form

Create a new one-page Web site for a community education program. Add necessary text, and create a form area and decide on a layout method. Use drop-down boxes to add prompting text instructing visitors to choose the class, time, and location (or other options). Include text boxes for necessary personal information. Include control buttons to reset and submit the form. Preview the page. Save and close the site and the browser window.

## •• 3: Laying Out a Form for a Computer Repair Shop

Create a new one-page site for a computer repair shop. Plan and create a survey that asks customers about their recent experiences with your business. Do not use a table for layout. Include text boxes for the visitor to enter his or her first and last name, address, phone number, and e-mail. Add three or four questions using check boxes or radio buttons (or both). Include a text area for additional information. Include control buttons to reset and submit the form. Use indentation, styles, and other techniques to format and lay out your form so that it is readable. Preview the form in a browser window. Save and close the site and the browser window.

## •• 4: Creating a Movie Fan Site

**Make It Personal**

You want to create a Web site that includes trivia questions about your favorite movie. Create a one-page site using a blank page or a CSS layout and a preformatted style sheet. Create a form area and use a table to lay out the form. Use at least one drop-down box and one text area (for example, to ask visitors to describe their favorite scene), and use radio buttons and check boxes to create a form with at least six trivia questions. Include control buttons to reset and submit the form. Preview and test the form, save the page and style sheet, then close the site.

## •• 5: Creating a Form for Online Shopping

**Working Together**

A custom T-shirt company wants to create a form for ordering shirts. Working as a team with several of your classmates, you are to plan and create the form. Each team member should contribute to planning the form purpose, page layout, and question types needed. As a group, decide on the fields you will need, and decide the best form control for each field. Start by creating a site folder, and add a page using a CSS layout. Create and attach a style sheet using a preformatted style sheet. Create a form area and groups for each question type, then add the necessary fields, labels, values, and prompting text. Include control buttons to reset and submit the form. Preview the page and test the form. Save and close the pages and style sheet, then close the site.

# 8 | Testing and Publishing Your Web Site

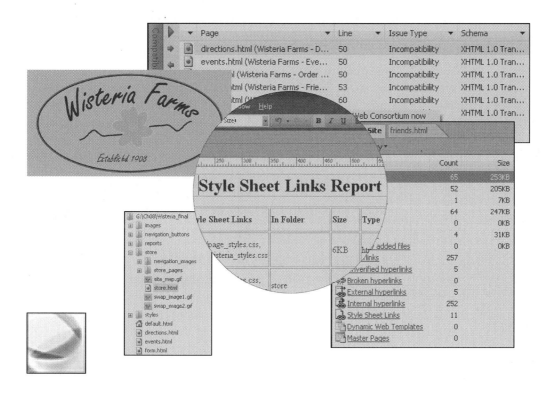

## Objectives

You will have mastered the material in this chapter when you can:

- Use Site Summary to check site problems
- Use Site Summary to fix site problems
- Organize the site folder contents
- Verify hyperlinks
- Save a report as an HTML file
- Create an Accessibility report

- Create a Compatibility report
- Examine Web site hosting
- Define Web server types
- Optimize HTML files
- Set publishing options
- Publish files to a remote server
- Manage files on a remote server

# 8 | Testing and Publishing Your Site

## Introduction

Publishing a site is the process of posting the files to a Web server, where they are made available to site visitors over the Internet. Publishing a site makes it public; whether the site represents your business, a client, or is personal, you must ensure the accuracy of the links and site content to present a professional and easy-to-use site for your visitors.

Prior to publishing your site, you need to prepare the files for publishing. In Chapter 1 you learned to check the spelling on your site and to print individual pages to review them and check for accuracy. In every chapter, you have tested links, interactivity, and other features as you added them to your site. In addition, you also need to confirm that all internal and external links work, the CSS and HTML code is compatible with current standards and browsers, your site does not download too slowly, and that you have met accessibility standards. Expression Web has many tools that examine different areas of concern and generate reports. You can use reports to pinpoint and fix problems, or save a report as an HTML page so that you can print it out or send it to a colleague.

An important part of preparing your site for publication is to have it tested by other people. This phase is called **beta testing**. Publishers of software and Web sites must conduct beta testing to check for errors, vague instructions, or features that do not function as intended. Unlike reports, which analyze technical aspects of your site, beta testing relies on real people experiencing your site. Upon completing beta testing, you review the information that you gather from beta site testers and make changes to the site content, navigation, and layout based on the types of issues that are uncovered. Some site features, such as the color scheme, might not appeal to everybody, but there could be valid reasons for not making changes; for example, the colors used may match the company's other marketing materials. Tester feedback on usability and vague content are almost always addressed.

Site testing is an ongoing process. After initially publishing your site, you will need to recheck the site periodically to ensure that site visitors receive accurate information, then publish necessary corrections to site pages. You must test your site any time you add, remove, or edit page content.

When publishing your site, you decide how and where the site will be published. If you have created the site on behalf of a client, the client might have access to a Web server that can host the files. You can sign up for fee-based hosting services if you do not have access to your own Web server. Before you make any decisions on how to publish the site, you will need to research costs, size limitations, and other factors to ensure that the published site meets your needs or those of your client.

**BTW**

**Web Accessibility**
See Appendix B for more information about accessibility and assistive technology.

## Project — Farm Stand Web Site

You have finished creating the Web site for your client, Wisteria Farms, a farm stand and grocery store in Dilton, New Hampshire. An additional page has been added to the site, listing links to other businesses. The site layout, formatting, and content have been approved by the client, and you are ready to prepare the site for publication. You have saved the reviewed, final site files in a new folder to keep them separate from the work in progress files you were working with earlier.

The project in this chapter shows you how to use Expression Web to create reports and make publishing decisions in order to publish the site to a beta testing folder, as shown in Figure 8–1. You will generate reports for a site summary, adherence to accessibility standards, and compatibility with various HTML and CSS versions. You will save a report as an HTML file. You will learn about Web site hosting and Web servers and set publishing options. Finally, you will publish the site to a remote server to make it available for beta testing.

**Figure 8–1**

## Overview

As you read this chapter, you will learn how to prepare the Web site shown in Figure 8–1 for publication by performing these general tasks:

- Run a Site Summary report
- Save a report as an HTML file
- Create Accessibility and Compatibility reports
- Set up a remote site
- Optimize HTML files for improved download times
- Publish files
- Manage files

**Plan Ahead**

**General Project Guidelines**

When preparing a site for publication, you should have it reviewed by others, such as your colleague(s) or client(s), to make sure the navigation is consistent and works properly, the content is accurate, and the layout is consistent and attractive. In addition, Expression Web has tools that can help you verify the technical functionality of the site, identifying potential issues such as missing information, slow pages, or broken links.

1. **Examine the site's technical aspects.** Using the Expression Web Site Summary tool and reports for accessibility and compatibility are necessary steps when preparing your site for publication. You can view information about the entire site or check individual pages.

2. **Determine which issues to fix.** Some of the issues identified by Expression Web summaries and reports might be things that you do not want to or cannot change. For example, if a report indicates that a certain page will download slowly over a dial-up connection, you might decide that value of the behaviors or images you have added to the page is greater than the potential inconvenience to the few site visitors who are still using a dial-up Internet connection. You *must* fix issues such as a broken hyperlink or a page that is not linked to other site pages.

3. **Assess hosting options.** Signing up with a Web site hosting service involves research and analysis. You must consider the physical needs of the site, such as overall size, types of images supported, and necessary interactions with a database. In addition, determine how you will access the server to make site changes or view reports on traffic or other aspects, and the service provider's file size limits and costs.

4. **Initiate the site publication.** Deciding that your site is ready to be published is an important step. Although you can always make changes to the site content, be careful to only publish the pages that are verified and approved for publication. If you are unsure about a page, and if not publishing does not cause problems with your site, mark it as Do Not Publish until you are certain the page is ready for publication. Keep the site pages synchronized (updated among users) as you and your colleagues work on them.

# Running and Reviewing a Site Summary Report

Reports within Expression Web include Site Summary, CSS, Accessibility, and Compatibility. You learned about the CSS report, which checks for unused or conflicting style rules, in Chapter 4. To run a report, you access the required report type from the site menu. A Site Summary report provides details on three different categories of information: Files, Shared Content, and Problems; more information on these categories is provided in Table 8–1. You will examine the Accessibility and Compatibility reports later in this chapter.

| Table 8–1 Site Summary Categories | | |
|---|---|---|
| **Category** | **Report Names** | **Used To** |
| Files | All Files, Recently Added Files, Recently Changed Files, and Older Files | Locate files and file information; filter files that were created or changed before or after a certain date to determine which files may need to be updated for content, formatting, or style. |
| Shared Content | Dynamic Web Templates, Master Pages, and Style Sheet Links | Ensure that all of your pages are attached to the correct templates and style sheets for consistency. |
| Problems | Unlinked Files, Slow Pages, and Hyperlinks | Locate potential problems that you must address to ensure a satisfactory experience for your site visitors. |

**BTW**

**Master Pages**
Master pages, like dynamic Web templates, are used to create consistent page layout and formatting. Master pages are used with .aspx files, which contain page content that is generated by a site event, such as a search or form request.

You can save any report as an HTML page, which allows you to maintain a record of errors and issues that you have fixed, share report data with colleagues, and create printed copies of reports. Point to Print on the File menu, then click Print to print any HTML report.

## To Start Expression Web and Open a Site and Page

If you are using a computer to step through the project in this chapter, and you want your screens to match the figures in this book, you should change your computer's resolution to 1024 × 768. For information about how to change a computer's resolution, read Appendix F.

The following steps, which assume Windows Vista is running, start Expression Web based on a typical installation, and open the site folder and a page. You may need to ask your instructor how to start Expression Web for your computer.

**Note:** If you are using Window XP, see Appendix E for alternate steps.

**1** Click the Start button on the Windows Vista taskbar to display the Start menu.

**2** Click All Programs at the bottom of the left pane on the Start menu to display the All Programs list.

**3** Click Microsoft Expression on the All Programs list to display the Microsoft Expression list.

**4** Click Microsoft Expression Web 2 to start Expression Web.

**5** Click File on the menu bar to open the File menu, then click Open Site to display the Open Site dialog box.

**6** Navigate to the data files.

**7** Click the Wisteria_final folder, then click the Open button to open the site in Expression Web (Figure 8–2).

**8** Click Task Panes on the menu bar, then click Reset Workspace Layout.

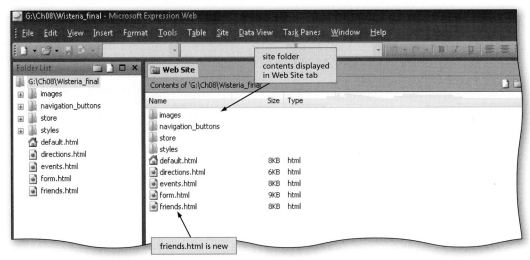

**Figure 8–2**

## To Run a Site Summary Report

When you run a Site Summary report, the report information is displayed in the Web Site tab. The Reports toolbar appears at the top of the Web Site tab, which contains a button arrow that allows you to change to another report view. You can also use Reports toolbar options to set the date that defines an older file or the size that is used to determine a slow page. The following steps run the Site Summary report for the Wisteria site. While the report runs, information about the report appears in the status bar. When the report is complete, the results will appear in the Web Site tab.

- Point to Reports on the Site menu, then click Site Summary to view the site report in the Web Site tab (Figure 8–3).

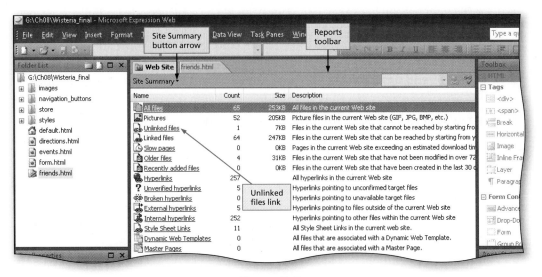

**Figure 8–3**

**2**

- Click the Unlinked files link to view the unlinked file report (Figure 8–4).

🔍 **Experiment**

- Click other options in the Site Summary list to view the details. To return to the site summary, click the *report type* button arrow on the Reports tool-bar, then click Site Summary.

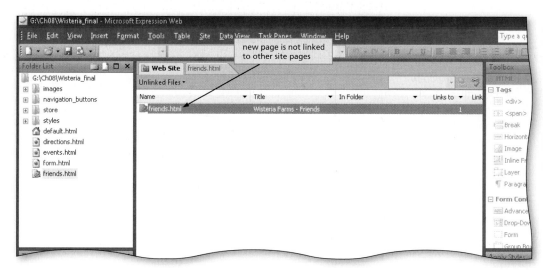

**Figure 8–4**

## To Fix an Unlinked File

Site visitors will be unable to access a page that is unlinked to any other site files. The following steps add an interactive button to the main navigation area for the friends.html page by copying and pasting an existing navigation button, editing its label and link, then copying the new button to all pages in the site.

**1**

- Double-click the default.html page in the Folder List to open it (Figure 8–5).

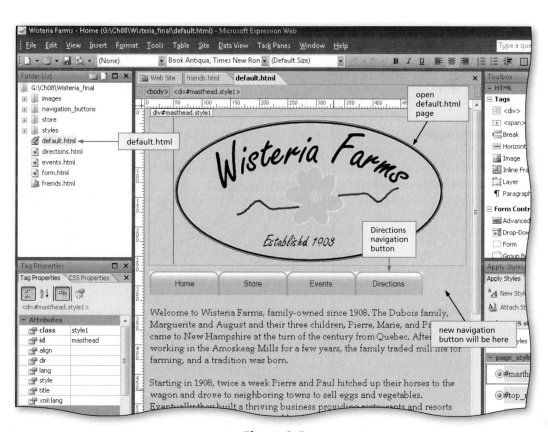

**Figure 8–5**

- Click the Directions navigation button to select it.

- Press CTRL+C to copy the Directions navigation button to the Clipboard, then click to the right of the button to place the insertion point.

- Press CTRL+V to paste a copy of the Directions navigation button (Figure 8–6).

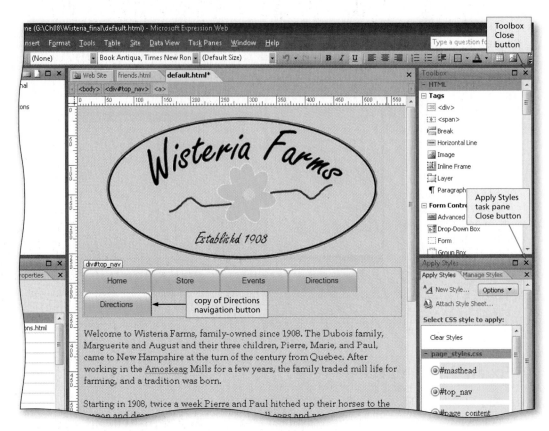

**Figure 8–6**

- Click the Toolbox Close button to close the Toolbox.

- Click the Apply Styles task pane Close button to close the task pane (Figure 8–7).

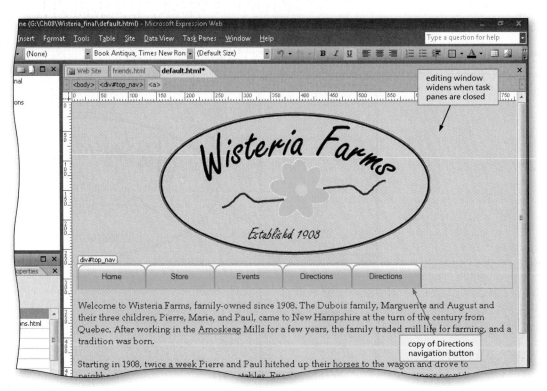

**Figure 8–7**

- Double-click the copy of the Directions navigation button to open the Interactive Buttons dialog box.

- Select the text in the Text text box, then type `Friends` to edit the button label.

- Select the text in the Link text box, then type `friends.html` to edit the button link (Figure 8–8).

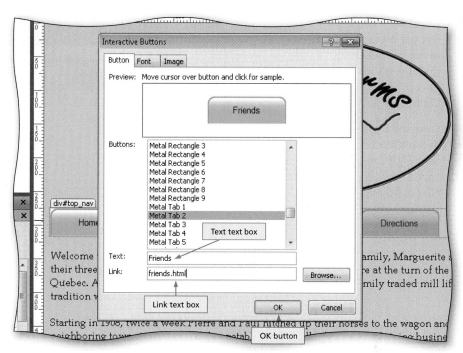

**Figure 8–8**

- Click the OK button to close the Interactive Buttons dialog box and update the new navigation button (Figure 8–9).

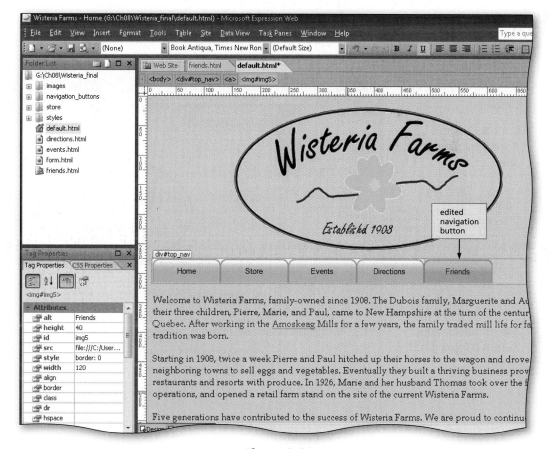

**Figure 8–9**

**6**

- Click the Friends navigation button to select it if necessary, then press CTRL+C to copy it to the Clipboard.

- Save and close the default.html page, then click OK in the Save Embedded Files dialog box (Figure 8–10).

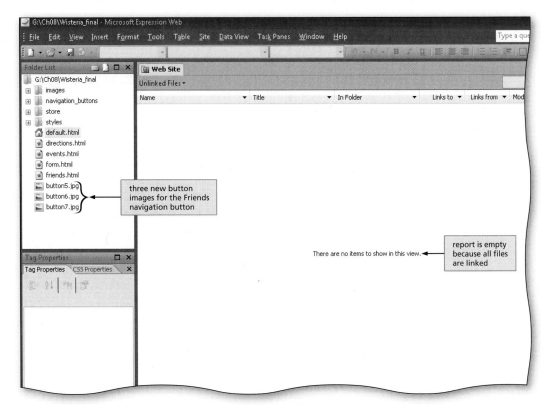

**Figure 8–10**

**7**

- Click the store folder plus sign to view the contents.

- Double-click the store.html page to open it.

- Click to the right of the Directions navigation button to position the insertion point, then press CTRL+V to paste the Friends navigation button (Figure 8–11).

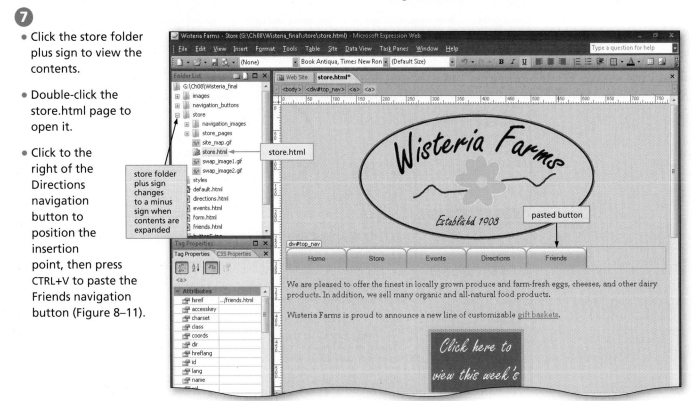

**Figure 8–11**

**8**

- Save and close the store.html page, and save the new embedded button images.

- Repeat Step 7 to paste the new Friends navigation button into the directions.html, events.html, form.html, and friends.html pages.

- Save and close all open pages, and save the new button images (Figure 8–12).

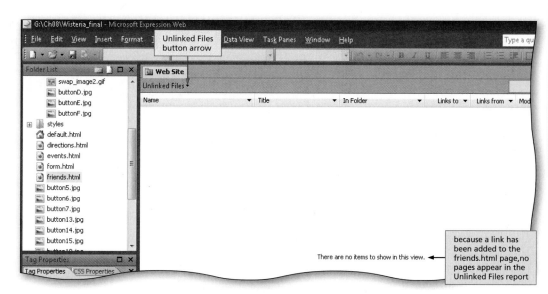

**Figure 8–12**

**Other Ways**

1. Right-click button to open shortcut menu, then click Copy to copy button to Clipboard.

2. Right-click where insertion point is positioned to open shortcut menu, then click Paste to paste copied button from Clipboard.

## To Organize Site Folder Contents

Keeping your site folder organized makes it easier for you to locate files. The following steps move the newly created image files for the Friends navigation button into folders.

**1**

- Click the Folders View button at the bottom of the Web Site tab to display the contents of the site folder (Figure 8–13).

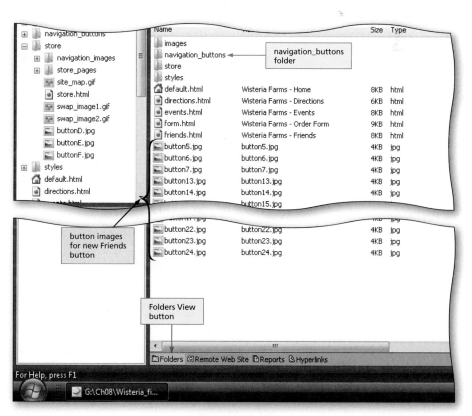

**Figure 8–13**

* Click the bottom JPEG image, press and hold SHIFT, scroll, then click the top JPEG image in the site folder to select all of the navigation button image files.

* Drag the selected files to the navigation_buttons folder to move them (Figure 8–14).

**Q&A**

I get a dialog box that says the folder contains a file with a duplicate name.

Because the button image files are named automatically, some of the filenames might be identical to filenames from buttons created during previous work on the site. Click the OK button, then rename any affected buttons (for example, by adding an "a" at the end of the filename). Click the Yes button in the Rename dialog box to allow Expression Web to rename any links to the image name, then move the renamed image files to the navigation_buttons folder.

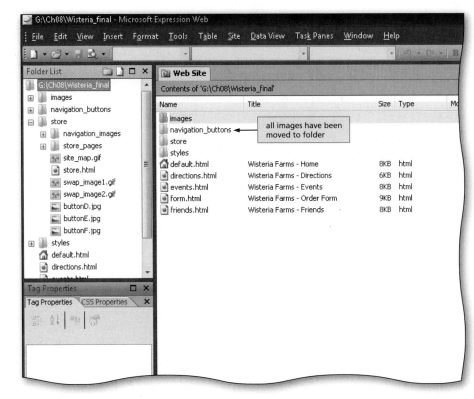

**Figure 8–14**

* Click the store folder plus sign to view its contents in the Folders List (Figure 8–15).

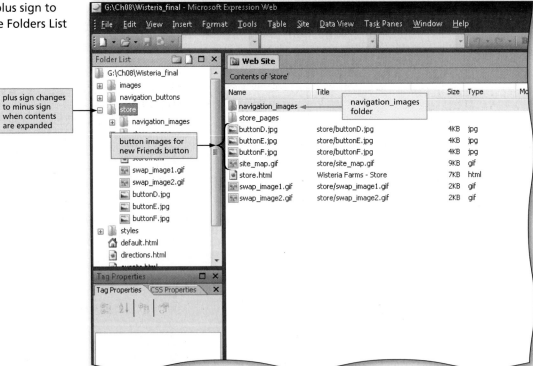

**Figure 8–15**

**4**

- Click the three JPEG images, press and hold SHIFT, then click the top JPEG image in the site folder to select all of the navigation button image files.

- Drag the selected files to the navigation_images folder to move them (Figure 8–16).

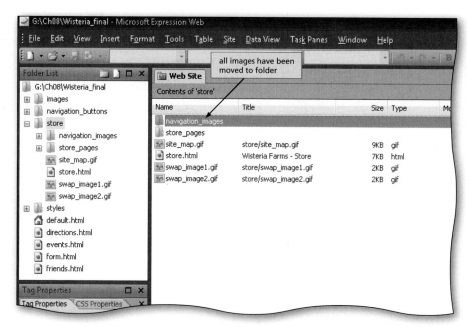

**Figure 8–16**

## To Verify External Hyperlinks

One way to verify all of the external hyperlinks in a site is to review all site pages, click each instance of an external link, and make sure that the link works. This can be time-consuming and can cause errors, especially because links can change on an external site after you have checked them manually. The following steps use Expression Web to verify each of the external hyperlinks in the site at once, then fix a broken link. As the report runs, information about the report appears in the status bar. When the report is complete, the results will appear in the Web Site tab.

**1**

- Click the Reports View button at the bottom of the Web Site tab to view the Unlinked file report.

- Click the Unlinked Files button arrow on the Reports toolbar, then click Site Summary to return to the site summary (Figure 8–17).

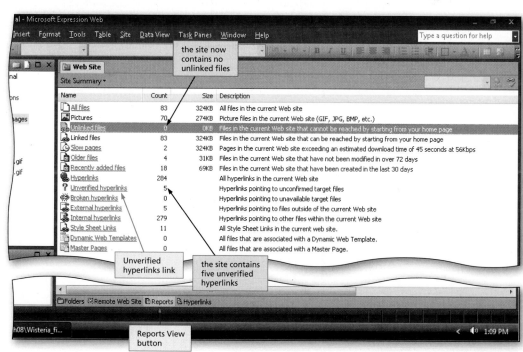

**Figure 8–17**

• Click the Unverified
  hyperlinks link to
  open the Reports
  View dialog box
  (Figure 8–18).

**Q&A**

The Reports View
dialog box does not
open for me.

Clicking the Don't
ask me this again
check box in the
Reports View dialog
box will automati-
cally run the report
to verify hyperlinks
when the Unverified
hyperlinks link is
clicked. If the dialog
box does not open
for you, skip Step 3.

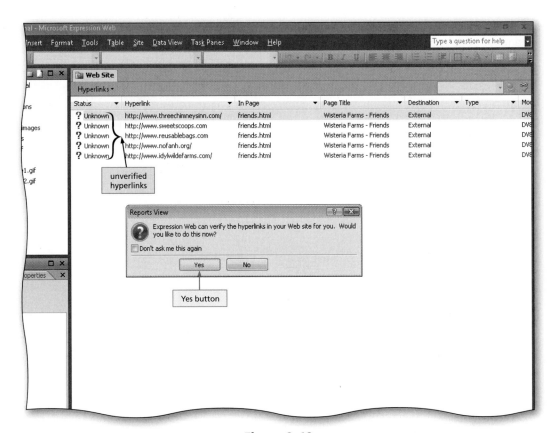

**Figure 8–18**

• Click the Yes button
  to verify the links
  (Figure 8–19).

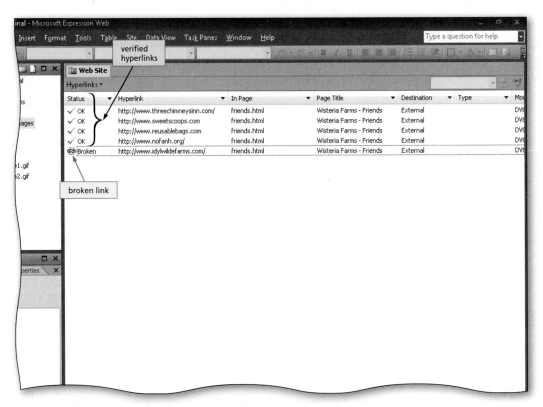

**Figure 8–19**

**4**

- Double-click the broken link to open the Edit Hyperlink dialog box (Figure 8–20).

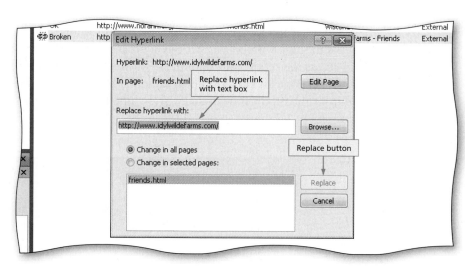

**Figure 8–20**

**5**

- In the Replace hyperlink with text box, delete the s so that the link reads, www.idylwildefarm.com, then click the Replace button to change the link's status to Unknown (Figure 8–21).

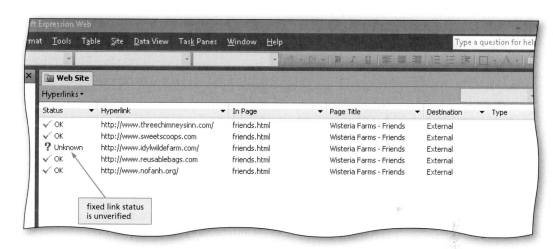

**Figure 8–21**

**6**

- Right-click the unknown link to open the shortcut menu, then click Verify Hyperlink to verify the corrected link (Figure 8–22).

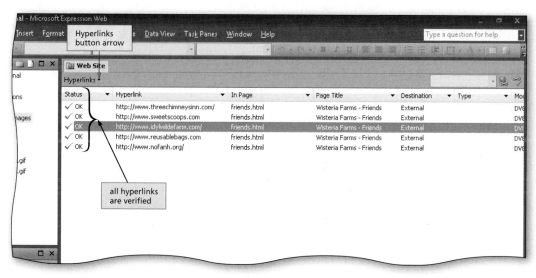

**Figure 8–22**

## To Save a Report as an HTML Page

Saving a report as a file allows you to reference the report information as a checklist of things that you must fix, or to generate a file to share with colleagues. Saving it as an HTML page allows it to be reopened in Expression Web so that you can access the report information as you work on the site. HTML files can easily be shared with others; when you send someone an HTML file, it will open by default in a browser, allowing the recipient to view the information and print the report if he or she wishes. The following steps show the style sheet links for all pages and save the report as an HTML page.

**1**

- Click the Hyperlinks button arrow, then click Site Summary to return to the site summary (Figure 8–23).

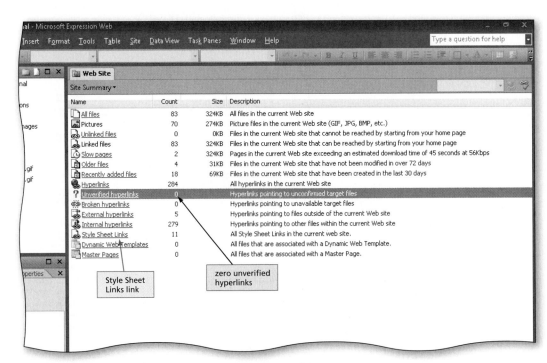

**Figure 8–23**

**2**

- Click the Style Sheet Links link to view the style sheet links report (Figure 8–24).

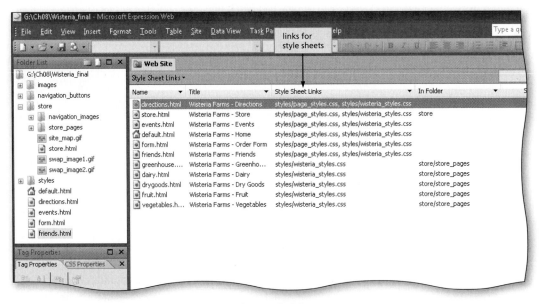

**Figure 8–24**

**3**

- Click Save As on the File menu to open the Save As dialog box (Figure 8–25).

**Figure 8–25**

**4**

- Click the New Folder button to insert a new, untitled folder (Figure 8–26).

**Q&A** My dialog box is different.

If your dialog box shows a Folders List below the folders button, click the Folders button. Use the scroll bar to see any additional content.

**Figure 8–26**

- Type `reports`, then press ENTER to name the new folder.
- Click the Open button to open the new folder (Figure 8–27).
- Click the Save button to save the report with the default name to the reports folder.

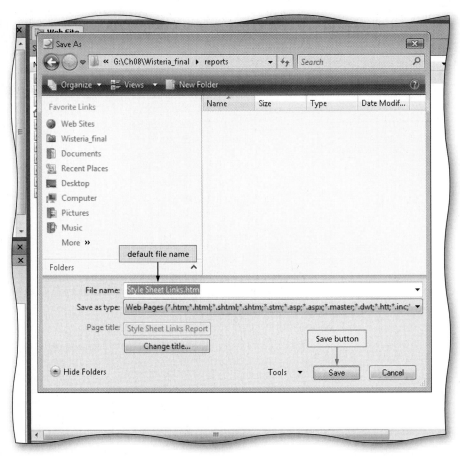

**Figure 8–27**

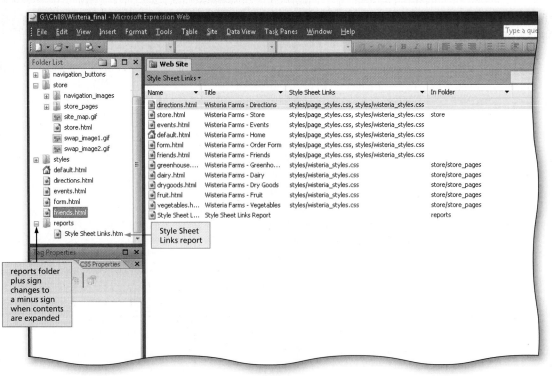

- In the Folder List, click the reports folder plus sign to expand the contents (Figure 8–28).

reports folder plus sign changes to a minus sign when contents are expanded

**Figure 8–28**

**7**

- In the Folder List, double-click the Style Sheet Links. htm file to open the HTML copy of the report (Figure 8–29).

- Right-click the Style Sheet Links.htm page tab, then close the HTML copy of the report.

**Experiment**

- Click Print on the File menu to view a hard copy of the report.

**Figure 8–29**

**Other Ways**

1. Press CTRL+S to open Save As dialog box.

2. In Accessibility or Compatibility task pane, click Generate HTML Report button to create HTML version of information; save as a new file.

**Plan Ahead**

**Determine which issues to fix.**

With the exception of misspellings or broken links, some issues that are revealed by running a site report will be things that you are unable to fix, that you might decide not to fix, or that you decide to change at a later date. You must balance the severity of the errors against the needs of the site — considerations will include the value of content, images, and behaviors that contribute to a file size, and any deadlines imposed by your client or business needs. While it is important to make your site work well for visitors with slower connections, such as dial-up over a telephone modem, the reality is that most visitors will have a faster connection, such as a cable modem. If a page with a video demonstrating a product is identified as having a slow download time, you might decide not to fix it if the video is necessary to the site or page content.

# Running and Reviewing an Accessibility Report

**BTW**

**Optimizing Your Site for Mobile Devices**
Making sites compatible with mobile devices requires modified screen size, input methods, and supported image file types. Some companies create modified versions of sites specifically for mobile device users.

Although most of your site visitors likely will be viewing your Web pages on a full-featured PC, some will not. Visitors with disabilities might use assistive technologies for accessing the Web, and increasing numbers of people are using mobile devices such as cell phones for Web access. Designing your site to meet the browsing needs of these two groups increases the potential audience for your site and keeps your site compliant with current accessibility standards. Adhering to accessibility standards also protects you from potential lawsuits from groups who protect the rights of those with disabilities. Accessibility standards are developed to make information available to those with visual, hearing, motor, and cognitive disabilities.

As mentioned in previous chapters, the World Wide Web Consortium (W3C) has published guidelines for site accessibility, called the **Web Content Accessibility Guidelines (WCAG)**. In addition, Section 508 of the U.S. Rehabilitation Act outlines accessibility standards for information and technology provided by the U.S. Federal Government. The Accessibility Checker allows you to specify the priority level of WCAG standards (1 or 2), and to check for Section 508 compatibility. The W3C Web site is located at www.w3.org. To see the W3C rule about an accessibility error, click the hyperlink in the Checkpoint column to access the W3C Web site and display more information about the WCAG standard and how to fix the error.

**BTW**

**WCAG Priority**
Expression Web can check for Priority 1 (must comply) or Priority 2 (should comply). In addition, there is a third priority level that outlines things developers may choose to comply with. Expression Web does not check for Priority 3.

Throughout the development of the Wisteria site, you have made decisions that help you achieve accessibility requirements, such as adding alternate text to images, using headings and captions in a table, and adding labels to the form. You can test the accessibility of each page individually to view and make adjustments in a focused, efficient manner, or test the site at once if you are fairly certain that there are not many accessibility issues in your site.

The **Accessibility Checker** is the dialog box in which you select the WCAG priorities, pages to check, and other information. In the Accessibility Checker you can also choose the type of information to display. The Errors check box displays the items that you must fix; the Warnings check box displays items that you might want to fix or check; and the Manual Checklist check box displays items that you need to check manually.

Figure 8–30 shows the Accessibility task pane with errors displayed and a link to the WCAG standard at the W3C Web site describing the error.

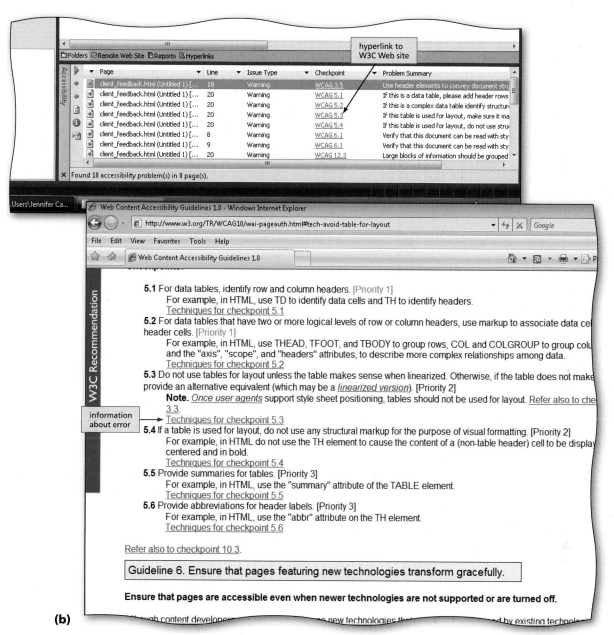

**(a)**

**(b)**

**Figure 8–30**

## To Create an Accessibility Report

The Accessibility task pane is similar to the CSS Reports task pane you worked with in Chapter 4. When you create a report, the results appear in the bottom of the Web Site pane. You can check each error individually or choose to ignore errors. The following steps generate an Accessibility report for the Wisteria site pages.

- Click Accessibility Reports on the Tools menu to open the Accessibility Checker dialog box (Figure 8–31).

**Q&A**

My options in the Check for and Show sections are different.

Depending on past usage, you may have different options selected. If necessary, click the WCAG Priority 1 check box and the WCAG Priority 2 check box in the Check for section to select them, then click the Errors and Warnings check boxes in the Show section to select them.

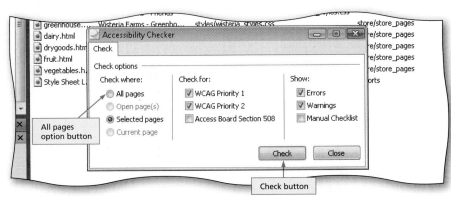

**Figure 8–31**

- Click the All pages option button to select it.

- Click the Check button to create the report and open it in the Accessibility task pane (Figure 8–32).

- Click the Accessibility task pane Close button to close the task pane.

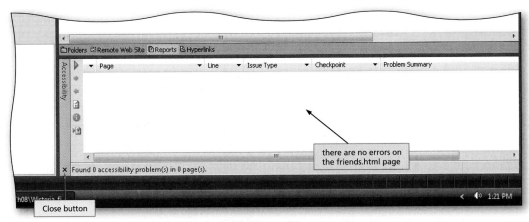

**Figure 8–32**

**BTW**

**Testing with Other Browsers**
You should check your site with a range of browsers, such as Mozilla Firefox, Safari, Opera, and Google Chrome by downloading the browser software and using the Preview in Browser button or opening the default.html page in the browser window and navigating through the site.

# Running and Reviewing a Compatibility Report

Because Web site visitors use a range of browsers for viewing Web sites, it is important to ensure that the pages you create work and appear as intended in various browsers. Compatibility reports check the HTML and CSS pages in your site for potential issues when your site is viewed with different browsers, which may use different types of HTML and CSS specifications.

The Microsoft Expression Web Compatibility report allows you to check compatibility with the latest versions of Windows Internet Explorer, as well as different versions of CSS, HTML, and XHTML. You should also check your site using other resolutions, or screen sizes, to make sure that viewers with differently sized monitors have a similar experience.

## To Create a Compatibility Report

Like the Accessibility report, the Compatibility report appears in a Compatibility task pane. For each potential error, the error type and status, as well as the page and line number of the HTML code of the location, are shown. You can click on an error to view it in HTML Code view. The following steps generate a Compatibility report for the Wisteria site. The report reveals an error related to centering a table. You have already corrected this error on other site pages by creating a CSS style rule, and you will correct it the same way on the friends.html page.

**1**

- Click Compatibility Reports on the Tools menu to open the Compatibility Checker dialog box (Figure 8–33).

My options in the Check HTML/XHTML compatibility with and Check CSS compatibility with sections are different.

Depending on past usage, you may have different options selected. If necessary, click the Check HTML/XHTML compatibility with box arrow, click Internet Explorer 7.0 to select it, click the Check CSS compatibility with box arrow, then click CSS 2.1 to select it.

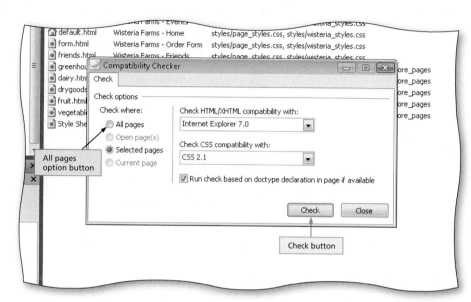

**Figure 8–33**

**2**

- Click the All pages option button to select it.

- Click the Check button to create the report and open it in the Compatibility task pane (Figure 8–34).

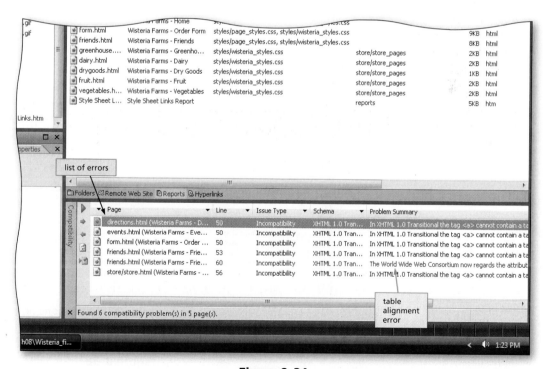

**Figure 8–34**

**3**

- Position the pointer over the alignment error to view more details on a ScreenTip (Figure 8–35).

**Q&A**

My task pane shows different errors.

Depending on the settings you choose in the Compatibility Checker, your version of Expression Web, or changes you have made to the site, your task pane may show additional errors.

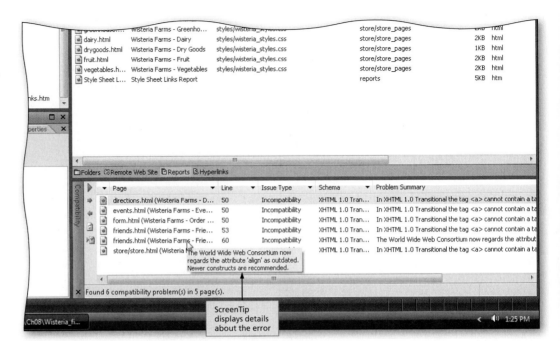

**Experiment**

- Run the Compatibility report with other CSS and HTML versions selected to verify that no other errors are found.

**Figure 8–35**

**4**

- Double-click the error to open the page in Code view and highlight the incompatible code (Figure 8–36).

- Select the code in Code view, then press DELETE to remove the code.

- Press CTRL+S to save the page.

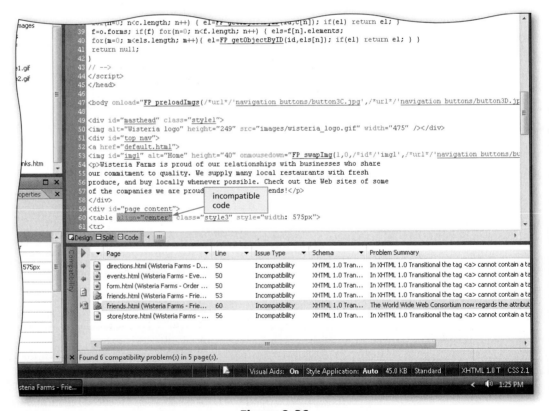

**Figure 8–36**

**5**

- Click the Show Design View button to switch to Design view (Figure 8–37).

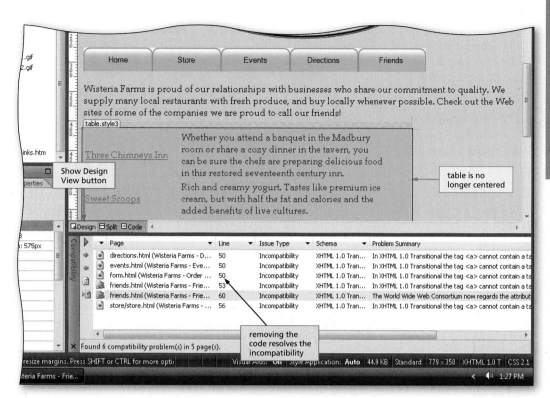

**Figure 8–37**

**6**

- Click Apply Styles on the Task Panes menu to open the Apply Styles task pane (Figure 8–38).

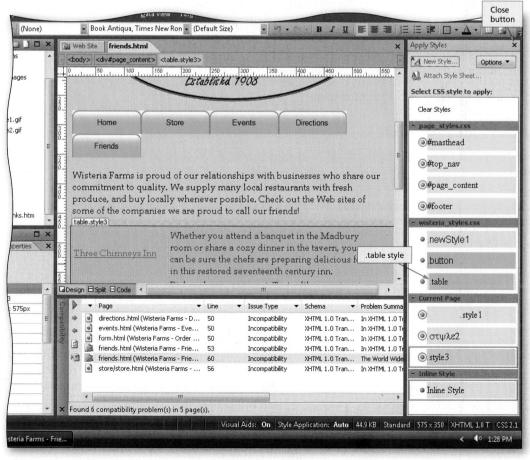

**Figure 8–38**

**7**

- Click anywhere in the table, then click the table tag on the Quick Tag Selector to select the table.

- Click the .table style in the Apply Styles task pane to apply it to the table.

- Click the Refresh Changed Results button in the Compatibility task pane to rerun the report and make sure there are no new errors introduced by your changes.

- Click the Apply Styles task pane Close button to close the task pane and view the changes to the table (Figure 8–39).

- Click the Compatibility task pane Close button to close the task pane.

- Save and close the friends.html page

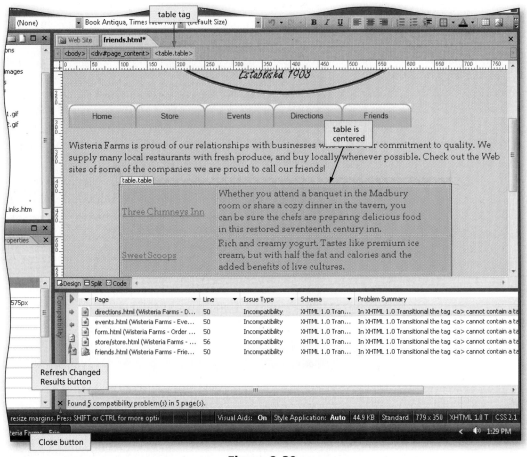

**Figure 8–39**

## Understanding Web Site Hosting

**BTW**

**Appendix C**
Appendix C covers additional information on selecting a host and publishing a site to a remote server.

A **Web server** is defined as either a software program that responds to requests from browsers (such as forms or searches), or the computer that **hosts**, or stores, site files or programs. A Web host is a company that runs multiple Web sites and Web servers and charges the owners of the sites to use these services. A large company might have its own dedicated, secure Web servers, supported by its own IT staff, which it can use to maintain the site content, update security settings, and keep track of site traffic.

Smaller companies rely on Web site hosts, also called **virtual hosts**, to allow them space on a server to store the necessary programs and files and to keep the connection to the Internet open and secure at all times. Some smaller companies, such as those conducting business on the Web, need access to their product and sales databases and secure payment processing to ensure that customers can complete transactions. You can perform an online search to find companies offering virtual hosting with a range of products and services. Your **Internet Service Provider (ISP)**, which provides your connection to the Internet, might offer limited hosting services that would be adequate for a small business. Some ISPs offer upgraded services with more advanced hosting capabilities.

When researching a Web hosting service, an important consideration is the **uptime**, or percentage of time the Internet connection remains open. If a server needs to be restarted or maintained, the Web site host might experience a small amount of planned downtime. During the downtime, if a customer attempts to access a site on the server, he or she will receive an error message. Reviews from current customers can help determine if the uptime is satisfactory, if most of the downtime is planned and pre-announced, and if the host has the capability to alert customers that the site is currently down and when it will be available again.

Hosts typically specify the types of files and overall size of the site you may have, according to your service agreement. Your agreement with the host also will specify additional requirements such as a database service. Hosts support various methods of publishing to their servers. You should look for a method that is compatible with Expression Web, as discussed in Table 8–2. You should also ask what types of reports are available to help you track site traffic and if there are any restrictions related to logging into your site to change files. Fees for site hosting are usually billed on a monthly or annual basis.

**BTW**

**Search Engine Optimization (SEO)**
SEO refers to adjustments to page content, page titles, and code to make the site and site pages appear higher in a query results list when viewed in a search engine. There are companies who specialize in SEO and can be hired for this purpose.

---

**Assess hosting options.**
Review the technical requirements of the site as well as customer reviews. Do an Internet search on the site host to see if there are any negative reviews about uptime, the ability to make changes, or the availability of reports. Make sure the hosting fees will meet your long-term budget needs.

**Plan Ahead**

## Defining Web Server Types

Before you can publish your site, you need to choose a host server and gather information about the server location and your account, including your account ID. Expression Web publishing supports four different server options, as outlined in Table 8–2.

**BTW**

**Securing a Domain Name**
A domain name is the address, or URL, of your site, such as *www.sitename.com*. You must purchase and register a domain name for your site; many Web hosting companies offer this service.

**Table 8–2 Expression Web Server Types**

| Server Type | Used For |
| --- | --- |
| FrontPage Server Extensions | Publishing sites that were created using Microsoft FrontPage, which was the software predecessor to the first version of Expression Web. The FrontPage server extensions must be installed on the Web server to which you are publishing your files. |
| WebDAV (Web-based Distributed Authoring and Versioning) | Allowing groups to use workflow and collaboration features in cases where there are multiple programmers responsible for creating and verifying HTML pages in the site. Not a very common option and might not be supported by your Web host. |
| FTP (File Transfer Protocol) | Publishing a site from a local computer to a remote server. This is the most common method of site publishing, but it requires knowledge of the location and access to an FTP server, and the file path for the folder to which you will publish your site. |
| File System | Posting site files to a folder on your computer or on a network folder to which you have access. Often used to back up a site before publishing it remotely. |

# Setting Publishing Options

Expression Web has three options for transferring files between the local folder (the original folder containing the site pages you created in Expression Web) and the remote folder (the folder on the server, computer, or FTP site that contains your published files). No matter where the remote folder is located, even if it is on the same local network, flash, or hard drive, *remote* indicates the location of the published files, and not that the folder is necessarily in a different location, such as a separate Web server. If you were publishing to an FTP site or Web server, you would have to know the address of the site, server, or folder to specify it in the Remote Web Site Properties dialog box.

The **local to remote** publishing option uploads all of the site pages from the local folder to the remote folder. This is the most common option and is what is used for the initial publication of your site, as well as for transferring updated or new site files. You might choose the **remote to local** publishing option if you need to re-create the original site files because they have been lost, deleted, or corrupted. The **synchronize** option looks at the files in both the remote and local locations, and replaces any files in either location that have an earlier save date. In some situations, site files are being worked on by multiple Web designers, each of whom has a copy of the entire site on their local computer and who has been posting updates. Each designer must use synchronization to update the files he or she has been working on to ensure that everyone has the latest version.

Before you make your site live to the public, make sure you have accomplished the following:

1. Review the Site Summary to view potential problems and the site's technical aspects.

2. Run reports to verify that the site meets current accessibility and compatibility requirements.

3. Organize your site files and optimize the HTML pages to streamline the organization and content of your site.

4. Conduct a beta test on the site to uncover vague or nonfunctioning site aspects and gain a human perspective.

5. Research and determine Web hosting options and find one that meets the needs of the site and your client.

6. Determine the URL (Web address) and register it. This will be the location to which you publish your site files in the Remote Web Site Properties dialog box.

7. Maintain the site content as necessary to keep your site current and functioning.

**Plan Ahead**

> **Initiate the site publication.**
> After the site content, links, and technical aspects have been approved by you and any other necessary individuals (such as colleagues, the client, members of your design team), you are ready to publish the site. You can decide to publish the site all at once or to withhold certain pages from the published site. After the site is published, you should keep the files up-to-date and synchronized.

## To Set Publishing Options

The following steps publish the site to a new remote folder in the data files in order to perform site beta testing. If you had access to an FTP server or Web site server, you could also post your files live to be available to the public. However, making the site content live would also give the impression that the business example used in this chapter is real and could confuse visitors who would like to make contact with the business.

**①**

- Click Publish Site on the File menu to open the Remote Web Site Properties dialog box.

- Click the File System option button to publish the site to a folder on your computer or network (Figure 8–40).

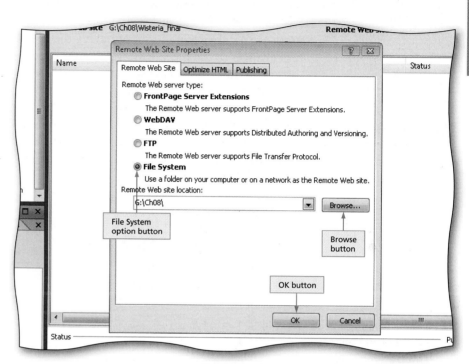

**Figure 8–40**

**②**

- Click the Browse button to open the New Publish Location dialog box.

- Navigate to the data files folder.

- Click the New Folder button to insert a new, untitled folder.

- Type Wisteria_published, then press ENTER to name the folder.

- Click the Open button to finish specifying the save location. (Figure 8–41).

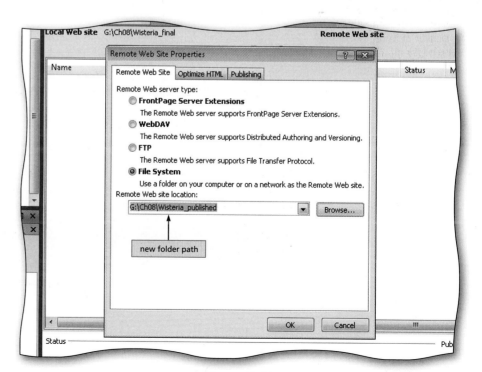

**Figure 8–41**

# Optimizing HTML

After publishing your Web site page(s), you can perform HTML optimization. HTML optimization refers to changes made to the remote version of HTML page(s) during the publishing process that remove unnecessary code or content, such as comments inserted into the HTML code. These changes streamline page download time by decreasing the file size of your page. If you have an HTML page into which many comments were inserted in Code view, such as to keep track of changes made and by whom in a site with many HTML programmers, optimizing the HTML content of a page can make significant changes to the speed with which your page downloads in a visitor's browser, thereby increasing the visitor's satisfaction with your site.

## To Optimize HTML

The following steps optimize the HTML files for the published site by removing unnecessary codes.

1

- Click the Optimize HTML tab in the Remote Web Site Properties dialog box to display the optimization options.

- Click the When publishing, optimize HTML by removing the following elements check box to allow you to specify which elements to remove (Figure 8–42).

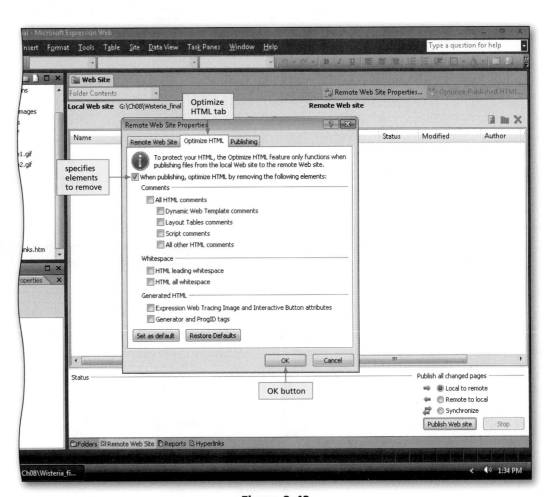

**Figure 8–42**

**2**

- Click all of the subsequent check boxes to select them.

- Click the OK button to optimize the HTML pages in the site and view the site in Remote Web Site view (Figure 8–43).

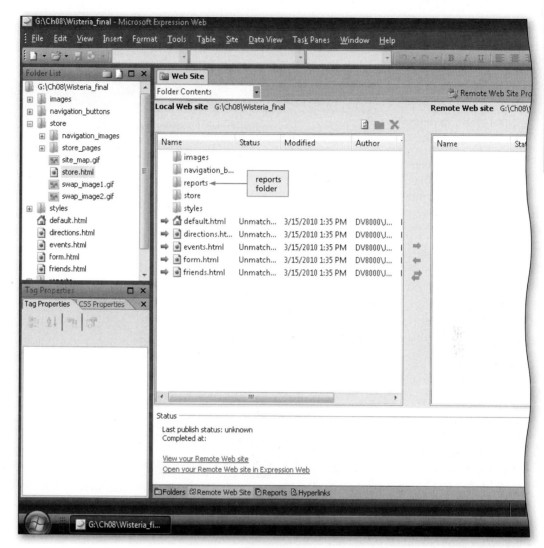

**Figure 8–43**

**Other Ways**

1. Click Optimize HTML on Tools menu to open Optimize HTML tab of Remote Web Site Properties dialog box if dialog box is closed.

## To Publish Files to a Remote Folder

The following steps publish the optimized Wisteria HTML files to the new folder to make them available for beta testing, then display the publication log. You will not publish the report, as it is not a part of the site contents.

- Double-click the reports folder in the Local Web site pane to view its content.

- Right-click the Style Sheet Links.htm file in the Local Web site pane to open the shortcut menu.

- Click Don't Publish on the shortcut menu to specify that Style Sheet Links.htm file will not publish at this time (Figure 8–44).

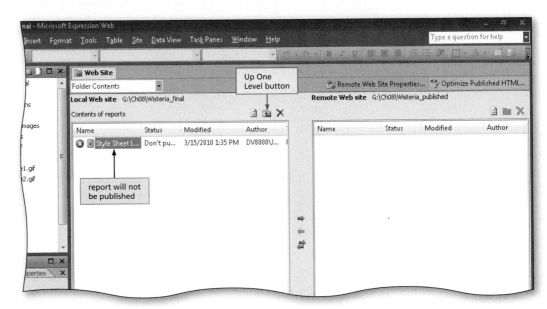

**Figure 8–44**

- Click the Up One Level button to view the contents of the site folder.

- Click the Local to remote option button to select it if necessary (Figure 8–45).

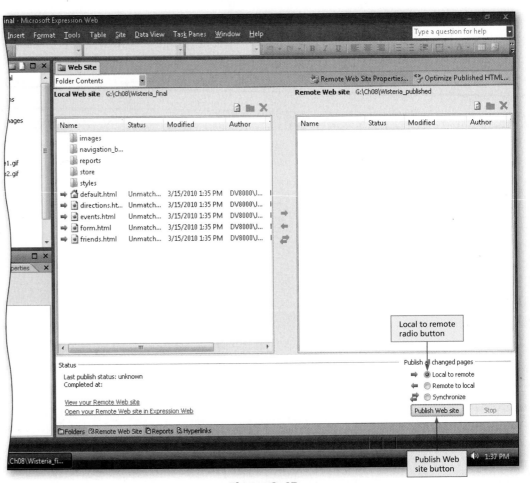

**Figure 8–45**

• Click the Publish
Web site button
to start the
publication
(Figure 8–46).

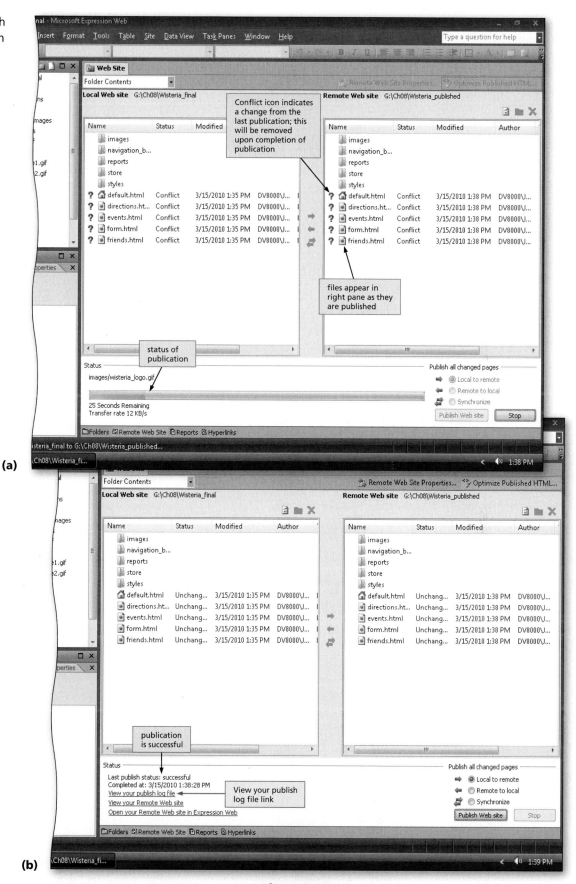

**Figure 8–46**

- Click the View your publish log file link to open the publication log (Figure 8–47).

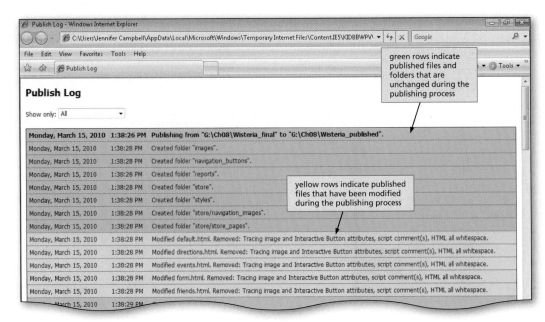

**Figure 8–47**

## To Manage Files on a Remote Server

The following steps change the directions.html page, synchronize the remote and local folder contents, view the folder contents of the remote site, then view the published site in a browser.

- Double-click the directions.html page to open it (Figure 8–48).

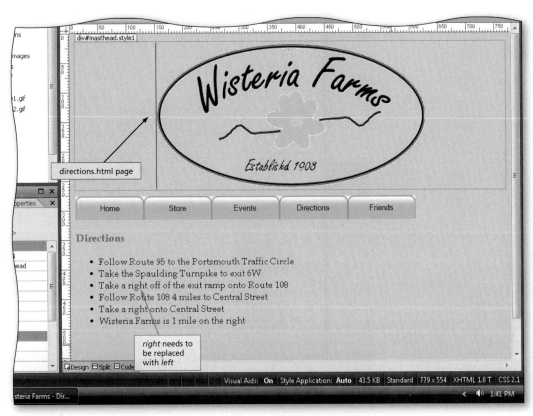

**Figure 8–48**

**2**

- In the third bullet, select the word, right, then type `left` (Figure 8–49).

- Save and close the directions.html page.

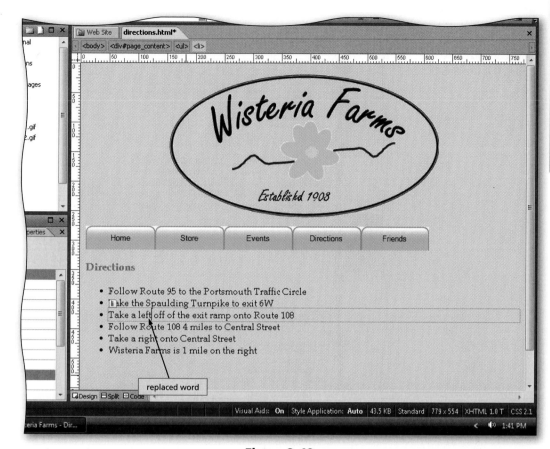

replaced word

**Figure 8–49**

**3**

- Click the Synchronize option button to select it (Figure 8–50).

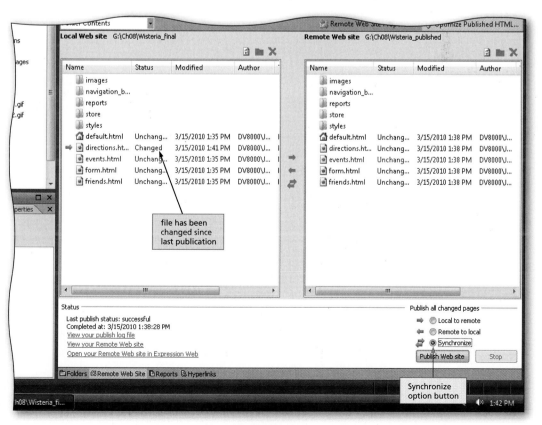

file has been changed since last publication

Synchronize option button

**Figure 8–50**

**4**

- Click the Publish Web site button to synchronize the site files (Figure 8–51).

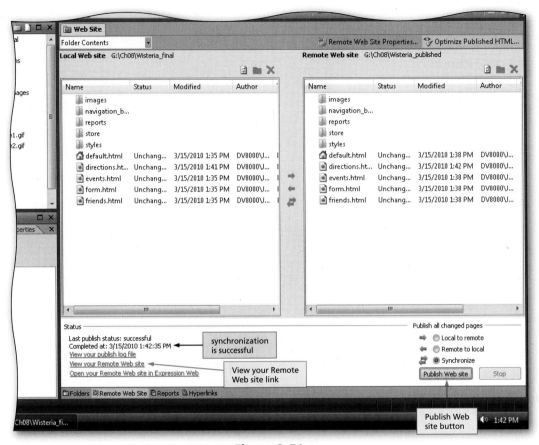

**Figure 8–51**

**5**

- Click the View your Remote Web site link to open the site file folder in a new window (Figure 8–52).

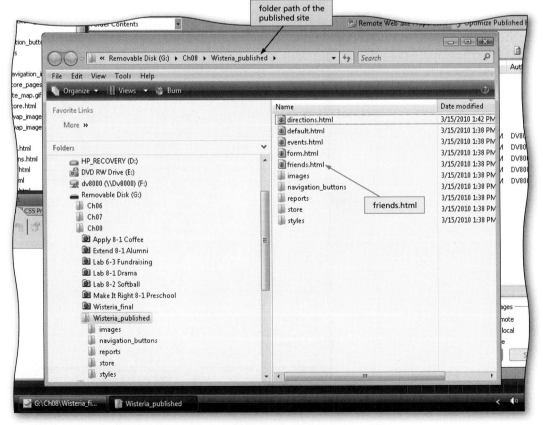

**Figure 8–52**

**6**

- Double-click the friends.html page to open it in a browser window (Figure 8–53).

**Q&A** At the top of my browser window, there is a message saying that ActiveX content has been blocked.

Because of your security settings, interactive features might be blocked automatically. Click the message at the top of the browser window, click Allow Blocked Content, then click the Yes button in the alert box to allow ActiveX controls for this site, or ask your instructor or technical support person for permission and assistance.

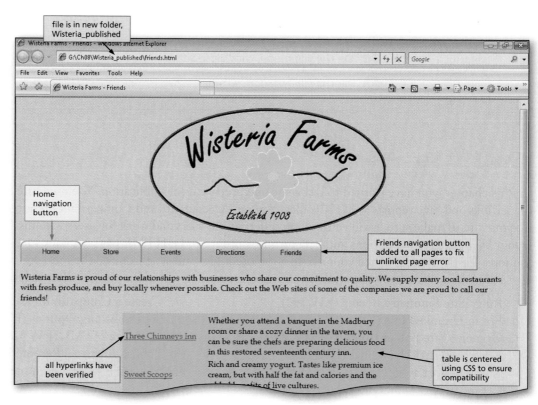

Figure 8–53

**7**

- Click the Home navigation button to open the default.html page in the browser window (Figure 8–54).

- Click the Close button on the browser title bar to close the browser window.

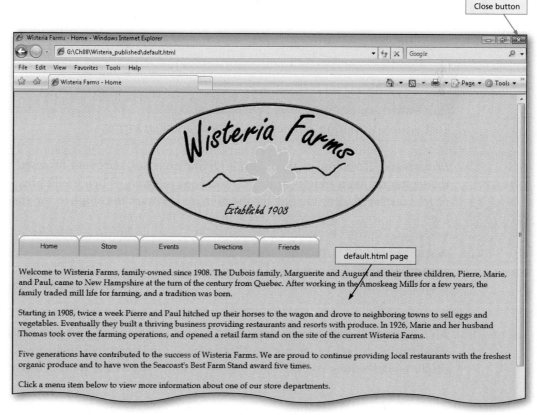

Figure 8–54

## To Close a Site and Quit Expression Web

**1** On the File menu, click Close Site.

**2** On the File menu, click Exit.

# Chapter Summary

In this chapter, you have learned to test a site and prepare it for publication. You used Site Summary to verify hyperlinks and save reports as HTML files. You ran Accessibility and Compatibility reports, and made changes to your site to make sure it will run well on different browsers and work for users with disabilities. You learned about Web site hosting options and beta testing, optimized the HTML pages in your site, and specified publishing options. Lastly, you published your site to a remote folder and synchronized the local and remote site files.

The items listed below include all the new Expression Web skills you have learned in this chapter.

1. Run a Site Summary Report (EW 502)
2. Fix an Unlinked File (EW 503)
3. Organize Site Folder Contents (EW 507)
4. Verify External Hyperlinks (EW 509)
5. Save a Report as an HTML Page (EW 512)
6. Create an Accessibility Report (EW 518)
7. Create a Compatibility Report (EW 519)
8. Set Publishing Options (EW 525)
9. Optimize HTML (EW 526)
10. Publish Files to a Remote Folder (EW 528)
11. Manage Files on a Remote Server (EW 530)

If you have a SAM user profile, you may have access to hands-on instruction, practice, and assessment. Log in to your SAM account (http://sam2007.course.com) to launch any assigned training activities or exams that relate to the skills covered in this chapter.

## Learn It Online

**Test your knowledge of chapter content and key terms.**

*Instructions:* To complete the Learn It Online exercises, start your browser, click the Address bar, and then enter the Web address `scsite.com/ew2/learn`. When the Expression Web Learn It Online page is displayed, click the link for the exercise you want to complete and then read the instructions.

### Chapter Reinforcement TF, MC, and SA
A series of true/false, multiple choice, and short answer questions that test your knowledge of the chapter content.

### Flash Cards
An interactive learning environment where you identify chapter key terms associated with displayed definitions.

### Practice Test
A series of multiple choice questions that test your knowledge of chapter content and key terms.

### Who Wants To Be a Computer Genius?
An interactive game that challenges your knowledge of chapter content in the style of the television quiz show.

### Wheel of Terms
An interactive game that challenges your knowledge of chapter key terms in the style of the television show *Wheel of Fortune*.

### Crossword Puzzle Challenge
A crossword puzzle that challenges your knowledge of key terms presented in the chapter.

# Apply Your Knowledge

Reinforce the skills and apply the concepts you learned in this chapter.

## Preparing a Coffee Shop Site for Publication

*Instructions:* Start Expression Web. Open the site, Apply 8-1 Coffee, from the Data Files for Students. See the inside back cover of this book for instructions for downloading the Data Files for Students, or see your instructor for information about accessing the required files.

You will test the site and publish it to a remote server, as shown in Figure 8–55.

**Figure 8–55**

*Perform the following tasks:*

1. Open the default.html page.

2. Point to Reports on the Site menu, then click Site Summary to open the summary in the Web Site tab.

3. Click the Broken hyperlinks link to view the report and click the No button in the Reports View dialog box.

4. Double-click the first broken hyperlink on the list to open the Edit Hyperlink dialog box.

5. Type `directions/directions.html` in the Replace hyperlink with text box, click the Change in all pages option button to select it if necessary, then click the Replace button to fix the broken links.

*Continued >*

**Apply Your Knowledge** *continued*

6. Right-click the first external hyperlink in the list, then click Verify Hyperlink on the shortcut menu to verify the link and change its status to OK. (*Hint:* The external hyperlinks start with http://.)

7. Right-click the second external hyperlink in the list, then click Verify Hyperlink on the shortcut menu to verify the link.

8. Click the Hyperlinks button arrow on the Reports toolbar, then click Site Summary to return to the summary.

9. Click the Internal hyperlinks link to view the report.

10. Click Save As on the File menu to open the Save As dialog box.

11. Click the New Folder button to insert a new folder, type reports, then press ENTER.

12. Click the Open button to open the reports folder.

13. Select the default filename in the File name text box, then type HyperlinksMM-DD-YYYY.htm. (*Hint:* Replace MM-DD-YYYY with today's date, separated by hyphens.) Click the Save button to save the report.

14. Click Accessibility Reports on the Tools menu to open the Accessibility Checker dialog box.

15. Click the All pages option button, then click the Check button to open the Accessibility task pane and confirm that there are no compatibility problems.

16. Click the Accessibility task pane Close button to close the task pane.

17. Click Compatibility Reports on the Tools menu to open the Compatibility Checker dialog box.

18. Click the All pages option button, then click the Check button to open the Compatibility task pane and confirm that there are no compatibility problems.

19. Click the Compatibility task pane Close button to close the task pane.

20. Click Publish Site on the File menu to open the Remote Web Site Properties dialog box.

21. Click the Browse button to open the New Publish Location dialog box, navigate to the data files, then click the New Folder button.

22. Type Coffee_published as the folder name, press ENTER, then click the Open button to specify the new folder as the publish location.

23. Click the Optimize HTML tab, click the When publishing, optimize HTML by removing the following elements check box, click the All HTML comments check box, then click the OK button.

24. Double-click the reports folder in the Local Web site pane to open it. Right-click the HyperlinksMM-DD-YYYY.htm file, then click Don't Publish on the shortcut menu.

25. Click the Up One Level button above the Local Web site pane to view the site folder contents.

26. Click the Publish Web site button to publish the site.

27. Click the default.html page tab to display the page. Click after the words, Garcia's Coffee Shop, in the page content area, then type located in Acton, Massachusetts. Save and close the default.html page.

28. Click the Synchronize option button, then click the Publish Web site button to update the remote site with the changes made to the local page.

29. Change the site properties, as specified by your instructor. Save the site with the filename Apply 8-1 Coffee Site, then submit the revised site in the format specified by your instructor.

30. Close the site.

# Extend Your Knowledge

Extend the skills you learned in this chapter and experiment with new skills. You may need to use Help to complete the assignment.

## Publishing an Alumni Web Site

*Instructions:* Start Expression Web. Open the site, Extend 8-1 Alumni, from the Data Files for Students. See the inside back cover of this book for instructions for downloading the Data Files for Students, or see your instructor for information about accessing the required files.

You will test the site and also verify the page titles before publishing the site shown in Figure 8–56.

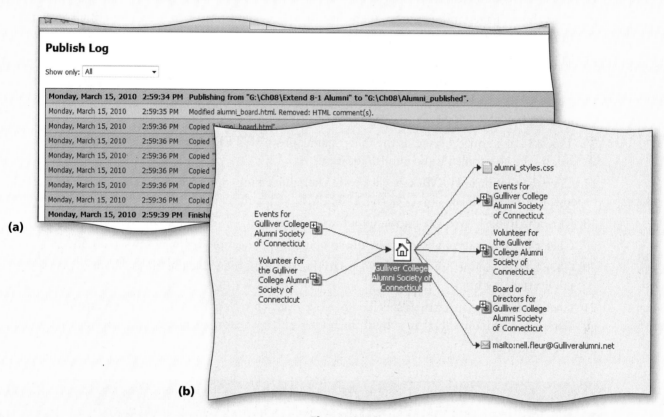

**Figure 8–56**

*Perform the following tasks:*

1. Point to Reports on the Site menu, then click Site Summary to open the summary in the Web Site tab.

2. Click the Hyperlinks View button at the bottom of the Web Site tab to switch to hyperlink view.

3. Click default.html in the Folder List to view the hyperlinks from the default.html page.

4. Right-click a blank area of the Web Site tab, then click Show Page Titles on the shortcut menu. Position the pointer over the Untitled 1 page to view the ScreenTip that indicates the untitled page is volunteer.html.

5. Double-click volunteer.html in the Folder List to open the page.

*Continued >*

6. Click Properties on the File menu to open the Page Properties dialog box. Type Volunteer for the Gulliver College Alumni Society of Connecticut in the Title text box to re-title the page, then click the OK button.

7. Save and close the volunteer.html page, then click the Web Site tab if necessary.

8. Click Accessibility Reports on the Tools menu to open the Accessibility Checker dialog box.

9. Click the All pages option button, then click the Check button to open the Accessibility task pane and confirm that there are no accessibility problems to address at this time.

10. Click the Accessibility task pane Close button to close the task pane.

11. Click Compatibility Reports on the Tools menu to open the Compatibility Checker dialog box.

12. Click the All pages option button, then click the Check button to open the Compatibility task pane and confirm that there are no compatibility problems.

13. Click the Compatibility task pane Close button to close the task pane.

14. Click Publish Site on the File menu to open the Remote Web Site Properties dialog box.

15. Click the Browse button to open the New Publish Location dialog box, navigate to the data files, then click the New Folder button.

16. Type Alumni_published as the folder name, press ENTER, then click the Open button to specify the new folder as the publish location.

17. Click the Optimize HTML tab, click the When publishing, optimize HTML by removing the following elements check box, click the All HTML comments check box, then click the OK button.

18. Click the Publish Web site button to publish the site.

19. Click the View your publish log file link to open the publication log in a browser window.

20. Click Save As on the File menu, navigate to the data files, then save the file as Alumni_publication_log.html.

21. Change the site properties, as specified by your instructor. Save the site with the filename Extend 8-1 Alumni Site, then submit the revised site in the format specified by your instructor.

22. Close the site.

## Make It Right

Analyze a site and correct all errors and/or improve the design.

### Fixing Errors in a Preschool Web Site

*Instructions:* Start Expression Web. Open the Web site, Make It Right 8-1 Preschool, from the Data Files for Students. See the inside back cover of this book for instructions for downloading the Data Files for Students, or see your instructor for information about accessing the required files.

You will view the site summary for testing the Web site below and fix an unlinked file and a compatibility issue, as shown in Figure 8–57.

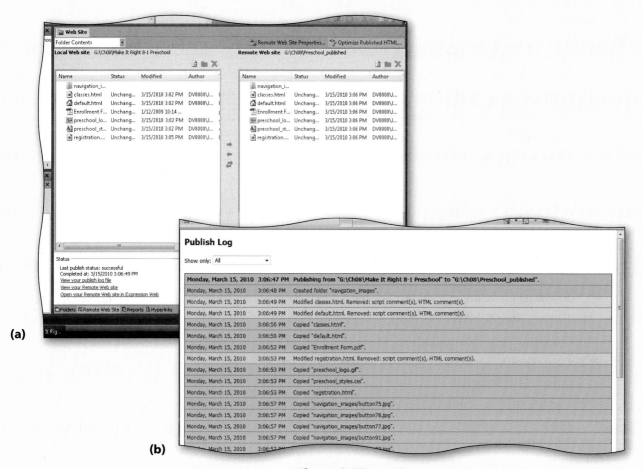

(a)

(b)

**Figure 8–57**

1. Point to Reports on the Site menu, then click Site Summary to open the summary in the Web Site tab.

2. Click the Unlinked files link and observe that there is one unlinked file, Enrollment Form.pdf.

3. Double-click the file, registration.html, in the Folder List to open it.

4. To create a link between registration.html and Enrollment Form.pdf, select the word, Applications, under the heading, Application Submission.

5. Press CTRL+K to open the Insert Hyperlink dialog box, click Enrollment Form.pdf, then click the OK button.

6. Save and close the registration.html page.

7. Click Accessibility Reports on the Tools menu to open the Accessibility Checker dialog box.

8. Click the All pages option button, then click the Check button to open the Accessibility task pane and confirm that there are no accessibility issues.

9. Click the Accessibility task pane Close button to close the task pane.

10. Click Compatibility Reports on the Tools menu to open the Compatibility Checker dialog box.

11. Click the All pages option button, then click the Check button to open the Compatibility task pane and confirm that there are no compatibility issues.

12. Double-click the second error on the list, then click the Design View button to view the page element with the error.

*Continued >*

**Make It Right** *continued*

13. Click the Style list arrow (*Hint*: It has heading 5 selected.), then click (None) to remove the style and return the div name to "caption."

14. Click the Font Size list arrow, then click small to add compatible formatting to the caption.

15. Save and close the page, then click the Refresh Changed Results button on the Compatibility task pane.

16. Click the Compatibility task pane Close button to close the task pane.

17. Click Publish Site on the File menu to open the Remote Web Site Properties dialog box.

18. Click the Browse button to open the New Publish Location dialog box, navigate to the data files, then click the New Folder button.

19. Type `Preschool_published` as the folder name, press ENTER, then click the Open button to specify the new folder as the publish location.

20. Click the Optimize HTML tab, click the When publishing, optimize HTML by removing the following elements check box, click the All HTML comments check box, then click the OK button.

21. Click the Publish Web Site button to publish the site.

22. Click the View your publish log file link to open the publication log in a browser window.

23. Click Save As on the File menu, navigate to the data files, then save the file as Preschool_ publication_log.html.

24. Change the site properties, as specified by your instructor. Save the site with the filename Make It Right 8-1 Preschool Site, then submit the revised site in the format specified by your instructor.

25. Close the site.

## In the Lab

Design and/or format a Web site using the guidelines, concepts, and skills presented in this chapter. Labs are listed in order of increasing difficulty.

### Lab 1: Use Site Summary to Verify Page Titles and Hyperlinks
*Problem:* You will view the Site Summary of the Web site shown in Figure 8–58 and use the reports to verify the page titles and external hyperlinks.

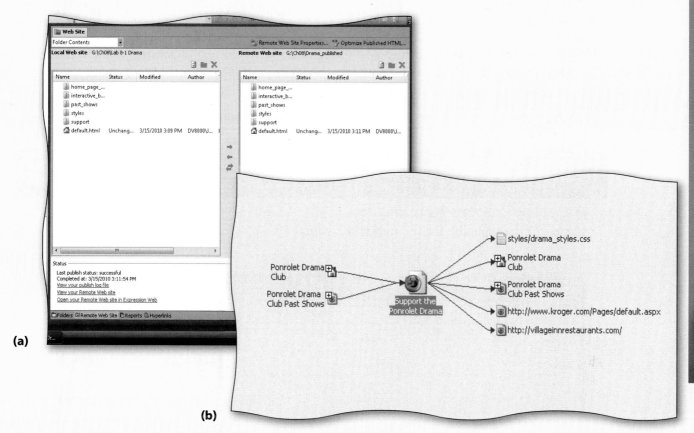

**(a)**

**(b)**

**Figure 8–58**

*Instructions:*

1. Start Expression Web.

2. Open the Web site, Lab 8-1 Drama, from the Data Files for Students.

3. View the Site Summary.

4. Click the Unverified hyperlinks link, then click the Yes button in the Reports View dialog box, if necessary.

5. Return to the Site Summary.

6. Click the Hyperlinks button at the bottom of the Web Site pane, then click the default.html page in the Folder List to view the hyperlinks for the page. Show page titles if necessary.

7. In the Folder List, expand the support folder, then open the support.html page.

8. Open the Page Properties dialog box, then change the page title to Support the Ponrolet Drama Club. Click the OK button to close the dialog box.

9. Save and close the support.html page.

10. Run a compatibility report on all pages in the site.

11. Run an accessibility report on all pages in the site.

*Continued >*

**In the Lab** *continued*

12. Open the Remote Web Site Properties dialog box. Specify the publish location as a new folder, called Drama_published, located in the data files, then close the dialog box.

13. Publish the Web site.

14. Submit the site in the format specified by your instructor, then close the site.

## In the Lab

### Lab 2: Publish a Sports Team Web Site

*Problem:* You will publish the site shown in Figure 8–59.

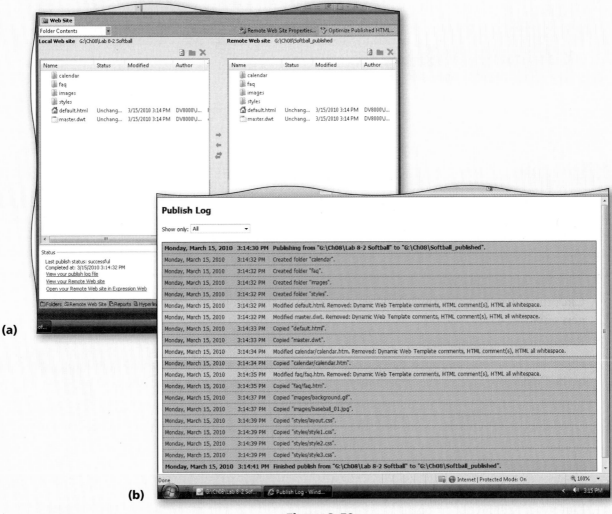

**(a)**

**(b)**

**Figure 8–59**

*Instructions:* Start Expression Web. Open the Web site, Lab 8-2 Softball, from the Data Files for Students. See the inside back cover of this book for instructions for downloading the Data Files for Students, or see your instructor for information about accessing the required files.

*Perform the following tasks.*

1. Display the Site Summary in the Web Site tab.

2. Click the Unverified hyperlinks link, then verify the external hyperlink.

3. Run a Compatibility report on all pages in the site to confirm that there are no compatibility issues.

4. Run an Accessibility report on all pages in the site to confirm that there are no accessibility issues.

5. Open the Remote Web Site Properties dialog box. Specify the publish location as a new folder, called Softball_published, located in the data files.

6. Click the Optimize HTML tab, select all of the check boxes, then close the dialog box.

7. Publish the Web site.

8. View the publish log file, then save the HTML file for the log as Softball_publication_log to the data files folder.

9. Submit the site in the format specified by your instructor, then close the site.

# In the Lab

## Lab 3: Synchronize Local and Remote Site Folders

*Problem:* You will publish, modify, then synchronize the site files for the remote and local site folders shown in Figure 8–60.

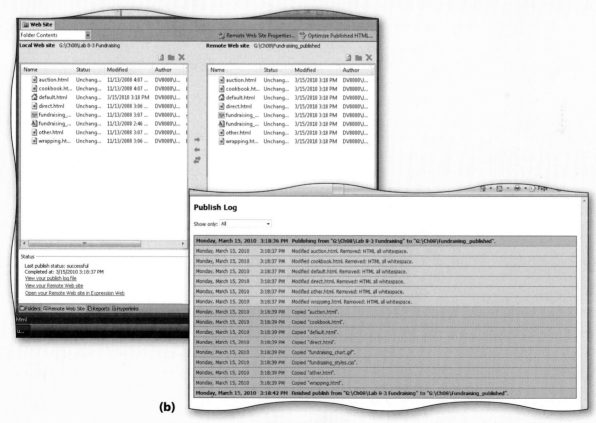

**(a)**

**(b)**

**Figure 8–60**

*Continued >*

**In the Lab** *continued*

*Instructions:*

Start Expression Web. Open the Web site, Lab 8-3 Fundraising, from the Data Files for Students. See the inside back cover of this book for instructions for downloading the Data Files for Students, or see your instructor for information about accessing the required files.

*Perform the following tasks.*

1. Open the Remote Web Site Properties dialog box. Specify the publish location as a new folder, called Fundraising_published, located in the data files.

2. Click the Optimize HTML tab, select all of the check boxes, then close the dialog box.

3. Publish the Web site.

4. Open the default.html page from the local site folder in Expression Web.

5. Change the street number from 443 to 1443, then save and close the default.html page.

6. Click the Synchronize option button, then publish the Web site.

7. View the publish log file, then save the HTML file for the log as Fundraising_publication_log to the data files folder.

8. Submit the site in the format specified by your instructor, then close the site.

## Cases and Places

Apply your creative thinking and problem solving skills to design and implement a solution.

● Easier    ●●More Difficult

### ● 1: Researching Web Site Hosts

Create a one-page Web site on Web hosts. Add a table with four rows and six columns. Designate the top row as a header row. Enter the following in the top row: Site Name; Cost; Maximum Size; Reporting Tools; Unique Feature; and Security. Conduct an Internet search on Web site hosts, then choose three to compare. Fill in the table with the information you have found.

### ● 2: Running a Compatibility Report

Create a new three-page Web site for a used record and CD store. Add a navigation area for the pages using interactive buttons. Add text, formatting, and an image to the home page. Do not add alternate text to the image. Run a Compatibility report. Fix the error by adding alternate text to the image. (*Hint*: Double-click the image to open the Picture Properties dialog box, then type in the Alternate Text text box.) Fix any other errors, then save and close the site and the browser window.

### ●● 3: Testing a Site Created Using a Dynamic Web Template

Create a new site for a florist using a dynamic Web template. Add text, formatting, and images to the home page and one other page; include at least three external hyperlinks. Run a Site Summary report. Verify the external hyperlinks. Save two reports as HTML files. Run a compatibility test, then preview the site in two different browsers and at different screen resolutions. Close the browser windows and the site.

### ●● 4: Creating an Accessible Web Site

**Make It Personal**

Create a new Web site for your favorite sports team. Add three pages using CSS layouts, then attach a preformatted style sheet to the pages. Add content, links, and images to the home page. Add a form to another page. On the third page, make a bulleted list that outlines four ways that you made your site accessible (if necessary, do an Internet search on creating accessible Web sites to get ideas). Run an Accessibility report. Save the pages and style sheets. Optimize the HTML code on your site pages. Publish the site to a new folder, change one of the pages, then synchronize the pages.

### ●● 5: Beta Testing a Site

**Working Together**

Open any multi-page Web site that your group or a team member has created, or create a new one. Working as a team with several of your classmates, outline a plan for beta testing the site. Each team member should contribute to the plan. Run Compatibility and Accessibility reports, then publish the site to a new folder. As a group, test the published site, and make a list of three things to change. Make the changes to the HTML files that are in the published site folder, then synchronize the remote and local site folders.

# 9 Building a Web Site with CSS-Based Templates

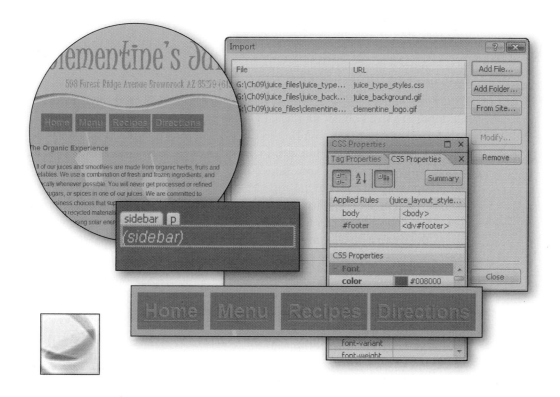

## Objectives

You will have mastered the material in this chapter when you can:

- Create a new dynamic Web template
- Import files into a site
- Add a background image
- Create ID-based styles
- Design list-based navigation
- Use descendent selectors
- Create CSS-based rollover images

- Add a sidebar
- Enhance readability using typography
- Specify line length and height
- Add a drop cap style
- Apply a dynamic Web template to a new page

# 9 | Building a Web Site with CSS-Based Templates

## Introduction

In this chapter you will learn about several advanced Expression Web design techniques that increase your site's appeal and usability. These tools also make it easier to expand your site, adding new pages as it grows. You used preformatted, multi-page dynamic Web templates to create Web sites in Chapter 3. Creating your own dynamic Web template allows you to create pages that share the same layout, formatting, and styles. Pages are distinguished by changing text and images that are in defined editable regions, such as a page content div, a sidebar, or an image.

Importing style sheets and image files into your site embeds them into the site folder, making them available for use in your site. Using CSS (cascading style sheets), you can create styles that will enhance your site pages. In this chapter, you will expand the CSS skills you learned in previous chapters to create ID-based styles for new elements. A **sidebar** is a fixed object that usually appears on the left or right of a block of text and includes related text. ID-based styles can also be used to convert an unordered (bulleted) list to a navigation area. Adding rollover styles to the navigation list items allows them to change when the pointer is positioned over them.

**Typography** refers to the appearance of text. Typography can include text formatting you have used in previous chapters, such as font families, font sizes, and font colors; you can use CSS to determine these aspects of typography, as well as line length, line height, and drop caps. A **drop cap** is a style that makes the first letter of a paragraph distinct by changing the color, font, size, or a combination of attributes.

## Project — Juice Bar Web Site

Your client, Clementine's Juice Bar, wants you to create a new Web site from scratch. You will create a dynamic Web template that can be attached to pages as the site expands. You will enhance the template using CSS to make your site standards compliant, as well as to make it easier to apply style and layout changes at a later date.

The project in this chapter shows you how to use Expression Web to create the site shown in Figure 9–1. You will create a new Web site, add pages, import image files and a style sheet, and create a dynamic Web template. Steps for creating the template will include adding a background image, a list-based navigation area, a logo, a sidebar, and the application of styles such as rollovers, drop caps, and other typography settings. You will attach the dynamic Web template to the other site pages.

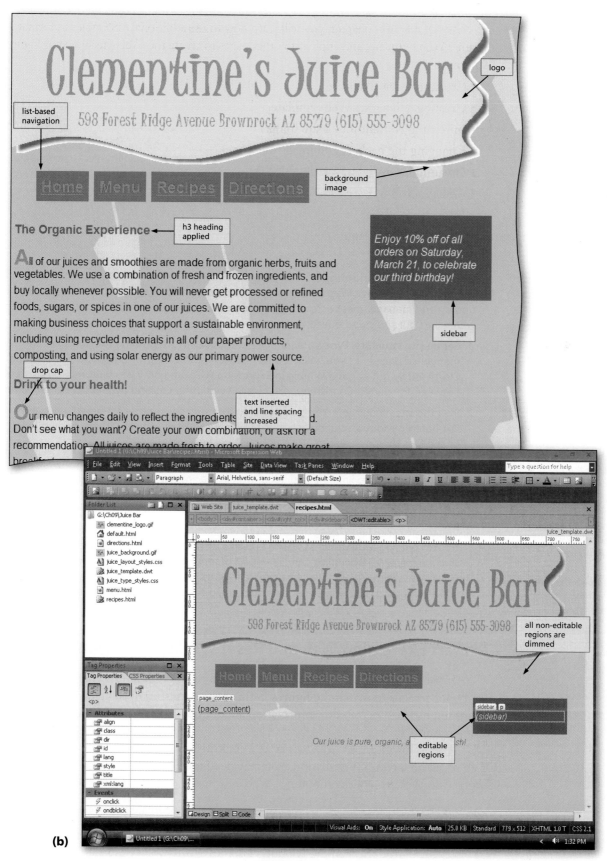

**Figure 9–1**

# Overview

As you read this chapter, you will learn how to use additional CSS styles to format a dynamic Web template, and apply it to other pages to create the Web site shown in Figure 9–1 by performing these general tasks:

- Creating a new Web site
- Creating a dynamic Web template
- Importing content into a site folder
- Changing the background image of a page
- Creating list-based navigation
- Adding a rollover style
- Inserting a sidebar
- Specifying typography

**Plan Ahead**

---

**General Project Guidelines**

Using CSS and dynamic Web templates, you can create multi-page sites that are easy to update and manage, meet accessibility standards, and include formatting and elements that will make your site stand out to visitors.

1. **Set up site structure.** When planning a multi-page site, determine the approximate number of page links you will need for the navigation area, whether you will be using CSS-based layout pages available in Expression Web, and how you will create consistency between the pages. Consistency can be achieved using CSS and dynamic Web templates.

2. **Plan the site navigation.** You can create an ID-based style to use list-based navigation. List-based navigation can be enhanced to create rollover effects without adding the image files that are created when using interactive buttons.

3. **Improve the site readability and visual interest using typography and CSS.** Specify the line length and height to limit the number of words on a line and add space between the lines. Both the line height and length affect the readability of your page. Elements such as a sidebar and drop caps can add visual interest to your page by calling out specific text or characters.

4. **Create site consistency using dynamic Web templates.** A dynamic Web template allows you to add common formatting, as well as objects such as navigation, logos, and backgrounds, that are managed by editing one file instead of making the same change on multiple pages. Determine which elements will be editable regions, allowing for content customization, while protecting other page elements from being edited outside of the template.

---

## To Start Expression Web and Reset Workspace Layout

If you are using a computer to step through the project in this chapter, and you want your screens to match the figures in this book, you should change your computer's resolution to $1024 \times 768$. For information about how to change a computer's resolution, read Appendix F.

The following steps, which assume Windows Vista is running, start Expression Web based on a typical installation. You may need to ask your instructor how to start Expression Web for your computer.

**Note:** If you are using Window XP, see Appendix E for alternate steps.

**1** Click the Start button on the Windows Vista taskbar to display the Start menu.

**2** Click All Programs at the bottom of the left pane on the Start menu to display the All Programs list.

**3** Click Microsoft Expression on the All Programs list to display the Microsoft Expression list.

**4** Click Microsoft Expression Web 2 to start Expression Web.

**5** Click Task Panes on the menu bar, then click Reset Workspace Layout.

**Set up site structure.**

To create a multi-page Web site with blank pages to which you will attach CSS and/or dynamic Web templates, first create a new Web site, determine the approximate number of page links you will need for the navigational area, then add pages that are blank or that use CSS-based layouts. Use the default.html page to add content: elements such as text, images, backgrounds, navigation, and sidebar elements that will be consistent for all pages. Once the page is complete, you can save it as a dynamic Web template, define the editable regions, and attach the template to the other site pages.

**Plan Ahead**

## To Create a New Web Site and Add Web Pages

The following steps create the Juice Bar Web site folder and add pages.

**1**

- Point to New on the File menu, then click Web Site to open the New dialog box.

- Click One Page Web Site, then click the Browse button to open the New Web Site Location dialog box.

- Navigate to the flash drive where your Data Files for Students are located, then click the Open button.

- Type `Juice Bar` in the Specify the location of the new Web site text box (Figure 9–2).

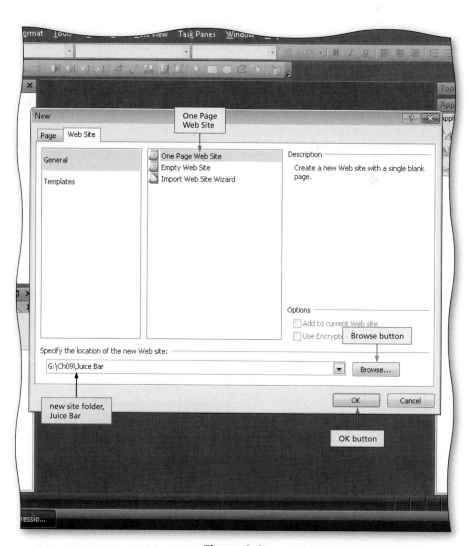

**Figure 9–2**

**2**

• Click the OK button to open the site folder and a blank page, default.html, in Expression Web (Figure 9–3).

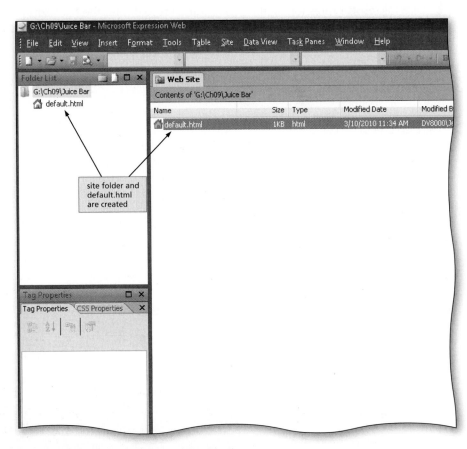

**Figure 9–3**

**3**

• Click the New Document button on the Common toolbar to insert a new, blank page (Figure 9–4).

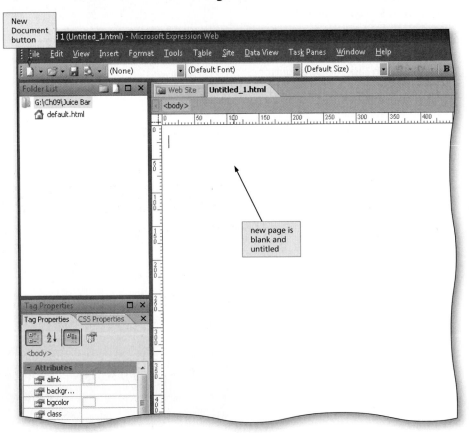

**Figure 9–4**

**4**

- Press CTRL+S to open the Save As dialog box.

- Type recipes.html in the File name text box to specify the page name (Figure 9–5).

**Figure 9–5**

**5**

- Click the Save button to save the new page (Figure 9–6).

- Right-click the recipes.html tab to display the shortcut menu, then click Close to close the recipes.html page.

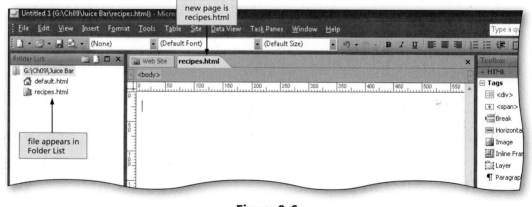

**Figure 9–6**

**6**

- Repeat Steps 3 through 5 to insert, save, and close two more blank pages: directions.html and menu.html (Figure 9–7).

**Other Ways**

1. Click New button arrow on Common toolbar, then click Web Site to open New dialog box.

2. Press CTRL+N to insert new, blank HTML page.

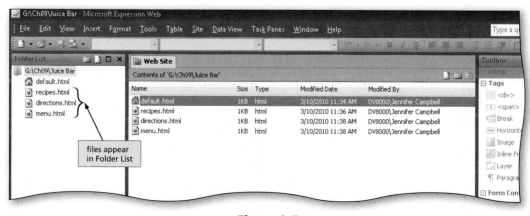

**Figure 9–7**

# Creating a New Dynamic Web Template

A new dynamic Web template looks like a blank HTML page and can be edited using the same tools. You can add a new page based on a CSS layout and save it as a dynamic Web template. You can use CSS and other formatting techniques to specify the layout and typography of the page, as well as to add common images, such as a logo and page background. Once the dynamic Web template layout and formatting have been finished, you will define the editable regions.

## To Create a New Dynamic Web Template

The following steps create a new page based on a CSS layout, then save it as a dynamic Web template that you will edit to create the basis for all other site pages.

- Point to New on the File menu, then click Page to open the New dialog box.

- Click CSS Layouts to display the page layout options.

- Click the second Header, nav, 2 columns, footer option to select a layout with a narrower right column (Figure 9–8).

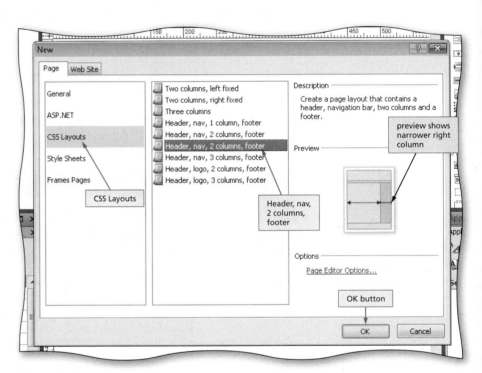

**Figure 9–8**

- Click the OK button to open the page and the associated style sheet in Expression Web (Figure 9–9).

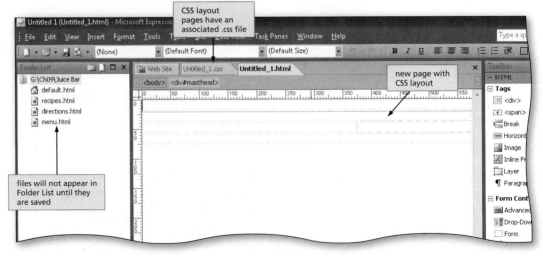

**Figure 9–9**

**3**

- Press CTRL+S to open the Save As dialog box.

- Type `juice_template.dwt` in the File name text box, then click the Save button to save the page as a template and open the Save As dialog box for the style sheet.

- Type `juice_layout_styles.css` in the File name text box (Figure 9–10).

**Figure 9–10**

**4**

- Click the Save button to save the new style sheet (Figure 9–11).

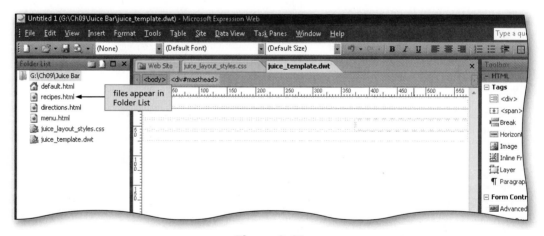

**Figure 9–11**

**Other Ways**

1. Point to New on File menu, click Dynamic Web Template to open new, blank dynamic Web template page.

# Importing Files

In previous chapters, when you have needed image files stored outside of the site folder, you have added them using the Insert menu, then saved a copy in the site folder by clicking OK in the Save Embedded Files dialog box. Importing a file or multiple files at once embeds them into your site folder, allowing you to use them as necessary without importing them individually.

In addition to image files, you can import style sheets that you created in other projects and reuse them. Once you have imported the style sheet, you can modify it as

**BTW**

**Reusing Style Sheets**
In addition to using preformatted style sheets provided by Expression Web, you can reuse a style sheet created for a different site. Modify fonts, colors, and layout to fit the new site.

necessary, which saves you time because you do not have to create a new style sheet from scratch. You are not limited to importing files; you can import an entire folder or Web site folder at once. In order to import a Web site, the site or the parts of the site that you want to import must be saved as a **Personal Web Package**. A Personal Web Package exports the files and folder structure in a single file with the extension .fwp. When importing a Personal Web Package, Expression Web allows you to choose which files and folders within the Personal Web Package you want to import.

## To Import Files into a Site

The following steps import the background image, the company logo, and a previously created style sheet that specifies the type styles you will use in the juice bar site.

- Point to Import on the File menu, then click File to open the Import dialog box (Figure 9–12).

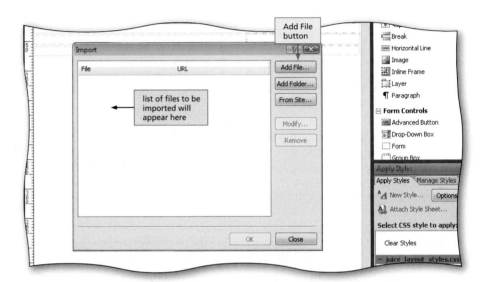

**Figure 9–12**

- Click the Add File button to open the Add File to Import List dialog box.

- Navigate to the Data Files, then double-click the juice_files folder to display its contents.

- Press and hold CTRL, then click the files clementine_logo.gif, juice_background.gif, and juice_type_styles.css to select them (Figure 9–13).

### Experiment

- Try importing an entire folder at once. Delete the folder and its contents from the site folder after you have done so.

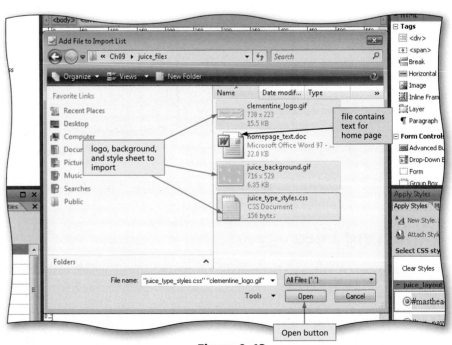

**Figure 9–13**

**3**

- Click the Open button to close the Add File to Import List dialog box and view the files in the Import dialog box (Figure 9–14).

**Q&A**

Why should I not select the homepage_text.doc file?

This is a Microsoft Word file that contains text for the home page. Later in the chapter you will open it in Microsoft Word and copy and paste it to the default.html page.

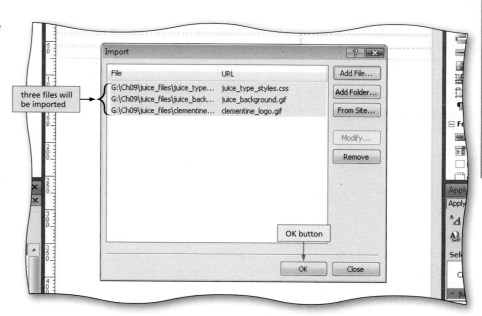

**Figure 9–14**

**4**

- Click the OK button to close the Import dialog box and embed the files in the site folder (Figure 9–15).

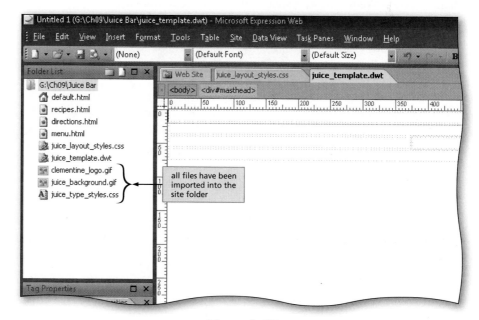

**Figure 9–15**

# Adding Background Images

A background image is one that appears behind the content of a Web page. It can repeat to create a consistent backdrop or attach itself to a specific position on the page to add visual interest to your site. A good background image is one that does not distract from the page content. It should be subtle enough to provide contrast between the background and the page text and should fit in with the other color choices of your page.

There are many different ways to add a **background image**. You can use the Page Properties dialog box to add a **tiled image**, one that is repeated both horizontally and

**BTW**

**Watermarks**

A watermark is a fixed image that appears (often faded) in the background of a printed page or Web page. To create a watermark on a Web page, use a combination of the background-image, background-repeat, and background-attachment CSS rules to insert a single instance of the image in a fixed location.

vertically to fill the page, to a specific page. You can also use the CSS background-image rule to specify the background image, and use other CSS rules to determine whether the image repeats or is in a fixed location. Options include repeating the image vertically or horizontally, displaying the image at a certain percentage or number of pixels, placing it once in the center of the page, or positioning it relative to the top, right, left, or bottom of the page. You can add a background image to a div by creating a class-based style and applying it to the div, or modifying the style of the div itself to include a background image. If you want the background image to display behind all of the page elements, modify the body style to include the background image.

When adding a background image, as with any image, you need to consider the impact of the file size on the page and on your site folder. A large file size will slow the download time of your page. Another consideration is the value of adding the image — what does it add to the page? Is the image required as part of company branding or to set a certain mood?

## To Add a Background Image to a Page

The following steps create a style rule to the juice_layout_styles.css that specifies a repeated background image using the juice_background.gif file. Because the dynamic Web template you are creating is based on this style sheet, changes you make to the style sheet will affect the template.

- Click the <body> tag on the Quick Tag Selector to select the entire body of the template page, then scroll in the Apply Styles task pane, if necessary, to see the body style in the task pane (Figure 9–16).

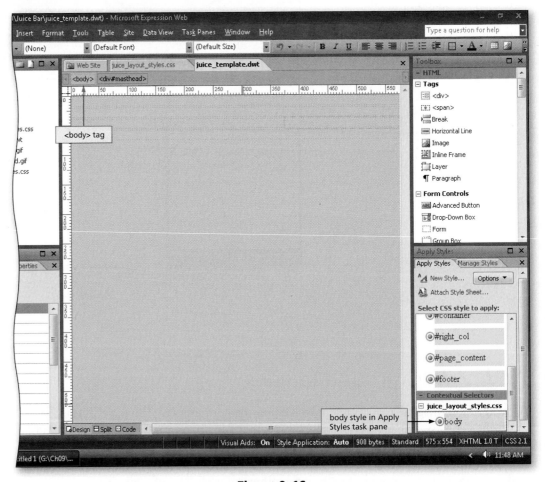

**Figure 9–16**

- Click the body style arrow in the Apply Styles task pane, then click Modify Style to open the Modify Style dialog box.

- Click Background in the Category list to display the background options (Figure 9–17).

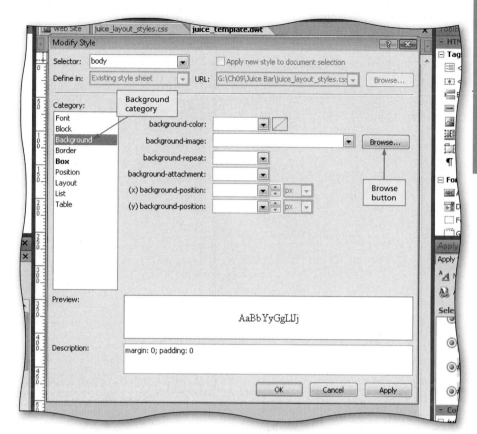

**Figure 9–17**

**3**

- Click the Browse button to open the Picture dialog box.

- Click the juice_background.gif file to select it (Figure 9–18).

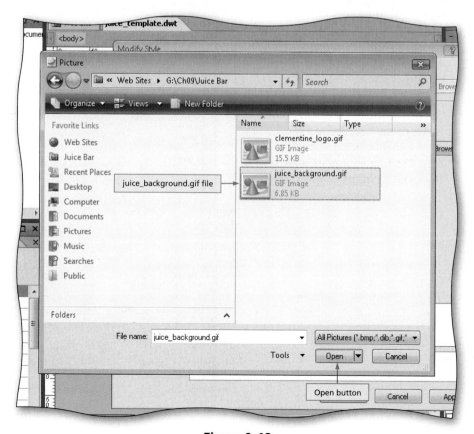

**Figure 9–18**

• Click the Open button to close the Picture dialog box (Figure 9–19).

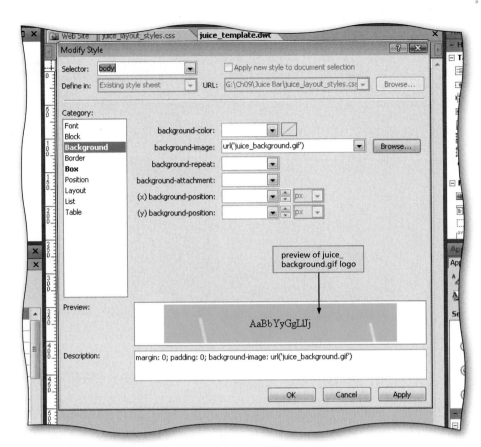

**Figure 9–19**

• Click the background-repeat box arrow, then click repeat to specify that the image will repeat (Figure 9–20).

 **Experiment**

• Experiment with different repeat options to see the changes in the effect of the background image. After experimenting, repeat Step 4 so that your page matches the example in the chapter.

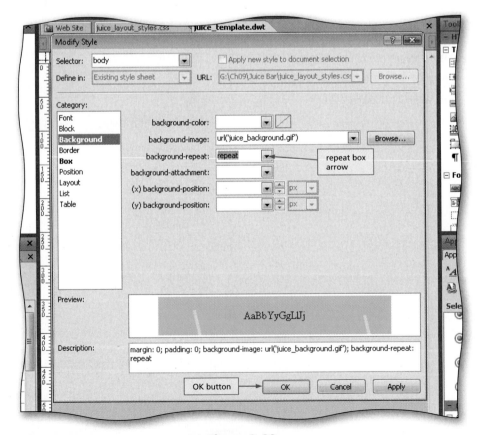

**Figure 9–20**

5

- Click the OK button to close the Modify Style dialog box, then click a blank area of the page to deselect the body.

- Click Save All on the File menu to save the changes to the default.html page and the style sheet (Figure 9–21).

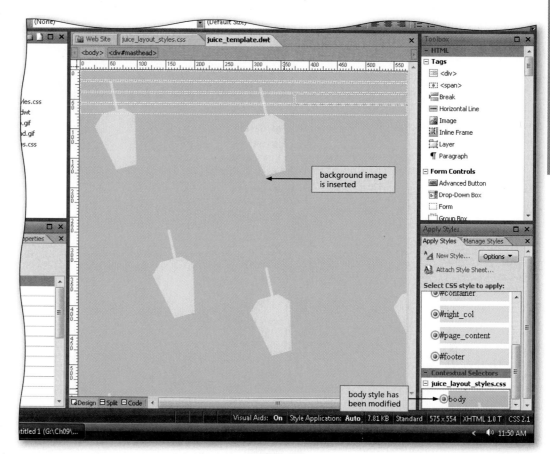

**Figure 9–21**

## To Add Page Content

The following steps insert the company logo into the masthead and apply transparency to the white logo border, add text to the footer, format the footer, and attach the style sheet you imported earlier. The footer and masthead will be the same on each page of the Web site. Although you will close the Apply Styles task pane, you can modify the footer properties using the CSS Properties task pane.

**1**

- Click in the masthead div at the top of the juice_template.dwt to position the insertion point (Figure 9–22).

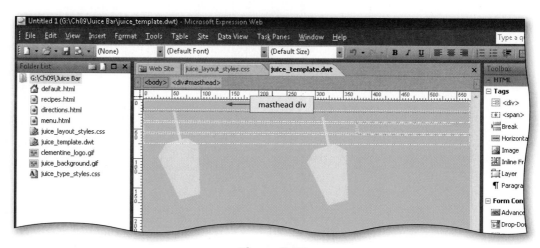

**Figure 9–22**

- Point to Picture on the Insert menu, then click From File to open the Picture dialog box.

- If necessary, navigate to the Juice Bar site folder.

- Click clementine_logo.gif to select it (Figure 9–23).

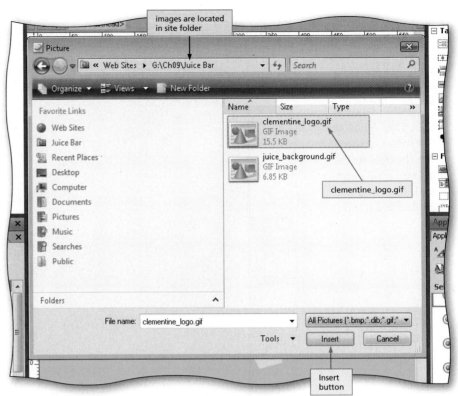

**Figure 9–23**

**3**

- Click the Insert button to open the Accessibility Properties dialog box.

- Type Clementine's Juice Bar logo in the Alternate text text box (Figure 9–24).

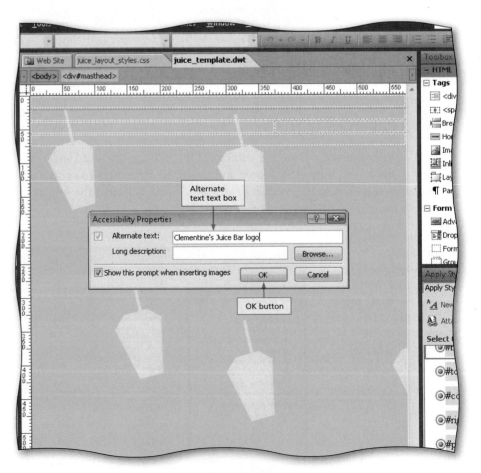

**Figure 9–24**

**4**

- Click the OK button to insert the logo at the top of the home page (Figure 9–25).

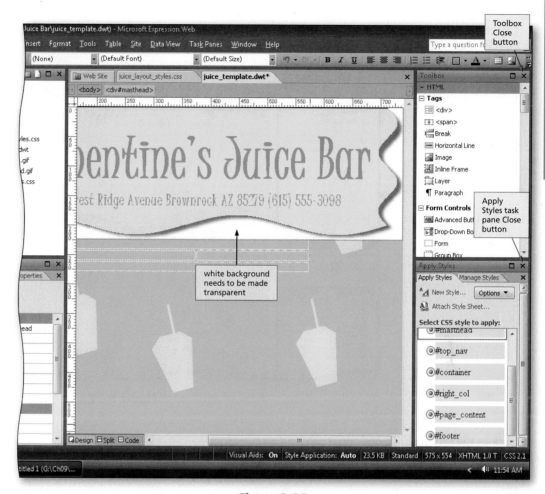

**Figure 9–25**

**5**

- Click the Apply Styles task pane Close button, then click the Toolbox Close button to display more of the Design Window.

- Right-click the Common toolbar, then click Pictures to open the Pictures toolbar.

- Click the logo to select it (Figure 9–26).

**Q&A**

My Pictures toolbar is not docked.

Drag the toolbar up under the Common toolbar to dock it.

**Figure 9–26**

- Click the Set Transparent Color button on the Pictures toolbar to turn the pointer into a brush, then click the white area of the logo to make it transparent (Figure 9–27).

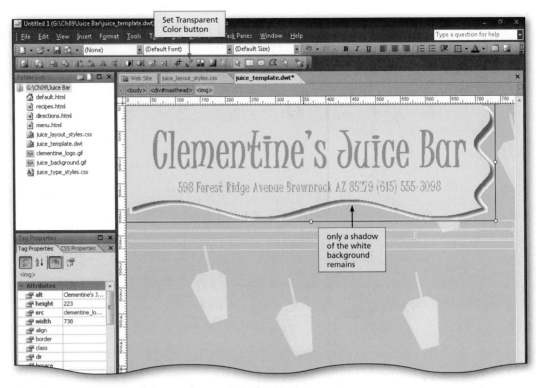

**Figure 9–27**

- Click in the footer div to position the insertion point.

- Type Our juice is pure, organic, and always fresh! (Figure 9–28).

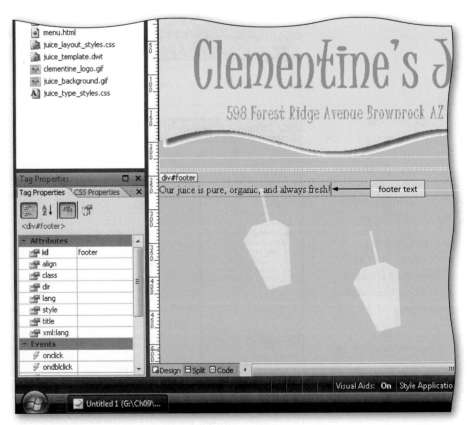

**Figure 9–28**

**8**

- Click the CSS Properties tab in the Tag Properties pane to display the CSS formatting options.

- Click color to display the color box arrow, click the color box arrow, then click the Green color box to change the font color to green.

- Click font-style to display the font-style box arrow, click the font-style box arrow, then click italic to change the font to italic (Figure 9–29).

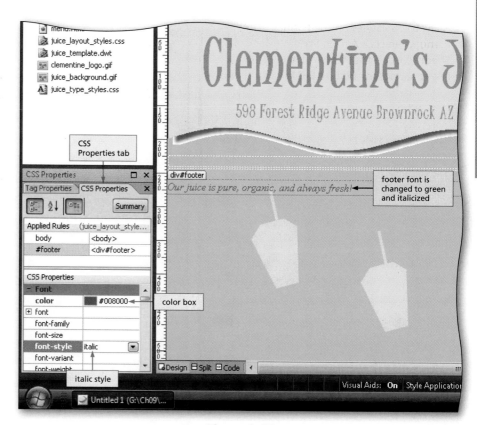

**Figure 9–29**

**9**

- In the CSS Properties list, scroll to the Block category, click text-align to display the text-align box arrow, click the text-align box arrow, then click center to center the footer text (Figure 9–30).

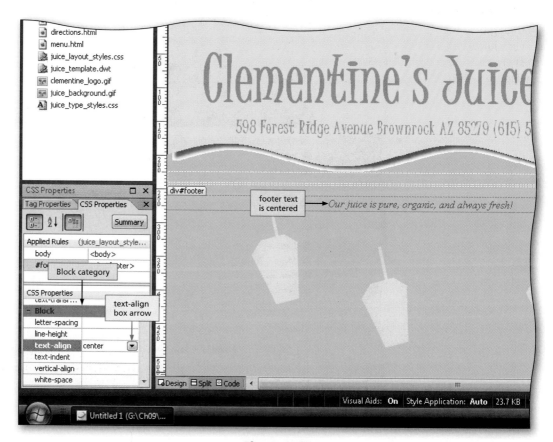

**Figure 9–30**

**10**

- Point to CSS Styles on the Format menu, then click Attach Style Sheet to open the Attach Style Sheet dialog box (Figure 9–31).

**Figure 9–31**

**11**

- Click the Browse button to open the Select Style Sheet dialog box, then click juice_type_styles.css to select it (Figure 9–32).

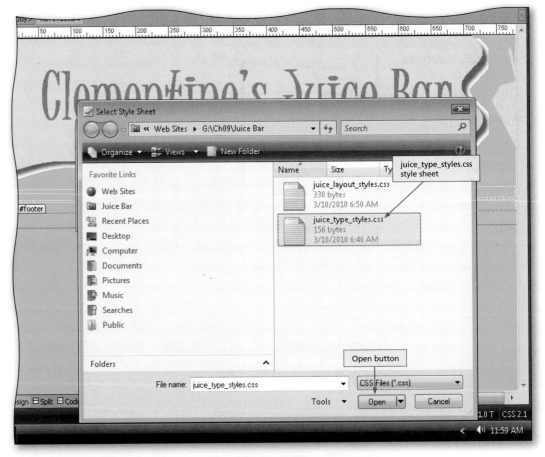

**Figure 9–32**

- Click the Open button to select the style sheet.

- Click the OK button to close the Attach Style Sheet dialog box and attach the style sheet (Figure 9–33).

- Click Save All on the File menu to save changes to all pages, then click OK to save the embedded files if necessary.

- Click Close in the Microsoft Expression Web dialog box to confirm 5 of 5 files updated.

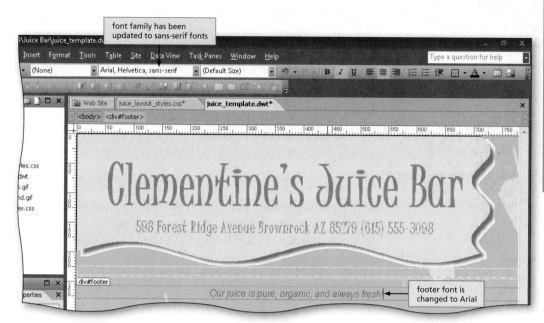

**Figure 9–33**

**Plan the site navigation.**
Determine which pages need to be in the primary site navigation area and how you want the navigation to appear. Adding interactive buttons, as you have done in previous chapters, adds visual interest to the site page and can have effects added, such as rollovers. Creating a list-based navigation area using an ID-based style is simpler than an image-based navigation area because there are no associated button images with the links, and adding a page to the list will automatically add any associated styles to the list item, link, and states such as hover or visited.

**Plan Ahead**

# Creating ID-Based Styles

As you previously learned, ID-based styles are applied to elements that only appear once on a page, such as the masthead, a footer, or a navigation area. A CSS-based layout page includes ID-based styles to define divs for page elements. You can create your own ID-based styles using the New Style dialog box. ID-based styles are always preceded by a pound symbol, also known as a number sign (#), whereas class-based styles, which can be applied to headers, body text, hyperlinks, or other elements that are able to repeat on a page, are preceded by a period (.).

**BTW**

**Print Style Sheets**
A print style sheet sets the rules for how a page will look when printed. Print style sheets can define changes to the Web page, such as removing an image or changing the font and page size to make the printed page more readable.

An ID-based style element can also have what are called **descendent selectors**. Descendent selectors are subcategories of items or actions that further define how the ID-based element appears. An example of a descendent selector is a list item, which is a sub-element of an unordered list. Another example is a hover rule, which adds a rollover effect that changes the appearance of a hyperlink when the mouse pointer is positioned (or hovered) over it.

**BTW**

**Web Accessibility**
See Appendix B for more information about accessibility and assistive technology.

## Using List-Based Navigation

Instead of a navigation area that uses image-based interactive buttons, you can use **list-based navigation** as a site navigation tool. List-based navigation is simply an unordered list (such as a bulleted list). An unordered list is easily read by assistive technologies, so it meets accessibility requirements. In previous chapters you used bullets and line breaks to separate unordered list items; however, you can present unordered list items side by side, use ID-based CSS rules and descendent selectors to add spaces between the items, and use rollover effects, such as changes to font color and background, to make your navigation list interactive. Figure 9–34 shows a list-based navigation area, including the levels of descendent selectors from left to right: navigation area, unordered list, list item, and hyperlink.

**Figure 9–34**

## To Create a List-Based Navigation Area

The following steps insert a bulleted list in the navigation div, type the text that will appear for each hyperlink, and add the hyperlinks to the other site pages.

- Click in the top_nav div to position the insertion point.

- Click the Bullets button on the Common toolbar to start a bulleted list (Figure 9–35).

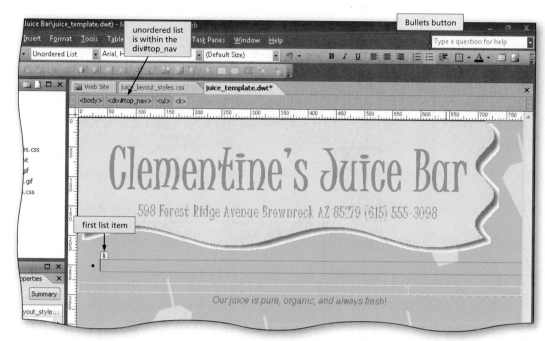

**Figure 9–35**

- Type Home, then press ENTER.

- Type Menu, then press ENTER.

- Type Recipes, then press ENTER.

- Type Directions (Figure 9–36).

**Figure 9–36**

- Select the word, Home, after the first bullet.

- Press CTRL+K to open the Insert Hyperlink dialog box.

- Click default.html to select it as the target of the link (Figure 9–37).

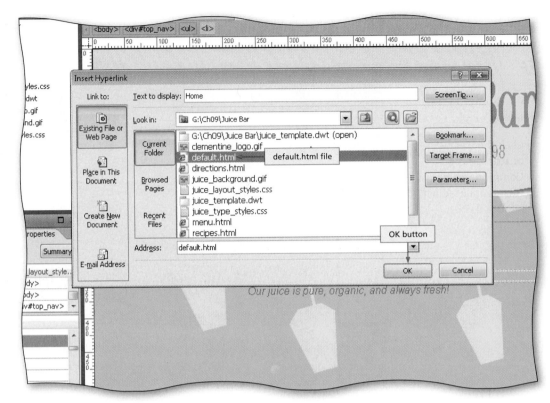

**Figure 9–37**

④

- Click the OK button to insert the hyperlink (Figure 9–38).

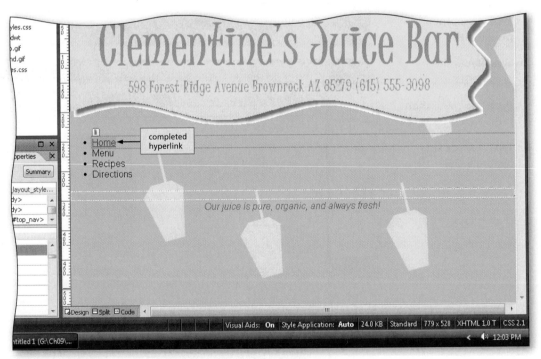

**Figure 9–38**

- Repeat Steps 3 and 4 to add a hyperlink from the word, Menu, to the menu.html page.

- Repeat Steps 3 and 4 to add a hyperlink from the word, Recipes, to the recipes.html page.

- Repeat Steps 3 and 4 to add a hyperlink from the word, Directions, to the directions.html page (Figure 9–39).

- Press CTRL+S to save the page.

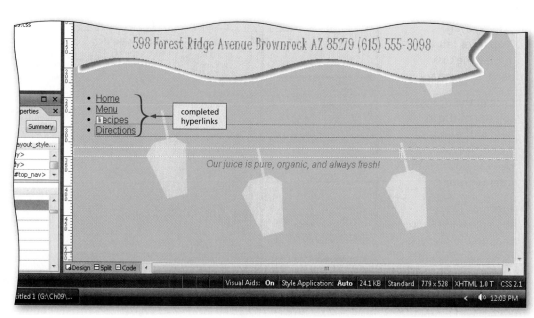

**Figure 9–39**

## To Add CSS Rules to the List

The following steps convert the list into an ID-based navigation list; use CSS to add styles to the list, list items, and hyperlinks; and create rollovers.

**1**

- Click the <ul> tag on the Quick Tag Selector to select the entire bulleted list (Figure 9–40).

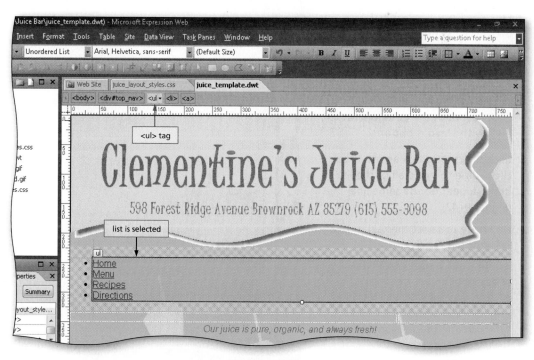

**Figure 9–40**

- Click the Tag Properties tab to display the task pane, if necessary.

- Click in the right column of the id field in the Tag Properties task pane to position the insertion point.

- Type navlist, then press ENTER to change the div type to a navigation list (Figure 9–41).

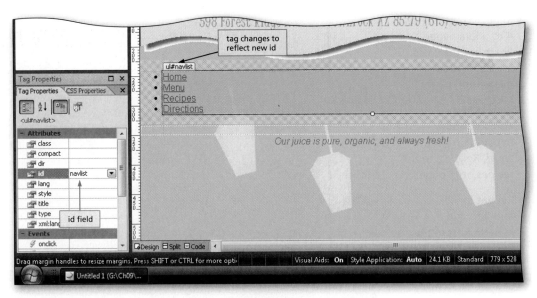

**Figure 9–41**

**③**

- Click New Style on the Format menu to open the New Style dialog box.

- Select the text in the Selector text box then type #navlist li to specify that the new style will be applied to each list item in the navigation list.

- Click the Define in box arrow, then click Existing style sheet to select it.

- Click the URL box arrow, then click juice_layout_styles.css to select it.

- Click Layout in the Category list to display the layout options.

- Click the display box arrow, then click inline to make all of the list items appear on the same line (Figure 9–42).

**Q&A**

Do I have to select the text in the Selector text box?

Yes. By default, Expression Web adds a period (.) at the beginning of each new style name, indicating that it will be a class-based style. When creating an id-based style, select both the default style name (typically *newstyle1*) and the period before it. When creating a class-based style, such as a drop cap, do not select the period.

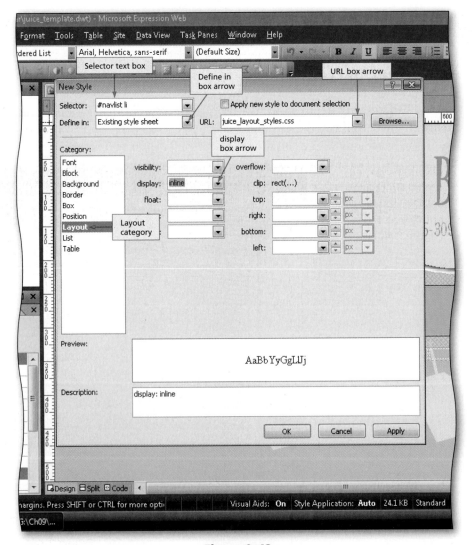

**Figure 9–42**

**4**

- Click List in the Category list to display the list options.

- Click the list-style-type box arrow, then click none to remove the bullet icons for the list items (Figure 9–43).

 **Experiment**

- Choose other options from the list-style-type box arrow menu to see the effects. When you are done, repeat Step 4 so that your page matches the chapter example.

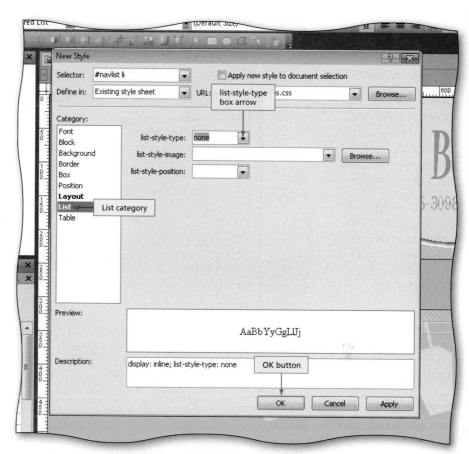

**Figure 9–43**

**5**

- Click the OK button to close the New Style dialog box and apply the list changes (Figure 9–44).

**Figure 9–44**

- Click between the word, Home, and the word, Menu, then press SPACEBAR to insert a space.

- Click between the word, Menu, and the word, Recipes, then press SPACEBAR to insert a space.

- Click between the word, Recipes, and the word, Directions, then press SPACEBAR to insert a space (Figure 9–45).

- Click Save All on the File menu to save the changes to both default.html and juice_layout_styles.css at once, then click the OK button to save the embedded styles if necessary.

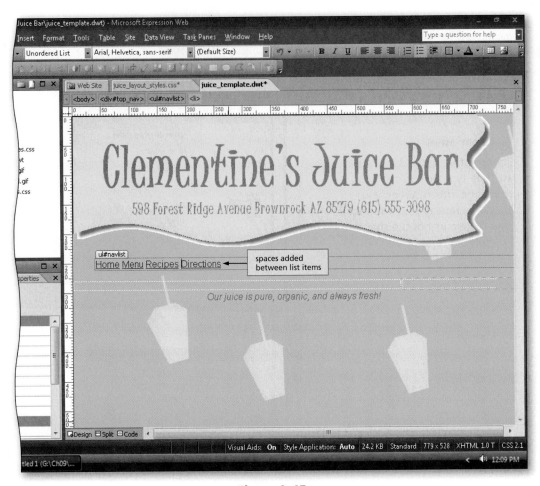

**Figure 9–45**

## To Create Rollovers

The following steps add spacing between the list items (a property) and change the font and background properties of the hyperlinks (a:link property) by creating ID-based styles. When you create the style for the hyperlink, you will also define the a:visited property at the same time in the New Style dialog box. Setting the a:visited property to be the same as the a:link property means that after a link has been clicked, it appears the same as before it was clicked. Then you will add a hover property (a:hover) to create the rollover effect.

**1**

- Click New Style on the Format menu to open the New Style dialog box.

- Select the text in the Selector text box, then type `#navlist a` to specify that the new style will be applied to each list item.

- Click Box in the Category list to display the layout options.

- Type `8` in the padding top text box to add 8 pixels of space between each list item and the div border (Figure 9–46).

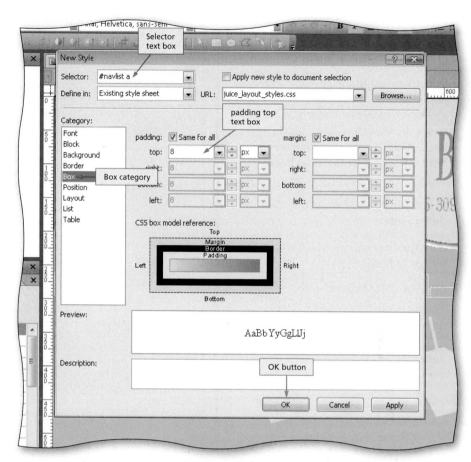

**Figure 9–46**

**2**

- Click the OK button to close the New Style dialog box and see the padding (Figure 9–47).

**Figure 9–47**

**3**

- Click New Style on the Format menu to open the New Style dialog box.

- Select the text in the Selector text box, then type `#navlist a:link, #navlist a:visited` to specify that the new style will be applied to each hyperlink text both before and after it has been clicked.

- Click the font-size box arrow, then click x-large.

- Click the font-weight box arrow, then click bold.

- Click the color box arrow to display the palette (Figure 9–48).

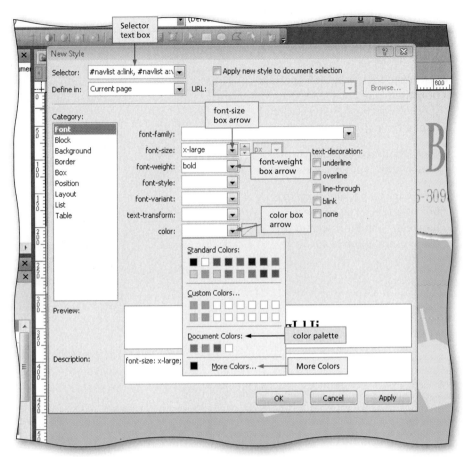

**Figure 9–48**

**4**

- Click More Colors to open the More Colors dialog box.

- Click the hexagon with the value FF,50,50 to change the font color (Figure 9–49).

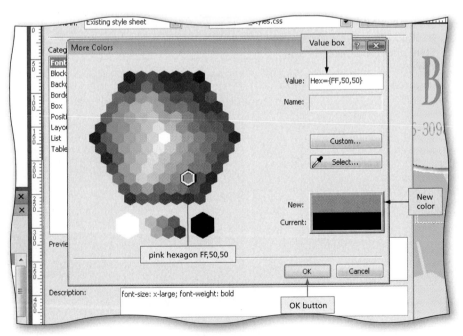

**Figure 9–49**

**5**

- Click the OK button to close the More Colors dialog box.

- Click Background in the Category list to display the background options.

- Click the background-color box arrow to display the palette (Figure 9–50).

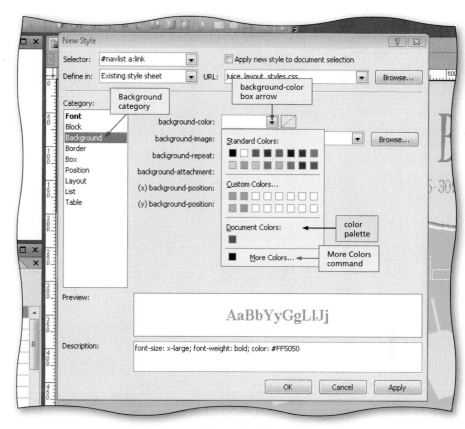

**Figure 9–50**

**6**

- Click More Colors to open the More Colors dialog box.

- Click the hexagon with the value 33,99,33 to select it (Figure 9–51).

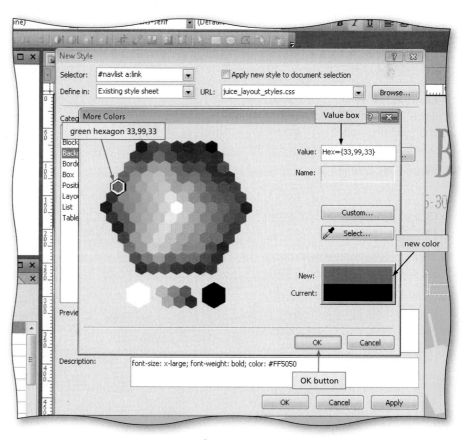

**Figure 9–51**

● Click the OK button to close the More Colors dialog box.

● Click the OK button to close the New Style dialog box and apply the new styles to the navigation list (Figure 9–52).

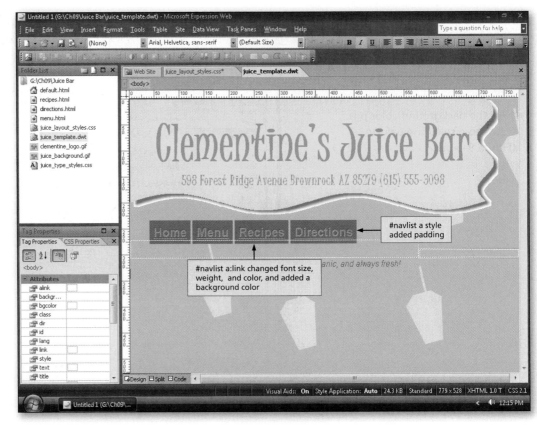

**Figure 9–52**

● Click New Style on the Format menu to open the New Style dialog box.

● Select the text in the Selector text box, then type `#navlist a: hover` to specify that the new style will be applied when the pointer is positioned over the link.

● Click the font-size box arrow, then click x-large.

● Click the font-weight box arrow, then click bold.

● Click the color box arrow to display the palette (Figure 9–53).

● Click the dark green color box under the Document Colors heading to change the font color.

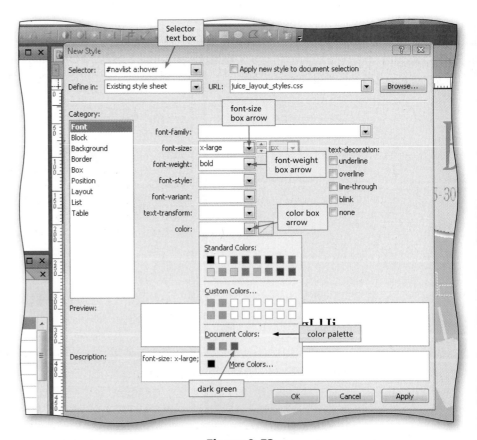

**Figure 9–53**

**9**

- Click Background in the Category list to display the background options.

- Click the background-color box arrow to display the palette.

- Click the pink color box under the Document Colors heading to change the background color (Figure 9–54).

- Click the OK button to close the New Style dialog box.

- Click Save All on the File menu to save default.html and juice_layout_styles.css.

### Experiment

- Choose other options for the hover style, including font size, font style, and others. When you are done, repeat Steps 8 and 9 so that your page matches the chapter example.

**Q&A**

Should I preview the page in a browser to view the effects?

You cannot preview a dynamic Web template in a browser. If you want to make any changes after the template is applied to other pages, any changes that you make to the template will automatically be applied to the attached pages.

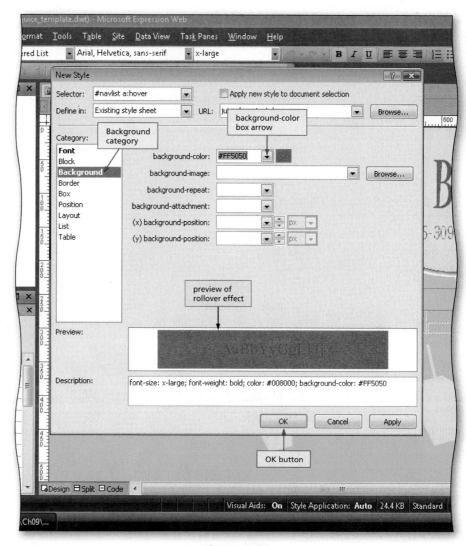

**Figure 9–54**

---

**Improve the site's readability and visual interest using typography and CSS.**
Creating elements and using typography effects make your site more appealing to visitors and improve the readability of the page content. A sidebar element can provide additional information about the page content or serve as a location for information that changes regularly, such as a description of a weekly special. Break up long blocks of page content by adding heading styles and drop caps.

**Plan Ahead**

# Adding Sidebars

Sidebars are ID-based page elements. Sidebars are often used in long articles or interviews in print-based newsletters and newspapers. As used in print publications, sidebars are boxes containing information related to the primary page content, usually text. In the sidebar element on a Web page, you can add text, an image, or a list of related links. The Clementine Juice Bar could use a sidebar for various purposes, such as to display a mission statement or description of a new product, or to spotlight the employee of the month. You can position

**BTW**

**Pull Quotes**
Similar to sidebars, pull quotes are text boxes used to add visual and content interest to an article or page. Pull quotes take an actual quote of text from the page content and set it in a box with a different font, background, or other settings. Pull quotes use the <blockquote> tag.

sidebars on one side or the other of the page, or add them to the center of two columns of text and have the column text wrap around the sidebar. You can resize the height and width to reshape the sidebar however best fits your style and page layout.

When creating a sidebar, you can convert a div into a sidebar in the Tag Properties task pane. The sidebar can be a specific height, or it can be adjusted to fit its contents. When setting the height, use the overflow property to determine where any extra text will appear. If you set the overflow as auto, Expression Web will add scroll bars that the user can drag to view the content that does not fit in the box; when using the auto setting, scroll bars do not appear if there is no overflow. Setting the overflow property as visible means that overflow text will appear on the page outside of the box, which is not attractive.

## To Add a Sidebar Element

Recall that the template you used to create the site has a two-column layout. The following steps insert a div in the right column, then convert it to a sidebar. In the New Style dialog box, you will create an ID-based style for the sidebar element with scroll bars and position it to the right of the page.

- Click in the right_col div to position the insertion point (Figure 9–55).

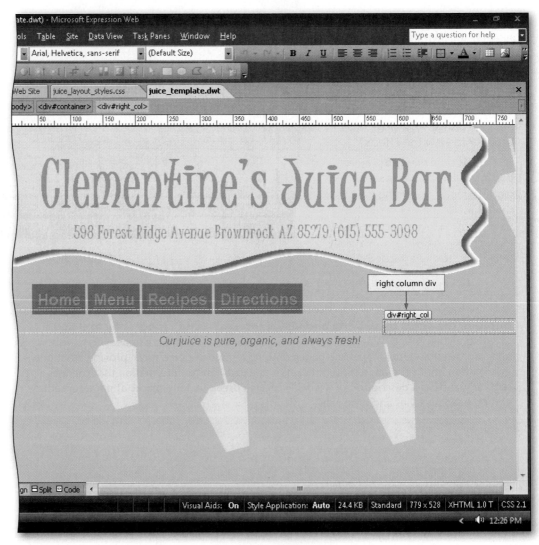

**Figure 9–55**

**2**

- Point to HTML on the Insert menu, then click div to insert a div within the right_col div (Figure 9–56).

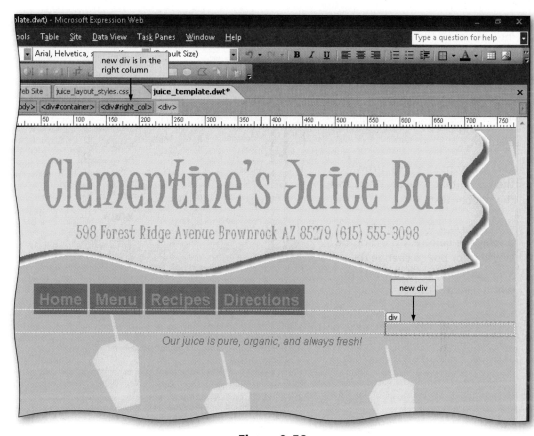

**Figure 9–56**

**3**

- Click in the right column of the id text box in the Tag Properties task pane to position the insertion point.

- Type sidebar, then press ENTER to change the div to a sidebar (Figure 9–57).

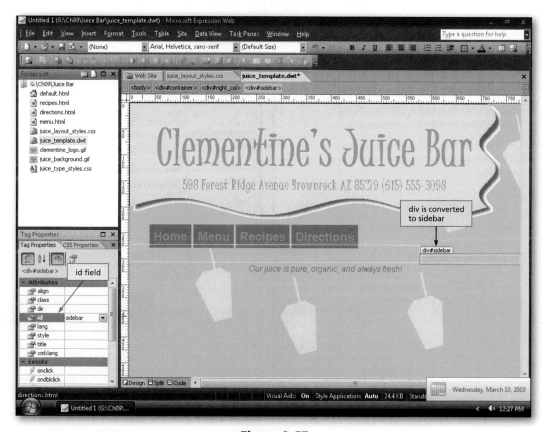

**Figure 9–57**

- Click New Style on the Format menu to open the New Style dialog box.

- Select the text in the Selector text box, then type #sidebar to specify that the new style will be applied to the new sidebar element.

- Click the font-style box arrow, then click italic to apply italics to the sidebar text.

- Click the color box arrow to display the palette, then click the White color box to change the font color of the sidebar text to white (Figure 9–58).

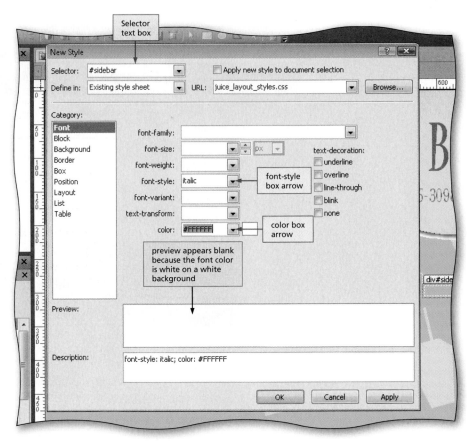

**Figure 9–58**

- Click Background in the Category list to display the background options.

- Click the background-color box arrow to display the palette, then click the Green color box to change the background of the sidebar box to green (Figure 9–59).

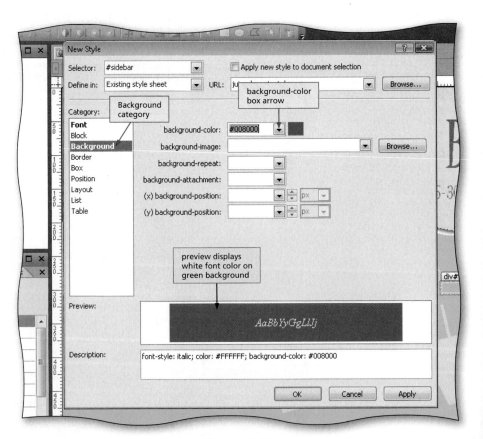

**Figure 9–59**

**6**

- Click Box in the Category list to display the spacing options around the box.

- Click in the padding top text box, then type 6 to insert 6 pixels of space between the sidebar text and the outside border of the sidebar.

- Click in the margin top text box, then type 6 to insert 6 pixels of space between the sidebar border and the page content (Figure 9–60).

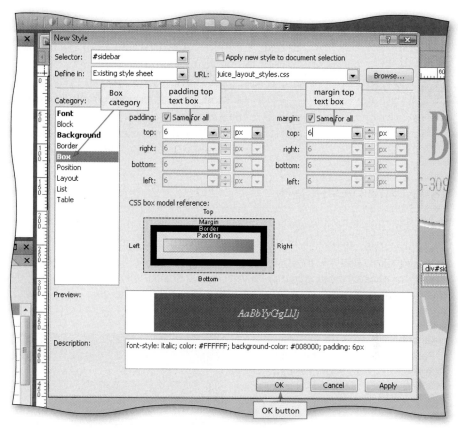

**Figure 9–60**

**7**

- Click the OK button to close the New Style dialog box and apply the changes to the sidebar div (Figure 9–61).

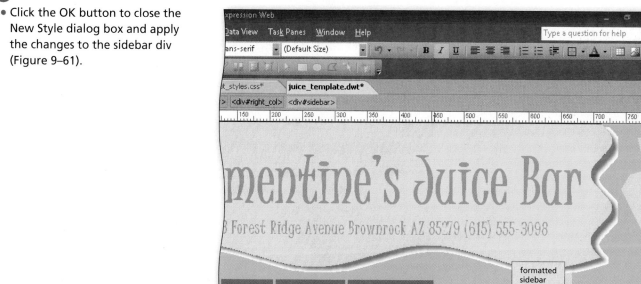

**Figure 9–61**

# Using Typography to Improve Readability

Typography can make the difference between a visually dense page and one that is easy to read and follow. A page where all of the text is the same font size and style is difficult to read; often, visitors will skip reading the entire page. Using header styles to distinguish text levels, such as titles, subtitles, and body text, is an important typography skill.

In addition, you can use typography to further increase the readability of your text by setting a line length and height. The easiest way to specify line length is to set the width of the content div. To add line spacing, change the style of the body text to add pixels of blank space that will automatically be added between lines of text as it wraps in your text.

## To Specify Line Height

The line-height property measures the height of the entire line of text, including the text. You can set the height as a fixed pixel height or as a percentage of the font size. A percentage allows for adjustments to the font size made by style changes or settings in the visitor's browser. A line height of 100% stacks the lines of text right on top of one another without spacing, so you should always specify a percentage over 100%. The following steps modify the style of the page content div to add space to the line height.

- Click Apply Styles on the Task Panes menu to open the Apply Styles task pane (Figure 9–62).

**Figure 9–62**

**2**

- Click the #page_content style box arrow in the Apply Styles task pane to view the menu.

- Click Modify Style to open the Modify Style dialog box.

- Click Block in the Category list to view paragraph spacing options.

- Type 150 in the line-height text box to specify that the line height will be 150% of the font size.

- Click the line-height Measurements box arrow, then click % to specify that the line-height will be measured as a percentage instead of pixels (Figure 9–63).

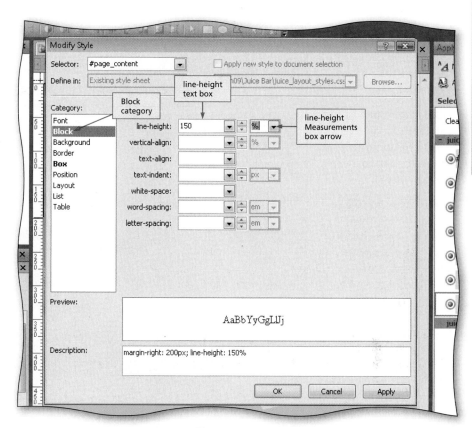

**Figure 9–63**

**3**

- Click Box in the Category list to view padding and margin options.

- Type 6 in the padding top box, then type 12 in the margin top box (Figure 9–64).

 Why are there 200 pixels of space in the right margin?

To make room for the right column sidebar, there are 200 pixels of space between the outside of the container that includes the page content and right column divs.

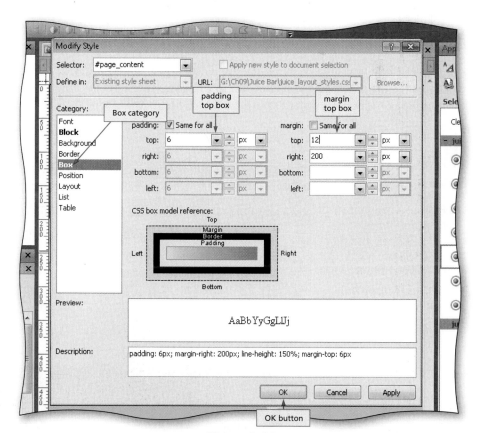

**Figure 9–64**

- Click the OK button to close the Modify Style dialog box and see the effect of the style change.

- Click the Apply Styles task pane Close button to close the task pane (Figure 9–65).

- Press CTRL+S to save the template, then click the OK button to save the embedded style sheet.

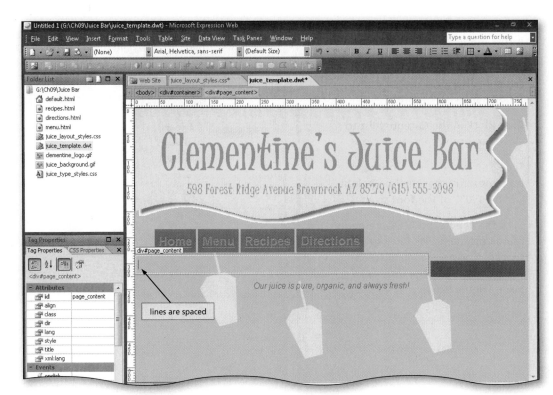

**Figure 9–65**

## To Specify Line Length

The following steps change the line length by changing the width of the page content div. You can modify the style for the div to a specific pixel width. In this case, you want the container that includes both the sidebar and page content areas to be a bit wider than the width of the logo, so you will view the width of the logo, then drag the div sizing handle to 800 pixels.

- Click the logo to select it.

- Position the pointer over the right sizing handle of the logo to view the ScreenTip, which reads 738 pixels (Figure 9–66).

**Figure 9–66**

**2**

- Click in the page_ content div to display the related tags on the Quick Tag Selector bar.

- Click the div#container tag on the Quick Tag Selector bar to select the entire div (Figure 9–67).

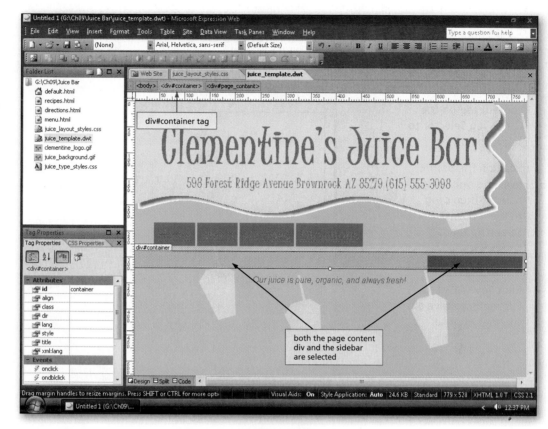

**Figure 9–67**

**3**

- Position the pointer over the right sizing handle, then drag to the left until the ScreenTip reads 750 pixels (Figure 9–68).

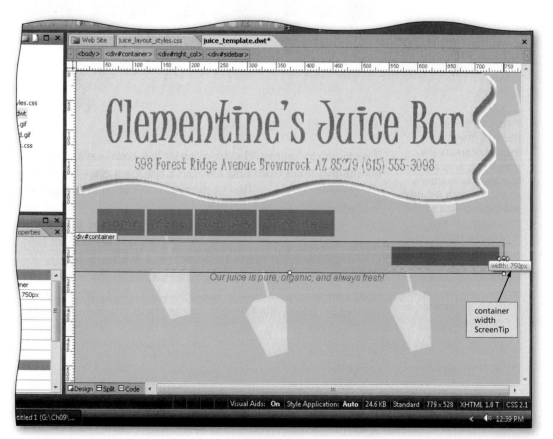

**Figure 9–68**

**4**

- Click anywhere in the page_content div to position the insertion point.

- Click the div#page_content tag on the Quick Tag Selector to select the div.

- Position the pointer over the right sizing handle, then drag to the left until the ScreenTip reads 500 pixels (Figure 9–69).

- Click Save All on the File menu to save all changes at once.

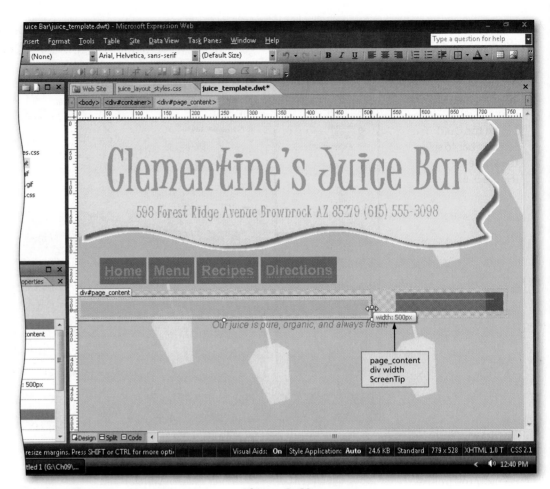

**Figure 9–69**

**BTW**

**First Letter Pseudo Class**
Instead of creating a class-based drop cap style that must be manually applied to each instance, you could create a style that automatically applies the style to the first letter of every paragraph in the body text. However, this is not widely supported by all browsers, so it should be avoided.

## Adding Drop Cap Styles

The main reason to add a drop cap style is to add visual interest to paragraphs and to distinguish them from one another. Creating a class-based drop cap style allows you to choose whether to apply it to the first letter in each paragraph of body text or only to the first paragraph under a header.

In printed pages that use drop caps, often the font used varies considerably from the body font, such as using a fancy scripted font for the drop cap. However, on Web pages, you should restrict the drop cap style to a Web-safe font or font family to ensure that it will be clearly readable in all browsers. One option is to use a sans-serif font family for the body text and a serif font as the drop cap style. Other ways to safely distinguish the drop cap are to change the font color or apply italics, bold, or both.

# To Add a Drop Cap Style

The following steps create a class-based drop cap style and apply it to the text on the default.html page. You decide to keep the font family the same but increase the font size and add color and bolding to create an attractive drop cap.

- Click New Style on the Format menu to open the New Style dialog box.

- Type dropcap in the Selector text box to name the new style.

- Click the font-family box arrow, then click Arial, Helvetica, sans-serif.

- Click the font-size box arrow, then click xx-large.

- Click the font-weight box arrow, then click bold.

- Click the color box arrow to view the palette (Figure 9–70).

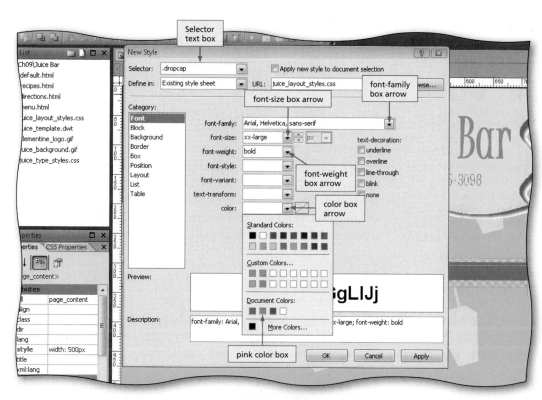

**Figure 9–70**

- Click the pink color box under the Document Colors headings to select it (Figure 9–71).

- Click the OK button in the New Style dialog box to close it.

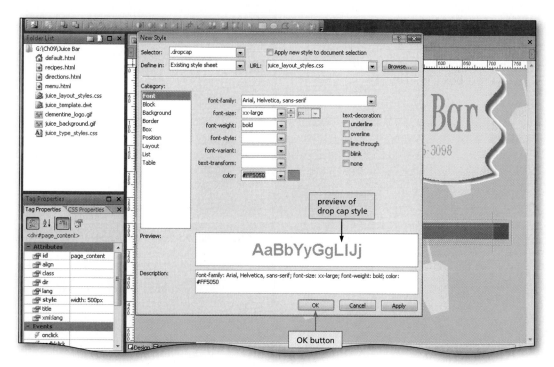

**Figure 9–71**

**Plan Ahead**

> **Create site consistency using dynamic Web templates.**
> Attaching dynamic Web templates to site pages makes your job easier as a Web designer, because only the content areas that you designate as editable regions need to be modified on each page. If you update the site to contain a new page, you only have to make the navigation change in the dynamic Web template itself; the navigation areas on the other site pages will update automatically.

**BTW**

**Quick Reference**
For a table that lists how to complete the tasks covered in this book using the mouse, shortcut menu, and keyboard, see the Quick Reference Summary at the back of this book, or visit the Expression Web 2 Quick Reference Web page (scsite.com/ew2/qr).

# Defining Editable Regions

Whereas common elements on a dynamic Web template usually include logos, footers, the navigation area, and style sheets, the editable regions are the areas of an HTML page that use a dynamic Web template that can be modified for each page. Common editable regions include sidebars, page content divs, and image placeholders. Like other Web elements, such as HTML file names, editable region names cannot contain spaces or special characters. You can convert an existing div into an editable region or create and add a new editable region. When you create a dynamic Web template, one editable region, doctitle, is automatically created in order to allow you to name each page with a different title.

## To Define Editable Regions

The following steps define the page's editable regions. When you define the editable regions, by default Expression Web uses the region name as placeholder text, which indicates to anyone editing the site using the template what should go in there. You can replace the placeholder text with other instructions if you wish.

**1**
- Right-click the page_content div to display the shortcut menu, then click Manage Editable Regions to open the Editable Regions dialog box.

- Type `page_content` in the Region name text box (Figure 9–72).

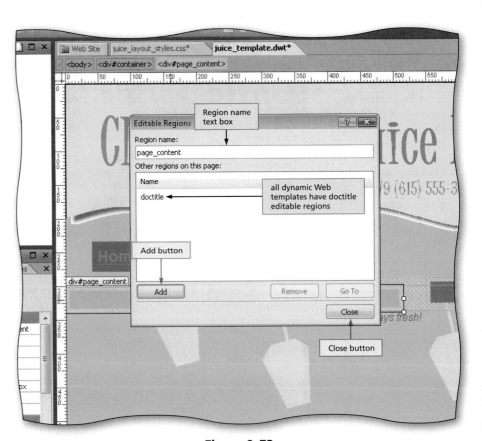

**Figure 9–72**

**2**

- Click the Add button to convert the div to an editable region named page_content.

- Click the Close button to view the page_content editable region (Figure 9–73).

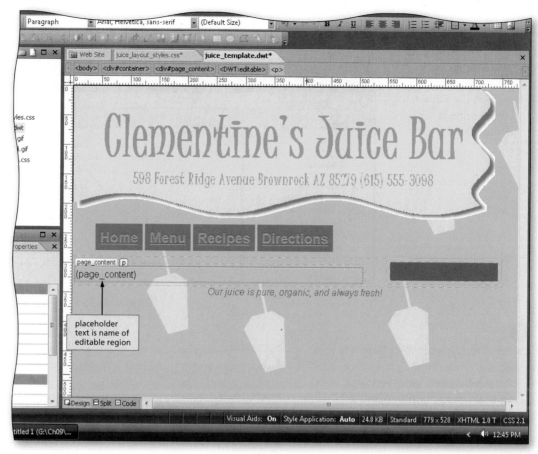

**Figure 9–73**

**3**

- Repeat Steps 1 and 2 to mark the sidebar div as an editable region.

- Click the Close button to view the sidebar editable region (Figure 9–74).

- Press CTRL+S to save the template, then click the OK button to save the embedded style sheet.

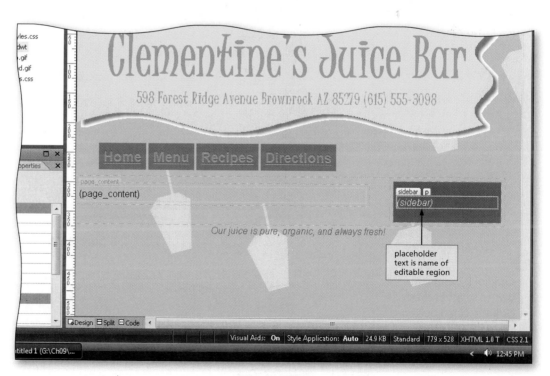

**Figure 9–74**

## To Attach a Dynamic Web Template to Existing Pages

The following steps attach the juice_template.dwt to the site pages.

**1**

- Double-click the default.html page in the Folder List to open it (Figure 9–75).

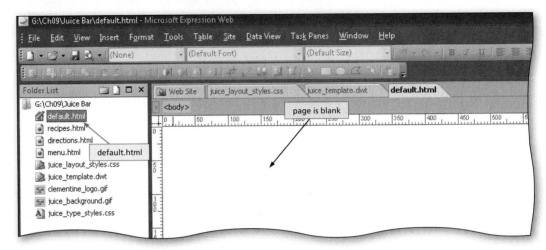

**Figure 9–75**

**2**

- Point to Dynamic Web Template on the Format menu, then click Attach Dynamic Web Template to open the Attach Dynamic Web Template dialog box (Figure 9–76).

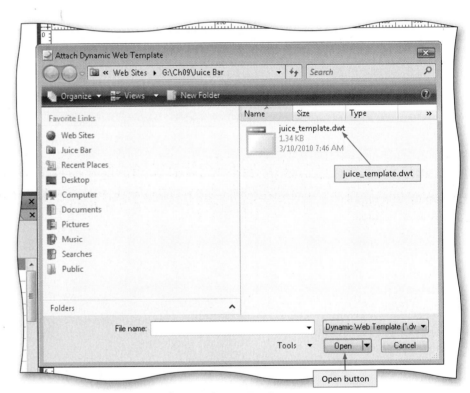

**Figure 9–76**

**3**

- Click juice_template. dwt to select it, then click the Open button to attach the template to the default. html page and open the first alert box (Figure 9–77).

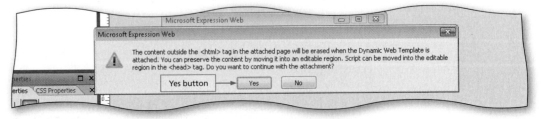

**Figure 9–77**

**4**

- Click the Yes button to overwrite any content on the default.html page and open the second alert box (Figure 9–78).

Why does this dialog box open?

Anytime an existing page is modified by applying a dynamic Web template to it, this dialog box will open, warning that any content will be overwritten. There is no content on any of the HTML pages in this site.

**Figure 9–78**

**5**

- Click the Close button to verify that the page has been updated (Figure 9–79).

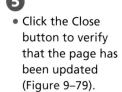

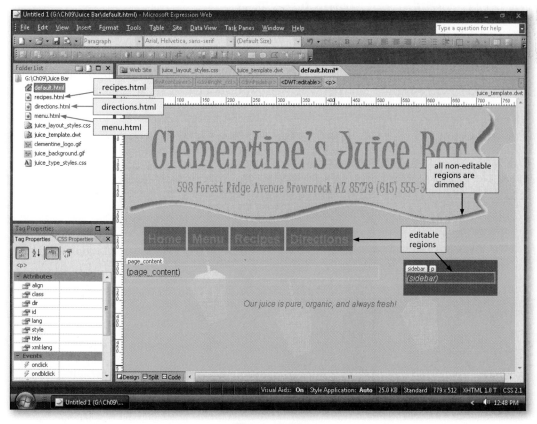

**Figure 9–79**

**6**

- Repeat Steps 1 through 4 to attach juice_template.dwt to the menu.html, directions.html, and recipes.html pages (Figure 9–80).

- Click Save All on the File menu to save all pages at once.

- Close the recipes.html, menu.html, and directions.html pages by right-clicking the page tab, then clicking Close.

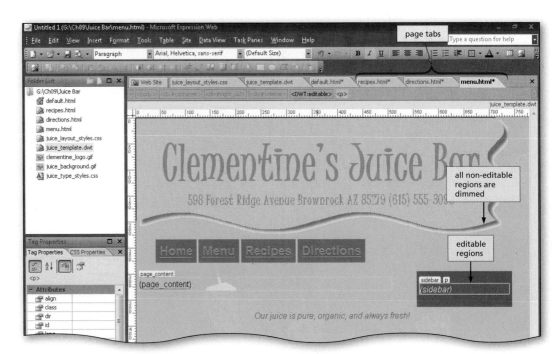

**Figure 9–80**

| Other Ways | |
|---|---|
| 1. Drag dynamic Web template from Folder List | to open page in Design window to attach it. |

## To Insert and Format Home Page Text

The following steps copy text from a Microsoft Word document, insert text into the page_content editable region on the default.html page, without copying the formatting from the source, then apply formatting such as heading and dropcap styles. You will also insert text in the sidebar by typing. You will be able to see the effects of the line height changes in the page_content div, as well as the font choices made for the sidebar.

**1**

- Click the Start button on the taskbar, point to All Programs, click Microsoft Office, then click Microsoft Office Word 2007 to start Microsoft Word (Figure 9–81).

**Q&A** What if I don't have Word 2007?

If you have another version of Word you can use that, or use any text editor.

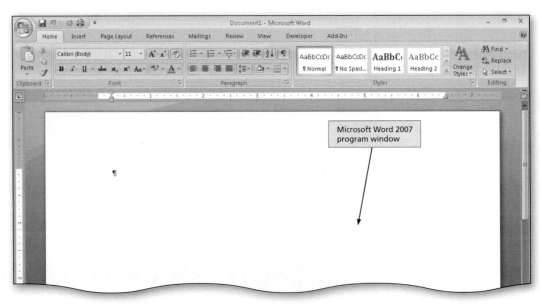

**Figure 9–81**

**2**

- Press CTRL+O to open the Open dialog box.

- Navigate to the location where your data files are stored.

- Double-click the juice_files folder to open it.

- Click the homepage_text.doc file (Figure 9–82).

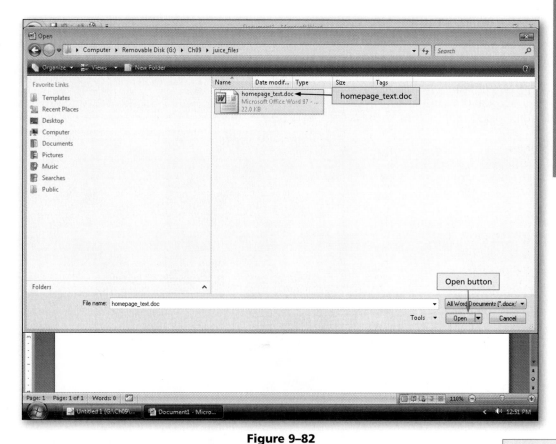

**Figure 9–82**

**3**

- Click the Open button to open the file in Word (Figure 9–83).

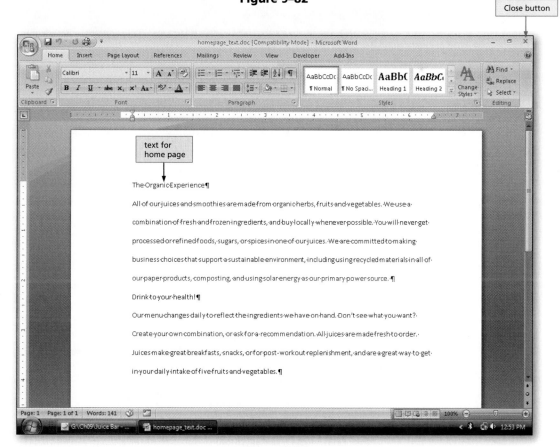

**Figure 9–83**

- Press CTRL+A to select all of the content.

- Press CTRL+C to copy the content to the Clipboard.

- Click the Close button to close the file and quit Microsoft Word.

- Click in the page_content div to position the insertion point, then select the placeholder text (Figure 9–84).

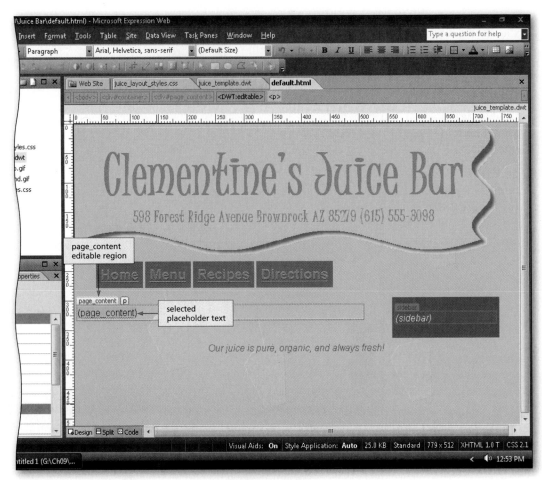

**Figure 9–84**

- Click Edit on the menu bar and then click Paste Text to open the Paste Text dialog box.

- Click Normal paragraphs without line breaks (Figure 9–85).

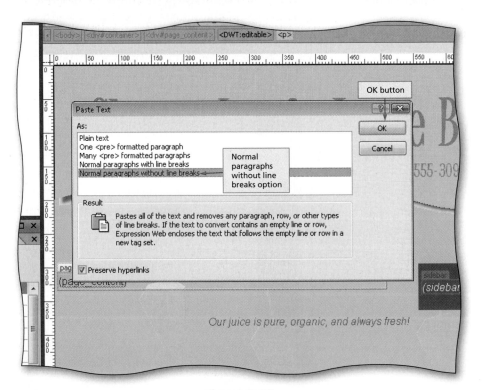

**Figure 9–85**

**6**
- Click the OK button to insert the text (Figure 9–86).

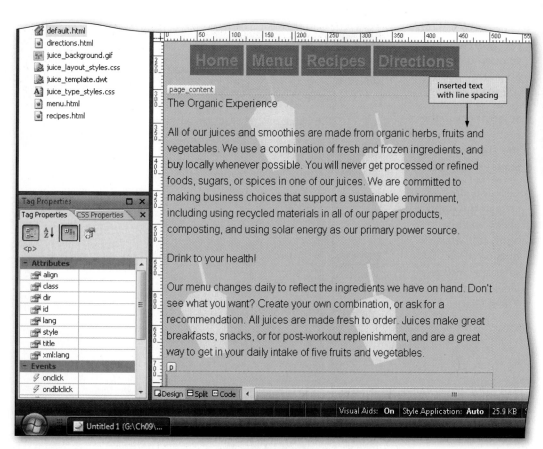

**Figure 9–86**

**7**
- Click in the words, The Organic Experience, then click the visual aid to select the div.

- Click the Style box arrow, then click Heading 3<h3> to apply a heading level to the selected text.

- Click in the words, Drink to your health!, then click the visual aid to select the div.

- Click the Style box arrow, then click Heading 3<h3> to apply a heading level to the text (Figure 9–87).

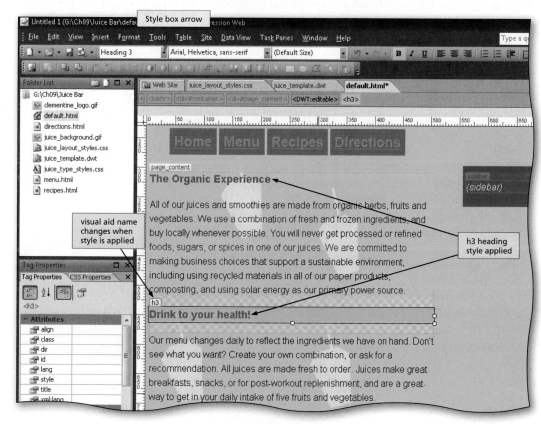

**Figure 9–87**

- Click Apply Styles on the Task Panes menu to open the Apply Styles task pane, if necessary.

- Select the A in the first word, All, under the The Organic Experience heading.

- Click the .dropcap style in the Apply Styles text box to apply it, then click outside of the selected word to view the drop cap effect (Figure 9–88).

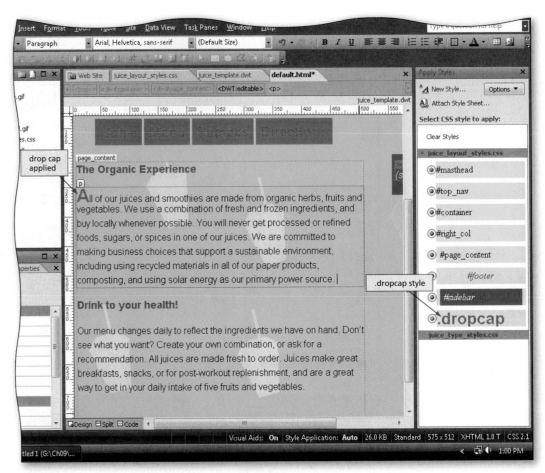

**Figure 9–88**

- Repeat Step 8 to apply the .dropcap style to the O in the word, Our, under the Drink to your health! heading (Figure 9–89).

### Experiment

- Apply the drop cap style to the first word in each paragraph to see the effect. When you are done, press CTRL+Z to undo the changes until your page matches the chapter example.

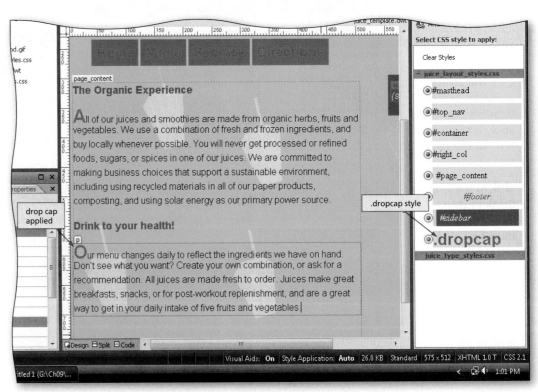

**Figure 9–89**

- Scroll to the right if necessary to view the sidebar.

- Click in the sidebar div to position the insertion point, then select the placeholder text (Figure 9–90).

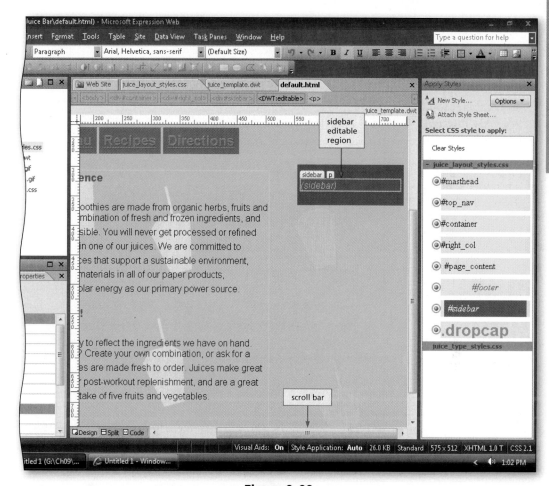

**Figure 9–90**

11
- Type Enjoy 10% off of all orders on Saturday, March 21, to celebrate our third birthday! in the sidebar div (Figure 9–91).

- Click Save All on the File menu to save changes to all pages and style sheets at once, then click the OK button to save the embedded style sheets if necessary.

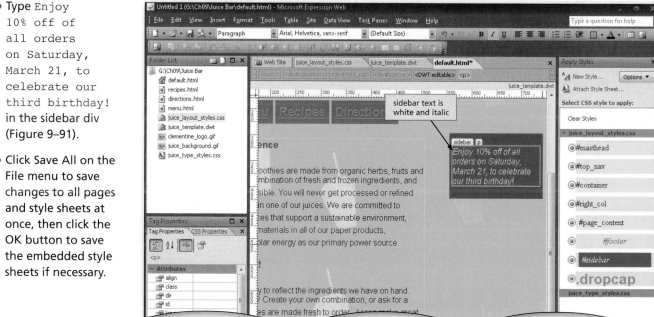

**Figure 9–91**

## To Preview a Web Page in a Browser

The following steps preview the default.html page in a browser.

**1**

- Click the Preview in Browser button arrow, then click Windows Internet Explorer 7.0 (800 × 600) to open the page in a browser window (Figure 9–92).

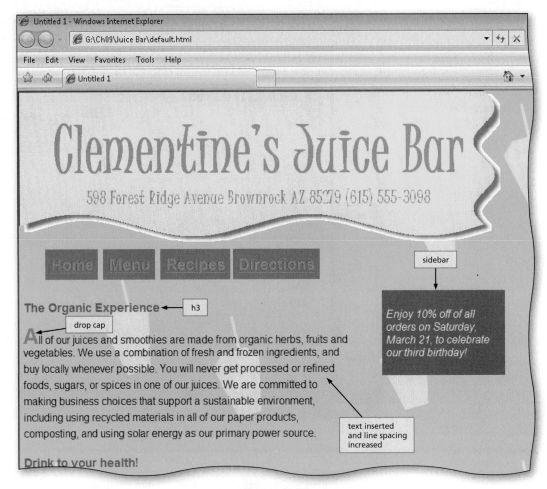

**Figure 9–92**

**2**

- Scroll to view the footer (Figure 9–93).

- Click the Close button to close the browser window.

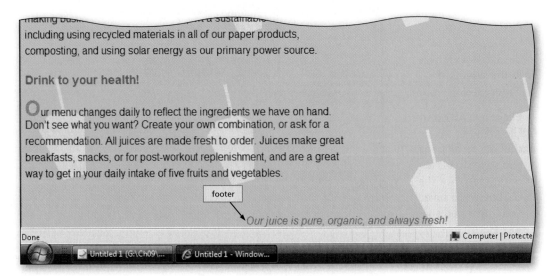

**Figure 9–93**

## To Close a Site and Quit Expression Web

**1** On the File menu, click Close Site.

**2** On the File menu, click Exit.

# Chapter Summary

In this chapter, you expanded on your CSS skills by creating and modifying ID-based elements such as sidebars, and creating class-based CSS rules for drop caps. You imported image and CSS files into your site folder for use in the new site you built. After creating a bulleted list, you learned to convert it into a navigation list and modify the list, hyperlink, and hover properties using descendent selectors to create a list-based navigation area with rollovers. When your page was complete, you converted it to a dynamic Web template, to which you added editable regions, then applied the template to other site pages to create a consistent, easy-to-update site.

The items listed below include all the new Expression Web skills you have learned in this chapter.

1. Create a New Web Site and Add Web Pages (EW 551)
2. Create a New Dynamic Web Template (EW 554)
3. Import Files into a Site (EW 556)
4. Add a Background Image to a Page (EW 558)
5. Add Page Content (EW 561)
6. Create a List-Based Navigation Area (EW 569)
7. Add CSS Rules to the List (EW 571)
8. Create Rollovers (EW 574)
9. Add a Sidebar Element (EW 580)
10. Specify Line Height (EW 584)
11. Specify Line Length (EW 586)
12. Add a Drop Cap Style (EW 589)
13. Define Editable Regions (EW 590)
14. Attach a Dynamic Web Template to Existing Pages (EW 592)
15. Insert and Format Home Page Text (EW 594)
16. Preview a Web Page in a Browser (EW 600)

 If you have a SAM user profile, you may have access to hands-on instruction, practice, and assessment. Log in to your SAM account (http://sam2007.course.com) to launch any assigned training activities or exams that relate to the skills covered in this chapter.

# Learn It Online

Test your knowledge of chapter content and key terms.

*Instructions:* To complete the Learn It Online exercises, start your browser, click the Address bar, and then enter the Web address `scsite.com/ew2/learn`. When the Expression Web Learn It Online page is displayed, click the link for the exercise you want to complete and then read the instructions.

### Chapter Reinforcement TF, MC, and SA
A series of true/false, multiple choice, and short answer questions that test your knowledge of the chapter content.

### Flash Cards
An interactive learning environment where you identify chapter key terms associated with displayed definitions.

### Practice Test
A series of multiple choice questions that test your knowledge of chapter content and key terms.

### Who Wants To Be a Computer Genius?
An interactive game that challenges your knowledge of chapter content in the style of a television quiz show.

### Wheel of Terms
An interactive game that challenges your knowledge of chapter key terms in the style of the television show *Wheel of Fortune*.

### Crossword Puzzle Challenge
A crossword puzzle that challenges your knowledge of key terms presented in the chapter.

# Apply Your Knowledge

Reinforce the skills and apply the concepts you learned in this chapter.

### Creating a Rare Books Store Dynamic Web Template
*Instructions:* Start Expression Web. You will create a new one-page Web site, modify it, and save it as a dynamic Web template, as shown in Figure 9–94. You will add a background image, a list-based navigation area, and ID-based styles. You will specify typography settings, including line height and a drop cap, then save the page as a dynamic Web template and apply it to other site pages.

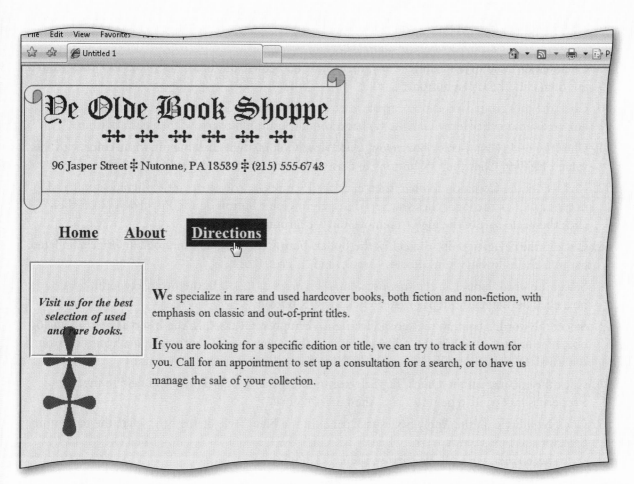

**Figure 9–94**

*Perform the following tasks:*

1. Point to New on the File menu, click Web Site, then click One Page Web Site.

2. Navigate to the drive and folder where you save your data files, type Apply 9-1 Bookshop in the Specify the location of the new Web site text box, then click the OK button.

3. Point to New on the File menu, then click Page. In the New dialog box, click CSS Layouts, click the first Header, nav, 2 columns, footer option (with the narrow column on the left side of the page), then click the OK button.

4. Save the new page as bookshop_template.dwt and the new CSS as bookshop_styles.css.

5. Point to Import on the File menu, then click File. In the Import dialog box, click the Add File button.

6. In the Add File to Import List dialog box, navigate to the data files, then double-click the bookshop_files folder. Press and hold CTRL, click each file to select both, click the Open button, then click the OK button to close all dialog boxes and embed the image files.

7. Click in the masthead to position the insertion point. Click Picture on the Insert menu, click From File, click the bookshop_logo file from the site folder, then click the Insert button. In the Accessibility Properties dialog box, type Ye Olde Book Shoppe logo, then click the OK button.

8. Click the <body> tag on the Quick Tag Selector, click the body style button arrow in the Apply Styles task pane, then click Modify Style. (*Hint:* Click Reset Workspace Layout on the Task Panes menu if necessary to open the necessary task panes.)

*Continued >*

*Apply Your Knowledge continued*

9. Click Background in the Category list, then click the Browse button. Click bookshop_background.gif, then click the Open button.

10. Click the background-repeat box arrow, then click no-repeat. Click the (x) background-position box arrow, then click left. Click the (y) background-position box arrow, then click bottom.

11. Click the background-color box arrow, click More Colors, then click the off-white color with the value FF,FF,99. Click the OK buttons to close the More Colors and Modify Style dialog boxes.

12. Right-click the Common toolbar, then click the Pictures button to open the Pictures toolbar if necessary. Click the logo, click the Set Transparent Color button on the Pictures toolbar, then click the white part of the logo to remove the background.

13. Click in the navigation div, then click the Bullets button on the Common toolbar. Type a bulleted list with the following items: Home, About, and Directions.

14. Select the word, Home, in the first list item, then press CTRL+K. In the Insert Hyperlink dialog box, click the default.html page, then click the OK button.

15. Select the word, About, in the second list item, then press CTRL+K. In the Insert Hyperlink dialog box, type about.html in the Address text box, then click the OK button. Add a hyperlink from the word, Directions, to directions.html. (*Hint:* You will create these pages later.)

16. Click the <ul> tag on the Quick Tag Selector to select the list. Click in the id field in the Tag Properties task pane, type navlist, then press ENTER.

17. Click New Style on the Apply Styles task pane. In the New Style dialog box, select the text in the Selector text box, then type #navlist li. Click the Define in box arrow, then click Existing style sheet. Click the URL box arrow, then click bookshop_styles.css.

18. Click Layout in the Category list, click the display box arrow, then click inline to make the list items appear on one line. Click List in the Category list, click the list-style-type box arrow, then click none to indicate that no bullets will separate the list items. Click the OK button to close the dialog box, then use the SPACEBAR to add spaces between each item.

19. Open the New Style dialog box, select the text in the Selector text box, then type #navlist a in the Selector text box to create a style that adds spaces around the list items. In the Box category, type 8 in the padding and margin top text boxes, then click the OK button.

20. Open the New Style dialog box, select the text in the Selector text box, then type #navlist a:link in the Selector text box to create a style that specifies the font and background of each list item. Click the font-size box arrow, click x-large, click the font-weight box arrow, then click bold. Click the color box arrow, then click More Colors. Click the brown hexagon on the bottom row with the value 66,33,00, then click the OK button in the More Colors and New Style dialog boxes.

21. Open the New Style dialog box, select the text in the Selector text box, then type #navlist a:hover in the Selector text box. Click the font-size box arrow, click x-large, click the font-weight box arrow, then click bold. Click the color box arrow, then click More Colors. Click the hexagon with the value FF,FF,99, then click the OK button. In the Background category, click the background-color box arrow, then click More Colors. Click the hexagon with the value 66,33,00, then click the OK button in the More Colors and New Style dialog boxes.

22. Click the bookshop_styles.css page tab to display it. Click at the end of the line, #navlist a:link (*Hint:* click before the brace, { ). Type #navlist a:visited.

23. In the template page, click in the left_col div. Double-click div in the Toolbox. Click in the id text box in the Tag Properties task pane, type sidebar, then press ENTER.

24. Open the New Style dialog box, select the text in the Selector text box, then type #sidebar in the Selector text box to create a style for the sidebar element. Click the font-size box arrow, click large, click the font-weight box arrow, then click bold. Click the font-style box arrow, then click

italic. Click the color box arrow, then click More Colors. Click the hexagon with the value 66,33,00, then click the OK button. In the Block category, click the text-align box arrow, then click center. In the Border category, click the border-style top box arrow, then click groove. In the Box category, type 6 in the padding top text box, type 12 in the margin top text box, then click the OK button.

25. Click the #page_content style button arrow, then click Modify Style. Click the font-size box arrow, then click large. Click the color box arrow, then click More Colors. Click the hexagon with the value 66,33,00. In the Block category, type 150 in the line-height text box. Click the line-height Measurements box arrow, then click %. Click the OK button to close the Modify Style dialog box.

26. Open the New Style dialog box, then type dropcap in the Selector text box. Click the font-size box arrow, then click x-large. Click the font-weight box arrow, then click bold. Click the OK button in the New Style box to close it.

27. Click in the footer div, then click the #footer tag to select it. Press DELETE to remove the footer.

28. Click in the page content div. Position the pointer over the right sizing handle, then drag to the right until the width is 600 pixels.

29. Click Save All on the File menu. Preview the page in a browser window, then close the browser window.

30. Right-click the page_content div, then click Manage Editable Regions. In the Editable Regions dialog box, type page_content in the Region name text box, then click the Add button. Click the Close button.

31. Repeat Step 30 to mark the sidebar div as an editable region. Save the template.

32. Open the default.html page. Point to Dynamic Web Template on the Format menu, then click Attach Dynamic Web Template. In the Attach Dynamic Web Template dialog box, click the bookshop.dwt, then click the Open button.

33. Click in the sidebar, then type Visit us for the best selection of used and rare books.

34. Click in the page_content div, then type We specialize in rare and used hardcover books, both fiction and non-fiction, with emphasis on classic and out-of-print titles.

   If you are looking for a specific edition or title, we can try to track it down for you. Call for an appointment to set up a consultation for a search, or to have us manage the sale of your collection.

35. Apply the .dropcap style to the first letter in each of the two paragraphs.

36. Point to New on the File menu, then click Create from Dynamic Web Template. In the Attach Dynamic Web Template dialog box, click the bookshop_template.dwt, then click the Open button. Save the page as about.html. Create another new page, directions.html, based on bookshop_template.dwt.

37. Change the site properties, as specified by your instructor. Submit the revised site in the format specified by your instructor. Save all pages, then close the site.

## Extend Your Knowledge

Extend the skills you learned in this chapter and experiment with new skills. You may need to use Help to complete the assignment.

### Creating a Craft Web Site Template

*Instructions:* Start Expression Web. You will create a new one-page Web site, modify it, and save it as a dynamic Web template, as shown in Figure 9–95. You will add a background image, a list-based navigation area, and id-based styles. You will create a rollover style for the navigation links that uses images. You will specify typography settings, including line height and a drop cap, then save the page as a dynamic Web template and apply it to other site pages.

**Figure 9–95**

*Perform the following tasks:*

1. Point to New on the File menu, click Web Site, then click One Page Web Site.

2. Navigate to the drive and folder where you save your data files, type `Extend 9-1 My Girl` in the Specify the location of the new Web site text box, then click the OK button.

3. Point to New on the File menu, then click Page. In the New dialog box, click CSS Layouts, click the first Header, nav 1, one column, footer option, then click the OK button. Save the new page as mygirl_template.dwt and the new CSS as mygirl_layout_styles.css.

4. Point to Import on the File menu, then click File. In the Import dialog box, click the Add File button.

5. In the Add File to Import List dialog box, navigate to the Data Files, then double-click the mygirl_files folder. Select all image files (*Hint:* Do not select the mygirl_homepage.doc file.), click the Open button, then click the OK button to close the dialog box and embed the image files.

6. Click in the masthead to position the insertion point, then drag the mygirl_logo file from the Folder List to the masthead. In the Accessibility Properties dialog box, type `My Girl Custom and Unique Accessories and Clothing logo`, then click the OK button.

7. Click the #page-content button arrow in the Apply Styles task pane, then click Modify Style. Click the font-size box arrow, then click large. In the Block category, type `150` in the line-height text box, click the line-height Measurements box arrow, then click %.

8. Click Background in the Category list, then click the Browse button next to the background-image text box. Click mygirl_background.gif, then click the Open button. Click the background-repeat box arrow, then click repeat. Click the OK button to close the Modify Style dialog box.

9. Click in the navigation div, then click the Bullets button on the Common toolbar. Type a bulleted list with the following items: `Home`, `Bows`, `Headbands`, and `Clothing`.

10. Select the word, Home, in the first list item, then press CTRL+K. In the Insert Hyperlink dialog box, click the default.html page, then click the OK button.

11. Select the word, Bows, in the second list item, then press CTRL+K. In the Insert Hyperlink dialog box, type `bows.html` in the Address text box, then click the OK button. Add a hyperlink from the word, Headbands, to headbands.html, and the word, Clothing, to clothing.html.

12. Click the <ul> tag on the Quick Tag Selector to select the list. Click in the id field in the Tag Properties task pane, type `navlist`, then press ENTER.

13. Click New Style on the Apply Styles task pane. In the New Style dialog box, select the text in the Selector text box, then type `#navlist li`. Click the Define in box arrow, then click Existing style sheet. Click the URL box arrow, then click mygirl_layout _styles.css.

14. Click Layout in the Category list, click the display box arrow, then click inline. Click List in the Category list, click the list-style-type box arrow, then click none. Click the OK button to close the dialog box, then use the SPACEBAR to add spaces between each item.

15. Open the New Style dialog box, select the text in the Selector text box, then type `#navlist a`. In the Box category, type `24` in the padding top text box, then click the OK button.

16. Open the New Style dialog box, select the text in the Selector text box then type `#navlist a:link`. Click the font-size box arrow, click xx-large, click the font-weight box arrow, then click bold. Click the color box arrow, then click More Colors. Click the hexagon with the value FF,66,99, then click the OK buttons to close the More Colors and New Style dialog boxes.

17. Click the mygirl_layout_styles.css page tab to display it. Click at the end of the line, #navlist a:link (*Hint:* Click before the brace, { ). Type `, #navlist a:visited`.

18. Click at the end of the style sheet code, press ENTER, then use a combination of typing and the shortcut menus to create the rule:

```
#navlist a:hover {
font-size: xx-large;
color: white;
font-weight: bold;
background-image:url('bow_rollover.jpg')
}
```

19. Save all open pages at once, then click the mygirl_template.dwt page tab.

*Continued >*

**Extend Your Knowledge** *continued*

20. Open the New Style dialog box, then type `dropcap` in the Selector text box. Click the font-size box arrow, then click x-large. Click the font-weight box arrow, then click bold. Click the OK button in the New Style dialog box to close it.

21. Click in the footer div, then type `My Girl donates 5% of every sale to Cradles to Crayons.` Select the words, Cradles to Crayons. Press CTRL+K, type `http://cradlestocrayons.org` in the Address text box, then click the OK button.

22. Click the #footer button arrow in the Apply Styles task pane, then click Modify Style. Click the font-size box arrow, then click large. Click the font-style list arrow, then click italic. Click the color box arrow, then click More Colors. Click the hexagon with the value FF,66,99, then click the OK buttons to close the More Colors and Modify Style dialog boxes.

23. Click in the page content div. Position the pointer over the right sizing handle, then drag to the left until the width is 775 pixels.

24. Preview the page in a browser window and test the rollovers.

25. Right-click the page_content div, then click Manage Editable Regions. In the Editable Regions dialog box, type `page_content` in the Region name text box, then click the Add button. Click the Close button, then save all open pages.

26. Open the default.html page. Point to Dynamic Web Template on the Format menu, then click Attach Dynamic Web Template. In the Attach Dynamic Web Template dialog box, click the mygirl_template.dwt, then click the Open button.

27. Click the Start button on the task bar, point to All Programs, click Microsoft Office, then click Microsoft Office Word 2007. Press CTRL+O to open the Open dialog box, then navigate to the Data Files. Double-click the mygirl_files folder. Click the mygirl_homepage.doc file. Click the Open button. Press CTRL+A, then press CTRL+C. Click the Close button to close the file and quit Microsoft Word.

28. Click in the #page_content div. Click Edit on the menu bar and then click to Paste Text to open the Paste Text dialog box. Click Normal paragraphs with line breaks, then click the OK button to insert the text.

29. Click in the words, Welcome to My Girl, then click the visual aid. Click the Style box arrow, then click heading 2. Apply the heading 2 style to the words, Shipping Information.

30. Apply the .dropcap style to the first letters in each of the paragraphs.

31. Point to New on the File menu, then click Create from Dynamic Web Template. In the Attach Dynamic Web Template dialog box, click the mygirl_template.dwt, then click the Open button. Save the page as bows.html. Create two other new pages, headbands.html and clothing.html, based on mygirl_template.dwt.

32. Change the site properties, as specified by your instructor. Submit the revised site in the format specified by your instructor. Save all pages, then close the site.

## Make It Right

Analyze a site and correct all errors and/or improve the design.

### Modifying and Attaching a Dynamic Web Template

*Instructions:* Start Expression Web. Open the Web site, Make It Right 9-1 Photo, from the Data Files for Students. See the inside back cover of this book for instructions for downloading the Data Files for Students, or see your instructor for information about accessing the required files. You will fix a template by adding list-based navigation and typography, then attach it to create the page shown in Figure 9–96.

**Figure 9–96**

*Perform the following tasks:*

1. Open the photo_template.dwt.

2. Click in the navigation div. Select the word, Home, in the first list item, then press CTRL+K. In the Insert Hyperlink dialog box, click the default.html page, then click the OK button.

3. Select the word, Background, in the second list item, then press CTRL+K. In the Insert Hyperlink dialog box, type `background.html` in the Address text box, then click the OK button. Add a hyperlink from the word, References, to references.html and a hyperlink from the word, Gallery, to gallery.html.

4. Click the <ul> tag on the Quick Tag Selector to select the list. Click in the id field in the Tag Properties task pane, type `navlist`, then press ENTER.

5. Click New Style on the Apply Styles task pane. In the New Style dialog box, select the text in the Selector text box, then type `#navlist li`. Click the Define in box arrow, then click Existing style sheet. Click the URL box arrow, then click photo_styles.css.

6. Click Layout in the Category list, click the display box arrow, then click inline. Click List in the Category list, click the list-style-type box arrow, then click none. Click the OK button to close the dialog box, then use the SPACEBAR to add spaces between each item.

7. Open the New Style dialog box, select the text in the Selector text box, then type `#navlist a`. In the Box category, type `12` in the padding and margin top text boxes, then click the OK button.

8. Open the New Style dialog box, select the text in the Selector text box, then type `#navlist a:link`. Click the font-size box arrow, then click x-large. Click the font-weight box arrow, then click bold. Click the color box arrow, then click Black. In the Background category, click the background-color box arrow, then click White. Click the OK button.

9. Open the New Style dialog box, select the text in the Selector text box, then type `#navlist a:hover`. Click the font-size box arrow, click x-large, click the font-weight box arrow, then click bold. Click the color box arrow, then click White. In the Background category, click the background-color box arrow, then click Black. Click the OK button.

*Continued >*

**Make It Right** *continued*

10. Click the Photo_styles.css page tab to display it. Click at the end of the line, #navlist a:link (*Hint:* Click before the brace, { ). Type, `#navlist a:visited`.

11. Click the #page_content style button arrow, then click Modify Style. Click the font-size box arrow, then click large. In the Block category, type `150` in the line-height text box, click the line-height Measurements box arrow, then click %. In the Box category, type `6` in the padding top text box, type `24` in the margin top text box, then click the OK button.

12. Open the New Style dialog box, then type `dropcap` in the Selector text box. Click the font-size box arrow, then click xx-large. Click the font-weight box arrow, then click bold. Click the OK button in the New Style dialog box to close it.

13. Right-click the page_content div, then click Manage Editable Regions. In the Editable Regions dialog box, type `page_content` in the Region name text box, then click the Add button. Click the Close button

14. Repeat step 13 to mark the sidebar div as an editable region.

15. Save all pages, then preview the page in a browser window.

16. Open the default.html page. Point to Dynamic Web Template on the Format menu, then click Attach Dynamic Web Template. In the Attach Dynamic Web Template dialog box, click the photo_template.dwt, then click the Open button.

17. Click in the sidebar, then type `In the month of December, all sitting fees for family portraits will be donated to the Toys for Tots program.`

18. Click in the page content div, then type `Quiet moments, small miracles, and nature's beauty. Those are the images that move me. No subject is too small to be captured by a camera and made into a work of art. Contact me to see more of my work.`

    `Mike Johnston`

    `(214) 555-9067`

19. Apply the .dropcap style to the Q in the first paragraph.

20. Add a mailto: link from the words, Contact me, to mike@mikesphotosonline.biz.

21. Point to New on the File menu, then click Create from Dynamic Web Template. In the Attach Dynamic Web Template dialog box, click the photo_template.dwt, then click the Open button. Save the page as background.html. Create two more new pages, references.html and gallery.html, based on photo_template.dwt.

22. Change the site properties, as specified by your instructor. Submit the revised site in the format specified by your instructor. Save all pages, then close the site.

## In the Lab

Design and/or format a Web site using the guidelines, concepts, and skills presented in this chapter. Labs are listed in order of increasing difficulty.

### Lab 1: Create a Template from an Existing Page

*Problem:* You are working on a Web site for you client, a band. You will create a template based on one of the pages, then use CSS rules to modify the template page. You will define the editable regions, then attach the template to the default.html page to create the page shown in Figure 9–97.

**Figure 9–97**

*Instructions:*

1. Start Expression Web, then open the Web site Lab 9-1 Band from the Data Files.

2. Open the band_template.html page. Click the body tag on the Quick Tag Selector. Open the Modify Style dialog box for the body style.

3. Modify the body style by changing the font-family to Arial, Helvetica, sans-serif; the font-size to large. Click in the background-color text box, type #CFCF9E to specify a custom background color; then close the Modify Style dialog box.

4. Open the Modify Style dialog box for the #page-content style. In the Block category, change the line-height to 150%. In the Box category, change the padding and margins to 10 pixels each. Close the Modify Style dialog box.

5. In the navigation div, add a hyperlink from the word, Home, in the first list item, to the default. html page. Add a hyperlink from the word, Gigs, to gigs.html, and the word, Music, to music.html.

6. Select the entire list. Change the id field in the Tag Properties task pane to navlist.

7. Open the New Style dialog box and create a new style called #navlist li. Save it to the band_styles.css style sheet. In the Layout category, change the display to click inline. In the List category change the list-style-type to none. Close the dialog box, then use the SPACEBAR to add spaces between each item.

8. Open the New Style dialog box and create a new style called #navlist a. In the Box category, change the padding and margin to 10, then click the OK button.

9. Open the New Style dialog box and create a new style called #navlist a:link. Change the font-size to x-large. To specify the font color, open the More Colors dialog box. Click the hexagon with the value 99,CC,FF. In the Background category, specify the background as black, then close the New Style dialog box.

*Continued >*

**In the Lab** *continued*

10. Open the band_styles.css. Click at the end of the line, #navlist a:link (*Hint:* Click before the brace, { }). Type `#navlist a:visited`.

11. Open the New Style dialog box and create a new style called #navlist a:hover. Change the font-size to x-large. Specify the font-color as black. In the Background category, open the More Colors dialog box. Click the hexagon with the value 99,CC,FF, then close the New Style dialog box.

12. Modify the footer style so that it is bold and centered.

13. Save the file as band_template.dwt.

14. Specify that the page_content div is an editable region.

15. Attach the band_template.dwt to the default.html page.

16. Type `We are excited to be opening the Saturday Showcase Concert at the fourth annual Oxbow Music Festival. We'll be playing songs from our new album.` in the page_content div on the default.html page.

17. Create two new pages, gigs.html and music.html, based on band_template.dwt.

18. Change the site properties, as specified by your instructor. Submit the revised site in the format specified by your instructor. Save all pages, then close the site.

## In the Lab

### Lab 2: Create a Travel Agency Template

*Problem:* Your client, a travel agency, has asked you to create a template for its new site. You will create a new template file, then use CSS rules to format and create the template page. You will define the editable regions, then attach the template to the default.html page to create the page shown in Figure 9–98.

**Figure 9–98**

*Instructions:*

1. Start Expression Web, then create a new one-page Web site called Lab 9-2 Travel.

2. Add a new page with the CSS Layout, Header, nav, one column, footer. Save the new page as travel_template.dwt and the new CSS as travel _styles.css.

3. Open the Import dialog box, then click the Add File button. In the Add File to Import List dialog box, navigate to the data files, then open the travel_files folder. Select all files, then close the dialog boxes.

4. Insert the travel_logo file into the masthead. In the Accessibility Properties dialog box, type `Alpine Travel logo`, then click close the dialog box.

5. Display the Pictures toolbar, if necessary. Select the logo, click the Set Transparent Color button on the Pictures toolbar, and click the light blue outside logo area to make it transparent.

6. Open the Modify Style dialog box for the #page-content style. Change the font-size to large and the color to the hexagon with the value 33,66,99. In the Block category, change the line-height to 150 %. In the Box category, change the padding and margins to 12 pixels. Close the Modify Style dialog box.

7. Display the travel_styles.css page. Under the gray text, /*CSS Layout*/, add the following style for the body by typing and using prompts:

```
body {
    background-image: url('travel_background.gif');
    background-repeat: repeat;
}
```

8. In the navigation div, type a bulleted list with the following items: `Home`, `Ski`, `Snowboard`, and `Winter Wonderland`.

9. Add a hyperlink from the word, Home, in the first list item to the default.html page. Add a hyperlink from the word, Ski, to ski.html; from the word, Snowboard, to snowboard.html; and the words, Winter Wonderland, to wonderland.html.

10. Select the entire list. Change the id field in the Tag Properties task pane to navlist.

11. Open the New Style dialog box and create a new style called #navlist li. Save it to the travel_styles.css style sheet. In the Layout category, change the display to click inline. In the List category, change the list-style-type to none. Close the dialog box, then use the SPACEBAR to add spaces between each item.

12. Open the New Style dialog box and create a new style called #navlist a. In the Box category, change the padding and margin to 12, then click the OK button.

13. Open the New Style dialog box and create a new style called #navlist a:link. Change the font-size to xx-large, then change the font-weight to bold. To specify the font color, open the More Colors dialog box. Click the hexagon with the value 33,66,99. In the Background category, specify the background as white, then click the OK button.

14. Open the travel_styles.css. Click at the end of the line, #navlist a:link (*Hint:* Click before the brace, {}). Type #navlist a:visited.

15. Open the New Style dialog box and create a new style called #navlist a:hover. Change the font-size to xx-large, then change the font-weight to bold. Specify the font-color as white. In the Background category, choose the color with the value 33,66,99.

16. Click in the page content div. Use the right sizing handle to change the width to 800 pixels. Change the footer to 800 pixels wide as well.

*Continued >*

**In the Lab** *continued*

17. Click in the footer div, then type

    ```
    Alpine Travel
    Horizon, MT 59632
    (406) 555-SNOW
    ```

18. Modify the footer style so that it is bold, centered, and the font color has the value 33,66,99.

19. Specify that the page_content div is an editable region.

20. Attach the travel_template.dwt to the default.html page.

21. Type `Welcome to Alpine Travel. We specialize in getaway packages for the snow adventurer. Travel, accommodations, car and equipment rentals, dining, lessons, and more!` in the page_content div on the default.html page.

22. Create three new pages, ski.html, snowboard.html, and wonderland.html, based on travel_template.dwt.

23. Change the site properties, as specified by your instructor. Submit the revised site in the format specified by your instructor. Save all pages, then close the site.

# In the Lab

## Lab 3: Create a Template for an Editor

*Problem:* You have a business providing freelance editorial services to local businesses and publishers. You will create a new template file, then use CSS rules to format and create the template page using ID-based and class-based styles. You will define the editable regions, then attach the template to the default.html page to create the page shown in Figure 9–99.

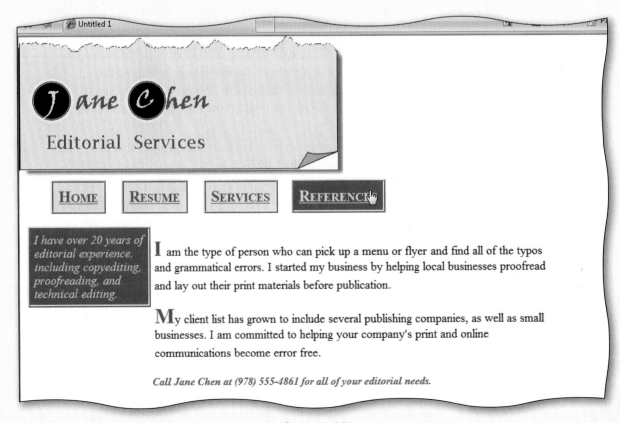

**Figure 9–99**

*Instructions:*

1. Start Expression Web, then create a new one-page Web site called Lab 9-3 Editor.

2. Add a new page with the CSS Layout, Header, nav, 2 columns, footer (with the narrow column on the left side of the page). Save the new page as editor_template.dwt and the new CSS as editor_styles.css.

3. Import the file editor_logo.gif from the editor_files folder in the Data Files.

4. Insert the editor_logo file into the masthead. In the Accessibility Properties dialog box, type `Jane Chen Editorial Services logo`, then close the dialog box.

5. Open the Modify Style dialog box for the #page-content style. Change the font-size to large. In the Block category, change the line-height to 150 %. In the Box category, change the padding to 8 and the top margin to 24 pixels. Close the Modify Style dialog box.

6. In the navigation div, type a bulleted list with the following items: `Home`, `Resume`, `Services`, and `References`.

7. Add a hyperlink from the word, Home, in the first list item to the default.html page. Add a hyperlink from the word, Resume, to resume.html; from the word, Services, to services.html; and the word, References, to references.html.

8. Select the entire list. Change the id field in the Tag Properties task pane to navlist.

9. Open the New Style dialog box and create a new style called #navlist li. Save it to the editor_styles.css style sheet. In the Layout category, change the display to inline. In the List category, change the list-style-type to none. Close the dialog box, then use the SPACEBAR to add spaces between each item.

10. Open the New Style dialog box and create a new style called #navlist a. In the Box category, change the padding and margin to 8, then click the OK button.

11. Open the New Style dialog box and create a new style called #navlist a:link. Change the font-size to x-large, change the font-weight to bold, then change the font-variant to small-caps. Change the font color to teal. In the Border category, change the border to ridge. In the Background category, specify the background-color by opening the More Colors dialog box. Click the hexagon with the value FF,FF,99, then close the dialog boxes.

12. Open the editor_styles.css. Click at the end of the line, #navlist a:link (*Hint:* Click before the brace, { }). Type `, #navlist a:visited` (*Hint:* be sure to type a comma between the style names to separate them.).

13. In the editor_styles.css, copy the style for #navlist a:link, click at the end of the style code, then paste it. (*Hint:* Select everything from the style name to the end brace.) Change the style name from #navlist a:link, #navlist a:visited to `#navlist a:hover`. Select the color value, 00,80,80, then type `#FFFF99`. Select the background-color value, FF,FF,99, then type `teal`.

14. Add a new div in the left_col div. Change the id field in the Tag Properties task pane to sidebar.

15. Open the New Style dialog box and create style called `#sidebar`. Change the font-size to large, then change the font-style to italic. Specify the font color as having a value of FF,FF,99. In the Background category, change the background-color to teal.

16. In the Border category, change the border to ridge. In the Box category, type 6 in the padding top text box, then type 12 in the margin top text box.

17. Click in the footer div, then type `Call Jane Chen at (978) 555-4861 for all of your editorial needs.`

18. Modify the footer style so that it is bold, italic, and the font color is teal. In the Block category, specify the text-align as center. In the Box category, add 12 pixels of margin space to the top.

*Continued >*

**In the Lab** *continued*

19. Drag the sizing handles to adjust the page_content div to 600 px wide, the footer to 815 pixels wide, and the sidebar to 170 pixels wide.

20. Add a new style for a drop cap that uses xx-large font size, has a bold font-weight, and is teal.

21. Specify that the page_content div and sidebar are editable regions.

22. Attach the editor_template.dwt to the default.html page.

23. Type `I am the type of person who can pick up a menu or flyer and find all of the typos and grammatical errors. I started my business by helping local businesses proofread and lay out their print materials before publication.`

    `My client list has grown to include several publishing companies, as well as small businesses. I am committed to helping your company's print and online communications become error free.` in the page_content div on the default.html page.

24. Apply the drop cap style to the first letters in each paragraph.

25. Type `I have over 20 years of editorial experience, including copyediting, proofreading, and technical editing.` in the sidebar div on the default.html page.

26. Create three new pages, resume.html, services.html, and references.html, based on editor_template.dwt.

27. Change the site properties, as specified by your instructor. Submit the revised site in the format specified by your instructor. Save all pages, then close the site.

# Cases and Places

Apply your creative thinking and problem solving skills to design and implement a solution.

**•** EASIER **••** MORE DIFFICULT

**• 1: Creating a List-Based Navigation**

Plan a new Web site for a knitting supply store by determining the number, title, and filenames for all of the pages in the site. Create a new empty Web site, then add a Web page based on a CSS layout. Save the new page as the default.html page. In the navigation area, create a bulleted list with at least three items and add hyperlinks using the planned site pages' filenames. Create an id-based style for the navigation list. Use descendent selectors to make the list appear on one line, without bullets or other separating icons. Use CSS to style the list items, hyperlink text, and hover state to create a list-based navigation area that uses rollovers.

**• 2: Converting an Existing Web Page to a Dynamic Web Template**

Open a Web site you have created in another chapter. Choose one of the site pages to save as a dynamic Web template. Before saving it as a template, modify the styles, background, and other page elements as you like. Modify the template by adding editable regions, then attach it to other site pages or add new site pages based on the template. Make at least two changes to the template, save the template, then verify that the updates were made to the other site pages.

**•• 3: Modifying a Dynamic Web Template**

Create a new, one-page Web site for a pre-owned sports equipment shop using one of Expression Web's dynamic Web templates. Open the dynamic Web template and add a drop cap style. Add a new div somewhere on the page, then define it as an editable region. Change at least two styles, such as changing the page background color or font-family, by modifying the body style. Save the changes to the template, then open the default.html page. Add text to the editable regions, then apply the drop cap style. Preview the page in a browser. Save and close the site and the browser window.

**•• 4: Using CSS to Create a Template for an Entrepreneurial Site**

**Make It Personal**

You want to design a site for a business you would like to start. You will plan a dynamic Web template for the Web site. Create logos and write text that will be imported into the site folder. Plan the names and numbers of site pages, and the layout of the pages. Create a new Web site, and add a blank page using a CSS layout. Import the files you created into the site. Create at least one id-based style and one class-based style. Add the appropriate text, images, and formatting to create the default.html page, including a list-based navigation area that includes links to the filenames of the other site pages you will add. Preview the page. Save it as a dynamic Web template and determine the editable regions. Add the rest of the site pages by creating them based on the dynamic Web template. Save and close the site.

**•• 5: Creating a Bike Messenger Company Web Site**

**Working Together**

Your client is a bike messenger company. Working as a team with several of your classmates, you are to plan and create a dynamic Web template for their Web site. Each team member should contribute to creating logos or writing text that will be imported into the site folder. As a group, plan the names and numbers of site pages, and the layout of the pages. Create a new Web site and add a blank page using a CSS layout. Import the files you created into the site. Create at least one id-based style and one class-based style. Add the appropriate text, images, and formatting to create the default.html page, including a list-based navigation area that includes links to the filenames of the other site pages you will add. Preview the page. Save it as a dynamic Web template and determine the editable regions. Add the rest of the site pages by creating them based on the dynamic Web template. Save and close the site.

## Web Site Marketing Feature

# Marketing and Maintaining a Web Site

## Objectives

You will have mastered the material in this special feature when you can:

- Identify online and offline marketing tools

- Discuss post-publishing Web site review and maintenance

- Describe site performance evaluation and Web analytics

# Introduction

You have worked hard to plan, develop, and publish your Web site, and now you are ready to reap the rewards! Whether your site is a personal, organizational, or e-commerce site, you can maximize those rewards by focusing on three ongoing tasks:

- generating visitor traffic to your site
- maintaining and, when necessary, updating site content
- evaluating your site's overall performance

Generating visitor traffic involves developing the right mix of offline and online promotional tools that can increase traffic to your site and that will fit within your budget constraints. The task of maintaining and updating your new site to keep pace with the dynamic technological environment and visitor expectations can be challenging. Two effective tools you can use to manage this task are a formal post-publishing review process and Web analytics technologies.

To help drive visitor traffic to your site, you can use a number of online tools, such as optimizing your site for search tool indexing or purchasing online ads that appear on other Web sites' pages. Additionally, you shouldn't overlook the power of traditional offline marketing tools, such as word of mouth, to promote your site and drive traffic to it.

# Online Marketing Tools

Online tools for driving traffic to a Web site abound and range from the simple and low cost, such as adding search key words and carefully written titles to your Web pages to increase accessibility by search engines, to more costly and sophisticated tools, such as participation in online advertising networks or sponsoring an affiliate marketing program. The mix of online marketing tools you choose depends on the type of site you publish and your marketing budget.

For example, a mix of low-cost online marketing tools, such as designing for search engine optimization and exchanging links with other sites, might be preferable for promoting a personal site where cost can be a major issue. An e-commerce site, however, likely has a marketing budget and can afford to supplement low-cost online marketing tools with more expensive tools, such as participation in a search engine paid placement program or purchasing online ads through an advertising network.

## Search Engine Optimization (SEO)

You are likely quite familiar with **search engines**, online tools that use robots or spiders to crawl the Web looking for Web pages to add to their indexes. Google and Live Search are examples of popular search engines. You can type specific keywords or phrases into a search engine's search text box and then click a button to search its index. The search engine then returns a list of Web pages relevant to the keywords, generally with the most likely relevant pages at or near the top of the list. For this reason, many search engine users focus on just those pages at or near the top of the list. **Search engine optimization**, or **SEO**, involves techniques you can use to make it easier for search engines to index your Web pages and to position your pages in the most desirable position in the search results list — at or near the top of the list.

Search engines use a variety of methods to index Web pages and then determine the indexed pages' relevance to specific keywords. Despite the variety and complexity of search engine methodologies, you can still follow a few common sense techniques, such as those listed below, to make it easier for a variety of search engines using different methodologies to index, describe, and list your pages.

**BTW**

**Meta and Title Tags**
Meta and title tags are located within the <head> and </head> tags on a Web page.

- use **HTML meta tags** to add keywords and a description to each of your Web pages, as shown in Figure SF 3–1
- use the **HTML title tag** to add a page title — the text that appears on the browser's title bar — that reflects the page's content, and where possible, keywords, as shown in Figure 3–1
- format page headings and subheadings with HTML heading tags (h1 through h6) and CSS styles
- add internal links on the home page for important subsidiary pages
- add a site map to summarize internal links
- write page text clearly and succinctly
- emphasize critical keywords within Web page text using bold or italic formatting

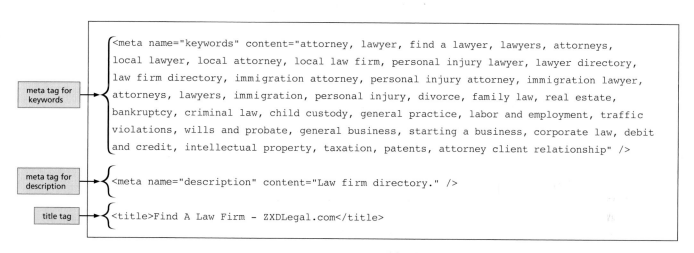

meta tag for keywords

```
<meta name="keywords" content="attorney, lawyer, find a lawyer, lawyers, attorneys,
local lawyer, local attorney, local law firm, personal injury lawyer, lawyer directory,
law firm directory, immigration attorney, personal injury attorney, immigration lawyer,
attorneys, lawyers, immigration, personal injury, divorce, family law, real estate,
bankruptcy, criminal law, child custody, general practice, labor and employment, traffic
violations, wills and probate, general business, starting a business, corporate law, debit
and credit, intellectual property, taxation, patents, attorney client relationship" />
```

meta tag for description

```
<meta name="description" content="Law firm directory." />
```

title tag

```
<title>Find A Law Firm - ZXDLegal.com</title>
```

**Figure SF 3–1**

Professional marketers specializing in online marketing often offer Web site SEO evaluation services. If you publish an e-commerce site, you might choose to hire a marketing firm that offers SEO services to help you optimize your Web pages for search engine indexing and search results placement by applying the above and other techniques. For more information about SEO techniques and examples of SEO marketing companies, visit **scsite.com/ew2/websources** and click a link under Special Feature 3, SEO.

## Search Tool Submission

Search tools include search engines, such as Google or Live Search, noted in the previous section, and **search directories**, such as Yahoo! or the DMOZ Open Directory Project. To locate a specific Web page using a directory, visitors drill down through a hierarchy of category links until they reach a list of specific pages. Unlike search engines, which create their indexes by crawling the Web and looking for new pages, a traditional directory's index is created by human editors. Today, in addition to using human editors, most directories partner with search engines to build their indexes.

Major search engines and directories also allow site owners to submit their Web site's information for inclusion in the search tools' indexes. Manually submitting your Web site's information can get your site indexed more quickly. You can take the time to visit various search tools and submit your site's information; alternatively, you can hire a marketing company that offers search tool submission services to do the work for you. Figure SF 3–2 illustrates the Live Search submission page.

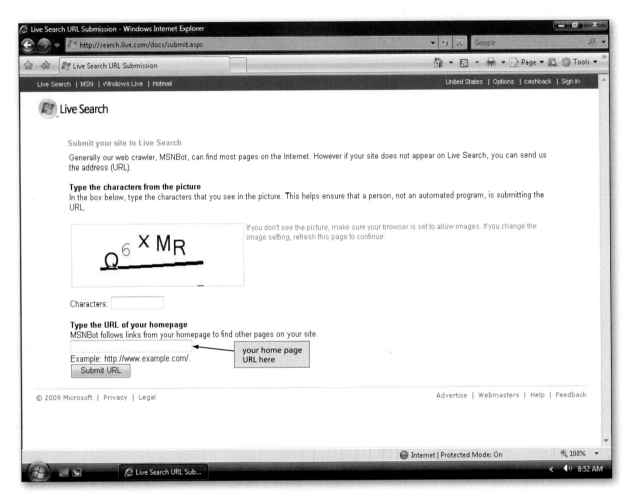

**Figure SF 3–2**

For more information about manual search tool submission, visit **scsite.com/ew2/ websources** and click a link under Special Feature 3, Search Tool Submission.

## Search Tool Paid Placement Programs

Search tool **paid placement programs**, sometimes called **sponsored listings** or **pay-per-click** programs, allow you to create online ads for your site that appear in a prominent place on a search results list page — often above or to the right of the search results list, as shown in the Figure SF 3–3.

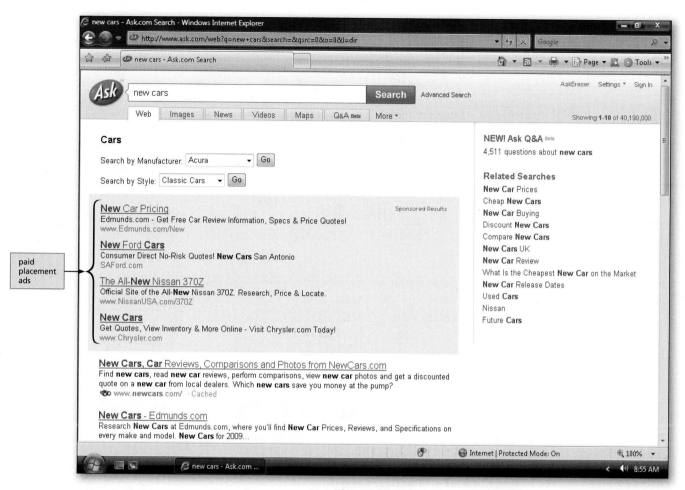

paid
placement
ads

**Figure SF 3–3**

While the details of individual paid placement programs vary, in general you sign up for a program by submitting an ad title, a brief description of your site, your URL, and a list of important keywords. The addition of your Web site ad on a search results page is triggered by a search based on one or more keywords from your keyword set. You pay a fee to the search tool each time a searcher clicks through to your Web site using the search tool ad. The Google Adwords (Figure SF 3–4), Yahoo! Sponsored Search (Figure SF 3–5), and Microsoft Search Advertising on Live Search programs are examples of paid placement programs.

**Figure SF 3–4**

**Figure SF 3–5**

For more information about search tool paid placement, visit **scsite.com/ew2/ websources** and click a link under Special Feature 3, Search Tool Paid Placement.

## Link Exchange

A free or low-cost Web site promotion option is to exchange **reciprocal links** with other Web sites. For example, a bed and breakfast site might add links to local entertainment venues and restaurants in return for those businesses adding links to the bed and breakfast site on their sites.

One option is to participate in a **link exchange program** that offers its members a wide range of reciprocal linking choices. Some link exchange programs are free to members, and some are fee based. Carefully review any link exchange program in which you might be interested to make certain that the program provides high-quality, relevant reciprocal links.

## Online Ads and Advertising Networks

In addition to search tool paid placement ads, many online businesses, called **advertisers**, purchase Web page advertising — for example, banner ads, sidebar ads, pop-up and pop-under ads, and rich media ads — to promote their Web sites.

A **banner ad** (Figure SF 3–6) is a horizontal ad in the shape of a rectangle, while a **sidebar ad** (Figure SF 3–6) is a vertical rectangular ad. Both banner and sidebar ads appear on a Web page, whereas pop-up (Figure SF 3–7) or pop-under ads open in their own window in front of or behind the open browser window. **Rich media ads**, sometimes called Flash ads (Figure SF 3–8), are multimedia ads offering eye-catching video or animation often including sound.

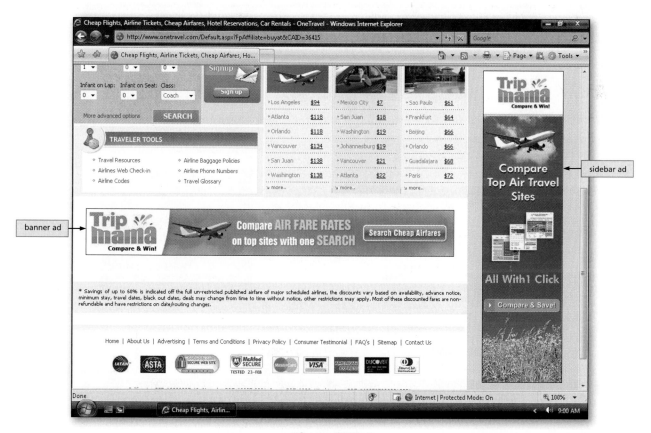

**Figure SF 3–6**

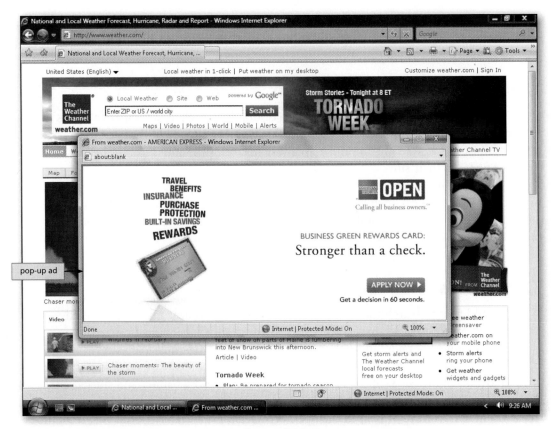

**Figure SF 3–7**

**Figure SF 3–8**

A Web site that hosts another site's online ad is called the ad's **publisher**. An **online advertising network** is a business that matches advertisers with publishers. Typically, advertisers' ads are stored on the advertising network's servers. The ads are then downloaded with the publishers' pages when the pages are requested by a visitor's browser.

Most online ads are clickable, meaning that visitors use the ads to click through to advertisers' Web sites. Online ad fees might be based, in part, on the number of ad **click-throughs** and/or on the number of **impressions**, the number of times an ad is viewed. For more information about online advertising, visit **scsite.com/ew2/websources** and click a link under Special Feature 3, Online Advertising.

## Affiliate Marketing Programs

An **affiliate marketing program** is a very popular type of online advertising program. An affiliate program drives traffic to an advertiser's Web site by paying a commission or fee to other sites, called publishers, who host affiliate program links to the advertiser's site.

When a visitor to a publisher's site clicks an affiliate program link, he or she is directed to the advertiser's site. The advertiser then pays a commission or fee to the publisher based on purchases or some other action that the visitor takes at the advertiser's site. The Amazon.com Associates program (Figure SF 3–9) is an example of a successful affiliate program. Other well-known and diverse e-commerce companies that use affiliate marketing programs to promote their Web sites include Network Solutions (domain names, Web hosting), 1-800-Flowers.com (flowers, gifts), and Edmunds.com (auto industry information).

**BTW**

**Affiliate Programs**
While an affiliate program is a marketing tool for a Web site advertiser, it is a revenue generation tool for a Web site publisher.

**Figure SF 3–9**

An **affiliate management network** is a business that brings together affiliate marketing program advertisers with willing publishers and then manages the entire process, including reviewing visitor click-throughs and handling commission or fee payments. For more information about affiliate marketing programs and affiliate management networks, visit **scsite.com/ew2/websources** and click a link under Special Feature 3, Affiliate Marketing.

## Business Blogs

A **business blog** is a chronological online diary or journal, usually published by a business's owner or a key member of a business's management team. Publishing a business blog allows a company to promote its business and Web site by discussing ideas with and soliciting feedback from customers, potential customers, and other interested parties.

For more information about business blogs, visit **scsite.com/ew2/websources** and click a link under Special Feature 3, Business Blogs.

## Permission-Based E-Mail Advertising and Newsletters

**Permission-based e-mail advertising messages** and **newsletters** can be cost-effective ways to drive traffic to your Web site and, for an e-commerce site, help you stay in touch with customers while promoting your products and services. Unsolicited e-mail, or **spam**, clogs e-mail inboxes everywhere and is very unpopular. Permission-based e-mail advertising and newsletters, also called **opt-in e-mail advertising**, is unlike spam because recipients are required to formally agree — or opt-in — to receiving the advertising e-mail messages or newsletters. Figure SF 3–10 illustrates a permission-based newsletter.

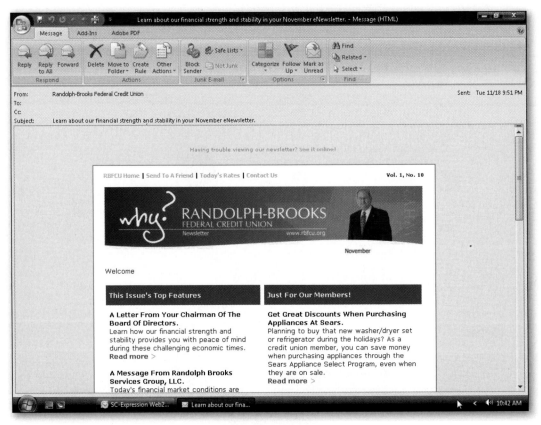

**Figure SF 3–10**

For more information about permission-based e-mail advertising, visit **scsite.com/ew2/websources** and click a link under Special Feature 3, Permission-Based E-Mail.

# Offline Print and Word-of-Mouth Advertising Tools

Print and word-of-mouth advertising can be effective offline techniques for promoting your Web site. For example, if you publish an e-commerce site and have a marketing budget, you can consider purchasing print ads in newspapers and magazines to promote your Web site. Remember to add your Web site's URL to any print materials that you publish, such as business cards, letterhead stationery, or brochures.

Do not underestimate the value of simple, old-fashioned **word-of-mouth** advertising — telling friends, family, coworkers, and other interested parties about your Web site and encouraging them to spread the word to *their* friends, family, and coworkers, and so on and so on. Word-of-mouth advertising can be a free, helpful way to drive traffic to all types of Web sites.

In addition to driving site traffic, the post-publishing work of maintaining a Web site and evaluating how well the site performs against goals and objectives is truly never finished.

# Web Site Maintenance

The Web is a dynamic environment in which information moves quickly, technologies advance rapidly, and site visitors' expectations are becoming increasingly sophisticated. To maintain a successful Web site in this environment, it is a good idea to develop a formal plan for regular post-publishing review and maintenance of your site. A post-publishing review ensures that all site features work correctly, links are not broken, content is current, and the site continues to meet visitors' needs and expectations.

You should plan to review and update your site's content, as necessary, to keep the content fresh and relevant. Including a Web page element, such as an e-mail link, that allows site visitors to offer feedback on their experience at your site is a good way to gather information about potential updates to your site.

You should also plan to test your site's navigation system on a regular basis in order to add new links, as necessary, and to avoid exposing visitors to the nuisance of broken links. Additionally, as part of your site's ongoing review and maintenance, you should evaluate and incorporate, as appropriate, any new technologies that might enhance your site visitors' experiences at your site.

# Web Site Performance Evaluation

Early in the Web site design process, you should have determined the overall goals and objectives for your site. Now that the site is published, it is important to evaluate, on an ongoing basis, whether your site is satisfying those goals and objectives.

To evaluate the performance of your Web site, you can establish measurable performance standards, often called **benchmarks**, to which you can compare actual performance. For example, suppose you have published an informational site and one of the goals for the site is to reach a large target audience. To evaluate the site's performance, you might set a benchmark for the number of visitors to the site over a specific period of time; then, at the end of the time period, you can compare the actual number of site visitors against the benchmark. Two popular tools you can use to both develop benchmarks and then evaluate site performance against those benchmarks are Web server log analysis and Web analytics.

BTW **Changing Goals and Objectives**
After an evaluation of performance benchmarks, you might find it necessary to modify the goals and objectives upon which the original benchmarks were based. Then develop new benchmarks, and reevaluate them.

## Web Server Log Analysis

Web server activities, such as a browser's request for a Web page, generate an entry in a server log. **Web server log analysis software** is used by marketers and large organizations to translate the raw data from server logs into useful information for Web site performance evaluation, such as the:

- IP address of the computer requesting the Web page
- URL of the link the visitor clicked to request the Web page
- date and time of the Web page request
- type of browser making the request
- path the visitor takes from Web page to Web page at the site

Web server log analysis is often part of a package of Web analytics products and services offered by marketers.

## Web Analytics

**Web analytics** products and services combine a variety of elements, including server log analysis, tracking cookies (small text files stored on a site visitor's computer), and other customer information supplied by a business, to paint a picture of how visitors behave at a Web site. Commonly used Web analytic measurements include:

- **unique visitors:** the number of individual site visitors during a specific period of time; a measure of the relative success at efforts to drive traffic to a site
- **repeat visitors:** the number of individual visitors who visit a site more than once during a specific time period; a measure of visitor satisfaction with a site
- **conversion rate:** for an e-commerce site, the rate at which visitors (shoppers) are converted into buyers; conversion rate can be a measure of the effectiveness of the shopping cart checkout process
- **page views:** the number of visitors to specific pages at a site; a measure of page popularity
- **click-stream analysis:** how visitors move from page to page at a site; a measure of the effectiveness of a site's navigation system

Marketers, such as VisiStat or WebTrends, provide a variety of Web analytics products and services. Figure SF 3–11 illustrates a sample VisiStat Web analytics report.

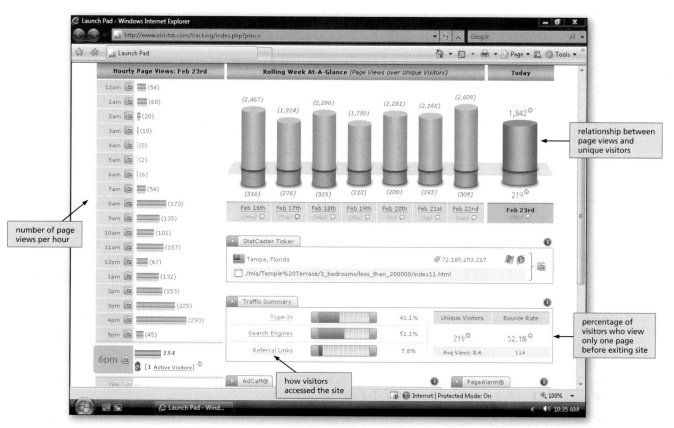

**Figure SF 3-11**

Benchmarking, Web server log analysis, and Web analytics are great tools, but they should always be combined with Web site owner and management expertise to create a more complete picture of a Web site's performance. To learn more about Web site performance evaluation, visit **scsite.com/ew2/websources** and click a link under Special Feature 3, Performance Evaluation.

## Feature Summary

In this special feature, you learned how to use online and offline tools to promote your Web site. Online tools include search engine optimization of your Web pages, manual search tool submission, search tool paid placement, link exchange, online ads, affiliate marketing programs, business blogging, and permission-based e-mail and newsletters. Offline tools include print media advertising and old-fashioned word of mouth.

You also learned about the significance of reviewing, testing, and updating Web site content on a regular basis. Additionally, you learned about the importance of establishing standards or benchmarks for Web site performance and then using technologies and management expertise to evaluate actual site performance against established benchmarks.

## In the Lab

Use Live Search, Google, or another search tool of your choice to locate relevant Web sites as you work through the following exercises.

### Lab 1: Researching Paid Placement Programs
*Problem:* You are looking for ways to promote the Boon Mountain Resort Web site you created in Chapter 1. A friend suggests that you explore participation in a search tool paid placement program.

*Continued >*

**In the Lab** *continued*

*Instructions:*   Review the Google Adwords, Yahoo! Sponsored Search, and Microsoft Search Advertising on Live Search paid placement programs. You can find links to these sites by visiting **scsite.com/ew2/ websources** and clicking a link under Special Feature 3, Search Tool Paid Placement. Compare the policies and procedures for the three paid placement programs. Then select the program that you think is the best choice for the Boon Mountain Resort Web site search engine advertising.

1. Using a word processing program, create a report that contains the following elements:

   a. a summary of your research and the reasons for your choice of program

   b. information for a paid placement ad for Boon Mountain resort that includes a title, description, URL, and other required information following the program's guidelines

   c. a list of appropriate keywords, following program guidelines

   d. estimated cost for each click-through action

2. Save your report as Lab SF 3-1 Paid Placement. At the discretion of your instructor, print your report.

## In the Lab

### Lab 2: Promoting an Informational Web Site

*Problem:*   You recently published an informational Web site focusing on ski conditions in your state. The goal of your site is to share information about weather, snow conditions, and special skiing events with other skiers. You cannot afford to spend much money to promote your site and are looking for free or low-cost site promotion options.

*Instructions:*   Use search tools and the information in this special feature to identify effective free or low-cost options for promoting the site.

1. Write a report that summarizes your promotion plan, including a list of the options you choose and how they will help promote your site.

2. Save your report as Lab SF 3-2 Site Promotion. At the direction of your instructor, print the report.

## In the Lab

### Lab 3: Evaluating Site Performance

*Problem*:   Your B2C beaded jewelry Web site has been in operation for six months. Online sales have increased every month, but you are still not quite sure how well your site is actually performing. You need help in evaluating your site's performance.

*Instructions*:   Use search tools and the information in this special feature to create at least three measurable performance benchmarks for your site. (You may assume any additional information about your B2C beaded jewelry business not detailed in these instructions.) Next, evaluate services and costs for at least three marketing companies that offer Web analytics and performance evaluation tools. Choose the marketing company that, in your opinion, offers the best selection of services and costs for your site.

1. Write a report that explains the performance benchmarks you have created and how the benchmarks will help you evaluate your Web site's performance.

2. Include in your report a summary of the services provided and costs for those services for each reviewed marketing company. Discuss the reasons for your choice of the specific marketing company that will provide you with Web analytics and performance evaluation products and services.

3. Save your report as Lab SF 3-3 Performance Evaluation. At the direction of your instructor, print the report.

## Appendix A
# Using Microsoft Expression Web 2 Help

## Introduction

You might have a question about how to use a specific Expression Web feature, or perhaps you want to learn more about the different features offered by Expression Web for creating, editing, and publishing Web pages. You can get answers on specific questions or browse available Help topics in the **Expression Web 2 Help window**. In the Help window, you can follow hyperlinks from the category list on the Help system starting page to a specific Help topic page, browse Help topics from a separate Table of Contents pane, or perform a keyword search to locate a specific Help topic.

To open the Expression Web 2 Help window, click the Microsoft Expression Web Help command on the Help menu. The Help window (Figure A–1) contains standard Windows Vista operating system window features, including a title bar and the Minimize, Maximize or Restore Down, and Close buttons. Additionally, the Help window contains a customizable **toolbar**, a **search bar**, a **content pane**, and a **Table of Contents pane** that you can show or hide as needed.

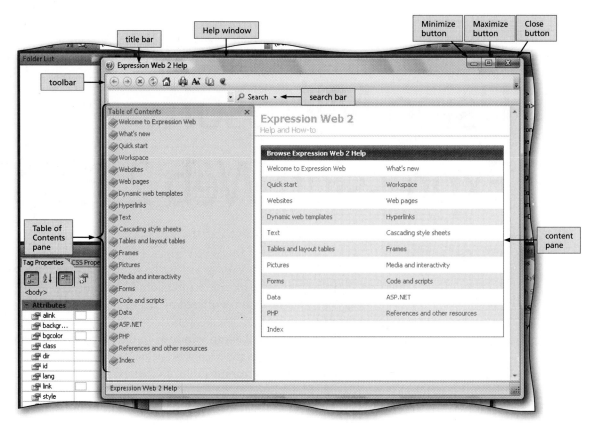

**Figure A–1**

## To Open the Expression Web 2 Help Window

The following steps open the Expression Web 2 Help window using a menu command.

• Start Expression Web, if necessary. Click Help on the menu bar to open the Help menu (Figure A–2).

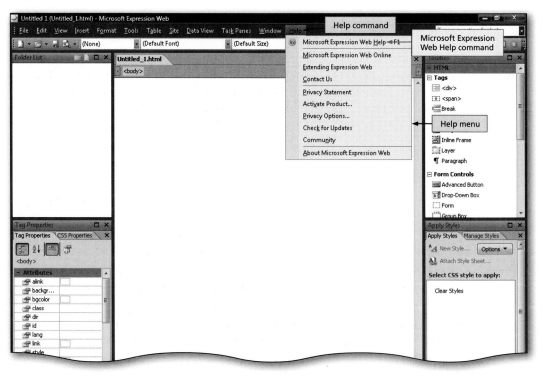

**Figure A–2**

**2**

- Click the Microsoft Expression Web Help command to open the Expression Web 2 Help window (Figure A–3).

**Q&A**

Can I resize the Help window?

You can resize the Help window by clicking the Maximize button on the Help window title bar to enlarge the window to fill the screen. You can then click the Restore Down button on the Help window title bar to restore the window to its previous size. You can also resize the Help window using the mouse pointer. If you position the mouse pointer on the left, right, top, or bottom boundary of the Help window, the mouse pointer becomes a sizing pointer. Drag the boundary to resize the window. You can also drag the sizing icon in the lower-right corner of the window to size the window proportionally.

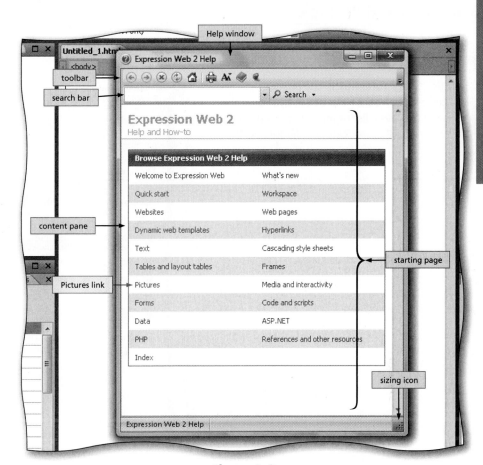

**Figure A–3**

**Other Ways**

1. Press F1
2. Click the Microsoft Expression Web Help button on the Standard toolbar

# The Expression Web 2 Help Window

By default, each time you open the Help window, it opens in a small window that is positioned on top of the Expression Web program window, as shown in Figure A–3. At the top of the Help window is the window's title bar with the name of the window and the Minimize, Maximize, and Close buttons. Below the title bar are a toolbar, a search bar, and a content pane that displays a starting page in the Browse Expression Web 2 Help box.

# Browsing Help Topics

When you open the Help window, the content pane contains the Help starting page or table of contents, which is a list of links to general Help topic categories. You can click a Help topic category link to jump to a list of individual Help topics within the category. Then click an individual Help topic link to view the topic details. As you click a link on the starting page, the linked page appears in the content pane. This page generally contains a list of subcategory links and might also include a list of individual Help topic links. You can click a topic link, if available, or continue to drill down through the subcategory links to view the detail page for a specific Help topic. As you browse, the Help system retains a browsing history of followed links that change color from blue to purple.

**BTW**

**Expression Web Online**
To learn more about working with Expression Web, click the Microsoft Expression Web Online or Community commands on the Help menu to visit the Expression Web site. On the Expression Web site you will find links to online tutorials, software documentation, discussion forums, and other useful information.

## To Browse Help Topics

The following steps jump to a specific Help topic by following links from the Help window starting page.

• Click the Pictures link in the Browse Expression Web 2 Help box in the content pane to view a list of individual Help topics within the Pictures category (Figure A–4).

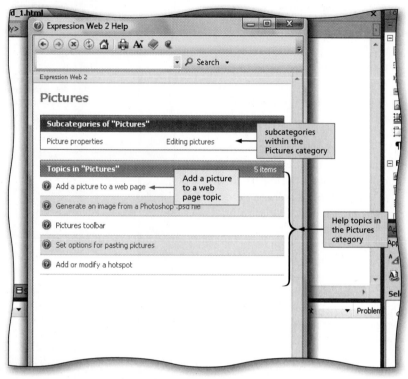

**Figure A–4**

• Click the Add a picture to a web page topic link to view the specific Help topic (Figure A–5).

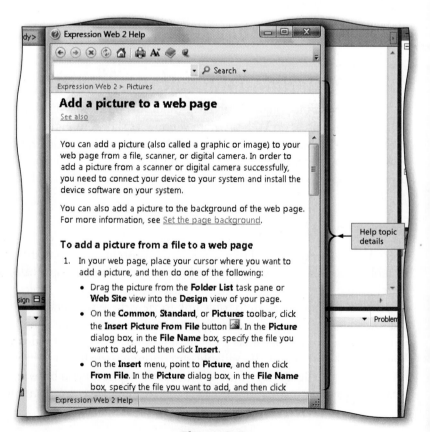

**Figure A–5**

**3**

- Scroll to view the entire Add a picture to a web page topic.

- Click the Set the size of a picture link, near the bottom of the Help topic page, to view that related topic (Figure A–6).

- Observe the breadcrumb trail above the content pane (Figure A–6).

**Q&A**

What is a breadcrumb trail?

A breadcrumb trail is a horizontal list of links that identifies the click path from a starting page to the current page. A breadcrumb trail, similar to the one above the content pane in Figure A–5, is frequently added to Web pages to provide an additional navigation tool. The Help system provides a breadcrumb trail above the content pane to make it easy to navigate back to a previous Help category's list of topics or back to the starting page. You can click a link in the breadcrumb trail to jump back to that page.

- Click the Pictures link in the breadcrumb trail above the content pane to return to list of related topics in the Pictures category.

- Click the Expression Web 2 link in the breadcrumb trail above the content pane to return to the Help starting page.

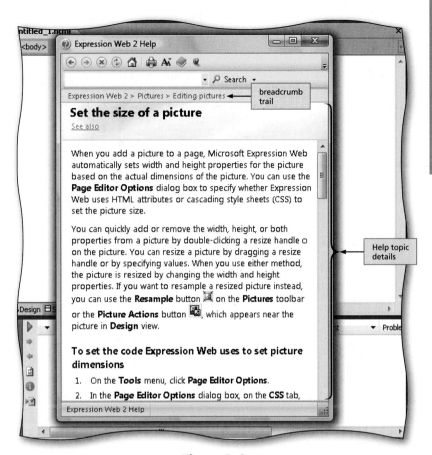

Figure A–6

## The Toolbar

The Help toolbar, located at the top of the Help window, contains 10 buttons, as shown in Figures A–7 and A–8.

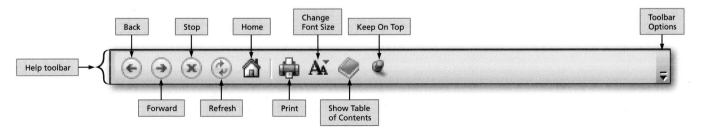

Figure A–7

The first six buttons — Back, Forward, Stop, Refresh, Home, and Print — are similar to toolbar buttons found in most Web browsers, such as Microsoft Internet Explorer.

- **Back** and **Forward buttons** — click the Back and Forward buttons to navigate between previous or next Help topics in the Help system browsing history during the current Help session.
- **Stop button** — click the Stop button to halt the display of a Help topic.
- **Refresh button** — click the Refresh button to redisplay the current Help topic.
- **Home button** — click the Home button to return to the Help starting page.
- **Print button** — click the Print button to open the Print dialog box and print the current Help topic.

The last button, the **Toolbar Options button**, allows you to customize the toolbar by adding or removing buttons. The remaining three buttons — the **Change Font Size**, **Show Table of Contents**, and **Keep On Top buttons** — allow you to increase or decrease the font size of the Help text, show the Table of Contents pane, and keep the Help window on top of the active Expression Web software window, respectively.

The Show Table of Contents and Keep On Top buttons are toggle switches that turn on or off a Help window feature. When you click the Show Table of Contents button to display the Table of Contents pane, the Show Table of Contents button becomes the **Hide Table of Contents button**. Similarly, the Keep On Top button becomes the **Not On Top button** when clicked. When the Not On Top button is active, the Expression Web Help window moves behind the active Expression Web software window. Figure A–8 illustrates the toolbar with active Hide Table of Contents and Not On Top buttons.

**Figure A–8**

When you want to browse Help topics but still be able to see the Help topics table of contents, you can show the hidden Table of Contents pane by clicking the Show Table of Contents button on the toolbar. Clicking a Help category link in the Table of Contents pane displays a list of related Help topics in the pane. Clicking a specific Help topic link in the Table of Contents pane displays the Help topic's details in the content pane.

## To Browse Help Topics Using the Table of Contents Pane

The following steps show the hidden Table of Contents pane and follow links in the pane to view a specific Help topic.

**1**

• Click the Show Table of Contents Pane button on the Help window toolbar to display the pane (Figure A–9).

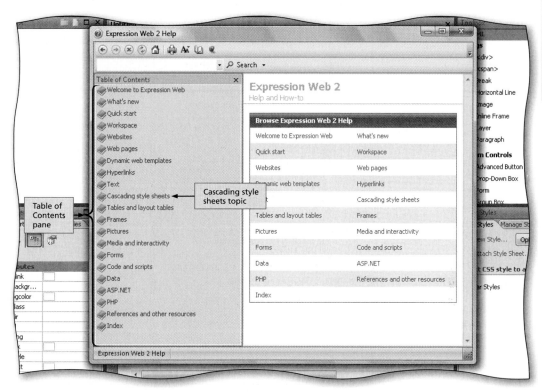

**Figure A–9**

**2**

• Click the Cascading style sheets category link in the Table of Contents pane to expand the Table of Contents and display links to help on specific CSS topics (Figure A–10).

**Figure A–10**

- Click the Cascading style sheets overview Help topic link in the Table of Contents pane to view the topic details in the content pane (Figure A–11).
- Click the Home button on the Help toolbar to display the Help window starting page in the content pane.
- Click the Hide Table of Contents button on the toolbar to hide the Table of Contents pane.

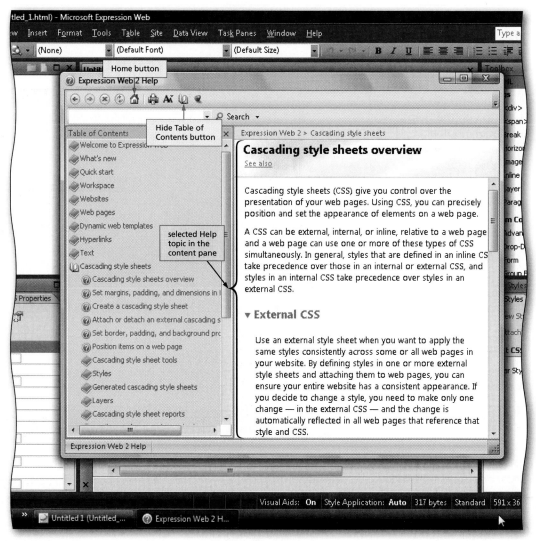

**Figure A–11**

## The Search Bar

You can search the Expression Web Help topics by performing a keyword search using the search bar located below the toolbar. The search bar contains a **search text box** in which you type your search keywords or phrases and a **Search button** you can click to perform the search.

**BTW**

**Help Index**
You can click the Index link in the Help window starting page or Table of Contents pane to view an alphabetized index of Help topics.

## To Search Help Topics Using the Search Bar

The following steps search for a specific Help topic by typing keywords in the search bar text box and then clicking the Search button.

**1**

- Type `layout tables` in the search bar text box (Figure A–12).

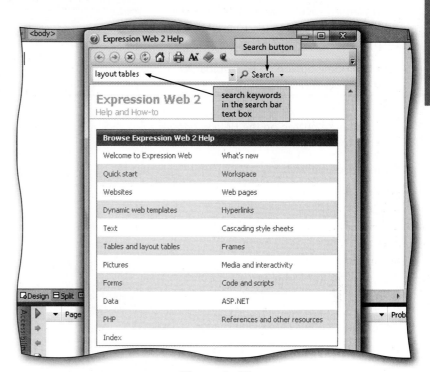

**Figure A–12**

**2**

- Click the Search button to search for and display a list of Help topics related to the keywords, layout, and tables (Figure A–13).

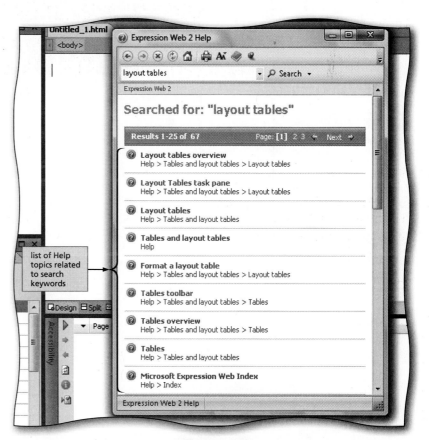

**Figure A–13**

**3**

- Click the Layout tables overview Help topic link in the content pane to view the Help topic (Figure A–14).

- With your instructor's permission, click the Print button on the toolbar to print the Help topic.

- Click the Home button on the toolbar to view the Help window starting page in the content pane.

- Click the Close button on the Help window title bar to close the Help window.

- Close Expression Web.

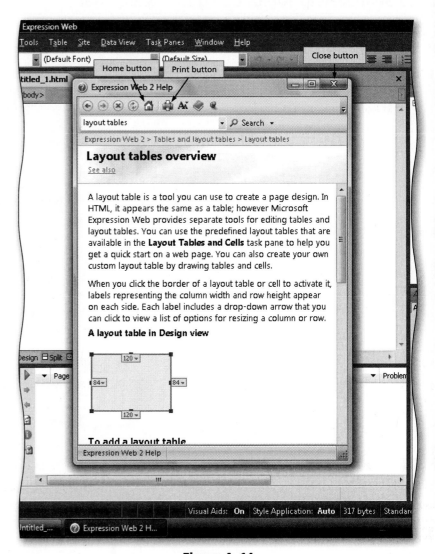

**Figure A–14**

**Other Ways**

1. Type search keywords in the Type a question for help text box in the upper-right corner of the Expression Web window

**Other Ways**

1. Press ALT+F4 to close the Help window

# Using Help

## 1 Browsing Help Topics

*Instructions*:    Use the Help window starting page and the Table of Contents pane to browse for specific Help topics. Print individual Help topics at the direction of your instructor.

1. Press the F1 keyboard shortcut key to open the Help window. Use the Browse Expression Web 2 category links to view the alphabetized index of Help topics. Find three Help topics about publishing a Web site. Review the Help topics and create a brief outline you can use to explain Web site publishing issues covered by the Help topics. Close the Help window.

2. Open the Help window using the method of your choice and show the Table of Contents pane. Use the Table of Contents pane to browse the Help topics for information on selecting and pasting text. Use the breadcrumb trail to return to the starting page. Hide the Table of Contents pane and close the Help window using the ALT+F4 keyboard shortcut keys.

## 2 Searching for Specific Help Topics

*Instructions*:    Use the Expression Web Type a question for Help box and the Help window search bar to search for specific Help topics. Print individual Help topics at the direction of your instructor.

1. Type the keyword phrase `attaching a style sheet` in the Type a question for help text box in the Expression Web window to view relevant Help topics. Follow a link to a specific Help topic. Close the Help window.

2. Open the Help window using the method of your choice and then use the search bar to search for Help topics about bulleted or numbered lists. Review at least two specific Help topics related to bulleted or numbered lists. Be prepared to discuss the topics with your classmates. Close the Help window.

3. Using the search method of your choice, search the Help system for a list of useful keyboard shortcut keys. Write down 10 keyboard shortcuts you think will be most useful to you. Close the Help window.

## 3 Using the Help Window Toolbar

*Instructions*:    Use the Help window toolbar to move between Help topics, refresh the current Help topic, change the font size of the current Help topic, move the Help window behind the Expression Web window, and restore the Help window on top of the Expression Web window.

1. Open the Help window using the method of your choice and view three help topics of your choice.

2. Click the Back and Forward buttons on the toolbar to move back and forward between the recently viewed Help topics.

3. Click the Refresh button on the toolbar to reload the current Help topic.

4. Click the Maximize button on the Help window title bar to resize the Help window. Then click the Change Font Size button on the toolbar to view a menu of font sizes; click Larger in the menu to change the font size. Click the Change Font Size button on the toolbar and click Medium to return to the default font size. Then click the Restore Down button on the Help window title bar to resize the window to its previous smaller size.

5. Click the Keep On Top button on the toolbar and then activate the Expression Web window to move the Help window behind the Expression Web window. Click the Expression Web 2 Help button on the taskbar to again view the Help window on top of the Expression Web window. Click the Not On Top button on the toolbar to keep the Help window in its default location on top of the Expression Web window. Close the Help window.

## Appendix B
# Web Standards and Accessibility

## Introduction

The application of Web standards and accessibility guidelines in the development and creation of your Web pages can enhance your Web pages' usability and cross-browser compatibility. Additionally, the application of Web standards and accessibility guidelines can make your pages' content accessible by visitors with disabilities.

## Web Standards

A **standard** is a generally accepted principle, rule, guideline, or technology that defines how to perform a task or measures the quality and consistency of the task's output. Industries from electrical engineering to accounting use standards, rules, and guidelines to ensure consistent high-quality output or technological performance. Two examples of **technology standards** include the IEEE 802.20 standard for deploying mobile broadband wireless across networks and the Hypertext Transfer Protocol (HTTP) standard for transmitting Web pages over the Internet.

**Web standards** encompass the guidelines and technologies developed to ensure the cross-browser compatibility of Web pages and the general usability and accessibility of those pages. Since the mid-1990s, the World Wide Web Consortium, or W3C (Figure B–1), has been establishing Web standards while coalitions such as the Web Standards Project and the Web Standards Group promote the use of those standards across the Web development community.

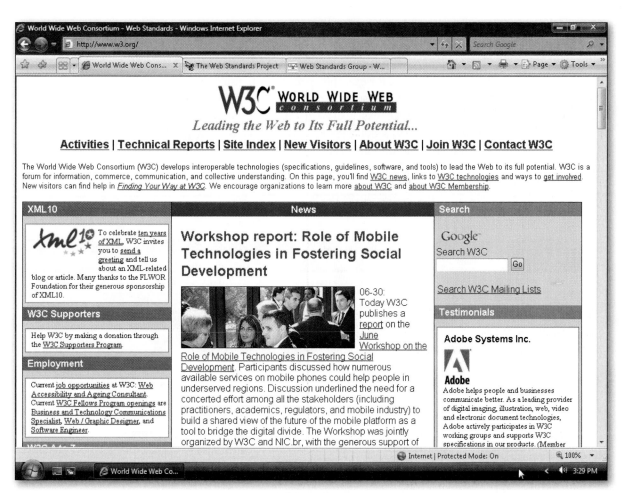

**Figure B–1**

Current Web technology standards developed by the W3C include the markup languages that define the arrangement and content of Web page elements (HTML 4.01, XHTML 1.1, XML) and Cascading Style Sheets (CSS) that control the layout and formatting of Web page elements. The development of Web standards is an ongoing process. For example, the W3C and related interested groups are currently working on the standards for HTML 5, the fifth major revision of the HTML standard.

To create standards-compliant Web pages, you should create your Web pages using valid HTML or XHTML markup and use CSS to lay out and format Web page content. Expression Web contains features such as CSS compatibility reporting that help you create standards-compliant Web pages. Ensuring that your Web pages comply with standards can be beneficial in many ways. For example, standards-compliant Web pages are easier to maintain, are compatible with current and future browser technologies, download faster, and provide content that is accessible by all users, including those with disabilities.

For more information about the W3C, the Web Standards Project, the Web Standards Group, or other Web standards topics, visit **scsite.com/ew2/websources** and click a link under Appendix B, Web Standards.

# Web Accessibility

The goal of **Web accessibility guidelines** is to ensure that all Web page content is available to people with disabilities; for example, people with visual impairments who typically use assistive technologies, such as screen readers, to access Web pages.

The W3C **Web Accessibility Initiative** (Figure B–2) and **Section 508** of the U.S. Rehabilitation Act of 1973 define current Web accessibility guidelines. Two examples of Web accessibility guidelines are: (1) always add a text equivalent for a non-text element, such as a picture; and (2) never use color alone to identify a hyperlink. Expression Web has features, such as the Accessibility task pane (Figure B–3), to help you find and solve accessibility problems with your Web pages.

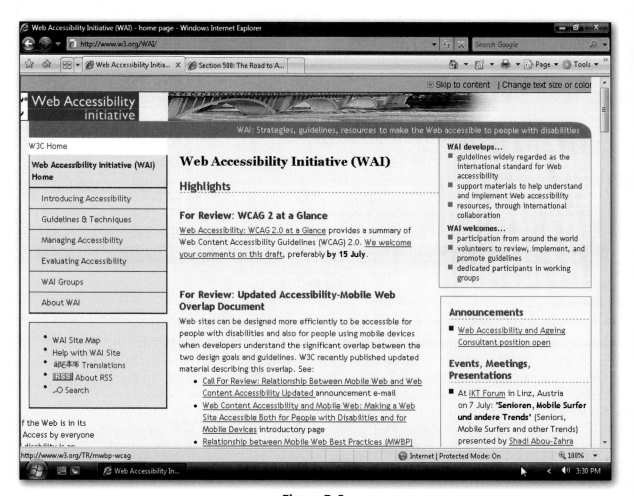

**Figure B–2**

Although the terms *Web usability* and *Web accessibility* are sometimes used interchangeably, incorporating all aspects of good Web design — structure, layout, color, and so forth — with Web standards to create your Web pages improves the usability of those pages for everyone who visits them. Web accessibility issues focus on making Web content accessible to visitors with disabilities. For more information about the Web Accessibility Initiative, Section 508, and other Web accessibility topics, visit **scsite.com/ ew2/websources** and click a link under Appendix B, Web Accessibility.

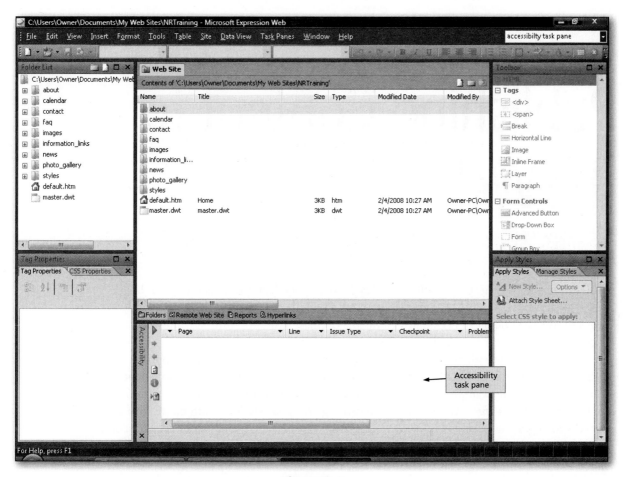

**Figure B–3**

**Appendix C**
# Publishing Content to the Web

## Introduction

**Publishing**, or copying, your Web site's files — Web pages, graphics, and other related files — to a Web server allows you to share your site with others. In order to publish your Web site so that others can access it, you need a domain name for your site and access to space on a Web server.

A **domain name** identifies your Web site and is part of the Uniform Resource Locator (URL) that a visitor types in his or her Web browser's address bar to download your site's pages. For example, the domain name for the Microsoft Web site is *microsoft.com* and the site's URL is *www.microsoft.com*. You can register your site's domain name with an **accredited registrar**, such as GoDaddy, Network Solutions (Figure C–1), or register.com, for a small annual fee.

**Figure C–1**

For more information about the Domain Name System (DNS) and registering domain names, visit **scsite.com/ew2/websources** and click a link under Appendix C, Domain Name System.

A **Web server** is a computer (and its software) that stores Web pages and then "serves up" the pages upon request from a Web browser. **Web server space** is available from a variety of sources. For example, your school might make Web server space available for students and faculty, or you might be able to acquire server space from your **Internet Service Provider (ISP)**, either as part of your Internet connection service or for an additional fee. Additionally, thousands of companies, such as Yahoo! Small Business (Figure C–2), bluehost, Microsoft Office Live Small Business, and Rackspace offer **Web hosting services** for all types of Web sites — from small one- or two-page personal sites to large, multipage e-commerce sites. Some Web hosting providers might also offer a number of additional services, such as e-mail accounts, shopping cart add-ons, Web site marketing services, and so forth.

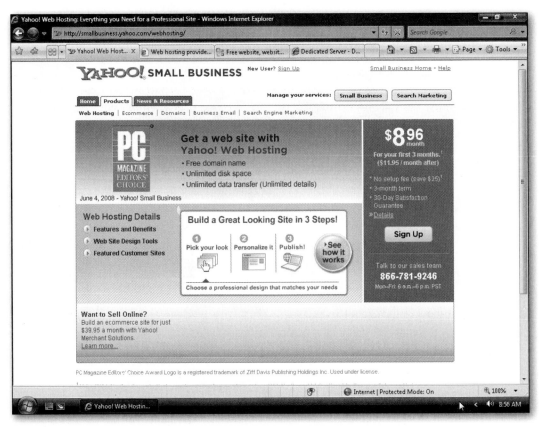

**Figure C–2**

Web hosting fees vary depending on a number of factors, such as the:

- Type of site (personal or business)
- Amount of server space required
- Number of pages at the site
- Number of e-mail accounts
- Anticipated level of traffic to the site
- Level of customer support you need

Many Web hosting companies also offer domain name registration services. Some Web hosting companies that cater to personal or small business Web sites might offer free Web hosting in exchange for posting advertising banners on the site's pages.

Before selecting a Web hosting service provider, you should first identify the amount of server space and bandwidth required for your Web site, plus the number of e-mail accounts and the types of services you require. Next, you should evaluate a number of service providers to compare prices for those services that you require. Other important considerations in your evaluation include comparing the service providers' server types and the availability of server-side functions, such as the ASP.NET Framework for Web pages built using ASP.NET tools or FrontPage Server Extensions for existing FrontPage sites updated in Expression Web. Additionally, you should consider how each service provider handles customer support, server backup and downtime, and whether disaster recovery plans and procedures are in place.

Finally, before publishing your site's files to a Web server, you should contact the network system administrator or technical support staff at your service provider (school, ISP, or Web hosting company) for specific instructions on how to upload your files, including the path to the server, your username, and your password.

To explore service providers that offer a variety of services and different levels of customer support, visit **scsite.com/ew2/websources** and click a link under Appendix C, Web Hosting Services.

# Publishing Your Site Using Expression Web

Expression Web provides features that allow you to copy your Web site files to or from a variety of sources and destinations, such as a **temporary staging server**, a **live Web server**, a folder on your computer's hard drive, or a storage device on your local network. Copying or publishing your Web site files to a temporary staging server allows you to test your site before it goes "live." As noted earlier, publishing your tested Web site files to a live or production server makes the site accessible by visitors using a Web browser. Publishing your Web site files to a folder on your hard drive, to a removable storage device, or to a network storage device allows you to create a backup of your site's files.

## Setting the Remote Web Site Properties

The first time you publish your Web site files using Expression Web, you must set the properties for the remote Web site. To do this, you can click the Publish Site command on the File menu to switch to Remote Web Site view and, at the same time, open the Remote Web Site Properties dialog box.

The Remote Web Site tab in the Remote Web Site Properties dialog box (Figure C–3) provides options for selecting the server-supported technology to be used in publishing site files and a text box for specifying the destination location. The four server-supported technologies are:

- **FrontPage Server Extensions** — server-side software that uses the HTTP or HTTPS protocols to transmit Web pages over the Internet and enables interactive Web page features for pages originally created using Microsoft FrontPage

- **WebDAV (Web-based Distributed Authoring and Versioning)** — an extension of the HTTP protocol that allows individuals within a workgroup to check in and check out Web site files for editing

- **FTP (File Transfer Protocol)** — the most commonly used technology for transferring files over the Internet

- **File System** — a method of publishing between storage devices on the same computer or network

Figure C–3 illustrates the Remote Web Site tab with the File System option selected and a CD drive as the destination location. These options allow publishing the Web site's files to a CD to create a backup copy of the files that can be stored in a secure off-site location.

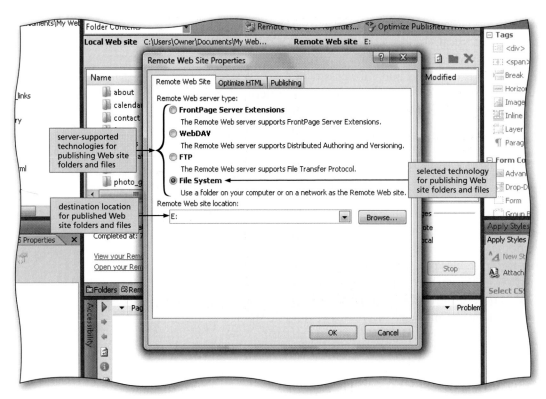

**Figure C–3**

The Optimize HTML tab (Figure C–4) contains options for removing unnecessary HTML code to create smaller, faster-loading pages, and the Publishing tab (Figure C–5) offers options for publishing only those files that have changed or all Web site files.

**Figure C–4**

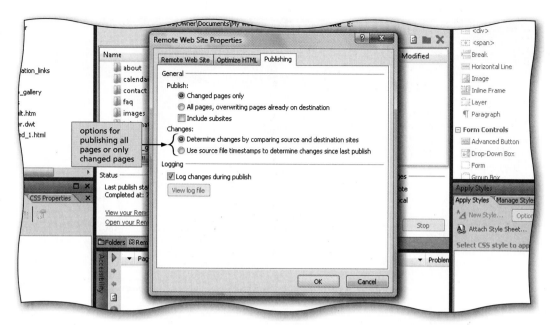

**Figure C–5**

After specifying the server type and location and setting any additional options in the Remote Web Site Properties dialog box, click OK to close the dialog box and view the open site's folders and files in Remote Web Site view.

Once you set the remote site properties for a Web site, opening the site and clicking the Publish Site command on the File menu displays the local site's files and folders and the remote site's files and folders, if any, in Remote Web Site view; the Remote Web Site Properties dialog box does *not* automatically open. To open the Remote Web Site Properties dialog box and reset the remote site properties while in Remote Web Site view, click the Remote Web Site Properties link above the view panes.

## Remote Web Site View

**Remote Web Site view** allows you to see the folders and files in the **Local Web Site pane** and the published files in the **Remote Web Site pane**. You may be tempted to think of a local Web site as a site stored on your computer or network server and the remote Web site as a site stored on a hosting company's or ISP's Web server. However, the terms *local Web site* and *remote Web site* refer only to the source and destination of the Web site files to be published and not the physical location of the storage devices involved.

The *local Web site* is always the Web site you opened in Expression Web, no matter where the site's files are physically stored; for example, the local Web site files might be physically located on your local computer's hard drive, a network storage device, a staging Web server, or a live Web server. The *remote Web site* is always the destination for the published files, which also might be a staging Web server, a live Web server, a folder on your hard drive, a network storage device, or a removable storage device.

In the Remote Web Site view shown in Figure C–6, the local Web site (the source) is a Web site stored on a computer's hard drive, and the remote Web site (the destination) is a copy of the Web site's folders and files stored on a CD in a CD drive on the same computer.

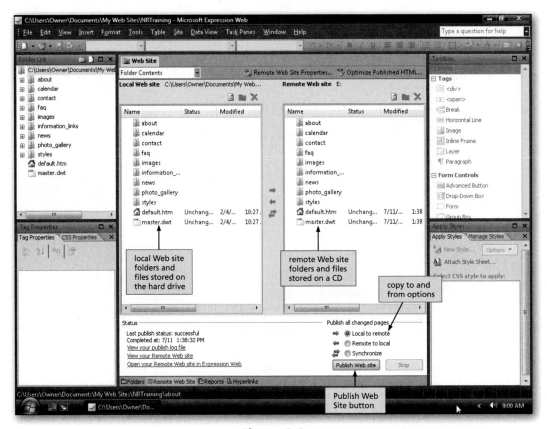

**Figure C–6**

You can set an option in Remote Web Site view to publish files to or from the local Web site and the remote Web site or to synchronize files between the two sites. After you set the desired **Local to remote**, **Remote to local**, or **Synchronize** option located in the lower-right corner below the view panes, click the Publish Web Site button to copy the files. You can also publish a file or folder by dragging it from the Local Web Site pane to the Remote Web Site pane or vice versa.

By default, the first time you publish a site, all files are copied. If you do not want to copy a specific file, right-click the filename in the appropriate pane and click the Don't Publish command on the shortcut menu. When republishing pages to an already published site, by default only changed pages are published. To republish all pages, even those that have not changed, you must set the *All pages, overwriting pages already on destination* option in the Publishing tab in the Remote Web Site Properties dialog box.

As you learned in the previous section, the File Transfer Protocol (FTP) is a commonly used technology for copying files from one location to another over the Internet. While FTP is a server type option in the Remote Web Site Properties dialog box, some Web developers might prefer to use FTP client software, rather than Expression Web, to publish their files.

# Publishing Your Site Using FTP Client Software

Another convenient way to publish your Web site is to use an FTP client to copy the site's files from one location to another. **FTP client software** provides a familiar graphical user interface of menu commands and toolbar buttons to help you quickly publish your Web site's files using FTP. FTP client examples include CuteFTP (Figure C–7), FileZilla, and SmartFTP.

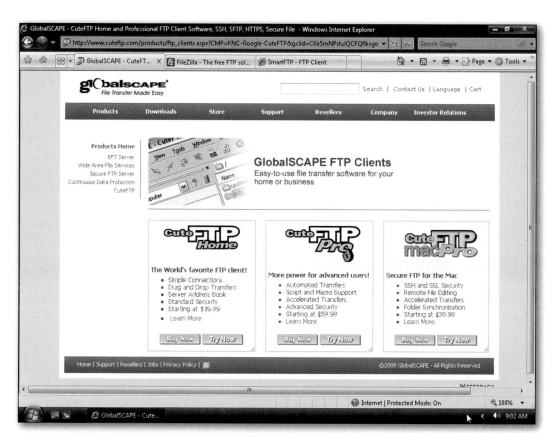

**Figure C–7**

Before using an FTP client to publish to a remote Web server, you must set up the location, username, and password to access the server using the FTP client's site manager feature. Then you open the remote Web site and view the local and remote Web sites' folders and files at the same time in side-by-side panes, as shown in Figure C–8. Figure C–8 illustrates a Web site's folders and files stored on a computer's hard drive and published to a remote Web server using CuteFTP client software. CuteFTP client software allows you to select and then copy one or more folders and files to or from the local and the remote Web sites using a menu command, a toolbar button, or drag and drop.

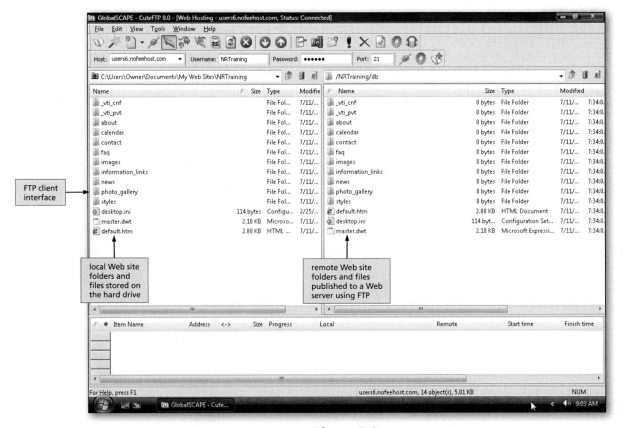

FTP client interface

local Web site folders and files stored on the hard drive

remote Web site folders and files published to a Web server using FTP

**Figure C–8**

## Appendix D
# Microsoft
# Expression Studio 2

## Introduction

Microsoft Expression Studio 2 is a family of five related software products — Expression Web 2, Expression Design 2, Expression Media 2, Expression Blend 2, and Expression Encoder 2 — used by Web developers to create standards-compliant Web pages. In addition to creating Web pages, the Expression Studio products help developers import, create, and edit vector and bitmap graphics, manage digital files, create interactive Web-based applications, and produce audio and video content for Web-based applications.

## Expression Web

A **WYSIWYG (What You See Is What You Get) editor** is software that automatically inserts markup language tags as you work with the software's graphical interface, including menu commands, toolbar buttons, and task panes, to create and edit a Web page. **Expression Web**, which you learn about in the chapters of this text, is a WYSIWYG editor used by both novice and professional Web developers to create standards-compliant Web pages. Expression Web is the replacement software for Microsoft FrontPage, which is no longer supported by Microsoft.

Expression Web (Figure D–1) provides easy-to-use Web site and page templates for the beginner while also delivering more sophisticated tools required by Web development professionals, such as Cascading Style Sheets for layout and formatting and a feature for Web standards compliance testing.

**Figure D–1**

# Expression Design

**Vector graphics** are images created by drawing shapes and lines, while **raster graphics**, also called **bitmaps**, are images created one pixel at a time. An example of a vector graphic is a company logo created by combining different drawing shapes and lines. Examples of bitmaps include animated images and photographs.

**Expression Design** (Figure D–2) is software you can use to import, create, and edit vector graphics and bitmaps. Expression Design includes features that let you apply special effects to graphics, combine vector graphics with bitmaps, and convert bitmaps into vector graphics and vice versa. Expression Design also offers tools for exporting graphics into Expression Web and Expression Blend.

**Figure D–2**

# Expression Media

Web developers frequently need to access digital media files stored in a variety of locations, such as a hard disk, multiple CDs or DVDs, or shared network folders. Managing hundreds of digital media files stored in a variety of locations can be challenging and time consuming. For example, it may be very difficult to locate a specific audio or video file or compare two or more similar image files when having to search through hundreds of files stored in various locations.

**Expression Media** is software you can use to import and catalog information about digital media files that are stored in a variety of locations. Only the file's information is imported — the file itself remains in its original location. Expression Media (Figure D–3) also provides tools to browse or search the media catalogs, organize and classify files, annotate and rename files, review images in a list or as thumbnails, edit images, listen to audio files, and watch movie and video files.

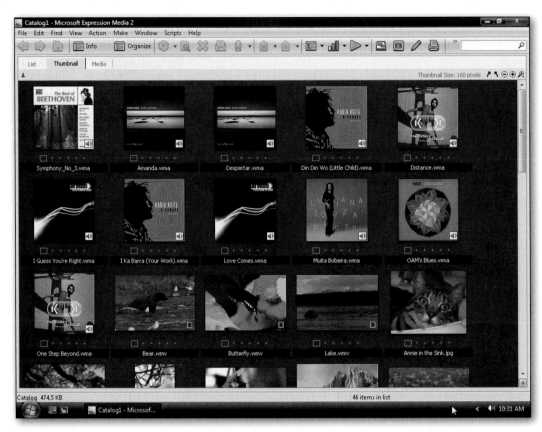

**Figure D–3**

# Expression Blend

**Expression Blend** is software designed for professional developers who need to create graphical user interfaces (GUIs) for Windows desktop applications using the Microsoft .NET Framework platform.

Expression Blend can also be used to create GUIs for rich interactive applications using XAML (Extensible Application Markup Language) and the Microsoft Silverlight plug-in technologies. A **rich interactive application**, or **RIA**, is a Web-based application with multimedia content. Silverlight (Figure D–4) is a browser plug-in that works with different browsers and different operating systems to display the multimedia content included in RIAs.

**Figure D–4**

Expression Blend (Figure D–5) provides tools for professional developers to combine images, animation, video, audio, text, and controls, such as buttons, list boxes, and scroll bars, in creating rich content for desktop or Web-based applications.

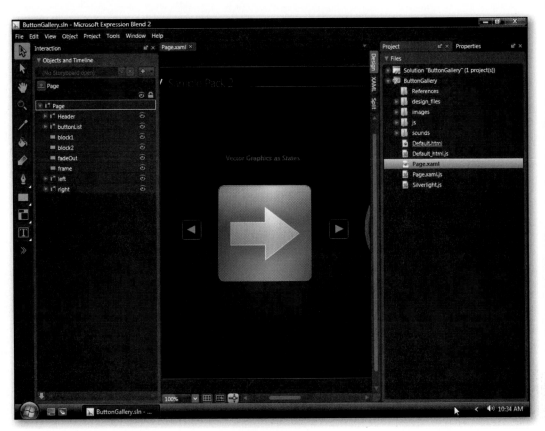

**Figure D–5**

For more information about the Microsoft .NET Framework, XAML, or Microsoft Silverlight, visit **scsite.com/ew2/websources** and click a link under Appendix D, Microsoft Platforms.

## Expression Encoder

**Encoding software** is used to compress audio and video files and output the files in a specific audio or video format. **Expression Encoder** (Figure D–6) is encoding software designed specifically to work with Silverlight technologies.

A variety of audio and video file formats can be imported into Expression Encoder, including AVI, WMV, WMA, MPEG2, and QuickTime files. The encoded files are output as WMV or WMA files for use with the Silverlight and Microsoft DirectShow multimedia technologies. Expression Encoder is integrated with Expression Media; files can be dragged from Expression Media and dropped into Expression Encoder.

**Figure D–6**

For more information about the five individual software products that make up Expression Studio, visit **scsite.com/ew2/websources** and click a link under Appendix D, Expression Studio 2.

## Appendix E
# Using Expression Web in Windows XP

The step-by-step instructions and illustrations in this text are based on Expression Web running in the Windows Vista operating system environment. If you are running Expression Web in the Windows XP operating system environment, your instructor might modify certain step-by-step instructions as necessary to perform tasks.

You also will see some variances between the desktop, the Windows taskbar and Start menu, the Expression Web window, and Expression Web dialog boxes on your screen with the illustrations in this text, including the:

- Default Windows color scheme and desktop background
- Size and color of the Minimize, Maximize, Restore Down, and Close buttons on the Expression Web title bar
- Program's title text color on the title bar
- Taskbar color and the Start button size and shape
- Start menu colors, arrangement, contents, and style
- Dialog box colors, boundary style, and, in some instances, dialog box content

This appendix illustrates examples of these differences by showing how to start Expression Web and then open and close an existing Web site.

## To Start Expression Web

The following steps, which assume Windows XP is running, start Expression Web based on a typical installation. Your instructor might provide alternate instructions for starting Expression Web on your computer.

 **1**

- Click the Start button on the Windows XP taskbar to display the Start menu.

- Point to All Programs on the Start menu to display the All Programs submenu.

- Point to Microsoft Expression on the All Programs sub-menu to display the Microsoft Expression 2 command (Figure E–1).

**Figure E–1**

**2**

- Click Microsoft Expression Web 2 to start Expression Web.

- If the Expression Web window is not maximized, click the Maximize button to the left of the Close button on the Expression Web title bar to maximize the window (Figure E–2).

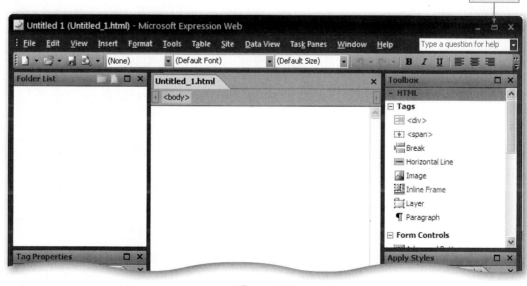

**Figure E–2**

| Other Ways | |
|---|---|
| 1. Double-click the Expression Web icon on the desktop, if one is present | 2. Click Microsoft Expression Web 2 on the Start menu, if present |

## To Open an Existing Web Site

The following steps close the Untitled_1.htm page, if necessary, and open the Boon Mountain Resort Web site data file from the USB flash drive where you save your data files. Your drive and folder information will likely differ from what is shown in the figure.

- Click File on the menu bar.

- Click Close to close the Untitled_1. html page (Figure E–3).

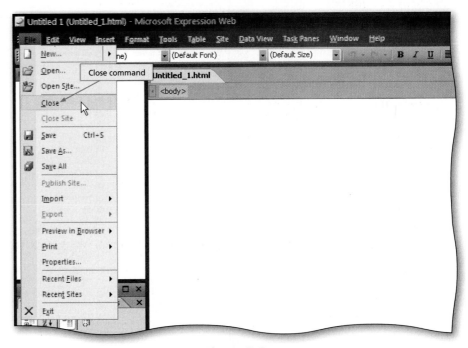

**Figure E–3**

- With your USB flash drive connected to one of the computer's USB ports, click File on the menu bar.

- Point to Open Site on the File menu (Figure E–4).

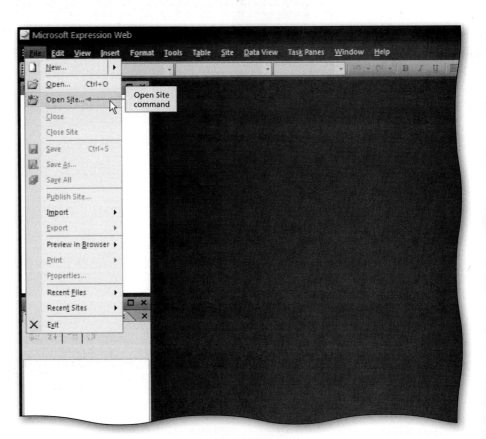

**Figure E–4**

**3**

- Click Open Site to display the Open Site dialog box.

- Click the Look in box arrow to view the list of available drives.

- Click the USB flash drive to select it and view its contents.

**Q&A**

How do I locate the site to open if I am not using a USB flash drive?

Use the same process, but select your device or network folder from the Look in list.

- Double-click the data file folder, if necessary, to open it.

**Figure E–5**

- Click boonmountainresortfinal to select the site name (Figure E–5).

**4**

- Click the Open button to open the site and all of its files and folders in the Expression Web window (Figure E–6).

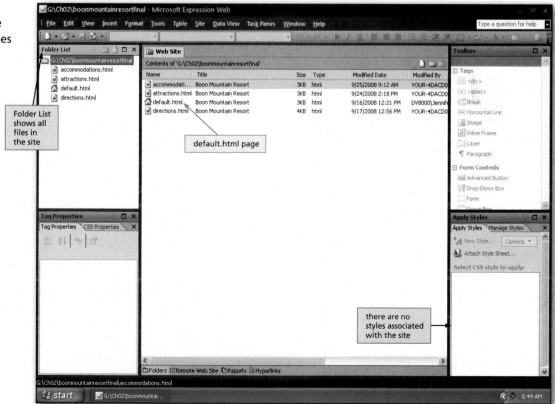

**Figure E–6**

## To Close a Web Site

The following steps close the Boon Mountain Resort Web site and the Expression Web program.

- Click File on the menu bar to open the File menu.

- Click Close Site to close the boonmountainresortfinal Web site (Figure E–7).

- Click the Close button on the Expression Web title bar.

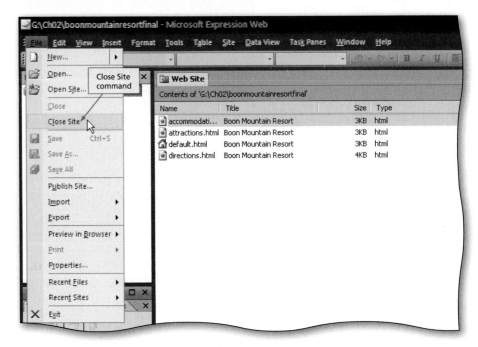

**Figure E–7**

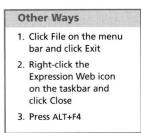

**Other Ways**

1. Click File on the menu bar and click Exit

2. Right-click the Expression Web icon on the taskbar and click Close

3. Press ALT+F4

## Appendix F
# Changing Screen Resolution

A **pixel** (short for picture element) is a single point of light on a computer screen. **Screen resolution** is a setting that determines the number of pixels necessary to display the program windows, pictures, text, and icons you see on your screen. Screen resolution usually is stated as the two numbers that represent the width and height of the pixels. For example, a screen with a 1024 × 768 screen resolution, the most common resolution used today, displays 1,024 pixels in width and 768 pixels in height; the screen illustrations in this book were created using the 1024 × 768 screen resolution. Other less common screen resolutions include the 800 × 600, 1152 × 720, 1280 × 768, and 1440 × 900 screen resolutions.

When you increase the screen resolution, you see more information on the screen, but the size of the information (text characters, toolbar buttons, dialog boxes, icons, pictures, and so forth) decreases; this might make the information more difficult to see for certain users. Alternatively, if you decrease the screen resolution, the size of the information increases, resulting in less visible area in which to view the information. Decreasing the screen resolution might, therefore, cause desktop icons to overlap or program toolbar buttons to be hidden.

Toolbars, buttons, and other elements can look different or appear in various locations in the program window when viewed at different screen resolutions. Variations in monitor shapes and sizes can also cause two screens set at the same resolution to look slightly different.

## To Change the Screen Resolution

The following steps change your screen resolution to 1024 × 768 to match the illustrations in this text.

- Click the Show desktop button on the taskbar, if necessary, to minimize all open windows so that the Windows Vista desktop appears.

- Right-click the Windows Vista desktop to display the Windows Vista desktop shortcut menu (Figure F–1).

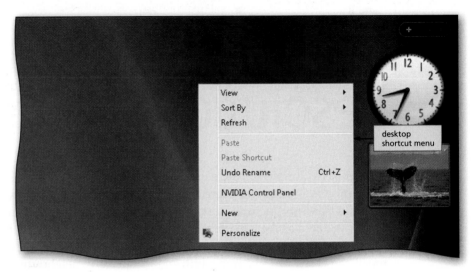

**Figure F–1**

- Click the Personalize command on the shortcut menu to open the Personalization window (Figure F–2).

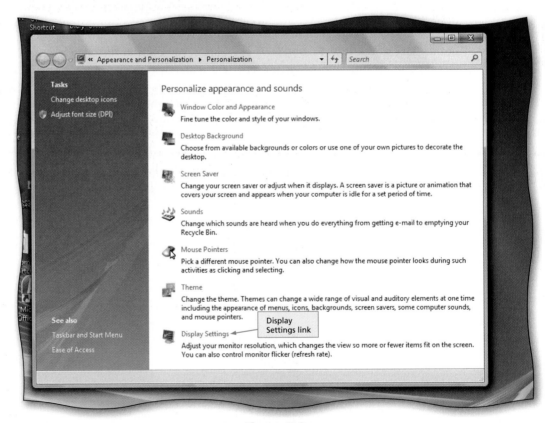

**Figure F–2**

**3**

- Click the Display Settings link in the Personalization window to open the Display Settings dialog box (Figure F–3).

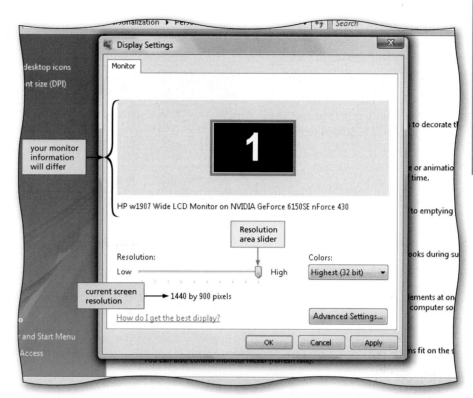

**Figure F–3**

**4**

- Drag the Resolution area slider to the left or right until the screen resolution is set to 1024 by 768 pixels (Figure F–4).

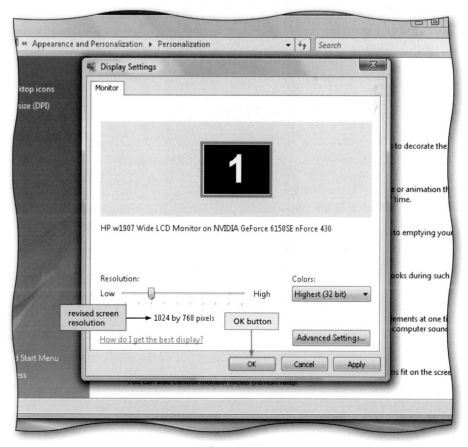

**Figure F–4**

- Click the OK button to close the Display Settings dialog box and change the screen resolution settings.

- Click the Yes button in the Display Settings dialog box to accept the new 1024 × 786 screen resolution (Figure F–5).

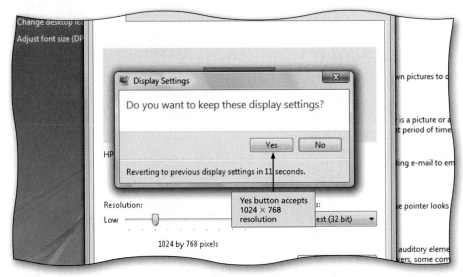

**Figure F–5**

- Click the Close button on the Personalize window title bar to close the window (Figure F–6).

- Observe any changes to the appearance of the desktop as a result of the new 1024 × 786 screen resolution.

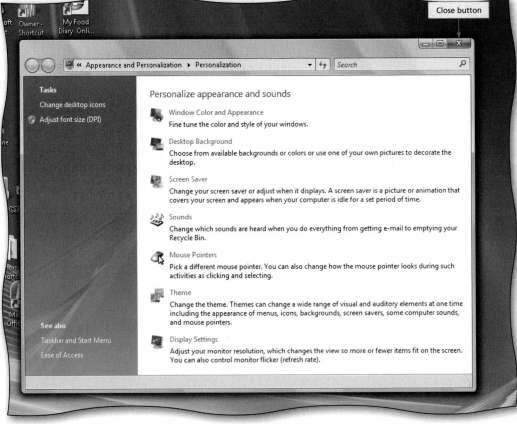

**Figure F–6**

# Index

Note: Page numbers in **boldface** type indicate key terms.

Special Characters, * (asterisk), EW 30

## A

accessibility, EW 75–76, APP 14–15
Accessibility Checker, **EW 516**
Accessibility Checker dialog box, EW 518
Accessibility Properties dialog box, EW 306, EW 327, EW 400, EW 406
Accessibility reports, EW 516–518
accredited registrars, **APP 16,** APP 21–22
ActiveX controls, **EW 372**
 allowing, EW 533
Add Choice dialog box, EW 393, EW 394
advertisers, **EW 625**
advertising. *See* marketing Web sites
advertising business model, EW 424
affiliate management networks, **EW 627,** EW 627–628
affiliate marketing programs, **EW 627,** EW 627–628
aligning images, EW 94
alignment, **EW 233**
all-in-one e-commerce solutions, **EW 437,** EW 437–438
alternate text, **EW 75,** EW 75–76
aspect ratio, **EW 89,** EW 89–93
ASP.NET controls, EW 550
asterisk (*), EW 30
Attach Style Sheet dialog box, EW 269, EW 270, EW 280, EW 281, EW 313, EW 314–315
attaching style sheets, **EW 242,** EW 268–270
 multiple style sheets, EW 280–282
 preformatted style sheets, EW 314–315

## B

Back button, Help toolbar, APP 5, **APP 6**
back office operations, **EW 429**
background images, **EW 557,** EW 557–567
 adding page content, EW 561–567

adding to pages, EW 558–561
 data tables, EW 316
BACKSPACE key, editing text, EW 183
balance, **EW 232,** EW 232–233
banner ads, **EW 625**
behaviors, **EW 368**
 helpful vs. annoying, identifying, EW 390
 jump menu, EW 390, EW 391–396
 status bar, EW 396–398
 swap image, EW 398–404
Behaviors task pane, EW 392
benchmarks, **EW 629**
beveling images, EW 99
bitmaps, **APP 26**
bookmarks, **EW 121,** EW 121–122
 adding, EW 122–126, EW 133–135
 browsers, EW 121
 copying and pasting, EW 128–129
 planning, EW 122
 testing, EW 126–127
borders, images, **EW 95,** EW 95–96
breadcrumb trail, APP 5
brightness, images, EW 99
Browse dialog box, EW 401
browsers, EW 48
 bookmarks, EW 121
 interactivity. *See* interactive buttons
 previewing in, EW 54–55
 previewing pages, EW 600
 testing sites with other browsers, EW 518
bulleted lists, **EW 25,** EW 25–27
business blogs, **EW 628**
business models, **EW 424**
 e-commerce, EW 424–428
business-to-business (B2B) business model, **EW 425,** EW 425–426
business-to-consumer (B2C) business model, **EW 425**
business-to-employee (B2E) business model, **EW 428**
business-to-government (B2G) business model, **EW 427,** EW 427–428
buttons. *See also specific button names*
 control, EW 454
 Help toolbar, APP 5, APP 6
 interactive (rollover). *See* interactive buttons
 option (radio). *See* radio buttons

Search, APP 8
Submit. *See* Submit buttons
view, EW 8

## C

Call Script behavior, EW 390
caption(s), data tables, **EW 316**
Caption Properties dialog box, EW 318, EW 319
card not present/card holder not present risk, **EW 434**
cascading, **EW 193**
Cascading Style Sheets (CSSs), EW 241–289, **EW 242**
 comments, EW 265
 creating external style sheets, EW 260–261
 CSS Properties task pane, EW 256–259
 CSS reports, EW 286–287
 CSS-based templates. *See* templates
 defining ID-based styles, EW 249–253
 entering CSS code, EW 265–270
 font families, EW 262–265
 positioning content using class-based styles, EW 254–256
 pre-built CSS layouts. *See* pre-built CSS layouts
 prioritizing rules, EW 246
 saving styles, EW 244
 site readability, EW 579
 speed, EW 259
 style sheets. *See* style sheets
 style types, EW 245
 syntax, EW 244–245
cell(s), data tables, **EW 302**
 adding and arranging content, EW 323
 adjusting margins, EW 319
 changing properties, EW 320–322
 inserting images, EW 326–329
 merging, EW 336, EW 337
 properties, EW 319–322
 splitting, EW 336, EW 338–339
 text entry, EW 323–326
Cell Properties dialog box, EW 322
centering text, EW 36
Change Font Size button, Help toolbar, **APP 6**
Change Property/Restore behavior, EW 390

character length, text box controls, EW 454

chargebacks, **EW 433**

check boxes, EW 453
 adding, EW 465–467
 setting values, EW 465

Check Browser behavior, EW 390

Check Plug-In behavior, EW 390

checkout process, **EW 430**

class(es), CSS, EW 245

class-based style(s), positioning content, EW 254–256

class-based style rules, **EW 245**

click-stream analysis, **EW 630**

click-throughs, **EW 627**

Clipboard, **EW 103**, EW 103–112
 copying images to other pages, EW 103–106

closing
 Microsoft Word, EW 182
 task panes, EW 85–87
 Web pages, EW 57
 Web sites in Windows XP, APP 36

Code view, **EW 48**, EW 49–51
 modifying pages, EW 266–268

colors
 custom, EW 15
 fonts, EW 37–38
 images, EW 99
 sorting information, EW 246
 Web design, EW 228–230

columns, data tables, **EW 302**
 adding, EW 329–333
 distributing, EW 345–346
 filling using Table Fill command, EW 333–336

commands. *See also specific command names*
 editing, EW 183
 toggle, EW 51

comments, CSS files, EW 265

Common toolbar, **EW 7**

Compatibility reports, EW 518–522

compression, **EW 75**

conserving ink and toner, EW 55

consistency, templates, EW 590

consumer-to-business (C2B) business model, **EW 427**

consumer-to-consumer (C2C) business model, **EW 426**

content
 adding and arranging in table cells, EW 323
 adding to pages, EW 561–567
 completing, pre-built CSS layouts, EW 276–280
 positioning using class-based styles, EW 254–256

contrast
 color schemes, EW 228
 images, EW 99

control buttons, EW 454

conversion rate, **EW 630**

converting text to tables, EW 342–346

copying
 images to other pages, EW 103–106
 interactive buttons, EW 379

copying and pasting
 internal links, EW 128–129
 navigation area, EW 385–386
 text from other pages, EW 274–280

cropping, EW 99, **EW 107,** EW 107–112

CSS(s). *See* Cascading Style Sheets (CSSs); style sheets

CSS Properties task pane, EW 256–258

CSS reports, EW 286–287

CSS Reports dialog box, EW 287

CSS Reports task pane, EW 287

CSS-based templates. *See* templates

custom colors, EW 15

customer support, e-commerce Web sites, EW 435

**D**

data, **EW 445**

data tables, **EW 302, EW 316,** EW 316–348
 adding content, EW 323
 adding rows and columns, EW 329–333
 arranging content, EW 323
 background images, EW 316
 captions, EW 316
 cells. *See* cells, data tables
 columns. *See* columns, data tables
 converting text to table, EW 342–346
 designing, EW 340
 formatting text, EW 340–341

header rows, EW 319
 images, EW 326–329
 inserting, EW 316–319
 navigation shortcuts, EW 323
 planning structure, EW 309
 rows. *See* rows, data tables
 saving default settings, EW 316
 splitting cells, EW 338–339
 table and cell properties, EW 319–322
 Table AutoFormat, EW 346–348
 Table Fill command, EW 333–336
 text entry, EW 323–326
 title rows, EW 336

database(s), **EW 442**, EW 445–446

database management systems, **EW 442**

declarations, **EW 194**

default site name, EW 159

DELETE key, editing text, EW 183

deleting. *See also* removing
 folders, EW 166
 Web pages, EW 164–165

delineating text, **EW 342**

descendent selectors, **EW 568**

Design view, EW 48

designing. *See also* Web design
 data tables, EW 340

discount rate, **EW 433**

displaying. *See also* viewing
 pages, inline frames, EW 349
 ruler, EW 87–88

distributing columns, **EW 345**

div(s) (<div> tags), **EW 20,** EW 20–23, EW 29
 heading styles, EW 34

division-based layout, **EW 20**

docking toolbars, EW 563

domain names, **APP 16**

drop caps, **EW 548**, EW 588–589

drop ship, **EW 434**

drop-down boxes, EW 453, **EW 458,** EW 458–462
 adding, EW 459–462
 assigning values, EW 458

duplicate filenames, EW 508

duplicating. *See* copying

dynamic Web templates, **EW 152,** EW 189–193, EW 372
 attaching to existing pages, EW 592–594

creating, EW 172, EW 189,
 EW 554–555
global changes, EW 190–193
previewing, EW 579

**E**

e-business. *See* e-commerce *entries*
e-commerce, EW 423–439, **EW 424**
 business models, EW 424–428
 role in today's business environment,
  EW 424
 Web hosting, EW 438
 Web sites. *See* e-commerce Web sites
e-commerce business models, **EW 424,**
 EW 424–428
e-commerce Web sites, EW 429–436
 all-in-one e-commerce solution,
  EW 437–438
 customer support, EW 435
 merchant accounts, EW 433–434
 order fulfillment, EW 434–435
 payment gateways, EW 432
 payment processors, EW 432
 product catalog, EW 429–430
 shopping cart, EW 430–432
 third-party payment processors,
  EW 436–437
 transaction security, EW 435–436
EDI (Electronic Data Interchange)
 systems, EW 424
Edit Hyperlink dialog box, EW 381,
 EW 393–394, EW 511
editable regions, **EW 172,** EW 590–591
editing interactive buttons, EW 380–382
editing text, EW 182–189
 finding and replacing text,
  EW 186–189
editing window, **EW 8**
EFT (electronic funds transfer)
 system, EW 424
electronic commerce. *See* e-commerce
 Web sites; e-commerce
Electronic Data Interchange (EDI)
 systems, EW 424
electronic funds transfer (EFT)
 system, EW 424
element(s)
 copying and pasting from other
  pages, EW 274–276
 CSS, EW 245

reusing, EW 378
 Web site e-commerce, EW 429–436
element-based style rules, **EW 245**
e-mail links, EW 135–138
 forms versus, EW 122, EW 135
embedding images, **EW 74**
encoding software, **APP 30,** APP 30–31
encryption, EW 445
enhancing images, EW 98–112
 cropping, EW 107–112
 transparency, EW 99–103
entry pages, **EW 222**
express checkout, EW 431
Expression Blend, **APP 28,** APP 28–30
Expression Design, **APP 26,**
 APP 26–27
Expression Encoder, **APP 30,**
 APP 30–31
Expression Media, **APP 27,** APP 27–28
Expression Web, EW 2, **APP 25,**
 APP 25–26
 quitting, EW 57–58
 starting, EW 6, EW 77, EW 246,
  EW 305, EW 371, EW 447,
  EW 501, EW 550–551
 starting in Windows XP, APP 33
 using in Windows XP, APP 32–36
Expression Web Help, EW 354,
 EW 373, APP 1–11
 browsing topics, APP 3–5
 content pane, APP 1
 index, APP 8
 opening window, APP 2–3
 resizing window, APP 3
 search bar, APP 8–10
 search pane, APP 1
 Table of Contents pane, APP 1,
  APP 7–8
 toolbar, APP 1, APP 5–6
Expression Web Online, APP 3
Expression Web 2 Help window,
 EW 55, EW 193, **APP 1,** APP 1–11
 browsing topics, APP 3–5
 content pane, APP 1
 index, APP 8
 opening window, APP 2–3
 resizing window, APP 3
 search bar, APP 8–10
 search pane, APP 1

Table of Contents pane, APP 1,
 APP 7–8
 toolbar, APP 1, APP 5–6
Extensible Hypertext Markup
 Language (XHTML), **EW 48**
Extensible Stylesheet Language
 (XSL), EW 244
external links, **EW 122,** EW 130–133
 adding, EW 130–131, EW 135–137,
  EW 478–481
 e-mail links, EW 135–138
 planning, EW 122
 ScreenTips, EW 137–138
 testing, EW 132–133
 verifying, EW 509–511
external style sheets, **EW 194,**
 EW 244
 creating, EW 260–261
extranets, **EW 424**

**F**

field values, **EW 445**
fieldset tags, **EW 462**
file(s)
 excluding from publication, EW 524
 importing, EW 555–557
 managing on remote servers,
  EW 530–533
 naming, EW 10, EW 156
 older, viewing, EW 500
 publishing to remote folders,
  EW 528–530
 unlinked, fixing, EW 503–507
file extensions, EW 5, EW 163
file formats, **EW 75**
File menu, EW 247
file size
 adjusting, EW 106
 compression, EW 118
File System, EW 523, **APP 19**
File Transfer Protocol (FTP),
 EW 523, **APP 19**
 FTP client software, publishing Web
  sites, APP 23–24
file upload controls, EW 454
filenames
 duplicate, EW 508
 home page, changing, EW 524
 naming files, EW 10, EW 156

finding and replacing text, EW 186–189
first letter pseudo class drop caps, EW 588
flipping images, EW 99
focal point, **EW 233**
folders
  adding, EW 167–168
  deleting, EW 166
  for images, creating, EW 118–121
  naming, EW 10, EW 156
  organizing button images into, EW 387–389
  organizing contents, EW 507–509
  remote, publishing files to, EW 528–530
  renaming, EW 161–162
font(s), **EW 235**
  changing, EW 34–45
  color, EW 37–38
  interactive buttons, EW 372
  monospace, EW 262
  sans serif, EW 262
  serif and sans serif, EW 235
  size, EW 39–40
  Web-safe, EW 262
font families, **EW 262,** EW 262–265
  creating, EW 262–265
form(s), EW 441–483, **EW 442**
  dividing, EW 444
  email links versus, EW 135
  planning and designing, EW 446–447
  rearranging using tables, EW 444
  testing, EW 481–482
form area, **EW 442**
  creating, EW 450–451
form controls, **EW 442,** EW 446–472
  adding, EW 453–472
  data input, EW 454
  form structure, EW 446–453
  labels, EW 464
  required, EW 464
  types, EW 453–454
form fields, **EW 442**
form handlers, **EW 442**
  specifying, EW 472–473
format
  planning for, EW 31
  text elements, EW 31
formatting, **EW 30,** EW 30–45
  centering text, EW 36
  font characteristics, EW 36–38

font choice, EW 43–45
font sizes, EW 36–43
heading styles, EW 33–35
Quick Tag Selector, EW 31–32
removing, EW 177, EW 244
Forward button, Help toolbar, APP 5, **APP 6**
frames, EW 233
  inline. *See* inline frames
  laying out Web pages, EW 354
framesets, **EW 354**
FrontPage Server Extensions, EW 523, **APP 19**
FTP (File Transfer Protocol), EW 523, **APP 19**
FTP client software, publishing Web sites, **APP 23,** APP 23–24
fulfillment houses, **EW 434**

## G

GIF (Graphics Interchange Format) format, EW 75
Go To URL behavior, EW 390
goals, Web sites, EW 219
  modifying, EW 629
Google Checkout, EW 431
graphics, EW 72. *See also* background images; image(s)
Graphics Interchange Format (GIF) format, EW 75
group boxes, **EW 446,** EW 454, **EW 462,** EW 462–464
  creating, EW 463–464
  radio buttons, EW 468

## H

header rows, data tables, **EW 319**
headings, **EW 30**
  styles, EW 33–35
Help system. *See* Expression Web Help; Expression Web 2 Help window
hierarchical structure, **EW 223**
high resolution, **EW 74**
Home button, Help toolbar, APP 5, **APP 6**
home pages, **EW 10**
  changing filename, EW 524
  inserting and formatting text, EW 594–599

hosting, **EW 522,** EW 522–523
  assessing options, EW 523
  virtual hosts, EW 522
  Web server types, EW 523
hotspots, **EW 368**
.htm file extension, EW 5
HTML (Hypertext Markup Language), **EW 48**
  optimizing, EW 526–527
  saving reports as HTML pages, EW 512–515
.html file extension, EW 5
HTML meta tags, **EW 621**
HTML tags, EW 48, EW 621
HTML title tags, **EW 621**
hyperlinks, **EW 72.** *See also* bookmarks; external links; link(s); mailto links
Hypertext Markup Language (HTML). *See* HTML (Hypertext Markup Language)

## I

ID(s), CSS, EW 245
ID-based style(s), EW 567–568
  defining, EW 249–253
ID-based style rules, **EW 245**
I-frames. *See* inline frames
image(s), **EW 72**
  accessibility, EW 75–76
  aligning, EW 94
  background. *See* background images
  beveling, EW 99
  bitmaps, APP 26
  borders, EW 95–96
  brightness, EW 99
  button, organizing into folders, EW 387–389
  changing dimensions, EW 405
  color, EW 99
  contrast, EW 99
  creating folder for, EW 118–121
  cropping, EW 99, EW 107–112
  embedding, EW 74
  enhancing, EW 98–112
  from external devices, EW 75
  flipping, EW 99
  inserting, EW 80–83
  inserting in cells, EW 326–329
  layering, EW 99

margins, EW 95, EW 97–98

planning for, EW 76

positioning, EW 93–98

raster graphics, APP 26

resampling, EW 89, EW 99

resizing, EW 89–93

rotating, EW 99

sources, EW 74

technical considerations, EW 74–75

templates, EW 154

tiled, EW 557–558

vector graphics, APP 26

watermarks, EW 558

Web-ready, EW 236

image maps, **EW 368,** EW 404–409

importing files, EW 555–557

impressions, **EW 627**

indenting, **EW 41**

indent size, EW 41

text, EW 41

index, Expression Web Help, APP 8

information, **EW 445**

inheritance, **EW 245**

ink, conserving, EW 55

inline frames, **EW 302,** EW 348–353

creating, EW 349–351

displaying pages, EW 349

security, EW 348

targeting links, EW 352–353

inline styles, **EW 194,** EW 244

Insert Hyperlink dialog box,
EW 283–284, EW 408

Insert Table dialog box, EW 317

Intellisense, **EW 265**

interactive buttons, **EW 368.** *See also*
dynamic Web templates

creating, EW 373–378

duplicating, EW 379

editing, EW 380–382

fonts, EW 372

organizing into folders, EW 387–389

testing, EW 382–384

uses, EW 378

Interactive Buttons dialog box,
EW 374–376, EW 380

interactivity, EW 367–409, **EW 368**

behaviors. *See* behaviors

buttons. *See* interactive buttons

definition, EW 368

overview, EW 370

internal links. *See* bookmarks

internal style sheets, **EW 194,** EW 244

Internet connection, speed, EW 112

Internet Service Providers (ISPs),
**EW 522, APP 17**

intranets, **EW 424**

inventory, virtual, EW 434

ISPs (Internet Service Providers),
APP 17

italicizing text, EW 42–43

**J**

JavaScript, **EW 368**

Joint Photographic Experts Group
(JPEG) format, EW 75

jump menu(s), **EW 368,** EW 390,
EW 391–396

Jump Menu dialog box, EW 393,
EW 395

Jump Menu/Go behavior, EW 390

**K**

keyboard shortcuts, table navigation,
EW 323

keywords, **EW 14**

spelling, EW 15

**L**

labels, **EW 464**

layering images, EW 99

layout(s). *See* page layout; pre-built
CSS layouts; workspace layout

layout tables, EW 233, **EW 354**

legends, **EW 446**

Length dialog box, EW 258–259

line breaks, extra, removing, EW 177

line height, specifying, EW 584–586

line length, specifying, EW 586–588

linear structure, **EW 222**

link(s), **EW 72,** EW 121–138

adding to pages, EW 283–284

external. *See* external links; mailto
links

fixing unlinked files, EW 503–507

internal. *See* bookmarks

planning, EW 122

reciprocal, EW 625

targeting, inline frames, EW 352–353

link exchange programs, **EW 625**

list-based navigation, **EW 568,**
EW 568–579

adding CSS rules to list, EW 571–574

creating list-based navigation area,
EW 569–571

rollovers, EW 574–579

selecting style names, EW 572

live Web servers, **APP 19**

Local to remote option, **EW 524**

Remote Web Site view, APP 22

Local Web Site pane, Remote Web
Site view, **APP 21**

lossless compression, EW 75

lossy compression, **EW 75**

**M**

mailto links, **EW 122,** EW 135–138

planning, EW 122

ScreenTips, EW 137–138

margins, images, **EW 95,** EW 97–98

marketing Web sites, EW 620–629

affiliate marketing programs,
EW 627–628

business blogs, EW 628

link exchange, EW 625

newsletters, EW 628

online ads, EW 625–627

paid placement programs,
EW 622–625

permission-based e-mail advertising,
EW 628

print advertising, EW 629

search tool submission, EW 621–622

SEO, EW 620–621

spam, EW 628

word-of-mouth advertising, EW 629

master pages, EW 501

masthead, **EW 20**

menu(s), jump, EW 390, EW 391–396

menu bar, **EW 7**

merchant accounts, **EW 423,**
EW 433–434

merging cells, data tables, **EW 336,**
EW 337

meta tags, EW 621

metadata, EW 160

Microsoft Expression Studio 2, **EW 2,**
APP 25–31

Expression Blend, APP 28–30

Expression Design, APP 26–27

Expression Encoder, APP 30–31
Expression Media, APP 27–28
Expression Web, APP 25–26
Microsoft Expression Web 2, **EW 2.**
    *See also* Expression Web
Microsoft Word, closing, EW 182
mobile devices, making sites
    compatible with, EW 516
Modify Style dialog box, EW 249–251,
    EW 252–253
monospace fonts, **EW 262**
multimedia, EW 236
multiple items, selecting, EW 453
multiple style sheets, attaching,
    EW 280–282

**N**

naming files and folders, EW 10,
    EW 156
navigation
  list-based, EW 568–579
  planning, EW 373, EW 567
  site pages without links in primary
    navigation area, EW 405
navigation area, **EW 20**
  access to site pages without links in
    primary navigation area, EW 405
  copying and pasting, EW 385–386
  list-based, creating, EW 569–571
navigation bar, updating, EW 163
navigation system, **EW 224,**
    EW 224–226
navigational links. *See* bookmarks;
    external links; link(s); mailto links
New dialog box, EW 271–272,
    EW 305, EW 310
New Style dialog box, EW 254–256
New submenu, EW 260
New Web Site dialog box, EW 306
newsletters, **EW 628**
Not on Top button, Help toolbar,
    **APP 6**

**O**

objectives, Web sites, EW 219,
    EW 629
older files, viewing, EW 500
online advertising networks, **EW 627**
Open Browser Window behavior,
    EW 390

Open Site dialog box, EW 247
opening
  existing Web sites in Windows XP,
    APP 34–35
  Expression Web Help window,
    APP 2–3
  Web pages, EW 14, EW 248
  Web sites, EW 77–80, EW 247–248,
    EW 501–502
optimizing HYML, EW 526–527
opt-in e-mail advertising, **EW 628**
option buttons. *See* radio buttons
order fulfillment, EW 434–435

**P**

<p> tags, EW 23–25, EW 28
padding, EW 95
page description, **EW 14**
Page Editor Options dialog box,
    EW 263–265
page layout, EW 19
  division-based, EW 20
  planning for, EW 19
page properties, setting, EW 14–19
Page Properties dialog box, EW 15–18
page title, **EW 14**
page views, **EW 630**
paid placement programs, **EW 622,**
    EW 622–625
paragraph text, EW 23–25
passwords, text box controls, EW 454
Paste Text dialog box, EW 279
pasting. *See also* copying and pasting
    text, EW 177–181
payment gateways, **EW 432**
payment processors, **EW 432**
PayPal Express, EW 431
pay-per-click programs, **EW 622,**
    EW 622–625
permission-based e-mail advertising
    messages, **EW 628**
Personal Web Packages, **EW 556**
Picture dialog box, EW 306, EW 327,
    EW 399, EW 406
Picture Properties dialog box, EW 328
pixels, **EW 74, APP 37**
pixilated images, **EW 74**
placeholders, **EW 76, EW 156,**
    EW 156–159
Play Sound behavior, EW 390

Popup Message behavior, EW 390
Portable Network Graphic (PNG)
    format, EW 75
portfolios, **EW 152**
  planning, EW 154
positioning
  content using class-based styles,
    EW 254–256
  images, EW 93–98
pre-built CSS layouts, EW 271–289
  adding hyperlinks, EW 283–284
  attaching multiple style sheets,
    EW 280–282
  completing page content, EW 276–280
  copying and pasting elements,
    EW 274–276
  CSS reports, EW 286–287
  organizing style sheets, EW 284–286
  previewing sites, EW 288–289
  using, EW 271–274
preformatted style sheets, EW 309–315
  attaching, EW 314–315
  creating new style sheets, EW 310–313
Preload Images behavior, EW 390
previewing
  dynamic Web templates, EW 579
  Web pages in browsers, EW 600
  Web sites, EW 54–55, EW 138–139,
    EW 203, EW 288–289
primary goals, **EW 219**
primary key, **EW 445**
print advertising, EW 629
Print button, Help toolbar, APP 5,
    **APP 6**
Print Preview feature, EW 56
printing
  style sheets, EW 567
  Web pages, EW 55–56
privacy issues, personal Web sites,
    EW 152
product catalogs, **EW 429,**
    EW 429–430
prompting text, **EW 442**
properties, **EW 194**
proportions, **EW 89,** EW 89–93
proximity, **EW 233**
publishers, **EW 627**
publishing, **APP 16,** APP 16–24
  defining Web server types, EW 523
  excluding files from publication,
    EW 524

initiating publication, EW 524
publishing files to remote folders,
 EW 528–530
Remote Web Site view, APP 21–22
setting options, EW 524–525
setting publishing options, EW 525
setting remote Web site properties,
 APP 19–21
using Expression Web, APP 19–22
using FTP software, APP 23–24
pull quotes, EW 579
Push buttons. *See* Submit buttons

## Q

quick tag(s), **EW 51**
Quick Tag Selector, EW 31–32,
 EW 51–52
Quick Tag Selector bar, **EW 8**
quitting Expression Web, EW 57–58

## R

radio buttons, EW 442, EW 454,
 **EW 464,** EW 464–465
 adding, EW 469–471
 group boxes, EW 468
 setting values, EW 465
raster graphics, **APP 26**
readability
 styles, EW 579
 typography, EW 579, EW 584–588
reciprocal links, **EW 625**
records, **EW 445**
Refresh button, Help toolbar, APP 5,
 **APP 6**
registrars, accredited, APP 16
Rehabilitation Act, Section 508 of,
 APP 14
Remote to local option, **EW 524**
 Remote Web Site view, APP 22
remote Web site, setting properties,
 APP 19–21
Remote Web Site pane, Remote Web
 Site view, **APP 21**
Remote Web Site view, **APP 21,**
 APP 21–22
removing. *See also* deleting
 extra line breaks, EW 177
 formatting, EW 177, EW 244

renaming
 folders, EW 161–162
 Web pages, EW 162–163
repeat visitors, **EW 630**
replacing
 template placeholder text,
  EW 172–176
 text, EW 186–189
reports
 Accessibility, EW 516–518
 Compatibility, EW 518–522
 CSS, EW 286–287
 Site Summary. *See* Site Summary
  reports
Reports View dialog box, failure to
 open, EW 510
resampling images, **EW 89,** EW 99
resetting workspace layout, EW 9,
 EW 77, EW 550, EW 551
resizing
 Expression Web Help window, APP 3
 images, EW 89–93
resolution, **EW 74**
 changing, APP 37–40
Restore command, EW 390
reusing elements, EW 378
RIAs (rich interactive applications),
 **APP 28**
rich interactive applications (RIAs),
 **APP 28**
rich media ads, EW 625, EW 627
rollover(s), EW 574–579
rollover buttons. *See* interactive
 buttons
rotating images, EW 99
rows, data tables, **EW 302**
 adding, EW 329–333
 distributing, EW 345–346
 filling using Table Fill command,
  EW 333
 header rows, EW 319
 new, creating, EW 336–337
 title rows, EW 336
rule(s), CSS, prioritizing, EW 246
ruler, displaying, EW 87–88
running Site Summary reports,
 EW 502–503

## S

sans serif fonts, **EW 262**
Save As dialog box, EW 273, EW 311
saving
 data table default settings, EW 316
 reports as HTML pages,
  EW 512–515
 styles, EW 244
 Web pages, EW 30
screen resolution, **APP 37**
 changing, APP 37–40
ScreenTips, **EW 137**
 mailto links, EW 137–138
search bar, Expression Web Help,
 **APP 1,** APP 8–10
search boxes, EW 122
Search button, **APP 8**
search directories, **EW 621,**
 EW 621–622
search engine(s), **EW 620**
search engine optimization (SEO),
 EW 523, **EW 620,** EW 620–621
search text box, **APP 8**
search tool paid placement programs,
 EW 622–625
secondary goals, **EW 219**
Section 508, **APP 14**
security
 e-commerce Web site transactions,
  EW 435–436
 inline frames, EW 348
Select Style Sheet dialog box, EW 269,
 EW 281, EW 313, EW 314
selecting
 multiple items, EW 453
 style names, EW 572
selectors, **EW 194**
 descendent, EW 568
SEO (search engine optimization),
 EW 523, **EW 620,** EW 620–621
serifs, **EW 235**
server(s). *See* Web server *entries*
server-side Web technologies, APP 18
Set Text behavior, EW 390
Set Text of Status Bar dialog box,
 EW 397
setting page properties, EW 14–19
shopping carts, **EW 430,** EW 430–432

shortcuts, editing, EW 183

Show Table of Contents button, Help toolbar, **APP 6**

sidebar(s), **EW 548,** EW 579–583

sidebar ads, **EW 625**

Site Summary reports, EW 500–515

  categories, EW 501

  determining which issues to fix, EW 515

  fixing unlinked files, EW 503–507

  organizing site folder contents, EW 507–509

  running, EW 502–503

  saving as HTML page, EW 512–515

  verifying external hyperlinks, EW 509–511

size. *See also* resizing

  files. *See* file size

  fonts, EW 39–40

  indents, EW 41

spam, **EW 628**

specificity, **EW 193**

specifying

  line height, EW 584–586

  line length, EW 586–588

speed

  CSSs, EW 259

  Internet connection, EW 112

spell checker, **EW 45,** EW 45–47

spelling keywords, EW 15

splash pages, **EW 222**

Split Cells dialog box, EW 338

Split view, **EW 48,** EW 49–51

splitting cells, data tables, **EW 336,** EW 338–339

sponsored listings, **EW 622,** EW 622–625

standards, **APP 12**

starting Expression Web, EW 6, EW 77, EW 246, EW 305, EW 371, EW 447, EW 501, EW 550–551

  in Windows XP, APP 33

status bar, **EW 8**

status bar behaviors, **EW 396,** EW 396–398

Stop button, Help toolbar, APP 5, **APP 6**

striping, **EW 340**

structure of forms, form controls, EW 446–453

structure of site, EW 160–171, **EW 222–223**

  adding folders, EW 167–168

  adding Web pages, EW 169–171

  deleting folders, EW 166

  deleting Web pages, EW 164–165

  hierarchical, EW 223

  linear, EW 222

  modifying, EW 163–171

  planning, EW 160

  renaming folders, EW 161–162

  renaming Web pages, EW 162–163

  setting up, EW 551

  webbed, EW 223

style(s). *See also* Cascading Style Sheets (CSSs); style sheets

  adding to navigation list, EW 571–574

  applying, EW 201–202

  applying to table text, EW 340–341

  creating, EW 198–201

  headings, EW 33–35

  ID-based, EW 567–568

  inline, EW 194, EW 244

  modifying, EW 195–197

  modifying using CSS Properties task pane, EW 256–259

  planning, EW 195

  saving, EW 244

  selecting style names, EW 572

  Submit buttons, EW 475–478

  syntax of rules, EW 194

  text, EW 20, **EW 20**

style sheets, **EW 193, EW 242.** *See also* Cascading Style Sheets (CSSs); pre-built CSS layouts

  attaching. *See* attaching style sheets

  external, EW 194, EW 244, EW 260–261

  internal, EW 194, EW 244

  multiple, attaching, EW 280–282

  organizing, EW 284–286

  preformatted. *See* preformatted style sheets

  printing, EW 567

  reusing, EW 556

  types, EW 194

  user-defined, EW 260

subfolders, EW 160

Submit buttons, **EW 442,** EW 472–482

  adding, EW 4730475

  adding links, EW 478–481

creating and applying new style, EW 475–478

  form handlers, EW 472–473

  testing, EW 481–482

subscription business model, EW 424

subsidiary pages, **EW 221**

swap image behaviors, **EW 398,** EW 398–404

  adding, EW 399–402

  modifying, EW 402–404

Swap Image/Restore behavior, EW 390

Swap Images dialog box, EW 401

Synchronize option, **EW 524**

  Remote Web Site view, APP 22, **APP 22**

syntax, CSS, EW 244–245

### T

tab order, setting, EW 446

table(s)

  creating, EW 452–453

  data. *See* data tables

  layout, EW 354

  rearranging forms using, EW 444

Table AutoFormat, **EW 346,** EW 346–348

Table Fill command, **EW 333,** EW 333–336

Table of Contents pane, Expression Web Help, **APP 1,** APP 7–8

Table Properties dialog box, EW 320, EW 322, EW 345

Tables toolbar, adding rows and columns, EW 329–333

target audience, **EW 220**

targeting links, inline frames, EW 352–353

task panes, **EW 8,** EW 84–88

  closing, EW 85–87

technology standards, **APP 12**

templates, EW 547–601

  dynamic, creating, EW 554–555

  site consistency, EW 590

  Web. *See* dynamic Web templates; Web templates

temporary staging servers, **APP 19**

testing interactive buttons, EW 382–384

text, EW 172–189. *See also* font(s); font families
alternate, EW 75–76
centering, EW 36
content, EW 19
converting to table, EW 342–346
copying and pasting from other pages, EW 274–280
delineating, EW 342
editing, EW 182–189
finding and replacing, EW 186–189
formatting. *See* formatting
indenting, EW 41
inserting and formatting for home page, EW 594–599
italicizing, EW 42–43
pasting, EW 177–181
placeholder, replacing, EW 172–176
planning content, EW 172
planning for, EW 19
specifying line height, EW 584–586
specifying line length, EW 586–588
spell checking, EW 45–47
tables, applying styles, EW 340–341
writing, EW 234–235
text area, **EW 454**
adding, EW 471–472
text box controls, **EW 454,** EW 454–458
adding, EW 454–457
assigning properties, EW 457–458
character length, EW 454
passwords, EW 454
text elements, format, EW 31
text entry, EW 20–29
bulleted lists, EW 25–27
data tables, EW 323–326
<div> tags, EW 20–23
paragraph text, EW 23–25
text wrapping, **EW 93**
third-party logistics providers, **EW 434**
third-party payment processors, **EW 436,** EW 436–438
thumbnails, **EW 112,** EW 112–121
creating, EW 113–118
tiled images, **EW 557–558**
title bar, **EW 7**
title rows, data tables, **EW 336**
title tags, EW 621

toggle commands, EW 51
toner, conserving, EW 55
toolbar(s), EW 8–9
docking, EW 563
Expression Web Help, APP 1, **APP 1,** APP 5–6
Toolbar Options button, Help toolbar, APP 5, **APP 6**
tracer lines, data tables, **EW 316**
transaction security, e-commerce Web sites, EW 435–436
transparency, images, EW 99–103
typography, **EW 548**
site readability, EW 579, EW 584–588

**U**

undoing changes, EW 96
unique visitors, **EW 630**
unlinked files, fixing, EW 503–507
updating navigation bar, EW 163
uptime, **EW 523**
usability testing, **EW 226**
USB flash drives, EW 12
user-defined style sheets, EW 260

**V**

values, **EW 194, EW 445**
drop-down boxes, EW 458
vector graphics, **APP 26**
verifying external links, EW 509–511
view(s), EW 48–53
Code view, EW 49–51
quick tags, EW 51
Split view, EW 49–51
visual aids, EW 51, EW 52–53
view buttons, **EW 8**
viewing. *See also* displaying
older files, EW 500
virtual hosts, **EW 522**
virtual inventory, **EW 434**
virtual storefront business model, EW 424
visual aids, EW 51

**W**

watermarks, EW 558
W3C (World Wide Web Consortium), EW 19

WCAG (Web Content Accessibility Guidelines), **EW 516,** EW 516–517
Web accessibility guidelines, **APP 14**
Web Accessibility Initiative, **APP 14**
Web analytics, **EW 630,** EW 630–631
Web browsers. *See* browsers; interactive buttons
Web Content Accessibility Guidelines (WCAG), **EW 516,** EW 516–517
Web design, EW 217–237
alignment, EW 233
balance, EW 232–233
color schemes, EW 228–230
focal point, EW 233
navigation system, EW 224–226
page length and content positioning, EW 230–231
page types, EW 220–222
pre- and post-publishing testing, EW 237
proximity, EW 233
purpose of site, EW 219
site structure, EW 222–223
target audience, EW 110
Web-ready images and multimedia, EW 236
writing text, EW 234–235
Web hosting, e-commerce, EW 438
Web hosting services, **APP 17**
Web page(s). *See also* home pages; page *entries*
adding, EW 169–171
closing, EW 57
creating from another page, EW 448–450
deleting, EW 164–165
description, EW 14
displaying using inline frames, EW 349
editable regions, EW 172, EW 590–591
existing, attaching dynamic Web templates, EW 592–594
layout. *See* page layout
length and content positioning, EW 230–231
modifying in Code view, EW 266–268
opening, EW 14, EW 248
renaming, EW 162–163
saving, EW 30

setting page properties, EW 14–19
splash (entry), EW 222
subsidiary, EW 221
title, EW 14
Web page tab, **EW 8**
Web server(s), **EW 522, APP 17**
  remote, managing files on,
    EW 530–533
  types, EW 523
Web server log analysis software,
  **EW 630**
Web server space, **APP 17**
Web site(s), **EW 2**
  accommodating future growth,
    EW 550
  closing in Windows XP, APP 36
  creating, EW 10–13
  default name, EW 159
  existing, opening in Windows XP,
    APP 34–35
  hosting, EW 522–523
  maintenance, EW 629
  opening, EW 77–80, EW 247–248,
    EW 501–502
  performance evaluation. *See* Web site
    performance valuation
  pre- and post-publishing testing,
    EW 237
  previewing, EW 138–139, EW 203,
    EW 288–289
  structure. *See* structure of site
  technical aspects, EW 502

Web site goal, **EW 219**
Web site objectives, **EW 219**
Web site performance valuation,
  EW 629–631
  Web analytics, EW 630–631
  Web server log analysis, EW 630
Web standards, EW 19, **APP 12,**
  APP 12–13
Web templates, **EW 152,** EW 154–159
  creating new Web site, EW 157–159
  dynamic. *See* dynamic Web templates
  images, EW 154
  replacing placeholder text,
    EW 172–176
  styles and style sheets, EW 193–204
  types, EW 155
Web-based Distributed Authoring and
  Versioning (WebDAV), EW 523,
  **APP 19**
webbed structure, **EW 223**
WebDAV (Web-based Distributed
  Authoring and Versioning),
  EW 523, **APP 19**
Web-ready images, EW 236
Web-safe fonts, EW 262
Web-safe palette, EW 230
What You See Is What You Get
  (WYSIWYG) design interface,
  **EW 2**
What You See Is What You Get
  (WYSIWYG) editor, **APP 25**

white space, EW 24
Windows XP
  closing Web sites, APP 36
  opening existing Web sites, APP 34–35
  using Expression Web in, APP 32–36
word-of-mouth advertising, **EW 629**
workspace, EW 7–8
workspace layout
  adjusting, EW 84–88
  resetting, EW 9, EW 77, EW 246,
    EW 305, EW 371, EW 550,
    EW 551
  task panes, EW 84–88
workspace window, EW 7–8
World Wide Web Consortium
  (W3C), EW 19
  WCAG, EW 516–517
WYSIWYG (What You See Is What
  You Get) design interface, **EW 2**
WYSIWYG (What You See Is What
  You Get) editor, **APP 25**

**X**

XHTML (Extensible Hypertext
  Markup Language), **EW 48**
XSL (Extensible Stylesheet Language),
  EW 244

# Quick Reference Summary

In the Microsoft Expression Web 2 program, you can accomplish a task in a number of ways. The following table provides a quick reference to each task presented in this textbook. The first column identifies the task. The second column indicates the page number on which the task is discussed in the book. The subsequent four columns list the different ways the task in column one can be carried out.

## Microsoft Expression Web Quick Reference Summary

| Task | Page Number | Mouse | Menu Bar | Shortcut Menu | Keyboard Shortcut |
|------|-------------|-------|----------|---------------|-------------------|
| Add a Background Image to a Page | EW 558 | body tag on Quick Tag Selector \| Modify Style link in Apply Styles task pane \| Background in the Category list \| Browse button \| select background image \| Open button \| OK button | File \| Properties \| Formatting tab \| Background picture check box \| Browse button \| select background image \| Open button \| OK button | | |
| Add a Form Control | EW 455 | Double-click *form control* in Toolbox OR Drag *form control* from Toolbox to page | | Right-click *form control* in Toolbox, then click Insert | |
| Add a Sidebar Element | EW 580 | *div* tag on Quick Tag Selector \| type navlist in id field in Tag Properties task pane \| ENTER | | | |
| Add a Submit Button | EW 473 | Double-click Input(Submit) in Toolbox OR Drag Input(Submit) from Toolbox to page | | Right-click Input (Submit) in Toolbox, then click Insert | |
| Add Folder | EW 167 | New Folder button on Folder List | File \| New \| Folder | | |
| Assign Properties to a Form Control | EW 457 | | Format \| Properties | Right-click *form control* on page, then click Form Field Properties | |
| Attach a Dynamic Web Template to Existing Pages | EW 592 | | Format \| Dynamic Web Template \| Attach Dynamic Web Template | | |
| Behavior, Insert | EW 391 | Click the Insert button in the Behaviors task pane, then click the Behavior to add | | | |
| Behavior, Modify | EW 402 | Double-click behavior in Behaviors task pane to open *behavior* dialog box | | | |
| Bold | EW 30 | Bold button on Common toolbar | Format \| Font | Font | CTRL+B |

**Microsoft Expression Web Quick Reference Summary** *(continued)*

| Task | Page Number | Mouse | Menu Bar | Shortcut Menu | Keyboard Shortcut |
|---|---|---|---|---|---|
| **Bookmark, Insert** | EW 133 | | Insert \| Bookmark | | CTRL+G |
| **Bullets** | EW 25 | Bullets button on Common toolbar | Format \| Bullets and Numbering | | |
| **Caption, Add to Table** | EW 317 | | Table \| Insert \| Caption | Insert \| Caption | |
| **Cell Properties, Change** | EW 320 | | Table \| Table Properties | Cell Properties | |
| **Cell, Split** | EW 338 | Split Cells button on Tables toolbar | Table \| Modify \| Split Cells | Modify \| Split Cells | |
| **Cells, Merge** | EW 338 | Merge Cells button on Tables toolbar | Table \| Modify \| Merge Cells | Modify \| Merge Cells | |
| **Center Text** | EW 36 | Center button on Common toolbar | Format \| Paragraph | | CTRL+E |
| **Close Page** | EW 57 | Close button on editing window | File \| Close | Close | CTRL+W |
| **Close Site** | EW 57 | | File \| Close Site | | |
| **Copy** | EW 103 | | Edit \| Copy | Copy | CTRL+C |
| **Create a Compatibility Report** | EW 519 | | Tools \| Compatibility Reports | | |
| **Create a Form Area** | EW 450 | Double-click Form in Toolbox | | Right-click Form in Toolbox, then click Insert | |
| **Create a List-Based Navigation Area** | EW 569 | Click Bullets button on Common toolbar \| type navigation list \| add hyperlink to each list item \| ul tag on Quick Tag Selector \| type navlist in id field in Tag Properties task pane \| ENTER | | | |
| **Create a New Dynamic Web Template** | EW 554 | | File \| New \| Create from Dynamic Web Template | | CTRL+S, type *filename*.dwt in File name text box, then press ENTER |
| **Create an Accessibility Report** | EW 518 | | Tools \| Accessibility Reports | | |
| **Crop an Image** | EW 107 | Crop button on Common toolbar \| drag cropping handles \| Crop button on Common toolbar again | | | |
| **CSS Layout Page, New** | EW 271 | | File \| New \| Page \| CSS Layouts | | |
| **CSS Report, Run** | EW 286 | | Tools \| CSS Reports | | |
| **Define Editable Regions** | EW 590 | | Format \| Dynamic Web Template \| Manage Editable Regions | Manage Editable Regions | |
| **Delete File or Folder** | EW 166 | | Edit \| Delete | Delete | DELETE |
| **Delete Text (Left of Insertion Point)** | EW 183 | | | | BACKSPACE |
| **Delete Text (Right of Insertion Point)** | EW 183 | | | | DELETE |

## Microsoft Expression Web Quick Reference Summary *(continued)*

| Task | Page Number | Mouse | Menu Bar | Shortcut Menu | Keyboard Shortcut |
|------|-------------|-------|----------|---------------|-------------------|
| E-mail Link, Add | EW 135 | | Insert \| Hyperlink | Hyperlink | CTRL+K |
| Find Text | EW 186 | | Edit \| Find | | CTRL+F |
| Font | EW 44 | Font box arrow on Common toolbar | Format \| Font | Font | |
| Font Color | EW 37 | Font Color arrow on Common toolbar | Format \| Font | Font | |
| Font Family, Create | EW 262 | | Tools \| Page Editor Options \| Font Families tab | | |
| Font Size | EW 39 | Font Size box arrow on Common toolbar | Format \| Font | Font | |
| Heading Style, Add | EW 33 | Style box arrow on Common toolbar | | | |
| Hotspot, Add | EW 405 | *Shape* Hotspot button on the Pictures toolbar \| draw hotspot shape | | | |
| Hyperlink, Insert | EW 122 | | Insert \| Hyperlink | Hyperlink | CTRL+K |
| Image, Align | EW 94 | Double-click image to open Picture Properties dialog box | Format \| Properties \| Appearance tab | Picture Properties \| Appearance tab | |
| Image, Insert | EW 80 | Insert Picture from File button on Common toolbar | Insert \| Picture \| From File | | |
| Image Margins, Modify | EW 97 | Drag margin border Or Double-click image to open the Picture Properties dialog box | Format \| Properties \| Appearance tab | Picture Properties \| Appearance tab | |
| Image, Resize | EW 89 | Drag corner resize Or Double-click image to open Picture Properties dialog box | Format \| Properties \| Appearance tab | Picture Properties \| Appearance tab | |
| Images, Borders and Padding | EW 95 | Borders button arrow on Common toolbar | Format \| Borders and Shading | | Hold SHIFT \| drag blue lines around graphic |
| Import Files into a Site | EW 556 | | File \| Import \| File | | |
| Indent Text | EW 41 | Increase Indent Position button on Common toolbar | Format \| Paragraph | | CTRL+M |
| Inline Frame, Add Link | EW 352 | Set Initial Page button in I-frame | | | |
| Inline Frame, Insert | EW 349 | Double-click Inline Frame button in Toolbox | Insert \| HTML \| Inline Frame | | |
| Interactive Button, Create | EW 373 | | Insert \| Interactive Button | | |
| Interactive Button, Edit | EW 380 | Double-click to open Interactive Buttons dialog box | | Button Properties | |
| Italics | EW 30 | Italics button on Common toolbar | Format \| Font | Font | CTRL+I |
| New Folder, Create | EW 118 | New Folder button on Folder List title bar | File \| New \| Folder | New Folder | |
| New Web Page | EW 169 | | File \| New \| Page | | CTRL+N |
| Optimize HTML | EW 526 | | Tools \| Optimize HTML | | |
| Page Properties, Set | EW 15 | | File \| Properties | Page Properties | |
| Paste | EW 103 | | Edit \| Paste | Paste | CTRL+V |

## Microsoft Expression Web Quick Reference Summary *(continued)*

| Task | Page Number | Mouse | Menu Bar | Shortcut Menu | Keyboard Shortcut |
|------|-------------|-------|----------|---------------|-------------------|
| **Paste Formatted Text** | EW 177 | | Edit \| Paste | | CTRL+V |
| **Paste Unformatted Text** | EW 177 | | Edit \| Paste Text | | |
| **Preview Site** | EW 54 | Preview in *browser* button arrow on Common toolbar \| *browser* | File \| Preview in Browser \| *browser* | | F12 |
| **Print** | EW 56 | | File \| Print \| Print | | CTRL+P |
| **Publish Files to a Remote Folder** | EW 528 | | File \| Publish Site | | |
| **Quick Tag Selector, Use** | EW 31 | Tag on Quick Tag Selector bar | | | |
| **Quit Expression Web** | EW 58 | Close button on program window title bar | File \| Exit | | |
| **Remove Formatting** | EW 177 | Paste Options button below pasted text \| Remove Formatting | Format \| Remove Formatting | | CTRL+SHIFT+Z |
| **Rename File or Folder** | EW 161 | Click the file or folder twice \| type new name | | Rename | |
| **Replace Template Text** | EW 172 | Select tag on Quick Tag Selector bar \| type replacement text | | | |
| **Replace Text** | EW 183 | | Edit \| Replace | | CTRL+H |
| **Reset Workspace Layout** | EW 9 | | Task Panes \| Reset Workspace Layout | | |
| **Rulers, Show or Hide** | EW 87 | | View \| Ruler and Grid \| Show Ruler | | |
| **Run a Site Summary Report** | EW 502 | | Site \| Reports \| Site Summary | | |
| **Save a Report as an HTML Page** | EW 512 | | File \| Save As | | CTRL+S |
| **Save Web Page** | EW 36 | Save button on Common toolbar | File \| Save | Save | CTRL+S |
| **ScreenTip, Add to Hyperlink** | EW 137 | | Insert \| Hyperlink | Hyperlink Properties | CTRL+K |
| **Select Paragraph** | EW 183 | Triple-click paragraph | | | |
| **Select Text (One Character at a Time)** | EW 183 | | | | SHIFT \| left or right arrow |
| **Select Text (One Word at a Time)** | EW 183 | | | | CTRL+SHIFT \| left or right arrow |
| **Select Word** | EW 183 | Double-click word | | | |
| **Set Publishing Options** | EW 525 | | File \| Publish Site | | |

Microsoft Expression Web Quick Reference Summary *(continued)*

| Task | Page Number | Mouse | Menu Bar | Shortcut Menu | Keyboard Shortcut |
|------|-------------|-------|----------|---------------|-------------------|
| **Specify Line Height** | EW 584 | *div* tag on Quick Tag Selector \| *style* list arrow in Apply Styles task pane \| Modify Style \| Block in Category list \| line height percentage in line-height text box \| line-height Measurements box arrow, then click % \| OK button | | | |
| **Specify Line Width** | EW 586 | Drag left or right resize handle of content div to adjust to desired line length | | | |
| **Spell Check** | EW 46 | | Tools \| Spelling \| Spelling | | F7 |
| **Style, Apply** | EW 201 | *Style* button in Apply Styles task pane | | | |
| **Style, Create Code** | EW 266 | Type first letter(s) of selector name or value, then double-click selector from shortcut menu | | | |
| **Style, Create New** | EW 198 | New Style link in Apply Styles task pane | Format \| New Style | New Style | |
| **Style, Modify** | EW 195 | *Style* button arrow in Apply Styles task pane \| Modify Style | | Modify Style | |
| **Style, New** | EW 254 | New Style link in Apply Styles task pane | Format \| New Style | | |
| **Style Sheet, Attach** | EW 268 | Attach Style Sheet link in Apply Styles task pane | Format \| CSS Styles \| Attach Style Sheet | | |
| **Style Sheet, New** | EW 260 | | File \| New \| CSS | | |
| **Style Sheet, New from Preformatted** | EW 310 | | File \| New \| Page \| Style Sheets | | |
| **Switch Views** | EW 49 | Show *view type* View button at bottom of editing window | View \| Page \| *view* | | |
| **Table AutoFormat** | EW 347 | Table AutoFormat button on Tables toolbar | Table \| Modify \| Table AutoFormat | Modify \| Table AutoFormat | |
| **Table Column, Add** | EW 330 | Column to the Left button on Tables toolbar Or Column to the Right button on Tables toolbar | Table \| Insert \| Column to the Left Or Table \| Insert \| Column to the Right | Insert \| Column to the Left Or Insert \| Column to the Right | |
| **Table Column, Delete** | EW 330 | Delete Cells button on Tables toolbar | Table \| Delete \| Delete Columns | Delete \| Delete Columns | CTRL+X |
| **Table, Convert to Text** | EW 342 | | Table \| Convert \| Table to Text | Modify \| Split Cells | |
| **Table, Fill** | EW 334 | | Table \| Fill \| Down Or Table \| Fill \| Right | | |
| **Table, New** | EW 316 | Insert Table button on Common toolbar | Table \| Insert Table | | |
| **Table, New from Text** | EW 342 | | Table \| Convert \| Text to Table | | |
| **Table Properties, Change** | EW 320 | | Table \| Table Properties | Table Properties | |
| **Table Row, Add** | EW 330 | Row Above button on Tables toolbar Or Row Below button on Tables toolbar | Table \| Insert \| Row Above Or Table \| Insert \| Row Below | Insert \| Row Above Or Insert \| Row Below | |

**Microsoft Expression Web Quick Reference Summary** *(continued)*

| Task | Page Number | Mouse | Menu Bar | Shortcut Menu | Keyboard Shortcut |
|------|-------------|-------|----------|---------------|-------------------|
| **Table Row, Delete** | EW 330 | Delete Cells button on Tables toolbar | Table \| Delete \| Delete Rows | Delete \| Delete Rows | CTRL+X |
| **Tag, Add** | EW 20 | Double-click tag in Toolbox<br>Or<br>Drag tag from Toolbox to desired location<br>Or<br><div> button on Common toolbar | Insert \| HTML \| *tag* | | |
| **Task Pane, Close** | EW 85 | Close button on title bar | Task Panes \| task pane name | Close | |
| **Task Pane, Dock** | EW 84 | Drag title bar to edge of window | | Dock | |
| **Task Pane, Maximize** | EW 84 | Maximize Window button on task pane title bar | | | |
| **Task Pane, Open** | EW 84 | | Task Panes \| task pane name | | |
| **Task Pane, Undock** | EW 84 | Drag title bar to blank area | | Float | |
| **Thumbnail, Create** | EW 113 | Auto Thumbnail button on Pictures toolbar | | Auto Thumbnail | CTRL+T |
| **Transparency, Set Around an Image** | EW 99 | Set Transparent Color button on Common toolbar | | | |
| **Undo Action** | EW 21 | Undo button on Common toolbar | Edit \| Undo | | CTRL+Z |
| **Visual Aids, Show or Hide** | EW 52 | Double-click Visual Aids button on status bar | View \| Visual Aids \| Show | | CTRL+/ |
| **Web Page, Delete** | EW 164 | | Edit \| Delete | Delete | DELETE |
| **Web Page, Open** | EW 14 | Open button arrow on Common toolbar \| Open<br>Or<br>Double-click page in Folder List or Web Site tab | File \| Open | | CTRL+O |
| **Web Page, Rename (Folder List)** | EW 162 | Click name in Folder List twice \| type new name | | Rename | |
| **Web Site, Create From Template** | EW 157 | | File \| New \| Web Site | | |
| **Web Site, Open** | EW 6 | Open button arrow on Common toolbar \| Open Site | File \| Open Site | | |